D0008453

# THE PROPHETS

abraham j. heschel

# THE
# PROPHETS

HARPER**PERENNIAL** MODERN**CLASSICS**

HARPER**PERENNIAL** 🔵 MODERN**CLASSICS**

The Revised Standard Version has been used throughout, interspersed occasion-
ally with the author's translation. Some paragraphs in this volume are taken from
*God in Search of Man* by Abraham J. Heschel published by Farrar, Straus and
Cudahy, New York, 1955.

A hardcover edition of this book was published in 1962 by Harper & Row,
Publishers.

HarperCollins books may be purchased for educational, business, or sales promo-
tional use. For information please write: Special Markets Department, Harper-
Collins Publishers Inc., 10 East 53rd Street, New York, NY 10022.

First Harper paperback edition (Volume I) published 1969. (Volume I includes
the first 281 pages of *The Prophets.*)
First Harper paperback edition (Volume II) published 1971. (Volume II includes
the second half of *The Prophets.*)
First Perennial Classics edition published 2001.
Perennial Classics are published by Perennial, an imprint of HarperCollins
Publishers.

Library of Congress Cataloging-in-Publication Data

Heschel, Abraham Joshua.
    The Prophets / Abraham J. Heschel. — 1st Perennial classics ed.
      p.  cm. — (Perennial classics)
    Originally published: 1st ed. New York : Harper & Row, 1962.
    Includes bibliographical references and indexes.
    ISBN 0-06-093699-1    ISBN 978-0-06-093699-0
    1. Bible. O.T. Prophets—Criticism, interpretation, etc.  2. Prophets.
  I. Title.  II. Perennial classic.

HS1505.2. H4   2001
224.'06—dc21                        2001024817

12 11 10     FG/RRD    30 29 28 27 26 25 24 23 22 21

## ABBREVIATIONS USED IN THE FOOTNOTES

*AASOR*   Annual of the American Schools of Oriental Research

*ANET*    J. B. Pritchard, ed., *Ancient Near Eastern Texts Relating to the Old Testament* (2nd ed.; Princeton, 1950)

*ERE*     J. Hastings, ed., *Encyclopedia of Religion and Ethics*

*(H.)*    Hebrew; used to denote verses in the Hebrew Bible when the numbering differs from RSV

*HUCA*    Hebrew Union College Annual, Cincinnati, Ohio

*JBL*     Journal of Biblical Literature

*MGWJ*    *Monatsschrift für die Geschichte und Wissenschaft des Judentums*

*ThWBNT*  *Theologisches Wörterbuch zum Neuen Testament*

*ZAW*     *Zeitschrift für die Alttestamentliche Wissenschaft*

*ZDMG*    *Zeitschrift der Deutschen Morgenländischen Gesellschaft*

# Contents

# II

# Introduction to the Perennial Classics Edition

"What manner of man is the prophet?" asks my father in the opening pages of *The Prophets*. A person of agony, whose "life and soul are at stake in what he says," yet who is also able to perceive "the silent sigh" of human anguish. In the common imagination, we think of prophets as people who foretell the future, who warn of divine punishment for sin, who demand social justice. Such moderation fails to understand that "God is raging in the prophet's words." While we may all criticize injustices in our society, they remain tolerable, while to the prophet "injustice assumes almost cosmic proportions." Why the indignation, the outrage? Is the prophet's reaction not out of proportion?

Yet it is precisely the passion of the prophet that is central. For my father, the importance of prophecy lies not only in the message, but in the role of the prophet as a witness, someone who is able to make God audible and to reveal not only God's will, but inner life. To be a prophet, he writes, is to be in fellowship with the feelings of God, to experience communion with the divine consciousness. The prophet hears God's voice and looks at the world from God's perspective.

That, indeed, is the starting-point of most religious people, but too often they are distracted, confusing the message with the messenger. For example, the Talmud states, "Since the day that the Temple was destroyed the Holy One blessed be He has nothing in this world but the four cubits of halakha alone." (Berachot 8a). For many Jewish thinkers, the passage teaches the centrality of halakha; for my father, the passage is to be read as an expression of regret. Halakha, no more than any other religion's central teaching, is the vehicle to God, not a substitute for God; a challenge, not a panacea. Similarly, he writes that prayer must be subversive, an affront to our complacency rather than a confirmation of our values: "To the prophet satiety of conscience is prudery and flight from responsibility."

The prophets were not simply biblical figures my father studied, but models for his life. One of the most vivid memories of my childhood is the Saturday night my father left home to join Dr. Martin Luther King, Jr., in the 1965 Voting Rights march from Selma to Montgomery. I remember kissing him goodbye and wondering if I would ever see him again. Alabama was a horror: I saw its vicious sheriffs on TV beating black demonstrators, turning German shepherds and water cannons against black children. Even the police were on the side of evil. Two weeks before my father left, the Alabama State Troopers had viciously beaten peaceful demonstrators on the Edmund Pettus Bridge—a day known as Bloody Sunday.

The greatness of that Selma march continues to reverberate because it was not simply a political event, but an extraordinary moral and religious event as well. For my father, the march was a deeply spiritual occasion. When he came home, he said, "I felt my legs were praying." His only regret, he later wrote, was that "Jewish religious institutions have again missed a great opportunity, namely, to interpret a Civil Rights movement in terms of Judaism. The vast number of Jews participating actively in it are totally unaware of what the movement means in terms of the prophetic traditions."

What are those prophetic traditions? My father's book on the prophets began as a study of prophetic subjectivity. The prophet was not simply a messenger from God, conveying a teaching that would inspire people to do justice and warn them of the consequences of failing to heed that message. The overriding importance of the prophets was not the content of their message, but the kind of religious experience they exemplified.

The religious experience of the prophets has long been a conundrum in biblical studies. Biblical scholarship, as it took shape in Germany in the mid-nineteenth century, was dominated by liberal Protestant theologians whose work on the prophets was colored by their religious polemics. They argued that the prophetic teachings constituted the zenith of Israel's religious development and that post–prophetic era Judaism was a period of decline and degeneration into narrow-minded nationalism and legalism. Theologically, German Protestants argued, the true heir of the prophetic tradition was not Judaism, but Christianity. The spirit of the prophetic tradition was kept alive in the teachings of Jesus, not those of the rabbis.

In the early twentieth century, Christian biblical scholars began to distinguish between the teachings of the prophets and the personalities of the prophets. While the teachings were linked to those of Jesus, the prophetic personality was increasingly described in disparaging terms—not unlike the disparagement of mystics, who were frequently derided by scholars as hysterics. The German biblical scholar Gustav Hölscher defined the prophets as ecstatics who had learned about altered states of consciousness from pagan Canaanite religious personalities. In their state of ecstasy, the prophets, according to Hölscher, saw themselves not as mere messengers of God, but spoke as God and identified themselves with God. Other scholars have also emphasized the prophet's full absorption into God, or else have presented the prophet as a mere mouthpiece for God's message.

For my father, such understandings of the prophets are without foundation in the biblical text and came into being because scholars lacked the appropriate conceptual tools to understand prophetic experience. None of the characteristic marks of ecstasy—frenzy, merging with God, self-extinction—are indicated in the prophetic literature. Rather, the prophets' experience of God, he suggests, is characterized as a communion with the divine consciousness, a sympathy with divine pathos, a deep concern by God for humanity. The prophets do not become absorbed into God, losing their own personalities, but share the divine pathos through their own sharply honed sympathy. Far from eradicating their own personalities, the prophets' own emotional experiences actively color their fellowship with the divine consciousness and their transmission of God's message.

*The Prophets,* first published in English in 1962, is an elaboration of my father's doctoral dissertation, "The Prophetic Consciousness," which he wrote at the University of Berlin at the age of twenty-five. He submitted the dissertation in 1932 and took his doctoral examinations just a few weeks after Hitler came to power. In order to receive a Ph.D., his dissertation had to be published, but in Nazi Germany that was not easy for a Jewish student. My father's dissertation finally appeared in 1935, published by the Krakow Academy of Sciences. The book was very well received, earning glowing reviews in academic journals in Europe and the United States. German biblical scholars, however, were not uniformly enthusiastic. The book appeared at a time when numerous German Protestants wanted to eliminate the Hebrew scriptures from the Christian Bible, on the grounds that it was a Jewish book. Others insisted that it be retained because it was an anti-Jewish book, on the grounds that the prophets are constantly denouncing the sins of Israel.

My father lived in Nazi Germany, fleeing just at the last minute. His mother and three of his sisters, all living in Poland, were murdered by the Nazis. For him, those experiences resulted in both a deepened commitment to his faith and a heightened sensitivity to the suffering of all people. Hitler and his followers came to power not with machine guns, but with words, he used to say, and they did so with a debased view of human beings rooted in contempt for God. You cannot worship God, he writes, and look with contempt at a human being as if he or she were an animal. In particular, he held German Christian religious leaders responsible for the widespread collaboration with the Nazi regime and their failure to provide theological tools for opposing anti-Semitism.

Thankfully, my father escaped Europe, "plucked like a brand from the fire," as he wrote. He arrived in the United States in March of 1940. His escape was facilitated by Julian Morgenstern, president of the Hebrew Union College, where my father taught for five years before becoming a professor at the Jewish Theological Seminary in New York City.

My father's formative years were spent in a world that no longer exists. Born in Warsaw in 1907, he was the youngest child of two special parents. His father was a Hasidic rebbe, known as the Pelzovizner rebbe, whose congregation consisted primarily of impoverished Jews. His mother was someone of such piety that people would come to ask her to pray on their behalf, as they might ask a rebbe. My father's family was a kind of royalty in the Jewish world and encompassed many of the most distinguished Hasidic leaders and thinkers. As a child, my father was treated with the deference accorded a prince: adults would rise when he entered the room, knowing that one day he would become a rebbe. He was considered an "illuy," or genius, and when he was still a little boy, he would be lifted onto tables to deliver learned orations on Jewish texts. The people around him lived with intense piety and religious observance, and he felt grateful, as he said much later, that he grew up surrounded by people of spiritual nobility.

In his late teens, my father decided to pursue secular studies, and he completed a course of study at a gymnasium, or secondary school, in Vilna. There he also became a member of a group of Yiddish poets who called themselves Jung Vilna, and he published a small volume of poetry. From Vilna he went to Berlin, where he studied at the University; at the Reform movement's Hochschule für die Wissenschaft des Judentums, where the new scientific approach to Jewish texts was practiced; and at the Orthodox rabbinical seminary. In Berlin, which was the intellectual center of Europe at the time, my father discovered that his professors at the University were in dire need of Jewish understandings of the Bible. He used to tell me about the professor who explained Isaiah's use of the expression "comfort ye, comfort ye my people" as the result of a scribal error: a scribe copying the text had forgotten he had already written down the phrase and wrote it a second time. Imagine, my father used to say, shaking his head, such an utter lack of sensitivity to biblical poetry.

My father's introduction of the term "divine pathos" as the central theological element of prophetic teaching was drawn from a rabbinic concept: "zoreḥ gavoha," a higher, divine need. God is not the detached, unmoved mover of the Aristotelian tradition, he insisted, but is "the most moved mover," deeply affected by human deeds. Divine pathos indicates a constant involvement of God in human history but insists that the involvement is an emotional engagement: God suffers when human beings are hurt, so that when I hurt another person, I injure God.

Hence the prophet is neither a messenger, an oracle, a seer, nor an ecstatic, but a witness to the divine pathos, one who bears testimony to God's concern for human beings. My father emphasized that God is not simply a topic of human interest, but that we are objects of divine concern. Being gripped by the anguish experienced by God in response to human affliction leaves the prophet overwhelmed and tormented. Facing callousness and indifference, the prophet does not perceive God as a source of comfort and reassurance, but as an incessant demand: "While the world is at ease and asleep, the prophet feels the blast from heaven."

Shortly after publishing *The Prophets*, my father became active in the anti-war movement, and in 1965 he founded an organization, Clergy and Laymen Concerned About Vietnam. As much as the Selma march was for him a religious experience, religion without indignation at political evils was impossible. Justice is not simply an idea or a norm, but a divine passion. Echoing the prophetic language, my father declared, "To speak about God and remain silent on Vietnam is blasphemous." If we are to follow, however modestly, the teachings of prophetic sympathy and divine pathos, then religion must be understood as the opposite of callousness. The opposite of good, he wrote, is not evil; the opposite of good is indifference. Indeed, our very humanity depends upon our compassion. In speaking out against the war, he said, "Remember that the blood of the innocent cries forever. Should that blood stop to cry, humanity would cease to be." Hearing the silent anguish is not limited to the prophets, but devolves upon all of us: "Few are guilty, but all are responsible," my father writes in the early pages of *The Prophets.*

My father was devastated by the war in Southeast Asia. He had many sleepless nights toward the end of his life (he died in December 1972) and was consumed by efforts to bring an end to the slaughter. Among his close friends, Daniel and Philip Berrigan, two Catholic priests, went to jail in protest, while William Sloane Coffin, the Protestant chaplain at Yale, was indicted for conspiracy to encourage draft-card burning. My father did not engage in civil disobedience, feeling he could be more effective in the anti-war movement out of jail. He spoke at numerous protest rallies and raised the issue of Vietnam when he lectured and taught. Students in his classes heard about the war as they learned about the prophets.

One of the distinguishing features of my father's leadership was his critique of his own community. As much as he spoke against racism and the war, he was equally critical of Jewish religious institutions: "On every Sabbath multitudes of Jews gather in the synagogues, and they often depart as they have entered." Prayer had become vicarious, delegated to rabbis and cantors who failed to inspire because they "do not know the language of the soul." He found fault as much with Orthodox as with Reform and Conservative branches of Judaism, as much with educators as with lay leaders. Too much money had been spent on demographic surveys and not enough on education, while educators themselves should make their goal "reverence for learning and the learning of reverence." Worship had lost its fear and trembling and had become a social occasion, rather than a moment of holiness. Society was disintegrating, and Judaism was conforming, failing to convey its resources of integrity. Judaism, he wrote, had become a platitude, when it should be spiritual effrontery. The modern Jew had become a messenger who had forgotten the message.

Such criticism did not always make my father welcome in the Jewish community. To this day, many Jews prefer a message that is secular, not religious; one that presents Jews as victims, not actors with responsibilities to the political arena; and one that praises Judaism, not criticizes it. My father did not tell his audience what they wanted to hear, but told them what they needed to improve. Like the prophets, for whom evil was never the climax of history, my father's message was sometimes harsh, but always held out a vision and a hope: "There is bound to come a renewal of our sense of wonder and radical amazement, a revival of reverence, an emergence of a sense of ultimate embarrassment, and ultimate indebtedness."

—Susannah Heschel

# Introduction

This book is about some of the most disturbing people who have ever lived: the men whose inspiration brought the Bible into being—the men whose image is our refuge in distress, and whose voice and vision sustain our faith.

The significance of Israel's prophets lies not only in what they said but also in what they were. We cannot fully understand what they meant to say to us unless we have some degree of awareness of what happened to them. The moments that passed in their lives are not now available and cannot become the object of scientific analysis. All we have is the consciousness of those moments as preserved in words.

My aim therefore is to attain an understanding of the prophet through an analysis and description of his *consciousness,* to relate what came to pass in his life—facing man, being faced by God—as reflected and affirmed in his mind. By consciousness, in other words, I mean here not only the perception of particular moments of inspiration, but also the totality of impressions, thoughts, and feelings which make up the prophet's being.

By insisting on the absolutely objective and supernatural nature of prophecy, dogmatic theology has disregarded the prophet's part in the prophetic act. Stressing revelation, it has ignored the response;

isolating inspiration, it has lost sight of the human situation. In contrast with what may be called "pan-theology," psychologists have sought to deduce prophecy entirely from the inner life of the prophets. Reducing it to a subjective personal phenomenon, they have disregarded the prophet's awareness of his confrontation with facts not derived from his own mind.

A rejection of both extremes must spring from the realization that the words of the prophets testify to a situation that defies both pan-theology and pan-psychology. Careful analysis shows that this situation is composed of revelation and response, of receptivity and spontaneity, of event and experience. I maintain, therefore, that the marks of the personal element are to be traced, not outside the prophet's act, but within it.

The prophet is a person, not a microphone. He is endowed with a mission, with the power of a word not his own that accounts for his greatness—but also with temperament, concern, character, and individuality. As there was no resisting the impact of divine inspiration, so at times there was no resisting the vortex of his own temperament. The word of God reverberated in the voice of man.

The prophet's task is to convey a divine view, yet as a person he *is* a point of view. He speaks from the perspective of God as perceived from the perspective of his own situation. We must seek to understand not only the views he expounded but also the attitudes he embodied: his own position, feeling, response—not only what he said but also what he lived; the private, the intimate dimension of the word, the subjective side of the message.

In the prophets of Israel we may trace similarities and parallels to personalities to be encountered elsewhere, since indeed the religion of the Hebrews shared much with other Semitic religions. It is therefore important to compare them with other types of men of ancient history who made similar claims. Yet the more difficult question is: What are the features that set the prophets of Israel apart? What constitutes their uniqueness?

The prophet is not only a prophet. He is also poet, preacher, patriot, statesman, social critic, moralist. There has been a tendency to see the essence and chief significance of prophecy in the display of one or another of these aspects. Yet this is a misapprehension of the intrinsic nature of prophecy.

The first objective of our inquiry should not be to see the prophet as an example of a species, but rather to ascertain the characteristics that set him apart as well as those he shares with others. In order to meet him truly as a prophet, the mind must shed certain habits of inquiry; traps and decoys of convenient patterns are to be avoided. The most assured way of missing the goal is an approach carried on with the preconceived certainty of being able to explain him. To explain the prophet in terms of a neat set of preconceived notions would be putting the cart before the horse. Explanation, when regarded as the only goal of inquiry, becomes a substitute for understanding. Imperceptibly it becomes the beginning rather than the end of perception.

The bias which so many scholars share and which may be defined as a principle—namely, that nothing is to be recognized as a datum unless it can be qualified *a priori* as capable of explanation—besides being pretentious and questionable, obstructs the view of much of reality and seriously affects our power to gain a pristine insight into what we face.

Confining attention to what is given in the literary sources, i.e., the prophetic books, I have sought to gain some insight into the minds of the prophets and to understand the decisive moments of their existence from that perspective.* It was not my intention in this study to pass judgment on the truth of their claim to have received revelation, nor to solve the enigma of prophecy by means of psychological or sociological explanations, nor yet to discover the conditions of its possibility or suggest means of its verification. The intention was

---

*The destruction of Jerusalem in 587 marks the end of the classical era in the history of prophecy, and the understanding of the prophetic figures who emerged during the exile raises problems of a special kind. This book deals with the classical or literary prophets of the eighth and seventh centuries B.C.E. Of other prophets there is only occasional mention, with the exception of Second Isaiah, whose message illumines many of the enigmas in the words and intentions of his predecessors.

to illumine the prophets' claim; not to explain their consciousness, but to understand it. By unveiling the decisive features of their awareness, the essential structure of experience as reflected in that consciousness may become manifest.

What I have aimed at is an understanding of what it means to think, feel, respond, and act as a prophet. It was not part of the task to go beyond his consciousness in order to explore the subconscious or reach out to the antecedent conditionings and experiences within the inner life of the individual. A surmise of what lies beyond and below the threshold of the prophet's consciousness can never be a substitute for the understanding of what is displayed in consciousness itself. Nor is it possible to confirm what he affirms. We may arrive at some knowledge of what stirred the prophet as a prophet—of the ideas by which he was moved at particular moments; we cannot prove the realities and events which preceded these moments.

The inquiry, then, was aimed, not at psychological motives to be looked for in the preprophetic background of the prophet's life, but at motives which are consciously given, even if not explicitly stated, and which constitute or at least reflect the decisive categories or the structural forms of prophetic thinking.

The procedure employed in an inquiry for gaining such insight was the method of pure reflection. Observation, inspection, tackling and probing, the sheer seeing of what we face, serve to introduce us to the realness of the phenomenon and sharpen our ability to formulate questions conducive to the discovery of what is unique about it. Indeed, it requires much effort to learn which questions should not be asked and which claims must not be entertained. What impairs our sight are habits of seeing as well as the mental concomitants of seeing. Our sight is suffused with knowing, instead of feeling painfully the lack of knowing what we see. The principle to be kept in mind is to know what we see rather than to see what we know.

Rather than blame things for being obscure, we should blame ourselves for being biased and prisoners of self-induced repetitiveness. One must forget many clichés in order to behold a single image. Insight is the beginning of perceptions to come rather than the extension of perceptions gone by. Conventional seeing, operating as it does with patterns and coherences, is a way of seeing the present in the past tense. Insight is an attempt to think in the present.

Insight is a breakthrough, requiring much intellectual dismantling and dislocation. It begins with a mental interim, with the cultivation of a feeling for the unfamiliar, unparalleled, incredible. It is in being involved with a phenomenon, being intimately engaged to it, courting it, as it were, that after much perplexity and embarrassment we come upon *insight*—upon a way of seeing the phenomenon from within. Insight is accompanied by a sense of surprise. What has been closed is suddenly disclosed. It entails genuine perception, seeing anew. He who thinks that we can see the same object twice has never seen. Paradoxically, insight is knowledge at first sight.

Such an inquiry must suspend personal beliefs or even any intent to inquire—e.g., whether the event happened in fact as it did to their minds. It is my claim that, regardless of whether or not their experience was of the real, it is possible to analyze the form and content of that experience. The process and result of such an inquiry represent the essential part of this book as composed a good many years ago.* While I still maintain the soundness of the method described above, which in important aspects reflects the method of phenomenology, I have long since become wary of impartiality, which is itself a way of being partial. The prophet's existence is either irrelevant or relevant. If irrelevant, I cannot truly be involved in it; if relevant, then my impartiality is but a pretense. Reflection may succeed in isolating an object; reflection itself cannot be isolated. Reflection is part of a situation.

The situation of a person immersed in the prophets' words is one of being exposed to a ceaseless shattering of indifference, and one needs a skull of stone to remain callous to such blows.

I cannot remain indifferent to the question whether a decision I reach may prove fatal to my existence—whether to inhale the next

---

* *Die Prophetie,* published by the Polish Academy of Sciences, Krakow, 1936, and by Erich Reiss, Berlin, 1936. For further details of the method employed, see the preface to that volume, pp. 1–6, as well as discussion throughout the present work.

breath in order to survive. Perhaps this is the issue that frightens the prophets. A people may be dying without being aware of it; a people may be able to survive, yet refuse to make use of their ability.

To comprehend what phenomena are, it is important to suspend judgment and think in detachment; to comprehend what phenomena mean, it is necessary to suspend indifference and be involved. To examine their essence requires a process of reflection. Such reflection, however, sets up a gulf between the phenomena and ourselves. Reducing them to dead objects of the mind, it deprives them of the power to affect us, to speak to us, to transcend our attitudes and conceptions.

While the structure and the bare content of prophetic consciousness may be made accessible by an attitude of pure reflection, in which the concern for their truth and validity is suspended, the sheer force of what is disclosed in such reflection quietly corrodes the hardness of self-detachment. The magic of the process seems to be stronger than any asceticism of the intellect. Thus in the course of listening to their words one cannot long retain the security of a prudent, impartial observer. The prophets do not offer reflections about ideas in general. Their words are onslaughts, scuttling illusions of false security, challenging evasions, calling faith to account, questioning prudence and impartiality. One may be equally afraid to submit to their strange certainties and to resist their tremendous claims because of incredulity or impotence of spirit. Reflection about the prophets gives way to communion with the prophets.

Pure reflection may be sufficient for the clarification of what the prophet's consciousness asserts—but not for what his existence involves. For such understanding it is not enough to have the prophets in mind; we must think as if we were inside their minds. For them to be alive and present to us we must think, not *about,* but *in* the prophets, with their concern and their heart. Their existence involves us. Unless their concern strikes us, pains us, exalts us, we do not really sense it. Such involvement requires accord, receptivity, hearing, sheer surrender to their impact. Its intellectual rewards include moments in which the mind peels off, as it were, its not-knowing. Thought is like touch, comprehending by being comprehended.

In probing their consciousness we are not interested only in the inward life, in emotion and reflection as such. We are interested in restoring the world of the prophets: terrifying in its absurdity and defiance of its Maker, tottering at the brink of disaster, with the voice of God imploring man to turn to Him. It is not a world devoid of meaning that evokes the prophet's consternation, but a world deaf to meaning. And yet the consternation is but a prelude. He always begins with a message of doom and concludes with a message of hope and redemption. Does this mean that no human wickedness can prevail over God's almighty love? Does this mean that His stillness is stronger than the turmoil of human crimes, that His desire for peace is stronger than man's passion for violence?

Prophecy is not simply the application of timeless standards to particular human situations, but rather an interpretation of a particular moment in history, a divine understanding of a human situation. Prophecy, then, may be described as *exegesis of existence from a divine perspective*. Understanding prophecy is an understanding of an understanding rather than an understanding of knowledge; it is exegesis of exegesis. It involves sharing the perspective from which the original understanding is done. To interpret prophecy from any other perspective—such as sociology or psychology—is like interpreting poetry from the perspective of the economic interests of the poet.

The spirit of such exegesis makes it incongruous for our inquiry to take refuge in the personal question (however vital): What do the prophets mean to us? The only sensible way of asking the personal question is to be guided by another, more audacious question: What do the prophets mean to God? All other questions are absurd unless this one question is meaningful. For prophecy is a sham unless it is experienced as a word of God swooping down on man and converting him into a prophet.

Proper exegesis is an effort to understand the philosopher in terms and categories of philosophy, the poet in terms and categories of poetry, and the prophet in terms and categories of prophecy.

Prophecy is a way of thinking as well as a way of living. It is upon the right understanding of the terms and categories of prophetic thinking that the success of our inquiry depends.

To rediscover some of these terms and categories requires careful exploration of the kinds of questions a prophet asks, and the sort of premises about God, the world, and man he takes for granted. Indeed, the most important outcome of the inquiry has been for me the discovery of the *intellectual relevance of the prophets.*

What drove me to study the prophets?

In the academic environment in which I spent my student years philosophy had become an isolated, self-subsisting, self-indulgent entity, a *Ding an sich,* encouraging suspicion instead of love of wisdom. The answers offered were unrelated to the problems, indifferent to the travail of a person who became aware of man's suspended sensitivity in the face of stupendous challenge, indifferent to a situation in which good and evil became irrelevant, in which man became increasingly callous to catastrophe and ready to suspend the principle of truth. I was slowly led to the realization that some of the terms, motivations, and concerns which dominate our thinking may prove destructive of the roots of human responsibility and treasonable to the ultimate ground of human solidarity. The challenge we are all exposed to, and the dreadful shame that shatters our capacity for inner peace, defy the ways and patterns of our thinking. One is forced to admit that some of the causes and motives of our thinking have led our existence astray, that speculative prosperity is no answer to spiritual bankruptcy. It was the realization that the right coins were not available in the common currency that drove me to study the thought of the prophets.

Every mind operates with presuppositions or premises as well as within a particular way of thinking. In the face of the tragic failure of the modern mind, incapable of preventing its own destruction, it became clear to me that the most important philosophical problem of the twentieth century was to find a new set of presuppositions or premises, a different way of thinking.

I have tried to elucidate some of the presuppositions that lie at the root of prophetic theology, the fundamental attitudes of prophetic religion, and to call attention to how they differ from certain presuppositions and attitudes that prevail in other systems of theology and religion. While stressing the centrality of pathos, a term which takes on major importance in the course of the discussion, I have tried not to lose sight of the ethos and logos in their teaching.

Disregarding derivative and subordinate circumstances and focusing attention upon the fundamental motives which give coherence and integral unity to the prophetic personality, I have been led to distinguish in the consciousness of the prophet between what happened *to* him and what happened *in* him—between the transcendent and the spontaneous—as well as between content and form. The structure of prophetic consciousness as ascertained in the analysis was disclosed as consisting, on the transcendent level, of pathos (content of inspiration) and event (form), and on the personal level, of sympathy (content of inner experience) and the sense of being overpowered (form of inner experience).

The prophet was an individual who said No to his society, condemning its habits and assumptions, its complacency, waywardness, and syncretism. He was often compelled to proclaim the very opposite of what his heart expected. His fundamental objective was to reconcile man and God. Why do the two need reconciliation? Perhaps it is due to man's false sense of sovereignty, to his abuse of freedom, to his aggressive, sprawling pride, resenting God's involvement in history.

Prophecy ceased; the prophets endure and can only be ignored at the risk of our own despair. It is for us to decide whether freedom is self-assertion or response to a demand; whether the ultimate situation is conflict or concern.

ABRAHAM J. HESCHEL

*Jewish Theological Seminary*
*New York City*
*August, 1962*

# THE PROPHETS

# I

# 1

# What Manner of Man
# Is the Prophet?

### Sensitivity to Evil

What manner of man is the prophet? A student of philosophy who turns from the discourses of the great metaphysicians to the orations of the prophets may feel as if he were going from the realm of the sublime to an area of trivialities. Instead of dealing with the timeless issues of being and becoming, of matter and form, of definitions and demonstrations, he is thrown into orations about widows and orphans, about the corruption of judges and affairs of the market place. Instead of showing us a way through the elegant mansions of the mind, the prophets take us to the slums. The world is a proud place, full of beauty, but the prophets are scandalized, and rave as if the whole world were a slum. They make much ado about paltry things, lavishing excessive language upon trifling subjects. What if somewhere in ancient Palestine poor people have not been treated properly by the rich? So what if some old women found pleasure and edification in worshiping "the Queen of Heaven"? Why such immoderate excitement? Why such intense indignation?

The things that horrified the prophets are even now daily occurrences all over the world. There is no society to which Amos' words would not apply.

> *Hear this, you who trample upon the needy,*
> *And bring the poor of the land to an end,*
> *Saying: When will the new moon be over*
> *That we may sell grain?*
> *And the Sabbath,*
> *That we may offer wheat for sale,*
> *That we may make the ephah small and the shekel great,*
> *And deal deceitfully with false balances,*
> *That we may buy the poor for silver,*
> *And the needy for a pair of sandals,*
> *And sell the refuse of the wheat?*
>
> *Amos 8:4–6*

Indeed, the sort of crimes and even the amount of delinquency that fill the prophets of Israel with dismay do not go beyond that which we regard as normal, as typical ingredients of social dynamics. To us a single act of injustice—cheating in business, exploitation of the poor—is slight; to the prophets, a disaster. To us injustice is injurious to the welfare of the people; to the prophets it is a deathblow to existence: to us, an episode; to them, a catastrophe, a threat to the world.

Their breathless impatience with injustice may strike us as hysteria. We ourselves witness continually acts of injustice, manifestations of hypocrisy, falsehood, outrage, misery, but we rarely grow indignant or overly excited. To the prophets even a minor injustice assumes cosmic proportions.

> *The Lord has sworn by the pride of Jacob:*
> *Surely I will never forget any of their deeds.*
> *Shall not the land tremble on this account,*
> *And every one mourn who dwells in it,*
> *And all of it rise like the Nile,*
> *Be tossed about and sink again, like the Nile of Egypt?*
>
> *Amos 8:7–8*

> *Be appalled, O heavens, at this,*
> *Be shocked, be utterly desolate, says the Lord.*

> *For My people have committed two evils:*
> *They have forsaken Me,*
> *The fountain of living waters,*
> *And hewed out cisterns for themselves,*
> *Broken cisterns,*
> *That can hold no water.*
>
> *Jeremiah 2:12–13*

They speak and act as if the sky were about to collapse because Israel has become unfaithful to God.

Is not the vastness of their indignation and the vastness of God's anger in disproportion to its cause? How should one explain such moral and religious excitability, such extreme impetuosity?

It seems incongruous and absurd that because of some minor acts of injustice inflicted on the insignificant, powerless poor, the glorious city of Jerusalem should be destroyed and the whole nation go to exile. Did not the prophet magnify the guilt?

The prophet's words are outbursts of violent emotions. His rebuke is harsh and relentless. But if such deep sensitivity to evil is to be called hysterical, what name should be given to the abysmal indifference to evil which the prophet bewails?

> *They drink wine in bowls,*
> *And anoint themselves with the finest oils,*
> *But they are not grieved over the ruin of Joseph!*
>
> *Amos 6:6*

The niggardliness of our moral comprehensions, the incapacity to sense the depth of misery caused by our own failures, is a fact which no subterfuge can elude. Our eyes are witness to the callousness and cruelty of man, but our heart tries to obliterate the memories, to calm the nerves, and to silence our conscience.

The prophet is a man who feels fiercely. God has thrust a burden upon his soul, and he is bowed and stunned at man's fierce greed. Frightful is the agony of man; no human voice can convey its full terror. Prophecy is the voice that God has lent to the silent agony, a voice to the plundered poor, to the profaned riches of the world. It is a form of living, a crossing point of God and man. God is raging in the prophet's words.

## THE IMPORTANCE OF TRIVIALITIES

"Human affairs are hardly worth considering in earnest, and yet we must be in earnest about them—a sad necessity constrains us," says Plato in a mood of melancholy. He apologizes later for his "low opinion of mankind" which, he explains, emerged from comparing men with the gods. "Let us grant, if you wish, that the human race is not to be despised, but is worthy of some considerations."*

"The gods attend to great matters; they neglect small ones," Cicero maintains.† According to Aristotle, the gods are not concerned at all with the dispensation of good and bad fortune or external things.‡ To the prophet, however, no subject is as worthy of consideration as the plight of man. Indeed, God Himself is described as reflecting over the plight of man rather than as contemplating eternal ideas. His mind is preoccupied with man, with the concrete actualities of history rather than with the timeless issues of thought. In the prophet's message nothing that has bearing upon good and evil is small or trite in the eyes of God (see pp. 464 f.).

Man is rebellious and full of iniquity, and yet so cherished is he that God, the Creator of heaven and earth, is saddened when forsaken by him. Profound and intimate is God's love for man, and yet harsh and dreadful can be His wrath. Of what paltry worth is human might—yet human compassion is divinely precious. Ugly though the behavior of man is, yet may man's return to God make of his way a highway of God.

## LUMINOUS AND EXPLOSIVE

"Really great works," writes Flaubert, "have a serene look. Through small openings one perceives precipices; down at the bottom

---

* *Laws*, VII, 803.
† *De Natura Deorum*, II, 167.
‡ *Magna Moralia*, II, 8, 1207, 1208, 1209.

there is darkness, vertigo; but above the whole soars something singularly sweet. That is the ideal of light, the smiling of the sun; and how calm it is, calm and strong! . . . The highest and hardest thing in art seems to me to be to create a state of reverie.''*

The very opposite applies to the words of the prophet. They suggest a disquietude sometimes amounting to agony. Yet there are interludes when one perceives an eternity of love hovering over moments of anguish; at the bottom there is light, fascination, but above the whole soar thunder and lightning.

The prophet's use of emotional and imaginative language, concrete in diction, rhythmical in movement, artistic in form, marks his style as poetic. Yet it is not the sort of poetry that takes its origin, to use Wordsworth's phrase, "from emotion recollected in tranquility." Far from reflecting a state of inner harmony or poise, its style is charged with agitation, anguish, and a spirit of nonacceptance. The prophet's concern is not with nature but with history, and history is devoid of poise.

Authentic utterance derives from a moment of identification of a person and a word; its significance depends upon the urgency and magnitude of its theme. The prophet's theme is, first of all, the very life of a whole people, and his identification lasts more than a moment. He is one not only with what he says; he is involved with his people in what his words foreshadow. This is the secret of the prophet's style: his life and soul are at stake in what he says and in what is going to happen to what he says. It is an involvement that echoes on. What is more, both theme and identification are seen in three dimensions. Not only the prophet and the people, but God Himself is involved in what the words convey.

Prophetic utterance is rarely cryptic, suspended between God and man; it is urging, alarming, forcing onward, as if the words gushed forth from the heart of God, seeking entrance to the heart and mind of man, carrying a summons as well as an involvement. Gran-

*Quoted by F. Kaufmann, *Thomas Mann, The World as Will and Representation* (Boston, 1957), p. 272.

deur, not dignity, is important. The language is luminous and explosive, firm and contingent, harsh and compassionate, a fusion of contradictions.

The prophet seldom tells a story, but casts events. He rarely sings, but castigates. He does more than translate reality into a poetic key: he is a preacher whose purpose is not self-expression or "the purgation of emotions," but communication. His images must not shine, they must burn.

The prophet is intent on intensifying responsibility, is impatient of excuse, contemptuous of pretense and self-pity. His tone, rarely sweet or caressing, is frequently consoling and disburdening; his words are often slashing, even horrid—designed to shock rather than to edify.

The mouth of the prophet is "a sharp sword." He is "a polished arrow" taken out of the quiver of God (Isa. 49:2).

> *Tremble, you women who are at ease,*
> *Shudder, you complacent ones;*
> *Strip, and make yourselves bare,*
> *Gird sackcloth upon your loins.*
> *Isaiah 32:11*

Reading the words of the prophets is a strain on the emotions, wrenching one's conscience from the state of suspended animation.

## THE HIGHEST GOOD

Those who have a sense of beauty know that a stone sculptured by an artist's poetic hands has an air of loveliness; that a beam charmingly placed utters a song. The prophet's ear, however, is attuned to a cry imperceptible to others. A clean house or a city architecturally distinguished may yet fill the prophet with distress.

> *Woe to him who heaps up what is not his own, . . .*
> *Woe to him who gets evil gain for his house, . . .*
> *For the stone cries out from the wall,*

*And the beam from the woodwork responds.*
*Woe to him who builds a town with blood,*
*And founds a city on iniquity!*
*Habakkuk 2:6, 9, 11–12*

These words contradict most men's conceptions: the builders of great cities have always been envied and acclaimed; neither violence nor exploitation could dim the splendor of the metropolis. "Woe to him . . ."? Human justice will not exact its due, nor will pangs of conscience disturb intoxication with success, for deep in our hearts is the temptation to worship the imposing, the illustrious, the ostentatious. Had a poet come to Samaria, the capital of the Northern Kingdom, he would have written songs exalting its magnificent edifices, its beautiful temples and worldly monuments. But when Amos of Tekoa came to Samaria, he spoke not of the magnificence of palaces, but of moral confusion and oppression. Dismay filled the prophet:

*I abhor the pride of Jacob,*
*And hate his palaces,*

he cried out in the name of the Lord (Amos 6:8). Was Amos, then, not sensitive to beauty?

What is the highest good? Three things ancient society cherished above all else: wisdom, wealth, and might. To the prophets, such infatuation was ludicrous and idolatrous. Assyria would be punished for her arrogant boasting:

*By the strength of my hand I have done it,*
*And by my wisdom, for I have understanding; . . .*
*Isaiah 10:13*

And about their own people, because "their hearts are far from Me, . . . the wisdom of the wise men shall perish" (Isa. 29:13, 14).

*The wise men shall be put to shame,*
*They shall be dismayed and taken;*
*Lo, they have rejected the word of the Lord,*
*What wisdom is in them?*
*Jeremiah 8:9*

Ephraim has said,

> *Ah, but I am rich,*
> *I have gained wealth for myself;*
> *But all his riches can never offset*
> *The guilt he has incurred. . . .*
> *Because you have trusted in your chariots*
> *And in the multitude of your warriors,*
> *Therefore the tumult of war shall arise among your people,*
> *And all your fortresses shall be destroyed, . . .*
>
> Hosea 12:8; 10:13, 14

Thus says the Lord: "Let not the wise man glory in his wisdom, let not the mighty man glory in his might, let not the rich man glory in his riches; but let him who glories, glory in this, that he understands and knows Me, that I am the Lord Who practice kindness, justice, and righteousness in the earth; for in these things I delight, says the Lord" (Jer. 9:23–24 [H. 9:22–23]).

This message was expressed with astounding finality by a later prophet: "This is the word of the Lord . . . : Not by might, nor by power, but by My spirit . . ." (Zech. 4:6).

## ONE OCTAVE TOO HIGH

We and the prophet have no language in common. To us the moral state of society, for all its stains and spots, seems fair and trim; to the prophet it is dreadful. So many deeds of charity are done, so much decency radiates day and night; yet to the prophet satiety of the conscience is prudery and flight from responsibility. Our standards are modest; our sense of injustice tolerable, timid; our moral indignation impermanent; yet human violence is interminable, unbearable, permanent. To us life is often serene, in the prophet's eye the world reels in confusion. The prophet makes no concession to man's capacity. Exhibiting little understanding for human weakness, he seems unable to extenuate the culpability of man.

Who could bear living in a state of disgust day and night? The conscience builds its confines, is subject to fatigue, longs for comfort, lulling, soothing. Yet those who are hurt, and He Who inhabits eternity, neither slumber nor sleep.

The prophet is sleepless and grave. The frankincense of charity fails to sweeten cruelties. Pomp, the scent of piety, mixed with ruthlessness, is sickening to him who is sleepless and grave.

Perhaps the prophet knew more about the secret obscenity of sheer unfairness, about the unnoticed malignancy of established patterns of indifference, than men whose knowledge depends solely on intelligence and observation.

> *The Lord made it known to me and I knew;*
> *Then Thou didst show me their evil deeds.*
> *Jeremiah 11:18*

The prophet's ear perceives the silent sigh.

In the Upanishads the physical world is devoid of value—unreal, a sham, an illusion, a dream—but in the Bible the physical world is real, the creation of God. Power, offspring, wealth, prosperity—all are blessings to be cherished, yet the thriving and boasting man, his triumphs and might, are regarded as frothy, tawdry, devoid of substance.

> *Behold, the nations are like a drop from a bucket,*
> *And are accounted as the dust on the scales; . . .*
> *All the nations are as nothing before Him,*
> *They are accounted by Him as less than nothing and emptiness.*
> *Isaiah 40:15, 17*

Civilization may come to an end, and the human species disappear. This world, no mere shadow of ideas in an upper sphere, is real, but not absolute; the world's reality is contingent upon compatibility with God. While others are intoxicated with the here and now, the prophet has a vision of an end.

> *I looked on the earth, and lo, it was waste and void;*
> *To the heavens, and they had no light.*

*I looked on the mountains, and lo, they were quaking,*
*All the hills moved to and fro.*
*I looked, and lo, there was no man;*
*All the birds of the air had fled.*
*I looked, and lo the fruitful land was a desert;*
*All its cities were laid in ruins*
*Before the Lord, before His fierce anger.*

*Jeremiah 4:23–26*

The prophet is human, yet he employs notes one octave too high for our ears. He experiences moments that defy our understanding. He is neither "a singing saint" nor "a moralizing poet," but an assaulter of the mind. Often his words begin to burn where conscience ends.

## AN ICONOCLAST

The prophet is an iconoclast, challenging the apparently holy, revered, and awesome. Beliefs cherished as certainties, institutions endowed with supreme sanctity, he exposes as scandalous pretensions.

To many a devout believer Jeremiah's words must have sounded blasphemous.

*To what purpose does frankincense come to Me from Sheba,*
*Or sweet cane from a distant land?*
*Your burnt offerings are not acceptable,*
*Nor your sacrifices pleasing to Me.*

*Jeremiah 6:20*

*Thus says the Lord of hosts, the God of Israel: Add your burnt offerings to your sacrifices, and eat the flesh. For in the day that I brought them out of the land of Egypt, I did not speak to your fathers or command them concerning burnt offerings and sacrifices. But this command I gave them: Obey My voice and I will be your God, and you shall be My people; and walk in all the way that I command you, that it may be well with you.*

*Jeremiah 7:21–23*

The prophet knew that religion could distort what the Lord demanded of man, that priests themselves had committed perjury by bearing false witness, condoning violence, tolerating hatred, calling for ceremonies instead of bursting forth with wrath and indignation at cruelty, deceit, idolatry, and violence.

To the people, religion was Temple, priesthood, incense: "This is the Temple of the Lord, the Temple of the Lord, the Temple of the Lord" (Jer. 7:4). Such piety Jeremiah brands as fraud and illusion. "Behold you trust in deceptive words to no avail," he calls (Jer. 7:8). Worship preceded or followed by evil acts becomes an absurdity. The holy place is doomed when people indulge in unholy deeds.

*Will you steal, murder, commit adultery, swear falsely, burn incense to Baal, and go after other gods that you have not known, and then come and stand before Me in this house, which is called by My name, and say, We are delivered!—only to go on doing all these abominations? Has this house, which is called by My name, become a den of robbers in your eyes? Behold, I Myself have seen it, says the Lord. Go now to My place that was in Shiloh, where I made My name dwell at first, and see what I did to it for the wickedness of My people Israel. And now, because you have done all these things, says the Lord, and when I spoke to you persistently you did not listen, and when I called you, you did not answer, therefore I will do to the house which is called by My name, and in which you trust, and to the place which I gave to you and to your fathers, as I did to Shiloh. And I will cast you out of My sight, as I cast out all your kinsmen, all the offspring of Ephraim.*

*Jeremiah, 7:9–15*

The prophet's message sounds incredible. In the pagan world the greatness, power, and survival of a god depended upon the greatness, power, and survival of the people, upon the city and shrine dedicated to his cult. The more triumphs the king achieved or the more countries he conquered, the greater was the god. A god who would let enemies destroy his shrine or conquer the people who worshiped him would commit suicide.

A tribal god was petitioned to slay the tribe's enemies because he was conceived as the god of that tribe and not as the god of the enemies. When the Roman armies were defeated in battle, the people, indignant, did not hesitate to wreck the images of their god.

The prophets of Israel proclaim that the enemy may be God's instrument in history. The God of Israel calls the archenemy of His people "Assyria, the rod of My anger" (Isa. 10:5; cf. 13:5; 5:26; 7:18; 8:7). "Nebuchadnezzar, the king of Babylon, My servant" whom I will bring "against this land and its inhabitants" (Jer. 25:9; 27:6; 43:10). Instead of cursing the enemy, the prophets condemn their own nation.

What gave them the strength to "demythologize" precious certainties, to attack what was holy, to hurl blasphemies at priest and king, to stand up against all in the name of God? The prophets must have been shattered by some cataclysmic experience in order to be able to shatter others.

## AUSTERITY AND COMPASSION

The words of the prophet are stern, sour, stinging. But behind his austerity is love and compassion for mankind. Ezekiel sets forth what all other prophets imply: "Have I any pleasure in the death of the wicked, says the Lord God, and not rather than he should turn from his way and life?" (Ezek. 18:23.) Indeed, every prediction of disaster is in itself an exhortation to repentance. The prophet is sent not only to upbraid, but also to "strengthen the weak hands and make firm the feeble knees" (Isa. 35:3). Almost every prophet brings consolation, promise, and the hope of reconciliation along with censure and castigation. He begins with *a message of doom;* he concludes with *a message of hope.**

The prominent theme is exhortation, not mere prediction. While

---

*See *Sifre Deuteronomy,* 342, beginning. Some modern scholars maintain that the pre-exilic prophets had no message except one of doom, that true prophecy is essentially prophecy of woe. Yet such a view can be maintained only by declaring, often on insufficient grounds, that numerous passages are interpolations. See H. H. Rowley, *The Servant of the Lord* (London, 1952), p. 125.

it is true that foretelling is an important ingredient and may serve as a sign of the prophet's authority (Deut. 18:22; Isa. 41:22; 43:9), his essential task is to declare the word of God to the here and now; to disclose the future in order to illumine what is involved in the present.*

## SWEEPING ALLEGATIONS

If justice means giving every person what he deserves, the scope and severity of the accusations by the prophets of Israel hardly confirmed that principle. The prophets were unfair to the people of Israel. Their sweeping allegations, overstatements, and generalizations defied standards of accuracy. Some of the exaggerations reach the unbelievable.

> *Run to and fro through the streets of Jerusalem,*
> *Look and take note!*
> *Search her squares to see*
> *If you can find a man,*
> *One who does justice*
> *And seeks truth; . . .*
> *But they all alike had broken the yoke,*
> *They had burst the bonds. . . .*
> *From the least to the greatest of them,*
> *Every one is greedy for unjust gain;*
> *And from prophet to priest,*
> *Every one deals falsely. . . .*
> *There is nothing but oppression within her.*
> *Jeremiah 5:1, 5; 6:13; 8:10; 6:6*

In contrast to Amos, whose main theme is condemnation of the rich for the oppresion of the poor, Hosea does not single out a particular section of the community.

*See the divergent views of R. H. Charles, *Critical and Exegetical Commentary on the Book of Daniel* (Oxford, 1929), p. xxvi, and A. Guillaume, *Prophecy and Divination* (London, 1938), pp. 111 f. See also H. H. Rowley, *loc. cit.*

*There is no truth, no love, and no knowledge of God in the land;*
*Swearing and lying, killing and stealing, and committing adultery,*
*They break all bonds, and blood touches blood.*

*Hosea 4:1–2*

Isaiah calls Judah a "sinful nation, . . . laden with iniquity" (1:4), "rebellious children" (30:1), "a people of unclean lips" (6:5). Indeed, the prophets have occasionally limited the guilt to the elders, princes, and priests, implying the innocence of those not involved in leadership. The assurance given in the name of the Lord,

> *Tell the righteous that all shall be well with them, . . .*
> *Woe to the wicked! It shall be ill with him,*
> *For what his hands have done shall be done to him,*

is emphatically addressed to the righteous men in Israel, spoken of in the plural, as well as to the wicked individual in Israel, spoken of in the singular (Isa. 3:10–11). The exclamation in the name of the Lord, "Wicked men are found among My people!" (Jer. 5:26), betrays, it seems, a more sober appraisal of the situation and may be kept in mind as a modification of the numerous extravagant qualifications uttered by the prophets *in their own names.*\*

Great orators in Rome had frequently manifested courage in publicly condemning the abuse of power by individuals. But the prophets challenge the whole country: kings, priests, false prophets, and the entire nation. The historical accounts in the books of Kings would certainly have referred to the moral corruption, had it been as grave as the prophets maintain.

In terms of statistics the prophets' statements are grossly inaccurate. Yet their concern is not with facts, but with the meaning of facts.

---

\*Rhetorical exaggeration is a frequent mode of the biblical style of writing. Rabbi Simeon ben Gamliel, who lived in Palestine in the first half of the second century A.D., asserted that Scripture employs hyperbolic phrases, citing Deut. 1:28 as an example, *Sifre Deuteronomy*, p. 25. A similar view was expressed by Rabbi Ammi of the third century, *Tamid* 29a. Cf. also E. König, *Stilistik, Rhetorik, Poetik in Bezug auf die Biblische Literatur* (Leipzig, 1900), p. 69; C. Douglas, *Overstatement in the New Testament* (New York, 1931), pp. 3–36.

The significance of human deeds, the true image of man's existence, cannot be expressed by statistics. The rabbis were not guilty of exaggeration in asserting, "Whoever destroys a single soul should be considered the same as one who has destroyed a whole world. And whoever saves one single soul is to be considered the same as one who has saved the whole world."

Extremely minute, yet vital entities formerly unknown to the mind were suddenly disclosed by the microscope. What seems to be exaggeration is often only a deeper penetration, for the prophets see the world from the point of view of God, as transcendent, not immanent truth.

Modern thought tends to extenuate personal responsibility. Understanding the complexity of human nature, the interrelationship of individual and society, of consciousness and the subconscious, we find it difficult to isolate the deed from those circumstances in which it was done. But new insights may obscure essential vision, and man's conscience grows scales: excuses, pretense, self-pity. Guilt may disappear; no crime is absolute, no sin devoid of apology. Within the limits of the human mind, relativity is true and merciful. Yet the mind's scope embraces but a fragment of society, a few instants of history; it thinks of what has happened, it is unable to imagine what might have happened.

## FEW ARE GUILTY, ALL ARE RESPONSIBLE

What was happening in Israel surpassed its intrinsic significance. Israel's history comprised a drama of God and all men. God's kingship and man's hope were at stake in Jerusalem. God was alone in the world, unknown or discarded. The countries of the world were full of abominations, violence, falsehood. Here was one land, one people, cherished and chosen for the purpose of transforming the world. *This* people's failure was most serious. The Beloved of God worshiped the Baalim (Hos. 11:1–2); the vineyard of the Lord yielded wild grapes (Isa. 5:2); Israel, holy to the Lord, "defiled My land, made My heritage an abomination" (Jer. 2:3, 7).

Defining truth as the conformity of assertion to facts, we may censure the prophets for being inaccurate, incongruous, even absurd; defining truth as reality reflected in the mind, we see *prophetic* truth as reality reflected in God's mind, the world *sub specie dei*.

Prophetic accusations are perhaps more easily understood in the light of the book of Job's thesis that men might judge a human being just and pure, whom God, Who finds angels imperfect, would not.*

> *Can mortal man be righteous before God?*
> *Can a man be pure before His Maker?*
> *Even in His servants He puts no trust,*
> *His angels He charges with error;*
> *How much more those who dwell in houses of clay,*
> *Whose foundation is in the dust,*
> *Who are crushed before the moth. . . .*
> *What is man, that he can be clean?*
> *Or he that is born of a woman, that he can be righteous?*
> *Behold God puts no trust in His holy ones,*
> *The heavens are not clean in His sight;*
> *How much less one who is abominable and corrupt,*
> *A man who drinks iniquity like water!*
>
> Job 4:17–19; 15:14–16

"For there is no man who does not sin" (I Kings 8:46). "Surely there is not a righteous man on earth who does good and never sins" (Eccles. 7:20).

It is with a bitter sense of the tremendous contrast between God's righteousness and man's failure that the psalmist prays:

> *Enter not into judgment with Thy servant;*
> *For no man living is righteous before Thee.*
>
> Psalm 143:2

Men are greatly praised when worthy of being reproved. Only a strong heart can bear bitter invectives.

---

*Eliphaz' thesis is accepted by Job (9:2); see also 25:4.

Above all, the prophets remind us of the moral state of a people: Few are guilty, but all are responsible. If we admit that the individual is in some measure conditioned or affected by the spirit of society, an individual's crime discloses society's corruption. In a community not indifferent to suffering, uncompromisingly impatient with cruelty and falsehood, continually concerned for God and every man, crime would be infrequent rather than common.

## THE BLAST FROM HEAVEN

To a person endowed with prophetic sight, everyone else appears blind; to a person whose ear perceives God's voice, everyone else appears deaf. No one is just; no knowing is strong enough, no trust complete enough. The prophet hates the approximate, he shuns the middle of the road. Man must live on the summit to avoid the abyss. There is nothing to hold to except God. Carried away by the challenge, the demand to straighten out man's ways, the prophet is strange, one-sided, an unbearable extremist.

Others may suffer from the terror of cosmic aloneness; the prophet is overwhelmed by the grandeur of divine presence. He is incapable of isolating the world. There is an interaction between man and God which to disregard is an act of insolence. Isolation is a fairy tale.

Where an idea is the father of faith, faith must conform to the ideas of the given system. In the Bible the realness of God came first, and the task was how to live in a way compatible with His presence. Man's coexistence with God determines the course of history.

The prophet disdains those for whom God's presence is comfort and security; to him it is a challenge, an incessant demand. God is compassion, not compromise; justice, though not inclemency. The prophet's predictions can always be proved wrong by a change in man's conduct, but never the certainty that God is full of compassion.

The prophet's word is a scream in the night. While the world is at ease and asleep, the prophet feels the blast from heaven.

## THE COALITION OF CALLOUSNESS AND AUTHORITY

The prophet faces a coalition of callousness and established authority, and undertakes to stop a mighty stream with mere words. Had the purpose been to express great ideas, prophecy would have had to be acclaimed as a triumph. Yet the purpose of prophecy is to conquer callousness, to change the inner man as well as to revolutionize history.

It is embarrassing to be a prophet. There are so many pretenders, predicting peace and prosperity, offering cheerful words, adding strength to self-reliance, while the prophet predicts disaster, pestilence, agony, and destruction. People need exhortations to courage, endurance, confidence, fighting spirit, but Jeremiah proclaims: You are about to die if you do not have a change of heart and cease being callous to the word of God. He sends shudders over the whole city, at a time when the will to fight is most important.

By the standards of ancient religions, the great prophets were rather unimpressive. The paraphernalia of nimbus and evidence, such as miracles, were not at their disposal.*

## LONELINESS AND MISERY

None of the prophets seems enamored with being a prophet nor proud of his attainment. What drove Jeremiah, for instance, to being a prophet?

*Very few miracles are ascribed to the prophets; see Isa. 38:7–8. Miracles have no probative value; see Deut. 13:1–3. What is offered to Ahaz (Isa. 7:11) is a sign rather than a miracle. On the meaning of this passage, see M. Buber, *The Prophetic Faith* (New York, 1949), p. 138.

Of Samuel it is reported that he called upon the Lord, and the Lord sent thunder and rain that day; and all the people greatly feared the Lord and Samuel (I Sam. 12:18). Gideon (Judg. 6:36–40) and Elijah (I Kings 18:36–38) implored God for miraculous signs. The miracle of the sundial (Isa. 38:1–8) was not performed for the purpose of verification. Miracles did not always have the power to put an end to uncertainty, since the magicians were able to duplicate them (see Exod. 8:7 [H. 7:11, 22]). The only medium of the prophet was the word or the symbolic act to illustrate its content. Even predictions of things to come did not always serve to verify the prophet's word.

*Cursed be the day*
*On which I was born! . . .*
*Because He did not kill me in the womb;*
*So my mother would have been my grave, . . .*
*Why did I come forth out of the womb*
*To see toil and sorrow,*
*And spend my days in shame?*
*Jeremiah 20:14, 17, 18*

Over the life of a prophet words are invisibly inscribed: All flattery abandon, ye who enter here. To be a prophet is both a distinction and an affliction. The mission he performs is distasteful to him and repugnant to others; no reward is promised him and no reward could temper its bitterness. The prophet bears scorn and reproach (Jer. 15:15). He is stigmatized as a madman by his contemporaries, and, by some modern scholars, as abnormal.

*They hate him who reproves in the gate,*
*They abhor him who speaks the truth.*
*Amos 5:10*

Loneliness and misery were only part of the reward that prophecy brought to Jeremiah: "I sat alone because Thy hand was upon me" (15:17). Mocked, reproached, and persecuted, he would think of casting away his task:

*If I say, I will not mention Him,*
*Or speak any more in His name,*
*There is my heart as it were a burning fire*
*Shut up in my bones,*
*And I am weary with holding it in,*
*And I cannot.*
*Jeremiah 20:9*

Jeremiah, when chosen to become a prophet, was told by the Lord: "And I, behold, I make you this day a fortified city, an iron pillar, and bronze walls, against the whole land, against the kings of

Judah, its princes, its priests, and the people of the land" (Jer. 1:18). And later he was reassured: "They will fight against you, but they shall not prevail over you" (Jer. 15:20).

The prophet is a lonely man. He alienates the wicked as well as the pious, the cynics as well as the believers, the priests and the princes, the judges and the false prophets. But to be a prophet means to challenge and to defy and to cast out fear.

The life of a prophet is not futile. People may remain deaf to a prophet's admonitions; they cannot remain callous to a prophet's existence. At the very beginning of his career, Ezekiel was told not to entertain any illusions about the effectiveness of his mission:

> *And you, son of man, be not afraid of them, nor be afraid of their words, though briers and thorns are with you and you sit upon scorpions; be not afraid of their words, nor be dismayed at their looks, . . . Behold, I have made your face hard against their faces, and your forehead hard against their foreheads. Like adamant harder than flint have I made your forehead; fear them not, nor be dismayed at their looks, . . . The people also are impudent and stubborn: I send you to them; and you shall say to them, Thus says the Lord God. And whether they hear or refuse to hear . . . they will know that there has been a prophet among them.*
>
> Ezekiel 2:6; 3:8–9; 2:4–5; cf. 3:27

The prophet's duty is to speak to the people, "whether they hear or refuse to hear." A grave responsibility rests upon the prophet:

> *If the watchman sees the sword coming and does not blow the trumpet, so that the people are not warned, and the sword comes, and takes any one of them; that man is taken away in his iniquity, but his blood I will require at the watchman's hand. So you, son of man, I have made a watchman for the house of Israel; whenever you hear a word from My mouth, you shall give them warning from Me.*
>
> Ezekiel 33:6–7; cf. 3:16–21

The main vocation of a prophet is "to declare to Jacob his transgression and to Israel his sin" (Mic. 3:8), to let the people know "that it is evil and bitter . . . to forsake . . . God" (Jer. 2:19), and to call upon them to return. But do they attain their end? Publicly Jeremiah declared to the people:

*For twenty-three years . . . the word of the Lord has come to me, and I have spoken persistently to you, but you have not listened. You have neither listened nor inclined your ears to hear, although the Lord persistently sent to you all his servants the prophets, saying, Turn now, every one of you, from his evil way and wrong doings. . . . Yet you have not listened to Me, says the Lord.*

*Jeremiah 25:3–7*

Yet being a prophet is also joy, elation, delight:

*Thy words were found, and I ate them;*
*Thy words became to me a joy*
*The delight of my heart;*
*For I am called by Thy name,*
*O Lord, God of hosts.*

*Jeremiah 15:16*

## THE PEOPLE'S TOLERANCE

The striking surprise is that prophets of Israel were tolerated at all by their people. To the patriots, they seemed pernicious; to the pious multitude, blasphemous; to the men in authority, seditious.

*Cry aloud, spare not,*
*Lift up your voice like a trumpet;*
*Declare to My people their transgression,*
*To the house of Jacob their sins.*

*Isaiah 58:1*

In the language of Jeremiah, the prophet's word is fire, and the people wood, "and the fire shall devour them" (Jer. 5:14; cf. Hos. 6:5).

How could the people endure men who proclaimed in the name of God,

> *I will send a fire upon Judah,*
> *And it shall devour the strongholds of Jerusalem!*
>
> Amos 2:5

> *Zion shall be plowed as a field;*
> *Jerusalem shall become a heap of ruins,*
> *And the mountain of the house a wooded height!*
>
> Jeremiah 26:18; cf. Micah 3:12

It must have sounded like treason when Amos called upon the enemies of Israel to witness the wickedness of Samaria.

> *Proclaim to the strongholds in Assyria,*
> *And to the strongholds in the land of Egypt,*
> *And say: "Assemble yourselves upon the mountains of Samaria,*
> *And see the great tumults within her,*
> *And the oppressions in her midst!"*
>
> Amos 3:9

It is strange, indeed, that a people to whom the names of Sodom and Gomorrah were charged with extreme insult would brook a prophet who did not hesitate to address his audience as "you rulers of Sodom . . . you people of Gomorrah" (Isa. 1:10).

> *And on that day, says the Lord God,*
> *I will make the sun go down at noon,*
> *And darken the earth in broad daylight.*
> *I will turn your feasts into mourning,*
> *And all your songs into lamentation; I will bring sackcloth*
>    *upon all loins,*
> *And baldness on every head; I will make it like the mourning*
>    *for an only son,*
> *And the end of it like a bitter day.*
>
> Amos 8:9–10

## AN ASSAYER, MESSENGER, WITNESS

The prophet is a watchman (Hos. 9:8), a servant (Amos 3:7; Jer. 25:4; 26:5), a messenger of God (Hag. 1:13), "an assayer and tester" of the people's ways (Jer. 6:27, RSV); "whenever you hear a word from My mouth, you shall give them warning from Me" (Ezek. 3:17). The prophet's eye is directed to the contemporary scene; the society and its conduct are the main theme of his speeches. Yet his ear is inclined to God. He is a person struck by the glory and presence of God, overpowered by the hand of God. Yet his true greatness is his ability to hold God and man in a single thought.

The spiritual status of a diviner, not to be confused with a prophet, is higher than that of his fellow man; the diviner is regarded as more exalted than other members of his society. However, the measure of such superiority is that of individuality. In contrast, the prophet feels himself placed not only above other members of his own society; he is placed in a relationship transcending his own total community, and even the realm of other nations and kingdoms. The measure of his superiority is that of universality. This is why the essence of his eminence is not adequately described by the term *charisma*. Not the fact of his having been affected, but the fact of his having received a power to affect others is supreme in his existence. His sense of election and personal endowment is overshadowed by his sense of a history-shaping power. Jeremiah, for example, was appointed "a prophet to the nations" (1:5). He was told:

> *See, I have set you this day over nations and over kingdoms,*
> *To pluck up and to break down,*
> *To destroy and to overthrow,*
> *To build and to plant.*
>
> Jeremiah 1:10

It is common to characterize the prophet as a messenger of God, thus to differentiate him from the tellers of fortune, givers of oracles, seers, and ecstatics. Such a characterization expresses only one aspect of his consciousness. The prophet claims to be far more than a messenger. He is a person who stands in the presence of God (Jer. 15:19), who stands "in the council of the Lord" (Jer. 23:18), who is a participant, as it were, in the council of God, not a bearer of dispatches whose function is limited to being sent on errands. He is a counselor as well as a messenger.

> *Surely the Lord God does nothing*
> *Without revealing His secret*
> *To His servants the prophets,*
>
> *Amos 3:7*

When the secret revealed is one of woe, the prophet does not hesitate to challenge the intention of the Lord:

> *O Lord God, forgive, I beseech Thee!*
> *How can Jacob stand?*
> *He is so small!*
>
> *Amos 7:2*

When the lives of others are at stake, the prophet does not say, "Thy will be done!" but rather, "Thy will be changed."

> *The Lord repented concerning this;*
> *It shall not be, said the Lord.*
>
> *Amos 7:3*

It is impossible for us to intuit the grandeur of the prophetic consciousness. A person to whom the spirit of God comes, becomes radically transformed; he is "turned into another man" (I Sam. 10:6). The vastness and gravity of the power bestowed upon the prophet seem to burst the normal confines of human consciousness. The gift he is blessed with is not a skill, but rather the gift of being guided and restrained, of being moved and curbed. His mission is to speak, yet in the vision of consecration Ezekiel, for example, was forewarned of the inability to speak. "Cords will be placed upon you . . . and I will make your tongue cleave to the roof of your mouth, so that you shall be dumb and unable to reprove them; . . . But when I speak with you, I will open your mouth, and you shall say to them, Thus says the Lord God" (Ezek. 3:25–27).

As a witness, the prophet is more than a messenger. As a messenger, his task is to deliver the word; as a witness, he must bear testimony that the word is divine.

The words the prophet utters are not offered as souvenirs. His speech to the people is not a reminiscence, a report, hearsay. The prophet not only conveys; he reveals. He almost does unto others what God does unto him. In speaking, the prophet reveals God. This is the marvel of a prophet's work: in his words, *the invisible God becomes audible*. He does not prove or argue. The thought he has to convey is more than language can contain. Divine power bursts in the words. The authority of the prophet is in the Presence his words reveal.

There are no proofs for the existence of the God of Abraham. There are only witnesses. The greatness of the prophet lies not only in the ideas he expressed, but also in the moments he experienced. The prophet is a witness, and his words a testimony—to *His* power and judgment, to *His* justice and mercy.

The contradictions in the prophetic message seem perplexing. The book of Amos, out of which come the words, "The end has come upon My people Israel" (8:2) and "Fallen no more to rise is the virgin Israel" (5:2), concludes with the prediction:

> *I will restore the fortunes of My people Israel,*
> *And they shall rebuild the ruined cities and inhabit them;*
> *They shall plant vineyards and drink their wine,*
> *And they shall make gardens and eat their fruit.*
> *I will plant them upon their land,*
> *And they shall never again be plucked up*
> *Out of the land which I have given them,*
> *Says the Lord your God.*
>
> Amos 9:14–15

What hidden bond exists between the word of wrath and the word of compassion, between "consuming fire" and "everlasting love"?

Does the apparent contradiction within the assertions of a prophet destroy the validity of his message? It would if prophecy dealt only with laws or principles. But the prophet deals with relations between God and man, where contradiction is inevitable. Escape from God and return to Him are inextricable parts of man's existence. Conformity to logical standards is not characteristic of man's conduct, which is why contradiction is inherent in prophecy.

We will have to look for prophetic coherence, not *in what* the prophet says but *of Whom* he speaks. Indeed, not even the word of God is the ultimate object and theme of his consciousness. The ultimate object and theme of his consciousness is God, of Whom the prophet knows that above His judgment and above His anger stands His mercy.

The prophetic utterance has, therefore, no finality. It does not set forth a comprehensive law, but a single perspective. It is expressed *ad hoc,* often *ad hominem,* and must not be generalized.

## THE PRIMARY CONTENT OF EXPERIENCE

What is the primary content of prophetic experience, the thought immediately felt, the motive directly present to the prophet's mind? What are the facts of consciousness that stirred him so deeply? Is it a sense of anxiety about the fate and future of the people or of the state? An impulse of patriotism? Is it personal irritation at the violation of moral laws and standards, a spontaneous reaction of the conscience against what is wrong or evil? Moral indignation?

In a stricken hour comes the word of the prophet. There is tension between God and man. What does the word say? What does the prophet feel? The prophet is not only a censurer and accuser, but also a defender and consoler. Indeed, the attitude he takes to the tension that obtains between God and the people is characterized by a dichotomy. In the presence of God he takes the part of the people. In the presence of the people he takes the part of God.

It would be wrong to maintain that the prophet is a person who plays the role of "the third party," offering his good offices to bring about reconciliation. His view is oblique. God is the focal point of his thought, and the world is seen as reflected in God. Indeed, the main task of prophetic thinking is to bring the world into divine focus. This, then, explains his way of thinking. He does not take a direct approach to things. It is not a straight line, spanning subject and object, but rather a triangle—through God to the object. An expression of a purely personal feeling betrays itself seldom, in isolated instances. The prophet is endowed with the insight that enables him to say, not I love or I condemn, but God loves or God condemns.

The prophet does not judge the people by timeless norms, but from the point of view of God. Prophecy proclaims what happened to God as well as what will happen to the people. In judging human affairs, it unfolds a divine situation. Sin is not only the violation of a law, it is as if sin were as much a loss to God as to man. God's role is not spectatorship but involvement. He and man meet mysteriously in the human deed. The prophet cannot say Man without thinking God.

Therefore, the prophetic speeches are not factual pronouncements. What we hear is not objective criticism or the cold proclamation of doom. The style of legal, objective utterance is alien to the prophet. He dwells upon God's inner motives, not only upon His historical decisions. He discloses *a divine pathos,* not just a divine judgment. The pages of the prophetic writings are filled with echoes of divine love and disappointment, mercy and indignation. The God of Israel is never impersonal.

This divine pathos is the key to inspired prophecy. God is involved in the life of man. A personal relationship binds Him to Israel; there is an interweaving of the divine in the affairs of the nation. The divine commandments are not mere recommendations for man, but express divine concern, which, realized or repudiated, is of personal importance to Him. The reaction of the divine self (Amos 6:8; Jer. 5:9; 51:14), its manifestations in the form of love, mercy, disappointment, or anger convey the profound intensity of the divine inwardness.

From the descriptions later in this book of the part pathos plays in the lives and messages of the great prophets, we will discover its meaning as a conception and as an object of experience.*

## THE PROPHET'S RESPONSE

In view of the insistence by the prophets of Israel upon the divine origin of their utterances, one inclines to agree with the ancient conception of the prophet as a mere mouthpiece of God. A careful analysis, however, compels us to reject the characterization of prophetic inspiration as a mere act of passive and unconscious receptivity (see pp. 456 f.). What, indeed, was the nature of the prophet's transmission of what he perceived? Was it an impersonal reproduction of an inspired message, a mere copy of the contents of inspiration, or did prophetic experience involve participation of the person in the act of transmission or even inspiration? Is prophecy to be thought of as a technical activity like divination? Is the prophet a person whose consciousness, in consequence of divine influence, utterly dissolves in surrender to the divine word, so that all spontaneous response and reaction is excluded?

The conception of the prophets as nothing but mouthpieces, the assumption that their hearts remain unaffected, would almost compel us to apply to them the words that Jeremiah used of the people:

> *Thou art near in their mouth*
> *And far from their heart.*
> *Jeremiah 12:2*

The prophet is not a mouthpiece, but a person; not an instrument, but a partner, an associate of God. Emotional detachment would be understandable only if there were a command which required the suppression of emotion, forbidding one to serve God "with all your heart, with all your soul, with all your might." God, we are told, asks not only for "works," for action, but above all for love, awe, and fear.

---

*See especially pp. 297 f. and the Appendix: A Note on the Meaning of Pathos, p. 627.

We are called upon to "wash" our hearts (Jer. 4:14), to remove "the foreskin" of the heart (Jer. 4:4), to return with the whole heart (Jer. 3:10). "You will seek Me and find Me, when you seek Me with all your heart" (Jer. 29:13). The new covenant which the Lord will make with the house of Israel will be written upon their hearts (Jer. 31:31–34).

The prophet is no hireling who performs his duty in the employ of the Lord. The usual descriptions or definitions of prophecy fade to insignificance when applied, for example, to Jeremiah. "A religious experience," "communion with God," "a perception of His voice"—such terms hardly convey what happened to his soul: the overwhelming impact of the divine pathos upon his mind and heart, completely involving and gripping his personality in its depths, and the unrelieved distress which sprang from his intimate involvement. The task of the prophet is to convey the word of God. Yet the word is aglow with the pathos. One cannot understand the word without sensing the pathos. And one could not impassion others and remain unstirred. The prophet should not be regarded as an ambassador who must be dispassionate in order to be effective.

An analysis of prophetic utterances shows that the fundamental experience of the prophet is a fellowship with the feelings of God, a *sympathy with the divine pathos,* a communion with the divine consciousness which comes about through the prophet's reflection of, or participation in, the divine pathos. The typical prophetic state of mind is one of being taken up into the heart of the divine pathos. Sympathy is the prophet's answer to inspiration, the correlative to revelation.

Prophetic sympathy is a response to transcendent sensibility. It is not, like love, an attraction to the divine Being, but the assimilation of the prophet's emotional life to the divine, an assimilation of function, not of being. The emotional experience of the prophet becomes the focal point for the prophet's understanding of God. He lives not only his personal life, but also the life of God. The prophet hears God's voice and feels His heart. He tries to impart the pathos of the message together with its logos. As an imparter his soul overflows, speaking as he does out of the fullness of his sympathy.

# 2

# Amos

## Amos and His Contemporaries

Under the long and brilliant reign of Jeroboam II (*ca.* 786–746 B.C.E.), the Northern Kingdom, also called the Kingdom of Israel, reached the summit of its material power and prosperity, expanding its territory northward at the expense of Hamath and Damascus, and

SELECTED BIBLIOGRAPHY: W. R. Harper, *A Critical and Exegetical Commentary on Amos and Hosea* ("The International Critical Commentary" [New York, 1915]); R. S. Cripps, *A Critical and Exegetical Commentary on the Book of Amos* (London, 1929); K. Cramer, *Amos, Versuch einer theologischen Interpretation* (Stuttgart, 1930); J. Morgenstern, *Amos Studies* (Cincinnati, 1941); A. Neher, *Amos: contribution à l'étude du prophétisme* (Paris, 1950); S. Spiegel, *Amos versus Amaziah* (New York, 1957); Y. Kaufmann, *The Religion of Israel*, VI (Heb.; Jerusalem, 1954), 56–92; (Eng.; translated and abridged by M. Greenberg [Chicago, 1960]), pp. 363 ff.; A. B. Ehrlich, *Randglossen zur Hebräischen Bibel*, vol. V. (Leipzig, 1912). For the history of the period see A. T. Olmstead, *History of Assyria* (New York, 1923), pp. 175 ff.; R. W. Rogers, *A History of Babylonia and Assyria*, II (New York, 1900), 104 ff.; *Cambridge Modern History*, III (Cambridge, 1907 ff.), 32–87; H. R. Hall, *The Ancient History of the Near East* (London, 1950), pp. 461–494; G. Contenau, *Everyday Life in Babylon and Assyria* (London, 1954); L. W. King, *A History of Babylon* (New York, 1919), pp. 270 ff.; M. Noth, *The History of Israel* (New York, 1958); J. Bright, *A History of Israel* (Philadelphia, 1959); W. F. Albright, "The Biblical Period," *The Jews*, vol. I, ed. by L. Finkelstein (New York, 1949); *idem, Archeology and the Religion of Israel* (Baltimore, 1953); *idem, From the Stone Age to Christianity* (2nd ed.; New York, 1957).

southward at the expense of Judah. During this entire period Assyria was weak, and Syria on the decline; Jeroboam took advantage of the weakness of both to extend his dominion, foster commerce, and accumulate wealth.

When Amos appeared in the North there was pride (6:13–14), plenty, and splendor in the land, elegance in the cities, and might in the palaces. The rich had their summer and winter palaces adorned with costly ivory (3:15), gorgeous couches with damask pillows (3:12), on which they reclined at their sumptuous feasts. They planted pleasant vineyards, anointed themselves with precious oils (6:4–6; 5:11); their women, compared by Amos to the fat cows of Bashan, were addicted to wine (4:1). At the same time there was no justice in the land (3:10), the poor were afflicted, exploited, even sold into slavery (2:6–8; 5:11), and the judges were corrupt (5:12). In the midst of this atmosphere arose Amos, a shepherd, to exclaim:

> *Woe to those who are at ease in Zion,*
> *And to those who feel secure on the mountain of Samaria,*
> *The notable men of the first of the nations,*
> *To whom the house of Israel come!*
> *Pass over to Calneh, and see;*
> *And thence go to Hamath the great;*
> *Then go down to Gath of the Philistines.*
> *Are they better than these kingdoms?*
> *Or is their territory greater than your territory,*
> *O you who put far away the evil day,*
> *And bring near the seat of violence?*
> *Woe to those who lie upon beds of ivory,*
> *And stretch themselves upon their couches,*
> *And eat lambs from the flock,*
> *And calves from the midst of the stall;*
> *Who sing idle songs to the sound of the harp,*
> *And like David invent for themselves instruments of music;*
> *Who drink wine in bowls,*
> *And anoint themselves with the finest oils,*

*But are not grieved over the ruin of Joseph!*
*Therefore they shall now be the first of those to go into exile,*
*And the revelry of those who stretch themselves shall pass away.*

*Amos 6:1–7*

Amos was working as a shepherd and dresser of sycamore trees when he was suddenly overwhelmed by God and called to be a prophet.* Although his home was in Tekoa, a village southeast of Bethlehem in the Kingdom of Judah, his utterances were all directed against the Kingdom in the North, against Samaria, Bethel, and the rulers of the land.

> *Fallen, no more to rise,*
> *Is the virgin Israel;*
> *Forsaken on her land,*
> *With none to raise her up.*
>
> *Amos 5:2*

"The end has come upon My people Israel," the Lord said to him in a vision (8:2).

What is the nature of Him whose word overwhelmed the herdsman Amos? Is His grandeur like a towering mountain? Is His majesty comparable to an inscrutable constellation? Is He sublime as the morning and mysterious as darkness? All comparisons fade to insignificance when confronted with what a person such as Amos asserted:

> *For lo, He who forms the mountains, and creates the wind,*
> *And declares to man what is his thought;*
> *Who makes the morning darkness,*
> *And treads on the heights of the earth—*
> *The Lord, the God of hosts, is His name. . . .*
> *He who made the Pleiades and Orion,*
> *And turns deep darkness into the morning,*
> *And darkens the day into night,*

---

*According to J. Morgenstern, *Amos Studies*, I (Cincinnati, 1941), 161–179, Amos began his prophetic activity in 752/1.

*Who calls for the waters of the sea,*
*And pours them out upon the surface of the earth,*
*The Lord is His name,*
*Who makes destruction flash forth against the strong,*
*So that destruction comes upon the fortress.*

*Amos 4:13; 5:8–9*

When Amos called upon the people to "seek the Lord and live" (5:6), he meant literally what he said. His words raged, proclaiming God's loathing for all men to know (6:8; 5:21).

## GOD AND THE NATIONS

*The Lord roars from Zion,*
*And utters His voice from Jerusalem;*
*The pastures of the shepherds mourn,*
*And the top of Carmel withers.*
*Amos 1:2; cf. Joel 3:16 [H. 4:16]\**

These words are strange and inexplicable to us. Most of us who care for the world bewail God's dreadful silence, while Amos appears smitten by God's mighty voice. He did not hear a whisper, "a still small voice," but a voice like a lion's roaring that drives shepherd and flock into panic.

What had provoked the anger of the Lord? What had happened to shatter His silence? The answer is given in an account of events that happened in the world of which Amos was a part. Two things stand out in the prophet's condemnation: the absence of loyalty and the absence of pity. Tyre had violated a treaty, "the covenant of brotherhood," and Edom had "pursued his brother with the sword, and cast off all pity, and his anger tore perpetually, and he kept his wrath for ever." Syria, ruled from its capital in Damascus, had tortured and slaughtered the people of Gilead "with threshing sledges of iron." Amos recalled how Philistia, ruled from Gaza, its capital, had carried

*On the voice of God as thunder, see Pss. 18:14; 29:3–9.

a whole people into captivity, selling them into slavery, in order to make some money; how the Ammonites had ripped up women with child in Gilead in order to annex a strip of territory. He ended with Moab, how they had burned the bones of the king of Edom into lime. This act of vandalism had not even the poor excuse of being profitable: it brought nothing but the gratification of hate (1:3–2:3).

## THE ANGER OF THE LORD

Yet the anger of the Lord was directed not only at the nations, but also at the people He had chosen. The people of Judah had rejected the Torah of the Lord, and had not kept His statutes (2:4). And the people of Israel, the Northern Kingdom (the creditors),

> . . . *sell the righteous\* for silver,*
> *And the needy for a pair of shoes—*
> *They that trample the head of the poor into the dust of the earth,*
> *And turn aside the way of the afflicted.*
>
> Amos 2:6, 7; cf. 5:11

Man may remain callous, but God cannot keep silent. Terrible is His voice, because He has a heart.

> *The Lord has sworn by the pride of Jacob:*
> *Surely I will never forget any of their deeds. . . .*
> *I will make the sun go down at noon,*
> *And darken the earth in broad daylight.*
> *I will turn your feasts into mourning,*
> *And all your songs into lamentation;*
> *I will bring sackcloth upon all loins,*
> *And baldness on every head;*
> *I will make it like the mourning for an only son,*
> *And the end of it like a bitter day.*
>
> Amos 8:7, 9–10

---

\*Probably "the innocent." Debtors were sold into slavery because they could not pay some trifling debts.

It was not only iniquity that had aroused the anger of the Lord; it was also piety, upon which His words fell like a thunderbolt. Sacrifice and ritual were regarded as the way that leads to the Creator. The men and the institutions dedicated to sacrificial worship were powerful and revered. Came a "dresser of sycamores" from the wilderness of Judah and proclaimed the word of God:

> *Even though you offer Me your burnt offerings and cereal offerings,*
> *I will not accept them,*
> *And the peace offerings of your fatted beasts*
> *I will not look upon.*
> *Take away from Me the noise of your songs;*
> *To the melody of your harps I will not listen.*
> *But let justice well up as waters,*
> *And righteousness as a mighty stream.*
>
> *Amos 5:22–24*

The juxtaposition of observing the laws of the Sabbath while waiting for the day to come to an end and of dealing "deceitfully with false balances" (8:5) strikes home a melancholy irony, easily lost on the modern reader. Man is waiting for the day of sanctity to come to an end so that cheating and exploitation can be resumed. This is a stunning condemnation. We are ready to judge a ritual act on its own merit. Properly performed, its value is undisputed. Yet, the prophet speaks with derision of those who combine ritual with iniquity.

The prophet's invectives could not be tolerated by his people. And when he went so far as to predict in public that the king of Israel would die by the sword and that the people of Israel would be led away captive, the outraged priest of Bethel, Amaziah, said to Amos: "Go, flee away to the land of Judah . . . ; never again prophesy at Bethel, for it is the king's sanctuary and it is a temple of the kingdom" (7:12–13).

But the prophet retorted:

> *I am no prophet, nor a prophet's son; but I am a herdsman, and a dresser of sycamore trees, and the Lord took me from following the flock, and the Lord said to me, Go, prophesy to my people Israel.*

> *Now therefore hear the word of the Lord.*
> *You say, Do not prophesy against Israel,*
> *And do not preach against the house of Isaac.*
> *Therefore thus says the Lord:*
> *Your wife shall be a harlot in the city,*
> *And your sons and your daughters shall fall by the sword,*
> *And your land shall be parceled out by line;*
> *You yourself shall die in an unclean land,*
> *And Israel shall surely go into exile away from its land.*
>
> *Amos 7:14–17*

## A Redeemer Pained by the People's Failure

What were the grounds on which Amos in the name of God doomed the nations? Judah was condemned

> *Because they have rejected the Torah of the Lord,*
> *And have not kept His statutes.*
>
> *Amos 2:4*

Yet the nations were not, like Israel, condemned for internal transgressions, but for international crimes, although there was no law in existence governing international relations. Amos, however, presupposes the conception of a law which was not embodied in a contract, the conception of right and wrong which precedes every contract, since all contracts derive their validity from it. Here a conception of law was expressed which was binding for all men, though it was not formally proclaimed; and there was a Lawgiver capable of enforcing it and coercing transgressors.

Did Amos speak as a champion of ethics? Was it in the name of the moral law that the shepherd of Tekoa left his sheep to proclaim his message in Samaria? Amos insisted that it was God whose call he followed and whose living word he carried.

There *is* a living God who cares. Justice is more than an idea or a norm. Justice is a divine concern. What obtains between God and His people is not only a covenant of mutual obligations, but also a relationship of mutual concern. The message of God is not an impersonal accusation, but the utterance of a Redeemer who is pained by the misdeeds, the thanklessness of those whom He has redeemed. His words are plaintive and disconsolate.

> *I brought you up out of the land of Egypt,*
> *And led you forty years in the wilderness,*
> *To possess the land of the Amorite.*
> *And I raised up some of your sons for prophets,*
> *And some of your young men for Nazirites.*
> *Is it not indeed so, O people of Israel? . . .*
> *But you made the Nazirites drink wine,*
> *And commanded the prophets,*
> *Saying, You shall not prophesy.*
>
> Amos 2:10–12

## ICONOCLASM

The most beautiful face lends itself to caricature, to a ludicrous exaggeration of some of its features. And the sublime ideas of biblical faith are equally subject to caricature. As examples may be cited the idea of "the people of the Lord" and the idea of "the day of the Lord."

From the beginnings of Israelite religion the belief that God had chosen this particular people to carry out His mission has been both a cornerstone of Hebrew faith and a refuge in moments of distress. And yet, the prophets felt that to many of their contemporaries this cornerstone was a stumbling block; this refuge, an escape. They had to remind the people that chosenness must not be mistaken as divine favoritism or immunity from chastisement, but, on the contrary, that it meant being more seriously exposed to divine judgment and chastisement.

*Hear this word that the Lord has spoken against you, O people of Israel, against the whole family which I brought up out of the land of Egypt:*

> *You only have I known\**
> *Of all the families of the earth;*

*On the meaning of the term in Hosea see pp. 70 ff.

> *Therefore I will punish you*
> *For all your iniquities.*
>
> *Amos 3:1–2*

Does chosenness mean that God is exclusively concerned with Israel? Does the Exodus from Egypt imply that God is involved only in the history of Israel and is totally oblivious of the fate of other nations?

> *Are you not like the Ethiopians to Me,*
> *O people of Israel? says the Lord.*
> *Did I not bring up Israel from the land of Egypt,*
> *And the Philistines from Caphtor and the Syrians from Kir?*
>
> *Amos 9:7*

The nations chosen for this comparison were not distinguished for might and prestige—countries such as Egypt or Assyria—but rather, nations which were despised and disliked. The color of the Ethiopians is black, and in those days many of them were sold on the slave markets. The Philistines were the archenemies of Israel, and the Syrians continued to be a menace to the Northern Kingdom. The God of Israel is the God of all nations, and all men's history is His concern.

There was a belief in the coming of "a day of the Lord," when God would triumph over all His enemies and establish His rule in the world. In the eyes of the multitude, that belief promised salvation for Israel, regardless of her conduct. The day of the Lord was seen as a day of punishment for pagans only rather than for all nations, Israel included.

> *Woe to you who desire the day of the Lord!*
> *Why would you have the day of the Lord?*
> *It is darkness, and not light;*
> *As if a man fled from a lion,*
> *And a bear met him;*
> *Or went into the house and leaned with his hand against the wall,*
> *And a serpent bit him.*

*Is not the day of the Lord darkness, and not light,*
*And gloom with no brightness in it?*

*Amos 5:18–20*

Amos tried to convey the sense of disappointment, God's aversion against the people. Indeed, what God demands of man is expressed not only in terms of action, but also in terms of passion. "I hate and abhor your feasts!" (5:21), says God. "Hate evil and love good" (5:15) is the great demand.

Is it conceivable that the prophet set forth God's powerful pathos in inner detachment? Does not the very fact of his conveying the pathos to the people imply an inner identification with it? We know that standing before God, Amos pleaded for the people. What, then, was his feeling when he stood before the people?

> *Does a lion roar in the forest,*
> *When he has no prey?*
> *Does a young lion cry out from his den*
> *If he has taken nothing?*
> *Does a bird fall in a snare on the earth,*
> *When there is no trap for it?*
> *Does a snare spring up from the ground,*
> *When it has taken nothing?*
> *Is a trumpet blown in a city,*
> *And the people are not afraid?*
> *Does evil befall a city,*
> *Unless the Lord has done it?*
> *Surely the Lord God does nothing,*
> *Without revealing His secret*
> *To His servants the prophets.*
> *The lion has roared;*
> *Who will not fear?*
> *The Lord God has spoken;*
> *Who can but prophesy?*

*Amos 3:4–8*

Amos, a prophet to whom the call of God came as a surprise and stayed on as dismay, is startled. The voice of God is compared with the roar of a lion about to fall upon its prey; Israel, God's chosen people, is the prey. And no one hears, no one trembles. All save the prophet are deaf and complacent. Yet Amos' reaction is not fear* but the inner compulsion to convey what the voice proclaims; not escape for shelter, but identification with the voice.

It seems amazing that in the book of Amos, which proclaims that God's supreme concern is righteousness and that His essential demand of man is to establish justice, God is compared with a lion in search of its prey. To Amos the good is not apart from God. At times God's call is, "Seek Me"; at other times, "Seek the good." He who seeks a lion will end as a victim, but Amos hears that Israel can live only in seeking God.

> *For thus says the Lord to the house of Israel:*
> *Seek Me and live; . . .*
> *Seek good, and not evil,*
> *That you may live; . . .*
> *Hate evil, and love good,*
> *And establish justice in the gate; . . .*
> *Amos 5:4; 5:14, 15*

## THE LORD REPENTED

The majority of scholars and theologians interpret the message of Amos as the application by the Deity of stern, mechanical justice.†
Such a view disregards the powerful expression of divine inwardness in the message of the prophet.

Had the Lord been a God of stern, mechanical justice, then long ago He might have repudiated His covenant and cast Israel off. He had a deep affection for His people, and had known them more inti-

---

*J. Wellhausen, *Die kleinen Propheten* (Berlin, 1892), and W. Nowack, *Die kleinen Propheten* (Göttingen, 1897), emend the text "who can but prophesy" to "who shall not fear." Sellin rejects this emendation as a remarkable misunderstanding of Amos' train of thought.

†Morgenstern, *op. cit.*, pp. 418 f.

mately than any of the other nations (3:2). Israel proved faithless, but again and again God had overlooked and forgiven, hoping that Israel might see the error of her way and repent. Again and again, He had sent into Israel warning portents, that Israel might take heed and return to Him. He sent upon them one calamity after another, "yet you did not return to Me."

The song of lament (see below) concerning the obduracy of the people, with its recurrent refrain, five times repeated, "yet you did not return to Me," (4:6–13), is an expression of God's mercy and of His disappointment.

Harsh is God's intolerance of injustice, but the gate of repentance remains open. When shown in a vision the imminent destruction of Israel by locust or by fire, Amos has no arguments to offer in his attempt to save his people. He does not question God's justice; he appeals to God's mercy:

> *O Lord God, forgive, I beseech Thee!*
> *How can Jacob stand?*
> *He is so small!*
> *The Lord repented concerning this;*
> *It shall not be, said the Lord.*
> *Amos 7:2–3; cf. 7:5–6*

"The Lord repented" not because the people are innocent, but because they are small. His judgment is never final. There is always a dimension of God's pervading affection where compassion prevails over justice, where mercy is a perpetual possibility:

> *It may be that the Lord, the God of hosts,*
> *Will be gracious to the remnant of Joseph.** 
> *Amos 5:15*

## AN ENCOUNTER WILL SAVE

*I gave you cleanness of teeth in all your cities,*
*And lack of bread in all your places,*

---

*It is a striking fact that while God's aversion is expressed in the first person, the testimony to His love is to be found only in the words of the prophet.

*Yet you did not return to Me, says the Lord.*
*And I also withheld the rain from you. . . .*
*I would send rain upon one city,*
*And send no rain upon another city; . . .*
*Yet you did not return to Me, says the Lord.*
*I smote you with blight and mildew; . . .*
*Your fig trees and your olive trees the locust devoured;*
*Yet you did not return to Me, says the Lord.*
*I sent among you a pestilence after the manner of Egypt;*
*I slew your young men with the sword; . . .*
*Yet you did not return to Me, says the Lord.*
*I overthrew some of you,*
*As when God overthrew Sodom and Gomorrah,*
*And you were as a brand plucked out of the burning;*
*Yet you did not return to Me, says the Lord.*
*Therefore thus I will do to you, O Israel;*
*Because I will do this to you,*
*Prepare to meet your God, O Israel!*
*For lo, He Who forms the mountains, and creates the wind,*
*And declares to man what is His thought; \**
*Who makes the morning darkness,*
*And treads on the heights of the earth—*
*The Lord, the God of hosts, is His name!*

*Amos 4:6–13*

*Prepare to meet your God, O Israel.* What will be the nature of that meeting? The verse is generally understood by commentators as predicting a punishment more severe than any of those which had been described.[†]

The long tale of infliction sets forth clearly the futility of chastisement. The soul is incapable of remorse. However, if hunger, drought,

---

\*Or "purpose," see I Kings 18:27. The Vulgate: *Et annuntians homini eloquium suum;* cf. Amos 3:7.

[†]See, e.g., R. S. Cripps, *A Critical and Exegetical Commentary on the Book of Amos* (London, 1929), pp. 176, 296 f. According to Rashi and Kimhi, in their *Commentaries, ad loc.,* it is a call to repentance.

blight, locust, pestilence, slaying of sons, and destruction of cities have had no effect, what should the next action be? Another more bitter infliction would contradict the central thesis of the tale.

It could also mean a prediction of total destruction, and this would be consonant with other statements in Amos (7:8; 8:2). However, had this been his intention, the prophet would have said, "Prepare for the day of the Lord," signifying extreme disaster (5:18).

Moreover, according to the common interpretation, "to prepare" in this verse means "to prepare for disaster," and "to meet" means "to head for disaster." In biblical usage the Hebrew term "to meet" (*likrath*) denotes either to go to a place to receive favorably a person upon arrival, or to oppose someone in battle; it does not mean to head for disaster. The term "to prepare" denotes to prepare for war or for a constructive achievement, not to prepare for defeat.

Amos' primary mission is not to predict, but to exhort and to persuade (cf. 5:4, 6, 14). Israel has failed to seek Him, so He will go out to meet Israel. Indeed, both terms in this verse occur in the Hebrew Bible in connection with a divine encounter.

Prior to the theophany at Sinai, the people of Israel are told, *"Be prepared"* (Exod. 19:11, 15); Moses is told, *"Be prepared"* (Exod. 34:2). In the hope of receiving a word of God, Balaam said to Balak, "Perhaps the Lord will come *to meet* me" (Num. 23:3).* Significantly, the following verse in the Aramaic translation begins with the words: "For, lo, *He is revealing Himself* Who formed the mountains. . . ." Israel has a rendezvous with God. Castigation failed; an encounter will save.

This seems to be Amos' premise: God does not leave man in the dark; He communicates His thought to man.

> *For lo, He Who forms the mountains, and creates the wind,*
> *And declares to man what is His thought; . . .*
> *The Lord, the God of hosts, is His name!*
>
> *Amos 4:13*

---

*In rabbinic literature, the necessity of preparation for prayer is derived from this verse; see *Tosefta Berachoth*, II, 18; *Bab. Berachoth*, 51b; *Shabbath* 10a.

Indeed, the prophecy of Amos that begins with a message of doom concludes with a vision of hope (9:11 ff.).*

Amos is so overwhelmed by his inspiration that there is little differentiation in his message between revelation and response. Conveying the word of God, he rarely (5:1–2, 15; 7:2, 5) adds his own word. There is no explicit statement of his sympathy, but only intimations of inner identifications and agreement.†

> *Do two walk together,*
> *Unless they have made an appointment? . . .*
> *Surely the Lord God does nothing,*
> *Without revealing His secret*
> *To His servants the prophets.*
>
> Amos 3:3, 7

These lines suggest a relation of *intimacy,* characteristic of those who are in close contact with one another and who have opened their hearts or their minds to such a degree that they deeply know and understand one another. Intimacy, however, never becomes familiarity. God is the Lord, and the prophets are His servants.

The prophet regards himself as one who walks together with God. God and he have agreed.

It is in the light of such sympathy, of such inner identification with the divine disappointment and aversion, that the spirit of Amos can be understood.

Amos' compassion for his people is profound. When beholding a vision of how "the Lord God was calling for a judgment by fire . . . it devoured the land," he prayed for mercy (7:4 ff.). And yet he also identified himself with God's threat of doom for the whole people. This is the burden of a prophet: compassion for man and sympathy for God.

---

*Amos' authorship of 9:8 ff. is maintained by Y. Kaufmann, *The Religion of Israel,* p. 368 (Heb.; vol. III, pt. I, pp. 88 f.).

†Cf. the correspondence between the divine exclamation "I hate your feasts" (5:21), and the prophetic admonition, "Hate the evil" (5:14).

# 3

# Hosea

## HOSEA AND HIS TIMES

Hosea's prophecy dealt primarily with the Northern Kingdom of Israel—its religion, morals, and politics—and his favorite name for the land was Ephraim. "Hosea was the prophet of the decline and fall of the Northern Kingdom, and stood in the same relation to Ephraim in the eighth century as that in which Jeremiah stood to Judah a century and a half later."*

We know that Hosea was married, the father of three children, and well acquainted with agricultural life. From his use of certain striking figures of speech it has been suggested that he was a baker, lived as a farmer on the land, was associated with the priesthood and the sanctuaries, had a strongly developed sex instinct which he vigorously

SELECTED BIBLIOGRAPHY: W. R. Harper, *A Critical and Exegetical Commentary on Amos and Hosea* (New York, 1915); E. Sellin, *Das Zwölfprophetenbuch* ("*Kommentar zum Alten Testament*" [2nd ed.; Leipzig, 1929]); S. L. Brown, *The Book of Hosea* ("Westminster Commentary" [London, 1932]); Y. Kaufmann, *The Religion of Israel* (Heb.; Jerusalem, 1954), VI, 93–146; (Eng.; Chicago, 1960), pp. 368 ff.; A. B. Ehrlich, *Randglossen zur Hebräischen Bibel,* vol. V (Leipzig, 1912); A. Wünsche, *Der Prophet Hosea* (Leipzig, 1868); H. L. Ginsberg, "Hosea's Ephraim, More Fool Than Knave," *JBL,* LXXX (1961), 339 f.
*S. L. Brown, *The Book of Hosea* (London, 1932), p. xvi.

repressed. With the same right we could suggest that he was a lover of the desert and an expert on lions, panthers, and bears.

According to the superscription of his book, Hosea began his prophetic activity in the prosperous days of the reign of Jeroboam II (786–746 B.C.E.) and lived through the period of anarchy which followed Jeroboam's death. Some scholars assume that he ceased to prophesy before 734, the year of the Syro-Ephraimitic war against Judah, while others maintain that he continued to be active until after the fall of Samaria in 722 and that he predicted the return of the population from captivity (chs. 11 and 13).

For many generations Israel and Judah were not disturbed by any power greater than the small countries in the area. This relatively peaceful situation came to an end in the middle of the ninth century when Assyria emerged as an empire and began to lead many expeditions across the Euphrates, compelling most of the states of Syria as well as the Northern Kingdom of Israel to submit to her sovereignty and to pay tribute. These expeditions, nightmares of extreme ruthlessness, enriched Assyria with plunder of gold, silver, and slaves.

The history of the following two centuries is but the story of the expansion of Assyria, and later of Babylonia, and the subjugation of western Asia. Subject states were spared complete extinction only on condition of submitting to severe terms of probation to test their fidelity to Assyria's rule. Such fidelity, however, was hard to bear. As soon as the invader departed, local kings would reassert themselves, and would seek to throw off the hated yoke.

The reign of Tiglath-pileser III (745–727 B.C.E.) saw the emergence of Assyria as a world empire. Tiglath-pileser resumed the policy of expansion toward the west, and by incessant wars subjugated peoples and countries, reducing them to vassals. He also introduced a new policy of conquest. Hitherto the westward incursions had ended in the exaction of booty, slaves, and annual tribute. Tiglath-pileser began the policy of deporting conquered populations from their homeland and of placing other exiles from distant areas in the evacuated territories, thus eliminating any effective rebellion. The record of the Assyrian policy is one of untold suffering and destruction, resulting in the downfall of the Kingdoms of Northern Syria (Arpad, Hamath, etc.), of Damascus (732), of the Northern Kingdom of Israel (721), of Judah (587), and even of Egypt (663). In 743, Tiglath-pileser embarked upon a campaign to subjugate the lands to the west. A coalition, according to conjecture headed by Uzziah, failed to stem the advance of the Assyrian army.

Assyria has been characterized as the nest of the bird of prey whence "set forth the most terrible expeditions which have ever flooded the world with blood. Ashur was its god, plunder its morality, cruelty and terror its means. No people was ever more abject than those of Ashur; no sovereigns were ever more despotic, more covetous, more vindictive, more pitiless, more proud of their crimes. Assyria sums up within herself all the vices. Aside from bravery, she offers not a single virtue."[*]

During the period of Tiglath-pileser, the Kingdom of Israel was in a state of anarchy. Within ten years following Jeroboam's death she had five kings, three of whom seized the throne by violence. The fall of Arpad in 740 was the signal for the prompt appearance of messengers from nearly all the neighboring states, including King Hiram of Tyre and King Rezin of Damascus, with presents of gold and silver, of ivory and purple robes. In the Northern Kingdom of Israel, Menahem (745–738 B.C.E.), who had usurped the throne, became a vassal of Assyria.[†]

The rulers felt relatively secure under Assyria's protection, but the hour of judgment was at hand. Hosea sounded an alarm, proclaiming the word of God:

> *Ephraim shall become a desolation*
> *In the day of punishment;* . . .
> *Upon them I will pour out*
> *My wrath like water.*
> *Ephraim is oppressed, crushed in judgment,* . . .

[*]De Morgan, quoted by A. T. Olmstead, *History of Assyria* (New York, 1923), p. 645.
[†]*ANET*, p. 283.

> *Therefore I am like a moth to Ephraim,*
> *And like dry rot to the house of Judah.*
>
> *Hosea 5:9–12*

Menahem remained king for six years, owing to the support of Assyria. Yet the pro-Assyrian policy evoked apparently strong opposition. Menahem's son, Pekahiah (*ca.* 738–737 B.C.E.) was murdered by Pekah (737–732 B.C.E.) son of Remaliah, who, after taking over the rule of the Kingdom, took part in the formation of an alliance between the small states of western Asia directed against Assyria, and hoping for support from Egypt.*

## POLITICAL PROMISCUITY

> *O Ephraim, you have played the harlot,*
> *Israel is defiled.*
>
> *Hosea 5:3; cf. 6:10; 9:1*

At times Hosea employed the term "harlot" in a figurative sense, in the sense of political promiscuity. The Northern Kingdom was in those days a hotbed of plots and intrigues, with constant military revolts and usurpations. King Zechariah, Jeroboam's son, had been slain by Shallum ben Jabesh; but the usurper had fallen a month later to Menahem, who only after much bloodshed had been able to establish his position. Hosea's horrified reaction was: "A vulture is over the house of the Lord!" (8:1.)

For Hosea, there was no legitimate king in the country at all. Kingship derived its prerogatives from a divine election; but of the kings who emerged from violence and rebellion, the word proclaims:

> *They made kings, but not through Me,*
> *They set up princes, but without My knowledge.*
>
> *Hosea 8:4*

---

*Referring apparently to Hoshea (732–724 B.C.E.), the last king of Samaria, who, though a vassal of Shalmaneser V, turned to Egypt for help (see II Kings 17:3–4); the prophet condemned him for mendacity and violence—they had made a treaty (*berith*) with Assyria, but they were taking oil to Egypt (12:1 [H. 12:2]).

Nor was corruption only in high places. All the people engaged in the numerous conspiracies were practicing fraud: first acting furtively like thieves, then roaming abroad like bandits. Like an oven their hearts burned with intrigue:

> *All of them are hot as an oven,*
> *And they devour their rulers.*
> *All their kings have fallen;*
> *And none of them calls upon Me.*
> *Hosea 7:7*

In addition to multiplying "falsehood and violence" (12:1), the various political factions, pro-Egyptian or pro-Assyrian, seeking to gain power or protection with the aid of foreign states, made the country a ready prey for the appetites of Assyria and Egypt.

> *Ephraim is like a dove,*
> *Silly and without sense,*
> *Calling to Egypt, going to Assyria, . . .*
> *They make a bargain with Assyria,*
> *And oil is carried to Egypt.*
> *Hosea 7:11; 12:1 [H. 12:2];*
> *cf. 8:13; 9:3, 6*

The political game of hiring allies among the nations was both perilous and blasphemous, with Israel lying between the mighty Assyrian empire and an ambitious Egypt. Far from being a cure for Israel's weakness, taking advantage of the shifting political constellation could have had only the opposite effect.

> *For they sow the wind,*
> *And they shall reap the whirlwind.*
> *The standing grain has no heads,*
> *It shall yield no meal;*
> *If it were to yield,*
> *Aliens would devour it.*
> *Israel is swallowed up;*

> *Already they are among the nations*
> *As a useless vessel.*
>
> *Hosea 8:7–8*

In addition, an alliance with Assyria would have meant more than partnership in arms. It was Assyria's policy to require from her allies and tributaries recognition of her supreme god. Thus Israel was being led to the brink of the abyss.

Egypt, though not an abyss, could be like an earthquake. The central manifestation of the love and omnipotence of God, cherished and remembered in Israel, was the exodus from Egypt (11:1).

> *I am the Lord your God*
> *From the land of Egypt;*
> *You know no God but Me,*
> *And besides Me there is no savior.*
>
> *Hosea 13:4*

But reliance on Assyria and Egypt would end in exile rather than security.

> *They shall return to the land of Egypt,*
> *And Assyria shall be their king,*
> *Because they have refused to return to Me.*
> *Hosea 11:5; cf. 9:3, 6, 15; also 8:13*

Ephraim had given bitter provocation (12:14 [H. 12:15]); the judgment was inevitable and would not be long delayed. "Samaria shall bear her guilt, because she has rebelled against her God" (13:16 [H. 14:1]).

And yet the fall of Samaria was not the final phase in God's relationship to Israel. His love for Israel was ineradicable. He could not give up the people He loved (11:8). Hosea was sent primarily, not to announce doom, but to effect return and reconciliation.

> *Return, O Israel, to the Lord your God,*
> *For you have stumbled because of your iniquity.*
> *Take with you words*

*And return to the Lord;*
*Say to Him,*
*Take away all iniquity;*
*Accept that which is good,*
*Our lips will replace the offering of bullocks.*
*Assyria shall not save us,*
*We will not ride upon horses;*
*We will say no more, "Our God,"*
*To the work of our hands.*
*In Thee the orphan finds mercy.*

*The children of Israel shall return and seek the Lord their God, and David their king; and they shall come in fear to the Lord and to His goodness in the latter days.*

*I will be as the dew to Israel;*
*He shall blossom as the lily, . . .*
*His shoots shall spread out;*
*His beauty shall be like the olive.*
     *Hosea 14:1–4 [H. 14:2–4];*
         *3:5; 14:5–6 [H. 14:6–7]*

## TENSION BETWEEN ANGER AND COMPASSION

What had Amos left undone, which Hosea must now do? Amos had proclaimed the righteousness of God, His iron will to let justice prevail. Hosea came to spell out the astonishing fact of God's love for man. God is not only the Lord Who demands justice; He is also a God Who is in love with His people.

There is a tone of divine nostalgia for the early days of God's relationship with Israel.

*Like grapes in the wilderness,*
*I found Israel;*
*Like the first fruit on the fig tree,*
*In its first season*

> *I saw your fathers. . . .*
> *When Israel was a child, I loved him,*
> *And out of Egypt I called My son.*
> *Hosea 9:10; 11:1*

Yet the more He called them, the more they went from Him.

> *It was I Who taught Ephraim to walk,*
> *I took them up in My arms;*
> *But they did not know that I healed them.*
> *I led them with cords of compassion,*
> *With the bands of love;*
> *I became to them as One Who eases the yoke on their jaws,*
> *I bent down to them and fed them gently.*
> *Hosea 11:3–4*

In the face of God's passionate love, the prophet is haunted by the scandal of Israel's desertion. "Israel has forgotten his Maker" (8:14). The voice of God's offended majesty fills his whole being.

> *She did not know*
> *That it was I Who gave her*
> *The grain, the wine, and the oil,*
> *And Who lavished upon her silver*
> *And gold which they used for Baal.*
> *Hosea 2:8 [H. 2:10]*

She went after the Baalim "and forgot Me, says the Lord" (2:13 [H. 2:15]).

The fertility of nature is an astounding wonder. To the non-Hebrew population of Palestine, or Canaan, a land surrounded by desert, the mystery of growth, the marvel of spring, remained a perpetual surprise. There were powers behind all this—the local gods of the land, called the Baalim, who were regarded as the givers of wool and flax, of oil and wine, of grain, vines, and fig trees (2:5, 12 [H. 2:7, 14]).

The conquest of Canaan by Israel was a process extending over several centuries. The Hebrews did not destroy the Canaanites (see Ps. 106:34), but merely occupied parts of the land, while other parts remained in the hands of the Canaanites. For some time there was constant warfare between the two groups, but gradually hostilities ceased, and the Hebrews began to mingle

> . . . *with the nations,*
> *And learned to do as they did.*
> *They served their idols,*
> *Which became a snare to them.*
> *They sacrificed their sons*
> *And their daughters to the demons;*
> *They poured out innocent blood,*
> *The blood of their sons and daughters,*
> *Whom they sacrificed to the idols of Canaan;*
> *And the land was polluted with blood.*
> *Thus they became unclean by their acts,*
> *And played the harlot in the doings.*
>
> *Psalms 106:35–39*

Without abandoning the cult of the God of their Fathers, the Hebrews worshiped the gods of the land they had conquered, sacrificing on the tops of the mountains and making offerings "upon the hills, under oak, poplar, and terebinth, because their shade is good" (4:13). The rites included sacred prostitution (4:14) as well as intoxication. It was the worship of a god of the land rather than of the Creator of heaven and earth; a god who in return for the blessings of fertility demanded the gifts of incense and the excitements of the flesh rather than a God Who in return for all blessings demanded righteousness and justice, love and mercy, faithfulness and attachment, Who was the Lord of nature everywhere as well as the Master of history at all times.

"They . . . make for themselves molten images" and sacrifice to them (13:2 f.). They do not realize their stupidity. "Men kiss calves" (13:2). "A people without understanding shall come to ruin" (4:14).

> *My people are destroyed for lack of knowledge;*
> *Because you have rejected knowledge,*
> *I reject you from being a priest to Me.*
>
> Hosea 4:6

What fascination did the cult of Baal and Ashtoreth hold for the people? Pagan gods not only appeal to the imagination and are beloved by poets and painters alike; they are more comprehensible than the invisible God of Abraham. The conception of one God Who created heaven and earth is hard on the imagination. There is such multiplicity and variety of beings, there are thousands of communities, millions of human beings, countless numbers of days and nights—and only one God? Pagan gods, moreover, are more easily approached and appeased. "Men and gods are of one race: and both from the self-same mother we draw our breath; . . . in some measure we come near at least to the Immortals, either in respect of mind or our outward form."*

The serenity of the people, who felt safe in the enthusiastic worship of both God and the Baalim, was shattered by the prophet, whose words fell like the blows of a hammer over their heads:

> *I am the Lord your God*
> *From the land of Egypt;*
> *You know no God but Me,*
> *And besides Me there is no savior.*
> *It was I who knew you in the wilderness,*
> *In the land of drought;*
> *But when they had fed to the full,*
> *They were filled, and their heart was lifted up;*
> *Therefore they forgot Me.*

---

*Pindar, *Nemean Odes,* VI, 1–2, 6–8. Despite long periods of eclipse, the pagan gods survived in Christian Europe during the Middle Ages. Jesus may become an Orpheus, "Jupiter may appear as one of the Evangelists, Perseus as a St. George, Saturn as God the Father." The glorification of the gods, particularly strong during the Renaissance, persisted in spite of protests and warnings of the Church against those who kept alive the memory of the gods. See J. Seznec, *The Survival of the Pagan Gods* (New York, 1961), pp. 213, 263.

> *So I will be to them like a lion,*
> *Like a leopard I will lurk beside the way.*
> *I will fall upon them like a bear robbed of her cubs,*
> *I will tear open their breast,*
> *And there I will devour them like a lion,*
> *As a wild beast would rend them.*
>
> *Hosea 13:4–8*

How deeply Hosea must have sensed the pathos of God to have been able to convey such dreadful words against his own people whom he loved so deeply. These words, however, were neither a final judgment nor an actual prediction. Their true intention was to impart the intensity of divine anger. And yet that anger did not express all that God felt about the people. Intense is His anger, but profound is His compassion. It is as if there were a dramatic tension in God.

Hosea describes a divine soliloquy in which the Lord considers withholding the execution of His judgment, waiting for Israel to acknowledge her guilt and to return.

> *I will return again to My place,*
> *Until they acknowledge their guilt and seek My face,*
> *And in their distress they seek Me, saying,*
> *Come, let us return to the Lord;*
> *For He has torn, that He may heal us;*
> *He has stricken, and He will bind us up.*
> *After two days He will revive us;*
> *On the third day He will raise us up,*
> *That we may live before Him.*
> *Let us know, let us press on to know the Lord;*
> *His going forth is sure as the dawn;*
> *He will come to us as the showers,*
> *As the spring rains that water the earth.*
>
> *Hosea 5:15–6:3*

However, the soliloquy continues, there is little hope that such return will take place. Israel is erratic, and her love is fleeting. God's anxiety comes to expression:

*What shall I do with you, O Ephraim?*
*What shall I do with you, O Judah?*
*Your love is like a morning cloud,*
*Like the dew that goes early away.*
*Therefore I have hewn them by the prophets,*
*I have slain them by the words of My mouth, . . .*

*Hosea 6:4–5*

## HOSEA SEES A DRAMA

Amos knows God as the selfless and exalted Being Whose sensibilities and concern for justice are painted by the sinful transgressions of Israel. The emotions suggested in his prophecies are not spontaneous. Apart from the active emotion of disdain, these emotions are reactive, provoked by human deeds: resistance and abhorrence leading to rejection. The exciting cause of the divine intervention in the course of history is furnished by human conduct: the relationship between God and Israel is upset by the provocations of man. We hear but sparingly of a positive spontaneous emotion welling up in the depths of the divine Being.

It is Hosea who flashes a glimpse into the inner life of God as He ponders His relationship to Israel. In parables and in lyrical outbursts the decisive motive behind God's strategy in history is declared. The decisive motive is love.

God is conceived, not as the self-detached Ruler, but as the sensitive Consort to Whom deception comes and Who nevertheless goes on pleading for loyalty, uttering a longing for a reunion, a passionate desire for reconciliation. Of all the prophets, only Jeremiah has sensed a wider scale of personal relations, a more intense subjectivity. Hosea has given us a supreme expression of the vision of the subjective God so typical for prophetic awareness.

*How shall I give you up, O Ephraim!*
*How shall I surrender you, O Israel!*
*How can I make you like Admah!*

*How can I treat you like Zeboiim!*
*My heart is turned within Me,*
*My compassion grows like a flame.*
*I will not execute My fierce anger,*
*I will not again destroy Ephraim;*
*For I am God and not man,*
*The Holy One in your midst,*
*And I will not come to destroy.*

*Hosea 11:8–9*

Hosea centralizes the various incidental reactions. Where Amos sees episodes, Hosea sees a drama. Going beyond the description of momentary conditions, Hosea reaches an awareness of the basic feeling, of the latent subjective meaning in all individual announcements and decisions. We hear not merely of an incidental pathos, but also of the cardinal, fundamental emotion; not merely of particular attitudes, but also of the constitutive relationship between God and Israel. Over and above the immediate and contingent emotional reaction of the Lord we are informed about an eternal and basic disposition. The historically conditioned expressions of pathos and the immediate situation between God and man are set in the light of the eternal background. At the beginning "when Israel was a child I loved him" (11:1).

The traits of pathos announced by Amos recur verbally in the prophecies of Hosea. The pathos of repugnance receives important variations of tone. It is expressed as abhorrence ("My God will abhor them," 9:17), as hatred ("Every evil of theirs is in Gilgal; / There I began to hate them. / Because of the wickedness of their deeds . . . ," 9:15), as anger ("Upon them I will pour out / My wrath like water," 5:10; cf. 8:5; 13:11, 14). Also the detestation of the aristocracy and their palaces which we find in Amos is known to Hosea:

*For Israel has forgotten his Maker,*
*And built palaces; . . .*

*Hosea 8:14*

The modulation of the divine feelings toward repentance, found in Amos, is expressed most stirringly: "My heart is turned within me" (11:8; cf. 12:6). But it is also said: "Compassion remains hid from Me" (13:14).

A new factor not found in Amos is the sense of tenderness and mercy. Hosea is able to express as no other prophet the love of God for Israel in its most varied forms—as compassion (11:8), as a mother's tenderness (1:6–8; 2:3, 6, 21, 25; 11:1), as love between husband and wife (3:1 ff.).* From the perspective of the fundamental disposition of love, it is understandable that healing and reconciliation, not harm and destruction, finally prevail. The central idea put before the people is not a divine repugnance to cultic worship in general, but the provocation caused by idolatry as well as God's plea for a renewal of the covenant (2:16 ff [H. 2:18 ff.]).

### EMOTIONAL SOLIDARITY

*Hear the word of the Lord, O people of Israel;*
*For the Lord has a controversy with the inhabitants of the land.*
*There is no truth or love, and no understanding for God in the land.*

*Hosea 4:1*

Whose part does the prophet take in the divine–human controversy?

The theme of Hosea's prophecy is apostasy. Most of his utterances are variations on the same theme. It is remarkable in his treatment that the subject of preoccupation is not the apostate, the backslider, but God the abandoned One. Hosea never tries to plead for the people or to dwell upon the reasons for the people's alienation from God. He has only one perspective: the divine partner. As a result there is little understanding on his part for the weakness of man. The words which Hosea flings at the people engaged in celebrating a harvest festival are stern and gloomy:

---

*A counterpart to the song of love (ch. 11) is the song of wrath (ch. 8; cf. 13:11), but again and again a cadence of reconciliation is heard (14:4 [H. 14:5]).

*Do not rejoice, Israel, like the peoples,*
*For you have played the harlot, forsaking your God. . . .*
*The days of visitation have come,*
*The days of recompense have come.*

*Hosea 9:1, 7*

Hosea's emotional solidarity with God is apparent throughout the book. In a survey of the history of Israel (9:10–17), in which past and present are contrasted and the imminent catastrophe is depicted, Hosea does not implore mercy for the people; instead, his sympathy with divine wrath rings in the harsh words:

*Give them, O Lord—*
*What wilt Thou give?*
*Give them a miscarrying womb*
*And dry breasts.*

*Hosea 9:14*

Hosea's prophecy, in which the essence of God's relationship to Israel is celebrated as love, tenderness, and nostalgia, contains also expressions of terrifying vehemence.

*I will be like a lion to Ephraim,*
*Like a young lion to the house of Judah.*
*I, even I, will rend and go away,*
*I will carry off, and none shall rescue.*
*Hosea 5:14; cf. 13:7–8*

How does one reconcile the tenderness of divine love with the vehemence of divine punishment? Clearly it is not a love that is exclusive and that ignores the wickedness of the beloved, forgiving carelessly every fault. Here is a love grown bitter with the waywardness of man. The Lord is in love with Israel, but He also has a passionate love of right and a burning hatred of wrong.

## LONGING FOR REUNION

God's relationship to Israel is most commonly described as a covenant. The word "covenant" conveys the permanence, steadfastness, and mutuality rather than the personal depth of that relationship. Is the covenant a tether, a chain, or is it a living intercourse?

In the domain of imagination the most powerful reality is love between man and woman. Man is even in love with an image of that love, but it is the image of a love spiced with temptation rather than a love phrased in service and depth-understanding; a love that happens rather than a love that continues; the image of tension rather than of peace; the image of a moment rather than of permanence; the image of fire rather than of light. But God said, "Let there be light."

To Hosea, marriage is the image for the relationship of God and Israel. This is one of the boldest conceptions of religious thinking. It may lack the excitement of adventure, but it has the aura of sublimity. It involves restraint, bringing with it duties and responsibilities, but it also endows with a nobility that is a synonym for eternity. Israel is the consort of God.*

Hosea's direct purpose, however, is not to celebrate the grandeur of that relationship, but rather to expose any implication of disturbance which that relationship may have for the life of God. Idolatry is adultery. More than objective falsehood, it is a betrayal of God; more than stupidity, it is lewdness. Israel is like a wanton wife, the Lord like a faithful, loving, but forsaken husband. The strain of disillusionment rings in the sharp and threatening words:

> *Plead with your mother, plead—*
> *For she is not my wife,*
> *And I am not her husband—*
> *That she put away her harlotry from her face,*
> *And her adultery from between her breasts; . . .*
> *Hosea 2:2 [H. 2:4]*

The prophet announces the intention of the Lord to repudiate the people, to devastate the land, to

---

*Hosea's conception of Israel as the consort of God represents one of the most important ideas in the history of Judaism (cf. Isa. 49:14–15; 62:5), and foreshadows the traditional interpretation of the Song of Songs.

> ... *make her like a wilderness,*
> *And set her like a parched land,*
> *And slay her with thirst.*
>                 *Hosea 2:3 [H. 2:5]*

It is the utterance of a pathos—not a decree, not a decision.

Yet stronger than jealousy is God's longing for reunion and His hope for Israel's return. The day will come when "you will call Me 'my husband,' . . . and I will betroth you to Me for ever; I will betroth you to Me in righteousness and in justice, in love and in mercy. I will betroth you to Me in faithfulness, and you shall know the Lord" (2:16, 19–20 [H. 2:18, 21–22]). The reconciliation will take effect as a new betrothal. And these will be the gift and dowry for the bride: righteousness, justice, kindness, mercy. The pathos of love, expressed first in the bitterness of disillusionment, finds its climax in the hope of reconciliation. "I will heal their backsliding, I will love them freely, for Mine anger has turned from him" (14:4 [H. 14:5]).

## HOW TO SHARE DISILLUSIONMENT

All images, parables, and symbols fade when applied to God. Even the description of God as the Consort of Israel fails to convey the love of God. A husband publicly betrayed by his wife is prevented by law and by emotion from renewing his marital life with her. But God's love is greater than law and emotion.

The pathos that moved the soul of Hosea possessed, in contrast to its elementary manifestations proclaimed by Amos, a complex structure. He was struck by the whole drama of God's relationship to Israel, a drama composed of various acts and stages. What would have made it possible for Hosea to attain an inner identification with all stages of the divine pathos? A mere knowledge of what has come to pass between God and Israel would have enabled him to have genuine sympathy for the present emotion, the disillusionment, but not for the whole gamut of experience, for all stages of the inner drama that preceded the present. The scope of sympathy is limited. One must share the experiences, or similar experiences, in order to share the emotional reactions to them. Moreover, disillusionment is a feeling the intensity of which is dependent upon the nature and depth of the emotional attitudes; one must have shared the love in order to share the disillusionment. Only a revival, one by one, of past happenings, together with the reactions they called forth, would enable the prophet to experience sympathy for the drama. For this purpose, the full story was re-enacted in the personal life of the prophet, and the variety of divine pathos experienced and shared in the privacy of his own destiny: love, frustration, reconciliation.

## HOSEA'S MARRIAGE

Hosea was told by the Lord to marry a girl named Gomer, the daughter of Diblaim, whom he loved.* For a time they were happy in their mutual affection. Three children were born, to whom Hosea gave symbolic names.† Subsequently, however, he discovered that Gomer had been unfaithful and had given herself to many lovers. She could not remain his wife. She then left him, or was sent away by him. That was the legal way: to expel the woman who became an adulteress. The husband was not allowed to live with her. "No pity for the

---

*The phrase 'esheth zenunim does not connote a harlot, which is called 'ishah zonah or simply zonah, but, as Ehrlich pointed out, a person who is disposed to become a harlot, a woman filled with the spirit of whoredom (Randglossen zur Hebräischen Bibel, V, 163). According to another view, the term denotes a woman who took part in the Canaanite fertility cult. See H. W. Wolff, "Hoseas geistige Heimat," Theologische Literaturzeitung (1956), pp. 83 ff. "In the course of the marriage Gomer's disposition revealed itself. Under the impression of this painful experience, Hosea describes his wife as she had become at the time of writing, i.e., after the birth of the three children mentioned in ch. 1." (H. Guthe in E. Kautzsch, Die Heilige Schrift des Alten Testaments [4th ed.; Tübingen, 1923–1924.]). The supposition that Hosea had married a harlot spoils the sense of the incident, which is meant to symbolize the historical relationship between God and Israel, the latter having been at the outset an obedient people.

†The first, a son, he called Yezreel, in token of the coming destruction of the dynasty of Jehu; the second, a daughter, and the third, another son, he named "Not-Pitied" and "Not-My-People," respectively, as signs of the Lord's rejection of Israel (1:2–9).

children, because they are children of harlotry; . . . she that conceived them had acted shamefully" (2:4 f.).*

But God's way is higher than the legal way. The Lord said to Hosea: "Bring Gomer back to your home, renew your love for her, even as the Lord loves the people of Israel, though they turn to other gods" (3:1). Hosea did bring her from the slavery into which she had fallen; the marriage was renewed. God cannot abandon Israel. He will not forsake her in spite of her faithlessness.

The account of this strange incident has been a puzzle to commentators.† They have found it morally repugnant that God should have commanded a prophet to marry or even to remarry an adulterous woman. The suggestion has been made, therefore, that the incident took place in a vision or a dream and was never carried out in real life, or that the story was told as a parable or allegory. The first view is advanced by Ibn Ezra, Maimonides,‡ and Kimhi,§ while the second view is expressed by the *Targum*, Rashi, and Hieronymus. Against these views and in favor of a literal understanding of the narrative, it is argued (*a*) that what is morally and religiously objectionable in actual practice becomes no more defensible by being presented as vision or parable; (*b*) that no indication is given by the prophet that this is vision or parable and not fact; (*c*) that the name Gomer bath Diblaim yields no symbolic significance; (*d*) that no symbolic significance can be attached to the fact that the second child is a girl rather than a boy; (*e*) that the literal view suits the realism of early prophecy better than the supposition that it is a product of literary imagination; (*f*) that the prophets were accustomed to giving symbolic names to real children; (*g*) that it would be strange for Hosea to tell such a story of his wife

---

*On the marriage of Hosea, cf. H. H. Rowley, *The Servant of the Lord* (London, 1952), p. 115, n. 1; W. R. Harper, *Amos and Hosea*, pp. 208 f.; cf. also R. Gordis, "Hosea's Marriage and Message," *HUCA*, XXV (1954), 9–34. Cf. H. L. Ginsberg, "Studies in Hosea 1–3," *Y. Kaufmann Jubilee Volume* (Jerusalem, 1960), pp. 50 ff.

†It is taken as a real event in Babylonian Talmud, *Pesahim* 87a–b; see also M. Friedmann, ed., *Seder Eliahu Rabba*, p. 187.

‡*The Guide of the Perplexed*, II, 46.

§H. Cohen, ed., *Commentary on Hosea* (New York, 1929). Cf. *Midrash Agada*, ed. Buber (Wien, 1894), p. 40.

if false or, if he were unmarried, about himself; and (h) that a real experience such as this furnishes the best explanation of Hosea's message—it was the outcome of the sufferings of his own heart.* The nonliteral view has rightly been rejected by most modern scholars, who maintain that the narrative contains a report of actual events in the life of Hosea.

Some commentators question Hosea's claim that the marriage was concluded in obedience to a divine command. The prophet, they maintain, married Gomer under ordinary circumstances without suspecting what was to happen. Gomer went astray. As the prophet brooded over the tragedy in his own household, and wondered how God could bring such an experience upon him, he came to regard his marriage as having been ordained by divine Providence, and so proclaimed it to have taken place in fulfillment of a divine word which had gone forth to him.†

The idea behind this theory is that Hosea's claim to have been commanded by God originated in his own mind and that he never experienced a moment which would have entitled him to say, "And the Lord said to me, Go again, love a woman who is beloved of a paramour and is an adulteress" (3:10). Thus, what Hosea gave out as a divine call was due to his own impulse. But this theory reflects upon the integrity of the prophet. It imputes to Hosea a pretension with which false prophets are charged—the giving out as divine words the thoughts of their own mind—for Hosea proclaimed that in entering upon his marriage he was following a divine command. Apart from other objections, therefore, "this modern psychological theory is in any case to be rejected since it does not do justice to the integrality of

*See E. Sellin, *Einleitung in das Alte Testament* (4th ed.; Leipzig, 1910), p. 109. See also Allwohn, *Die Ehe des Propheten Hosea im psychoanalytischer Beleuchtung* (Gressen, 1926), pp. 35 ff.; K. Budde, *"Der Abschnitt Hosea 1–3 und seine grundlegende religionsgeschichtliche Bedeutung,"* in *Alttestamentliche Forschungen, Sonderheft der theologischen Studien und Kritiken,* I (Stuttgart, 1925).

†Wellhausen, Smith, *et al.* According to others Hosea's wife was corrupted by the immorality of the public cult. Then the prophet, as a result of his disillusionment in love, reached the position of fundamental world denial.

the whole and arbitrarily changes the words of the prophet."* Our rationalistic prejudice gives us no right to maintain that what the prophet described as a divine call was actually pretension and the product of hindsight.

In addition to the historical and psychological problem, the question of the meaning of the marriage has often been discussed. Some scholars maintain that the purpose of the marriage was to teach through demonstration: to let the people recognize in this conjugal affair, played out before their gaze, a picture of their own conduct and fate. The impulse to this theory comes from the fact that the prophets of Israel often performed symbolic acts in order to demonstrate dramatically their message to the public.†

The facts to be dramatized were the following: betrayal by the wife, the naming of the children, the repudiation of the wife, the taking her back, and perhaps also the sorrow of the prophet. Publicly to dramatize a wife's adultery comes close to popularizing infidelity, and the moral didactic effect of such a dramatization would be highly questionable.

It is also unlikely that the prophet's repudiation of his wife was meant to demonstrate to the public God's actual rejection of the people. Hosea never proclaimed, but only threatened, the rejection of Israel; in that case the symbol would have been in contradiction to historical realities. Even the taking back of the wife cannot have been meant as an example. In Hosea's view, the reconciliation of God and people was to be attained only through penitence and conversion (14:1 f. [H. 14:2 f.]). But nothing is said in the story about Gomer's conversion, and it is not to be supposed that the prophet would have offered the people a symbolic picture inconsistent with his own exhortations. Nor does it seem plausible that so emotional and sensitive a personality as Hosea's should have contracted a marriage which was meant purely for public instruction. To play for years that sort of the-

*See H. Gressmann in H. Schmidt, *Die Schriften des Alten Testaments,* II (1), 263.

†See G. Fohrer, *Die symbolischen Handlungen der Propheten* (Zurich, 1953).

atrical role—and it should be remembered that he had three children by Gomer—would have been for Hosea a public vivisection of his own fate, a martyrdom, and something comparable with cultic prostitution. Nor is it likely that the sorrow of Hosea was meant to represent symbolically to the people the pain of God's deception.

It has been suggested that drama took its origin, not from the imitation of men, but from the desire to imitate the actions of divine beings. This theory seems to receive confirmation from the development of the drama in Egypt as well as among many American Indian tribes. The actors are masked to represent the appropriate deities. This implies, to the primitive mind, that the actor is, for the time being, the deity whom he represents. However, only those deities can be represented with whom the actor believes he can be identified. The Greek drama was closely connected with the cult of Dionysus. "Athene and Zeus and Poseidon have no drama because no one, in his wildest moments, believed he could become and be Athene or Zeus or Poseidon. It is indeed only in the orgiastic religions that these splendid moments of conviction could come, and, for Greece at least, only in an orgiastic religion did the drama take its rise."*

To the prophets of Israel the idea of a human being copying or imitating the inner life of God would have appeared as the height of absurdity. For man to play God, to believe himself to be God, would have been horrible blasphemy. Moreover, the purpose of symbolic acts was to anticipate or to forecast the future—such as the doom of the state, the captivity of the people, or their return to the land. In contrast, the symbolic function of Hosea's marriage would have been to re-enact the past. Yet the sins of the past were known. What purpose would be served by illustrating what was notorious?

## THE MARRIAGE AN ACT OF SYMPATHY

It seems absurd to assume that the prophet's marriage was performed for effect, as a mere demonstration, as an act intended for

---

*J. Harrison, *Prolegomena to the Study of Greek Religion* (Cambridge, 1908), p. 568.

public information. One must not reduce the fullness of an act to its operational meaning. We cannot adequately understand a person by the impressions he produces in other people. A person is not a puppet, and martyrdom is not a masquerade. One thing is clear: the primarily given and immediate spiritual datum in the story of the marriage is the prophet's experience. The event stirred and shocked the life of Hosea regardless of its effect upon public opinion. It concerned him personally at the deepest level and had a meaning of the highest significance for his own life.

As time went by, Hosea became aware of the fact that his personal fate was a mirror of the divine pathos, that his sorrow echoed the sorrow of God. In this fellow suffering as an act of sympathy with the divine pathos the prophet probably saw the meaning of the marriage which he had contracted at the divine behest.

The marriage of Hosea was no symbolic representation of real facts, no act of re-creating or repeating events in the history of Israel or experiences in the inner life of God. Its meaning was not objective, inherent in the marriage, but subjective, evocative. Only by living through in his own life what the divine Consort of Israel experienced, was the prophet able to attain sympathy for the divine situation. The marriage was a lesson, an illustration, rather than a symbol or a sacrament. Its purpose was not to demonstrate divine attitudes to the people, but to educate Hosea himself in the understanding of divine sensibility.

The tragic disturbance in the relationship between God and Israel must have determined decisively his attitude and outlook. Hosea, who again and again emphasized the unchanging devotion of God to Israel, was not simply an advocate of the people. His mind was powerfully affected by the embitterment of God, echoed in his own sympathetic experience.

A difference of opinion exists concerning the origin of the parable which expresses the relationship between God and Israel by the symbol of marriage. It has been sought in Canaanite religion, in the Baal and Ashtoreth cult.* However, "the idea of a marriage of Baal with the soil could not be conclusively shown to exist in Canaanite thought."† Although there are similarities in the God-Israel and Baal-land marriage symbolism, there are also unmistakable differences between the two ideas. In the first place, in Canaanite religion the relationship between the god and the land remains foremost, whereas in the religion of Israel, the people appear instead of the land. In the second place, the Canaanite view emphasizes primarily the sensuous, naturalistic aspect, whereas the prophetic idea alludes to the emotional and legal bond.‡

That the idea which lies behind this parable of marriage derives from the doctrine of the covenant between God and Israel is entirely plausible.

## DAATH ELOHIM

Hosea's central complaint against the people is that they do not know God. He employs the verb "to know" with striking frequency, and coins the expression *daath elohim,* usually rendered as "knowledge of God." The verb *yada* does not always mean simply "to know," "to be acquainted with." In most Semitic languages it signifies sexual union as well as mental and spiritual activity. In Hebrew *yada* means more than the possession of abstract concepts. Knowledge compasses inner appropriation, feeling, a reception into the soul.§ It involves both an intellectual and an emotional act.

An analysis of the usage of the verb in biblical Hebrew leads to

---

*E. Sellin, *Das Zwölfprophetenbuch* (Leipzig, 1929), p. 24.
†J. Ziegler, *Die Liebe Gottes bei den Propheten* (Münster, 1930), p. 67.
‡*Ibid.,* p. 68.
§See the fine study by E. Braumann, "Yada *und seine Derivate,*" ZAW, XXVIII (1908), 125, who justly remarks that "*daath hashem* in Hosea denotes especially the fulfilment of the conjugal intercourse between Israel and the Lord." See also S. Mowinckel, *Die Erkenntnis Gottes bei den alttestamentlichen Propheten* (Oslo, 1941); W. Reiss, *"Gott erkennen" im Sprachgebrauch des Alten Testaments* (Bonn, 1951); W. Zimmerli, *Erkenntnis Gottes nach dem Buche Ezekiel* (Zurich, 1954). Cf. J. Pederson, *Israel,* I–II (London and Copenhagen, 1926), 109.

the conclusion that it often, though not always, denotes an act involving concern, inner engagement, dedication, or attachment to a person. It also means to have sympathy, pity, or affection for someone. In a number of passages it is inaccurate to translate *yada* with "to know." Let us cite a few examples:

1. After relating that the people of Israel groaned under their bondage in Egypt and cried out for help, the book of Exodus says that "their cry under bondage came up to God. And God heard their groaning, and God remembered His covenant with Abraham, with Isaac, and with Jacob. And God saw the people of Israel and God *knew* their condition" (Exod. 2:24–25). What the text means is: and He *had pity*. In the same story we read: "Then the Lord said, I have seen the affliction of My people who are in Egypt, and have heard their cry because of their taskmasters; I *know* their sufferings" (Exod. 3:7). What the text means is: I *have sympathy for*, I *am affected by*, their sufferings.

2. Israel is told: "You shall not oppress a stranger; you *know* the heart of a stranger, for you were strangers in the land of Egypt" (Exod. 23:9). The correct meaning is: You *have sympathy*, or a *feeling*, for the heart of a stranger. "A righteous man *has regard* for the life of his beast, but the mercy of the wicked is cruel" (Prov. 12:10). The correct meaning is: he *has a feeling* (or *sympathy*) for his beast.

> *Who can stand before His indignation?*
> *Who can endure the heat of His anger?*
> *His wrath is poured out like fire,*
> *And the rocks are broken asunder by Him.*
> *The Lord is good,*
> *A stronghold in the day of trouble;*
> *He knows those who take refuge in Him.*
> *But with an overflowing flood*
> *He will make a full end of His adversaries,*
> *And will pursue His enemies into darkness.*
> *Nahum 1:6–8*

The correct meaning is: He *has pity on.*

> *I will rejoice and be glad for Thy steadfast love,*
> *Because Thou hast seen my affliction,*
> *Thou hast seen the troubles of my soul.*
>
> Psalm 31:7

The true meaning is: Thou *hast a feeling* (or *pity*) for.

3. Joseph is viceroy over Egypt. He saves her people from starvation and changes the entire system of land tenure in the country. Such a position and such activities must have made him the most famous man in the country. Then, after Joseph died, we are told: "There arose a new king over Egypt, who did *not know* Joseph" (Exod. 1:8). In what sense is the verb used here? To have meant he *did not know* him personally would be a platitude; to have meant he *did not know of* him would be ludicrous. What is probably meant is that he *did not care* for Joseph; he disliked him.

4. Of the sons of Eli, the high priest at the central sanctuary of Shiloh and judge over Israel, I Sam. 2:12 records that "they were base men; they knew not the Lord." Knowledge in the sense of information they must have had; what they lacked was an inner commitment or an emotional attachment. "Adam *yada* Eve his wife, and she conceived and bore Cain" (Gen. 4:1). It is usually rendered "Adam *knew* Eve his wife." The word is used here as well as elsewhere in the Bible in a sense of intimate sexual relationship. It is, however, likely that the sense in which it is used here refers to a total relationship, emotional as well as sexual. A more accurate translation would be: "Adam *attached* himself to Eve his wife."*

The relationship between God and Israel, conceived by Hosea in terms of marital love, desertion, and the hope of new betrothal,

---

*"The Lord knows the way of the righteous, but the way of the wicked will perish" (Ps. 1:6). The psalmist does not mean that the Lord knows the way topographically; he means that the Lord is concerned about every step the righteous man takes. "The heart knows its own bitterness, and no stranger shares its joy" (Prov. 14:10). Here, too, "to know" means "to feel." What we know, a stranger can share; what we feel, no one can fully share. What we know is universal; what we feel is private. Cf. Ps. 131:2; Job 23:10; Isa. 43:2. See N. H. Snaith, *The Distinctive Ideas of the Old Testament* (London, 1947), p. 135.

calls not only for right action, but also for a feeling for each other on the part of those involved. It implies not only legal obligations, but also inner attitudes. In the light of his own complete emotional solidarity with God, Hosea seems to have seized upon the idea of sympathy as the essential religious requirement. The words *daath elohim* mean *sympathy for God,* attachment of the whole person, his love as well as his knowledge; an act of involvement, attachment or commitment to God. The biblical man knew of no bifurcation of mind and heart, thought and emotion. He saw the whole person in a human situation. "For I desire steadfast love and not sacrifice, *daath* of God, rather than burnt offerings" (6:6); *daath* corresponds to *hesed,* or love. What is desired is an inner identification with God rather than a mere dedication to ceremonies. Thus the expression *daath elohim* must be understood in the framework of Hosea's thinking of the God-Israel relationship as one of engagement, marriage, betrayal, and remarriage.

> *Their deeds do not permit them*
> *To return to their God.*
> *For the spirit of harlotry is within them*
> *And they know not the Lord. . . .*
> *They have dealt faithlessly with the Lord,*
> *For they have borne alien children.*
>
> *Hosea 5:4, 7*

As an antithesis to "the spirit of harlotry," knowledge of God must mean an intimate relation to, or a feeling for, God.

According to the analogy of sexual union to which this verb points, this sympathy must be understood to imply an emotional experience that is reciprocal. Just as in sexual reciprocal emotion, where the feeling of one person is in no sense an object to the other, where rather both persons share the same feeling, the structure of the sympathy implied in Hosea's hypothesis is not compassion for one another, but a suffering together, the act of sharing an inner experience.

The word, then, as we have seen, has an intellectual as well as an emotional meaning. In most passages, the intellectual component of *daath* is stressed; in Hosea, the emotional component seems to be primary. His *daath elohim* does not connote a knowledge *about* God, but an awareness *of* God, a sensitivity for what concerns Him, a concern for the divine person, not only for the divine will;* a concern that involves inwardness as well as action.

That the word *daath* in Hosea denotes an act involving complete engagement of the person may be inferred from the words in which God predicts the new relationship with His people (2:19–20 [H. 2:21–22]). Personal involvement, like the one that occurs when a man becomes engaged to a woman, seems to be regarded as the prerequisite for, or the essence of, the *daath* or "knowledge" of God. "I am the Lord your God from the land of Egypt; . . . It was I who *knew* you in the wilderness, in the land of drought" (13:4–5). What the prophet means is "I *cared* for you" or "I was *attached* to you."

Unlike the prophetic sympathy which arises in response to a revelation and the pathos it discloses, the general sympathy which Hosea requires of man is a constant solidarity, an emotional identification with God. It is the central religious postulate. The loss of *daath* is the cause of man's undoing (4:6).

The contrast between Amos and Hosea is seen both in what they condemn and in what they stress. To Amos, the principal sin is *injustice;* to Hosea, it is *idolatry.* Amos inveighs against evil *deeds;* Hosea attacks the absence of *inwardness.* In the words of Amos:

> *I hate, I despise your feasts,* . . .
> *I will not accept your* sacrifices. . . .
> *But let* justice *roll down like waters,*
> *And righteousness like a mighty stream.*
>                                              *Amos 5:21–24*

---

*Baudissin, *Archiv für die Religionswissenschaft,* XVIII, 226, explains the term to mean "to be concerned about the divine will," but this does not render its peculiar meaning.

In the words of Hosea:

> *For I desire* love [ḥesed] *and not sacrifice,*
> Attachment to God *rather than burnt offerings.*
> *Hosea 6:6*

In surveying the past, Amos dwells on what God has done (2:9 ff.); Hosea dwells on what God has felt for Israel (11:1–4). "You only have I known of all the families of the earth," in the words of Amos (3:2). "When Israel was a child, I loved him," in the words of Hosea (11:1). And again from Hosea: "There is no loyalty (*'emeth*), no love (*ḥesed*), and no knowledge of God in the land" (4:1).

# 4

# Isaiah
## (Isa. 1–39)

### PROSPERITY AND POWER

Under the long reign of Uzziah (*ca.* 783–742 B.C.E.), in fame second only to Solomon's, Judah reached the summit of its power. Uzziah built up the economic resources of the country as well as its military strength. He conquered the Philistines and the Arabians, and received tribute from the Ammonites; he fortified the country, reorganized and re-equipped the army. "In Jerusalem he made engines, invented by skilful men, to be on the towers and the corners, to shoot arrows and great stones" (II Chron. 26:15). His success as king, administrator, and commander in chief of the army made him ruler over the largest realm of Judah since the disruption of the Kingdom.

Uzziah's strength became his weakness. "He grew proud, to his destruction," and attempted to usurp the power of the priesthood,

SELECTED BIBLIOGRAPHY: B. Duhm, *Das Buch Jesaia* (*"Göttingen Handkommentar zum Alten Testament"* [9th ed.; Göttingen, 1922]); G. B. Gray, *A Critical and Exegetical Commentary on the Book of Isaiah* ("International Critical Commentary" [New York, 1912]); O. Procksch, *Isaia I* (*"Kommentar zum Alten Testament"* [Leipzig, 1930]); E. J. Kissane, *The Book of Isaiah*, vol. I (Dublin, 1941); Y. Kaufmann, *The Religion of Israel* (Heb.; Jerusalem, 1954), VI, 147–256; (Eng. trans., M. Greenberg [Chicago, 1960], pp. 378 ff.); A. B. Ehrlich, *Randglossen zur Hebräischen Bibel*, vol. IV (Leipzig, 1912).

even entering the Temple of the Lord to burn incense on the altar, a privilege reserved to the priest. Azariah, the chief priest, followed by eighty priests, "men of valor," pleaded with him:

"It is not for you, Uzziah, to burn incense to the Lord, but for the priests, the sons of Aaron, who are consecrated to burn incense. Go out of the sanctuary; for you have done wrong, and it will bring you no honor from the Lord God." This angered Uzziah, and as his anger mounted, leprosy broke out on his forehead. "And King Uzziah was a leper to the day of his death, and being a leper dwelt in a separate house, for he was excluded from the house of the Lord" (II Chron. 26:18–21).*

It was about 750 B.C.E. when Uzziah was stricken with leprosy, and his place in public was taken over by his son Jotham, officially designated as regent, though actual power seems to have remained with Uzziah. Under Jotham (d. *ca*. 735), Judah continued to be the most stable, prosperous, and powerful state in the area. Her wealth and military power placed her in the forefront of the anti-Assyrian movement when Tiglath-pileser III of Assyria invaded Syria in 743.

The increasing prosperity of Judah "was not canalized for the exclusive benefit of the aristocracy and the wealthy merchants, as was apparently true of the Northern Kingdom in the eighth century. . . . All private houses so far excavated reflect a surprisingly narrow range of variation in the social scale. . . . In other words, there was no period in Judah during which was such concentration of wealth in the hands of individuals as to destroy the social order."† The people made good use of the opportunities for commercial and industrial expansion.

## ISAIAH AND THE NORTHERN KINGDOM

The years in which Isaiah began his prophetic activity were the beginning of a most critical period for both Israel and Judah. He

*Cf. II Kings 15:3–5; Josephus, *Antiquities,* IX, 10, 4; J. Morgenstern, "The Sin of Uzziah," *HUCA,* XII–XIII (1937–1939), 1 ff.

†W. F. Albright, "The Biblical Period," in L. Finkelstein, ed., *The Jews* (New York, 1949), pp. 39 ff.

received his call to be a prophet in the year in which King Uzziah of Judah died (*ca.* 742), not long after the death of Jeroboam II of Israel (746) and the advent of Tiglath-pileser (745), under whom the Assyrians set themselves the tremendous task of conquering both Babylonia and Syria. Overpowering small states, plundering cities, deporting populations, the Assyrians became a menace that filled Syria and Palestine with terror. Soon Samaria in alliance with Damascus became involved in a treacherous adventure against Judah, which ended in their becoming prey to Assyria's aggression. The relative security of the preceding several centuries was rudely broken.

The future of Judah hung in the balance; Samaria was doomed. The message of Isaiah, particularly as received by him in his great vision, spelled the final judgment.

Amos and Hosea had devoted their ministries to trying to save the people of the Northern Kingdom. They had called for return, but met with no response. What was to be Isaiah's role in relation to Samaria?

Neither the words of the prophets nor the experience of disaster seemed to shake the self-reliance of the people of the Northern Kingdom. In pride and arrogance of heart they boasted:

> *The bricks have fallen,*
> *But we will build with hewn stones;*
> *The sycamores have been cut down,*
> *But we will put cedars in their place.*
> *Isaiah 9:10 [H. 9:9]*

All attempts to purify Samaria failed; its final destruction was proclaimed (17:1–11; 9:8–21 [H. 9:7–20]).

> *Through the wrath of the Lord of hosts*
> *The land is burned,*
> *And the people are like fuel for the fire; . . .*
> *Isaiah 9:19 [H. 9:18]*

The judgment will be carried out at the decree of the Lord.

> *He will raise a signal for a nation afar off,*
> *And whistle for it from the ends of the earth;*

*And lo, swiftly, speedily it comes!*
*None is weary, none stumbles,*
*None slumbers or sleeps,*
*Not a waistcloth is loose,*
*Not a sandal-thong is broken.*
*Their arrows are sharp,*
*All their bows bent,*
*Their horses' hoofs seem like flint,*
*And their wheels like the whirlwind.*
*Their roaring is like a lion,*
*Like young lions they roar;*
*They growl and seize their prey,*
*They carry it off, and none can rescue.*

*Isaiah 5:26–29*

The Northern Kingdom was doomed; Ephraim as a people would cease to exist (7:8); Isaiah had no role to play in its destiny (28:1–4). With few exceptions, his message was directed to Judah.

## SURRENDER TO ASSYRIA

King Jotham died about 735 and was succeeded by his son Ahaz (735–715 B.C.E.), who at once found himself embroiled in a serious crisis. The western states had accepted the dominion of Assyria only at the point of the sword. They hated the conquerors, and yielded only when crushed. The people hoped continually for an opportunity to free themselves from the bitter yoke, and the opposition did not long remain dormant. In the Kingdom of Israel a usurper named Pekah (737–732 B.C.E.), leader of an anti-Assyrian movement, came into power. Taking advantage of the Assyrian king's involvement in the east, Pekah together with Rezin of Damascus united against Assyria, and apparently they were joined by Askelon and Gaza, whose independence was threatened by Assyria. King Ahaz, who refused to join the anti-Assyrian coalition, found himself threatened by the allied kings whose combined forces subjected Jerusalem to a state of siege

(II Kings 15:37; 16:5; Isa. 7:1 ff.). The object of this undertaking was to depose King Ahaz and to replace him by a friend of their own, probably an Aramaean, who would bring the Kingdom of Judah into the anti-Assyria coalition. It would have meant the end of the dynasty of David.

The attack by the two superior enemies progressed well. The territory of Judah was devastated, Jerusalem was threatened; the Edomites and Philistines on the south, probably incited by the aggressors, annexed portions of Judah's territory (II Kings 10:5; II Chron. 28:16–18). King Ahaz as well as his people were in a state of panic. As Isaiah put it, "His heart and the heart of his people shook as the trees of the forest shake before the wind" (7:2). There seemed to be only one way to save the Kingdom: to implore powerful Assyria for aid. Assyria would save Jerusalem.

At that critical moment, probably in the year 735, while Jerusalem was besieged by the superior forces of the enemy, Isaiah conveyed the word of God to the king: "Take heed, be quiet, do not fear, and do not let your heart be faint, because of these two smoldering stumps of firebrands" who were planning to conquer Judah. "Thus says the Lord God: It shall not stand, it shall not come to pass." But Ahaz' fear was not allayed. In a final attempt to influence the king, Isaiah offered to confirm the divine authority of his words by a sign. "Ask a sign of the Lord your God; let it be deep as Sheol or high as heaven." But Ahaz said: "I will not ask, and I will not put the Lord to test" (7:1–12).

We have no right to question the king's sincerity. His refusal to ask for a sign was motivated by piety (cf. Deut. 6:16). Besieged and harassed by his enemies, he sent messengers to Tiglath-pileser III (745–727 B.C.E.), king of Assyria, saying: "I am your servant and your son. Come up, and rescue me from the hand of the king of Syria and from the hand of the king of Israel, who are attacking me" (II Kings 16:7).

No other ruler would have acted differently. The state was in peril, so he appealed to a great power for military aid. Isaiah offered words; Assyria had an army. To rely on God rather than on weapons would have been to subordinate political wisdom to faith. The issue was not to let faith in God be a guide in his personal life. The issue was to let faith be the guide in a public life: other people's lives were at stake, the future of the country was in peril. The king would have had to justify to his people a refusal to ask for help.

So Ahaz decided that it was more expedient to be "son and servant" to the king of Assyria than son and servant to the invisible God. He took refuge in a lie (cf. 28:15). The independence of Judah was surrendered to Assyria.

The appeal of Ahaz, accompanied by silver and gold from the treasuries of the Temple and the royal palace in Jerusalem, was accepted by Tiglath-pileser, though he hardly needed Ahaz' request for help as an incentive for his campaigns in Syria and Palestine. Having settled his difficulties in the east, he turned against the Kingdom of Israel and ravaged its northern territory. The whole of Galilee and Gilead together with a strip along the seacoast was made part of an Assyrian province, and the population deported. That was the first act in the Assyrian captivity. Samaria was left intact; the opposition, which presumably favored dependence upon Assyria, did away with Pekah and placed his assassin, Hoshea (732–724 B.C.E.), upon the throne. Hoshea paid tribute to Tiglath-pileser, and was recognized by him as a vassal king. Thereafter, according to his own account, Tiglath-pileser turned southward, capturing Askelon and Gaza, thus freeing Ahaz from the danger of his other enemies. In 734–732, he ravaged Syria and Palestine to the very borders of Egypt. Damascus was conquered, the king of Syria killed, his chief advisers impaled, his gardens and orchards hacked down, and the inhabitants deported. The whole west was turned into a series of Assyrian provinces.*

Ahaz, overawed by the triumphs of the Assyrian king, readily yielded to the glamour and prestige of the Assyrians in religion as well as in politics. In 732, he went to Damascus to pay homage to Tiglath-pileser. There he saw an altar, which he ordered copied and installed

*See *ANET,* pp. 281 f.; A. T. Olmstead, *History of Assyria* (New York, 1923), pp. 197 f.

in the Temple at Jerusalem (II Kings 16:10 ff.). He also made changes in the arrangements and furniture of the Temple "because of the king of Assyria" (II Kings 16:18). The altar made after the Assyrian pattern carried, it seems, the acknowledgment of Assyria's greatness in the realm of religion and was a public recognition of the power of the alien god.

## A Covenant with Death

Isaiah asked Ahaz to believe that it was neither Pekah nor Rezin nor even the mighty Tiglath-pileser who governed history. The world was in the hands of God, and it was folly to be terrified by "these two smoldering stumps of firebrands"; those powers were destined for destruction, and even the might of Assyria would not last forever. The right policy was neither to join the coalition nor to rely upon Assyria. The judgment over Judah was inevitable, and it was not to be averted by alliances, arms, or strategy. Accompanied by his son Shear-jashub—a symbolical name expressing the conviction that a remnant would turn to God and be saved—Isaiah appealed to the king to be calm. He also announced that a young woman would have a son and would call his name Immanuel—God is with us—and that before the boy reached the age of two or three years, the allied kings would have departed from the land. Then evil days would come upon Judah, such days as she had not seen since the secession of the Northern Kingdom. Egypt and Assyria would lay the land waste. But a remnant would return, and a reign of everlasting peace and justice be inaugurated.

Ahaz and the court were feeling secure owing to the treaty with Assyria, and were congratulating themselves on having so shrewdly frustrated their enemies. Scoffingly they said:

> *We have made a covenant with death,*
> *And with Sheol we have an agreement;*
> *When the overwhelming scourge passes through*
> *It will not come to us;*

> *For we have made lies our refuge,*
> *And in falsehood we have taken shelter.*
>
> *Isaiah 28:15*

But Isaiah was distressed at their cynicism and folly. The Lord had warned him "not to walk in the way of this people. . . . Do not call alliance* all that this people call alliance; do not fear what they fear" (8:11–12). In the name of God he proclaimed:

> *I will make justice the line,*
> *And righteousness the plummet;*
> *Hail will sweep away the refuge of lies,*
> *Waters will overwhelm the shelter.*
> *Then your covenant with death will be annulled,*
> *Your agreement with Sheol will not stand;*
> *When the overwhelming scourge passes through,*
> *You will be beaten down by it.*
>
> *Isaiah 28:17–18*

A gulf was separating prophet and king in their thinking and understanding. What seemed to be a terror to Ahaz was a trifle in Isaiah's eyes. The king, seeking to come to terms with the greatest power in the world, was ready to abandon religious principles in order to court the emperor's favor. The prophet who saw history as the stage for God's work, where kingdoms and empires rise for a time and vanish, perceived a design beyond the mists and shadows of the moment.

While others acclaimed Ahaz for having gained the most powerful protection, Isaiah insisted that Assyria would bring disaster. "Because this people have refused the waters of Shiloah that flow gently, . . . the Lord is bringing up against them the waters of the River, mighty and many, the king of Assyria and all his glory; it will rise over all its channels and go over all its banks; it will sweep on into Judah, it will overflow and pass on, reaching even to the neck; its

---

*See E. J. Kissane, *The Book of Isaiah*, I (Dublin, 1941), 103, and the reference to Neh. 4:2.

outspread wings will fill the breadth of your land, O Immanuel" (8:6–8).

When Tiglath-pileser died in 727, hopes of independence began to stir among the disgruntled vassals in the western part of the empire. Hoshea of Israel, after reaching an understanding with the Egyptian king, stopped payment of the annual tribute. In reprisal, Assyria sent her army against Samaria. Though Egypt failed to offer any aid, Samaria was able to hold out for three years. In 722, the city fell to Sargon II (722–705 B.C.E.); the Israelite monarch was overthrown and the population sent as captives to Assyria. The end of the Northern Kingdom filled the people of Judah with grief and consternation.

## JERUSALEM REJOICES, ISAIAH IS DISTRESSED

Ahaz was succeeded by his son Hezekiah (*ca.* 715–687 B.C.E.), whose marvelous career was predicted by Isaiah when the child was still an infant. Hezekiah was the opposite of his father. No king of Judah among his predecessors or his successors could, it was said, be compared to him (II Kings 18:5). His first act was to repair and to purge the Temple and its vessels, to reorganize the services of the priests and Levites (II Chron. 29:3–36).

Hezekiah must have realized the prudence of Ahaz in refusing to be involved in intrigues against Assyria. To be sure, Judah was a vassal and was paying substantial tribute to the Assyrian overlord. Yet hateful as this condition was, Hezekiah seemed to realize that to throw off the yoke of Assyria would mean to court disaster, and in spite of strong pressure brought to bear upon him by the vassal states in Syria and Palestine to join them in rebellion, he held aloof. He took no part in the abortive revolt instigated by the king of Hamath.

Gradually, however, the people became impatient with the policy of submission to Assyria, which meant perpetual tribute and perpetual strain. In an inscription belonging to the year 711, Sargon II refers to the rulers of Palestine, Judah, Edom, Moab, and others, who had to bring tributes and presents to "my lord Ashur," but who meditated on hostility and plotted evil, and were sending their tokens of homage to the king of Egypt, "a potentate incapable to save them," seeking an alliance with him.* Indeed, it was Egypt that began in those years to play a fateful role in the political decisions of Judah.

For a long time Egypt had lapsed into relative stagnation, punctuated by civil war, and had broken up into numerous small states, independent of each other. Assyrian kings looked with desire upon Egypt, so rich and seemingly so defenseless, and Tiglath-pileser III advanced to her very border. Assyria was in control of Gaza, the gateway to the land of the Pharaohs. Around 720, conditions changed. A powerful state called Ethiopia, with its capital Napata, the biblical Noph, came into being, whose ruler Shabako invaded Egypt, seized the throne, set up a strong, unified government, and inaugurated the Twenty-second Dynasty. Egypt began to carry on intrigues in southern Palestine against the Assyrian conqueror and sought to encourage the subjugated states to rebel against the enemy.† It would appear that an ambitious plan was conceived, at the instigation of Egyptian agents, by which the Philistines, Moab, Edom, and Judah were to join Ashdod in a simultaneous attack on the Assyrians. Egyptian envoys arrived in Jerusalem to try to induce Judah to join the alliance, promising military support.

Egypt had set herself up as the champion of the subjugated nations, and while her envoys were entertained in Jerusalem they seem to have been greeted as deliverers from the Assyrian yoke. The poor, oppressed, helpless people were waiting for God to deliver them.

At that moment Isaiah again interfered, addressing his people with words of comfort and warning. God has not forgotten them. He is looking on from His abode in heaven, watching the events. The moment of deliverance from Assyria has not yet arrived, nor will Ethiopia be the agent to bring about the oppressor's end. Another nation is to be chosen for this act, which will come about at God's appointed time (18:1 ff.).‡

---

*ANET, p. 287.

†J. H. Breasted, A History of Egypt (New York, 1912), pp. 547 f.

‡The prophecy probably belongs to the early years of the Ethiopian dynasty, see Kissane, op. cit., pp. 202 f.

To illustrate the futility of depending on Egypt (30:7) and the disaster to which the pro-Egyptian policy would lead, Isaiah walked about Jerusalem in the scanty garb of a slave—symbolic of what lay in store for the peoples of Egypt and Ethiopia. Not only would they fail to send effective aid to the rebel states of Palestine; they themselves would fall victims to the might of Assyria (ch. 20). It seems that Isaiah's advice was heeded. Judah did not take part in the battle of 711/713, led by Ashdod, which quickly collapsed.

As long as Sargon II reigned, no open break with Assyria was made. But when that king died and was succeeded by his greatly inferior son Sennacherib (705–681 B.C.E.), Hezekiah, evidently thinking the time propitious, formally refused tribute (II Kings 18:7), and took steps to defend his independence. Sargon had met his death in a battle that apparently ended in serious defeat for Assyria, and rebellion broke out at both extremities of the far-flung empire. In Babylon, Merodach-baladan rebelled, and with Elamite help, established himself as king (703). Looking for allies in his fight against Assyria, he sent envoys with letters and a gift to Hezekiah, ostensibly to congratulate him on his recovery from a serious illness. Hezekiah rejoiced over the distinguished visitors and showed them his treasure house and all his armory, trying to impress them with the wealth and strength of Judah. "There was nothing in his house nor in all his realm which Hezekiah did not show them." The object of this courtesy visit was to draw Judah into some compact against Assyria.

At that moment Isaiah appeared before Hezekiah, who seemed to be elated over the friendship of the Babylonian king, and denounced his enthusiasm for the new friend. He predicted that membership in the projected coalition would result in the destruction of the Kingdom and exile for the people. "Hear the word of the Lord of hosts: Behold, the days are coming, when all that is in your house, and that which your fathers have stored up till this day, shall be carried to Babylon; . . . Some of your own sons . . . shall be eunuchs in the palace of the king of Babylon . . ." (39:5–7).* Hezekiah again hesi-

---

*The date of this episode is uncertain, see J. Bright, *History of Israel* (Philadelphia, 1959), p. 269, n. 53; Albright, *op. cit.*, p. 43. It occurred either in 721–710 or in 704–703 B.C.E.

tated, but when the revolt spread throughout Palestine and Syria, and a powerful coalition of kingdoms was formed, Hezekiah not only joined the coalition, but seems to have become the leader of the insurrection. His envoys were dispatched to Egypt to negotiate a treaty (30:1–7; 31:1–3), carrying "their riches on the backs of asses, and their treasures on the humps of camels" (30:6). He was busy arranging his defences, providing arms, fortifying the walls of Jerusalem, and digging a tunnel through which water was brought underneath the hill of Jerusalem to a pool within the walls.

The decision to join the coalition against Assyria evoked

> . . . *joy and gladness,*
> *Slaying oxen and killing sheep,*
> *Eating flesh and drinking wine.*
> Isaiah 22:13

We can picture the scene. Jerusalem is tumultuous, exultant; the people are all on the housetops, shouting. The king speaks at a mass meeting in the square at the gate of the city. "Be strong and of good courage. Do not be afraid or dismayed before the king of Assyria and all the horde that is with him; for there is One greater with us than with him. With him is an arm of flesh; but with us is the Lord our God, to help us and to fight our battles" (II Chron. 32:7–8).

Jerusalem rejoices, and Isaiah is distressed. The people "looked to weapons" (22:8) as the source of security, rather than to Him Who is the true master of both nature and history. "You did not look to Him Who created it, or have regard for Him Who planned it long ago" (22:11).

Those who act as if there were no God, no divine order in history, are more foolish than one who would sow and plant, while completely disregarding the nature of the soil or the seasons of the year. They act as if man were alone, as if their deeds were carried out in the dark, as if there were no God Who saw, no God Who knew.

> *Woe to those who hide deep from the Lord their counsel,*
> *Whose deeds are in the dark,*

*And who say, Who sees us? Who knows us?*
*You turn things upside down!*
*Shall the potter be regarded as the clay;*
*That the thing made should say of its maker,*
*He did not make me;*
*Or the thing formed say of him who formed it,*
*He has no understanding?*

Isaiah 29:15–16

## IF YOU WILL NOT BELIEVE, YOU WILL NOT ABIDE

The policy adopted by Hezekiah was tactically the same as the one employed by his father. He turned to Egypt for protection against Assyria, just as his father, Ahaz, had turned to Assyria for protection against the Northern Kingdom and Syria. My enemy's enemy is my friend, was his belief. The king put his trust in the art of politics, carrying out his plan, disregarding God's plan; entering an alliance, but not in God's spirit; taking refuge in the protection of Pharaoh, and assuming that man could be relied upon.

Isaiah's utter distrust of worldly power, his disgust for the military boots, for "every garment rolled in blood" (9:5 [H. 9:4]), for the scepter and the pomp of the wicked rulers (14:5, 11), for their arrogance, pride, and insolence, made it impossible for him to approve of any military alliance. And above all, reliance on the arms of Egypt meant denial of God's power over history.

*Turn away from man,*
*In whose nostrils is breath,*
*For of what account is he? . . .*
*For the Lord is our Judge, the Lord is our Ruler,*
*The Lord is our King; He will save us. . . .*
*Woe to the rebellious children, says the Lord,*
*Who carry out a plan that is not from Me,*
*Who turn an alliance not of My spirit,*
*Adding sin to sin;* *

---

*See Kissane, *op. cit.,* p. 336.

*Who set out to go down to Egypt,*
*Without asking for My counsel,*
*To take refuge in the protection of Pharaoh,*
*To seek shelter in the shadow of Egypt!*
*Therefore shall the protection of Pharaoh turn to your shame,*
*The shelter in the shadow of Egypt to your humiliation. . . .*
                                    *Isaiah 2:22; 33:22; 30:1–2*

Isaiah predicted that the alliance with Egypt would not only prove "worthless and empty" and bring "shame and disgrace" (30:7, 5); it would end in disaster (30:12 ff.). The soldiers, the chariots, and the horses, even if they should be superior in number to those of the enemy, would prove of no avail.

*A thousand shall flee at the threat of one, . . .*
*Till you are left*
*Like a flagstaff on the top of a mountain,*
*Like a signal on a hill.*

                                    *Isaiah 30:17*

The efforts of those who try to oppose God's design are sinful and futile.

*For He is wise and brings disaster,*
*He does not call back His words,*
*But will arise against the house of the evildoers,*
*Against the helpers of those who work iniquity. . . .*
*Return ye to Him from Whom you have deeply revolted,*
  *O people of Israel.*

                                    *Isaiah 31:2, 6*

### AGAINST ALLIANCES

There were, we should like to suggest, three reasons for the prophet's opposition to any alliance with either Egypt or Assyria. (1) Reliance on a world power meant a demonstration of the belief that man rather than God, weapons rather than attachment to Him, determined the destiny of the nations. (2) Subservience to a nation such as Assyria meant accepting her gods and cults. (3) An alliance with Assyria meant an involvement in her military operations.

The history of Israel began in two acts of rejection: the rejection of Mesopotamia in the days of Abraham and the rejection of Egypt in the days of Moses. In both cases it was a rejection of political and spiritual sovereignty.* For many centuries the impact of both Mesopotamian and Egyptian religion on the religion of western Asia had been prodigious. The names and ideograms of Mesopotamian gods and goddesses were borrowed by Hurrians, Hittites, Amorites, and Canaanites alike. The cult of Mesopotamian deities like Dagan penetrated into southern Palestine. The cult of Ishtar of Nineveh was carried into places as far removed from Assyria as Egypt and southwestern Asia Minor.†

After settling in the land of Canaan, Israel had to face the political and religious challenge of minor city-states and local cults. For generations Israel remained secure from any direct involvement with either Mesopotamia or Egypt. The situation changed rapidly in the eighth century with the emergence of Assyria as an empire, intent upon conquering the small states in the Near East. In addition, Egypt, unwilling to permit the power of Assyria to extend to her very borders, began to assert her political and military influence in the same area. Caught in the contest between the two powers, the kings of Judah and the Northern Kingdom of Israel would turn either to Assyria for protection or, more often, to Egypt for protection against Assyria. The hard-won emancipation from Mesopotamia and Egypt that had been brought about in the days of Abraham and Moses faced a dangerous test in the days of Hosea, Isaiah, and Jeremiah.

The Assyrians were fanatically devout. In military campaigns the king assumed the role of the deputy of the god. The prowess and victories of the army were thought to reflect the power of the god Ashur. Assyria imposed the recognition of her gods as the overlords

*See E. A. Speiser, *New Horizons in Bible Study* (Baltimore, 1958), pp. 8 f.

†W. F. Albright, *From the Stone Age to Christianity* (2nd ed.; Baltimore, 1957), p. 212.

of the gods of the conquered peoples. Political subservience involved acceptance of her religious institutions. It was nearly impossible for a small vassal state to keep from being flooded with the idolatrous and superstitious practices under royal Assyrian protection. This explains the infiltration into Judah of all sorts of foreign cults and superstitions in the period in which she was a vassal of Assyria.

What did Isaiah propose in place of alliances?

> *In returning [ to God] and in rest you shall be saved;*
> *In quietness and in trust shall be your strength.*
>
> Isaiah 30:15

Isaiah's plea made little impression upon the government. Threatened as the state was by the aggressive might of Assyria, was it not more prudent to rely on Egyptian arms than to withdraw into quietness and trust in the Lord? "No," was the answer to Isaiah's plea. "We will speed upon horses! . . . We will ride upon swift steeds!" (30:16). But Isaiah continued to insist: Do not rely on horses! Do not trust in chariots because they are many or on horsemen because they are very strong! (31:1.) Look to the Holy One of Israel; consult the Lord!

> *The Egyptians are men, and not God;*
> *And their horses are flesh, and not spirit.*
> *When the Lord stretches out His hand,*
> *The helper will stumble, and he who is helped will fall,*
> *And they will all perish together.*
>
> Isaiah 31:3

Isaiah could not accept politics as a solution, since politics itself, with its arrogance and disregard of justice, was a problem. When mankind is, as we would say, spiritually sick, something more radical than political sagacity is needed to solve the problem of security. For the moment a clever alignment of states may be of help. In the long run, it is bound to prove futile.

Is it realistic to expect that nations would discard their horses and look to the Lord instead? Indeed, it is hard to learn how to live by faith. But Isaiah insisted that one cannot live without faith. "If you will not believe, you will not abide" (7:9). Faith is not an easy or convenient path. There are frustrations in store for him who expects God to succeed at every turn in history. But "he who believes will not be in haste" (28:16). Enduring strength is not in the mighty rivers, but in "the waters of Shiloah that flow gently" (8:6).

Politics is based on the power of the sword. But Isaiah was waiting for the day when nations "shall beat their swords into plowshares and their spears into pruning hooks." Alliances involve preparation for war, but Isaiah was horrified by the brutalities and carnage which war entails. In his boundless yearning he had a vision of the day when "nation shall not lift up sword against nation, neither shall they learn war any more" (2:4). War spawns death. But Isaiah was looking to the time when the Lord "will swallow up death for ever, and the Lord God will wipe away tears from all faces" (25:8; see p. 234). Israel's security lies in the covenant with God, not in covenants with Egypt or other nations. The mysterious power of faith maintains: God alone is true protection. Such power will not collapse in the hour of disaster: "I will wait for the Lord, Who is hiding His face from the house of Jacob, and I will hope in Him" (8:17). Never must a calamity shake Israel's trust.

> O Lord our God,
> Other lords besides Thee have imposed themselves upon us,
> But it is Thou alone upon Whom we call.
>
> Isaiah 26:13

## ASSYRIA SHALL FALL BY A SWORD NOT OF MAN

Assyria with all her might and triumph was but a tool in the hands of God for carrying out His work against sinful nations. But in her ruthlessness and arrogance she perpetrated dreadful crimes instead of manifesting justice.

> Ah, Assyria, the rod of My anger,
> The staff of My Fury!

*Against a godless nation I send him,*
*Against the people of My wrath I command him,*
*To take spoil and seize plunder,*
*To tread them down like the mire of the streets.*
*But he does not so intend,*
*His mind does not so think;*
*To cut off nations not a few;*
*For he says:*
*Are not my commanders all kings?*
*Is not Calno like Carchemish?*
*Is not Hamath like Arpad?*
*Is not Samaria like Damascus?*
*As my hand has reached to the kingdoms of the idols*
*Whose graven images were greater than those*
   *of Jerusalem and Samaria,*
*Shall I not do to Jerusalem and her idols*
*As I have done to Samaria and her images?*
                 *Isaiah 10:5–11*

While Assyria was at the height of her power, Isaiah proclaimed her downfall. His prediction was not the forecast of an isolated event, but part of a divine plan and purpose for Israel and all nations.

*The Lord of hosts has sworn:*
*As I have planned, so shall it be;*
*As I have purposed, so shall it stand.*
*I will break the Assyrian in My land,*
*And upon My mountains trample him under foot;*
*His yoke shall depart from them,*
*And his burden from their shoulder.*
*This is the purpose that is purposed*
*Concerning the whole earth;*
*This is the hand that is stretched out*
*Over all nations.*
                 *Isaiah 14:24–26*

The way in which the Lord carries out His plan remains inscrutable. But He employs human agents as well as "a sword not of man" to accomplish His designs.

> *Assyria shall fall by a sword, not of man;*
> *A sword, not of man, shall devour him; . . .*
> *His rock shall pass away through terror*
> *And his princes in panic shall desert the standard,*
> *Says the Lord Whose fire is in Zion,*
> *And Whose furnace is in Jerusalem . . .*

*The Lord will cause His majestic voice to be heard and the descending blow of His arm to be seen, in furious anger and a flame of devouring fire with a cloudburst and tempest and hailstones. The Assyrians will be terror-stricken at the voice of the Lord, when He smites with His rod.*
> Isaiah 31:8–9; 30:30–31*

Assyria's power was a phantom, "but the Lord of hosts, Him you shall regard as holy; let Him be your fear, let Him be your dread!" (8:13.) It was in such dread and fear that Isaiah proclaimed what the real problems were.

## SENNACHERIB'S INVASION OF JUDAH

About 703, Sennacherib embarked on a series of campaigns, and with quick blows overwhelmed the rebels. He first smashed the resistance of Merodach-baladan and his Elamite ally, and, having secured his border east of the Tigris, launched an expedition in 701 against Syria and Palestine. The very presence of the mighty monarch, or, in his own words, "the terror-inspiring splendor of my lordship" stunned the petty kingdoms. Most rulers quickly surrendered by offering their tribute, while others were easily overrun. A large Egyptian and Ethiopian army dispatched to relieve the beleaguered town of

---

*See also 17:12–14. "No serious argument has been advanced by those who deny" Isaiah authorship of 30:27–33; see Kissane, *op. cit.*, p. 336.

Ekron was defeated. Important as it might have been to invade Egypt, Sennacherib's army instead turned against Judah, the chief enemy in this entire campaign. There was nothing to hinder their entrance into Judah. Soon her valleys were filled with Assyrian chariots and horsemen (22:7), the country ravaged, forty-six fortified cities turned over to the pro-Assyrian kings of the Philistine cities, and their population deported. Sennacherib set up his headquarters in Lachish, Judah's strong frontier fortress, where he awaited Hezekiah's surrender.

Facing the possibility of complete disaster, Hezekiah sent a message to the king of Assyria at Lachish. "I have done wrong; withdraw from me; whatever you impose on me I will bear." An extremely heavy tribute was exacted, probably more than Jerusalem was able to bear (II Kings 18:14–16). Yet, Sennacherib apparently demanded still more: the surrender of Jerusalem. This was impossible to accept. Hezekiah, encouraged by Isaiah who predicted that Sennacherib would never capture the city, refused to open its gates. Jerusalem was besieged; Hezekiah, Sennacherib boasted, was shut up in his capital "like a bird in a cage." But the powerful fortress, whose defences had been strengthened in preparation for the revolt, withstood the enemy's onslaught.

We can visualize the events. In order to force the city to capitulate by breaking down public morale, an Assyrian official, Rabshakeh, meets the representatives of Hezekiah and addresses them within the hearing of the people crowded on top of the city wall. He starts out by maintaining that Judah can rely neither on Egypt's aid nor on God's protection. Egypt is but "a broken reed," and the God of Israel is angry at Hezekiah for having closed the cultic shrines all over the country, thus forcing the people to come to the one shrine in Jerusalem. Moreover, "has any of the gods of the nations delivered his land out of the hand of the king of Assyria?" The God of Israel is just as powerless against the might of Assyria, as the gods of the conquered nations have been. Scoffingly Rabshakeh maintains that Judah has no horses, and if she had, she could not make use of them for lack of skilled horsemen. Apparently echoing statements made by the prophets, Rabshakeh then states that it is the Lord, the God of Israel, who ordered Sennacherib to destroy Judah (II Kings 18:17 ff.; Isa. 36:4 ff.). Better to submit than to face defeat and deportation.

The plight of Jerusalem seemed desperate. All neighboring kingdoms either had surrendered or were crushed. The country was overrun by the enemy, Egyptian aid proved worthless. Jerusalem was alone. In that hour of distress and disgrace, Isaiah proclaimed the word that the Lord had spoken concerning Assyria.

> *She despises you, she scorns you—*
> *The virgin daughter of Zion;*
> *She wags her head behind you—*
> *The daughter of Jerusalem.*
> *Whom have you mocked and reviled?*
> *Against whom have you raised your voice*
> *And haughtily lifted your eyes?*
> *Against the Holy One of Israel!*
> *By your servants you have mocked the Lord,*
> *And you have said, With my many chariots*
> *I have gone up the heights of the mountains,*
> *To the far recesses of Lebanon;*
> *I felled its tallest cedars,*
> *Its choicest cypresses;*
> *I came to its remotest height,*
> *Its densest forest.*
> *I dug wells and drank waters,*
> *And I dried up with the sole of my foot*
> *All the streams of Egypt.*
> *Have you not heard*
> *That I determined it long ago?*
> *I planned from days of old*
> *What now I bring to pass,*
> *That you should make fortified cities*
> *Crash into heaps of ruins,*
> *While their inhabitants, shorn of strength,*

*Are dismayed and confounded,*
*And have become like plants of the field*
*And like tender grass,*
*Like grass on the housetops,*
*Blighted before it is grown.*
*I know your sitting down*
*And your going out and coming in,*
*And your raging against Me.*
*Because you have raged against Me*
*And your arrogance has come to My ears,*
*I will put My hooks in your nose*
*And My bit in your mouth,*
*And I will turn you back on the way*
*By which you came.*

*Isaiah 37:22–29*

Isaiah's prediction was vindicated by a miraculous event. A disastrous pestilence spread in the Assyrian camp, decimating the army. Sennacherib returned to Nineveh and was eventually murdered by his sons (II Kings 19:36–37).*

From 701 for about three-quarters of a century, until the downfall of the Assyrian empire, Judah continued to be a dependency of the Assyrian emperor, and was not involved in the political drama that took place close at hand. Under the reign of Sennacherib's son, Esarhaddon (681–669 B.C.E.), who conquered a great part of Egypt, and under Ashurbanipal (669–633?), Assyria reached the summit of her power.

## CONFUSIONS

As we have seen, Isaiah's primary concern is not Judah's foreign policy, but rather the inner state of the nation. In the period in which he begins his activity, there is prosperity in the land.

*See *ANET,* pp. 287 f.; L. Honor, *Sennacherib's Invasion of Palestine* (New York, 1926).

The king is astute, the priests are proud, and the market place is busy. Placid, happy, even gay, the people pursue their work and worship in their own way, and life is fair. Then again appears a prophet, hurling bitter words from the depth of a divine anguish. People buy, sell, celebrate, rejoice, but Isaiah is consumed with distress. He cannot bear the sight of a people's normal crimes: exploitation of the poor, worship of the gods. He, like the prophets before him, has a message of doom and a bitter look. Even things that are pretty are sickening to him.

> *Their land is filled with silver and gold,*
> *There is no end to their treasures;*
> *Their land is filled with horses,*
> *There is no end to their chariots.*
> *Isaiah 2:7*

What is the issue that haunts the prophet's soul? It is not a question, but a bitter exclamation: How marvelous is the world that God has created! And how horrible is the world that man has made!

The essence of blasphemy is confusion, and in the eyes of the prophet confusion is raging in the world.

The earth is full of the glory of God (6:3), but the land is filled with idols (2:8). Men are haughty and full of pride (2:11), yet "they bow down to the work of their hands, to what their own fingers have made" (2:8). They regard themselves as wise and shrewd (5:21), but are devoid of the simple insight with which even an animal is endowed—knowing whose he is (1:3).

Princes are scoundrels (1:23); judges are corrupt, acquitting the guilty for a bribe and depriving the innocent of his right (5:23). They do not defend the fatherless, and the widow's case does not come to them (1:23). The people are being crushed by the elders and princes, while the mansions of the wealthy contain the spoils of the poor (3:14 f.). And in spite of all this, the knave is called noble, and the churl is said to be honorable (cf. 32:5).

Jerusalem—destined to be the place from which the word of God (2:3), Him Who creates heaven and earth, went forth—even Jerusalem "the faithful city has become a harlot, she that was full of justice! Righteousness lodged in her, but now murderers" (1:21), graven images, and idols (10:10 f.). Indeed, the land that the Lord has given to His people is "filled with idols; they bow down to the work of their hands!" The house of Jacob is "full of diviners from the east and of soothsayers like the Philistines" (2:6–8).

The prophet is struck by man's interminable pride, by his soaring pretension. Things done by man are lofty, high, and brazen, even worshiped, while the exaltation of God is but a hope.

> *You turn things upside down!*
> *Shall the potter be regarded as the clay;*
> *That the thing made should say of its maker:*
> *"He did not make me";*
> *Or that the thing formed say of him who formed it:*
> *"He has no understanding"?*
>
> *Isaiah 29:16*

## THE ANGER OF THE LORD

The prophet knows that "the anger of the Lord is kindled against His people" (5:25). Visions of doom haunt the prophet's soul. The whole world is on the verge of disaster. The Lord is about to judge the nations, and His judgment will shake the world.

> *Behold, the name of the Lord comes from far,*
> *Burning with His anger, and in thick rising smoke;*
> *His lips are full of indignation,*
> *And His tongue is like a devouring fire;*
> *His breath is like an overflowing stream*
> *That reaches up to the neck;*
> *To sift the nations with the sieve of destruction,*
> *And to place on the jaws of the peoples a bridle that leads astray. . . .*
> *I will punish the world for its evil,*
> *And the wicked for their iniquity;*
> *I will put an end to the pride of the arrogant,*

*And lay low the haughtiness of the ruthless.*
*I will make men more rare than fine gold,*
*And mankind than the gold of Ophir.*
*Therefore I will make the heavens tremble,*
*And the earth will be shaken out of its place,*
*At the wrath of the Lord of hosts*
*In the day of His fierce anger.*

*Isaiah 30:27–28; 13:11–13*\*

God when silent may be disregarded, but when He rises to terrify the earth, men will enter the caverns of the rocks and the clefts of the cliffs "before the terror of the Lord . . . and the glory of his majesty" (Isa. 2:19, 21).

*Man shall be brought low, man shall be humbled,*
*And the eyes of the haughty shall be cast down,*
*But the Lord of hosts shall be exalted in justice,*
*And the Holy God show Himself holy in righteousness.*

*Isaiah 5:15–16*

Characteristic of the dreadful intensity of the divine anger is the phrase used repeatedly by Isaiah, describing it when kindled against Ephraim:

*As the tongue of fire devours the stubble,*
*As the dry grass sinks down in the flame,*
*So their root will be rottenness,*
*And their blossom go up like dust. . . .*
*For all this His anger is not turned away*
*And His hand is stretched out still. . . .*
*So the Lord cut off from Assyria head and tail,*
*Palm branch and reed in one day, . . .*
*The Lord . . . has no compassion on their fatherless and widows;*
*For everyone is godless and an evildoer,*

---

\*Some critics maintain that Isa. 13:1–14:2 was written on the occasion of the death of an Assyrian king (Sargon or Sennacherib) and that it was adapted by a later editor to the fall of Babylon.

*And every mouth speaks folly. . . .*
*Through the wrath of the Lord of hosts*
*The land is burned,*
*And the people are like fuel for the fire;*
*No man spares his brother.*

                    *Isaiah 5:24, 25; 9:14–19; cf. 9:20; 10:4*

Grim, foreboding, relentless is the account of the anger in action.

Listening to the prophet's words about the grandeur of God's anger, even the disparagers cannot dissemble their terror.

> *The sinners in Zion are afraid;*
> *Trembling has seized the godless:*
> *Who among us can dwell with the devouring fire?*
> *Who among us can dwell with everlasting burnings?*
> *Isaiah 33:14*

However, the destructiveness of God's power is not due to God's hostility to man, but to His concern for righteousness, to His intolerance of injustice. The human mind seems to have no sense for the true dimension of man's cruelty to man. God's anger is fierce because man's cruelty is infernal.

## DIVINE SORROW

Significantly, however, the speech that opens the book of Isaiah, and which sets the tone for all the utterances by this prophet, deals not with the anger, but with the sorrow of God. The prophet pleads with us to understand the plight of a father whom his children have abandoned.

> *Hear, O heavens, and give ear, O earth;*
> *For the Lord has spoken:*
> *Sons have I reared and brought up,*
> *But they have rebelled against Me.*
> *The ox knows its owner*
> *And the ass its master's crib;*

> *But Israel does not know,*
> *My people does not understand.*
>
> Isaiah 1:2–3

The prophet laments in his own words the children's desertion of their father:

> *They have forsaken the Lord,*
> *They have despised the Holy One of Israel.*
>
> Isaiah 1:4

But the sympathy for God's injured love overwhelms his whole being. What he feels about the size of God's sorrow and the enormous scandal of man's desertion of God is expressed in the two lines quoted above which introduced God's lamentation. "Hear, then, O house of David! Is it too little for you to weary men, that you weary my God also?" (7:13.) In different words addressed to the king, the prophet conveys his impression of the mood of God: As happened in the time of Noah and as is happening again, God's patience and longsuffering are exhausted. He is tired of man. He hates man's homage, his festivals, his celebrations. Man has become a burden and a sorrow for God.

> *What to Me is the multitude of your sacrifices?*
> *Says the Lord;*
> *I have had enough of burnt offerings of rams*
> *And the fat of fatted beasts;*
> *I do not delight in the blood of bulls,*
> *Or of lambs, or of he-goats.*
> *When you come to appear before Me,*
> *Who requires of you*
> *This trampling of My courts?*
> *Bring no more vain offerings;*
> *Incense is an abomination to Me.*
> *New moon and sabbath and the calling of assemblies—*
> *I cannot endure iniquity and solemn assembly.*
> *Your new moons and your appointed feasts*
> *My soul hates;*

*They have become a burden to Me,*
*That I am weary to bear.*
*When you spread forth your hands,*
*I will hide My eyes from you;*
*Even though you make many prayers,*
*I will not listen;*
*Your hands are full of blood.*

*Isaiah 1:11–15*

The weariness of God,* an important theoretical category in Isaiah's thinking, brings about a greater concealment of His personal involvement in history. It is a time in which divine anger becomes active in history.

*I Myself have commanded My consecrated ones,*
*Have summoned My mighty men to execute My anger.*

*Isaiah 13:3*

There is a shift of emphasis from pathos as an emotion to pathos in action. Pathos is spoken of in Isaiah more frequently in an instrumental than in a personal sense. An important element in his thinking is the conception that the world's great powers are instruments of the divine will. Not the elements of nature, but primarily the powers of history carry out the designs of God. (Cf. 5:26; 7:18; 9:10 f.). The shift of emphasis comes to expression in phrases which characterize historic events as reflecting divine situations. "Ah, Assyria, the rod of My anger, the staff of My indignation" (10:5); "the weapons of My indignation" (13:5). Pathos becomes an attribute in action or a sign of judgment, as in the phrase, "Against the people of My wrath do I send him [Assyria]" (10:6).

## THERE IS SORROW IN HIS ANGER

God's affection for Israel rings even in the denunciations. It is "My people" who do not understand (1:3). It is "My people" who

---

*The expression also occurs in Isa. 43:24.

are suppressed by "the elders and princes" (3:14). He is anxious to forgive, to wipe out their sins (1:18). They are His children (1:2), "rebellious children" (30:1).

God is more than Lord and Owner; He is Father (1:2–4; 30–31). But for all His love and compassion, He cannot tolerate the corruption of the leaders who succumb to bribes and run after gifts, who "do not defend the fatherless, and the widow's cause does not come to them" (1:23). "Your silver has become dross, your wine mixed with water" (1:22).

> *Therefore the Lord says,*
> *The Lord of hosts,*
> *The Mighty One of Israel:*
> *Ah, I will vent My wrath on My enemies,*
> *And avenge Myself on My foes.*
> *I will turn My hand against you*
> *And will smelt away your dross as with lye*
> *And remove all your alloy.*
> *And I will restore your judges as aforetime,*
> *And your counselors as at the beginning.*
> *Afterward you shall be called the city of righteousness,*
> *The faithful city.*
> *Zion shall be redeemed by justice,*
> *And those in her who repent, by righteousness.*
>
> Isaiah 1:24–27

There is sorrow in God's anger. It is an instrument of purification, and its exercise will not last forever. "For the Lord will have compassion on Jacob and will again choose Israel, and settle them in their own land, and the stranger shall join himself to them, and will cleave to the house of Jacob" (14:1). His mercy is not discarded, merely suspended. His anger lasts a moment, it does not endure forever.

> *In a very little while My indignation will come to an end. . . .*
> *Come, My people, enter your chambers,*

*And shut your doors behind you;*
*Hide yourselves for a little while*
*Until the indignation is past.*

*Isaiah 10:25; 26:20*

Anger is not His disposition, but a state He waits to overcome.

*Therefore the Lord waits to be gracious to you;*
*Therefore He exalts Himself to show mercy to you.*
*For the Lord is a God of justice*
*Blessed are all those who wait for Him.*

*Isaiah 30:18*

Isaiah also stresses the quality of zeal, which to him seems to explain the miracle of "the surviving remnant." "For out of Jerusalem shall go forth a remnant, and out of Mount Zion a band of survivors. The zeal of the Lord of hosts will accomplish this" (37:32). The throne of David will be established "with justice and with happiness. . . . The zeal of the Lord of hosts will accomplish this" (9:7 [H. 9:6]).*

## SYMPATHY FOR GOD

Isaiah is animated by a sense of dread and the awareness of the transcendent mystery and exclusiveness of God, and only secondarily by a sense of intimacy, sympathy, and involvement in the divine situation.† He calls Him "the King" (6:13); *ha'adon* (1:24; 3:1; 10:16, 33; 19:4), "the Lord *tsebaoth*," but also *'abir Israel*, "the Mighty One of Israel"; "Rock of Israel (30:29); "my God" (7:13); "my Beloved" (5:1). To Hosea, Israel is God's consort; to Isaiah, God's vineyard. Like Amos (1:2; 3:8, 12) and Hosea (5:14; 13:8), Isaiah uses the image of a lion to describe the might of the Lord.

---

*See Küchler, *"Der Gedanke des Eifers im Alten Testament,"* ZAW, XXVIII, 42 ff.

†A comparison between the "prophetic marriages" of Hosea and Isaiah is instructive. Hosea finds its meaning in sympathy; Isaiah, in the realization of a divine decision (8:3 ff.; 9:5 ff.).

*For thus said the Lord to me:*
*As a lion or a young lion growls over his prey,*
*And when a band of shepherds is called forth against him*
*Is not terrified by their shouting,*
*Or daunted at their noise,*
*So the Lord of hosts will come down*
*To fight upon Mount Zion and upon its hill.*

*Isaiah 31:4*

Isaiah's sympathy for God comes to expression in a parable describing the crisis in the relationship between God and Israel.

*I will sing of my Friend*
*The song of this love for His vineyard:*
*My Friend had a vineyard*
*On a very fertile hill.*
*He digged it, He cleared it of stones,*
*And planted it with choice vines;*
*He built a tower in the midst of it,*
*And hewed out a wine press in it;*
*He looked for it to yield grapes,*
*But it yielded sour grapes.*
*And now, O inhabitants of Jerusalem and men of Judah,*
*Judge, I pray you, between Me and My vineyard.*
*What more should I have done for My vineyard,*
*That I have not done for it?*
*Wherefore, when I looked for it to yield grapes,*
*Why did it yield sour grapes?*
*And now I will tell you*
*What I will do to My vineyard.*
*I will remove its hedge,*
*And it shall be devoured;*
*I will break down its wall,*
*And it shall be trampled down.*
*I will make it a waste;*
*It shall not be pruned or hoed,*

*It shall grow briers and thorns;*
*I will also command the clouds*
*That they rain no rain upon it.*
*For the vineyard of the Lord of hosts*
*Is the house of Israel,*
*And the men of Judah*
*Are His pleasant planting.*
*He looked for justice,*
*But behold, there is violence,*
*For righteousness,*
*There is outrage.*

*Isaiah 5:1–7*

In this song of the vineyard, the prophet speaks first in his own name (vss. 1–2), then as the voice of God (vss. 3–6), and again in his own name (vs. 7). What personal attitude is reflected in the prophet's words?

It is first the prophet's love of God, Who is called "my Friend" and for Whom he sings "a love song concerning His vineyard." He neither rebukes the people's ingratitude nor bewails their prospect of ruin and disgrace. The prophet's sympathy is for God Whose care for the vineyard had been of no avail. God's sorrow rather than the people's tragedy is the theme of this song.

The song contains a gentle allusion to the grief and the disappointment of God. He feels hurt at the thought of abandoning the vineyard He had rejoiced in, and in which He had placed so much hope and care. In another prophecy we hear the song of God's dream, in which is fondly conceived the preservation of the vineyard, and His joy at the thought of continuing to care for it.

*. . . A precious vineyard—sing to it!*
*I, the Lord, am its keeper;*
*Every moment I water it.*
*Lest any one harm it,*
*I guard it night and day;*
*I have no wrath.*

*Would that I had thorns and briers to battle!*
*I would set out against them,*
*I would burn them up together.*
*Or let them lay hold of My protection.*
*Let them make peace with Me,*
*Let them make peace with Me.*

*Isaiah 27:2–5*

## AT ONE WITH HIS PEOPLE

What was the purpose of planting the vineyard (5:1–7), of choosing the people? The vineyard was planted to yield righteousness and justice. Yet the fruit it yielded was violence and outrage, affecting God, arousing His anger.

*Their speech and their deeds are against the Lord,*
*Defying His glorious presence.*

*Isaiah 3:8*

Isaiah pleads for the meek and the poor, condemning the ruthless and the scoffers,

*. . . all who watch to do evil, . . .*
*Who by a word make a man out to be an offender,*
*And lay a snare for him who reproves in the gate,*
*And with an empty plea turn aside him who is in the right.*

*Isaiah 29:20, 21*

It is the moral corruption of the leaders that has shattered God's relationship to His people, and in a passage which seems to belong in the context of the parable of the vineyard we read:

*The Lord shall enter into judgment*
*With the elders and princes of His people:*
*It is you who have devoured the vineyard;*
*The spoil of the poor is in your homes.*

> *What do you mean by crushing My people,*
> *By grinding the face of the poor?*
>> *Isaiah 3:14–15*

However, it is not only the iniquity of others that upsets the prophet Isaiah. He feels polluted himself! "I am a man of unclean lips, and I dwell in the midst of a people of unclean lips" (6:5). Being unclean (literally: polluted) is a state of estrangement, a state in which one is kept away from the holy.

Isaiah, who flings bitter invectives against his contemporaries, identifies himself with his people (1:9) which are to be "my people" (3:12; cf. 8:10; 7:14). His castigation is an outcry of compassion. He sees his people all bruised and bleeding, with no one to dress their wounds.

> *The whole head is sick,*
> *The whole heart is faint.*
> *From the sole of the foot even to the head*
> *There is no soundness in it,*
> *But bruises and sores*
> *And bleeding wounds;*
> *They are not pressed out, or bound up,*
> *Or softened with oil.*
>> *Isaiah 1:5–6*

The Moabites, in the neighboring nation of Moab which had often been involved in hostilities with the Hebrews and entertained a contemptuous attitude toward them (Jer. 48:27; cf. Zeph. 2:8), are condemned by the prophets for their arrogance, boastfulness, and insolence (Isa. 16:6; cf. 25:10–12; Jer. 48:27).* And yet when Moab falls at the hands of the invader, Isaiah avers:

> *My heart cries out for Moab. . . .*
> *Let every one wail for Moab. Give counsel,*

---

*At a later date, the Moabites mocked and scorned the fugitives from Judah (Ezek. 28:8–11).

> *Grant justice; make your shade like night*
> *At the height of noon;*
> *Hide the outcasts,*
> *Betray not the fugitive;*
> *Let the outcasts of Moab*
> *Sojourn among you;*
> *Be a refuge to them*
> *From the destroyer . . .*
> *I weep with the weeping of Jazer. . . .*
> *I drench you with my tears.*
> >            Isaiah 15:5; 16:7; 16:3–4; 16:9\*

A similar appeal is made by Isaiah on behalf of an Arabian tribe:

> *To the thirsty bring water,*
> *Meet the fugitive with bread. . . .*
> *For they have fled from the swords,*
> *From the drawn sword,*
> *From the bent bow,*
> *And from the press of battle.*
> >            Isaiah 21:14–15

However, in the face of idolatry and corruption, seeing that his people "have rejected the Torah of the Lord of hosts," and "despised the word of the Holy One of Israel" (5:24), the prophet seems to have lost his sense of compassion. In a moment of anger he utters the astounding words "forgive them not!" (2:9).

Is Isaiah's heart made of stone? Does he feel no pity for the people whose ruin he predicts? Indeed, two sympathies dwell in a prophet's soul: sympathy for God and sympathy for the people. Speaking to

---

\*Some commentators insist that Isa. 15–16 is no elegy on Moab, but was originally "a mocking song, sung by the enemies of the Moabites. The signs of sympathy with the Moabites are mere expressions of sarcasm." The mocking song, which "originated among Bedouins who had at some time or other invaded and partly conquered the land of Moab" was later used by a prophet from Judah, not Isaiah. See A. H. Van Zyl, *The Moabites* (Leiden, 1960), pp. 20 ff. Cf., however, the argument advanced by Y. Kaufmann, *The Religion of Israel* (Eng.; Chicago, 1960), p. 382.

the people, he is emotionally at one with God; in the presence of God, beholding a vision, he is emotionally at one with the people. When told of the doom which threatens "this people," Isaiah exclaims with a voice of shock and protest, "How long, O Lord?" (6:11; cf. Jer. 4:14; Ps. 74:10).

Indeed, the stern visions of disaster which he beholds for Israel and other nations drive him into the depths of agony. This is how he describes what he felt when such a vision was told to him:

> *A stern vision is told to me;*
> *The plunderer plunders,*
> *The destroyer destroys. . . .*
> *My loins are filled with anguish,*
> *Pangs have seized me,*
> *Like the pangs of a woman in travail;*
> *I am bowed down so that I cannot hear,*
> *I am dismayed so that I cannot see.*
> *My mind reels, horror has appalled me;*
> *The twilight I longed for*
> *Has been turned for me into trembling.*
>
> *Isaiah 21:2–4*

Nothing vitiates the impact of a prophet so much as mockery, and it is the incredibility of his message that encourages cynicism:

> *Let Him make haste,*
> *Let Him speed His work*
> *That we may see it;*
> *Let the purpose of the Holy One of Israel draw near,*
> *And let it come, that we may know it!*
>
> *Isaiah 5:19*

Isaiah's contemporaries are frivolous and gay, while the prophet is shattered by his vision of the day of the Lord: "a day of tumult and trumpeting and turmoil," "battering down of walls," famine, flight, captivity. The prophet's grief is more than he can bear.

> *Therefore I said:*
> *Look away from me.*
> *Let me weep bitter tears.*
> *Do not labor to comfort me*
> *For the ruin of my people.*
> *Isaiah 22:4*

Even though he sees ruin and disaster in the days to come, he does not cease to implore mercy:

> *O Lord, be gracious to us; we wait for Thee.*
> *Be our arm every morning,*
> *Be our help in time of trouble.*
> *Isaiah 33:2*

Israel has forsaken the Lord, but the Lord will not forsake Israel; He will not discard them. But in order to redeem, He must first smelt away the dross as with lye and remove the alloy (1:25). Grim and dreadful will be the process of purification. There is no redemption without affliction. When the Lord smites a people, He is both "smiting and healing" (19:22). This sort of knowledge cannot help but darken the heart.

## THE VISION OF ISAIAH

*In the year that King Uzziah died I saw the Lord sitting upon a throne, high and lifted up; and His train filled the temple. Above Him stood the seraphim; each had six wings: with two he covered his face, and with two he covered his feet, and with two he flew. And one called to another and said:*

> *Holy, holy, holy is the Lord of hosts;*
> *The whole earth is full of His glory.*

*And the foundations of the thresholds shook at the voice of him who called, and the house was filled with smoke. And I said: Woe is me! For I am lost; for I am a man of unclean lips, and I dwell in the midst of a people of unclean lips; for my eyes have seen the King, the Lord of hosts!*

*Then flew one of the seraphim to me, having in his hand a burning coal which he had taken with tongs from the altar. And he touched my mouth, and said: Behold, this has touched your lips; your guilt is taken away, and your sin forgiven. And I heard the voice of the Lord saying, Whom shall I send, and who will go for us? Then I said, Here I am! Send me. And he said, Go, and say to this people:*

> *Hear and hear, but do not understand;*
> *See and see, but do not perceive.*
> *Make the heart of this people fat,*
> *And their ears heavy,*
> *And shut their eyes;*
> *Lest they see with their eyes,*
> *And hear with their ears,*
> *And understand with their hearts,*
> *And turn and be healed.*

*Then I said, How long, O Lord? And He said:*

> *Until cities lie waste without inhabitant,*
> *And houses without men,*
> *And the land is utterly desolate,*
> *And the Lord removes men far away,*
> *And the forsaken places are many in the midst of the land.*
> *And though a tenth remain in it,*
> *It will be burned again,*
> *Like a terebinth or an oak,*
> *Whose stump remains standing when it is felled.*
> *The holy seed is its stump.*

*Isaiah 6*

The mandate Isaiah receives is fraught with an appalling contradiction. He is told to be a prophet in order to thwart and to defeat the essential purpose of being a prophet. He is told to face his people while standing on his head. Did he not question his own faculties of seeing, hearing, and understanding when perceiving such a message? What gave him the certainty that it was God's voice speaking to him?

It is generally assumed that the mission of a prophet is to open the people's hearts, to enhance their understanding, and to bring about rather than to prevent their turning to God.

Was not Isaiah's entire ministry devoted to persuading, to exhorting, and to influencing his people? I venture to advance a hypothesis: that this perplexing prophecy can be understood only if it be applied to the Northern Kingdom.*

Punishment described in the Bible is of two kinds: physical and spiritual. It is the second kind which Isaiah is told about. The people (of the Northern Kingdom?) are to be deprived of sensitivity to God and of the ability to repent.

Events burst forth in history which evoke man's sense of wonder. But history moves also in a way which drains one's faith, one's inner sight. It is as if God acted to deprive man of his sense of wonder, withholding his understanding, enhancing his callousness.

The haunting words which reached Isaiah seem not only to contain the intention to inflict insensitivity, but also to declare that the people already are afflicted by a lack of sensitivity. The punishment of spiritual deprivation will be but an intensification or an extension of what they themselves had done to their own souls. For hardening of the heart is either due to man himself (Jer. 5:3; Isa. 44:18; Zech. 7:11–13; Josh. 11:20; I Sam. 6:6; Ps. 95:8) or comes about as punishment from above. The Bible has several references to God hardening the heart of man. (See pp. 244 ff.)

## Uncanny Indifference

Callousness is sovereign and smug; it clings to the soul and will not give in. The crack of doom is in the air, but the people, unperturbed, are carried away by a rage to be merry. *Carpe diem*—after all, death signifies merely the end of the opportunity to be merry.

---

*On the whole problem, cf. F. Hesse, *"Das Verstockungsproblem im Alten Testament," BZAW*, LXXIV (Berlin, 1955), 44 ff.; M. Buber, *The Prophetic Faith* (New York, 1949), pp. 130 f.; G. von Rad, *Theologie des Alten Testaments*, II (München, 1961), 162 ff.; M. M. Kaplan, "Isaiah 6:1–11," *JBL*, XLV (1926), 251–259.

*In that day the Lord God of hosts*
*Called for weeping and lamentation,*
*And baldness and girding with sackcloth;*
*And behold, joy and gladness,*
*Slaying oxen and killing sheep,*
*Eating flesh and drinking wine.*
*Let us eat and drink*
*For tomorrow we die!*
*The Lord of hosts has revealed in my ears:*
*Verily, this iniquity shall not be pardoned till you die,*
*Says the Lord God of hosts.*

*Isaiah 22:12–14*

The threat of scourge and doom does not frighten the scoffers, nor does the prophet's condemnation of their cherished beliefs as lies and falsehood shake their self-assurance. Frivolously they boast: "Evil shall not overtake or meet us" (Amos 9:10).

*We have made a covenant with death,*
*We have made a pact with Sheol.*
*The overwhelming scourge, when it passes,*
*Shall not come upon us.*
*For we have made lies our refuge,*
*We have taken shelter in falsehood.*

*Isaiah 28:15*

Obstinacy in an hour of imminent disaster is uncanny, irrational. Can a people whose plight is so grave remain deaf to the redeeming word of God? How shall one explain such a disposition?

In His effort to bring Israel back to His way, the Lord had tried to call upon the people, to confer favors upon them. Yet, "the more I called them, the more they went away from Me" (Hos. 11:2). "When the wicked is spared, he does not learn righteousness; in the land of uprightness he deals perversely and does not regard the majesty of the Lord" (Isa. 26:10). So He chastised them in order to make them repent, and chastisement proved to be no cure. The people were smitten and continued to rebel (1:5); they did not stop to ponder about the meaning of their suffering nor to "turn to Him who smote them, nor seek the Lord of hosts" (9:12; cf. 10:20).* How did the inhabitants of Samaria explain the calamity that overtook their land? They thought it was due to an error in politics rather than to a failure in their relation to God.

> In pride and in arrogance of heart [they boasted]:
> The bricks have fallen,
> But we will build with dressed stones;
> The sycamores have been cut down,
> But we will replace them with cedars.
>
> Isaiah 9:9–10 [H. 9:8–9]

Moved by compassion for his people, the prophet does not suppress his cry of anguish: "How long, O Lord?" (6:11). And yet, he could not fail to carry out his sad mission.

> Stupefy yourselves and be in a stupor,
> Blind yourselves and be blind!
> Be drunk, but not with wine;
> Stagger, but not with strong drink!
> For the Lord has poured out upon you
> A spirit of deep sleep,
> And has closed your eyes, the prophets,
> And covered your heads, the seers.
>
> Isaiah 29:9–10

How else could the prophet perform such a fateful task if not in overwhelming sympathy with the divine pathos? The prophet in speaking, as it seems, of what is supremely important, says to the people: "The vision of all this has become to you like the words of a book that is sealed. When men give it to one who can read, saying, Read this, he says, I cannot, for it is sealed. And when they give the book to one who cannot read, saying, Read this, he says, I cannot read" (29:11–12).

*See Rashi and Kimhi, Commentaries, ad loc.

On another occasion, however, Isaiah in beseeching the Lord for mercy describes the people's sobbing words to their God:

> O Lord, in distress they sought Thee,
> They poured out a prayer
> When Thy chastening was upon them.
> Like a woman with child,
> Who writhes and cries out in her pangs,
> When she is near her time,
> So have we been because of Thee, O Lord.
> We are with child, we writhe,
> We have, as it were, brought forth wind.
>
> Isaiah 26:16–18

## MY PEOPLE GO INTO EXILE FOR WANT OF KNOWLEDGE

Isaiah's primary mission is to his own people. Unlike the nations of the world, Israel is reprimanded not only for arrogance and moral iniquity, but also for idolatry and the abandonment of God. The Creator of heaven and earth is called by Isaiah "the Holy One of Israel." There is a unique and intimate relationship between God and His people, yet the people have gone astray.

A factual description of the state of religion in the time of Isaiah, based upon the data cited in his accusation, would speak of disregard and deviation, of disobedience and evasion. Yet Isaiah speaks of rebellion, rejection, and disdain.

> Ah, sinful nation,
> A people laden with iniquity,
> Offspring of evildoers,
> Sons who deal corruptly!
> They have forsaken the Lord,
> They have despised the Holy One of Israel,
> They are utterly estranged . . .
> They have despised the Torah of the Lord of hosts,
> They have contemned the word of the Holy One of Israel.
>
> Isaiah 1:4; 5:24

There is no contrition, no compunction, no regret. Instead there is pride, conceit, and complacency (32:9 ff.).

"Israel does not know, My people does not understand" (1:3) is, we have seen, the divine complaint with which the book of Isaiah begins. We are told again what Hosea had proclaimed: *My people go into exile for want of knowledge* (5:13). The sort of knowledge they lack is alluded to in

> *They do not regard the deeds of the Lord,*
> *Or see the work of His hands.*
> *Isaiah 5:12*

The people do not know how sick they are. Their leaders are "wise in their own eyes and shrewd in their own sight" (5:21). Does the wisdom of their leaders keep them from complete confusion?

> *Woe to those who call evil good*
> *And good evil,*
> *Who put darkness for light*
> *And light for darkness,*
> *Who put bitter for sweet*
> *And sweet for bitter!*
> *Isaiah 5:20*

Human wisdom and understanding have failed to save man from pride, presumption, and arrogance. It is in the face of such failure that Isaiah proclaims the intention of the Lord to discredit man's wisdom and shatter his understanding.

> *Therefore, behold I will again*
> *Do marvelous things with this people,*
> *Wonderful and marvelous;*
> *The wisdom of their wise shall perish,*
> *The understanding of their prudent men shall be hid.*
> *Isaiah 29:14*

What, then, is the hope? What will take the place of human wisdom?

## A REMNANT WILL RETURN

Neither words of persuasion nor threats of castigation will have any effect. Something greater than prophetic words, namely, an eschatological event, will be necessary to silence the arrogance of man.

> Behold the day of the Lord comes,
> Cruel, with wrath and fierce anger,
> To make the earth a desolation,
> And to destroy its sinners from it. . . .
> I will punish the world for its evil,
> And the wicked for their iniquity;
> I will put an end to the pride of the arrogant,
> And lay low the haughtiness of the ruthless.
>
> Isaiah 13:9, 11

If mankind's basic malady is callousness, will the extermination of arrogance bring about a cure? The extinction of evil is, indeed, but a part of the eschatological vision. Suffering does not redeem; it only makes one worthy of redemption; for the purpose of redemption is to initiate an age in which "those who err in spirit will come to understanding, and those who murmur will accept instruction" (29:24).

There is "a screen that is cast over all peoples, a veil that veils all nations." That screen, that veil, will be destroyed at the eschatological feast which the Lord of hosts will make for all peoples on Mt. Zion (25:6–7). Something new, an outburst of the Spirit, will initiate redemption.

> For the palace will be forsaken,
> The populous city deserted;
> The hill and the watchtower
> Will become dens for ever,
> A joy of wild asses,
> A pasture of flocks;
> Until the Spirit is poured upon us from on high. . . .
>
> Isaiah 32:14–15

Isaiah holds out two hopes for mankind. One is immediate, partial, historical: "A remnant will return!" The other is distant, final, eschatological: the transformation of the world *at the end of days.*

Isaiah had named one of his sons *Shear-jashub*, which means "a remnant will return," as God's living sign for a supreme hope (cf. 8:18). "A remnant will return, the remnant of Jacob, to the mighty God. For though your people Israel be as the sand of the sea, only a remnant of them will return" (10:21–22).

The type of man who will survive the ordeals of history is described by Isaiah as one

> *. . . who walks righteously and speaks uprightly;*
> *He who despises the gain of oppressions;*
> *Who shakes his hands, lest they hold a bribe;*
> *Who stops his ears from hearing of bloodshed,*
> *And shuts his eyes from looking upon evil.*
>
> Isaiah 33:15

But beyond the hope that a remnant will return lies the ultimate hope that the whole world will be transformed.

## ZION

Isaiah knew that disaster was bound to come, but also that a remnant would survive, that Zion would endure, and that through Israel and out of Zion redemption for all nations would flow. Unlike Jeremiah, Isaiah never predicted the destruction of Jerusalem.*

Over and above all the threats and denunciations uttered by Isaiah rises the more powerful certainty of God's lasting, indestructible attachment to His people and to Zion. His disengagement from Israel is inconceivable. Anger passes; His attachment will never pass. Prophetic messages of doom are ambivalent. He is "smiting and healing" (19:22). Prophecy always moves in a polarity, yet the tension of yes and no, of anger and love, of doom and redemption, is often dis-

---

*See G. von Rad, *op. cit.*, pp. 166 ff.

solved in the certainty of God's eternal attachment, as, for example, in the words of a postexilic prophet: "For thus said the Lord of hosts, after His glory sent me to the nations who plundered you, for he who touches you touches the apple of His eye" (Zech. 2:8 [H. 2:12]).

There are words spoken by Isaiah which are unrelated to any historic situation and which allude to that attachment not contingent upon human merit or conduct:

> *Ah, the thunder of many peoples,*
> *They thunder like the thundering of the sea!*
> *Ah, the roar of nations,*
> *They roar like the roaring of mighty waters!*
> *The nations roar like the roaring of many waters,*
> *But He will rebuke them, and they will flee far away,*
> *Chased like chaff on the mountains before the wind*
> *And whirling dust before the storm.*
> *At evening time, behold, terror!*
> *Before morning, they are no more!*
> *This is the portion of those who despoil us,*
> *And the lot of those who plunder us.*
>
> *Isaiah 17:12–14*

The covenant is not only with the people, but also with the land, with Jerusalem, with Zion. All hopes and visions of things to come are connected with these places.

> *Like birds hovering, so the Lord of hosts*
> *Will protect Jerusalem;*
> *He will protect and deliver it,*
> *He will spare and rescue it.*
>
> *Isaiah 31:5*

Zion is not only His chosen place, founded by the Lord, "and in her the afflicted of His people find refuge" (14:32); His design for the history of the nations is to be finished on Mt. Zion and in Jerusalem (10:12).

Zion is where at the end of days all the nations shall go to learn the ways of God.

> *For out of Zion shall go forth Torah*
> *And the word of the Lord from Jerusalem.*
> Isaiah 2:3; see also 4:5; 33:20;
> cf. Micah 4:14; Isaiah 40;
> 65:18; Zechariah 2

> *Thus says the Lord God:*
> *Behold, I have laid a foundation in Zion:*
> *A stone, a tested stone,*
> *A precious cornerstone,*
> *An indestructible foundation:*
> *He who believes will not be in haste.*
> Isaiah 28:16

Judah will succumb before the invaders, but when the period of oppression is ended Zion will be restored (16:4).

> *Then a throne shall be established in mercy,*
> *And there shall sit on it in truth,*
> *In the tent of David,*
> *A judge who seeks justice,*
> *And excels in righteousness.*
> Isaiah 16:5

And yet, God is above all a God of justice, not a mere patron. Thoughts that savor of content, the combination of iniquity and reliance on God, "Is not the Lord in the midst of us? No evil shall come upon us" (Mic. 3:11), the certainty that Jerusalem is indestructible, which Isaiah's contemporaries entertain, are, in his eyes, a refuge in a lie (28:15). "I have heard a decree of destruction from the Lord God of hosts upon the whole land" (28:22). The Lord Himself will fight His people.

> *I will distress Ariel. . . .*
> *I will encamp against you round about. . . .*

*Then deep from the earth you shall speak,*
*From low in the dust your word shall come;*
*Your voice shall come from the ground like the voice of a ghost,*
*Your speech shall whisper out of the dust.*

*Isaiah 29:2–4*

Israel is surrounded by enemies. Nations conspire and take counsel together to destroy her. Yet,

*He Who sits in the heavens laughs; . . .*
*Then He will speak to them in His wrath,*
*And terrify them in His fury, saying:*
*I have set My king*
*On Zion, My holy hill.*

*Psalm 2:4–6*

The divine sarcasm expressed by the psalmist rings in Isaiah's words:

*Take note, you peoples, and be dismayed;*
*Give ear, all you far countries;*
*Gird yourselves and be dismayed;*
*Gird yourselves and be dismayed.*
*Take counsel together, but it will come to nought;*
*Speak a word, but it will not stand,*
*For God is with us.*

*Isaiah 8:9–10; cf. 18:4*

# 5

# Micah

*Micah, a contemporary of Isaiah, apparently regarded the purpose of* his mission to be "to declare to Jacob his transgression and to Israel his sin" (3:8). He was the first prophet to predict the destruction of Jerusalem. It was in the days of Hezekiah (cf. Jer. 20:17 f.) that Micah expressed the dreadful words:

> *The Lord is coming forth out of His place,*
> *And will come down and tread upon the high places of the earth.*
> *The mountains will melt under Him*
> *And the valleys will be cleft,*
> *Like wax before the fire,*
> *Like waters poured down a steep place.*
> *All this for the transgression of Jacob.*
> *And for the sins of the house of Israel. . . .*
> *Zion shall be plowed as a field;*
> *Jerusalem shall become a heap of ruins,*
> *And the mountain of the house a wooded height.*
>
> *Micah 1:3–5; 3:12*

SELECTED BIBLIOGRAPHY: A. J. Tait, *The Prophecy of Micah* (New York, 1917); P. Haupt, *The Book of Micah* (Chicago, 1910).

Micah refers only by implication to the sin of idolatry, to the people who bow down to the work of their own hands, to the sorcerers and soothsayers. In his eyes the fatal sin is the sin of moral corruption. The rich men are full of violence, and the inhabitants speak lies: "Their tongue is deceitful in their mouth" (6:12).

The prophet directs his rebuke particularly against the "heads of the house of Jacob and the rulers of the house of Israel, who abhor justice and pervert all equity." It is because "they build Zion with blood and Jerusalem with wrong" (3:9–10) that Zion and Jerusalem will be destroyed.

Again and again he hurls bitter words at the leaders:

> It is not for you to know justice?—
> You who hate the good and love the evil,
> Who tear the skin from off My people,
> And their flesh from off their bones;
> Who eat the flesh of My people,
> And flay their skin from off them.
>
> Micah 3:1–3

Here, amidst a people who walk haughtily (2:3), stands a prophet who relentlessly predicts disaster and disgrace for the leaders as well as for the nation, maintaining that "her wound is incurable" (1:9), that the Lord is "devising evil" against the people: "It will be an evil time" (2:3). The heads of the people, he exclaims,

> . . . give judgment for a bribe,
> Its priests teach for hire,
> Its prophets divine for money.
> Yet they lean upon the Lord and say,
> Is not the Lord in the midst of us?
> No evil shall come upon us.
>
> Micah 3:11

"Do not preach," the prophet is told, "one should not preach of such things; disgrace will not overtake us" (2:6). But the prophet spells out his message:

> *You shall eat, but not be satisfied. . . .*
> *You shall sow, but not reap . . .*
> *That I may make you a desolation, . . .*
> *And you shall bear the reproach of My people.*
> Micah 6:14, 15, 16

To the soul of Micah, the taste of God's word is bitter. In his love for Zion and his people, he is tormented by the vision of the things to come:

> *For this I will lament and wail;*
> *I will go stripped and naked;*
> *I will make lamentation like the jackals,*
> *And mourning like the ostriches. . . .*
> *Because evil has come down from the Lord*
> *To the gate of Jerusalem.*
> Micah 1:8, 12

Micah does not question the justice of the severe punishment which he predicts for his people. Yet it is not in the name of justice that he speaks, but in the name of a God who "delights in steadfast love," "pardoning iniquity and passing over transgression" (7:18). In the name of the Lord he proclaims:

> *In anger and wrath I will execute judgment*
> *Upon the nations that did not obey.*
> Micah 5:15

Yet, there is reluctance and sorrow in that anger. It is as if God were apologizing for His severity, for His refusal to be complacent to iniquity. This is God's apology to Israel. He cannot forget "the treasures of wickedness in the house of the wicked" or "acquit the man with wicked scales and with a bag of deceitful weights" (6:10, 11).

God's sorrow and disappointment are set forth before the people.

> *Hear what the Lord says:*
> *Arise, plead your case before the mountains,*

*And let the hills hear your voice.*
*Hear, you mountains, the controversy of the Lord,*
*And you enduring foundations of the earth;*
*For the Lord has a controversy with His people,*
*And He will plead with Israel.*
*O My people, what have I done to you?*
*And in what have I wearied you? Answer Me!*
*For I brought you up from the land of Egypt,*
*And redeemed you from the house of bondage,*
*And I sent before you Moses, Aaron, and Miriam.*
*O My people, remember what Balak king of Moab devised,*
*And what Balaam the son of Beor answered him;*
*And what happened from Shittim unto Gilgal,*
*That you may know the righteous acts of the Lord.*

Micah 6:1–5

"Answer Me!" calls the voice of God. But who hears the call? "The voice of the Lord cries to the city" (6:9), but the city is complacent.

The prophet is a lonely man. His standards are too high, his stature too great, and his concern too intense for other men to share. Living on the highest peak, he has no company except God.

*Woe is me! For I have become*
*As when the summer fruit has been gathered,*
*As when the vintage has been gleaned:*
*There is no cluster to eat,*
*No first-ripe fig which my soul desires,*
*The godly man has perished from the earth,*
*And there is none upright among men;*
*They all lie in wait for blood,*
*And each hunts his brother with a net.*
*Their hands are upon what is evil, to do it diligently;*
*The prince and the judge ask for a bribe,*
*And the great man utters the evil desire of his soul;*
*Thus they weave it together.*

*The best of them is like a brier,*
*The most upright of them a thorn hedge.*
*The day of their watchmen, of their punishment, has come;*
*Now their confusion is at hand.*
*Put no trust in a neighbor,*
*Have no confidence in a friend;*
*Guard the doors of your mouth*
*From her who lies in your bosom;*
*For the son treats the father with contempt,*
*The daughter rises up against her mother,*
*The daughter-in-law against her mother-in-law;*
*A man's enemies are the men of his own house.*
*But as for me, I will look to the Lord,*
*I will wait for the God of my salvation;*
*My God will hear me.*

*Micah 7:1–7*

In spite of the gloom of his predictions, Micah insists that his message is for the good of his people. Though not openly calling for a repentance that would avert God's judgment, his words imply such a call. To those who oppose him, saying, "Do not preach," Micah responds:

*Should this be said, O house of Jacob?*
*Is the Spirit of the Lord impatient?*
*Are these His doings?*
*Do not my words do good to him who walks uprightly?*

*Micah 2:7*

Together with the word of doom, Micah proclaims the vision of redemption. God will forgive "the remnant of His inheritance," and will cast all their sins "into the depths of the sea" (7:18 f.), and every man shall sit "under his vine and under his fig tree, and none shall make them afraid" (4:4).

Among the great insights Micah has bequeathed to us is how to accept and to bear the anger of God. The strength of acceptance comes from the awareness that we have sinned against Him and from the certainty that anger does not mean God's abandonment of man forever. His anger passes, His faithfulness goes on forever. There is compassion in His anger; when we fall, we rise. Darkness is not dismal. When we sit in the darkness, God is our light.

> Rejoice not over me, O my enemy;
> When I fall, I shall rise;
> When I sit in darkness,
> The Lord will be a light to me.
> I will bear the indignation of the Lord,
> Because I have sinned against Him,
> Until He pleads my cause
> And executes judgment for me.
>
> *Micah 7:8–9*

In another great insight the prophet, speaking as an individual and in the first person singular, poses the most urgent question of religious existence: What is the way of true worship?

> With what shall I come before the Lord,
> And bow myself before God on high?
> Shall I come before Him with burnt offerings,
> With calves a year old?
> Will the Lord be pleased with thousands of rams,
> With ten thousands of rivers of oil?
> Shall I give my first-born for my transgression,
> The fruit of my body for the sin of my soul?
> He has showed you, O man, what is good;
> And what does the Lord require of you
> But to do justice, and to love kindness,
> And to walk humbly with your God?
>
> *Micah 6:6–8*

# 6

# Jeremiah

O land, land, land,
Hear the word of the Lord!

*Jeremiah 22:29*

*The call to be a prophet came to Jeremiah in the year 625* B.C.E.*, and* he was active during the reigns of the last kings of Judah—Josiah (640–609 B.C.E.), Jehoiakim (609–598 B.C.E.), Jehoiachin (598–597 B.C.E.), Zedekiah (597–587 B.C.E.)—and continued for some time after the fall of Jerusalem in 587 B.C.E.

*The word of the Lord came to me saying,*

> *Before I formed you in the womb I knew you,*
> *And before you were born I consecrated you;*
> *I appointed you a prophet to the nations.*

SELECTED BIBLIOGRAPHY: P. Volz, *Der Prophet Jeremia* (*"Kommentar zum Alten Testament"* [Leipzig, 1922]); W. Rudolph, *Jeremia* (*"Handbuch zum Alten Testament"* [Tübingen, 1947]); E. A. Leslie, *Jeremiah Chronologically Arranged, Translated, and Interpreted* (New York, 1954); A. C. Welch, *Jeremiah, His Time and His Work* (Oxford, 1954); *The Book of Jeremiah* ("The Expositor's Bible"), exegesis by J. P. Hyatt, exposition by S. R. Hopper (New York, 1956); S. D. Luzzatto, *Commentary on Jeremiah* (Heb.; Lemberg, 1876); Y. Kaufmann, *The Religion of Israel* (Heb.; Jerusalem, 1954), VII, 393–474; (Eng. trans., M. Greenberg [Chicago, 1960]), pp. 409 ff.; A. B. Ehrlich, *Randglossen zur Hebräischen Bibel*, vol. IV (Leipzig, 1912); J. Skinner, *Prophecy and Religion* (Cambridge, 1922); A. Malamat, "Jeremiah and the Last Two Kings of Judah," *Palestine Exploration Quarterly*, I (1951), 81–87.

*Then I said, Ah, Lord God! Behold, I do not know how to speak, for I am only a youth. But the Lord said to me,*

> *Do not say, I am only a youth;*
> *For to all to whom I send you, you shall go,*
> *And whatever I command you, you shall speak.*
> *Be not afraid of them,*
> *For I am with you to deliver you, says the Lord.*

*Then the Lord put forth His hand and touched my mouth; and the Lord said to me,*

> *Behold, I have put My words in your mouth,*
> *See, I have set you this day over nations and over kingdoms,*
> *To pluck up and to break down,*
> *To destroy and to overthrow,*
> *To build and to plant.*

*And the word of the Lord came to me, saying, Jeremiah, what do you see? And I said, I see a rod of almond. Then the Lord said to me, You have seen well, for I am watching over My word to perform it.*

*The word of the Lord came to me a second time, saying, What do you see? And I said, I see a boiling pot, facing away from the north. Then the Lord said to me, Out of the north evil shall break forth upon all the inhabitants of the land. For, lo, I am calling all the tribes of the kingdoms of the north, says the Lord; and they shall come and every one shall set his throne at the entrance of the gates of Jerusalem, against all its walls around about, and against all the cities of Judah. And I will utter My judgments against them, for all their wickedness in forsaking Me; they have burned incense to other gods, and worshiped the works of their own hands. But you, gird up your loins; arise, and say to them everything that I command you. Do not be dismayed by them, lest I dismay you before them. And I, behold, I make you this day a fortified city, an iron pillar, and bronze walls, against the whole land, against the kings of Judah, its princes, its priests, and the people of the land. They*

*will fight against you; but they shall not prevail against you, for I am
with you, says the Lord, to deliver you.*

*Jeremiah 1: 4–19*

## COMPLACENCY AND DISTRESS

Although Isaiah had insisted that Jerusalem would withstand the
onslaught of her enemies, Jeremiah, like Micah, was told that the enemies would overwhelm Jerusalem and all the fortified cities of Judah:
"Out of the north evil shall break forth" (1:14). They maintained that
the state of Judah had forfeited the privilege of God's protection.

And yet, Jeremiah did not think that evil was inevitable. Over
and above man's blindness stood the wonder of repentance, the open
gateway through which man could enter if he would. Jeremiah's call
was addressed to Israel as a whole as well as to every member of the
people (18:11):

> *Return, faithless Israel, says the Lord,*
> *I will not look on you in anger,*
> *For I am merciful, says the Lord.*
> *Jeremiah 3:12 [H. 3:11];*<br>*cf. 4:1; 25:5; 35:15\**

> *Like a basket full of birds,*
> *Their houses are full of treachery;*
> *Therefore they have become great and rich,*
> *They have grown fat and sleek.*
> *They know no bounds in deeds of wickedness;*
> *They judge not with justice*
> *The cause of the fatherless, . . .*
> *They do not defend the rights of the needy.*
> *Jeremiah 5:27–28*

Jeremiah, looking upon the garishness of Jerusalem, felt hurt by
the people's guilt and by the knowledge that they had a dreadful debt

---

\*On the refusal to return, see 5:3; 8:5; 22:27; 44:5.

to pay. The Lord's severe judgment would be meted out; He would not swerve aside. It was hard for God to deal harshly with His beloved people. Rather than inflict a penalty on the whole people, the Lord had tried to purify them:

> Behold, I will refine them and test them,
> For what else can I do, because of My dear people?
> > Jeremiah 9:7 [H. 9:6]

Yet, all attempts at purification were of no avail.

Filled with a sense of security, the people scorned the warnings of the true prophets, saying,

> The prophets will become wind;
> The word is not in them. . . .
> They are sure that the Lord . . . will do nothing,
> No evil will come upon us,
> Nor shall we see sword or famine.
> > Jeremiah 5:13; 5:12

Indeed,

> They are all stubbornly rebellious,
> Going about with slanders;
> They are bronze and iron,
> All of them act corruptly.
> The bellows blow fiercely,
> The lead is consumed by the fire;
> In vain the refining goes on,
> For the wicked are not removed.
> Refuse silver they are called,
> For the Lord has rejected them.
> > Jeremiah 6:28–30

Jeremiah's was a soul in pain, stern with gloom. To his wistful eye the city's walls seemed to reel. The days that were to come would be dreadful. He called, he urged his people to repent—and he failed. He screamed, wept, moaned—and was left with a terror in his soul.

## THE AGE OF WRATH

Utterances denoting the wrath of God, the intent and threat of destruction, are found more frequently and expressed more strongly in Jeremiah than in any other prophet. For this reason, Jeremiah has often been called a prophet of wrath.

However, it would be more significant to say that Jeremiah lived in an age of wrath. His contemporaries had no understanding of the portent of their times, of the way in which God was present at the time. They did not care for time. But a prophet has a responsibility for the moment, an openness to what the moment reveals. He is a person who knows what time it is. To Jeremiah his time was an emergency, one instant away from a cataclysmic event.

> *Cut off your hair and cast it away;*
> *Raise a lamentation on the bare heights,*
> *For the Lord has rejected and forsaken*
> *The generation of His wrath.*
> *Jeremiah 7:29*

Jeremiah hurled a dreadful word at his people, accusing them of provoking or exciting God's anger, an expression not used by earlier prophets (cf. 7:18–19; 11:17–18; 25:6; 44:3–8): "The sons of Israel and the sons of Judah . . . have done nothing but provoke Me to anger by the work of their hands, says the Lord. This city has aroused My anger and wrath, . . ." (32:30–32). The words he proclaimed are merciless: "Thus says the Lord God: Behold, My anger and My wrath will be poured out on this place, upon man and beast, upon the trees of the field and the fruit of the ground; it will burn and not be quenched" (7:20).

> *Behold, the storm of the Lord!*
> *Wrath has gone forth,*

*A whirling tempest;*
*It will burst upon the head of the wicked.*
*The anger of the Lord will not turn back*
*Until He has executed and accomplished*
*The intents of His mind.*
*In the latter days you will understand it clearly. . . .*
*A lion has gone up from his thicket,*
*A destroyer of nations has set out;*
*He has gone forth from his place*
*To make your land a waste;*
*Your cities will be ruins*
*Without inhabitant.*

*Jeremiah 23:19–20, cf. 30:23–24; 4:7, 5:6*

The days would come when

*the dead bodies of this people will be food for the birds of the air, and for*
*the beasts of the earth; and none will frighten them away. And I will*
*make to cease from the cities of Judah and from the streets of Jerusalem*
*the voice of mirth and the voice of gladness, the voice of the bridegroom*
*and the voice of the bride; for the land shall become a waste. . . . [Jerusa-*
*lem will be] a heap of ruins, a lair of jackals [and] the cities of Judah a*
*desolation, without inhabitant.*

*Jeremiah 7:33–34; 9:11*

## GOD'S LOVE OF ISRAEL

God's love of Israel is one of Israel's sacred certainties which Jeremiah, like Hosea and Isaiah before him, tried to instill in the minds of the people.

*Thus says the Lord;*
*The people who survived the sword*
*Found grace in the wilderness; . . .*
*With everlasting love have I loved you,*
*Therefore I have continued My faithfulness to you.*

*Jeremiah 31:2–3*

It was in love that God and Israel met.

>*The word of God came to me, saying: Go and proclaim in the hearing of Jerusalem, Thus says the Lord:*

>>*I remember the devotion of your youth,*
>>*Your love as a bride,*
>>*How you followed Me in the wilderness,*
>>*In a land not sown.*
>>*Israel was holy to the Lord,*
>>*The first fruits of His harvest.*
>>*All who would destroy him would be held guilty;*
>>*Punishment would come to them,*
>>*Says the Lord.*

>>>>>>*Jeremiah 2:1–3*

"Father!—To God Himself we cannot give a holier name," said Wordsworth. Child—God Himself does not use a more tender word. In spite of Israel's failure, the voice of God avers:

>>*For I am a father to Israel,*
>>*And Ephraim—he is My first-born.*

>>>>>>*Jeremiah 31:9*

Ephraim is "a precious son," "a darling child." Such was God's anticipation:

>>*I thought*
>>*How I would set you among My sons,*
>>*And give you a pleasant land,*
>>*The most glorious inheritance among the nations.*
>>*And I thought you would call me, "My Father,"*
>>*And would not turn from following Me.*

>>>>>>*Jeremiah 3:19; cf. 3:4*

Following the prophet Hosea, Jeremiah employed the analogy of married love to express the relationship of God and Israel. "I was their husband, says the Lord" (31:32).

*Surely, as a faithless wife leaves her husband,*
*So have you been faithless to Me, O house of Israel,*
*Says the Lord. . . .*
*If a man divorces his wife,*
*And she goes from him*
*And becomes another man's wife,*
*Will he return to her?*
*Would not that land be greatly polluted?*
*You have played the harlot with many lovers;*
*And would you return to Me?*
*Says the Lord.*
*Lift up your eyes to the bare heights and see!*
*Where have you not been lain with?*
*By the wayside you have sat awaiting lovers,*
*Like an Arab in the wilderness,*
*You have polluted the land*
*With your vile harlotry.*

*Jeremiah 3:20; 3:1–2*

## THE INNER TENSION

Jeremiah depicted the dramatic tension in the inner life of God. As in Abraham's debate with God over the threatened destruction of Sodom, there was an implied desire not to let the judgment fall upon Judah.

*Go to and fro in the streets of Jerusalem,*
*See, I entreat you, and know!*
*And look in its broad open places*
*To see whether you can find one*
*Who does justly,*
*Who practices faithfulness,*
*Says the Lord.*

*Jeremiah 5:1*

On account of their sins, the land would be subjected to devastation. Yet the judgment seemed to be painful to the Supreme Judge,

and Jeremiah tried to convey that God sought to justify His judgment.
The words of God betray an inner oscillation:

> *How can I pardon you?*
> *Your children have forsaken Me,*
> *Have sworn by those who are no gods.*
> *When I fed them to the full,*
> *They committed adultery*
> *And trooped to the houses of harlots.*
> *They were well-fed lusty stallions,*
> *Each neighing for his neighbor's wife.*
> *Shall I not punish them for these things?*
> *Says the Lord.*
> *Shall I not avenge Myself*
> *On a nation such as this? . . .*
> *They judge not with justice*
> *The cause of the fatherless, . . .*
> *They do not defend the rights of the needy.*
> *Shall I not punish them for these things?*
> *Says the Lord.*
> *Shall I not avenge Myself*
> *On a nation such as this? . . .*
> *Their tongue is a deadly arrow;*
> *It speaks deceitfully.*
> *With his mouth each speaks peaceably to his neighbor,*
> *But in his heart he plans an ambush for him.*
> *Shall I not punish them for these things?*
> *Says the Lord.*
> *Shall I not avenge Myself*
> *On a nation such as this?*
> > *Jeremiah 5:7–9, 28–29; 9:8–9 [H.9:7–8]*

"The Lord wrests the decision to judge from Himself: He would
at once forgive, He has attempted to do so by means of disciplinary
training, now He can no more forgive, He must avenge himself, . . .

He has been deceived, offended, betrayed: it is His own possession, with which He must part."*

## THE SORROW AND ANGUISH OF THE LORD

A great hope was Israel; "the first fruits" were a foretaste of a harvest of blessing.† But as time passed, God's hope was dashed. The people deserted their Redeemer and worshiped instead "the works of their own hands" (1:16). God's pain and disappointment ring throughout the book of Jeremiah. What a sublime paradox for the Creator of heaven and earth to implore the people so humbly:

> *Thus says the Lord:*
> *What wrong did your fathers find in Me,*
> *That they went far away from Me,*
> *And pursued what is worthless,*
> *And became worthless?*
>
> *Jeremiah 2:5*

The heart of melancholy beats in God's words: "My people have forgotten Me" (18:15); "they have forsaken Me" (2:13; cf. 1:16; 2:17, 19; 3:21; 5:7; 13:25; 16:11; 17:13; 19:4).

How much quiet tenderness, how much unsaid devotion is contained in the way in which the Lord of heaven and earth spoke of Israel: "My people," "My dear people" (bath 'ami).

> *For My people are foolish,*
> *They know Me not;*
> *They are stupid children,*
> *They have no understanding.*
>
> *Jeremiah 4:22*

---

*P. Volz, *Der Prophet Jeremia* (Leipzig, 1922), p. 60. See E. A. Leslie, *Jeremiah* (New York, 1954), p. 60, whose translation is the one quoted above.

†"The Lord once called you a green olive tree, fair with goodly fruit" (11:16; cf. 2:21).

"My people have been lost sheep" (50:6). "The shepherds who care for My people . . . have scattered My flock and have driven them away" (23:2). The false prophets "have healed the wound of My people lightly" (6:14). They did not proclaim "My words to My people" (23:22). They "make My people forget My name" (23:27), and "lead My people astray by their lies" (23:32).

There were moments of compassion and moments of anger. But God's attachment to Israel is eternal. It was "My people" when the blessing was proclaimed (12:1, 16; 30:3); it was "My people Israel" when their wickedness was condemned (7:12) or punishment announced. In regard to the external enemies of Israel, God said: "They have despised My people" (33:24).

As great as God's wrath is His anguish. Together with proclaiming the forthcoming disaster—"The people . . . shall be cast out in the streets of Jerusalem, victims of famine and sword, with none to bury them" (14:16)—the prophet was told by God:

> You shall say to them this word:
> Let my eyes run down with tears night and day,
> And let them not cease,
> For My dearly beloved people (bath 'ami)
>   is smitten with a great wound,
> With a very grievous blow.
>
> Jeremiah 14:17

Again and again the prophet brought God's word to His beloved people: mourn, grieve, sorrow, lament. A sense of delicacy prevented the prophet from spelling out the meaning of the word: Mourn My people for Me as well. . . .*

> Thus says the Lord: . . .
> O My dear people (bath 'ami), gird on sackcloth,
> And roll in ashes;
> Make mourning as for an only son,

*This was sensed by the rabbis of the second and third centuries. Cf. their interpretations of pertinent passages in Jeremiah, particularly in the Midrash on Lamentations.

*Most bitter lamentation,*
*For suddenly the destroyer will come upon us.*

*Jeremiah 6:22, 26*

These words are aglow with a divine pathos that can be reflected, but not pronounced: God is mourning Himself. "Thus says the Lord. Behold, what I have built I am breaking down, and what I have planted I am plucking up . . ." (45:4). God's sorrow rises again and again to unconcealed heights of expression.

*I have forsaken My house,*
*I have abandoned My heritage;*
*I have given the beloved of My soul*
*Into the hands of her enemies.*
*My heritage has become to Me*
*Like a lion in the forest,*
*She has lifted up her voice against Me;*
*Therefore I hate her.*
*Is My heritage to Me like a speckled bird of prey?*
*Are the birds of prey against her round about?*
*Go, assemble all the wild beasts;*
*Bring them to devour.*
*Many shepherds have destroyed My vineyard,*
*They have trampled down My portion,*
*They have made My pleasant portion*
*A desolate wilderness.*
*They have made it a desolation;*
*Desolate, it mourns to Me.*
*The whole land is made desolate,*
*But no man lays it to heart.*
*Upon all the bare heights in the desert*
*Destroyers have come;*
*For the sword of the Lord devours*
*From one end of the land to the other;*
*No flesh has peace.*
*They have sown wheat and have reaped thorns,*

*They have tired themselves out but profit nothing.*
*They shall be ashamed of their harvests*
*Because of the fierce anger of the Lord. . . .*
*Thus says the Lord;*
*A voice is heard in Ramah,*
*Lamentation and bitter weeping.*
*Rachel is weeping for her children;*
*She refuses to be comforted for her children,*
*Because they are not.*
*Thus says the Lord;*
*Keep your voice from weeping*
*And your eyes from tears;*
*For your work shall be rewarded, says the Lord,*
*And they shall come back from the land of the enemy.*
*There is hope for your future, says the Lord,*
*And your children shall come back to their own country.*

*Jeremiah 12:7–13; 31:15–17*

Israel's distress was more than a human tragedy. With Israel's distress came the affliction of God, His displacement, His homelessness in the land, in the world. And the prophet's prayer, "O save us," involved not only the fate of a people. It involved the fate of God in relation to the people. For Israel's desertion was not merely an injury to man; it was an insult to God. This was the voice of God Who felt shunned, pained, and offended:

*Have I been a wilderness to Israel,*
*Or a land of thick darkness?*
*Why then do My people say,*
*We are free,*
*We will come no more to Thee?*
*Can a maiden forget her ornaments,*
*Or a bride her attire?*
*Yet My people have forgotten Me*
*Days without number.*

*Jeremiah 2:31–32*

The Lord Who had dwelt in the midst of Israel was abandoning His dwelling place. But should Israel cease to be His home, then God, we might say, would be without a home in the world. He would not have left His people altogether, but He would be among them like a stranger, like a wayfarer, withholding His power to save. It is as if there were an inner wrestling in God.

> *O Thou hope of Israel,*
> *Its savior in time of trouble!*
> *Why shouldst Thou be like a stranger in the land,*
> *Like a wayfarer who turns aside to tarry for a night?*
> *Why shouldst Thou be like a man astounded?*
> *Like a mighty man who cannot save?*
> *Yet Thou, O Lord, art in the midst of us,*
> *And we are called by Thy name,*
> *Leave us not.*
>
> *Jeremiah 14:8–9*

When the calamity came, and death was "cutting off the children from the streets and the young men from the squares" (9:21 [H. 9:20]), He called upon the people to take up "weeping and wailing" (9:10 [H. 9:9]).

> *Thus says the Lord of hosts:*
> *Consider, and call for the mourning women to come;*
> *Let them make haste and raise a wailing over us,*
> *That our eyes may run down with tears,*
> *And our eyelids gush with water.*
>
> *Jeremiah 9:17–18 [H. 9:16–17]*

"Thus says the Lord of hosts: . . . raise a wailing *over us,* . . ." Does not the word of God mean: Cry for Israel and Me? The voice of God calling upon the people to weep, lament, and mourn, for the calamities are about to descend upon them, is itself a voice of grief, a voice of weeping.

> *O Lord, Thou hast deceived me,*
> *And I was deceived;*
> *Thou art stronger than I,*
> *And Thou hast prevailed.*
>
> *Jeremiah 20:7*

This standard rendition misses completely the meaning of the text and ascribes to Jeremiah a pitiful platitude ("Thou art stronger than I"). The proper rendition of Jeremiah's exclamation would be:

> *O Lord, Thou hast seduced me,*
> *And I am seduced;*
> *Thou hast raped me*
> *And I am overcome.*

The meaning of this extraordinary confession becomes clear when we consider what commentators have failed to notice, namely, the specific meaning of the individual words. The striking feature of the verse is the use of two verbs *patah* and *ḥazak*. The first term is used in the Bible and in the special sense of wrongfully inducing a woman to consent to prenuptial intercourse (Exod. 22:16 [H. 22:15]; cf. Hos. 2:14 [H. 2:16]; Job 31:9). The second term denotes the violent forcing of a woman to submit to extranuptial intercourse, which is thus performed against her will (Deut. 22:15; cf. Judg. 19:25; II Sam. 13:11). The first denotes seduction or enticement; the second, rape. Seduction is distinguished from rape in that it does not involve violence. The woman seduced has consented, although her consent may have been gained by allurements. The words used by Jeremiah to describe the impact of God upon his life are identical with the terms for seduction and rape in the legal terminology of the Bible.*

---

*The expression *patah* is often found in this meaning in the language of the Mishnah; *ḥazak* has gained a precise significance in the Talmud: the idea and the term have become of central importance for the notion of the right to property. As a consequence of its specification in this sense, the expression in the sense of sexual violation was supplanted by the term *'anas;* cf. *Ketuboth* 3, 4, where both terms occur. See also W. Rudolph, *Jeremia* (Tübingen, 1947), p. 113.

These terms used in immediate juxtaposition forcefully convey the complexity of the divine-human relationship: sweetness of enticement as well as violence of rape. Jeremiah, who like Hosea thought of the relationship between God and Israel in the image of love, interpreted his own involvement in the same image. This interpretation betrays an ambivalence in the prophet's understanding of his own experience.

The call to be a prophet is more than an invitation. It is first of all a feeling of being enticed, of acquiescence or willing surrender. But this winsome feeling is only one aspect of the experience. The other aspect is a sense of being ravished or carried away by violence, of yielding to overpowering force against one's own will. The prophet feels both the attraction and the coercion of God, the appeal and the pressure, the charm and the stress. He is conscious of both voluntary identification and forced capitulation.

This dialectic of what takes place in the prophetic consciousness points to the approach we have adopted in our analysis. Objectively considered, it is, on the one hand, the divine pathos which stirs and entices the prophet, and, on the other hand, unconditioned power which exercises sheer compulsion over the prophet. Subjectively, it is in consequence the willing response of sympathy to persuasion and also the sense of being utterly delivered up to the overwhelming power of God. A man whose message is doom for the people he loves not only forfeits his own capacity for joy, but also provokes the hostility and outrage of his contemporaries. The sights of woe, the anticipation of disaster, nearly crush his soul.

And yet, the life of Jeremiah was not all misery, tension or pressure. He also knew the bliss of being engaged to God, "the joy and delight" of being, as it were, a bride.

> *Thy words were found, and I ate them,*
> *Thy words became to me a joy,*
> *The delight of my heart,*
> *For I am called by Thy name,*
> *O Lord, God of hosts.*
>
> *Jeremiah 15:16*

The words "joy" and "delight" occur four other times in the book of Jeremiah, and always in connection with nuptial festivities (7:34; 16:9; 25:10; 33:11). The bearing of a name was a sign of betrothal. "Let us be called by your name," the unmarried women called to a man (Isa. 4:1). The prophet's situation was one of betrothal to the Lord, to the God of hosts.

## SYMPATHY FOR GOD

1. "I am full of the wrath *(ḥemah)* of God" (6:11), exclaims Jeremiah. He was filled with a blazing passion, and it was this emotional intensity which drove him to discharge God's woeful errands. The ultimate purpose of a prophet is not to be inspired, but to inspire the people; not to be filled with a passion, but to impassion the people with understanding for God. Yet the ears of this people were closed: "The word of the Lord is to them an object of scorn" (6:16). Jeremiah was filled to overflowing with the wrath of God, which he could neither suppress nor contain, and which poured itself out therefore upon innocent "children in the street and upon the gatherings of young men" (6:11). The wrath of God was not the threat of judgment being poured forth, but the upsurge of wrath in Jeremiah himself. The compulsion to pour it forth must not be regarded as an ecstatic compulsion, for up to this point Jeremiah had been able to contain his anger.*

From this confession on the part of the prophet, it is clear with what agitation and passionate concern he was accustomed to fulfill his vocation. Again and again Jeremiah proclaimed the pathos of wrath. His being filled with divine wrath was his sympathy with it. Jeremiah not only experienced such sympathy; he was fully conscious of his experience.

2. The prophet of wrath did not merely proclaim it; he lived it, and was conscious of it.

> *I did not sit in the company of merrymakers,*
> *Nor did I rejoice;*

*See D. P. Volz, *op. cit.,* p. 74.

*I sat alone, because Thy hand was upon me,*
*For Thou hadst filled me with indignation* [za'am].

*Jeremiah 15:17*

The question may be asked whether, to the mind of Jeremiah, his sympathy proceeded from an internal impulse or whether it was forced upon him from without. The phrase, "Thou hadst filled me with indignation," might justify the supposition that he experienced his agitation not as a personal response, but as an inoculated emotion, a state of being possessed. However, as we shall see, such a supposition is improbable.

According to Jer. 25:15–29, the prophet was told by the Lord: "Take from My hand this cup of wine of wrath *(ḥemah),* and make all the nations to whom I send you drink it. . . . Then you shall say to them, Thus says the Lord of hosts, the God of Israel: Drink, be drunk and vomit, fall and rise no more, because of the word I am sending among you." To drink of the divine wrath meant the same as to be doomed or to drink poison.* It would, therefore, be absurd to assume that Jeremiah drank or was filled with divine anger. It was the pathos that evoked in him an anger of sympathy.

3. Jeremiah's activity seemed both futile and distasteful. He tried to abstain from conveying his message to the people.

> *If I say, I will not mention Him;*
> *Or speak any more in His name,*
> *There is in my heart as it were a burning fire,*
> *Shut up in my bones,*
> *And I am weary with holding it in,*
> *And I cannot.*

*Jeremiah 20:9*

The key to the understanding of this passage may be found in the phrase, "I am weary of holding it in," which is almost identical

---

*To the Semitic mind, poison and wrath are integrally connected; see H. Gressmann, *Der Ursprung der Israelitisch-Juedischen Eschatologie* (Göttingen, 1905), pp. 130 f.

with the phrase in 6:11, quoted above, referring to the prophet's inability to suppress the divine wrath in him. In all likelihood the passage refers to the same theme, namely, the fire of wrath that glowed within him.

In the language of Jeremiah, fire is used in a twofold sense: as a symbol of destruction (21:14; 43:12; 48:45; 49:27; 50:32), and as a symbol of anger (4:4; 17:4; 21:12; cf. Deut. 32:22; Ezek. 21:31 [H. 21:36]; 22:31; 36:5; 38:19; Nah. 1:6; Ps. 39:3 [H. 39:4]; 79:5; 89:46 [H. 89:47]; Lam. 1:13; 2:4; Isa. 66:15). The identification of the divine word and fire has a double implication: the pathos, anger and its effect; and the threatened annihilation. The divine word moved in Jeremiah as fire because he lived through the experience of divine wrath. Just as the pathetic wrath of God could become a physical fire of destruction, so the wrathful word of the prophet could work itself out as a destructive fiery element.

The prophet was filled with a passion which demanded release; if he tried to contain it, its flame burned within him like a fever.* Jeremiah could not have felt it as a passion breathed into him by God. Biblical thought, as we have seen, regards every outburst of fire which comes from God over a people, a land, or an individual, as a destructive force. Jeremiah felt the divine wrath as springing up from within.

There are, then, two separate themes in this confession. The fire of anger as the condition of the prophet's soul, and the sense of compulsion to bring it to expression. His inner condition is one of sympathy with the divine anger, the emotional and passionate character of which is indicated by the fact that Jeremiah localized his passion in the heart, which, according to ancient Hebrew conceptions, is the seat of emotion and passion.

A further implication of this confession is that the prophetic sympathy was stronger than the will, the inner passion more powerful than the personal disposition.

---

*The idea of "the burning fire in the heart and the bones" is reminiscent of the hot fever which is described as a "fire in the bones"; cf. the expressions *qadachath* (Lev. 26:16; Deut. 28:22) and *'esh shel 'aṣamoth* in the Babylonian Talmud, *Gittin* 70a.

4. The prophet not only must learn to see how man behaves, but also must learn to sense God's feeling: His eternal love for Israel.

*Thus said the Lord to me, Go and buy a linen waistcloth, and put it on your loins, and do not dip it in water. So I bought a waistcloth according to the word of the Lord, and put it on my loins. And the word of the Lord came to me a second time, Take the waistcloth which you have bought, which is upon your loins, and arise, go to the Euphrates, and hide it there in a cleft of the rock. So I went, and hid it by the Euphrates, as the Lord commanded me. And after many days the Lord said to me, Arise, go to the Euphrates, and take from there the waistcloth which I commanded you to hide there. Then I went to the Euphrates, and dug, and I took the waistcloth from the place where I had hidden it. And behold, the waistcloth was spoiled; it was good for nothing.*

*Then the word of the Lord came to me: Thus says the Lord: Even so will I spoil the pride of Judah and the great pride of Jerusalem. This evil people, who refuse to hear My words, who stubbornly follow their own heart and have gone after other gods to serve them and worship them, shall be like this waistcloth, which is good for nothing. For as the waistcloth clings to the loins of a man, so I made the whole house of Israel and the whole house of Judah cling to Me, says the Lord, that they might be for Me a people, a name, a praise, and a glory, but they would not listen.*

*Jeremiah 13:1–11*

If the purpose of the story of the waistcloth were only to let the prophet see in a symbolic way the punishment of the people, he would not have been told to put it on his loins. But it is precisely this part of the story that seems to hold the central meaning of the act. The prophet must learn to feel for himself God's intimate attachment to Israel; he must not only know about it, but experience it from within. "For as the waistcloth clings to the loins of a man, so I made the whole house of Israel and the whole house of Judah cling to Me, . . . that they might be for Me a people, a name, a praise, and a glory, but they would not listen." Like Hosea in his marriage experience, Jeremiah must learn the grief of God in having to spoil what is intimately precious to Him.

Thus there are two aspects to the story. The first aspect is didactic: to convey to the prophet symbolically the decision to punish the people (the buying of the waistcloth and its rotting). The second aspect is sympathetic: to let the prophet feel what that decision means to the life and pathos of God. Indeed, the command to the prophet to wear the waistcloth before placing it in the cleft of a rock would be devoid of meaning if the purpose of the story were only to demonstrate to the prophet the punishment to come.

5. Of his inner condition Jeremiah said:

> *My heart is broken within me,*
> *All my bones are out of joint;*
> *I am like a drunken man,*
> *Like a man overcome by wine,*
> *Because of the Lord,*
> *And because of His holy words.*
> *Jeremiah 23:9*

What was the source of this dreadful condition? What emotion or what awareness brought this condition about? The prophet stated it briefly: "Because of the Lord, and because of His holy words." Had it been the sense of forthcoming disaster, or the awareness of the people's sins, he would have said, "Because of the people, and because of their fate or sins." What convulsed the prophet's whole being was God. His condition was a state of suffering in sympathy with the divine pathos.

The idea of drunkenness as a punishment occurs frequently in the book of Isaiah (25:15 ff.; 51:7, 39, 57; cf. Lam. 4:21; Isa. 63:6). Babel was the cup which contained the wine of destruction for the people. But the prophet was as far from describing himself as the bearer of annihilation as from describing himself as the object of punishment. Comparison with the speech about the wine of wrath (25:15) strongly suggests that in this confession, too, the prophet was thinking of an intoxication by the wrath of God.*

---

*As regards the verb *'abar,* cf. its meaning "to be angry" in the *hithpael;* Deut. 3:26; Ps. 78:21, 59, etc.; cf. also Num. 5:14.

This supposition is confirmed by the following consideration. The prophecies of Jeremiah that we have examined are variations of one and the same theme. The striking recurrence of the "motif" leads one to suppose that a fundamental experience was in question, about the meaning of which the prophet was often concerned. Verses 23:9; 20:9; 6:9; and 15:17 constitute a series of formulae in which we can detect the increasing clarity of the idea.

6. Jeremiah hated his prophetic mission. To a soul full of love, it was horrible to be a prophet of castigation and wrath. What rewards did he receive for carrying the appalling burden?

> *I have become a laughingstock all the days:*
> *Every one mocks me.*
> *For as often as I speak I have to cry out,*
> *Have to complain of violence and abuse,*
> *For the word of the Lord has become for me*
> *A reproach and derision all day long.*
>
> *Jeremiah 20:7–8*

In spite of public rejection, in spite of inner misery, he felt unable to discard the divine burden, unable to disengage himself from the divine pathos. He knew why he had to yield; he knew how to explain his inability to resist the terrible errand.

## SYMPATHY FOR ISRAEL

The modes of prophetic sympathy are determined by the modes of the divine pathos. The pathos of love and the pathos of anger awake corresponding tones in the heart of the prophet. In his confessions Jeremiah allows us to obtain a glimpse of the fervor of love as well as of the raging of anger against the people. Through insight into the nexus between prophetic emotion and divine pathos, it is possible to gain a clue to the meaning behind the conflicting and confusing emotions of Jeremiah's mind. His inconsolable grief over the destiny of the people is an expression of fellowship and love; the people's anguish is his anguish. However, his emotions are not simply an expression of instinctive attachment to his people or a feeling of personal involvement in their fate. At times Jeremiah even wished to abandon his people (19:1; cf. I Kings 19:3 ff.).

Ardent as was his love for the people, he was primarily driven by what God felt for Israel. Accord with divine pathos determined his attractions and aversions. Love involves an appreciation of what is precious in the beloved person. Israel was precious because it was the consort and the beloved of the Lord.

The prophet was fully conscious of his emotional nexus with God. It was the bidding of God that his compassion and lament were uttered.

> *Declare in Judah, and proclaim in Jerusalem, and say, . . .*
> *For this gird you with sackcloth,*
> *Lament and wail;*
> *For the fierce anger of the Lord*
> *Has not turned back from us.*
>
> *Jeremiah 4:5, 8; cf. 14:17*

Jeremiah loved his people. But he also trembled, knowing that God is just.

> *My anguish, my anguish! I writhe in pain!*
> *Oh, the walls of my heart!*
> *My heart is beating wildly;*
> *I cannot keep silent;*
> *For I hear the sound of the trumpet,*
> *The alarm of war,*
> *Disaster follows hard on disaster,*
> *The whole land is laid waste.*
> *Suddenly my tents are destroyed,*
> *My curtains in a moment.*
> *How long must I see the standard,*
> *And hear the sound of the trumpet?*
>
> *Jeremiah 4:19–21*

The prophet not only was a man concerned with right and wrong. He also had a soul of extreme sensitivity to human suffering.

In the midst of hurling the harshest words of impending doom, he was suddenly gripped by what was in store for his people:

> For I heard a cry as of a woman in travail,
> Anguish as of one bringing forth her first child,
> The cry of the daughter of Zion gasping for breath,
> Stretching out her hands,
> Woe is me! I am fainting before murderers.
>
> *Jeremiah 4:31*

Impassioned with a sense of the divine disturbance, Jeremiah could condemn with a vehemence that was at times terrifying and devoid of charity. But his own heart was rich in tenderness and sensitivity to other people's suffering. He terrified in order to save. The disaster he threatened would be a disaster to him, sorrow and excruciating anguish. He had implored and warned them, He knew that if the people should remain dead to his words, he would drown in his own tears.

> Hear and give ear; be not proud,
> For the Lord has spoken.
> Give glory to the Lord your God
> Before He brings darkness,
> Before your feet stumble
> On the twilight mountains,
> And while you look for light
> He turns it into gloom
> And makes it deep darkness.
> But if you will not listen,
> My soul will weep in secret for your pride;
> My eyes will weep bitterly and run down with tears,
> Because the Lord's flock has been taken captive.
>
> *Jeremiah 13:15–17*

This, indeed, was at the root of his anguish. Those whom he loved he was called upon to condemn. When the catastrophe came, and the enemy mercilessly killed men, women, and children, the prophet must have discovered that the agony was greater than the heart could feel, that his grief was more than his soul could weep for.

> *My grief is beyond healing*
> *My heart is sick within me. . . .*
> *For the wound of my beloved people is my heart wounded,*
> *I mourn, and dismay has taken hold on me.*
> *Is there no balm in Gilead?*
> *Is there no physician there?*
> *Why then has the health of my beloved people*
> *Not been restored?*
> *O that my head were waters,*
> *And my eyes a fountain of tears,*
> *That I might weep day and night*
> *For the slain of my beloved people! . . .*
> *Who will have pity on you, O Jerusalem,*
> *Or who will bemoan you?*
> *Who will turn aside*
> *To ask about your welfare?*
>
> *Jeremiah 8:18-9:1 [H. 8:18–23]; 15:5*

Instead of searching their own lives for the failures that brought down God's wrath on them, the people resented Jeremiah's prediction of doom, accusing him of ill-will, as if he were to blame for the disaster he predicted. Was Jeremiah an enemy of his people (15:10–11)?

Deeply hurt by the accusations, Jeremiah protested before God his innocence and his love of his people. The word of doom was not born in his heart (17:6).

> *Remember how I stood before Thee, . . .*
> *To turn away Thy wrath from them.*
>
> *Jeremiah 18:20*

Indeed, this was a part of the complexity of the prophet's inner existence. He was a person overwhelmed by sympathy for God and sympathy for man. Standing before the people he pleaded for God;

standing before God he pleaded for his people. The prediction of doom was contrary to his own feelings. When the false prophet Hananiah predicted that within two years' time the captives of Judah, together with the vessels of the Temple, which had been taken to Babylonia after the first Babylonian invasion, would be brought back to Jerusalem, Jeremiah exclaimed: "Amen! May the Lord do so; may the Lord make the words which you have prophesied come true" (28:6). In a moment of distress, while Babylon was waging war against Jerusalem, King Zedekiah turned to the prophet, saying: "Pray for us to the Lord our God" (37:3; cf. 7:16; 11:14; 14:11, 20–22; 18:20; 21:2).

Jeremiah prayed and pleaded for His people:

> We acknowledge our wickedness, O Lord,
> And the iniquity of our fathers,
> For we have sinned against Thee.
> Do not spurn us, for Thy name's sake;
> Do not dishonor Thy glorious throne.
> Remember and do not break Thy covenant with us.
> *Jeremiah 14:20–21*

God had a stake in the life of Israel. In spurning His people, He would dishonor the throne of His glory. Here, then, was a task of the prophet: to remind God of His own concern.

In pleading for his people, the prophet acknowledged their sins, recalled the covenant. Yet, the answer to his prayer was tinged with sadness: "Though Moses and Samuel stood before Me, My soul would not turn to this people. Send them out of My sight, and let them go!" (15:1.)

Awful as God's punishment would be, to be abandoned by Him would be incomparably worse. The prophet was haunted by the fear of ultimate calamity: God's rejection or loathing of the people. The plight of man was shrouded in what God felt about man. In his brooding about the situation of the people, Jeremiah's thought turned to God's soul and pathos.

*Hast Thou utterly rejected Judah?*
*Does Thy soul loathe Zion?*
*Why hast Thou smitten us*
*So that there is no healing for us?*
      *Jeremiah 14:19*

## THE POLARITY WITHIN

*See, I have set you this day over nations and over kingdoms,*
*To pluck up and to break down,*
*To destroy and to overthrow,*
*To build and to plant.*
      *Jeremiah 1:10*

Jeremiah was called to an office both sublime and appalling. First he had to castigate, foretell doom and destruction; only after that could he comfort, offer hope, build and plant. Because of the ordeals he would have to face and the strength he would need, he was told: "Gird up your loins; arise and say to them everything that I command you. Do not be dismayed by them, lest I dismay you before them" (1:17). In order to be able to rise above dismay, to be able to persevere in the spirit of defiance, he was suddenly transformed into the stark opposite of his usual self. "Behold, I make you this day a fortified city, an iron pillar, and bronze walls, against the whole land, against the kings of Judah, its princes, its priests, and the people of the land" (1:18). He succeeded, indeed, in offending, chafing, even alarming his contemporaries. Dashing the people's sense of security, he added insult to gloom by chiding them for what they revered. Having been enabled to withstand like a fortress all the attacks that came from without, Jeremiah's inner life never turned to bronze or iron.

The role of the prophet was ambiguous in the eyes of some of his contemporaries. The indignation that flowed from him, the anger he displayed, even when extrinsic to his mind, became so intimate a part of his soul that those exposed to it could easily mistake it as his own antipathy rather than as sympathy with divine anger, and could assume that he had his own ax to grind, that he was giving vent to personal hostility. It seems that Jeremiah was accused of feeling delight in anticipating the disaster which he had announced in the name of the Lord. He who loved his people, whose life was dedicated to saving his people, was regarded as an enemy. Over and above the agony of sensing the imminent disaster, his soul was bruised by calumny. What protection was there against such backbiting? No one could look into his heart, but everybody was hurt by his words. Only the Lord knew the truth.

> *Heal me, O Lord, and I shall be healed;*
> *Save me, and I shall be saved;*
> *For Thou art my praise. . . .*
> *I have not pressed Thee to send evil,*
> *Nor have I desired the day of disaster,*
> *Thou knowest;*
> *That which came out of my lips*
> *Was before Thy face.*
>
> *Jeremiah 17:14, 16*

Jeremiah was gentle and compassionate by nature, and the mission he had to carry out was, to him, distasteful in the extreme. It made him contentious, petulant, irascible. People he had prayed for turned out to be his enemies. "Woe is me, my mother, that you bore me, a man of strife and contention to the whole land! I have not lent, nor have I borrowed, yet all of them curse me. So let it be, O Lord, if I have not entreated Thee for their good, if I have not pleaded with Thee on behalf of the enemy in the time of trouble and in the time of distress!" (15:10–11). It seemed impossible to break through the wall of suspicion: "Can one break iron, iron from the north, and bronze?" (15:12.)

There were people who considered him a traitor. "You are telling a lie. The Lord our God did not send you . . . but Baruch . . . has set you against us, to deliver us into the hand of the Chaldeans [Babylonians], that they may kill us or take us into exile in Babylon" (42:2–3). The priests and the prophets pronounced him worthy of death

(26:11). Even the men of his own village, Anathoth, those closest to him, were in full cry after him, seeking to take his life (11:21; 12:6). The shock of discovering how those who spoke "fair words" to him were seeking his life came as a bolt of lightning to a soul riven with pain, tortured by visions of imminent disaster.

> *I was like a gentle lamb*
> *Led to the slaughter.*
> *I did not know it was against me*
> *They devised schemes, saying:*
> *Let us destroy the tree with its fruit,*
> *Let us cut him off from the land of the living,*
> *That his name be remembered no more.*
> *O Lord of hosts, Who judgest righteously,*
> *Who triest the heart and the mind,*
> *Let me see Thy vengeance upon them,*
> *For to Thee I have committed my cause.*
> *Jeremiah 11:19–20*

He was called upon to deny the charge of forsaking his country and of going to the enemy camp. "It is false; I am not deserting to the Chaldeans!" (37:14.) When Jeremiah became aware of a conspiracy to slay him (18:23), it was more than he could bear. There had been the promise at the time of his call to be a prophet: "They will fight against you; but they shall not prevail against you, for I am with you, says the Lord, to deliver you" (1:19).

At the crucial moment of history, Jeremiah was the hope, the anchor, and the promise. The slaying of Jeremiah would have meant the death blow to Israel as well, a collapse of God's mission.

It was not his vested interests, honor, or prestige that the prophet was fighting for. He was fighting for the physical survival of his people. Those members of the people who sought to destroy him must have been regarded by him as traitors, as a deadly menace to his prophetic mission. Since all attempts at persuasion had proved futile, and even the Lord's call was of no avail, what else was left for the prophet to do except to pray that his enemies be destroyed so that the whole people could be saved? (11:20; 12:3; 15:15; 17:18; 18:21)

Polarity of emotion is a striking fact in the life of Jeremiah. We encounter him in the pit of utter agony and at the height of extreme joy, carried away by divine wrath and aching with supreme compassion. There are words of railing accusation and denunciation; the lips that pleaded for mercy utter petitions for retribution, for the destruction of those who stand in the way of the people's accepting his prophetic word. Indeed, the commission he received at the time of his call endowed him with the power to carry out two opposite roles:

> *To pluck up and to break down,*
> *To destroy and to overthrow,*
> *To build and to plant.*
> *Jeremiah 1:10*

Aside from the moral problem involved in the harsh petitions, there is the personal problem. Do not such contrasts or opposing attitudes indicate a lack of integrity? Is not his pleading for the destruction of his opponents a collapse of his power of mercy? A way of comprehending these contradictions as being parts of a unified personality is to remember that the prophet's inner life was not wholly his own. His emotional situation reflected the divine relation to Israel: compassion as well as anger. What he felt was not always original with him. "Filled with the wrath of God," it was beyond his ability to weigh, measure, or control the outburst of anger. The actual occasion of such an outburst may at times have been a personal one; its possibility and intensity derived from sympathy. The tension of being caught, heart and soul, in two opposing currents of violent emotion, was more than a human being could bear.

> *Cursed be the day*
> *On which I was born!*
> *The day when my mother bore me,*
> *Let it not be blessed!*
> *Cursed be the man*

> *Who brought the news to my father,*
> *A son is born to you,*
> *Making him very glad . . .*
> *Because He did not kill me in the womb.*
> *So my mother would have been my grave,*
> *And her womb for ever great.*
> *Why did I come forth from the womb*
> *To see toil and sorrow,*
> *And spend my days in shame? . . .*
> *O that I had in the desert*
> *A wayfarers' lodging place,*
> *That I might leave my people*
> *And go away from them!*
> > *Jeremiah 20:14–15, 17–18;*
> > *9:2 [H. 9:1]*

## THE HYPERTROPHY OF SYMPATHY

Jeremiah seems to have suffered at times from a hypertrophy of sympathy for God. Inherent in sympathetic emotion is a tendency to become divorced from the occasion or the subject by which it was called forth. What starts out, for example, as a feeling of sadness in sympathy for a bereaved person, may become a condition of sadness as such, no longer associated with the particular person. It may also surpass in intensity the feeling of the person for whom one has sympathy. Sympathy may continue even when the bereaved person has found comfort and overcome his grief.

Jeremiah's sympathy seems at times to have become an independent pathos, even deviating from the divine pathos. Such deviation led to a conflict between the pathos of the Lord and the pathos of the prophet. Therefore, the Lord had to correct and enlighten him about the nonfinality of pathos. The anger had become the prophet's own, rather than remaining a true reflection of the divine pathos. Such excess of sympathy with the divine wrath shows the danger of a sympathy grown absolute. "Avenge me on my persecutors" (15:15), the prophet prayed. Adversaries endangered the preaching of God's word; the prophet lost patience. He exhorted God to depart from merciful longsuffering. Thus it developed that the prophet's indignation was stronger than God's anger, that the prophet's sympathy for the divine pathos went beyond the divine pathos. Divine forbearance and human indignation conflicted, and the prophet had to be told that God was concerned about the disciplining, not the destruction, of His adversaries; it was not the business of the prophet to recommend that the Lord punish, but that He test and purify (5:1, 4 f.; 6:9 f., 27 f.; 8:6).

In answer to Jeremiah's prayer, "Avenge me on my persecutors" (15:15), the Lord said to him:

> If you return, I will restore you,
> And you shall stand before Me.
> If you utter what is precious, and not what is base,
> You shall be as My mouth.
>
> *Jeremiah 15:19*

Instead of a modicum of satisfaction or a hint of understanding for the dreadful burden he faithfully bore, instead of a new promise of protection, aid, or solace, Jeremiah received a rebuke. The words he had dared to speak before the Lord were worthless; the state of mind he had exhibited was gently and implicitly condemned as apostasy. How often had he condemned the people and called upon them to repent and to return. Now he himself, the prophet, the servant, the watchman, was told by God to repent, to return.

The ambitendency of Jeremiah's invectives and maledictions characterized the prophet's mission from the start. His appointment, as we have seen, was

> To pluck up and to break down,
> To destroy and to overthrow,
> To build and to plant.
>
> *Jeremiah 1:10*

He offered both grief and rebirth, both doom and redemption.

> If you return, O Israel, says the Lord,
> To Me you should return.

*If you remove your abominations from My presence,*
*And do not waver;*
*If you swear, As the Lord lives,*
*In truth, in justice, and in uprightness,*
*Then nations shall bless themselves in Him,*
*And in Him shall they glory.*

*Jeremiah 4:1–2*

Beyond all indignation and imprecations lay the certainty that Israel as God's creation would abide, Israel would exist.

*Thus says the Lord,*
*Who gives the sun for light by day*
*And the fixed order of the moon*
*And the stars for light by night,*
*Who stirs up the sea so that its waves roar—*
*The Lord of hosts in His name.*
*If this fixed order departs*
*From before Me, says the Lord,*
*Then shall the descendants of Israel cease*
*From being a nation before Me for ever. . . .*
*Thus says the Lord:*
*Behold I will restore the fortunes of the tents of Jacob,*
*And have compassion on his dwellings;*
*The city shall be rebuilt upon its mound,*
*And the palace shall stand where it used to be.*

*Jeremiah 31:35–36; 30:18*

## PROPHECY NOT THE ONLY INSTRUMENT

There was no sense of guilt, no feeling of shame. Judah said, "I am innocent." But the Lord proclaimed: "Behold, I will bring you to judgment for saying, I have not sinned" (2:35). "Were they ashamed when they committed abominations? No, they were not at all ashamed; they did not know how to blush" (6:15; 8:12). The Lord implored His people: "Only acknowledge your guilt, that you rebelled against the Lord your God" (3:13). And the prophet enjoined the people: "Let us lie down in our shame, and let our dishonor cover us, for we have sinned against the Lord our God, we and our fathers . . ." (3:25).

> *I, the Lord, search the mind*
> *And try the heart,*
> *To give every man according to his ways,*
> *According to the fruit of his doings.*
> *Jeremiah 17:10; cf. 11:20; 20:12*

Jeremiah knew that the malady was not primarily in the wickedness of the deeds, but in "the stubbornness of their evil hearts" (3:17; 7:24; 9:14 [H. 9:13]; 11:8; 13:10; 14:14; 16:12; 18:12; 23:17); in their "evil thoughts" (4:14), not only in their evil manners. "This people has a stubborn and rebellious heart" (6:23). They are circumcised in body but "uncircumcised in heart" (9:26). "Remove the foreskin of your hearts" (4:4). "Wash your heart from wickedness" (4:14). "Where is the word of the Lord? Let it come" (17:15), they said. "The word of God is to them an object of scorn. . . . To whom shall I speak and give warning, that they may hear?" (6:10). In such despondency the prophet began to question the possibility of succeeding in his mission.

> *Can the Ethiopian change his skin*
> *Or the leopard his spots?*
> *Then also you can do good*
> *Who are accustomed to do evil. . . .*
> *The heart is deceitful above all things.*
> *And desperately corrupt;*
> *Who can understand it?*
> *Jeremiah 13:23; 17:9*

Man is unable to redeem himself, to cure the sickness of the heart. What hurts the soul, the soul adores. Can man be remade? A prophet can give man a new word, but not a new heart. It is God who must give man a heart to know that He is God (24:7).

Prophecy is not God's only instrument. What prophecy fails to bring about, the new covenant will accomplish: the complete transformation of every individual.

> *Behold, the days are coming, says the Lord, when I will make a new covenant with the house of Israel and the house of Judah, not like the covenant which I made with their fathers when I took them by the hand to bring them out of the land of Egypt, My covenant which they broke, though I was their husband, says the Lord. But this is the covenant which I will make with the house of Israel after those days, says the Lord: I will put My law within them, and I will write it upon their hearts; and I will be their God, and they shall be My people. And no longer shall each man teach his neighbor and each his brother, saying, Know the Lord, for they shall all know Me, from the least of them to the greatest, says the Lord; for I will forgive their iniquity, and I will remember their sin no more.*
>
> *Jeremiah 31:31–34 [H. 31:30–33];*
> *cf. Ezekiel 11:19 ff.; 36:26 f.*

For many years Jeremiah had predicted pestilence, slaughter, famine, and captivity (15:2). However, when calamity arrived, in the hour of panic and terror, when every face was turned pale with dark despair, the prophet came to instill hope, to comfort, to console.*

> *It is a time of distress for Jacob;*
> *Yet he shall be saved out of it. . . .*
> *Then fear not, O Jacob My servant, says the Lord,*
> *Nor be dismayed, O Israel;*
> *For lo, I will save you from afar,*
> *And your offspring from the land of captivity.*
> *Jacob shall return and have quiet and ease,*
> *And none shall make him afraid,*
> *For I am with you to save you, says the Lord.*
> *Jeremiah 30:7, 10–11*

---

*I do not share the view advanced by Rudolph, *Jeremiah*, p. 159, that chs. 30 and 31 date from the reign of King Josiah, and that the references to Judah (30:3–4, 8–9; 31:1, 23–30, 38–40) are insertions by a later editor.

The rule of Babylon shall pass, but God's covenant with Israel shall last forever. The day will come when "the people of Israel and the people of Judah shall come together, weeping as they come, and they shall seek the Lord their God. They shall ask the way to Zion, with faces turned toward it, saying, Come, let us join ourselves to the Lord in an everlasting covenant which will never be forgotten" (50:4–5). Jerusalem will dwell secure under the watchword, "The Lord is our vindication" (33:16).

The climax of Jeremiah's prophecy is the promise of a covenant which will mean not only complete forgiveness of sin (33:8; 50:20), but also a complete transformation of Israel. In time to come God will give Israel "one heart and one way" and make with them "an everlasting covenant" (32:39–40), which will never be violated (50:40).

## THE COLLAPSE OF ASSYRIA

During his last years Hezekiah had been completely under the influence of Isaiah. His death in 687/6 brought the twelve-year-old Manasseh to the beginning of his long reign (687/6–642 B.C.E.), during which the reforms that had been introduced by Hezekiah were abolished. All the high altars and shrines were restored. Manasseh remained a docile vassal of Nineveh, and even assisted Assyria's campaign against Egypt, which was conquered by the Assyrian army under Esarhaddon (681–669 B.C.E.) and Ashurbanipal (ca. 669–633 B.C.E.).

King Josiah (640–609 B.C.E.), who ascended the throne following the assassination of his father, Amon (642–640 B.C.E.), made a total break with the policy of Manasseh. The rapid decline of Assyrian power and influence made it easier for those who abhorred Manasseh's idolatry. Young King Josiah inaugurated a reformation which marks an epoch in the religious history of Israel. He undertook, first of all, a consistent purge of foreign cults and practices. Various solar and astral cults, mostly of Mesopotamian origin and imported into Judah in the wake of Assyrian dominion, as well as native cults—some introduced by Manasseh (II Kings 21:1–9), some of very long standing—were removed and destroyed (II Kings 23:4 ff.). Josiah further took advantage of Assyria's weakness to free his people from political dependence upon her.

The year in which Jeremiah received his call to be a prophet was a turning point in history. Ashurbanipal died in 633(?), leaving the Assyrian empire in a state of weakness, ripe for dissolution. During his reign Nineveh had lost her grip on the provinces; Egypt, Judah, and other states in Palestine and Syria regained their independence. Ashurbanipal's brutality and punitive raids into the territory of his neighbors had increased the hatred for Assyria to a passion.* For ages, Assyria had plundered all the peoples within her range. Wherever her name was known it was execrated. Now her end was approaching. Nineveh, the exultant city that said to herself, "I am, and there is no one else," was about to become a desolation, a dry waste like the desert. "Everyone who passes by her hisses and shakes his fist" (Zeph. 2:15).

> *Woe to the bloody city,*
> *All full of lies and booty—*
> *No end to the plunder! . . .*
> *Behold I am against you,*
> *Says the Lord of hosts,*
> *And will lift up your skirts over your face;*
> *I will let nations look on your nakedness,*
> *And kingdoms on your shame. . . .*
> *There is no assuaging your hurt,*
> *Your wound is grievous.*
> *All who hear the news of you*
> *Clap their hands over you.*
> *For upon whom has not come*
> *Your unceasing evil?*
>
> 

*Nahum 3:1, 5, 19;*
*cf. Ezekiel 31:3 ff.; 32:22 ff.*
> 

---

*ANET, pp. 291, 294.

On the other hand, God's compassion for "Nineveh, that great city, in which there are more than a hundred and twenty thousand persons who do not know their right hand from their left, and also much cattle," is the theme of the book of Jonah (4:11).

The death of Ashurbanipal, who like his predecessors was also ruler of Babylon, was the signal for a new revolt by the Babylonians, long held in subjugation by Assyria, and anxious to regain the power and prestige they once possessed and to restore to their city the glory of former times. At once we find Nabopolassar (626–605 B.C.E.) king of Babylon. With the change of rulers from Ashurbanipal to Nabopolassar, the hegemony of Assyria came to an end, and the leadership among the Semitic peoples of Asia passed to the Chaldeans, or Babylonians.

With Babylonia firmly in his possession, Nabopolassar joined the Median tribes and their king Cyaxares (ca. 625–585 B.C.E.) in the final assault upon Assyria. In the year 612, Nineveh fell before the onslaught. Briefly and almost contemptuously Nabopolassar wrote the epitaph of the overthrown empire: "I slaughtered the land of Subarum, I turned the hostile land into heaps and ruins." "The Assyrian, who since distant days has ruled over the peoples and with his heavy yoke had brought injury to the people of the Land, their feet from Akkad I turned back, their yoke I threw off."* The Assyrian kingdom disappeared from history, and there was no longer an Assyrian people. The dreaded empire collapsed with surprising speed, only a short time after she had reached the zenith of her power. Her strength suddenly flagged, and she fell prey to her enemies.

The Babylonians had emerged as a major power, and Josiah seems to have supported them in their plans to destroy the might of Assyria. Egypt, on the other hand, which two generations earlier had been the last great target of Assyrian aggression, was Assyria's sole ally in her death agony. Apprehensive of the growing might of new Babylonia, Egypt had been intermittently supporting Assyria against

*A. T. Olmstead, *History of Assyria* (New York, 1923), p. 640.

the Babylonians and their allies. At the same time, she began to nurture the hope of regaining possession of Palestine and Syria, which had once belonged to Egypt. So, at the outset of his reign, the Pharaoh Neco II (609–593 B.C.E.) marched into Palestine. While other local kings now almost independent were too dispirited to offer battle, Josiah, who by this time was practically independent and had no desire to come under the control of Assyria, tried to stop the Egyptians. The clash occurred in the year 609, near Megiddo, and ended in tragedy for Judah. Josiah was slain, and his army returned to Jerusalem, where his son Jehoahaz was proclaimed king. Neco, who now considered himself overlord of Judah, deposed the new king and deported him to Egypt. Jehoahaz' brother Johoiakim was placed on the throne as an Egyptian vassal, and the land was laid under heavy tribute. Judah's independence was ended. Neco was master of the erstwhile Assyrian provinces as far as the Euphrates.

As said above, the call to be a prophet came to Jeremiah during the reign of Josiah, in the year 625, but we do not know with any degree of certainty of public activity on the part of Jeremiah during Josiah's reign. He clashed with public authorities during the reign of Johoiakim (609–598 B.C.E.) when he delivered his message first in Topheth and then in the Temple court in Jerusalem. Pashur, the Temple officer, struck him publicly and put him in prison (19:14–20:3). Another such prophecy spoken in the Temple court announcing the destruction of the Temple as well as of the city of Jerusalem, enraged the priests, the false prophets, and the people. Jeremiah was put on trial and threatened with the penalty of death, but was saved by some officers.

The rise of Nebuchadnezzar (605/4–562 B.C.E.) brought the activity of Jeremiah to a climax. He was charged to write down in the form of a scroll all his prophecies since the days of Josiah (36:1 f.), the gist of which was the message: "The king of Babylon will certainly come and destroy this land" (36:29). Copied by his secretary, Baruch, these prophecies were read to the people by Baruch in the court of the Temple. The people were deeply moved by the prophet's message, and when the story of this episode reached the court, king and princes asked to hear it.

King Jehoiakim was a petty tyrant who shed much blood in Jerusalem (II Kings 24:4). Knowing the terrible temper of the king, who had already put one prophet to death (Jer. 26:23), the princes advised both Jeremiah and Baruch to hide. The king, to whom the prophecies were read, did not hesitate to cast into the fire Jeremiah's scroll, section by section. He ordered Jeremiah imprisoned, but the prophet could not be found (ch. 36). However, after some time he came out of hiding and resumed his public activity.

There could hardly be a greater incompatibility than that between Jeremiah and King Jehoiakim, whose chief interest was to enlarge his palace, apparently using forced labor to do so.

> *Woe to him who builds his house by unrighteousness,*
> *And his upper rooms by injustice;*
> *Who makes his neighbor serve him for nothing,*
> *And does not give him his wages;*
> *Who says, I will build myself a great house*
> *With spacious upper rooms,*
> *And cuts out windows for it,*
> *Paneling it with cedar,*
> *And painting it with vermilion.*
> *Do you think you are a king*
> *Because you compete in cedar?*
> *Did not your father eat and drink*
> *And do justice and righteousness?*
> *Then it was well with him.*
> *He judged the cause of the poor and needy;*
> *Then it was well.*
> *Is not this to know Me?*
> *Says the Lord.*
> *But you have eyes and heart*
> *Only for your dishonest gain,*
> *For shedding innocent blood,*

*And for practicing oppression and violence.*
*Therefore thus says the Lord*
*Concerning Jehoiakim the son of Josiah, king of Judah:*
*They shall not lament for him, saying,*
*Ah, my brother! or, Ah sister!*
*They shall not lament for him, saying,*
*Ah, lord! or, Ah his majesty!*
*With the burial of an ass he shall be buried,*
*Dragged and cast forth beyond the gates of Jerusalem.*

*Jeremiah 22:13–19*

## THE EMERGENCE OF THE BABYLONIAN EMPIRE

In 605, a change in the balance of power placed Judah in a new danger. The Egyptian Neco, determined to extend his dominion beyond the Euphrates into the northern part of Mesopotamia, put in the field an immense army and reached Carchemish, on the Euphrates, without opposition. Nebuchadnezzar, the son of Nabopolassar, gave battle, and won a crushing victory. Neco was undone and his army fled in confusion, pursued by Nebuchadnezzar; the latter might have overrun Egypt had he not been apprised of his father's sudden death, which compelled him to return to Babylon. A new Babylonian empire came into being, and for many years it was to dominate the Near East.

Judah was thrown into consternation by this turn of events (Jer. 46). Jehoiakim transferred his allegiance to Nebuchadnezzar and became his vassal (II Kings 24:1).

Quietly, however, Jehoiakim seems to have been convinced that the security of Judah was tied to the destiny of Egypt. He was therefore determined to throw off the Babylonian yoke. Many leading citizens apparently supported his policy. The only clear voice raised against such a fatal venture was that of Jeremiah who, like Isaiah in a similar crisis, warned the nation against such suicidal folly. Nebuchadnezzar, he proclaimed, had been designated by the Lord to carry out His will; Judah as well as many other lands would be in his hand (25:15 f.; 27:6). It was futile to resist him, and those who relied on

Egypt would be put to shame as were those who had once relied on Assyria (2:36 f.).

> *Thus says the Lord of hosts:*
> *Behold, evil is going forth*
> *From nation to nation,*
> *And a great tempest is stirring*
> *From the farthest parts of the earth! . . .*
> *Wail, you shepherds, and cry,*
> *And roll in ashes, you lords of the flock,*
> *For the days of your slaughter and dispersion have come,*
> *And you shall fall like choice rams.*
> *No refuge will remain for the shepherds,*
> *Nor escape for the lords of the flock.*
> *Hark, the cry of the shepherds,*
> *And the wail of the lords of the flock!*
> *For the Lord is despoiling their pasture,*
> *And the peaceful folds are devastated,*
> *Because of the fierce anger of the Lord.*
> *Like a lion He has left His covert,*
> *For their land has become a waste*
> *Because of the sword of the Lord,*
> *And because of his fierce anger.*
>
> *Jeremiah 25:32, 34–38*

At last the king omitted the payment of the tribute, and the issue was joined. Nebuchadnezzar, though occupied elsewhere, had no intention of tolerating such an act. Pending the time when he could act in person, he encouraged marauding nomadic hordes, friendly to the Babylonians, to ravage the land of Judah (II Kings 24:2; Jer. 35:11). Subsequently, in 597, he arrived in person at the head of an army to besiege Jerusalem. Before the Babylonian army laid siege to the capital, King Jehoiakim died, and his son, the new king Jehoiachin, a lad of eighteen years, realizing the hopelessness of the situation, decided to surrender before an assault should be undertaken. With his mother and the entire court he was carried into captivity, followed by seven thousand men capable of carrying arms and one thousand workers in iron, together with their families, and an enormous booty. A boy of twenty-one named Zedekiah was made king of Judah.

The eleven years (597–587 B.C.E.) of Zedekiah's reign were notable for a steady decline in Judah's power and for the desperate efforts of Jeremiah to avert the coming disaster. A ruler of good intentions, not entirely unresponsive to warnings of the prophet, whom he consulted on occasion on matters of state (37:3–10, 16–21; 38:14–28), Zedekiah felt himself helpless among his headstrong officials, and he was under their domination (38:5).

Meanwhile, the cherished holy vessels, the king Jehoiachin, and the upper class of Judean leaders were being kept in Babylonian exile. The king was a servant of Nebuchadnezzar. Patriots in Judah as well as in the neighboring kingdoms subject to Babylonian domination were clamoring for revolt, encouraged by diviners, soothsayers, and false prophets who announced that exile and the rule of Babylon would soon end. Egypt, to the south, continued to stir up revolt among the small states against the yoke of the Babylonians, and high officials in Jerusalem were ready to play the dangerous game, as had Hezekiah a century earlier. Emissaries from five kingdoms in the area came to Jerusalem to organize the rebellion. At that moment, Jeremiah, at the command of God, resorted to a strange and bold act. He harnessed a wooden yoke to his neck with thongs and bars, just as would be done to an ox when plowing or threshing, and thus the prophet appeared before the foreign statesmen proclaiming the word of God:

> *Thus says the Lord of hosts, the God of Israel: This is what you shall say to your masters: It is I Who by My great power and My outstretched arm have made the earth, with the men and animals that are on the earth, and I give it to whomever it seems right to Me. Now I have given all these lands into the hand of Nebuchadnezzar, the king of Babylon, my servant, and I have given him also the beasts of the field to serve him. All the nations shall serve him and his son and his grandson, until the time of his own land comes; then many nations and great kings shall make him their slave.*

*But if any nation or kingdom will not serve this Nebuchadnezzar king of Babylon, and put its neck under the yoke of the king of Babylon, I will punish that nation with the sword, with famine, and with pestilence, says the Lord, until I have consumed it by his hand. So do not listen to your prophets, your diviners, your dreamers, your soothsayers, or your sorcerers, who are saying to you, You shall not serve the king of Babylon. For it is a lie which they are prophesying to you, with the result that you will be removed far from your land, and I will drive you out, and you will perish. But any nation which will bring its neck under the yoke of the king of Babylon and serve him, I will leave on its own land, to till it and dwell there, says the Lord.*

*Jeremiah 27:4–11*

Jeremiah repeated the same stern warning to King Zedekiah as well as to the priests who were influenced by the prediction of the false prophets: "Bring your necks under the yoke of the king of Babylon, serve him and his people, and you will live" (27:12). The acceptance of Babylonian overlordship, unlike the submission to Assyria which Isaiah had called upon the people to reject, did not involve the danger of complete expulsion and national extinction.

## THE FALL OF JERUSALEM

In spite of historical experience, forced upon the people for close to one hundred and fifty years, many voices were raised in favor of rebellion against Babylon (28:1 ff.). In vain did Jeremiah plead for obedience to Nebuchadnezzar as the one into whose hands the Lord had transferred world rule (37:11 ff.).

Disregarding Jeremiah's warnings, Zedekiah yielded at the end to his leading officials and to the clamor of the people to take the insane step of renouncing his allegiance to Nebuchadnezzar, and sent ambassadors to Egypt seeking military protection against the Babylonians. Nebuchadnezzar had made a treaty *(berith)* with Zedekiah, which Zedekiah confirmed with an imprecatory oath; now, Zedekiah broke the treaty and his oath (Ezek. 17:13–21; II Chron. 36:13).

Nebuchadnezzar's reaction was swift. Early in 588 (or 589) his army arrived, placing Jerusalem under blockade and occupying the rest of the country.

While the Babylonian army was fighting Jerusalem, Jeremiah confronted the king, and declaring it to be the will of God that Jerusalem should fall to the Babylonians, demanded surrender to Babylonia (34:1–5; 21:3–7). Such a demand must have outraged both the devout and the zealots of Jerusalem. To surrender the holy city to a pagan conqueror! Jeremiah's advice was resented. Courageously the people continued to hold out, believing that just as God had delivered Jerusalem from Sennacherib, He would deliver it from Nebuchadnezzar.

Jeremiah's demand to surrender to Nebuchadnezzar was not primarily a plea to accept the foreign yoke as punishment for sins, but rather a call for understanding God's design to turn over the dominion of the entire area to the Babylonian empire, which was to last seventy years (24:7 ff.; 29:10 ff.). Even during his confinement in the court of the guard, while Jerusalem was besieged and doomed to be captured, Jeremiah proclaimed,

> *Thus says the Lord: In this place of which you say, it is a waste without man or beast, in the cities of Judah and the streets of Jerusalem that are desolate, without man or inhabitant or beast, there shall be heard again the voice of mirth and the voice of gladness, the voice of the bridegroom and the voice of the bride, the voices of those who sing, as they bring thank offerings to the house of the Lord;*

> > *Give thanks to the Lord of hosts,*
> > *For the Lord is good,*
> > *For his steadfast love endures for ever!*

> *For I will restore the fortunes of the land as at first, says the Lord.*
> > > *Jeremiah 33:10–11* *

---

*Compare Y. Kaufmann, *The Religion of Israel* (Eng.; Chicago, 1960), pp. 422 f.

Meanwhile an Egyptian army arrived from the southwest which forced the Babylonians to suspend the siege of Jerusalem for a time (37:5; 34:21). But Jeremiah persisted in predicting defeat, publicly discouraging the people from fighting, disparaging the effectiveness of Egyptian help, even advocating that the people and the army desert to the Babylonians.

Taking advantage of the temporary lifting of the siege, Jeremiah desired to go to his native town on a personal matter; he was arrested at the gate of Jerusalem and, accused of deserting to the Babylonians, was thrown into a dungeon cell (37:11–16). It was at the intervention of the king that he was transferred to the court of the guard and supplied with ample rations (37:17–21). There the prophet continued to express his seditious opinions: resistance to the Babylonians was futile, and dying was wrong. In the name of the Lord he appealed to individuals to leave the city and to surrender (21:8–10). The king's officers threw him into an empty cistern. It was an Ethiopian eunuch, Ebed-melech, who, with the king's permission, saved him from death by starvation (chs. 37–38). Jeremiah remained in the lighter captivity of the court prison until he was liberated at the capture of Jerusalem by the Babylonians.

Meanwhile, the Egyptian relief force was defeated and the siege of Jerusalem resumed. Zedekiah, whose only hope now was for a miracle from God, sent a delegation to Jeremiah, saying: "Pray for us. Perhaps the Lord will make the Babylonian king withdraw from us." But the prophet's answer was stern: Your resistance will get weaker. God Himself will fight against you "with outstretched hand and strong arm, in anger, in fury, and in great wrath." The city will be captured; some of the people shall die of pestilence, the rest will be carried away in captivity (see 21:44).

Jerusalem held out for one and one-half years, until famine decided the issue. In 587 the city fell. The holy city was plundered and burned by the conquerors: the Temple of Solomon went up in flames. The prophet who had served as a voice castigating the people was now, in sorrow, the voice of the people.

> *Woe is me because of my hurt!*
> *My wound is grievous.*
> *But I said: Truly this is an affliction,*
> *And I must bear it.*
> *My tent is destroyed,*
> *All my cords are broken;*
> *My children have gone from me,*
> *They are not;*
> *There is no one to spread my tent again,*
> *To set up my curtains.*
>
> *Jeremiah 10:19–20*

To us today, Zedekiah's rebellion against Nebuchadnezzar appears as a gross miscalculation of the political circumstances. Judah's defiance against a power that crushed Assyria was as foolhardy as her reliance on Egypt was self-deceptive. The new empire did not threaten Judah's existence and seems to have been satisfied with acknowledgment of its overlordship and the payment of tribute. Judah could have survived under Babylonian overlordship even more easily than it did under Assyrian or Egyptian tutelage.

Yet, it is not political sagacity that explains Jeremiah's opposition to the stand taken by the rulers of the kingdom, implying a reversal of the position taken by Isaiah when he had insisted that Judah should not capitulate to Assyria. The prophet does not see the world from the point of view of a political theory; he is a person who sees the world from the point of view of God; he sees the world through the eyes of God. To Jeremiah, the relationship to Nebuchadnezzar was much less important than the relationship to God.

Jeremiah was constantly exposed to the situation of God, and tirelessly attentive to the mood of the people, offering boldly the call, the challenge, and the warning, attempting to unravel the knots in the relationship between God and Israel.

He had seen like no other prophet "affliction under the rod of His wrath," but he was also imbued with the certainty of God's attachment, which surpasses His wrath. ". . . as I have watched over them to pluck up and break down, to overthrow, destroy, and bring evil, so I will watch over them to build and to plant, says the Lord" (31:28; see 1:10). "Behold, the days are coming, says the Lord, when I will raise up for David a righteous branch, and he shall reign as king and deal wisely, and shall execute justice and righteousness in the land. In his days Judah will be saved, and Israel will dwell securely. And this is the name by which He will be called: 'The Lord is our righteousness' " (23:5–6).

> *Their children shall be as they were of old,*
> *Their congregation shall be established before Me;*
> *I will punish all who oppress them.*
>
> *Jeremiah 30:20*

> *They shall come and sing aloud on the height of Zion,*
> *They shall be radiant over the goodness of the Lord . . .*
>
> *Jeremiah 31:12*

Nebuchadnezzar's soldiers burned the temple, the king's palace, the larger houses of Jerusalem. The walls were razed, most of the inhabitants were deported.

The Jerusalem man is busy destroying, God is erecting.

# 7

# Habakkuk

*The life of Habakkuk is unknown to us. Presumably the prophet* was a native of Judah who prophesied during the reign of Jehoiakim (609–598 B.C.E.), at the time of the triumphs of Nebuchadnezzar.

The world of Habakkuk is known to us through the little book that bears his name. What is that world like? It is a place in which "justice never goes forth" (1:4) except in perverted form.

> *O Lord, how long shall I cry for help,*
> *And Thou wilt not hear?*
> *Or cry to Thee, Violence!*
> *And Thou wilt not save?*
> *Why dost Thou make me see wrongs*
> *And look upon trouble?*
> *Destruction and violence are before me;*
> *Strife and contention arise.*
> *So the law is slacked*
> *And justice never goes forth.*

SELECTED BIBLIOGRAPHY: Stonehouse, *The Book of Habakkuk* (London, 1911); G. A. Smith, *The Book of the Twelve Prophets* (New York, 1929), pp. 117–160.

> For the wicked surround the righteous,
> So justice goes forth perverted.
>                                        Habakkuk 1:2–4

A startled, tormented man is Habakkuk. He is distressed at the fact that violence prevails and agonized by the thought that God tolerates evil. He prays, "How long?" He cries, "Why?"

His prayer and his cry do not remain unanswered. However, the response given to him is not the comfort of an explanation. The Voice that comes to him says,

> Look . . . see,
> Wonder and be astounded.
> For I am doing a work in your days
> That you would not believe if told.
> For lo, I am rousing the Chaldeans,
> That bitter and hasty nation,
> Who march through the breadth of the earth,
> To seize habitations not their own.
> Dread and terrible are they;
> Their justice and dignity proceed from themselves.
> Their horses are swifter than leopards,
> More fierce than the evening wolves;
> Their horsemen press proudly on,
> Yea, their horsemen come from afar;
> They fly like an eagle swift to devour.
> They all come for violence;
> Terror of them goes before them.
> They gather captives like sand.
> At kings they scoff,
> And of rulers they make sport.
> They laugh at every fortress,
> For they heap up earth and take it.
> Then they sweep by like the wind and go on,
> Guilty men, whose own might is their god!
>                                        Habakkuk 1:5–11 [H. 1:6–11]

The Voice does not explain why God should rouse the terrible Chaldeans to march through the breadth of the earth. On the contrary, the message represents another assault upon Habakkuk's understanding, adding mystery to amazement. While God's design is veiled in an enigma, it is the prophet who volunteers an explanation. The nations are guilty; punishment must follow the guilt. The Chaldeans are the instrument of God's justice.

> *O Lord, Thou hast ordained them as a judgment;*
> *And Thou, O Rock, hast established them for chastisement.*
> *Habakkuk 1:12*

Comforting as the thought is that crime does not go unpunished, it is a thought that gives rise to grave and bitter questions. Is this the way to let justice prevail? Should "guilty men, whose own might is their god" be the instrument to carry out the will of God? Is this the way of justice: that innocent men should perish so that the wicked may be punished?

> *Thou who art of purer eyes than to behold evil*
> *And canst not look on wrong,*
> *Why dost Thou look on faithless men,*
> *And art silent when the wicked swallows up*
> *The man more righteous than he?*
> *Habakkuk 1:13*

Justice is meaningless to the great powers of the world. Merciless are they, and absolutely worthless is man in their eyes. God, Who so loves man that He does not tire of uttering through the prophets His outrage at the wrongs done unto man, is now accused by Habakkuk of being responsible for the vitiation of man.

> *For Thou makest men like the fish of the sea,*
> *Like crawling things that have no ruler.*
> *Habakkuk 1:14*

The ruthless king

> *. . . brings all of them up with a book; . . .*
> *He gathers them in his seine;*
> *So he rejoices and exults.*
>
>                *Habakkuk 1:15*

Net and seine are his gods; to them he sacrifices and brings incense, "for by them he lives in luxury, and his food is rich."

> *His greed is as wide as Sheol;*
> *Like death he has never enough.*
> *He gathers for himself all nations,*
> *And collects as his own all peoples. . . .*
> *Is he then to keep on emptying his net,*
> *And mercilessly slaying nations for ever?*
>
>                *Habakkuk 2:5; 1:17*

There is darkness in the world and anguish in the heart. Should one abandon God and burn incense to net and seine? Should one abandon mercy?

In his anguish Habakkuk decides to wait for another encounter with God.

> *I will take my stand to watch*
> *And station myself on the tower,*
> *And look forth to see what He will say to me,*
> *And what I will answer concerning my complaint.*
>
>                *Habakkuk 2:1*

Two things he wishes to know: God's word and his own answer, for the first is meaningless without the second. This is the insight Habakkuk receives:

> *Write the vision;*
> *Make it plain upon tablets,*
> *So he may run who reads it.*
> *For still the vision awaits its time;*
> *It hastens to the end—it will not lie.*
> *If it seem slow, wait for it.*

> *It will surely come, it will not delay.*
> *Behold, he whose soul is puffed up in him shall fail,*
> *But the righteous shall live by his faith.*
>
> > Habakkuk 2:2–4

Habakkuk's vision remains unknown to us. Its content is not put into words. It clearly was a vision of redemption at the end of days. There is an answer to Habakkuk's question. It is an answer, not in terms of thought, but in terms of events. God's answer will happen, but it cannot be spelled out in words. The answer will surely come; "if it seem slow, wait for it." True, the interim is hard to bear; the righteous one is horrified by what he sees. To this the great answer is given: "The righteous shall live by his faith." It is an answer, again not in terms of thought, but in terms of existence. Prophetic faith is trust in Him, in whose presence stillness is a form of understanding.

> *The Lord is in His holy temple;*
> *Let all the earth keep silence before Him!*
>
> > Habakkuk 2:20

The book of Habakkuk concludes with a vision and a prayer. The prophet sees the future in the perfect tense and employs figures of nature as symbols of history. The great theophany has come: the Lord is arriving upon a chariot of victory. His glory covers the heavens, and the earth is full of His praise. But His appearance is dreadful. Before Him goes pestilence, and close behind follows plague. He bestrides the earth in indignation, trampling the nations in anger. He comes forth for the salvation of His people, of His anointed, to crush "the head from the house of the wicked" who rejoice in devouring the poor in secret. Dismay clutches at the prophet:

> *I hear, and my body trembles,*
> *My lips quiver at the sound;*
> *Rottenness enters into my bones,*
> *I tremble where I stand.*
> *I will quietly wait for the day of trouble*
> *To come upon people who invade us.*
>
> > Habakkuk 3:16

Habakkuk realizes and accepts the mystery of divine anger. He knows it is an instrument necessary for redemption. Humbly he prays: "In anger remember mercy" (3:2).

The prophet trembles, but he also has the power to wait on the Lord. However, the depth of his experience lies deeper than trust and faith. What the prophet faces is not his own faith. He faces God. To sense the living God is to sense infinite goodness, infinite wisdom, infinite beauty. Such a sensation is a sensation of joy. The world may be dismal; the wrath may turn the gardens into a desert; yet the prophet "will rejoice in the Lord." This, it seems, is Habakkuk's personal answer to the vision:

> *Though the fig tree do not blossom,*
> *Nor fruit be on the vines,*
> *The produce of the olive fail*
> *And the fields yield no food,*
> *The flock be cut off from the fold*
> *And there be no herd in the stalls,*
> *Yet I will rejoice in the Lord*
> *I will joy in the God of my salvation.*
> *Habakkuk 3:17–18*

# 8

# Second Isaiah

## ON THE EVE OF REDEMPTION

The Neo-Babylonian empire did not last long. It declined rapidly after the death of Nebuchadnezzar in the year 562 B.C.E. Cyrus, the Persian king of the little principality of Elam, succeeded in overpowering the two powers that had divided the Near Eastern world at the fall of Assyria. He defeated the king of the Median empire in 550 and the king of Babylonia in 539. Cyrus was now the head of the great Persian empire, and his power extended as far as the western coast of Asia Minor.

It was in this exciting period that a prophet arose who lifted the meaning of these events from the level of political history to the level of understanding world history as a drama of redemption. He proclaimed that the Lord was about to redeem His people, that Babylon would fall, and that Cyrus, who had been called and empowered by

SELECTED BIBLIOGRAPHY: J. Muilenburg, "Introduction and Exegesis to Isaiah, chs. 40–66," in G. A. Buttrick, ed., *The Interpreter's Bible,* V (Nashville, 1956), 381–773; M. Buber, *The Prophetic Faith* (New York, 1949); Y. Kaufmann, *The Religion of Israel,* IV (Heb.; Jerusalem, 1956), 51–156; C. C. Torrey, *The Second Isaiah* (New York, 1928); E. J. Kissane, *The Book of Isaiah,* vol. II (Dublin, 1943).

the Lord to carry out His will in history (41:5–7; 44:28; 45:1 f.), was destined to play an important part in the return of Israel to Zion and in the restoration of Jerusalem. The majestic words of this prophet, whose name is unknown, are found in the later chapters of the book of Isaiah (chs. 40–66). The message of Second Isaiah, as he is conventionally called, is of no age. It is prophecy tempered with human tears, mixed with a joy that heals all scars, clearing a way for understanding the future in spite of the present. No words have ever gone further in offering comfort when the sick world cries.

## MY RIGHT IS DISREGARDED BY GOD

The Lord had carried out His threat and punished without pity (Lam. 2:17). But what had His punishment accomplished? Devastation, famine, death, and distress; Jerusalem was destroyed, Israel in exile, and her sons were "like an antelope in a net" (51:20). The tormentors had said to Israel: "Bow down, that we may pass over," and she made her "back like the ground and like the street for them to pass over" (51:23). The exiles lived in continual fear "because of the fury of the oppressor when he sets himself to destroy" (51:13). Yet, even in distress, with the Temple destroyed, Jerusalem in ruins, and liberty lost, Israel remained faithful to her God. "The Lord is in the right, for I have rebelled against His word" (Lam. 1:18). "Is it not from the mouth of the Most High that good and evil come?" (Lam. 3:38). Why should a man complain about the punishment of his sins?

The suffering servant "opened not his mouth, like a lamb that is led to the slaughter" (53:7). Yet, Second Isaiah does not passively accept Zion's lot. Far from being silent, he challenges the Lord, putting the Lord in remembrance.

*For Zion's sake I will not keep silent,*
*And for Jerusalem's sake I will not rest,*
*Until her triumph goes forth as brightness,*

> *And her rescue as a burning torch. . . .*
> *Upon your walls, O Jerusalem,*
> *I have set watchmen;*
> *All the day and all the night*
> *They shall never be silent.*
> *You who put the Lord in remembrance,*
> *Take no rest. . . .*
> *Awake, awake, put on strength,*
> *O arm of the Lord.*
>
> *Isaiah 62:1, 6–7; 51:9*

The prophet voices his bewilderment at the silence of the Almighty.

> *O Lord, Thou art our Father;*
> *We are the clay, and Thou art our potter;*
> *We are all the work of Thy hand.*
> *Be not exceedingly angry, O Lord,*
> *And remember not iniquity for ever.*
> *Behold, consider, we are all Thy people.*
> *Thy holy cities have become a wilderness,*
> *Zion has become a wilderness,*
> *Jerusalem a desolation.*
> *Our holy and beautiful house,*
> *Where our fathers praised Thee,*
> *Has been burned by fire,*
> *All our pleasant places have become ruins.*
> *Wilt Thou restrain Thyself at these things, O Lord?*
> *Wilt Thou keep silent, and afflict us to the utmost? . . .*
> *Look down from heaven and see,*
> *From Thy holy and glorious habitation.*
> *Where are Thy zeal and Thy might?*
> *The yearning of Thy heart and Thy compassion*
> *Are withheld from me.*
>
> *Isaiah 64:8–12 [ H. 64:7–11]; 63:15*

More excruciating than the experience of suffering is the agony of sensing no meaning in suffering, the inability to say, "Thy rod and Thy staff, they comfort me." Can He Who "has destroyed without mercy all the habitations of Jacob," Who "has become like an enemy" (Lam. 2:2, 5), still be trusted as the God Who is our Father?

> *Zion said: The Lord has forsaken me,*
> *My Lord has forgotten me. . . .*
> *I have labored in vain,*
> *I have spent my strength for nothing and vanity. . . .*
> *My way is hid from the Lord,*
> *My right is disregarded by my God.*
> *Isaiah 49:14, 4; 40:27*

Israel's misery seemed out of all proportion to her guilt, and its justice belied by other facts of history.

Was this to be hailed as justice: agony for Israel and glory for Babylon? The beloved of God bruised and despised while the "mistress of kingdoms" (47:5) "felt secure in . . . wickedness" (47:10)? Was it not obvious that God did not care? Or was it beyond His power to save those for whom He cared? (See 59:1.)

To comfort is to throw a glimmer of meaning into a cave of wretchedness. Jerusalem—"she has none to comfort her" (Lam. 1:2, 9, 16, 17, 21). Who will condole with you? How may I comfort you? (51:19.) Why was Israel driven into exile? Why did Israel continue to be in exile?

## WHO TAUGHT HIM THE PATH OF JUSTICE?

In an atmosphere of bewilderment, confusion, and despondency, and speaking to

> *A people robbed and plundered, . . .*
> *All of them trapped in holes*
> *And hidden in prisons*
> *Isaiah 42:22*

the prophet first accepts the burden of the mystery of divine wisdom before attempting to illumine His ways.

> *For My thoughts are not your thoughts,*
> *Neither are your ways My ways, says the Lord.*
> *For as the heaven is higher than the earth,*
> *So are My ways higher than your ways*
> *And My thoughts than your thoughts.*
>
> Isaiah 55:8–9

Living in the certainty of a divine wisdom which defies human understanding, those who question Him expect the Lord to adjust His thought to their thoughts, His design to their conceptions. The prophet maintains that those who question Him try to enlighten Him; that those who contend with Him presume to instruct Him in "the path of justice," "the way of understanding." The overwhelming grandeur of His wisdom as manifested in the realm of nature should inspire humility when reflecting about His ways in the realm of history.

> *Who has measured the waters in the hollow of his hand,*
> *Marked off the heavens with a span,*
> *Enclosed the dust of the earth in a measure,*
> *Weighed the mountains in scales*
> *And the hills in a balance?*
> *Who has directed the Spirit of the Lord,*
> *Or as His counselor has instructed Him?*
> *Whom did He consult for his enlightenment,*
> *Who taught Him the path of justice,*
> *Who taught Him knowledge,*
> *Who showed Him the way of understanding? . . .*
> *Woe to him who strives with his Maker,*
> *An earthen vessel with the potters!*
> *Does the clay say to him who fashions it, What are you making?*
> *Or, Your work has no handles?*
> *Woe to him who says to a father, What are you begetting?*

*Or, to a woman, With what are you in travail? ...*
*Will you command Me concerning the work of My hands?*
                    *Isaiah 40:12–14; 45:9–11\**

## The Suffering Servant

God's thoughts are higher than human thoughts. Yet just as God may share the sufferings of man, so man may share the thoughts of God.

Amos had proclaimed:

> *You only have I known*
> *Of all the families of the earth;*
> *Therefore I will punish you*
> *For all your iniquities.*
>
>                    *Amos 3:2*

Second Isaiah would phrase the last words to read: "For all their iniquities." What Israel endured was not simply chastisement for her sins; her agony far exceeded her guilt. Indeed,

> *She has received from the Lord's hand*
> *Double for all her sins.*
>
>                    *Isaiah 40:2*

She is the suffering servant of the Lord.†

As a rule we reflect on the problem of suffering in relation to him who suffers. The prophet's message insists that suffering is not to be

---

*According to Rashi, in his *Commentary,* this passage contains an answer to the problem of why the Lord lets the wicked prosper and Israel suffer.

†The outstanding songs of the servant of the Lord are 42:1–4; 49:1–6; 50:4–9; 52:13–53:12. Perhaps no other problem in the Hebrew Bible has occupied the minds of scholars more than the identification and interpretation of the servant. For a survey of the vast literature, see C. R. North, *The Suffering Servant in Deutero-Isaiah* (Oxford, 1956). In the main, four theories have been proposed. The servant is (1) an anonymous contemporary of Second Isaiah; (2) Second Isaiah himself; (3) Israel; (4) a purely ideal or imaginary figure. To quote J. Muilenburg, in *The Interpreter's Bible,* V, 408, 411, "The servant is certainly Israel. . . . Israel, and Israel alone, is able to bear all

understood exclusively in terms of the sufferer's own situation. In Israel's agony, all nations are involved. Israel's suffering is not a penalty, but a privilege, a sacrifice; its endurance is a ritual, its meaning is to be disclosed to all men in the hour of Israel's redemption.

Deliverance, redemption, is what the Lord has in store for Israel, and through Israel for all men. Her suffering and agony are the birthpangs of salvation which, the prophet proclaims, is about to unfold. In answer to the prophet's fervent invocation (51:9), the Lord is about to bare His arm or His might before the eyes of all the nations. (Cf. 52:10 with 53:1.)

> *How beautiful upon the mountains*
> *Are the feet of him who brings good tidings,*
> *Who publishes peace, who brings good tidings of good,*
> *Who publishes salvation,*
> *Who says to Zion, Your God reigns.*
> *Hark, your watchmen lift up their voice,*
> *Together they sing for joy;*
> *For eye to eye they see*
> *The return of the Lord to Zion.*
> *Break forth together into singing,*
> *You waste places of Jerusalem;*
> *For the Lord has comforted His people,*
> *He has redeemed Jerusalem. . . .*
> *Behold, My servant shall prosper,*
> *He shall be exalted and lifted up,*
> *And shall be very high.*
> *As many were astonished at him—*
> *His appearance was so marred, beyond human semblance,*

---

that is said about the servant of the Lord. For the fundamental fact outweighing all others is the repeated equation of the two in the poems." See 41:8 ff.; 43:8–13; 44:1–2, 21; 45:4; 49:3. According to H. H. Rowley, *The Faith of Israel* (London, 1956), p. 122, "The servant is at once Israel and an individual, who both represents the whole community and carries to its supreme point the mission of the nation, while calling the whole people to enter into that mission, so that it shall be its mission and not merely his. . . . The servant is Israel today and tomorrow; but Israel may be all or a few or one of its members."

*And his form beyond that of the sons of men—*
*So shall he startle many nations;*
*Kings shall shut their mouths because of him;*
*For that which has not been told them they shall see,*
*And that which they have not heard they shall understand.*
*Who has believed what we have heard?*
*And to whom has the arm of the Lord been revealed?*
*For he grew up before Him like a young plant,*
*And like a root out of dry ground;*
*He had no form or comeliness that we should look at him,*
*And no beauty that we should desire him.*
*He was despised and rejected by men;*
*A man of sorrows, and acquainted with grief;*
*And as one from whom men hide their faces*
*He was despised, and we esteemed him not.*
*Surely he has borne our griefs*
*And carried our sorrows;*
*Yet we esteemed him stricken,*
*Smitten by God, and afflicted.*
*But he was wounded for our transgressions,*
*He was bruised for our iniquities;*
*Upon him was the chastisement that made us whole,*
*And with his stripes we are healed. . . .*
*And like a sheep that before its shearers is dumb,*
*So he opened not his mouth. . . .*
*By his knowledge shall the righteous one, My servant,*
*Make many to be accounted righteous;*
*And he shall bear their iniquities.*
*Therefore I will divide him a portion with the great,*
*And he shall divide the spoil with the strong;*
*Because he poured out his soul to death,*
*And was numbered with the transgressors;*
*Yet he bore the sin of many,*
*And made intercession for the transgressors.*

*Isaiah 52:7–9, 13; 53:5, 7, 11–12*

Suffering as chastisement is man's own responsibility; suffering as redemption is God's responsibility. It was He Who had chosen Israel as His servant; it was He Who had placed upon Israel the task of suffering for others. The meaning of her agony was shifted from the sphere of man to the sphere of God, from the moment to eternity.

## IN ALL THEIR AFFLICTION, HE WAS AFFLICTED

Israel's suffering is God's grief. In reflecting on what this people has endured, His words sound like pangs of remorse.

> *I was angry with My people,*
> *I profaned My heritage.*
> *Isaiah 47:6*

Not all the evils that befell Israel go back to the will of God. The Babylonians, who in His providence became the leading power in the world and into whose hand He handed over His people, "showed them no mercy"; on the aged they made their yoke "exceedingly heavy." While Israel suffered, the Lord restrained Himself. But the time of His restraint and silence is over. He can wait no longer for the display of His might and mercy.

> *For a long time I have kept silent,*
> *I have kept still and restrained Myself;*
> *Now I will cry out like a woman in travail,*
> *I will gasp and pant.*
> *Isaiah 42:14*

The allusion to the Lord as "a woman in travail," the boldest figure used by any prophet, conveys not only the sense of supreme urgency of His action, but also a sense of the deep intensity of His suffering. Of the person who cleaves to Him in love, the Lord says:

> *When he calls to Me, I will answer him;*
> *I will be with him in affliction.*
> *Psalm 91:15*

Of God's involvement in human suffering the prophet declares courageously:

> *In all their affliction He was afflicted . . .*
> *In His love and in His pity He redeemed them,*
> *He lifted them up and carried them all the days of old.*
>
> Isaiah 63:9

It is God's involvement in the suffering of man (see pp. 139 ff.) that explains this particular concern for the downtrodden and contrite. (Cf. 57:15.)

To extricate the people from despondency, to attach meaning to their past and present misery, was the task that the prophet and God had in common. "Comfort ye, comfort ye My people, says your God" (40:1). And also, "I, I am He that comforts you" (66:13). His comfort comes from compassion (49:13), and will bring about joy (51:3), deliverance from captivity, and the restoration of Zion and Jerusalem.

> *For soon My salvation will come,*
> *And My deliverance be revealed. . . .*
> *Israel is saved by the Lord*
> *With everlasting salvation. . . .*
> *Behold, the Lord has proclaimed*
> *To the end of the earth:*
> *Say to dear Zion,*
> *Behold, your salvation comes,*
> *Behold, His reward is with Him,*
> *His recompense before Him.*
> *They shall be called the holy people,*
> *The redeemed of the Lord;*
> *You shall be called Sought out,*
> *A city not forsaken.*
>
> Isaiah 56:1; 45:17; 62:11–12

## BECAUSE I LOVE YOU

Earlier prophets, absorbed in guilt and punishment, addressed Israel as "sinful nation, a people laden with iniquity" (Isa. 1:4); Second Isaiah, radiant with triumph and joy, addresses Israel as "you who pursue righteousness, you who seek the Lord" (51:1).

What Jeremiah proclaimed as the Lord's promise for the future, "I will put My teaching within them, and I will write it upon their hearts" (Jer. 31:33 [H. 31:32]), Second Isaiah seems to regard as fulfilled:

> *Hearken to me, you who know righteousness,*
> *The people in whose heart is My teaching.*
>
> *Isaiah 51:7*

"Deeply despised, abhorred by the nations, servant of rulers" (49:7), Israel is given the spirit to say to the world,

> *The Lord has called me from the womb, . . .*
> *And said to me, You are My servant,*
> *Israel, in whom I am glorified.*
>
> *Isaiah 49:1, 3*

Earlier, God was challenging Israel; now, Israel is questioning God. The task of the early prophets was to threaten and to shock; Second Isaiah's task is to give "power to the faint" and "strength to him who has no might" (40:29). They called upon Israel to mourn; he calls upon her to sing and to rejoice.

Israel's transgressions are trivial and insignificant when compared with God's love. Iniquities pass, even their memory may vanish in forgiveness, but God's love for Israel will never pass, will never vanish.

> *I, I am He*
> *Who blots out your transgressions for My own sake,*
> *And I will not remember your sins. . . .*
> *I have swept away your transgressions like a cloud,*
> *And your sins like mist;*
> *Return to Me, for I have redeemed you.*
>
> *Isaiah 43:25; 44:22*

There was no rejection on His part, He did not divorce His people (50:1). There was no detachment or personal alienation, but rather a spurious separation.

> *Your iniquities have made a separation*
> *Between you and your God,*
> *And your sins have hid His face from you*
> *So that he does not hear.*
>
> Isaiah 59:2

Sins affect His attitude temporarily; they cannot alter his relationship radically. God's love of Israel is eternal. Is it conceivable that sin, the work of man, should destroy what is intimately divine and eternal? For the reason of His eternal attachment is

> *Because you are precious in My eyes,*
> *And honored, and I love you. . . .*
> *For a brief moment I forsook you,*
> *But with great compassion I will gather you.*
> *In overflowing wrath for a moment*
> *I hid My face from you,*
> *But with everlasting love I will have compassion on you,*
> *Says the Lord, your Redeemer.*
> *Can a woman forget her suckling child,*
> *That she should have no compassion on the son of her womb?*
> *Even these may forget*
> *Yet I will not forget you*
> *For the mountains may depart*
> *And the hills be removed*
> *But My steadfast love shall not depart from you,*
> *And My covenant of peace shall not be removed,*
> *Says the Lord, Who has compassion on you.*
>
> Isaiah 43:4; 54:7–8; 49:15; 54:10

## THE LORD'S OATH

"For I am God, and there is no other" (45:22). The Father of all men is committed to all men. Second Isaiah not only conveys the Lord's invitation and commitment to every man on earth; he proclaims that God has sworn that all men will worship Him. Here is a

divine oath, not merely a hope. Here is a statement transcending all
doubts.

> *By Myself I have sworn,*
> *From My mouth has gone forth in righteousness*
> *A word that shall not return:*
> *To Me every knee shall bow,*
> *Every tongue shall swear.*
>
> *Isaiah 45:23*

While the coming salvation is the redemption of His people and
the restoration of Jerusalem and Zion, the end of His design is that

> *The glory of the Lord shall be revealed,*
> *And all flesh shall see it together.*
> *Isaiah 40:5*

It is the paradox of the human situation that those who do not
even know God are chosen by Him to be the instruments in enabling
men to know God. Cyrus, who did not know Him (45:4–5), is consecrated, called, and equipped for his great mission, so

> *. . . that men may know, from the rising of the sun*
> *And from the west, that there is none besides Me;*
> *I am the Lord, and there is no other.*
> *Isaiah 45:6*

Even as Cyrus may not know Him and is yet chosen to carry out
God's mission, the nations of the world who may not know Him are
waiting for God, for His teaching and redemption (42:4; 51:4–5).
Idolatry will disappear (42:16–17; 45:16–17). To all nations the call
goes forth:

> *Turn to Me and be saved,*
> *All the ends of the earth!*
> *Isaiah 45:22*

The Lord is coming "to gather all nations and tongues, and they
shall come and shall see My glory" (66:18), and they will all be His
servants.

*The foreigners who join themselves to the Lord,*
*To minister to Him, to love the name of the Lord,*
*And to be his servants,*
*Every one who keeps the Sabbath, and does not profane it,*
*And holds fast My covenant—*
*These I will bring to My holy mountain,*
*And make them joyful in My house of prayer;*
*Their burnt offerings and their sacrifices*
*Will be accepted on My altar;*
*For My house shall be a house of prayer*
*For all peoples.*

*Isaiah 56:6–7*

## A LIGHT TO THE NATIONS

In contrast to the books of earlier prophets where the word of God speaks of Israel in the third person, now the Voice speaks to Israel directly in the second person. It is not a prophet speaking in His name; it is predominantly God addressing Himself to the people; it is I, not He. Prophetic receptivity is shared by all. Meaning is manifest, insight is common. It is as if in fulfillment of Moses' prayer, "Would that all the Lord's people were prophets, that the Lord would put His spirit upon them!" (Num. 11:29), Israel is declared to be God's spokesman, or prophet (49:2). Just as the Lord said to Jeremiah, "I appointed you a prophet to the nations" (Jer. 1:5), He said to Israel, "I appointed you a light to the nations" (49:6). The term "servant of the Lord," used to designate the prophets (I Kings 14:18; 15:29; II Kings 9:7, 36; 14:25; 17:13, 23; 21:10; 24:2; Amos 3:7; Isa. 20:3; Jer. 7:25; 25:4; 26:5), is now applied to Israel.

"As for Me, this is My covenant with them, says the Lord: My spirit which is upon you, and My words which I have put in your mouth, shall not depart out of your mouth, or out of the mouth of your children, or out of the mouth of your children's children, says the Lord, from this time forth and for evermore" (59:21). "All your sons shall be taught by the Lord" (54:13).

> *I will pour My spirit upon your descendants,*
> *And My blessing on your offspring.*
> *I have put My words in your mouth,*
> *And hid you in the shadow of My hand,*
> *To plant heaven,*
> *To establish earth,*
> *Saying to Zion, You are My people.*
>     *Isaiah 44:3; 51:16; cf. Joel 2:28 [H. 3:1]*

Just as prior to the exile individual prophets addressed themselves to Israel, Israel now addresses herself to the nations. Like Jeremiah, Israel was called to her task from the earliest moment of her existence (Jer. 1:5).

> *Listen to me, O coastlands,*
> *Hearken, you peoples from afar.*
> *The Lord called me from the womb,*
> *From the body of my mother He named my name.*
> *He made my mouth like a sharp sword,*
> *In the shadow of His hand He hid me;*
> *He made me a polished arrow,*
> *In His quiver he hid me away.*
> *He said to me, You are My servant,*
> *Israel, in whom I will be glorified.*
>     *Isaiah 49:1–3*

Israel is more than an instrument in God's design. Israel is made to be "a witness to the peoples" (55:4). "You are My witnesses!" (44:8). Israel is called to be

> *A light to the nations,*
> *To open the eyes that are blind,*
> *To bring out the prisoners from the dungeon,*
> *From the prison those who sit in darkness.*
>     *Isaiah 42:6–7*

For the accomplishment of His grand design, the Lord waits for the help of man (cf. 63:5). This is the meaning of being His servant:

to be a light to the nations so that His salvation "may reach to the end of the earth" (49:6).

> *Behold My servant, whom I uphold,*
> *My chosen, in whom My soul delights;*
> *I have put My spirit upon him,*
> *He will bring forth justice to the nations.*
> *He will not cry or lift up his voice,*
> *Or make it heard in the street;*
> *A bruised reed he will not break,*
> *And a dimly burning wick he will not quench;*
> *He will faithfully bring forth justice.*
> *He will not fail or be discouraged*
> *Till he has established justice in the earth,*
> *And the coastlands wait for his teaching.*
>
> Isaiah 42:1–4

## THE WORD OF OUR GOD WILL STAND FOREVER

The grandeur and presence of God are strikingly apparent, heaven and earth are radiant with His glory. It is enough to lift up the eyes on high and see Who created these (40:26). Yet men are blind; spiritually, they live in a dungeon. Israel's destiny is, as we have seen, "to open the eyes that are blind." Yet the tragedy is that the servant himself fails to understand the meaning of his mission.

> *Who is blind but My servant,*
> *Or deaf as My messenger whom I send?*
> *Who is blind as My dedicated one,*
> *Or blind as the servant of the Lord?*
> *He sees many things, but does not observe them;*
> *His ears are open, but he does not hear.*
>
> Isaiah 42:19–20

There were those who though walking in the darkness trusted in the name of the Lord and relied on Him (50:10), while others, "stub-

born of heart," did not respond to the message of redemption proclaimed by the prophet (46:12), or even forsook the Lord and forgot
Zion (65:11). An extremely bitter, crushing cry bursts out of the
prophet:

> *We have all become like one who is unclean;*
> *All our righteous deeds are like a polluted garment.*
> *We all fade like a leaf,*
> *Our iniquities, like the wind, take us away.*
>
> *Isaiah 64:6\**

The prophet continues to stress the sharp contrast between the
Creator and His creation, the eternal and the evanescent, the thoughts
of God and the thoughts of man, the sublimity of the Lord and the
triviality of man (40:17, 22), heaven and earth (55:8–9), the reality
of God and the nothingness of idols, the everlastingness of His Word
and the impermanence of human kindness.

> *All flesh is grass,*
> *And all its kindness is like the flower in the field.*
> *The grass withers, the flower fades, . . .*
> *But the word of our God will stand for ever.*
>
> *Isaiah 40:6–8*

He stresses the contrast between the wisdom of God's works and
the limited worth of human deeds, the eternity of God's love and the
temporariness of His wrath (54:7–8), the marvel of God's presence
and the enigma of His silence.

> *Who are you that you are afraid of man who dies,*
> *Of the son of man who is made like grass, . . .*
> *And fear continually all the day*
> *Because of the fury of the oppressor,*
> *When he sets himself to destroy? . . .*
> *Truly, Thou art a God who hidest Thyself,*
> *O God of Israel, the Savior.*
>
> *Isaiah 51:12–13; 45:15*

---

\*See A. J. Heschel, *God in Search of Man* (New York, 1955), pp. 393 f.

Heaven, the most permanent and sublime part of God's creation, as well as the earth, mankind's dearest shelter, which according to Ecclesiastes (1:4) endures forever, are considered evanescent when compared with God's salvation.

> Lift up your eyes to the heaven,
> And look at the earth beneath;
> For the heaven will vanish like smoke,
> The earth will wear out like a garment,
> And they who dwell in it will die like gnats;
> But My salvation will be for ever,
> And My deliverance will never be ended.
>
> Isaiah 51:6

The deliverance of Israel and the return to Zion are depicted as an event of both universal and cosmic significance. From distant lands, nations will come to Zion and declare: "God is with you only, and there is no other" (45:14), and will sing to the Lord a new song (42:10–12).

Heaven and the depths of the earth, mountains and every tree in the forest will break forth into singing, "for the Lord has redeemed Jacob" (44:23).

"For behold, I create a new heaven and a new earth" (65:17; cf. 66:22). Salvation will come; "in its time I will hasten it" (60:22). "Those who wait for Me shall not be put to shame" (49:23).

# 9

# History

## THE IDOLATRY OF MIGHT

Why were so few voices raised in the ancient world in protest against the ruthlessness of man? Why are human beings so obsequious, ready to kill and ready to die at the call of kings and chieftains? Perhaps it is because they worship might, venerate those who command might, and are convinced that it is by force that man prevails. The splendor and the pride of kings blind the people. The Mesopotamian, for example, felt convinced that authorities were always right: "The command of the palace, like the command of Anu, cannot be altered. The king's word is right; his utterance, like that of a god, cannot be changed!"* The prophets repudiated the work as well as the power of man as an object of supreme adoration. They denounced "arrogant boasting" and "haughty pride" (Isa. 10:12), the kings who ruled the nations in anger, the oppressors (Isa. 14:4–6), the destroyers of nations, who went forth to inflict waste, ruin, and death (Jer. 4:7), the "guilty men, whose own might is their god" (Hab. 1:11).

*T. Jacobsen, in H. Frankfort, *et al.*, eds., *The Intellectual Adventure of Ancient Man* (Chicago, 1946), p. 203.

> *Their course is evil,*
> *Their might is not right.*
> *Jeremiah 23:10*

The end of public authority is to realize the moral law, a task for which both knowledge and understanding as well as the possession of power are indispensable means. Yet inherent in power is the tendency to breed conceit. ". . . one of the most striking and one of the most pervasive features of the prophetic polemic [is] the denunciation and distrust of power in all its forms and guises. The hunger of the powerful knows no satiety; the appetite grows on what it feeds. Power exalts itself and is incapable of yielding to any transcendent judgment; it 'listens to no voice' (Zeph. 3:2)."* It is the bitter irony of history that the common people, who are devoid of power and are the prospective victims of its abuse, are the first to become the ally of him who accumulates power. Power is spectacular, while its end, the moral law, is inconspicuous.

"Material force is the *ultima ratio* of political society everywhere. Arms alone can keep the peace."† This was and still remains the axiom with men everywhere. The sword is not only the source of security; it is also the symbol of honor and glory; it is bliss and song.

When the prophets appeared, they proclaimed that might is not supreme, that the sword is an abomination, that violence is obscene. The sword, they said, shall be destroyed.

> *They shall beat their swords into plowshares,*
> *And their spears into pruning hooks;*
> *Nation shall not lift up sword against nation,*
> *Neither shall they learn war any more.*
> *Isaiah 2:4*

The prophets, questioning man's infatuation with might, insisted not only on the immorality but also on the futility and absurdity of

---

*J. Muilenburg, *The Way of Israel* (New York, 1961), p. 89.
†John Henry Cardinal Newman, *Discussions and Arguments* (London, 1872), p. 203.

war. In a later era Napoleon, we are told, solemnly declared to his Minister of Education: "Do you know, Fontanes, what astonishes me most in this world? The inability of force to create anything. In the long run the sword is always beaten by the spirit."* Yet, the most astonishing thing in the world is the perennial disregard of the impotence of force. What is the ultimate profit of all the arms, alliances, and victories? Destruction, agony, death.

> *Peoples labor only for fire,*
> *Nations weary themselves for naught.*
> *Habakkuk 2:13*

Egypt and Mesopotamia were involved recurrently in a struggle for supremacy. At the same time, Mesopotamia was beset by internal conflicts between the rival peoples of Babylonia and Assyria. Those two countries carried on frequent wars against sedentary and migratory peoples in the Near East who were considered threats to the empires or who were simply tempting prey for the insatiable kings and warlords. They fell upon the quiet people in the villages, "all of them dwelling without walls, and having no bars or gates; to seize spoil and carry off plunder; . . . to carry away silver and gold, to take away cattle and goods" (Ezek. 38:11–13).

As it was in the age of the prophets, so it is in nearly every age: we all go mad, not only individually, but also nationally. We check manslaughter and isolated murders; we wage wars and slaughter whole peoples. Ferocity appears natural; generosity, superimposed. Since the natural often seems sacred, we seldom dare suppress or try to remake what has been called "all that fine belligerence within us." We measure manhood by the sword and are convinced that history is ultimately determined on the fields of battle. "There is no peace, says my God, for the wicked" (Isa. 57:21; cf. 48:22). "Perpetual peace is a dream—and not even a beautiful dream—and war is an integral part of God's ordering of the Universe. In war, Man's noblest virtues come into play: courage and renunciation, fidelity to

*J. C. Herold, *The Mind of Napoleon* (New York, 1955), p. 76.

duty and a readiness for sacrifice that does not stop short of offering up Life itself. Without war the world would become swamped in materialism."*

David at one time assembled at Jerusalem all officials of Israel—the officers, the commanders, the mighty men, and all the seasoned warriors. Then he rose to his feet and said: "Hear me, my brethren and my people. I had it in my heart to build a house of rest for the Ark of the covenant of the Lord, . . . and I made preparations for building. But God said to me: You may not build a house for My name, for you are a warrior and have shed blood. . . . It is Solomon your son who shall build my house . . ." (I Chron. 28:1–3, 6).†

The Chronicler did not regard the wars of David as wrong. Far from it; God was with David wherever he went, and his victories over the enemies assured security to Israel, so that "violent men shall waste them no more, as formerly," and established his throne forever (I Chron. 17:8–14). David's wars were regarded as a necessary evil, but the fierce doings David was involved in made him unfit to build the house for the Lord.

The prophets did not isolate the evil of war, and they seem to have regarded it as the extension of a condition that prevails even in time of peace.

Noise, fury, tumult are usually associated with battles of war, when nation seeks to destroy nation. The cheating, the cunning, the humiliations by which individuals seek to destroy each other are pursued discreetly, with no one feeling hurt, consciously, except the victim. The walls within which secret crimes are committed remain quiet. But to the ear of the prophet,

*H. von Moltke, as quoted by A. Toynbee, *War and Civilization* (New York, 1950), p. 16.
†The word of the Lord came to David through the prophet Nathan, commanding him not to build a Temple (II Sam. 7; I Chron. 17); but here a different reason is given. The statement in I Kings 5:3 that David had been too busy fighting to have time to erect the Temple is often characterized by modern interpreters as "abysmally lower" than the reason given in I Chron. These interpreters fail to observe that the reason mentioned in I Kings is contained in a communication sent by Solomon to Hiram, the king of Tyre.

> *The stone will cry out from the wall,* . . .
> *Woe to him who builds a town with blood,*
> *And founds a city on iniquity!*
> *Habakkuk 2:11–12*

Righteousness and peace are interdependent (cf. Ps. 85:10). "The effect of righteousness will be peace, And the result of righteousness quietness and trust for ever" (Isa. 32:17).

> *Woe to those who devise wickedness*
> *And work evil upon their beds!*
> *When the morning dawns, they perform it,*
> *Because it is in the power of their hand.*
> *They covet fields, and seize them;*
> *And houses, and take them away;*
> *They oppress a man and his house,*
> *A man and his inheritance.*
> *Micah 2:1–2*

Amos castigated the individuals "who store up violence and robbery in their strongholds" (3:10). "Your rich men are full of violence!" Micah exclaimed (6:12). The condemnation of violence (*hamas, shod, ʿoshek*) is a major theme in the prophets' speeches.

On the other hand, the denunciation of violence committed by private individuals applied a millionfold to the brutal wars of aggression waged by insatiable and arrogant empires. Although Assyria, for example, was used as a tool for the merited chastisement of other peoples, the prophets insisted that the guilt was the aggressor's. Amos cried out against the cruelties inflicted by the various nations upon each other—nations which, casting off all pity, pursued one another with the sword, ripping up women with child, slaughtering people, driving them into captivity, selling them into slavery (Amos 1:3, 13). On the day of battle, Hosea reminds us, cities were devastated by the conqueror, and mothers were dashed to pieces with their children (Hos. 10:14).

Isaiah was filled with disgust for the military boots, for every mantle rolled in blood (Isa. 9:5 [H. 9:4]), for the scepter and the pomp of the wicked rulers (Isa. 14:5, 11), for the arrogance, pride, and insolence of the rulers. Above all, Isaiah entertained extreme disgust for the Assyrians. The prophet's vehement denunciation of the individuals oppressing the poor and crushing the needy, and his sense of outrage at those who were accumulating dishonest gain applied even more to the brutalities suffered by entire communities at the hand of hostile armies and their leaders.

Assyria has often been called the most ruthless nation of antiquity. For ages she plundered all peoples within her reach, like a lion which "filled his caves with prey and his dens with torn flesh" (Nah. 2:12 [H. 2:13]). Her warfare abounded in atrocities; cutting off the heads of conquered peoples was a common procedure. The kings of Assyria boasted of towns destroyed, dismantled or burned, leveled as if by a hurricane or reduced to a heap of rubble. The victors took away everything they could carry. Upon capturing a city,

> the king's throne would be set up before the gates of the city and the prisoners would be paraded before him, led by the monarch of the captured town, who would undergo the most agonizing torture, such as having his eyes put out or confinement in a cage, until the king of Assyria set a term to his long-drawn agony. Sargon had the defeated king of Damascus burned alive before his eyes. The wives and daughters of the captured king were destined for the Assyrian harems and those who were not of noble blood were condemned to slavery. Meanwhile the soldiery had been massacring the population, and brought the heads of their victims into the king's presence, where they were counted up by the scribes. Not all the male prisoners were put to death, for the boys and craftsmen were led into captivity, where they would be assigned to the hardest tasks on the royal building projects, where the swamps which cover so much of Mesopotamia must have caused an enor-

mously high rate of mortality. The remainder of the population
were uprooted and sent to the other end of the Empire.*

Isaiah spoke to Israel as well as to "all . . . inhabitants of the
world" (Isa. 18:3). What went on in Israel on a small scale went on
in the world on a grand scale. The misdeeds of individuals who
deprived their fellow men of their rightful possessions—"Woe to
those who join house to house, who add field to field" (Isa. 5:8)—
were trifling compared to the crimes of Assyria. "The oppressor" (Isa.
14:4) tried to turn the world into a desert, overthrowing cities and
refusing to let his prisoners go home (Isa. 14:17). What a passion for
war, what a pleasure in destruction!

The great powers spread not only ruin and destruction, but also
guilt and moral corruption. In the case of Assyria, she was condemned
for her "countless harlotries," for betraying nations "with her harlotries, and peoples with her charms" (Nah. 3:4). The small nations were
first subdued and then forced to become allies, fellow travelers, sup-
plying soldiers, joining Assyria in the slaughter of other nations.† Seeking glory, booty, and power, vanquished kings became commanders
in Assyria's army, sharing her glories, partaking in the slaughter. It
was about such enticement that Habakkuk exclaimed:

> *Woe to him who makes his neighbors drink,*
> *Causing them to join him in his fury,*
> *Who makes them drunk,*
> *To gaze on their shame!*
> *You will be sated with contempt instead of glory, . . .*
> *Shame will come upon your glory! . . .*

---

*G. Contenau, *Everyday Life in Babylon and Assyria* (London, 1954), p. 148.
Assyrian art was "great only in portraying the dying agonies of men and of beasts. . . .
Nothing comparable is to be found in ancient art to the 'stele of the vultures' feeding
on the carrion of the vanquished." (R. H. Bainton, *Christian Attitudes toward War
and Peace* [New York, 1960], p. 19.) See also A. T. Olmstead, *History of Assyria* (New
York, 1923), p. 295; D. D. Luckenbill, *Ancient Records of Babylonia and Assyria,* I
(Chicago, 1926), 145; H. Schmokel, *Geschichte des alten Vorderasiens ("Handbuch der
Orientalistik,"* II, 3), pp. 252 f.

†The army of Assyria was composed of many nations, see Isa. 10:8; 13:4; 17:12;
22:6; for Babylonia, see Jer. 34:1.

*For the blood of men and violence to the earth,*
*To cities and all who dwell therein.*

> *Habakkuk 2:15–17*

A few decades later, after the downfall of Assyria, it was Babylonia whose might and splendor held many nations in her spell. A state of intoxication, a voluntary madness, overcame the world, eager to join and to aid the destroyer, accessories to aggression.

*Babylon was a golden cup in the hand of the Lord,*
*Making the whole earth drunk;*
*The nations drank of her wine,*
*Therefore the nations went mad.*

> *Jeremiah 51:7*

## There Is No Regard for Man

How ugly and weird the world is: drunk with lust for power, infatuated with war, merciless and sad.

*The envoys of peace weep bitterly,*
*The highways lie waste, . . .*
*Covenants are broken,*
*Witnesses are despised,*
*There is no regard for man.*

> *Isaiah 33:7–8\**

Of course, there is religion in the world. There are even men who worship the Righteous One:

*From the ends of the earth we hear songs of praise,*
*Of glory to the Righteous One.*
*But I say, I pine away,*
*I pine away. Woe is me!*

---

\*Both Driver and Kissane ascribe the poem to Isaiah; see E. J. Kissane, *The Book of Isaiah* (Dublin, 1941), p. 369.

> *For the treacherous deal treacherously,*
> *The treacherous deal very treacherously.* *
>
> > *Isaiah 24:16*

Before the fall of Assyria, nations lived in dread of that country, whose design was "to destroy and to cut off nations not a few" (Isa. 10:7). The tyrant says in his heart:

> *I will ascend to heaven;*
> *Above the stars of God I will set my throne on high. . . .*
> *I will ascend above the heights of the clouds,*
> *I will be like the Most High.*
>
> > *Isaiah 14:13–14*

The root of all evil is, according to Isaiah, man's false sense of sovereignty and, stemming from it, man's pride, arrogance, and presumption. Assyria said:

> *By the strength of my hand I have done it,*
> *And by my wisdom, for I have understanding;*
> *I have removed the boundaries of peoples,*
> *And have plundered their treasures;*
> *Like a bull I have brought down those who sat on thrones.*
> *My hand has found like a nest*
> *The wealth of the peoples;*
> *And as men gather eggs that have been forsaken*
> *So I have gathered all the earth;*
> *And there was none that moved a wing,*
> *Or opened the mouth, or chirped.*
>
> > *Isaiah 10:13–14*

Even little Moab, a tiny kingdom west of the Dead Sea, was full of arrogance, pride, insolence, and false boasts (Isa. 15:6).

---

*The meaning of the verse is uncertain. Most critics assign it to a time after the destruction of Jerusalem in 587. According to Kissane, *op. cit.*, p. 270, "the poem is just as applicable to the period of Isaiah as to any other period."

There is no limit to cruelty when man begins to think that he is the master. Such a claim is as dangerous as it is absurd.

> *Shall the ax boast over him who hews with it,*
> *Or the saw magnify itself against him who wields it?*
> *As if the rod should swing him who lifts it,*
> *Or as if the staff should lift him who is not wood!*
>
> Isaiah 10:15

Such presumption will not last forever. The design of the Lord is "to humble the pride of all glory, to dishonor all the honored of the earth" (Isa. 23:9).

> *Enter into the rock,*
> *And hide in the dust*
> *Before the terror of the Lord,*
> *Before the glory of His majesty.*
> *The naughtiness of man shall be brought low,*
> *And the pride of men shall be humbled;*
> *And the Lord alone shall be exalted*
> *In that day.*
> *For the Lord of hosts has a day*
> *Against all that is proud and haughty,*
> *Against all that is exalted and high;*
> *Against all the cedars of Lebanon,*
> *The high and exalted;*
> *And against all the oaks of Bashan;*
> *Against all the high mountains,*
> *And against all the lofty hills;*
> *Against every high tower,*
> *And against every fortified wall;*
> *Against all the ships of Tarshish,*
> *And against all the beautiful galleys;*
> *And the haughtiness of man shall be humbled,*

> *And the pride of men shall be brought low;*
> *And the Lord alone will be exalted in that day.*
> > *Isaiah 2:10–17*

## FOR NOT BY FORCE SHALL MAN PREVAIL

The prophets were the first men in history to regard a nation's reliance upon force as evil. Hosea condemned militarism as idolatrous.

> *Israel has forgotten his Maker*
> *And built palaces;*
> *Judah has multiplied fortified cities. . . .*
> *You have trusted in your chariots*
> *And in the multitude of your warriors, . . .*
> *[Israel has] gone up to Assyria,*
> *A wild ass wandering alone; . . .*
> *They hire allies among the nations. . . .*
> *When Ephraim saw his sickness,*
> *And Judah his wound,*
> *Then Ephraim went to Assyria,*
> *And sent to the great [?] king.* *
> *But he is not able to cure you*
> *Or heal your wound.*
> > *Hosea 8:14; 10:13; 8:9–10; 5:13*

Having anticipated Isaiah's vision of enduring peace, Hosea proclaimed in the name of the Lord: "I will not deliver them by bow, nor by sword, nor by war, nor by horses, nor by horsemen. . . . I will make for you a covenant on that day with the beasts of the field, the birds of the air, and the creeping things of the ground; I will abolish the bow, the sword, and war from the land, and I will make you lie down in safety" (Hos. 1:7; 2:18).

"The gods are on the side of the stronger," according to Tacitus.

---

*According to Rashi, the reference is to Hoshea and Ahaz; according to Kimhi, the reference is to Menahem and Ahaz.

The prophets proclaimed that the heart of God is on the side of the weaker. God's special concern is not for the mighty and the successful, but for the lowly and the downtrodden, for the stranger and the poor, for the widow and the orphan.

The heart of God goes out to the humble, to the vanquished, to those not cared for.

> *I will restore health to you,*
> *And your wounds I will heal, says the Lord,*
> *Because they have called you an outcast:*
> *It is Zion, for whom no one cares.*
> Jeremiah 30:17

> *The Lord has founded Zion,*
> *And in her the afflicted of His people find refuge. . . .*
> *The meek shall obtain fresh joy in the Lord,*
> *And the poor among men shall exult in the Holy One of Israel.*
> Isaiah 14:32; 29:19

"For not by force shall man prevail" (I Sam. 2:9). "The nations shall see and be ashamed of all their might" (Mic. 7:16). "Not by might, . . . says the Lord of hosts" (Zech. 4:6).

> *Some boast of chariots, and some of horses;*
> *But we boast of the name of the Lord our God. . . .*
> *His delight is not in the strength of the horse,*
> *Nor is His pleasure in the legs of a man.*
> *But the Lord takes pleasure in those who fear Him,*
> *In those who hope in His steadfast love.*
> Psalms 20:7; 147:10–11

> *This is the man to whom I will look,*
> *He that is humble and contrite in spirit,*
> *And trembles at My word. . . .*
> *For thus says the high and the lofty One*
> *Who inhabits eternity, Whose name is Holy:*
> *I dwell in the high and holy place,*

*And also with him who is a contrite and humble spirit.*
*To revive the spirit of the humble,*
*To revive the heart of the contrite . . .*
*Zion shall be redeemed by justice,*
*And those in her who repent, by righteousness.*
                              Isaiah 66:2; 57:15; 1:27

## THE PANTHEISM OF HISTORY

One must not confound biblical theology with the mystical view that God is all, and all is God. The prophets never taught that God and history are one, or that whatever happens below reflects the will of God above. Their vision is of man defying God, and God seeking man to reconcile with Him.

History is where God is defied, where justice suffers defeats. God's purpose is neither clearly apparent nor translatable into rational categories of order and design. There are only moments in which it is revealed.

God's power in history does not endure as a process; it occurs at extraordinary events.* There is a divine involvement and concern, involvement in what is done, for that which is. Even where His power is absent, His concern is present.

There was a moment when God looked at the universe made by Him and said: "It is good." But there was no moment in which God could have looked at history made by man and said: "It is good."†

To the ancient Greeks, a man's home is in nature, and the urgent problem is knowledge of nature, of cosmos. Because cosmos is the most comprehensive concept, all ideas, all problems can be under-

---

*On the distinction between process and event, see p. 551.
†On the significance of the prophetic understanding of history see M. Eliade, *Cosmos and History: The Myth of the Eternal Return* (New York, 1954); R. Niebuhr, *Faith and History* (New York, 1949), pp. 126 f.; *idem, The Self and the Dramas of History* (New York, 1955), pp. 75 ff.; J. P. Hyatt, *Prophetic Religion* (New York, 1947), pp. 76 ff.; E. Jacob, *Theology of the Old Testament* (New York, 1958); J. Muilenburg, *op. cit.*, pp. 74 ff. See also A. J. Heschel, *The Sabbath* (New York, 1951); J. Muilenburg, "The Biblical View of Time," *Harvard Theological Review*, LIV (1961), 225–252.

stood once the laws of the cosmos are discovered. Historic events are part of the species of natural events, just as man is but part of the animal species. The gods being themselves a part of nature have no power over history. The only thing that Herodotus would say about the divine power that ordains the course of history is that it rejoices in upsetting and disturbing things. "He was only repeating what every Greek knew: that the power of Zeus is manifested in the thunderbolt, that of Poseidon in the earthquake, that of Apollo in pestilence, and that of Aphrodite in the passion that destroyed at once the pride of Phaedra and the chastity of Hippolytus."*

To the prophets, man's home is in history, and their central concern is what is happening in history. Both nature and history are subject to God's dominion. Just as the word is the vessel for His revelation, history is the vessel for His action and the material for man's achievement.

## THE UNITY OF HISTORY

The prophet may be regarded as the first universal man in history; he is concerned with, and addresses himself to, all men. It was not an emperor, but a prophet, who first conceived of the unity of all men.

"The prophets who preceded you and me from ancient times," said Jeremiah to Hananiah, "prophesied . . . against many countries and great kingdoms" (Jer. 28:8).

Amos spoke in the name of Him who decides the destiny of all nations (Amos 9:7), and proclaimed His judgment over Damascus, Gaza, Tyre, Edom, the Ammonites, and Moab as well as over Israel and Judah (Amos 1:3–2:6). Isaiah proclaimed God's purpose and design "concerning the whole earth" (14:26), and actually addressed himself to "all you inhabitants of the world, you who dwell on the earth" (Isa. 18:3; cf. 33:13; 34:1), delivering special prophecies concerning Babylon, Moab, Damascus, Egypt, Tyre, and others (chs. 13–23). It

---

*R. G. Collingwood, *The Idea of History* (Oxford, 1946), p. 22; cf. Herodotus, *History,* I, 32.

is the God of Israel Who summons the mighty men to execute His designs (Isa. 13:3, 5), Who calls the nations of the world into judgment, and it is He Whom one day all nations shall worship in Zion (Isa. 2:2 ff.; 11:10; 18:7).

> *The Lord of hosts has sworn:*
> *As I have resolved*
> *So shall it be,*
> *As I have planned*
> *So shall it stand:*
> *I will break Assyria in My land,*
> *And trample him upon My mountains;*
> *His yoke shall depart from them,*
> *And his burden from their shoulder.*
> *This is the plan that is planned*
> *Concerning the whole earth,*
> *This is the hand that is stretched out*
> *Over all nations.*
> *For the Lord of hosts has planned,*
> *And who will annul it?*
> *His hand is stretched out,*
> *And who will turn it back? . . .*
> *Behold, the Lord, the Lord of hosts*
> *Will lop the boughs with terrifying power;*
> *The great in height will be hewn down,*
> *The lofty will be brought low.*
> *Isaiah 14:24–27; 10:33*

Jeremiah was appointed "a prophet to the nations" (Jer. 1:5), not merely to Israel, and like Isaiah he proclaimed prophecies concerning many nations.* He was told to give a charge to the envoys of the kings of Edom, Moab, Ammon, Tyre, and Sidon who had come to Jerusalem (Jer. 27:2 ff.): All nations are accountable to One God; they are declared to be full of guilt against the Holy One of Israel.

---

*See H. Bardtke, *"Jeremia der Fremdvölkerprophet,"* ZAW, LIII (1935), 20 ff.

"Every man is stupid and without knowledge" (Jer. 51:17). "The Lord has an indictment against the nations; He is entering into judgment with all flesh" (Jer. 25:31). All nations are made to drink the cup of wrath (Jer. 25:17 ff.; cf. 1:14). The nations cannot endure His indignation (Jer. 10:10). Jeremiah proclaimed: "At that time Jerusalem shall be called the throne of the Lord, and all nations shall gather to it, to the presence of the Lord in Jerusalem, and they shall no more stubbornly follow their own evil heart" (Jer. 3:17; cf. 4:2; 10:7).

In the words of a later prophet: "Have we not all one father? Has not one God created us? Why then are we faithless to one another, profaning the covenant of our fathers?" (Mal. 2:10.)

> *What then shall I do when God rises up?*
> *When He remembers, what shall I answer Him?*
> *Did not He Who made me in the womb make him?*
> *Did not One fashion us in the womb?*
>
> *Job 31:14–15*

Thus was born the idea of one history. The particular event or situation is related to Him Who rules over all nations. Just as the knowledge of nature was born with the discovery of principles determining all happenings in nature, so is consciousness of history the result of an awareness of One God judging all events in history.

## THE HUMAN EVENT AS A DIVINE EXPERIENCE

History is first of all what man does with power. To the prophets, power is a divine assignment; emperors are mere tools in the hand of God, and the word of the prophet is, according to Jeremiah, mightier than the power of kings.

> *See, I have set you this day over nations and over kingdoms,*
> *To pluck up and to break down,*
> *To destroy and to overthrow,*
> *To build and to plant.*
>
> *Jeremiah 1:10*

The Lord chooses agents from the ends of the earth (Isa. 5:20) through whom His will is carried out. He says of Cyrus, the king of Persia: "He is My shepherd, and he shall fulfill all My purpose" (Isa. 44:28), and of Assyria: "the rod of My anger, the staff of My fury" (Isa. 10:5), "the weapons of His indignation" (13:5). As an agent of God, Nebuchadnezzar is called God's servant (Jer. 25:9; 27:6; 43:10; cf. Ezek. 26:7). Egypt and Assyria are like tiny insects, comparable to a fly and a bee in the eyes of God. The Assyrian king may boast of his might, his army may invade the land of Judah, but the word of God proclaims:

> I will put My hook in your nose,
> And My bridle in your mouth,
> And I will turn you back
> On the way by which you came.
> The Assyrian shall fall by a sword, not of man,
> And a sword, not of man, shall devour him.
>
> Isaiah 31:8

To all men, both near and far, Isaiah addresses the word of God: "Acknowledge My might" (33:13). Assyria's masters are planning to conquer the whole earth (Isa. 5:25–29). Her greed is reckless, her weapons devastating, her armies formidable, crushing all resistance, sweeping to victories. No one seems to question her invincibility except Isaiah, who foresees the doom of the oppressor, the collapse of the monster.

> The people who walked in darkness
> Have seen a great light;
> Those who dwelt in gloom,
> Upon them a light shines, . . .
> For the yoke they endured,
> The staff on their shoulders,
> The rod of their oppressors,
> Thou hast broken as on the day of Midian.
> For every boot that tramped in tumult,

*And every mantle rolled in blood*
*Will be burned as fuel for the fire.*
　　　　*Isaiah 9:2, 4–5 [H. 9:1, 3–4]*

It is generally assumed that politics, warfare, and economic activities are the substance and the subject matter of history. To the prophets, God's judgment of man's conduct is the main issue; all else is marginal.

Others have considered history from the point of view of power, judging its course in terms of victory and defeat, of wealth and success; the prophets look at history from the point of view of justice, judging its course in terms of righteousness and corruption, of compassion and violence.*

To the modern historian, history is not the understanding of events, but rather the understanding of man's experience of events. What concerns the prophet is the human event as a divine experience. History to us is the record of human experience; to the prophet it is a record of God's experience.

There is nothing we forget as eagerly, as quickly, as the wickedness of man. The earth holds such a terrifying secret. Ruins are removed, the dead are buried, and the crimes forgotten. Bland complacency, splendid mansions, fortresses of cruel oblivion, top the graves. The dead have no voice, but God will disclose the secret of the earth.

*For behold, the Lord will go forth from His place,*
*To punish the iniquity of the inhabitants of the earth,*
*And the earth shall disclose the blood shed upon her,*
*And shall no longer cover up her slain.*

　　　　　　　　*Isaiah 26:21*

Human power is not the stuff of which history is made. For history is not what is displayed at the moment, but what is concealed in the mind of the Lord.

---

*A modern historian, e.g., relates that the Assyrian king Sennacherib, a ruler notable for his ruthlessness in war, "was followed by a sentimental son, who undid his father's work. . . . Had Assyria been more mercilessly consistent, the fall of the Assyrian

## THE CONTINGENCY OF CIVILIZATION

Of one thing men are sure: The earth is a steadfast thing, and the world will go on forever. One may doubt everything except that civilization will continue. But the prophet had no such certainty.

The prophet depicts the Lord when about to visit iniquities upon mankind.

> Behold the Lord will lay waste the earth and make it desolate,
> He will twist its surface and scatter its inhabitants. . . .
> The world languishes and withers,
> The heavens languish together with the earth. . . .
> The earth lies polluted under its inhabitants,
> For they have transgressed the laws,
> Violated the statutes, broken the everlasting covenant.
> Therefore a curse devours the earth,
> Its inhabitants suffer for their guilt;
> Therefore the inhabitants of the earth are scorched,
> Few men are left.
>
> Isaiah 24:1, 4–6

Dislike for the world or disparagement of civilization is alien to the prophet. His attachment to God calls upon him to be involved with humanity. Yet in the face of idle and false impositions, he announces the contingency and insecurity of civilization, the sickness and liability of man. Israel is under judgment; the covenant with God must not be taken as immunity from judgment.

> O Lord, Thou art my God,
> I will exalt Thee, I will praise Thy name,
> For Thou hast done marvelous things,
> Plans formed of old, faithful and sure.
> For Thou hast made the city a heap,
> The fortified city a ruin;

---

empire might have been indefinitely postponed." (A. T. Olmstead, *History of Assyria* [New York, 1923], p. 296; cf. pp. 294 f.)

> *The castle of the aliens is a city no more,*
> *It shall never be rebuilt.*
> *Therefore, strong peoples will glorify Thee,*
> *Cities of ruthless nations will fear Thee.*
> *Because Thou hast been a refuge to the poor,*
> *A refuge to the needy in his distress,*
> *A shelter from the storm, a shade from the heat.*
> *Though the fury of the ruthless be like a storm,*
> *Though the noise of the aliens be like heat in a dry land,*
> *Thou allayest heat by the shade of a cloud,*
> *The song of the mighty shall be subdued.*
>
> Isaiah 25:1–5

High over the scandals and illusions of triumphant tyrants rises the mighty voice:

> *I will punish the world for its evil,*
> *And the wicked for their iniquity;*
> *I will put an end to the pride of the arrogant,*
> *And humble the haughtiness of the tyrants. . . .*
> *For the ruthless shall come to nought,*
> *The scoffer shall vanish,*
> *And all who watch to do evil shall be cut off.*
>
> Isaiah 13:11; 29:20

## THE POLARITY OF HISTORY

Awareness of a problem means awareness of a conflict or a tension between two ideas, forces or situations. In this sense the prophets discovered the problem of history as a tension between what happens now and what may happen next. The future is no simple continuation of the present. Just as the present, in their eyes, represented a violation of what was established in the past (Israel's commitment to God), so may the future overturn the seeming solidity of what is being done in the present.

Moreover, the situation here and now is but a stage in the drama of history. Whatever happens now affects the past; it either shapes or distorts events that are going on. By history we do not mean the "gone" or the dead past, but the present in which past and future are interlocked. Sin is repudiation of history. Sacred events, sacred moments are commitments. The conscience stands still, but commitments go on.

Jeremiah was told to go to a potter's house where he would receive a revelation. "So I went down to the potter's house, and there he was working at his wheel. Whenever the vessel he was making went wrong, as clay is apt to do in a potter's hand, he would remake it in a different shape, such as he thought suitable. Thereupon the word of the Lord came to me: Am I not able to act toward you, O Israel, like this potter? You are in my hands as clay is in the hands of the potter" (Jer. 18:3–4).

Life is not as fate designs, nor is history a realm to be tyrannized by man. Events are not like rocks on the shore shaped by wind and water. Choice, design, is what determines the shape of events. God is at work on man, intent to fashion history in accord with Himself.

The tragic sense in man interprets a catastrophe as that which has to be, that which is fated to be. The relentless power of fate cannot be resisted. The greatest Greek drama rests on the interplay between fate and character, "between what man cannot change and what remains within his power."*

In contrast, Jeremiah was told: "If at any time I declare concerning a nation or a kingdom, that I will pluck up and break down and destroy it, and if that nation, concerning which I have spoken, turns from its evil, I will repent of the evil that I intended to do to it. And if at any time I declare concerning a nation or a kingdom that I will build and plant it, and if it does evil in My sight, not listening to My voice, then I will repent of the good which I had intended to do it . . ." (Jer. 18:7–8).

Sin is not a *cul de sac,* nor is guilt a final trap. Sin may be washed away by repentance and return, and beyond guilt is the dawn of for-

*W. C. Greene, *Moira* (Cambridge, 1944), p. 92.

giveness. The door is never locked, the threat of doom is not the last word.

Ultimately there is only one will by which history is shaped: the will of God; and there is only one factor upon which the shape of history depends: the moral conduct of the nations. The history of mankind moves between these two poles.*

## STRANGE IS HIS DEED, ALIEN IS HIS WORK

Strongly as Isaiah is convinced that history is not an arena where willful nations carry out their evil designs, but rather an area where God's will comes to expression, he also knows that not all history is a performance of God; that He often detaches Himself from the affairs of man; that His judgments are not always "wrought in the earth." The presence of God in history, the manifestation of His will in the affairs of the world, is the object of the prophet's longing. It is not mystical experience he yearns for in the night, but historical justice. Mystical experience is the illumination of an individual; historical justice is the illumination of all men, enabling the inhabitants of the world to learn righteousness.

> In the way of Thy judgments,
> O Lord, we wait for Thee;
> Thy name and the thought of Thee is the delight of our soul.
> My soul yearns for Thee in the night,
> My spirit within me earnestly seeks Thee.
> For as Thy judgments are wrought in the earth,
> The inhabitants of the world learn righteousness.
>
> Isaiah 26:8–9

To Isaiah, God is strength, song, salvation (Isa. 12:2), "a rock of refuge" (17:10); but He can also become "a stone of offence, a rock of stumbling, . . . a trap and a snare" (Isa. 8:14).

For the Lord is often passive, seemingly indifferent to Israel's

*See P. Volz, *Der Prophet Jeremia* (Leipzig, 1922), p. 191.

fate. He does not act at once; He does not always intervene, but He is watching the course of events. Thus the Lord said to Isaiah:

> *I will quietly look for My abode,*
> *Like clear heat in sunshine,*
> *Like a cloud of dew in the heat of harvest.*
>
> Isaiah 18:4

The summer heat and the dew promote the maturing of the grape. Destroyers and oppressors are allowed to continue until just before the fruit matures, when the branches together with the fruit will be ruthlessly cut off (Isa. 18:5–6).* "The Lord waits to be gracious to you" (Isa. 30:18). When the moment is ripe and His purpose complete,

> *Now I will arise, says the Lord,*
> *Now I will lift Myself up,*
> *Now I will be exalted.*
>
> Isaiah 33:10

God's ways are just, right, wise, but neither transparent nor immune to misunderstanding. There is an unfolding and a shrouding, a concealing within a disclosing, consoling as well as confusing.

It is hard to see how history and justice are always one. "The Lord will rise up . . . to do His deed—strange is His deed; to work His work—alien is His work" (Isa. 28:21). It is a dawn of meaning to some, and darkness to others. God is "wonderful in counsel, excellent in wisdom" (Isa. 28:29). Yet His work often stuns man's power of comprehension. He does

> *. . . marvelous things with this people,*
> *Wonderful and marvelous;*
> *The wisdom of their wise men shall fail,*
> *And the prudence of their prudent men shall be hid.*
>
> Isaiah 29:14

---

*See E. J. Kissane, *op. cit.*, p. 207.

What is unequivocal in God's wisdom becomes ambiguous to man's intelligence.

> *Whoever is wise, let him understand these things;*
> *Whoever is discerning, let him know them;*
> *For the ways of the Lord are right,*
> *The upright walk in them,*
> *But transgressors stumble in them.*
>
> *Hosea 14:9 [H. 14:10]*

Exceedingly intricate are His ways. Any attempt to formulate a theory, to stamp a dogma, to define God's itinerary through history, is a sham, fraught with pretension. In the realm of theology, shallowness is treason.

The psalmist is overwhelmed by the sublime grandeur of God's righteousness and the unfathomable depth of His judgments. They are like mighty mountains beyond the reach of man, like the abyss too deep to fathom. Only His love and faithfulness are everywhere.

> *Thy love, O Lord, extends to the heavens,*
> *Thy faithfulness to the clouds.*
> *Thy righteousness is like the mighty mountains,*
> *Thy judgments are like the great abyss.*
>
> *Psalm 36:5–6* *

Jeremiah is a person who stands "in the council of the Lord," but at the same time is exasperated by the mysterious remoteness of the Lord. God is his strength, stronghold, and refuge (Jer. 16:19), but at times God appears "like a man confused, like a mighty man who cannot save" (Jer. 14:9). At times Jeremiah sings of the joy and delight in being "called by Thy name" (Jer. 15:16), and at times he cries out, "Be not a terror to me!" (Jer. 17:17.) At times he maintains, "The Lord is with me a dread warrior, therefore my persecutors will stumble; they will not overcome me" (Jer. 20:11), and at times he exclaims, "Wilt Thou be to me like a deceitful brook? Like waters that fail?" (Jer. 15:18.)

*See Ibn Ezra, *Commentary, ad loc.*

It is one of the essential paradoxes of prophetic thinking that, although the prophet speaks continually of the people's guilt and of dreadful punishment in store for them, once the disaster comes he is stunned, puzzled, unable to justify completely the full measure of suffering.

> *Is Israel a slave? Is he a homeborn servant?*
> *Why then has he become a prey?*
> *The lions have roared against him,*
> *They have roared loudly.*
> *They have made his land a waste;*
> *His cities are in ruins, without inhabitant. . . .*
> *O Thou hope of Israel,*
> *Its savior in time of trouble,*
> *Why shouldst Thou be like a stranger in the land,*
> *Like a wayfarer who turns aside to tarry for a night?*
>
> *Jeremiah 2:14–15; 14:8*

In an imaginary dialogue with Israel, the Lord apologizes, as it were, for abandoning His people. The wrath is not of His own choice. It is the people who are responsible for it. The prophet hears "the cry of my dear people from the length and breadth of the Land": "Is the Lord not in Zion? Is her King not in her?" And to this God responds: "Why have they provoked Me to anger with their graven images and with their foreign idols?" (Jer. 8:19.)

For all the inner identification with God, the prophet is not always ready to accept divine judgment as final (Amos 7:2, 5). He does not hesitate to complain about God's way. Isaiah asks: "How long, O Lord?" (Isa. 6:11); and Habakkuk: "O Lord, how long shall I cry for help, and Thou wilt not hear?" (Hab. 1:2). Yet, once God acts and the scourge takes its bitter toll, the prophets are neither crushed nor resentful. Ill follows ill, woe succeeds woe, and no grumbling (cf. Lam. 2:20). "The Lord is in the right, for I have rebelled against His word" (Lam. 1:18).

"I have dealt you the blow of an enemy, the punishment of a merciless foe, because your guilt is great, because your sins are flagrant"

(Jer. 30:14). Oppressed and afflicted, Israel does not question God's judgment. Affliction only demonstrates God's power and justice.

"It is not so much the suffering as the senselessness of it that is unendurable," declared Nietzsche. Pain was the price the people had to pay for having been chosen and then having sinned. "The Lord has done what He purposed, has carried out His threat; as He ordained long ago . . ." (Lam. 2:17). Pain had a purpose: to purify the people; and the people did not despise the Lord's discipline, nor become weary of His reproof, "for the Lord reproves him whom He loves, as a father the son in whom he delights" (Prov. 3:11–12). "Know then in your heart that, as a man castigates his son, so the Lord your God castigates you" (Deut. 8:5). "Blessed is the man whom Thou dost chasten, O Lord . . ." (Ps. 93:12). Out of anguish comes the people's prayer:

> *Thou hast chastened me, and I was chastened,*
> *Like an untrained calf;*
> *Bring me back that I may be restored,*
> *For Thou art the Lord my God.*
> *For after I turned away I repented;*
> *After I was instructed, I smote upon my thigh;*
> *I was ashamed, I was confounded,*
> *Because I bore the disgrace of my youth.*
> *Jeremiah 31:18–19*

And yet, God is not absent even though His work may be silent. His presence in history does not continually come to expression in cataclysmic events. The ways in which He acts are perceptible at rare moments, but usually they are indiscernible—just as the work of him who tills the soil is only occasionally spectacular. He does not always plow or harrow; there are many small, inconspicuous labors to be carried out in order to achieve the main goal. In fact, the undramatic art of tilling the soil reflects God's counsel and wisdom.

> *Give ear, and hear my voice;*
> *Hearken, and hear my speech.*

*Is the ploughman continually plowing?*
*Does he continually break up and harrow his ground?*
*Does he not, when he has leveled its surface,*
*Scatter dill, sow cummin,*
*Plant wheat, corn and barley,*
*And spelt as the border?*
*For he is instructed aright;*
*His God teaches him.*
*Dill is not threshed with a sledge,*
*Nor is a cart wheel rolled over cummin;*
*But dill is beaten out with a stick,*
*And cummin with a rod.*
*Does one crush bread grain?*
*No, he does not thresh it for ever;*
*When he drives his cart wheel over it*
*With his horses, he does not crush it.*
*This also comes from the Lord of hosts;*
*He is wonderful in counsel,*
*And excellent in wisdom.*

*Isaiah 28:23–29*

The prophet is prepared for pain. One of the effects of his presence is to intensify the people's capacity for suffering, to rend the veil that lies between life and pain. And yet Jeremiah knew how shattering the outpouring of God's anger could be. "Chastise, O Lord, but in just measure; not in Thy anger, lest Thou bring me to nothing" (Jer. 10:24). In a moment of anguish he cried out:

*Why is my pain unceasing,*
*My wound incurable,*
*Refusing to be healed,*
*Wilt Thou be to me like a deceitful brook?*
*Like waters that fail?*

*Jeremiah 15:18*

Man is ready to accept a God Who is close at hand, Whose power is present, Whose judgment can be understood, Whose glory can be experienced. But the invisible God of Israel is hard on man, for His power is often absent, His judgment obscure, His glory concealed.

> *Am I a God close at hand,*
> *And not a God far off?*
> *Says the Lord.*
> *Can anyone hide himself in secret places*
> *Where I shall not see him?*
> *Do I not fill heaven and earth?*
> *Says the Lord.*
>
> *Jeremiah 23:23–24\**

Hopes are wrecked, faith is mocked. What must not happen, does. Is history, then, a distortion of what God wills, misrepresenting and defying His will? Or does God's itinerary in history lead through a maze of seeming contradictions? Is His design for justice woven of more threads than man comprehends? You shall be patient, for I the Lord your God am patient.

> *The anger of the Lord will not turn back*
> *Until he has executed and accomplished*
> *The intents of His mind.*
> In the latter days you will understand it clearly.
>
> *Jeremiah 23:20; cf. 30:24*

In the eyes of man, what comes about and what is still to come may be an age apart; in the eyes of God, they are one. The darkness of history, therefore, conceals a light. Beyond the mystery is meaning. And the meaning is destined to be disclosed.

## LIKE A STRANGER IN THE LAND

Perplexity is not alien to the prophets. Jeremiah continually proclaims that God's justice is revealed in the events of history, that the Lord is the Righteous Judge Who gives to every man according to his deeds (Jer. 17:10), that God's justice never rests until it reaches and

---

*These verses do not belong in the context of ch. 23.

defeats those who are wicked and defiant. This certainty is a stronghold in which his teaching is sheltered. However, experience and
observation lead him to the haunting realization that the magnificent
rock is not impregnable; what he is called upon to proclaim he finds
difficult to sustain.

Significantly, the question he raises is not why the righteous suffer, but rather why the wicked prosper.

> *Righteous art Thou, O Lord, when I complain to Thee;*
> *Yet I would plead my case before Thee.*
> *Why does the way of the wicked prosper?*
> *Why do all who are treacherous thrive?*
> *Thou plantest them, and they take root;*
> *They grow and bring forth fruit.*
>
> Jeremiah 12:1–2

The answer he is given is a rebuke; the issue that puzzles him is
minor compared with issues he may still face.*

> *If you have raced with men on foot, and they have wearied you,*
> *How will you compete with horses?*
> *And if in a safe land you fall down,*
> *How will you do in the jungle of Jordan?*
>
> Jeremiah 12:5†

Indeed, the greatest question of all regarding the problem of justice is yet to confront him. It is the question, "Why do the righteous
suffer?" Is suffering an index of guilt? Is it not a fact that suffering is
meted out beyond the measure of guilt? The land of Israel was
destroyed, and the misery seemed out of proportion to the guilt.

> *How long will the land mourn,*
> *The grass of every field wither?*
>
> Jeremiah 12:4

---

*Compare and contrast Jer. 2:18.

†Cf. Kimhi, *Commentary, ad loc.* It seems that vs. 5 follows directly vs. 2a. Vs. 6
follows 11:22. In the interpretation, I follow P. Volz, *op. cit.*, pp. 141 f.

*Behold, He snatches away; who can hinder Him?*
*Who will say to Him: What doest Thou?*

*Job 9:12*

## A History of Waiting for God

This is what the prophets discovered. *History is a nightmare.* There are more scandals, more acts of corruption, than are dreamed of in philosophy. It would be blasphemous to believe that what we witness is the end of God's creation. It is an act of evil to accept the state of evil as either inevitable or final. Others may be satisfied with improvement, the prophets insist upon redemption. The way man acts is a disgrace, and it must not go on forever. Together with condemnation, the prophets offer a promise. The heart of stone will be taken away, a heart of flesh will be given instead (Ezek. 11:19). Even the nature of the beasts will change to match the glory of the age. The end of days will be the end of fear, the end of war; idolatry will disappear, knowledge of God will prevail.

The inner history of Israel is a history of waiting for God, of waiting for His arrival. Just as Israel is certain of the reality of the Promised Land, so is she certain of the coming of "the promised day." She lives by a promise of "the day of the Lord," a day of judgment followed by salvation, when evil will be consumed and an age of glory will ensue.

In contrast to Amos, who stressed the aspect of judgment of the day, Isaiah unfolds the total vision of the darkness and the glory.

> *The earth staggers like a drunken man,*
> *It sways like a hut; . . .*
> *On that day the Lord will punish*
> *The host of heaven, in heaven,*
> *And the kings of the earth, on the earth.*
>
> *Isaiah 24:20–21*

Yet, following the judgment "it will be said on that day: Lo, this is our God; we have waited for Him, that He might save us. This is the

Lord; we have waited for Him; let us be glad and rejoice in His salvation" (Isa. 25:9).

In words contained in the book of Isaiah we hear of the time when "the terror of defeat and captivity will be merely a memory."

> *Your eyes will see the king in his beauty;*
> *They will behold a land that stretches afar.*
> *Your mind will muse on the terror:*
> *Where is he who counted, where is he who weighed the tribute?*
> *Where is he who counted the towers? . . .*
> *Your eyes will see Jerusalem,*
> *A quiet habitation, an immovable tent,*
> *Whose stakes will never be plucked up,*
> *Nor will any of its cords be broken.*
>
> Isaiah 33:17–20

The day will come when God "will destroy the covering that is cast over all peoples, the veil that is spread over all nations. He will swallow up death for ever, the Lord God will wipe away tears from all faces, the reproach of His people He will take away from all the earth; for the Lord has spoken" (Isa. 25:7–8). "Those who err in spirit will come to understanding, and those who murmur will accept instruction." (Isa. 29:24).

In a world where images are holy, where idols are both feared and adored, where paganism rules triumphantly, Isaiah predicts:

> *The idols shall utterly pass away!*
> *And the holes of the ground,*
> *From before the terror of the Lord,*
> *And from the glory of His majesty,*
> *When He rises to terrify the earth.*
> *In that day men will cast forth*
> *Their idols of silver and their idols of gold,*
> *Which they made for themselves to worship,*
> *To the moles and to the bats,*
> *To enter the caverns of the rocks,*

> *And the clefts of the cliffs,*
> *From before the terror of the Lord,*
> *And from the glory of His majesty,*
> *When He rises to terrify the earth.*
>
> Isaiah 2:18–21

"In that day men will regard their Maker, and their eyes will look to the Holy One of Israel; they will not have regard for the altars, the work of their hands, and they will not look to what their own fingers have made, either the Asherim or the altars of incense" (Isa. 17:7–8).

The people will be purified by suffering. "Though the Lord give you the bread of adversity and the water of affliction, yet your Teacher will not hide Himself any more, but your eyes shall see your Teacher, and your ears shall hear a word behind you saying: This is the way, walk in it, when you turn to the right or when you turn to the left" (Isa. 30:20–21).*

The promise made to Abraham will be fulfilled. "In you shall all the families of the earth be blessed" (Gen. 12:3).† Israel will flourish, and all nations will come to understanding.

> *Thus says the Lord, Who redeemed Abraham,*
> *  concerning Jacob:*
> *Jacob shall no more be ashamed,*
> *No more shall his face grow pale.*
> *For when he sees his children,*
> *The work of My hands in his midst,*
> *They will hallow My name;*
> *They will hallow the Holy One of Jacob,*
> *And will stand in awe of the God of Israel.*
> *And those who err in spirit will come to understanding,*
> *And those who murmur will accept instruction.*
>
> Isaiah 29:22–24

---

*Isaiah's authorship of this passage is maintained by Kissane, *op. cit.*, p. 337.

†Cf. Gen. 18:18; 22:18; 26:4; 28:14; see also C. R. North, *The Old Testament Interpretations of History* (London, 1946), p. 26.

## THEY SHALL NOT HURT OR DESTROY

The sword is the pride of man; arsenals, forts, and chariots lend supremacy to nations. War is the climax of human ingenuity, the object of supreme efforts: men slaughtering each other, cities battered into ruins. What is left behind is agony, death, and desolation. At the same time, men think very highly of themselves; "they are wise in their own hearts, shrewd in their own sight" (Isa. 5:21). Idols of silver and gold are what they worship. Nineveh, "the bloody city, all full of lies and booty," held the world in spell with her "countless harlotries," with her "graceful and deadly charms" (Nah. 3:1, 4).

Into a world fascinated with idolatry, drunk with power, bloated with arrogance, enters Isaiah's word that the swords will be beaten into plowshares, that nations will search, not for gold, power, or harlotries, but for God's word.

The power and splendor of Nineveh were unrivaled in the world. For centuries it was the city to which the eyes of the civilized world were turned. The immense tribute that flowed from many lands into the capital of the empire not only helped to maintain a huge army, but also lust, luster, and luxury.

Jerusalem, in contrast, was "a quiet habitation," little known to the nations except as a target for invaders. But in the vision of Isaiah the nations will no more turn their eyes to Nineveh, the seat of human power, but to Jerusalem, the seat of divine learning, eager to learn God's ways, eager to learn how to walk in His paths.

"In that day the root of Jesse shall stand as an ensign to the peoples; him shall the nations seek, and his dwellings shall be glorious" (Isa. 11:10).

> *It shall come to pass at the end of days*
> *That the mountain of the house of the Lord*
> *Shall be established as the highest of the mountains,*
> *And shall be raised above the hills,*
> *And all the nations shall flow to it.*
> *And many people shall come and say:*
> *Come, let us go up to the mountain of the Lord,*

> *To the house of the God of Jacob;*
> *That He may teach us His ways*
> *And that we may walk in His paths.*
> *For out of Zion shall go forth teaching,*
> *And the word of the Lord from Jerusalem.*
> *He shall judge between the nations,*
> *And shall decide for many peoples;*
> *And they shall beat their swords into plowshares,*
> *And their spears into pruning hooks.*
> *Nation shall not lift up sword against nation,*
> *Neither shall they learn war any more.*
>
> 

*Isaiah 2:2–4*
> 

What to us seems inconceivable, to Isaiah was a certainty: War will be abolished. They shall not learn war any more because they shall seek knowledge of the word of God. Passion for war will be subdued by a greater passion: the passion to discover God's ways.*

Had the prophets relied on human resources for justice and righteousness, on man's ability to fulfill all of God's demands, on man's power to achieve redemption, they would not have insisted upon the promise of messianic redemption, for messianism implies that any course of living, even the supreme efforts of man by himself, must fail in redeeming the world. In other words, human history is not sufficient unto itself. Man's conscience is timid, while the world is ablaze with agony. His perception of justice is shallow, often defective, and his judgment liable to deception.

> *There shall come forth a shoot from the stump of Jesse,*
> *And a branch shall grow out of his roots,*
> *And the Spirit of the Lord shall rest upon him,*
> *The spirit of wisdom and understanding,*
> *The spirit of counsel and might,*
> *The spirit of knowledge and the fear of the Lord.*
> *Through the fear of the Lord he will have supreme sensitivity.*

---

*The study by H. Gross, *Die Idee des ewigen und allgemeinen Weltfriedens* (Trier, 1946), reached the author after the completion of this manuscript.

*He shall not judge by what his eyes see,** 
*Or decide by what his ears hear;* 
*But with righteousness shall he judge the helpless,* 
*And decide with equity for the meek of the earth;* 
*And he shall smite the earth with the rod of his mouth,* 
*And with the breath of his lips he shall slay the wicked.* 
*Righteousness shall be the girdle of his waist,* 
*And faithfulness the girdle of his loins.* 
*The wolf shall dwell with the lamb,* 
*And the leopard shall lie down with the kid,* 
*And the calf and the lion and the fatling together,* 
*And a little child shall lead them.* 
*The cow and the bear shall feed;* 
*Their young shall lie down together;* 
*And the lion shall eat straw like the ox.* 
*The sucking child shall play over the hole of the asp,* 
*And the weaned child shall put his hand on the adder's den.* 
*They shall not hurt or destroy* 
*In all My holy mountain;* 
*For the earth shall be full of the knowledge of the Lord* 
*As the waters cover the sea.*

*Isaiah 11:1–9*

## BLESSED BE MY PEOPLE EGYPT

What is history? Wars, victories, and wars. So many dead. So many tears. So little regret. So many fears. And who could sit in judgment over the victims of cruelty when their horror turns to hatred? Is it easy to keep the horror of wickedness from turning into a hatred of the wicked? The world is drenched in blood, and the guilt is endless. Should not all hope be abandoned?

What saved the prophets from despair was their messianic vision and the idea of man's capacity for repentance. That vision and that idea affected their understanding of history.

---

*See 1 Sam. 16:7.

History is not a blind alley, and guilt is not an abyss. There is always a way that leads out of guilt: repentance, or turning to God. The prophet is a person who, living in dismay, has the power to transcend his dismay. Over all the darkness of experience hovers the vision of a different day. "In that day there shall be a highway from Egypt to Assyria; the Assyrian will come to Egypt, and the Egyptian into Assyria, and the Egyptians will worship with the Assyrians.* In that day Israel shall be a third with Egypt and Assyria, a blessing in the midst of the earth, which the Lord of hosts has blessed, saying, Blessed be My people Egypt, and Assyria, the work of My hands, and Israel, My inheritance" (Isa. 19:23–25).†

Egypt and Assyria are locked in deadly wars. Hating each other, they are both the enemies of Israel. Abominable are their idolatries, and frightful are their crimes. In the days of Abraham and Moses, as in the days of Isaiah, the repudiation of both Mesopotamia and Egypt was the very destiny of Israel. How does Isaiah, the son of a people which cherishes the privilege of being called by the Lord, "My people, the work of My hands," feel about Egypt and Assyria? The God of Israel is also the God of her enemies, without their knowing Him and despite their defying Him. The enmity between the nations will turn to friendship. They will live together when they worship together.‡

---

*See A. B. Ehrlich, *Randglossen zur Hebräischen Bibel,* IV (Leipzig, 1912), 73.

†Duhm, followed by many critics, maintains that 19:16–25 is postexilic. Assyria is taken to stand for Seleucid Syria, and Egypt for Ptolemaic Egypt. Others maintain that the prophecy belongs to Isaiah; see Y. Kaufmann, *The Religion of Israel* (Heb.), p. 226, n. 80; (Eng.), p. 350, n. 2; Kissane, *op. cit.,* pp. 209 f. For our purpose it matters little whether Isaiah or another composed this chapter.

‡A similar thought is found in Zech. 2:15: "Many nations shall join themselves to the Lord in that day, and shall be My people." Cf. Isa. 56:1–7: "My house shall be called a house of prayer for all peoples." See also I Kings 8:41–43; Isa. 45:20; 60:6–7; 66:18–19; Jer. 3:17; 4:2; 12:16; 16:19; Zeph. 3:9–10; Zech. 8:20–23; 14:16–21; Mal. 1:11; Ps. 22:28; 47:2; 65:3; 67:46; 68:3–33; 76:12; 96:7–8; 102:23; 117:1.

# 10

# Chastisement

## The Futility of Chastisement

The threat of punishment is one of the most prominent themes of the prophetic orations. Yet the prophets themselves seem to have questioned the efficacy of punishment. Punishment has three aims: retributive, deterrent, and reformatory.*

The divine intention, according to the prophets, is not primarily

---

*According to L. R. Farnell, *The Attributes of God* (Oxford, 1925), p. 174, the vindictive theory was first challenged by the humanitarian ethics and philosophy of the Greeks. He refers to Plato's theory of human punishment, the intention of which should be reformative and remedial only, and to Homer's suggestion, *Odyssey* 1, 31, that the gods send no evil to men, either in this life or in the next. However, according to Homer, the purpose of punishment is retributive and deterrent. For the Greeks, justice was the retribution that countered wrongdoing. Thus, "justice and revenge are not very different, indeed they coincide when vengeance is taken for wrongdoing. A product of this kind of justice is the *ius talionis* which was usual in early times and finds pregnant expression in the saying 'an eye for an eye, a tooth for a tooth.' This is to be traced among the Greeks also; for them, justice is retributive justice." (M. P. Nilsson, *Greek Piety* [Oxford, 1948], pp. 35 f.) The Greek word for punishment, *poine,* has a coercive element. "*Poine* overtakes the evildoer as a spirit of revenge, sometimes at the hand of others, sometimes through the dispensation of fate, generally through his own misdeeds." (*Encyclopaedia of Social Sciences,* XII, 712.) A combination of the retributive and the deterrent intentions of justice is found in Deut. 19:19 ff.; cf. K. F. Nägelsbach, *Die Homerische Theologie* (Nürnberg, 1861), p. 320.

retributive, to impose penalty in consequence of wrongdoing; but rather deterrent, to discourage transgression by fear of punishment; and reformatory, to repair, to refine, to make pure by affliction: God's purpose is not to destroy but to purify (cf. Isa. 27:7–8; 28:29), "to purge away your dross as with lye and remove all your alloy; . . . afterward you shall be called the city of righteousness, the faithful city" (Isa. 1:25–26; cf. 4:4). "Behold, I will refine them and test them, for what else can I do, because of My dear people?" (Jer. 9:7 [H. 9:6].) "I have tried you in the furnace of affliction," said a later prophet (Isa. 48:10). Through suffering lies the way to restoration and to the implanting of His will in the hearts of regenerated people (Isa. 1:26; Hos. 6; 10:12, 14; Jer. 24:7; 31:33 f.). In distress they may seek Him (Hos. 5:15).

The prophets, however, discovered that suffering does not necessarily bring about purification, nor is punishment effective as a deterrent. The futility of chastisement was a problem that occupied the minds of the prophets. Jeremiah, for example, knew that punishment is not the answer:

> *O Lord, do not thy eyes look for truth?*
> *Thou hast smitten them,*
> *But they felt no anguish;*
> *Thou hast consumed them,*
> *But they refused to take correction.*
> *They have made their faces harder than rock;*
> *They have refused to repent. . . .*
> *In vain have I smitten your children,*
> *They took no correction.*
>
> Jeremiah 5:3; 2:30

## THE STRANGE DISPARITY

The two staggering facts in the life of a prophet are: God's turning to him, and man's turning away from him. This is often his lot: to be chosen by God and to be rejected by the people. The word of God, so clear to him, is unintelligible to them.

*To whom will he impart knowledge,*
*And to whom will he convey a message?*
*Those who are weaned from the milk,*
*Those taken from the breast?*
*For it is precept upon precept, precept upon precept,*
*Line upon line, line upon line,*
*Here a little, there a little.*
*Nay, but by men of strange lips*
*And with an alien tongue*
*The Lord will speak to this people,*
*To whom He has said:*
*This is rest;*
*Give rest to the weary*
*And this is repose;*
*Yet they refused to hear.*
*Therefore the word of the Lord will be to them*
*Precept upon precept, precept upon precept,*
*Line upon line, line upon line,*
*Here a little, there a little;*
*That they may go, and fall backward,*
*And be broken, snared, and caught.*
                                        *Isaiah 28:9–13*

What baffles the prophet is the disparity between the power and impact of God and the immense indifference, unyieldingness, sluggishness, and inertia of the heart. God's thunderous voice is shaking heaven and earth, and man does not hear the faintest sound. The Lord roars like a lion (Amos 3:8). His word is like fire, like a hammer which breaks the rock in pieces (Jer. 23:29), and the people go about unmoved, undisturbed, unaware. What to the prophet is like the sun piercing the thickest cloud remains unnoticed by the people.

*Woe to those who call evil good,*
*And good evil,*
*Who put darkness for light,*
*And light for darkness,*

> *Who put bitter for sweet,*
> *And sweet for bitter.*
> $\qquad$ *Isaiah 5:20*

The prophet is scorched by the word of God—"There is in my heart as it were a burning fire shut up in my bones" (Jer. 21:9)—but the hearts of the people are asbestos, fireproof.

> *I have become a laughingstock all the day,*
> *Everyone mocks me. . . .*
> *The word of God has become for me*
> *A reproach and derision all day long.*
> *They refuse to hear the instruction of the Lord.*
> $\qquad$ *Jeremiah 20:7–8*

> *They say to the seers: See not!*
> *And to prophets: Prophesy not to us what is right!*
> *Speak to us smooth things,*
> *Prophesy illusions!*
> *Depart from the way, turn aside from the path,*
> *Let us hear no more of the Holy One of Israel!*
> $\qquad$ *Isaiah 30:10–11*

The prophet Amos was forbidden to appear in Bethel and Jeremiah was imprisoned because their message shocked those in power.

It was a major enigma that confronted the prophet: How is it possible not to see the majesty of the Lord (Isa. 26:10), not to sense that the whole earth is full of His glory (Isa. 6:3), not to understand God's sign in the happenings of history? What we call the irrational nature of man, they called hardness of heart.

> *O Lord, Thy hand is exalted,*
> *But they see not.*
> $\qquad$ *Isaiah 26:11*

It is a recurring complaint: "O foolish and senseless people, who have eyes, but see not, who have ears, but hear not" (Jer. 5:21; Ezek. 12:2; Isa. 43:8). "Sons who will not hear the instructions of the

Lord" (Isa. 30:9). "Like a stubborn heifer, Israel is stubborn" (Hos. 4:16). "Ephraim is like a dove, silly and without sense, calling to Egypt, going to Assyria" (Hos. 7:11). "My people are destroyed for lack of knowledge!" (Hos. 4:6.) "Their ears are closed, they cannot listen (Jer. 6:10). The Lord set watchmen over the people, saying: "Give heed to the sound of the trumpet!" But they said, "We will not give heed" (Jer. 6:17). How abysmal stubbornness can be. Man rears his own despots—idols, lies, perversions; he labors to prepare his own disaster. Is he insane?

## THE FAILURE OF FREEDOM

The central message of the prophets is the insistence that *the human situation can be understood only in conjunction with the divine situation*. The absurdity of isolating the human situation and treating it in disregard of the divine involvement is exemplified by the self-defeating course of man-made history.

Modern interpretations see history as the arena in which man reigns supreme, with the forces of nature as his only possible adversaries. Man is alone, free, and growing stronger. God is either nonexistent or unconcerned. It is human initiative that makes history, and it is primarily by force that constellations change. Man can attain his own salvation.

This view of history, starting with man's consciousness of freedom and sense of sovereignty, arrives at the antinomy of freedom and fate: the frustration and collapse of freedom. Man is not the master of his own destiny. Forces he cannot completely control emerge imperceptibly to stifle him and to defy his intentions, his plans, and his visions.

Prophetic reflection begins, we might say, with the abuse and consequent failure of freedom, with the irrationality of human conduct, and it points to God Who stands above history. Man-made history is not history's only dimension. The pathos and judgment of God transcend the human dimension. Great conquerors are seen as mere tools of His mysterious will. Man has choice, but not sovereignty.

History is not a meaningless conglomeration of neutral facts, but a drama unfolding the relationship between God and man. The drama is staged in time and encompasses the wide arena of human affairs. A battle is raging: man in his presumption undertakes to fashion history in disregard and defiance of God. The prophets witness the misery that man endures as well as man's wickedness that God endures, and even tolerates. But God is wrestling with man. History is where God is defied, where His judgment is enacted, and where His kingship is to be established. For it is of the realm of space, not of the realm of history, that the seraphim proclaim: "It is full of His glory." Only a sprinkling of His glory is found in history.

## THE SUSPENSION OF FREEDOM

The opposite of freedom is not determinism, but hardness of heart. Freedom presupposes openness of heart, of mind, of eye and ear.

According to Hegel, the history of the world is none other than the progress of the consciousness of freedom. With some qualification one might say in the spirit of the prophets that the history of the world with which they dealt was none other than the progress of the condition of hardness of heart.

Freedom is not a natural disposition, but God's precious gift to man. Those in whom viciousness becomes second nature, those in whom brutality is linked with haughtiness, forfeit their ability and therefore their right to receive that gift. Hardening of the heart is the suspension of freedom.* Sin becomes compulsory and self-destructive. Guilt and punishment become one.

In other words, the ability to understand, to see or to hear the divine significance of events, may be granted or withheld from man. One may see great wonders, but remain entirely insensitive. "You have seen all that the Lord did before your eyes in the land of Egypt . . . the great trials which *your eyes saw,* the signs, and those great wonders.

*See Maimonides, *Eight Chapters,* ch. 8.

But to this day the Lord *has not given you* a mind to understand, or *eyes to see,* or ears to hear" (Deut. 29:2–4 [H. 29:1–3]).

The normal soul is fit and pliable, open to truth, sensitive to God. But if the people "have eyes, but see not, have ears, but hear not," it is because of "a stubborn and rebellious heart" (Jer. 5:23). Sin has its cause in the hardness, stiffness, or the stubbornness of heart.* To be callous is to be blind to the presence of God in the world, blind to "the glory of His majesty" (Isa. 2:21). Such blindness results in pride, haughtiness, and arrogance.

Hardness of heart is a condition of which the person afflicted is unaware. Not knowing what ails him, he is unable to repent and to recover. However, when hardness is intensified from above, responsibility is assumed by God. He smites and He restores, bringing about a revival of sensitivity.

It seems that the only cure for willful hardness is to make it absolute. Half-callousness, paired with obstinate conceit, seeks no cure. When hardness is complete, it becomes despair, the end of conceit. Out of despair, out of total inability to believe, prayer bursts forth.

Prophets came and went; words had no effect, turbulent punishments, miseries, were of no avail. Man is of many minds. "The heart is deceitful above all things, and desperately corrupt; who can understand it?" (Jer. 17:9.) Where signs and words from without fail, despair within may succeed.

The dark fact of callousness, just like the luminous power of understanding, goes back to God who creates light as well as darkness in the heart of man. The weird miracle of callousness, resistance to God, may be due to an obstinacy imposed by God. Punishment and guilt become one.

While not denying that the people sin of their own free will, there

*In the Bible, callousness is the root of sin. There are many words to express it: "stubbornness of heart," "hardness of heart" (Deut. 29:18; Lam. 3:65); "brazen-faced and stiff-hearted" (Ezek. 2:4); "stubborn of heart" (Isa. 46:12); "uncircumcised in the heart" (Jer. 9:25). "The heart [of the godless] is gross like fat," exclaims the psalmist (119:70). The prophets continually reproach Israel for lack of sensibility (Isa. 42:20; 48:8; cf. Ps. 106:7; Prov. 28:14; 29:1; cf. also E. La B. Cherbonnier, *Hardness of Heart* [New York, 1955]).

is a subtle awareness of God's being involved in man's going astray, an involvement that adds bafflement to injury.

> *O Lord, why dost Thou make us err from Thy ways*
> *And harden our heart, so that we fear Thee not?*
> *Return for the sake of Thy servants,*
> *The tribes of Thy heritage.*
>
> *Isaiah 63:17*

One might ask: Do not these lines imply the thought that God shares in human responsibility and is involved in human guilt? It is a thought that may also be evoked by the words in God's speech to Job:

> [*The ostrich*] *deals cruelly with her young as if they were not hers.* . . .
> *Because God has made her forget wisdom,*
> *And given her no share of understanding.*
>
> *Job 39:16–17*

"Ah, Lord God, surely Thou hast utterly deceived this people and Jerusalem, saying: It shall be well with you; whereas the sword has reached their very life" (Jer. 4:10). In other words: Since Thou hast been patient with the false prophets who misled and persuaded the people that all is well, It is as If though Thou hast deceived them. The false prophets have led the people astray by insisting that there is no reason for anxiety; what the future holds in store is peace and prosperity. The leaders are responsible for the people. But who is responsible for the leaders? Witnessing the disaster that came upon Judah, Jeremiah exclaims: "For most of the people think that the Lord has spoken to those prophets, and they are confused as to whether to listen to me or to them, and the majority is inclined to follow them, because they are many."*

## NO WORD IS GOD'S LAST WORD

Agony is the final test. When all hopes are dashed and all conceit is shattered, man begins to miss what he has long spurned. In dark-

---

*Kimhi, *Commentary, ad loc.*

ness, God becomes near and clear. "He shall go through it suffering and hungry, and then when hungry he shall break out in anger and curse his king and his gods; He shall turn his face upwards, and look upon the earth, and behold distress and darkness, the gloom of darkness, and he will be thrust into thick darkness. But there will be no gloom for her that was in anguish. . . . The people that walked in darkness behold a great light; those who dwelt in a land of deep darkness, on them a light shines" (Isa. 8:21–9:2 [H. 8:21–9:1]).

When all pretensions are abandoned, one begins to feel the burden of guilt. It is easier to return from an extreme distance than from the complacency of a good conscience, from spurious proximity.

God smites and He restores, He hurts and He heals, He obstructs and He exposes hearts and eyes. Such exposing, the liquidation of Isaiah's first assignment (see above, p. 113) is perhaps alluded to in the words: "He has taken away the covering of Judah" (Isa. 22:8).

Isaiah's original charge must have early come to an end. Did he not insist that his mission was to "strengthen the weak hands and make firm the feeble knees" (Isa. 35:3)? And did he not appeal in words designed to bring about insight and understanding: "O house of Jacob, come let us walk in the light of the Lord" (Isa. 2:5)? "Wash yourselves, make yourselves clean, remove the evil of your doings from before My eyes" (1:16).

God is invisible, distant, dwelling in darkness (I Kings 8:12). His thoughts are not our thoughts; His ways in history are shrouded and perplexing. Prophecy is a moment of unshrouding, an opening of the eyes, a lifting of the curtain. Such moments are rare in history. "With their flocks and herds they shall go to seek the Lord, but they will not find Him; He has withdrawn from them" (Hos. 5:6). Moments did come when the prophets obtained no vision from the Lord (Lam. 2:9).

*We do not see our signs;*
*There is no longer any prophet.*
Psalm 74:9

What Isaiah suggested in terms of human insensitivity was expressed by Amos in terms of divine inaccessibility. Generation after generation, it was as if God had opened a door: in the prophets His word was revealed. Prophecy had become a commonplace, and the word wearisome, obtrusive. Not forever, the prophet is told. The Lord will shut the door, and the word will obtrude no more.

> *Behold, the days are coming, says the Lord,*
> *When I will send a famine on the land;*
> *Not a famine of bread, nor a thirst for water,*
> *But of hearing the words of the Lord.*
> *They shall wander from sea to sea, and from north to east;*
> *They shall run to and fro, to seek the word of the Lord,*
> *But they shall not find it.*
>
> *Amos 8:11–12*

And yet, the word of God never comes to an end. For this reason, prophetic predictions are seldom final. No word is God's final word. Judgment, far from being absolute, is conditional. A change in man's conduct brings about a change in God's judgment. No word is God's final word.

> *Yea, O people in Zion who dwell in Jerusalem; you shall weep no more. He will surely be gracious to you at the sound of your cry; when he hears it, he will answer you. And though the Lord give you the bread of adversity and the water of affliction, yet your Teacher will not hide himself any more, and your eyes shall see your Teacher. And your ears shall hear a word behind you, saying: This is the way, walk in it. . . . In that day the deaf shall hear the words of a book, and out of their gloom and darkness the eyes of the blind shall see. . . . Then the eyes of the blind shall be opened, and the ears of the deaf unstopped; then shall the lame man leap like a hart, and the tongue of the dumb sing for joy.*
>
> *Isaiah 30:19–21; 29:18; 35:5–6*

God's anger must not obscure His redeeming love.

> *Behold, God is my salvation;*
> *I will trust, and will not be afraid;*

*For the Lord God is my strength and my song,*
*And He has become my salvation.*

*Isaiah 12:2*

"We have waited for Him, that He might save us" (Isa. 25:9). And the day will surely come "when the Lord binds up the hurt of His people, and heals the wounds inflicted by His blow" (Isa. 30:26). He hurts, and He heals.

# 11

# Justice

## SACRIFICE

Sacred fire is burning on the altars in many lands. Animals are being offered to the glory of the gods. Priests burn incense, songs of solemn assemblies fill the air. Pilgrims are on the roads, pageantries in the sacred places. The atmosphere is thick with sanctity. In Israel, too, sacrifice is an essential act of worship. It is the experience of giving oneself vicariously to God and of being received by Him. And yet, the pre-exilic prophets uttered violent attacks on sacrifices (Amos 5:21–27; Hos. 6:6; Isa. 1:11–17; Mic. 6:6–8; Jer. 6:20; 7:21–23; Isa. 61:1–2; Pss. 40:7; 50:12–13). Samuel insisted: "Has the Lord as great delight in burnt offerings and sacrifices, as in obeying the voice of the Lord? Behold, to obey is better than sacrifice, and to hearken than the fat of rams" (I Sam. 15:22).* However, while Samuel stressed

---

*A sentence expressing a similar view is found in the *Instruction for King Meri-kare,* who ruled Egypt in the second half of the third millennium B.C.E. "More accept-able is the character of one upright of heart than the ox of the evildoer." (*ANET,* pp. 417 f.) For other statements in later literature which have a bearing upon the attitude of the prophets to animal sacrifice, see R. S. Cripps, *A Critical and Exegetical Commen-tary on the Book of Amos* (London, 1929), pp. 342 ff.; A. J. Heschel, *Theology of Ancient Judaism,* I (Heb.; London and New York, 1962), 33 ff.

the primacy of obedience over sacrifice, Amos and the prophets who followed him not only stressed the primacy of morality over sacrifice, but even proclaimed that the worth of worship, far from being absolute, is contingent upon moral living, and that when immorality prevails, worship is detestable. Questioning man's right to worship through offerings and songs, they maintained that the primary way of serving God is through love, justice, and righteousness.

This is a paradox to be sure, and like every paradox its opposite is a view that is orthodox. It contains both a negation and an affirmation, the negation being more intelligible than the affirmation. It is difficult for us today to appreciate the boldness and defiance contained in these pronouncements. The distinction between the holy and the profane, between the divine and the mundane, is the basis of religious thinking. A line is drawn between the interests of man and the demands of God. What is it that all gods demand? Sacrifice, incense, reverence for their power. Sacrifice, the strength and the measure of piety, acts wherein God and man meet—all this should be called obnoxious?

Of course, the prophets did not condemn the practice of sacrifice in itself; otherwise, we should have to conclude that Isaiah intended to discourage the practice of prayer (Isa. 1:14–15).* They did, however, claim that deeds of injustice vitiate both sacrifice and prayer. Men may not drown the cries of the oppressed with the noise of hymns, nor buy off the Lord with increased offerings. The prophets disparaged the cult when it became a substitute for righteousness. It is precisely the implied recognition of the value of the cult that lends force to their insistence that there is something far more precious than sacrifice.

These feasts and assemblies, offerings and rites, hallowed by the loyalty of many generations, had become the essence of piety. One cannot doubt the sacred authenticity of the cult. It had a place and a procedure of its own, a sacred nimbus, a mysterious glory. It differed

---

*For a long time the polemic of the prophets was taken to mean a radical rejection of the cult. In more recent studies it is maintained that the prophets merely criticized the abuse and absolutization of the cult. See the literature cited in R. Hentschke, *Die Stellung der vorexilischen Schriftpropheten zum Kultus* (Berlin, 1957), p. 1, n. 6.

from all other pursuits; exceptional, striking, set apart, it conferred unique blessings. In the sacrificial acts something happened, something sacred was evoked, conjured up, initiated; something was released or cast away. The person was transformed, a communion vital to man and precious to God established.

In the sacrifice of homage, God was a participant; in the sacrifice of expiation, God was a recipient. The sacrificial act was a form of personal association with God, a way of entering into communion with Him. In offering an animal, a person was offering himself vicariously. It had the power of atonement.*

How supremely certain ancient man was that sacrifice was what the gods most desired may be deduced from the fact that fathers did not hesitate to slaughter their own children on the altar. When Mesha, the king of the Moabites, was hard-pressed in war, he sacrificed his own son, who would have reigned as his successor, for a burnt offering upon the wall (II Kings 3:27).†

To add paradox to sacrilege: all this grandeur and solemnity are declared to be second rate, of minor importance, if not hateful to God, while deeds of kindness, worrying about the material needs of widows and orphans, commonplace things, platitudinous affairs, are exactly what the Lord of heaven and earth demands! To give up a thousand fertile vineyards for an acre of barren ground? To find the presence of God in the shape of righteousness?

What they attacked was, I repeat, supremely venerable: a sphere

---

*The original meaning of sacrifice is obscure; see R. de Vaux, *Ancient Israel* (New York, 1961), pp. 447 f., and the literature cited on pp. 548 f.

†The sacrificial cult was endowed with supreme "political" significance. It was the chief requirement for the security of the land and may be regarded as analogous to the cult of military defense in our own day. Both have their roots in the concern for security. Cease to appease the gods with offerings on the altars, and their anger will strike you down. Sacrifice is a way of preventing the attack. Even as late as the third century of our era "one of the commonest motives for the popular hatred felt toward Christians was the belief that, neglecting the sacrifices themselves and encouraging others to do likewise, they had aroused the fury of the gods against the Empire. In 410, after the capture of Rome by Alaric and his Goths, this prejudice had such power that Augustinus was compelled to answer it; in the first ten books of the *City of God*, he is engaged in showing that the Christians were not responsible for Rome's misfortunes." (A. M. J. Festugière, *Epicurus and His Gods* [Oxford, 1955], p. 54.)

unmistakably holy; a spirituality that had both form and substance, that was concrete and inspiring, an atmosphere overwhelming the believer—pageantry, scenery, mystery, spectacle, fragrance, song, and exaltation. In the experience of such captivating sanctity, who could question the presence of God in the shape of a temple?

> *Let us go to His dwelling place;*
> *Let us worship at His footstool!*
> *Arise, O Lord, and go to Thy resting place,*
> *Thou and the ark of Thy might.*
> *Let Thy priests be clothed with righteousness,*
> *And let Thy saints shout for joy. . . .*
> *For the Lord has chosen Zion;*
> *He has desired it for His habitation:*
> *This is My resting place forever;*
> *Here I will dwell, for I have desired it.*
> *Psalm 132:7–9, 13–14*

It is hard for us to imagine what entering a sanctuary or offering a sacrifice meant to ancient man. The sanctuary was holiness in perpetuity, a miracle in continuity; the divine was mirrored in the air, sowing blessing, closing gaps between the here and the beyond. In offering a sacrifice, man mingled with mystery, reached the summit of significance: sin was consumed, self abandoned, satisfaction was bestowed upon divinity. Is it possible for us today to conceive of the solemn joy of those whose offering was placed on the altar?

> *Then I will go to the altar of God,*
> *To God my exceeding joy;*
> *I will praise Thee with the lyre,*
> *O God, my God.*
> *Psalm 43:4; cf. Deut. 12:18–19;*
> *31:11; Exod. 34:23 f.; Isa. 1:12*

## GOD IS AT STAKE

Why should religion, the essence of which is worship of God, put such stress on justice for man? Does not the preoccupation with morality tend to divest religion of immediate devotion to God? Why should a worldly virtue like justice be so important to the Holy One of Israel? Did not the prophets overrate the worth of justice?

Perhaps the answer lies here: righteousness is not just a value; it is God's part of human life, *God's stake in human history*. Perhaps it is because the suffering of man is a blot upon God's conscience; because it is in relations between man and man that God is at stake. Or is it simply because the infamy of a wicked act is infinitely greater than we are able to imagine? People act as they please, doing what is vile, abusing the weak, not realizing that they are fighting God, affronting the divine, or that the oppression of man is a humiliation of God.

> *He who oppresses a poor man insults his Maker,*
> *He who is kind to the needy honors Him.*
> *Proverbs 14:31; cf. 17:5*

The universe is done. The greater masterpiece still undone, still in the process of being created, is history. For accomplishing His grand design, God needs the help of man. Man is and has the instrument of God, which he may or may not use in consonance with the grand design. Life is clay, and righteousness the mold in which God wants history to be shaped. But human beings, instead of fashioning the clay, deform the shape.

The world is full of iniquity, of injustice and idolatry. The people offer animals; the priests offer incense. But God needs mercy, righteousness; His needs cannot be satisfied in the temples, in space, but only in history, in time. It is within the realm of history that man is charged with God's mission.

Justice is not an ancient custom, a human convention, a value, but a transcendent demand, freighted with divine concern. It is not only a relationship between man and man, it is an *act* involving God, a divine need. Justice is His line, righteousness His plummet (Isa. 28:17). It is not one of His ways, but in all His ways. Its validity is not only universal, but also eternal, independent of will and experience.

People think that to be just is a virtue, deserving honor and rewards; that in doing righteousness one confers a favor on society.

No one expects to receive a reward for the habit of breathing. Justice is as much a necessity as breathing is, and a constant occupation.

## The *A Priori*

Power, omniscience, wisdom, infinitude, are the attributes that man associates with the Supreme Being. Justice is not necessarily regarded as an essential attribute of God, nor is charity considered in all religions an essential part of piety. The holy men of India, for example, stand aloof from moral issues, and the highest goal of Indian philosophy and piety is to shed the fetters of action by overcoming the inclination to be active. Indeed, books on religion in which no reference is made to morality are as common as books on morality in which no reference is made to religion.

Greek religion did not stress the connection between religion and morality.\* It offered no precepts for the regulation of human conduct. Each god had his appointed sphere within which he exercised control. The gods were jealous to avenge any infringement of their privileges. But the sinner was punished, not as a moral offender, but as a trespasser against a divine power. In the tragedies the gods were considered guarantors of human justice, which consisted primarily of submission to destiny; but the gods in turn were not required to observe justice in their conduct toward mortals.

Occasionally we find the belief that certain gods who were the sources of the skills and wisdom of man had also given laws to him. In popular Greek religion there was a belief that specific laws were revealed by a god; among Cretans it was said to have been Zeus, and in Lacedaemon, Apollo. According to Homer, Minos, the Cretan lawgiver, "went every ninth year to converse with his Olympian sire"; his laws were derived from Zeus.† The difference, however, is that the

---

\*In Homer, "cruelty, provided again it be not too petty, is thought little of, either in the dealings of one of the kings with the people under his sway or in the behaviour of the gods towards their subjects, mankind as a whole." (W. K. C. Guthrie, *The Greeks and Their Gods* [London, 1950], p. 119).

†Plato, *Laws*, 624, 630, 632 (see p. 594 f.).

laws, like the skills, are not regarded as being an expression of the personal will of the god; they are something that the gods have dealt out rather than something to which they remain personally committed.

There are few thoughts as deeply ingrained in the mind of biblical man as the thought of God's justice and righteousness. It is not an inference, but an *a priori* of biblical faith, self-evident; not an added attribute to His essence, but given with the very thought of God. It is inherent in His essence and identified with His ways.*

> *The rock, His work is perfect;*
> *For all His ways are justice.*
> *O God of faithfulness and without iniquity,*
> *Just and right is He.*
>
> > *Deuteronomy 32:4*
>
> *Righteous art Thou, O Lord,*
> *And right are Thy judgments.*
> > *Psalm 119:137*

God is the source of right (Deut. 1:17), judge of all the earth. It is inconceivable that He shall not do the right (Gen. 18:25), that He shall pervert justice (Job 8:3), or do wickedly (Job 34:12). "For the

---

*On the problem raised in Plato's *Euthyphro* and its relation to biblical thinking, see A. J. Heschel, *God in Search of Man* (New York, 1959), p. 17. The concern of the Deity in the administration of justice to the poor is found in other religions as well. Amon-Re, the Egyptian god, is addressed as he "who comes at the voice of the poor man. If I call to thee when I am distressed, thou comest and thou rescuest me. Thou givest breath [to] him who is weak; thou rescuest him who is imprisoned." (*ANET*, p. 380.) A moving prayer for a helpless client in the court of law who is bewildered by the demands of the administrators of justice has come down from Egypt: "O Amon, give thy ear to one who is alone in the court of justice, who is poor. . . . The court cheats him of silver and gold for the scribes of the mat as well as of clothing for the attendants. May it be found that Amon assumes his form as the vizier, in order to permit the poor man to get off. May it be found that the poor man is vindicated. May the poor man surpass the rich." (*ANET*, p. 380.) In a Babylonian hymn, Shamash the sun god is praised for punishing the unrighteous judge, the receiver of a bribe who perverts justice, and for being pleased with him who "intercedes for the weak." (G. R. Driver, in D. C. Simpson, ed., *The Psalmists* [London, 1926], p. 169.) See also J. Ferguson, *Moral Values in the Ancient World* (New York, 1959).

Lord is a God of justice" (Isa. 30:18). "The Lord is righteous, He loves righteousness" (Ps. 11:7). That "God is a righteous judge" is the incontestable premise of Jeremiah's question, "Why does the way of the wicked prosper?" (Jer. 12:1.)

## MISHPAT AND TSEDAKAH

The two key terms are *tsedakah (tsedek)* and *mishpat*. The word *mishpat* means the judgment given by the *shofet* (judge); hence the word can mean justice, norm, ordinance, legal right, law. The word *tsedakah* may be rendered by "righteousness." While legality and righteousness are not identical, they must always coincide, the second being reflected in the first.*

It is exceedingly difficult to establish the exact difference in meaning of the biblical terms *mishpat,* justice, and *tsedakah,* righteousness (which in parallelism are often used as variants). However, it seems that justice is a mode of action, righteousness a quality of the person. Significantly, the noun derived from *shafat* (to judge) is *shofet,* which came to mean a judge or arbitrator; while the noun from *tsadak* (to be just) is *tsaddik,* a righteous man.

Righteousness goes beyond justice. Justice is strict and exact, giving each person his due. Righteousness implies benevolence, kindness, generosity. Justice is form, a state of equilibrium; righteousness has a substantive associated meaning. Justice may be legal; righteousness is associated with a burning compassion for the oppressed. When you extend a loan to a poor man, "you shall not sleep in his pledge; when the sun goes down, you shall restore to him the pledge, that he may sleep in his cloak and bless you; and it shall be righteousness to you before the Lord your God" (Deut. 24: 10–13).†

---

*The word *mishpat* seems to imply *the ability to discern between good and evil.* Thus prayed King Solomon: "Give Thy servant an understanding heart to judge Thy people: to discern between good and evil" (I Kings 3:9; cf. 3:11).

†"Hear my prayer, O Lord. . . . Answer me in Thy *tsedakah*. Enter not into judgment *(mishpat)* with Thy servant; for no man living is righteous before Thee. For Thy name's sake, O Lord, preserve my life! In Thy *tsedakah* bring me out of trouble" (Ps. 143:1–2, 11). "He will judge the world with righteousness" (Ps. 98:9), namely,

It would be wrong to assume that there was a dichotomy of *mish-pat* and kindness; "Justice was not equal justice but a bias in favor of the poor. Justice always leaned toward mercy for the widows and the orphans."* Divine justice involves His being merciful, compassionate.

> *Therefore the Lord is waiting to be gracious to you;*
> *Therefore He exalts Himself to show mercy to you.*
> *For the Lord is a God of justice;*
> *Blessed are all those who wait for Him.*
>
> Isaiah 30:18

Justice dies when dehumanized, no matter how exactly it may be exercised. Justice dies when deified, for beyond all justice is God's compassion. The logic of justice may seem impersonal, yet the concern for justice is an act of love.

## INSPIRATION AS A MORAL ACT

If intense regard and concern for man is the mark of a moral act, then inspiration of the prophets in which God's regard and concern for man are disclosed and in which the prophet is entrusted with a mission to help the people, must be viewed as an eminently moral act. The moral aspect sets the prophetic act apart from intellectual, artistic, and mystical experiences.

In archaic religions the relationship between man and his gods and the relationship between man and his fellow men represented two areas unrelated to each other. Man owed certain duties toward the

---

with kindness. "They ask of Me righteous judgments" (Isa. 58:2) rather than strict justice. "They shall judge the people with righteous judgment" (Deut. 16:18) is hardly a tautology. "O Lord, according to all Thy righteousness [or righteous acts], let Thy anger and Thy wrath turn away from Thy city Jerusalem" (Dan. 9:16). The word *tsedakah* has often been rendered as *Strafgerechtigkeit,* though nowhere in the Bible is it used in this sense; see D. P. Volz, *Prophetengestalten* (Stuttgart, 1949), p. 188, n. 1.

*R. Niebuhr, *Pious and Secular America* (New York, 1958), p. 92. It is significant that particularly in later Hebrew the word *tsedakah* is linked with *ḥesed,* Jer. 9:29; Ps. 36:11; 40:11; 143:11 f.; see also Ps. 85:11.

gods—he must offer prayer and sacrifice, the neglect of which is sin—but these duties did not concern his relations to his fellow men. In performing the rites, in his search to share sanctity or to attain salvation, the religious man might experience the power and grandeur of the divine, the bestowal of grace, or the assumption of insight, but not the concern of the god for someone else.

Religious experience, in most cases, is a private affair in which a person becomes alive to what transpires between God and himself, not to what transpires between God and someone else; contact between God and man comes about, it is believed, for the benefit of the particular man. In contrast, prophetic inspiration is for the sake, for benefit, of a third party. It is not a private affair between prophet and God; its purpose is the illumination of the people rather than the illumination of the prophet. (See p. 462.)

The phenomenon of prophecy is predicated upon the assumption that man is both in need of, and entitled to, divine guidance. For God to reveal His word through the prophet to His people is an act of justice or an act of seeking to do justice. The purpose of prophecy is to maintain the covenant, to establish the right relationship between God and man.

## PERVERSION OF JUSTICE

The fact that filled the prophets with dismay was not the absence of adequate laws, but the absence of righteousness. Judges were active in the land, but their judgments were devoid of righteousness. The prophets were shocked not only by acts of injustice on the part of scoundrels but also by the perversion of justice on the part of the notables. When warped and garbled, justice yields strife and distrust.

> *Do horses run upon rock?*
> *Does one plow the sea with oxen?*
> *But you have turned justice into poison,*
> *The fruit of righteousness into wormwood. . . .*

*O you who turn justice to wormwood,*
*And cast down righteousness to the earth!*
    *Amos 6:12; 5:7; cf. Deuteronomy 29:17;*
*Jeremiah 8:14; 9:14; 23:15; Lamentations*
              *3:15, 19; Proverbs 5:4*

*They utter mere words;*
*With empty oaths they make covenants;*
*So judgment springs up like poisonous weeds*
*In the furrows of the field.*

                    *Hosea 10:4*

Israel was the vineyard that the Lord had planted. He looked for it to yield grapes, but it yielded wild grapes. He looked for it to yield justice, but it yielded perversion of justice; for righteousness, but it yielded outrage (Isa. 5:2).

The prophets consistently singled out the leaders, the kings, the princes, the false prophets, and the priests as the ones responsible for the sins of the community. (See Hos. 4:6, 8 f.; 7:3, 16; 9:15; Jer. 2:26.)

*Hear this, O priest!*
*Give heed, O house of Israel!*
*Hearken, O house of the king!*
*For the judgment pertains to you.*

                    *Hosea 5:1*

*The Lord enters into judgment*
*With the elders and princes of his people:*
*It is you who have devoured the vineyard,*
*The spoil of the poor is in your houses.*
*What do you mean by crushing the people,*
*By grinding the face of the poor?*
*Says the Lord of hosts.*

                    *Isaiah 3:14–15*

After declaring that no one in the streets of Jerusalem did justice or sought truth, Jeremiah added:

> *Then I said, These are only the poor,*
> *They have no sense;*
> *For they do not know the way of the Lord,*
> *The Torah of their God.*
> *I will go to the great,*
> *And will speak to them;*
> *For they know the way of the Lord,*
> *The Torah of their God.*
> *But they all alike had broken the yoke,*
> *They had burst the bonds.*
>
> Jeremiah 5:4–5

"The shepherds are stupid" (Jer. 10:21). "Thus says the Lord God: Behold, I am against the shepherds; I will require My sheep at their hand" (Ezek. 34:10).

## THE SENSE OF INJUSTICE

The prophets' preoccupation with justice and righteousness has its roots in a powerful awareness of injustice. That justice is a good thing, a fine goal, even a supreme ideal, is commonly accepted. What is lacking is a sense of the monstrosity of injustice. Moralists of all ages have been eloquent in singing the praises of virtue. The distinction of the prophets was in their remorseless unveiling of injustice and oppression, in their comprehension of social, political, and religious evils. They were not concerned with the definition, but with the predicament, of justice, with the fact that those called upon to apply it defied it.

Justice may be properly described as "the active process of remedying or preventing what should arouse the sense of injustice." What is uppermost in the prophets' mind is not justice, "an ideal relation or static condition or set of perceptual standards,"* but the presence of oppression and corruption. The urgency of justice was an urgency

---

*E. N. Cahn, *The Sense of Injustice* (New York, 1949), pp. 13 f.

of aiding and saving the victims of oppression. In the words of the psalmist:

> From the heavens Thou didst utter judgment
> The earth feared and was still,
> When God arose to establish judgment
> To save all the oppressed of the earth.
>
> Psalm 76:9–10

## NONSPECIALIZATION OF JUSTICE

Justice is scarce, injustice exceedingly common. The concern for justice is delegated to the judges, as if it were a matter for professionals or specialists. But to do justice is what God demands of every man: it is the supreme commandment, and one that cannot be fulfilled vicariously.

Righteousness must dwell not only in the places where justice is judicially administered. There are many ways of evading the law and escaping the arm of justice. Only a few acts of violence are brought to the attention of the courts. As a rule, those who know how to exploit are endowed with the skill to justify their acts, while those who are easily exploited possess no skill in pleading their own cause. Those who neither exploit nor are exploited are ready to fight when their own interests are harmed; they will not be involved when not personally affected. Who shall plead for the helpless? Who shall prevent the epidemic of injustice that no court of justice is capable of stopping?

In a sense, the calling of the prophet may be described as that of an advocate or champion, speaking for those who are too weak to plead their own cause. Indeed, the major activity of the prophets was *interference*, remonstrating about wrongs inflicted on other people, meddling in affairs which were seemingly neither their concern nor their responsibility. A prudent man is he who minds his own business, staying away from questions which do not involve his own interests, particularly when not authorized to step in—and prophets were given no mandate by the widows and orphans to plead their cause. The prophet is a person who is not tolerant of wrongs done to others, who resents other people's injuries. He even calls upon others to be the champions of the poor. It is to every member of Israel, not alone to the judges, that Isaiah directs his plea:

> *Seek justice,*
> *Undo oppression;*
> *Defend the fatherless,*
> *Plead for the widow.*
> *Isaiah 1:17*

To the king as well as to the people, the prophet proclaims: "Thus says the Lord: Do justice and righteousness, and deliver from the hand of the oppressor him who has been robbed. Do no wrong or violence to the alien, the fatherless, and the widow, nor shed innocent blood in this place" (Jer. 22:3). "Amend your ways and your doings; . . . execute justice one with another; . . . do not oppress the alien, the fatherless, or the widow" (Jer. 7:5 f.).

In the *Iliad* gods as well as men are indifferent to wrongs inflicted, not upon themselves, but on others.* Quite a number of homicides are mentioned. However, "outside the circle of the dead man's kinsmen and friends, there is no indication of any popular sentiment against ordinary homicide. Odysseus, in his character of Cretan refugee, had told a tale to Eumaeus in which he represented himself as the slayer of the son of Idomeneus. It would be hard to imagine a more cowardly murder than this. And yet Eumaeus receives the supposed murderer with all the respect due to a stranger in accordance with the prevailing customs. Several murderers are mentioned as living as honored members of communities to which they had come as exiles."†

---

*S. Ranulf, *The Jealousy of the Gods and Criminal Law at Athens,* I (Copenhagen and London, 1933–1934), 20 f.

†R. J. Bonner and G. Smith, *The Administration of Justice from Homer to Aristotle* (Chicago, 1930), I, 16; II, 39 ff.: "Advocates were generally drawn from the litigant's friends and relatives. In the course of time they tended to become professional, and the practice of paying advocates arose. Yet there was a law which forbade the paying of advocates in private suits. Although the law could not be enforced, it nevertheless embarrassed the advocate who could not claim relationship or close associ-

It was long after the time of the early prophets of Israel that a law of Solon's (d. 559 B.C.E.) was promulgated in Athens which presupposed the readiness of the citizens to interfere when wrongs were inflicted on others. Solon "believed that the best-governing state was that in which those who had suffered no wrong were as diligent in prosecuting and punishing the wrongdoers as those who had suffered wrong."* The first appearance of "advocates" was at a trial in 489 B.C.E. It was in Rome that the advocate, more through his oratorical art than through his knowledge of law, achieved outstanding eminence.†

An act of interfering in a case in which a wrong was inflicted upon someone else is reported from the time of David. After King David's sin with Bathsheba, the wife of Uriah, the prophet Nathan went to David and told him a parable.

*There were two men in a certain city, the one rich and the other poor. The rich man had very many flocks and herds; but the poor man had nothing but one little ewe lamb, which he had bought. And he brought it up, and it grew up with him and with his children; it used to eat of his morsel, and drink from his cup, and lie in his bosom, and it was like a daughter to him. Now there came a traveler to the rich man, and he was unwilling to take one of his own flock or herd to prepare for*

---

ation with the litigant." About the abuse of such persecutions, the so-called sycophants ("a happy compound of the common barretor, informer, pettifogger, busybody, rogue, liar, and slanderer"), see pp. 42 ff. Cf. R. J. Bonner, *Lawyers and Litigants in Ancient Athens* (Chicago, 1927), pp. 59 ff.; R. Pound, *The Lawyer from Antiquity to Modern Times* (St. Paul, 1953), p. 29.

*R. J. Bonner and G. Smith, *op. cit.*, I, 170.

†The institution of the advocate, of a person who pleads the cause of someone else, was one of the great revolutions in the history of legal theory and practice. The Egyptians believed that speeches of advocates would cloud the issues. In the words of the Greek historian-traveler Diodorus: "The cleverness of the speakers, the spell of their delivery, the tears of the accused, influence many persons to ignore the strict rules of law and the standards of truth." (Quoted by J. H. Wigmore, *A Panorama of the World's Legal Systems* [St. Paul, 1928], p. 31; on China and Japan, see pp. 178 and 485.) In Nuzi documents there seems to be provision for the appearance at the court of a representative or attorney or substitute with the right of arguing the case of another person. See E. A. Speiser in *AASOR*, X (1928–29), 63.

*the wayfarer who had come to him, but he took the poor man's lamb, and*
*prepared it for the man who had come to him. Then David's anger was*
*greatly kindled against the man; and he said to Nathan, As the Lord*
*lives, the man who has done this deserves to die; and he shall restore the*
*lamb fourfold, because he did this thing, and because he had no pity.*
*Thereupon Nathan said to David: You are the man.*

*II Samuel 12:1–6*

Ahab, the king of Israel (875–853 B.C.E.), insisted upon securing
the property of Naboth of Jezreel. When the latter refused to sell it,
he was put to death on false accusation. For this outrage, Elijah the
prophet said to Ahab: "Have you killed, and also taken possession? . . .
Thus says the Lord: In the place where the dogs licked up the blood
of Naboth shall dogs lick your own blood" (I Kings 21:1–19).

## THE LOVE OF KINDNESS

The demand is not only to respect justice in the sense of abstaining from doing injustice, but also to strive for it, to pursue it.

> Seek *the Lord, all you humble of the land,*
> *Who do His commands;*
> Seek *righteousness,* seek *humility;*
> *Perhaps you may be hidden*
> *On the day of the anger of the Lord.*
>
> *Zephaniah 2:3*

"Righteousness, and only righteousness you shall pursue"
(Deut. 16:20). The term "pursue" carries strong connotations of
effort, eagerness, persistence, inflexibility of purpose. This implies
more than merely respecting or following justice, walking in the way
of righteousness; righteousness may be hard to attain; it may escape
us if we do not pursue it. (See Isa. 16:5.)

> *Hearken to me, you who pursue righteousness,*
> *You who seek the Lord.*
>
> *Isaiah 51:1*

"You who pursue righteousness, you who seek the Lord"—what greater praise is possible than is given by the juxtaposition of these phrases?

The imperative includes more than doing; it asks for love;* beyond justice, it refers to good and evil. "Seek good and not evil. . . . Hate evil and love good and establish justice in the gate" (Amos 5:14, 15).

"It has been told you, O man, what is good, and what does the Lord require of you but *to do justice,* and *to love kindness (ḥesed),* and *to walk humbly with your God*" (Mic. 6:8)—*doing* justice as well as *loving* kindness. The prophets tried to excite fervor, to make *ḥesed* an object of love.

What the Lord requires of man is more than fulfilling one's duty. To love implies an insatiable thirst, a passionate craving. To love means to transfer the center of one's inner life from the ego to the object of one's love.

## THE INNER MAN

Is this all the prophet came to teach us—social justice? Are there no other demands to be satisfied, no other goals to be attained?

God not only asks for justice; He demands of man "to regard the deeds of the Lord, to see the work of His hands" (Isa. 5:12; cf. 22:11), "to walk in His paths" (Isa. 2:3).† "If you will not believe, you will not abide" (Isa. 7:11).

> *Give thanks to the Lord,*
> *Call upon His name,*
> *Make known His deeds among the nations,*
> *Proclaim that His name is exalted,*
> *Sing praises to the Lord, . . .*

---

*"For I the Lord love justice; I hate robbery and wrong" (Isa. 61:8; cf. Ps. 37:28). "He loves righteousness and justice" (Ps. 33:5). "For the Lord is righteous, He loves righteous deeds" (Ps. 11:7). "You love righteousness and hate wickedness" (Ps. 45:7). The Lord is called "lover of justice" (Ps. 99:4).

†On Hosea's demand for *daath elohim,* see pp. 70 ff.

> *Shout, sing for joy, . . .*
> *For great in your midst is the Holy One of Israel.*
> > *Isaiah 12:3–6*

It is not only action that God demands, it is not only disobedience to the law that the prophet decries.

> *They do not cry to Me from the heart.*
> > *Hosea 7:14*

> *This people draw near with their mouths*
> *And honor Me with their lips,*
> *While their hearts are far from Me;*
> *Their fear of Me is a commandment of men learned by rote.*
> > *Isaiah 29:13*

The fault is in the hearts, not alone in the deeds.

> *Their heart is false;*
> *Now they must bear their guilt.*
> > *Hosea 10:2*

> *Thou art near in their mouth,*
> *And far from their heart. . . .*
> *Break up your fallow ground,*
> *Sow not among thorns.*
> *Circumcise yourselves to the Lord,*
> *Remove the foreskin of your hearts,*
> *O men of Judah and inhabitants of Jerusalem.*
> > *Jeremiah 4:3–4*

Amos condemns the rich who revel in luxuries for not being pained or grieved over the afflictions of the people (6:6).

> *For the fool speaks folly,*
> *And his mind plots iniquity;*
> *To practice ungodliness,*
> *To utter error concerning the Lord,*

*To leave the craving of the hungry unsatisfied,*
*And to deprive the thirsty of drink.*

*Isaiah 32:6*

The Lord alone is holy; "let Him be your fear, let Him be your dread" (Isa. 8:13). To fear God is to be unafraid of man. For God alone is king, power, and promise. "Yet even now, says the Lord, return to Me with all your heart, with fasting, with weeping, and with mourning, and rend your hearts and not your garments" (Joel 2:13).

*Thus says the Lord:*
*Cursed is the man who trusts in man and makes flesh his arm,*
*Whose heart turns away from the Lord.*
*He is like a shrub in the desert,*
*And shall not see any good come.*
*He shall dwell in the parched places of the wilderness,*
*In an uninhabited salt land.*
*Blessed is the man who trusts in the Lord,*
*Whose trust is the Lord.*
*He is like a tree planted by water,*
*That sends out its roots by the stream,*
*And does not fear when heat comes,*
*For its leaves remain green,*
*And is not anxious in the year of drought,*
*For it does not cease to bear fruit.*

*Jeremiah 17:5–8*

## AN INTERPERSONAL RELATIONSHIP

If justice be the mere relationship of a person to what he deserves,* then why should it take precedence over the relationship of a person to what he desires? Obviously the situation of one who deserves contains an element not present in the situation of one who

---

*"Justice is the firm and continuous desire to render to everyone that which is due" *(Iustitia est constans et perpetua voluntas ius suum cuique tribuens)* is the opening statement in Justinian's *Institutiones.*

desires, namely, having a claim, being entitled to something. An individual's desire is his private affair, an individual's claim involves other selves. The claim of one person to attain justice is contingent upon the assumption that there is another person who has the responsibility to answer it. Justice, then, is an interpersonal relationship, implying both a claim and a responsibility.

Justice bespeaks a situation that transcends the individual, demanding from everyone a certain abnegation of self, defiance of self-interest, disregard of self-respect. The necessity of submitting to a law is derived from the necessity of identifying oneself with what concerns other individuals or the whole community of men. Justice is valid because of the community that unites all individuals. The sense of justice is outgoing, transitive, inclusive.

There is an interpersonal correlation of claim and responsibility, but there is also an inner personal correlation of right and duty. Ancient Israel "does not distinguish between right and duty," and *mishpat,* the word for justice, denotes what a person may claim as well as what he is bound to do to others. In other words, it signifies both *right and duty.**

Justice as an interpersonal relationship, involving a claim and a responsibility, a right and a duty, applies, according to the Bible, to both God and man. In its fundamental meaning, *mishpat* refers to all actions which contribute to maintaining the covenant, namely, the true relation between man and man, and between God and man.

Thus, justice in the Bible must not be taken in a legal sense as the administration of law according to the rules of law by a judge. "One constantly 'judges' in the daily life, because one must constantly act so as to uphold the covenant, i.e., the whole of the common life

---

*"He establishes the right of the fatherless or the widow" (Deut. 9:18); "the right of redemption by purchase is yours" (Jer. 32:7). "Thou hast maintained my right and my judgment" (Ps. 9:5). "Why do you say, O Jacob . . . my right is disregarded by my God?" (Isa. 40:27). A special *mishpat* obtains between parents and children (Exod. 21:9), between neighbors (Exod. 21:31), between rich and poor (Exod. 23:6), between Israel and God (Jer. 5:4–5).

of the community. Everything in which this kind of judging manifests itself is called *mishpat*."*

## A Grammar of Experience

Why and for what purpose was Abraham chosen to become a great and mighty nation, and to be a blessing to all the nations of the earth? Not because he knew how to build pyramids, altars, and temples, but "in order that he may charge his children and his household after him to keep the way of the Lord by doing righteousness and justice" (Gen. 18:18–19). Righteousness is foremost among the things God asks of man. "Thus says the Lord: Let not the wise man glory in his wisdom, let not the mighty man glory in his might, let not the rich man glory in his riches; but let him who glories, glory in this: that *he understands and knows Me, that I am the Lord Who does kindness, justice, and righteousness in the earth;* for in these things I delight, says the Lord" (Jer. 9:23–24).

This is sublime knowledge, sublime understanding, a new grammar of experience. What we encounter in the world is not neutral, impersonal being, things, forces, forms, colors. What we encounter is full of God's kindness, justice, and righteousness. "The earth is full of the kindness (*ḥesed*) of the Lord" (Ps. 33:5). "He is the Lord our God; His judgments are in all the earth" (Ps. 105:7). "The heavens declare His righteousness . . . and all the people behold His glory" (Pss. 50:6; 97:6). "Thy love, O Lord, extends to the heavens, Thy faithfulness to the clouds" (Ps. 36:6).

God's love and kindness indicate a road. It is a road not limited to a particular area in space nor to exceptional miraculous happenings. It is everywhere, at all times.

---

*J. Pedersen, *Israel,* I–II (London and Copenhagen, 1926), pp. 348 ff.; K. H. Fahlgren, *Sedaka* (Uppsala, 1932), pp. 120 ff.; N. H. Snaith, *The Distinctive Ideas of the Old Testament* (London, 1944), p. 76. In the book of Judges no mention is made of any judicial activity of Othniel, Gideon, or Jephtah. They maintained the covenant by serving at critical moments as leaders of the people, and assuring their victory and independence.

Kindness, justice, and righteousness are heaven's part in life. Its perception is the prophet's daily experience and the spring of joy. And this is why celebration is man's first response to life and being. Beauty and grandeur are not anonymous; they are outbursts of God's kindness.

In the passage quoted above (Jer. 9:23–24), knowledge of God is knowledge of what He does: kindness, justice, righteousness. In another passage, knowledge of God is equated with what man does: justice, righteousness. In exhorting King Jehoiakim, Jeremiah contrasts him with his father:

> *Did not your father eat and drink*
> *And do justice and righteousness?*
> *Then it was well with him.*
> *He judged the cause of the poor and needy;*
> *Then it was well.*
> *Is not this to know Me?*
> *Says the Lord.*
>
> Jeremiah 22:15–16

Here knowledge is not the same as thought, comprehension, gnosis or mystical participation in the ultimate essence. Knowledge of God is action toward man, sharing His concern for justice; sympathy in action.

Inner identification with God's will and concern is the goal of the new covenant:

> *I will put My Torah within them,*
> *And write it on their hearts;*
> *And I will be a God to them,*
> *And they to Me a people.*
>
> Jeremiah 31:32

The world is overwhelmingly rich; the human mind is incapable of paying attention to all its aspects. The painter sees the world in color, the sculptor in form; the musician perceives the world in sounds, and the economist in commodities. The prophet is a man who sees the world with the eyes of God, and in the sight of God even things of beauty or acts of ritual are an abomination when associated with injustice.

The world is overwhelmingly rich, but the prophet perceives the whole world in terms of justice or injustice. (See p. 8.)

## As a Mighty Stream

Justice is usually defined as giving every person his due.* It connotes a conformity, a congruence, a proportion of some kind. This is reflected in the numerical symbols employed by the Greeks to express as the essence of justice the relation of parity between two contraposited terms: the *dyad,* also the number 8, which has 2 for its root, because of its peculiar divisibility. The idea of a balancing of two sides against one another is expressed in the most common symbol of justice, namely, the *scales.*† When the *sword* is added to the scales, it is a symbol not only of power, but also of precision; it seeks not so much to strike as to cut clearly the matter of controversy into two equal parts.‡

In sharp contrast to these symbols, expressing calmness, congruence, and precision, stands the prophetic image:

> *Let justice roll down like waters,*
> *And righteousness like a mighty stream.*§
>
> Amos 5:24

One is uncertain of the exact meaning of this bold image. It seems to combine several ideas: a surging movement, a life-bringing substance, a dominant power.

A mighty stream, expressive of the vehemence of a never-ending,

---

*See Simonides in *Republic,* I, 331e, and Plato's refutation.
†Cf. Deut. 25:13 f.; 24:17: "You shall not pervert [or: incline] the justice due to the sojourner or to the fatherless." See also Prov. 16:11.
‡G. Del Vecchio, *Justice* (New York, 1953), pp. 169 ff.; cf. I Kings 3:24.
§R. S. Cripps: "as a never failing stream." Cf. "Then your peace would have been like a river, and your righteousness like the waves of the sea" (Isa. 48:18).

surging, fighting movement—as if obstacles had to be washed away for justice to be done. No rock is so hard that water cannot pierce it. "The mountain falls and crumbles away, the rock is removed from its place—the waters wear away the stones" (Job 14:18 f.). Justice is not a mere norm, but a fighting challenge, a restless drive.

Balancing is possible when the scales are unimpaired, and the judge's eyes sound. When the eyes are dim and the scales unsure, what is required is a power that will strike and change, heal and restore, like a mighty stream bringing life to the parched land. There is a thirst for righteousness that only a mighty stream can quench.

Righteousness as a mere tributary, feeding the immense stream of human interests, is easily exhausted and more easily abused. But righteousness is not a trickle; it is God's power in the world, a torrent, an impetuous drive, full of grandeur and majesty. The surge is choked, the sweep is blocked. Yet the mighty stream will break all dikes.

Justice, people seem to agree, is a principle, a norm, an ideal of the highest importance. We all insist that it ought to be—but it may not be. In the eyes of the prophets, justice is more than an idea or a norm: justice is charged with the omnipotence of God. What ought to be, shall be!

Righteousness is a vast and mighty stream because God is its unfailing source.

## EXALTATION IN JUSTICE

*But the Lord of hosts shall be exalted in justice,*
*The Holy One of Israel sanctified in righteousness.*
*Isaiah 5:16*

This is a staggering assertion. Why should His justice be the supreme manifestation of God? Is not wisdom or omnipotence a mode of manifestation more magnificent and more indicative of what we associate with the divine? It would have been more plausible to declare: The Lord of hosts is exalted in majesty, the Holy One of Israel is sanctified in omnipotence. Omnipotence is an attribute which no mortal shares with God, while justice is a quality to which human beings, too, lay claim; it is a quality devoid of sublimity and mystery, elementary and undistinguished.

Isaiah's declaration is humble compared with the words the Lord spoke to Job out of the whirlwind. How trite and prosaic are justice and righteousness when matched against the transcendent majesty and the crushing mystery of the Creator of the universe; a still, small voice compared with a thunderbolt. Job's answer to the words spoken out of the whirlwind was:

> *I had heard of Thee by the hearing of the ear,*
> *But now my eye sees Thee;*
> *Therefore I despise myself*
> *And repent in dust and ashes.*
>
> *Job 42:6*

In contrast, Isaiah was able to exclaim:

> *O house of Jacob,*
> *Come, let us walk*
> *In the light of the Lord.*
> *Isaiah 2:5*

Perhaps this is the deeper meaning of the words, "The Holy One of Israel is sanctified in righteousness." The holy is all mystery, inscrutable, dwelling in "thick darkness." Yet beyond the darkness is righteousness. Mystery is not the ultimate. Mystery is surpassed by meaning.

> *Cloud and deep darkness are round about Him;*
> *Righteousness and justice are the foundations of His throne.*
> *Psalm 97:2*

History, what happens here and now, is the decisive stage for God's manifestation. His glorious disclosure is not in a display of miracles, evoking fascination, but in establishing righteousness, evoking appreciation.

*Exalted\* is the Lord,*
*He who dwells on high,*
*He has filled Zion with justice and righteousness.*
*He will be the permanence of your times,*
*Abundance of salvation, wisdom, and knowledge.*
*The fear of the Lord is His treasure.*

*Isaiah 33:5–6*

The grandeur and majesty of God do not come to expression in the display of ultimate sovereignty and power, but rather in rendering righteousness and mercy. "He exalts Himself to show mercy to you" (Isa. 30:18).

*For Thou hast been a stronghold to the poor,*
*A stronghold to the needy in his distress.*

*Isaiah 25:4*

Isaiah's declaration does not speak about values, and its intention is not to assert that holiness and justice are very much alike, or that justice is holy, or that holiness is just.† Isaiah speaks about God, and his intention is to say that the Lord of heaven and earth, of nature and history, finds His true exaltation in justice. Isaiah does not pronounce a theory, he proclaims what is to come. He does not teach what ought to be, he predicts what shall be.

The importance of moral ideas was known to people everywhere. Yet linked with the awareness of their importance was an awareness of their impotence. The prophets proclaimed that justice is omnipotent, that right and wrong are dimensions of world history, not merely modes of conduct. The existence of the world is contingent upon right and wrong, and its secret is God's involvement in history.

History is a turmoil. Survival and perdition are equally possible. But justice will decide; righteousness will redeem.

*Zion shall be redeemed by justice,*
*And those in her who repent, by righteousness.*

*Isaiah 1:27*

---

\*Heb.: *nisgav;* cf. Isa. 2:11.
†See Plato, *Protagoras,* 331.

Justice will not fail. Addressing himself to Assyria while she is at the height of her power, the prophet exclaims:

> *Woe to you, destroyer,*
> *Who yourself have not been destroyed;*
> *You treacherous one,*
> *With whom none has dealt treacherously!*
> *You will be destroyed.*
> *When you have made an end of dealing treacherously,*
> *You will be dealt with treacherously.*
>
> *Isaiah 33:1*

If justice is but a category, a conformity, then injustice must be regarded as an irregularity, a deviation from a norm. But justice is like a mighty stream, and to defy it is to block God's almighty surge. The moralists discuss, suggest, counsel; the prophets proclaim, demand, insist.

To sum up, the image of scales conveys the idea of form, standard, balance, measure, stillness. The image of a mighty stream expresses content, substance, power, movement, vitality.

Justice represented as a blindfolded virgin, while conveying the essential thought of the rightful caution of the mind against illusions and partiality of the heart, conceives of the process of justice as a mechanical process, as if the life of man were devoid of individuality and uniqueness and could be adequately understood in terms of inexorable generalizations. There is a point at which strict justice is unjust.

Immutable justice—the principle *fiat justitia, pereat mundus*—raises justice to a position of supremacy, denying to any other principle the power to temper it, regarding it as an absolute; the world exists for the sake of maintaining justice rather than justice for the sake of maintaining the world. Carried to the extreme, the principle sets up a false dichotomy of world and justice, betraying the truth that the survival of the world is itself a requirement of justice.*

*The maxim is said to have been the motto of Emperor Ferdinand I (1503–1564) (T. H. Harbottle, *Dictionary of Quotations* [London, 1906], p. 70). According to B. Stevenson (*The Home Book of Quotations* [New York, 1944], p. 1030), the maxim *fiat justitia et ruant coeli* (let justice be done, though the heavens fall), was used for the

God's concern for justice grows out of His compassion for man. The prophets do not speak of a divine relationship to an absolute principle or idea, called justice. They are intoxicated with the awareness of God's relationship to His people and to all men.

Justice is not important for its own sake; the validity of justice and the motivation for its exercise lie in the blessings it brings to man. For justice, as stated above, is not an abstraction, a value. Justice exists in relation to a person, and is something done by a person. An act of injustice is condemned, not because the law is broken, but because a person has been hurt. What is the image of a person? A person is a being whose anguish may reach the heart of God. "You shall not afflict any widow or orphan. If you do afflict them, and they cry out to Me, I will surely hear their cry. . . . if he cries to Me, I will hear, for I am compassionate" (Exod. 22:22–23, 27).

When Cain murdered his brother Abel, the words denouncing his crime did not proclaim: "You have broken the law." Instead we read: "And . . . the Lord said: What have you done? The voice of your brother's blood is crying to Me from the ground" (Gen. 4:10).

## AUTONOMY OF THE MORAL LAW

For all the centrality of ethos in the prophetic understanding of God, it is incorrect to say, as is often done, that "justice to the Israelit-

---

first time in English literature by William Watson in 1601. (See also Büchmann, *Geflü-gelte Worte* [27th ed.; Berlin, 1925], p. 527.) The origin of the maxim is obscure. G. Del Vecchio in his *Justice* (p. 175), quoting the opinion by Salvatorelli and Hühn (*La Biblia* [Milan, 1915], p. 151) that it goes back to the prophets, assumes that the substance if not the letter of the maxim is derived from the Hebrew Bible. G. F. Moore (*Judaism in the First Centuries of the Christian Era*, II, 196), cites the maxim as a parallel to the statement by Rabbi Eliezer, son of Rabbi Jose the Galilean of the second century, that it is forbidden to arbitrate in a settlement. "But *let the law pierce the mountain* (let the law take its course). And so Moses' motto was: Let the law pierce the mountain. Aaron, however [loved peace and pursued peace and] made peace between man and man" (*Tosefta, Sanhedrin* I, 3; the words in parenthesis, *Bab. Sanhedrin*, 6b; see also *Yebamoth,* 92a). There is some difference, however, between a mountain to be pierced and the world to be destroyed. God, not justice, is alone ultimate, and His rule follows mercy as well as justice. Akiba's principle, "No pity is to be shown in a matter of law" (*Mishnah Kethuboth*, IX, 2) merely implies that pity must not enter ish mind was such an indispensable thing in the universe that it some-times seems to stand out as some irresistible power independent even of God, as something which God Himself needs obey."*

In an effort to prove the similarity of Judaism and Kantian ethics, it was often maintained that, according to Judaism, "the moral law is autonomous because it originates in the nature of the human mind alone. . . . That autonomy implies the absence of every extraneous will in the creation of morality, every external power. . . . This exalted purity and this dignity of the moral are independent of every sort of theistic notion, because they spring from the very nature of the human mind." "Ethical holiness may be thought of detached from religious holiness. It has value and dignity of its own, without reference to God, the ordainer of morality; that is, the moral idea has an existence inde-pendent of the recognition that it is actualized in God."†

The prophets did not conceive of the ethos as an autonomous idea, as a sovereign essence, higher in the scale of reality than God Himself, standing above him like a supreme force. God to them was more than a moral principle or a moral exemplar.

The central achievement of biblical religion was to remove the veil of anonymity from the workings of history. There are no ultimate laws, no eternal ideas. The Lord alone is ultimate and eternal. The laws are His creation, and the moral ideas are not entities apart from Him; they are His concern. Indeed, the personalization of the moral idea is the indispensable assumption of prophetic theology. Mercy, grace, repentance, forgiveness, all would be impossible if the moral principle were held to be superior to God. God's call to man, which resounds so frequently in the utterances of the prophets, presupposes an ethos based, not upon immutable principles, but rather upon His eternal concern. God's repenting a decision which was based on moral grounds clearly shows the supremacy of pathos.

---

the judicial process; it follows Exodus 23:3 ("nor shall you be partial to a poor man in his suit") and Leviticus 19:15. Hegel rephrased the maxim into the very different *fiat justitia ne pereat mundus.*

*M. Lazarus, *The Ethics of Judaism,* I (Philadelphia, 1900–1901), 135–136.
†*Ibid.,* II, 13.

Crime is not a violation of a law, but a sin against the living God. "Against Thee, Thee only have I sinned, and done that which is evil in Thy sight," confesses the psalmist (51:6). "If Thou, O Lord, shouldst mark iniquities, who could stand?" (Ps. 132:3.)

To identify God with the moral idea would be contrary to the very meaning of prophetic theology. God is not the mere guardian of the moral order. He is not an intermediary between a transcendental idea of the good and man. The prophet does not think of Him as a being whose function it is to supervise the moral order and to bring about the realization of an autonomous morality. As love cannot be identified with the values found in it, so the relation between God and man cannot be simply equated with the value of the moral idea. The pathos structure of divine ethos follows from the unlimited sovereignty of God. If the moral law were something absolute and final, it would represent a destiny to which God Himself would be subject. Far from being sovereign, God would then fall into dependence on rigid, objective norms.

## THE PRIMACY OF GOD'S INVOLVEMENT IN HISTORY

For a long time the importance of the prophets was seen to lie in the fact that they raised the religion of cult to a religion of morality.* Ethical monotheism was "their contribution to the spiritual growth of their race."† The religion introduced by the prophets was a sort of protestantism, directed against all sorts of "paganism" and ritualism, with the main emphasis placed upon faith. The image of the prophets was that of preachers of morals and spiritual religion as opposed to ceremonialism and ritual. This view has now been questioned. "The prophets have been isolated in too high a degree, and made makers of ideas which in reality were common Israelite stock, and modern scholars have in a one-sided way stressed certain ideas of the prophets

*G. Hölscher, *Die Profeten* (Leipzig, 1914), p. 188.
†A. Kuenen, *The Prophets and Prophecy in Israel* (London, 1877), p. 589.

which acquired importance for posterity, and to which there might be found a special connection in the nineteenth century."*

Ethical monotheism must not be regarded as the contribution of the classical prophets,† since it was known in Israel long before the time of Amos. Nor is "the primacy of morality" to be regarded as the chief characteristic of prophetic thought.

Divine ethos does not operate without pathos. Any thought of an objectivity, or a Platonic self-subsistence of ideas, be it the idea of beauty or of justice is alien to the prophets. God is all-personal, all-subject. His ethos and pathos are one.

The preoccupation with justice, the passion with which the prophets condemn injustice, is rooted in their sympathy with divine pathos. The chief characteristic of prophetic thought is the primacy of God's involvement in history. History is the domain with which the prophets' minds are occupied. They are moved by a responsibility for society, by a sensitivity to what the moment demands.

Since the prophets do not speak in the name of the moral law, it is inaccurate to characterize them as proclaimers of justice, or *mishpat*. It is more accurate to see them as proclaimers of God's pathos, speaking not for the idea of justice, but for the God of justice, for God's concern for justice. Divine concern remembered in sympathy is the stuff of which prophecy is made.

To the biblical mind the implication of goodness is mercy. Pathos, concern for the world, is the very ethos of God. This ethical

---

*See J. Pedersen, "The Role Played by Inspired Persons among the Israelites and the Arabs," in H. H. Rowley, ed., *Studies in Old Testament Prophecy* (Edinburgh, 1950), pp. 127 ff.; *"Die Auffassung vom Alten Testament,"* ZAW, XLIX (1931), 161 ff.

†This view, based upon the theory that the early popular religion of Israel was polytheistic or monolatristic and that only under the influence of the literary prophets was monotheism established, has been challenged by scholars. If the term "monotheist" means one who teaches the existence of only one God, the creator of everything, the source of justice, who is equally powerful in Egypt, in the desert, and in Palestine, who has no sexuality and no mythology," then Moses was a monotheist. (Cf. W. F. Albright, *From the Stone Age to Christianity* [Baltimore, 1940], p. 207.) See also Y. Kaufmann, *The Religion of Israel* (Eng.: Chicago, 1960), pp. 221 f. On the much debated controversy whether monotheism goes back to Moses or to the prophets, see B. Balscheit, *Alter und Aufkommen des Monotheismus in der Israelitischen Religion* (Berlin, 1938).

sensitivity of God—not the ethical in and for itself—is reflected in the prophets' declarations. Prophetic morality rests upon both a divine command and a divine concern. Its ultimate appeal is not to the reasonableness of the moral law, but to the fact that God has demanded it and that its fulfillment is a realization of His concern.

## INTIMATE RELATEDNESS

Is the prophetic message to be reduced to a simple, plausible prescription: *Do ut des,* "I give so that thou mayest give"? Be moral, and I shall make you happy, says the Lord.

What the prophets proclaim is God's intimate relatedness to man. It is this fact that puts all of life in a divine perspective, in which the rights of man become, as it were, divine prerogatives. Man stands under God's concern.

It is a thought staggering and hardly compatible with any rational approach to the understanding of God, that the Creator of heaven and earth should care about how an obscure individual man behaves toward poor widows and orphans. And if God is so powerful, and this concern so profound, why do the wicked prosper? (Cf. Jer. 12:1.)

Pathos is, indeed, *righteousness wrapped in mystery, togetherness in holy otherness.* Is the word of God irrational? But by what reason do we measure the word of God? By the reason expressed in our thoughts. But do we always understand our own thoughts? Can we always express what we mean? This, then, is our plight: What is most rational to the prophets seems irrational to us.

That incompatibility, however, is not ultimate. The goal is to establish compatibility, to refute idolatry and presumption that separate and antagonize man from what is supremely meaningful; to destroy illusions and to inspire realism.

God rules the world by justice and compassion, or love. These two ways are not divergent, but rather complementary, for it is out of compassion that justice is administered. But again and again His compassion, or love, is manifested in the world. Cain, slaying his brother, does not receive the punishment he deserves. Though justice would require that Abel's blood be avenged, Cain is granted divine pardon and protection.*

A father is disqualified to serve as a judge. Yet the judge of all men is also their Father. He would be unjust to His own nature were He to act in justice without being compassionate.

---

*Noticing that Gen., ch. 1, has *elohim* for God, not the Ineffable Name, while in ch. 2 both the Ineffable Name, the Tetragrammaton, and *elohim* occur, the rabbis remarked that in creating our world, God first intended to rule it according to the principle of strict justice (*middath ha-din*), but He realized that the world could not thus endure, so He associated mercy (*middath ha-rahamim*) with justice and made them to rule jointly. *Elohim* signifies strict justice; the Ineffable Name stands for mercy. It is maintained that when God acts according to mercy, the Ineffable Name is used, while *elohim* is used to signify His acting according to strict justice. Mercy has precedence over justice. Both justice and mercy as the main attributes of God's relation to man afford an insight into the polarity of God's dominion. Justice is a standard, mercy an attitude; justice is detachment, mercy attachment; justice is objective, mercy personal. God transcends both justice and mercy. See *"Yalkut Talmud Torah"* in J. Mann, *The Bible as Read and Preached in the Old Synagogue* (Heb.; Cincinnati, 1940), p. 271; Rashi, *Commentary* on Gen. 1:1; *Genesis Rabba*, 12, 15.

# THE PROPHETS

# II

# 1

# The Theology of Pathos

### UNDERSTANDING OF GOD

How should the question about the nature of the prophets' understanding of God be asked? The form in which the question is usually put—What is the prophets' idea of God?—is hardly adequate.

Having an idea of friendship is not the same as having a friend or living with a friend, and the story of a friendship cannot be fully told by what one friend thinks of the being and attributes of the other friend. The process of forming an idea is one of generalization, or arriving at a general notion from individual instances, and one of abstraction, or separating a partial aspect or quality from a total situation. Yet such a process implies a split between situation and idea, a disregard for the fullness of what transpires, and the danger of regarding the part as the whole. An idea or a theory of God can easily become a substitute for God, impressive to the mind when God as a living reality is absent from the soul.

The prophets had no theory or "idea" of God. What they had was an *understanding*. Their God-understanding was not the result of a theoretical inquiry, of a groping in the midst of alternatives about the being and attributes of God. To the prophets, God was overwhelmingly real and shatteringly present. They never spoke of Him as from a distance. They lived as witnesses, struck by the words of God, rather than as explorers engaged in an effort to ascertain the nature of God; their utterances were the unloading of a burden rather than glimpses obtained in the fog of groping.

The autonomy of ideas may result in their isolation or even in regarding them as independent, eternal, self-subsisting essences. To the prophets, the attributes of God were drives, challenges, commandments, rather than timeless notions detached from His Being. They did not offer an exposition of the nature of God, but rather an exposition of God's insight into man and His concern for man. They disclosed attitudes *of* God rather than ideas *about* God.

The bricks we collect in order to construct the biblical image of God are, as a rule, conceptual notions, such as goodness, justice, wisdom, unity. In terms of frequency of usage in biblical language, they are surpassed by statements referring to God's pathos, which, however, for a variety of reasons, has never been accorded proper recognition in the history of biblical theology.

Having described in the preceding chapters the place of the divine pathos in the thought of individual prophets, we shall now dwell on its general significance as a central category in prophetic theology.

The prophets, as said above, did not simply absorb the content of inspiration, they also claimed to understand its meaning, and sought to bring such meaning into coherence with all other knowledge they possessed. Moreover, inspiration was not their only source of knowledge. Together with receptivity to the word of God they were endowed with a receptivity to the presence of God. The presence and anxiety of God spoke to them out of manifestations of history. They had an intuitive grasp of hidden meanings, of an unspoken message.

A person's perception depends upon his experience, upon his assumptions, categories of thinking, degree of sensitivity, environment, and cultural atmosphere. A person will notice what he is conditioned to see. The prophet's perception was conditioned by his experience of inspiration.

By contrast to speculative knowledge, the pensive-intuitive attitude of the prophet to God, in which God is apprehended through His sensible manifestations, is to be characterized as *understanding*. Our intention of replacing in prophetology the traditional idea of knowledge of God by introduction of this new term is justified not only by the unsuitability of the former designation, but also by the usefulness of the latter. The prophets received their knowledge of God either through the moment of revelation or through intuitive contemplation of the surrounding world. In the first case, they received an inspiration as an expression of the divine Person; in the second, they sensed the signs of God's presence in history. They experienced the word as a living manifestation of God, and events in the world as effects of His activity. The given factor, whether the word* or the event, was for them an expression of the divine. In both cases their comprehension consisted of an understanding of God through His expression, an understanding which proceeds from expressions addressed to them as well as from unspoken signs of their divine source or motivation.

The point of departure of such understanding is any datum which is felt to be an "expression" of God, the course it takes is a meditation on the meaning of this expression, and the final result is an increased sensitivity to the presence of God—not an impersonal knowledge. The culmination of prophetic fellowship with God is insight and unanimity—not union.

Understanding of God is contingent upon the distinction between being and expression. Its quality depends upon one's relationship with the divine. Since the time of Descartes it has been asserted that the understanding of other selves takes place through analogy. While it is true that we do not experience a person independently of his bodily actions or expressions, yet through, and in connection with, these expressions, other selves are experienced with the same immediacy with which we experience our own selves. Our conviction as to their existence is based upon directly experienced fellow-

---

*P. Heinisch, *Das Wort im Alten Testament und im alten Orient, "Biblische Zeitfragen," 7–8* (Münster, 1922).

ship, not upon inference. To the prophet, knowledge of God was fellowship with Him, not attained by syllogism, analysis, or induction, but by living together.

For a neutral observer, the comprehension of the expressions of love that come from a person who is in love may at times be possible only by way of analogy. However, the person for whom these expressions are intended has an immediate understanding of what they mean. These expressions are not perceived apart from the beloved person; the beloved person is sensed in that person's expressions. And although their meaning is experienced through understanding, it is nevertheless no *circulus vitiosus* to say that the immediacy of the understanding is the result of the meaning. The intuitive knowledge which the beloved person possesses is a primary factor in the act of understanding. This important factor is, of course, not inferred from the act of understanding, but is a determinative element of the understanding itself. The directedness of the divine acts of expression to the prophet thus conditions the peculiar immediacy of his act of apprehension, which does not require analogy in order to be possible.

Even if the prophets had affirmed the essential unknowability of God, they would still have insisted on the possibility of understanding Him by reflective intuition.

## THE GOD OF PATHOS

Prophecy consists in the inspired communication of divine attitudes to the prophetic consciousness. As we have seen, the divine pathos is the ground-tone of all these attitudes. A central category of the prophetic understanding for God, it is echoed in almost every prophetic statement.

To the prophet, we have noted, God does not reveal himself in an abstract absoluteness, but in a personal and intimate relation to the world. He does not simply command and expect obedience; He is also moved and affected by what happens in the world, and reacts accordingly. Events and human actions arouse in Him joy or sorrow, pleasure or wrath. He is not conceived as judging the world in detachment. He reacts in an intimate and subjective manner, and thus determines the value of events. Quite obviously in the biblical view, man's deeds may move Him, affect Him, grieve Him or, on the other hand, gladden and please Him. This notion that God can be intimately affected, that He possesses not merely intelligence and will, but also pathos, basically defines the prophetic consciousness of God.

The God of the philosophers is like the Greek *anankē*, unknown and indifferent to man; He thinks, but does not speak; He is conscious of Himself, but oblivious of the world; while the God of Israel is a God Who loves, a God Who is known to, and concerned with, man. He not only rules the world in the majesty of His might and wisdom, but reacts intimately to the events of history. He does not judge men's deeds impassively and with aloofness; His judgment is imbued with the attitude of One to Whom those actions are of the most intimate and profound concern. God does not stand outside the range of human suffering and sorrow. He is personally involved in, even stirred by, the conduct and fate of man.

Pathos denotes, not an idea of goodness, but a living care; not an immutable example, but an outgoing challenge, a dynamic relation between God and man; not mere feeling or passive affection, but an act or attitude composed of various spiritual elements; no mere contemplative survey of the world, but a passionate summons.

## PATHOS AND PASSION

Did the prophets conceive of divine pathos as a passion such as may powerfully grip a human being?* By passion we mean drunkenness of the mind, an agitation of the soul devoid of reasoned purpose, operating blindly "either in the choice of its purpose, or, if this be supplied by reason, in its accomplishment; for it is an emotional convulsion which makes it impossible to exercise a free consideration of

---

*"By passions I mean desire, anger, fear, confidence, envy, joy, friendly feeling, hatred, longing, jealousy, pity; and generally those states of consciousness which are accompanied by pleasure or pain." (Aristotle, *Nicomachean Ethics*, 1105b, 20 ff.; cf. *Eudemian Ethics*, 1220b, 12 ff.).

principles and the determination of conduct in accordance with them."* In contrast, pathos was understood not as unreasoned emotion, but as an act formed with intention, depending on free will, the result of decision and determination. Even "in the moment of anger" (Jer. 18:7), what God intends is not that His anger should be executed, but that it should be annulled by the people's repentance. (See chapter "The Meaning and Mystery of Wrath.")

The divine reaction to human conduct does not operate automatically. Man's deeds do not necessitate but only occasion divine pathos. Man is not the immediate but merely the incidental cause of pathos in God, the *"occasio"* or *"causa occasionalis,"* which freely calls forth a pathetic state in God. There is no nexus of causality, but only one of contingence between human and divine attitudes, between human character and divine pathos. The decisive fact is that of divine freedom. Pathos is not an attribute but *a situation*.

On the other hand, the divine pathos is not an absolute force which exists regardless of man, something ultimate or eternal. It is rather a reaction to human history, an attitude called forth by man's conduct; a response, not a cause. Man is in a sense an agent, not only the recipient. It is within his power to evoke either the pathos of love or the pathos of anger.

## PATHOS AND ETHOS

God's pathos was not thought of as a sort of fever of the mind which, disregarding the standards of justice, culminates in irrational and irresponsible action. There is justice in all His ways, the Bible insists again and again.

There is no dichotomy of pathos and ethos, of motive and norm. They do not exist side by side, opposing each other; they involve and presuppose each other. It is because God is the source of justice that His pathos is ethical; and it is because God is absolutely personal—devoid of anything impersonal—that this ethos is full of pathos.

---

*Kant, *Critique of Judgment,* par. 29; cf. W. Wundt, *Einführung in die Psychologie* (Leipzig, 1922), pp. 31 ff.

Pathos, then, is not an attitude taken arbitrarily. Its inner law is the moral law; ethos is inherent in pathos. God is concerned about the world, and shares in its fate. Indeed, this is the essence of God's moral nature: His willingness to be intimately involved in the history of man. (See pp. 277 ff.)

## THE TRANSITIVE CHARACTER OF THE DIVINE PATHOS

The divine pathos is not merely intentional; it is also transitive. The gods of mythology are self-centered, egotistic. The cowardice of Ares, the incontinence of Aphrodite, the lusts of Zeus, the jealousy of the gods, are reflexive passions. Zeus is "hit by the dart of desire and is inflamed with passion" for Io, with whom he desires "to enjoy the pleasures of Cypris" so that his "eye may be eased of its desire."*

Pathos, on the other hand, is not a self-centered and self-contained state; it is always, in prophetic thinking, directed outward; it always expresses a relation to man. It is therefore not one of God's attributes as such. It has a transitive rather than a reflexive character, not separated from history.

## MAN'S RELEVANCE TO GOD

The theology of pathos brings about a shift in the understanding of man's ultimate problems. The prophet does not see the human situation in and by itself. The predicament of man is a predicament of God Who has a stake in the human situation. Sin, guilt, suffering, cannot be separated from the divine situation. The life of sin is more than a failure of man; it is a frustration to God. Thus, man's alienation from God is not the ultimate fact by which to measure man's situation. The divine pathos, the fact of God's participation in the predicament of man, is the elemental fact.

The essential meaning of pathos is, therefore, not to be seen in its psychological denotation, as standing for a state of the soul, but in

---

*Aeschylus, *Prometheus Bound,* 645 ff. Pindar speaks of the morbid sexual passion of Zeus and Poseidon, *The Olympian Odes,* 1, 40–45.

its theological connotation, signifying God as involved in history. He is engaged to Israel—and has a stake in its destiny. The profundity of this insight can be sensed only in the light of the prophets' awareness of the mystery and transcendence of God. For the biblical understanding of history, the idea of pathos is as central as the idea of man being an image of God is for the understanding of creation.

The biblical writers were aware of the paradox involved in God's relation to man. "Behold, to the Lord your God belong heaven and the heaven of heavens, the earth with all that is in it; yet the Lord set His heart in love upon your fathers and chose their descendants after them, you above all peoples, as at this day" (Deut. 10:14–15).

Never in history has man been taken as seriously as in prophetic thinking. Man is not only an image of God; he is a perpetual concern of God. The idea of pathos adds a new dimension to human existence. Whatever man does affects not only his own life, but also the life of God insofar as it is directed to man. The import of man raises him beyond the level of mere creature. He is a consort, a partner, a factor in the life of God.

## The God of Pathos and the Wholly Other

As a reaction to excessive rationalism and the complete disregard of the mystery and uniqueness of the divine, twentieth-century theologians have often tended to go to the other extreme. God is the Wholly Other; religion has to be demonic in order to be authentic, opposed to reason in order to be unique; and God must have nothing in common with His creation.*

The God of the prophets is not the Wholly Other, a strange, weird, uncanny Being, shrouded in unfathomable darkness, but the God of the covenant, Whose will they know and are called upon to convey. The God they proclaim is not the Remote One, but the One Who is involved, near, and concerned. The Silent One may be the antithesis of man, but prophecy is God meeting man.

---

*Otherness is not a unique category. Evil, Plato suggests, is somehow mere non-existence, or better, is "otherness," *heteroios* (*Parmenides,* 160–162).

The Wholly Other is the sharp antithesis to the consciousness of man. However, all being, anything that is given to the mind, stands over against the mind as otherness. What meets the biblical man is a transcendent relatedness, a divine claim and demand.

Absolute antithesis is alien to the Hebrew mind. That the Lord has made known His ways to Moses (Ps. 103:7) is a certainty basic to biblical consciousness.

Silence encloses Him; darkness is all around Him. Yet there is meaning beyond the darkness. God is *meaning beyond the mystery.*

> *Clouds and thick darkness are round about Him,*
> *Righteousness and justice are the foundation of His throne.*
> *Psalm 97:2*

The numinous is not the supreme category for the prophets, else they would not have attacked the sacred, that which the people revered and which was set apart as holy. The primary object of their religious consciousness was a pathos rather than a numen.

Pathos, far from being intrinsically irrational, is a state which the prophet is able to comprehend morally as well as emotionally.

What Abraham and the prophets encountered was not a numen, but the fullness of God's care. The moral law may be obscured, but never suspended. The very act of addressing Abraham was experienced as care. It was because of the experience of God's responding to him in his plea for Sodom (Gen. 18:23 ff.) that Abraham did not question the command to sacrifice his only son, and it was the certainty of God's love and mercy that enabled the prophets to accept His anger.

The holy in the Bible is not a synonym for the weird. "He blessed the seventh day and made it holy" (Gen. 2:3), not weird or terrible. The Wholly Other stands outside all relations to man, whereas the very genitive "the Holy One of Israel" suggests the relatedness of God. Terrifying in His grandeur and demand, the Holy One evokes a sense of unworthiness and contrition. The Holy is otherness as well as nonotherness. This is why it is possible to speak of God's holiness as a pattern for man.

## THE PROPHETIC SENSE OF LIFE

To the prophets, the gulf that separates man from God is transcended by His pathos. For all the impenetrability of His being, He is concerned with the world and relates Himself to it. The tragic antithesis between man and the gods is powerfully expressed in a well-known Babylonian prayer of a righteous sufferer:

> I myself was thinking only of prayer and supplication: supplication was my concern, sacrifice my rule; the day of worship of the gods was my delight, the day of my goddess' procession was my profit and my wealth. . . . I taught my hand to observe the divine ordinances. . . . Oh, that I only knew that these things are well pleasing to a god! *What appears beautiful to man is abominable to the god, and what is odious to man's heart is most pleasing to the god.* Who has learnt [to understand] the will of the gods in heaven, the gods' plan, full of wisdom, who can comprehend it? When have stupid mortals ever understood the ways of the gods?*

This is a powerful expression of despair. One knows the power of the gods, but, ignorant of their will, the mind cannot fathom what is good in their eyes. In fact, the gods and man contradict each other. There is no meeting, there is no knowledge of what counts most. "The god's anger, sickness, impurity, sin: it all amounts to the same thing. We offend God even when we ourselves neither know nor desire this; we are enemies of God, and indeed for no other reason than that He is our enemy."[†]

This prayer expresses the tragic sense of life. In sharp contrast, the prophetic sense of life knows of no such contradiction, of no such ultimate darkness.

---

*S. Langdon, *Babylonian Wisdom* (Paris, 1923), pp. 168 f. (Italics mine, A. J. H.) Cf. *ANET,* p. 435. At the end of the poem the gods have mercy on the sufferer and turn to him full of goodness.

†G. van der Leeuw, *Religion in Essence and Manifestation* (London, 1938), p. 520.

Underlying this contrast are two different conceptions of the nature of sin. There is an awareness in many religions of a blindly working guilt, of sin as a situation in which man is begotten, of sin which is involved in man's very being and stands far above the ability of the individual man. Sin is not conceived as something that happens, but as something that is and obtains regardless of man's relationship to the gods. "Since we are what we ought not to be, we also necessarily do what we ought not to do. Therefore we need a complete transformation of our mind and nature. That is the new birth. Although the guilt lies in action, *operari,* yet the root of the guilt lies in our *essentia* and *existentia,* for out of these the *operari* necessarily proceeds. Accordingly our own true sin is really original sin."*

The Mesopotamians, while they knew themselves to be subject to the decrees of the gods, had no reason to believe that these decrees were necessarily just. Hence their penitential prayers abound in self-accusations of faults and misdeeds, but lack the awareness of disobedience to the divine will; they are vibrant with despair but not with contrition, with regret but not with return.

To the prophets, sin is not an ultimate, irreducible or independent condition, but rather a disturbance in the relationship between God and man; it is an adverb not a noun, a condition that can be surmounted by man's return and God's forgiveness.

The divine pathos is like a bridge over the abyss that separates man from God. It implies that the relationship between God and man is not dialectic, characterized by opposition and tension. Man in his essence is not the antithesis of the divine, although in his actual existence he may be rebellious and defiant. The fact that the attitudes of man may affect the life of God, that God stands in an intimate relationship to the world, implies a certain analogy between Creator and creature. The prophets stress not only the discrepancy of God and man, but also the relationship of reciprocity, consisting of God's engagement to man, not only of man's commitment to God. The disparity between God and the world is overcome in God, not in man.

*Schopenhauer, *The World as Will and Idea,* Bk. II, ch. 48.

Confronted with an unconditional and absolute will of God, with eternity and perfection, man in his brittleness appears as a complete antithesis. But the prophets face a God of compassion, a God of concern and involvement, and it is in such concern that the divine and the human meet. Pathos is the focal point for eternity and history, the epitome of all relationships between God and man. Just because it is not a final reality, but a dynamic modality, does pathos make possible a living encounter between God and His people.

The uniqueness and wealth of meaning implied in the divine pathos, and its essential significance for the understanding of the religious situation, lead us to regard it as a theological category *sui generis.*

## PATHOS AND COVENANT

The decisive importance of the idea of divine pathos emerges clearly when we consider the possible forms in which God's relation to the world may present itself. A purely ethical monotheism in which God, the guardian of the moral order, keeps the world subject to the law, would restrict the scope of God's knowledge and concern to what is of ethical significance. God's relation to man would, in general, run along the lines of a universal principle. The divine pathos alone is able to break through this rigidity and create new dimensions for the unique, the specific, and the particular.

It is not law and order itself, but the living God Who created the universe and established its law and order, that stands supreme in biblical thought. This differs radically from the concept of law as supreme, a concept found, for example, in the Dharma of Mahayana Buddhism. Before the Torah, the covenant was.

In contrast to our civilization, the Hebrews lived in a world of the covenant rather than in a world of contracts. The idea of contract was unknown to them. The God of Israel "cares as little for contract and the cash nexus as He cares for mere slavish obedience and obsequiousness. His chosen sphere is that of covenant."* His relationship

*W. F. Lofthouse, "*Hen* and *Ḥesed* in the Old Testament," *ZAW* (1933), pp. 29 ff.

to His partner is one of benevolence and affection. The indispensable and living instrument holding the community of God and Israel together is the law.

Prophecy is a reminder that what obtains between God and man is not a contract but a covenant. Anterior to the covenant is love, the love of the fathers (Deut. 4:37; 10:15), and what obtains between God and Israel must be understood, not as a legal, but as a personal relationship, as participation, involvement, tension. God's life interacts with the life of the people. To live in the covenant is to partake of the fellowship of God and His people. Biblical religion is not what man does with his solitariness, but rather what man does with God's concern for all men.

The idea of divine pathos throws light on many types of relation between God and man unknown in apathetic religion. The covenant between God and Israel is an example. The category of divine pathos adds a new dimension to it. The covenant is an extraordinary act, establishing a reciprocal relation between God and man; it is conceived as a juridical commitment. Pathos, on the other hand, implies a constant concern and involvement; it is conceived as an emotional engagement. From the point of view of the unequivocal covenant-idea, only two forms of relationship between God and people are possible: the maintenance or the dissolution of the covenant. This rigid either-or is replaced by a dynamic multiplicity of forms of relationship implied in pathos.

## The Meaning of Pathos

The basic features emerging from the above analysis indicate that the divine pathos is not conceived of as an essential attribute of God, as something objective, as a finality with which man is confronted, but as an expression of God's will; it is a functional rather than a substantial reality; not an attribute, not an unchangeable quality, not an absolute content of divine Being, but rather a situation or the personal implication in His acts.

It is not a passion, an unreasoned emotion, but an act formed with intention, rooted in decision and determination; not an attitude taken arbitrarily, but one charged with ethos; not a reflexive, but a transitive act. To repeat, its essential meaning is not to be seen in its psychological denotation, as standing for a state of the soul, but in its theological connotation, signifying God as involved in history, as intimately affected by events in history, as living care.

Pathos means: God is never neutral, never beyond good and evil. He is always partial to justice. It is not a name for a human experience, but the name for an object of human experience. It is something the prophets meet with, something eventful, current, present in history as well as in nature.

The prophets never identify God's pathos with His essence, because for them the pathos is not something absolute, but a form of relation. Indeed, prophecy would be impossible were the divine pathos in its particular structure a necessary attribute of God. If the structure of the pathos were immutable and remained unchanged even after the people had "turned," prophecy would lose its function, which is precisely so to influence man as to bring about a change in the divine pathos of rejection and affliction.

In sum, the divine pathos is the unity of the eternal and the temporal, of meaning and mystery, of the metaphysical and the historical. It is the real basis of the relation between God and man, of the correlation of Creator and creation, of the dialogue between the Holy One of Israel and His people. The characteristic of the prophets is not foreknowledge of the future, but insight into the present pathos of God.

# Comparisons and Contrasts

## The Self-Sufficiency of God

The uniqueness of the prophetic theology of pathos can be better appreciated when compared with other theological outlooks. Indeed, the various conceptions of God as they have emerged in the history of religious thinking may be evaluated from the notion of pathos as a key perspective.

The idea of pathos is both a paradox and a mystery. He Who created All should be affected by what a tiny particle of His creation does or fails to do? Pathos is both a disclosure of His concern and a concealment of His power. The human mind may be inclined to associate the idea of God with absolute majesty, with unmitigated grandeur, with omnipotence and perfection. God is most commonly thought of as a First Cause that started the world's mechanism working, and which continues to function according to its own inherent laws and processes. It seems inconceivable that the Supreme Being should be involved in the affairs of human existence.

The idea of the Good was the God of Plato, and it was the meaning of the term "good" that determined his understanding of the concept of God. "The Good," says Plato, "differs in nature from everything else in that the being who possesses it always and in all respects has the most perfect sufficiency and is never in need of any other thing."*

If God is a Being of absolute self-sufficiency, then the entire world outside Him can in no way be relevant to Him. The obvious implication of such a concept is the principle that God has no need of a world, that there is nothing man can do to add to His excellence. "One who is self-sufficient can have no need of the service of others, nor of their affection, nor of social life, since he is capable of living alone. This is especially evident in the case of a god. Clearly, since he is in need of nothing, God cannot have need of friends, nor will he have any."†

Philosophical theologians have maintained, therefore, that while man is dependent upon the Supreme Being, the Supreme Being has no need of man, standing aloof from the affairs of man. Religion is a monologue, pure theotropism. (See p. 563.)

The most consistent exposition of the self-sufficiency of deities was developed by Epicurus as a reaction to the widely held belief that the gods were dependent upon man's sacrificial offerings as well as to excessive fear of the gods. To an infinite number of people religion remained a bondage which weighed heavily on their souls. "Undoubtedly," writes Theophrastus, "*desidaimonia* would seem to be a feeling of constant terror in regard to the divine power." People were oppressed by fear, lest by even an involuntary omission of ritual observance, they might have offended the divinity.‡

The Greeks have always regarded the gods as immortal and happy beings par excellence. Since the first condition for happiness is the absence of worry, which can be attained only by *ataraxia,* by living apart from the world, politics, and affairs, concern with which spoils tranquility and peace, it therefore appeared absurd, according to Epicurus, to assume that the gods should concern themselves with the affairs of men. What holds true for man, holds true for the gods.

---

* *Philebus,* 60c.
†Aristotle, *Eudemian Ethics,* VII, 1244b.
‡Theophrastus, *Characters,* XXVIII, beginning; cf. the famous reference to Epicurus in Lucretius, *De Rerum Natura,* I, 63.

The slightest concern for the government of the world or human affairs would upset their serenity and happiness. This, then, is the right conception of divine existence: existence without cares, like the existence of the sage who takes no interest in human affairs. Possessing everything necessary for their well-being, the gods live in interstellar space in a state of bliss and serenity, are indifferent to the world, and in no need of human worship.* "Blessed and immortal Nature knows no trouble herself nor does she cause trouble to anyone else, so that she is not a prey to feelings either of anger or benevolence; for all such things only belong to what is weak."† "The Divinity pays no heed to us"; for "what is blessed and incorruptible neither feels troubles itself nor causes them to others." (See p. 6.) Thus "anger and favor alike are excluded from the nature of a being at once blessed and immortal."‡

Similarly, the Supreme Being, according to the Hindu view, is not avid "to broadcast to everyone identical and correct notions concerning the nature and function of his divinity. He is not a jealous God. On the contrary, he permits and takes benign delight in all the differing illusions that beset the beclouded mind of *Homo Sapiens*. He welcomes and comprehends every kind of faith and creed. Though he is himself perfect love and inclined to all of his devotees, no matter what their plane of understanding, he is also and at the same time supremely indifferent, absolutely unconcerned."§

To the Deists of modern times, God's transcendence implies His complete detachment and apartness from the world. They deny that God stands in any personal relation to nature and man. The universe

---

*Diogenes Laertius, *Lives of Eminent Philosophers,* X, 193. G. Bailey, *Epicurus, the Extant Remains,* I (Oxford, 1926), 76–77; A. M. J. Festugière, *Epicurus and His Gods* (Oxford, 1955), pp. 57 f. The quality of the gods is often described in German literature as *"Olympische Ruhe."* At Olympus, the everlasting home of the gods, "no winds beat roughly, and neither rain nor snow can fall; but it abides in everlasting sunshine and in a great peacefulness of light, wherein the blessed gods are illumined for ever and ever." (Homer, *Odyssey,* VI, 42 ff.; see Büchmann, *Gefluegelte Worte* [27th ed.; Berlin, 1925], p. 78.)

†Sextus Empiricus, *Outlines of Pyrrhonism,* I, 155; III, 219.

‡Cicero, *De Natura Deorum,* I. 45.

§H. Zimmer, *Philosophies of India* (New York, 1956), p. 396.

bears to God the relation which the watch bears to the watchmaker. God brought the universe into being and imparted to it once and for all the driving force of its mechanism. Because His creation is perfect, no adjustment is ever necessary. Any belief in divine intervention in the natural course of the universe is precluded by the idea of the perfection of its Maker. God's relation to the moral world is similar. He is the author of the moral as well as of the physical law, but in each sphere equally remote from the particular cases in which they operate. Reward and punishment follow automatically in strict accordance with the principle of cause and effect, and there is neither need nor room for any special interposition of God in human affairs. Revelation is not thought of as a series of acts occurring in particular moments of history. It is a single act, the act by which God endowed man with his natural reason.

This conception was foreshadowed in Aristotle's doctrine of God as developed in the *Metaphysics*, Bk. Lambda. Deity, to him, is the unmoved mover, pure form, eternal, wholly actual, immutable, immovable, self-sufficient, and wholly separated from all else. It acts upon the world, not through its own activity, but through the longing for it which the world has; not as a mechanical, but as a final cause. Its only activity, resting purely within itself ( *actus purus*), is thought, and thought alone. What is divine thought about? Divine thought as pure form needs nothing else as an object, but has itself for its constant, unchanging content; it is thinking about thought, self-consciousness.

The contrast with prophetic thinking may be expressed in the following way. As we have seen, to Plato the relationship of things to the transcendent is signified by the participation ( *metexis*) of the phenomenon in the idea. The good differs in its nature from everything else in that it is never in need of anything else. The idea is stated even more explicitly by Aristotle: a god needing nothing, will not need a friend, nor have one. A self-sufficient being whose perfection is beyond all possibility of enhancement and diminution could not be in need of any being not itself. To the prophets, the relationship of the world to the transcendent is signified by the participation of God (pathos) in the world. Not self-sufficiency, but concern and involvement characterize His relation to the world.

The idea of the self-sufficiency of God became fused with the idea of the self-sufficiency of man. The certainty of man's capacity to find peace, perfection, and the meaning of existence gained increasing momentum with the advancement of technology. Man's fate, it was maintained, depended solely upon the development of his social awareness and the utilization of his own power. The course of history was regarded as a perpetual progress in cooperation, an increasing harmonization of interests. Man is too good to be in need of supernatural guidance.

Biblical religion begins with God addressing man, with His entering into covenant with man. God is in need of man.\* A Supreme Being, apathetic and indifferent to man, may denote an idea, but not the living God of Israel.

The prophets explicitly argued against those who said, "The Lord will not do good, nor will He do ill" (Zeph. 1:12). "The Lord does not see us, the Lord has forsaken the land" (Ezek. 8:12; cf. 9:9). "My way is hidden from the Lord, and my right is disregarded by my God" (Isa. 40:27; cf. 29:15; Pss. 10:4; 14:2; 94:7).

## TAO, THE WAY

The *Tao* ("the Way") of Lao-Tzu also forms an antithesis to the prophetic idea of God. *Tao*, the ultimate ground from which all things emanate, is a dark abysmal something, nameless and indefinite. *Tao* is the eternal silence, the everlasting calm, and the unchangeable law of cosmic order, immanent in all things. In accordance with *Tao*, freedom from desires is man's supreme virtue. Man must lay aside all desires and inclinations, surrender all lusts and passions, and imitate *Tao* in its potent and humble tranquility. Agitation and unrest must be avoided. Corresponding to this inner freedom from desires is the

---

\*See A. J. Heschel, *Man Is Not Alone* (New York, 1951), pp. 241 ff., and *The Theology of Ancient Judaism,* I (*Torah min hashamayim* [Heb.; London and New York]), 73 ff.

outward life of nonaction (*wei-wu-wei*), namely, the absence of action for particular ends. Quietism is the typical manner of a life in harmony with *Tao*.

"Heaven and earth do not act from any wish to be benevolent; they deal with all things as the dogs of grass are dealt with." The sages do not act from any wish to be benevolent; they deal with the people as the dogs of grass are dealt with."[*] Heaven, which comes into being after Tao,[†] does not strive nor speak; it does not call, and yet men come to It of themselves.[‡] Heaven has no feeling of kindness, but so it is that the greatest kindness comes from It. "The crash of thunder and the blustering wind both come without design."[§]

Absolute distance and aloofness characterize the Supreme Being in Confucianism, in which there is a reverent recognition of heaven as the source from which man derives his nature, although for the attainment of virtue little importance is attached to any communication between heaven and man.

God is essentially the moral order of the universe, an order operating in the phenomena of nature as well as in the course of history and the destinies of individuals. The order is impersonal, for heaven does not speak, nor does it hear what men say. It is "the something, not ourselves, that makes for righteousness." In the unvarying moral order "the destiny of men is determined in strict accordance with their conduct," and it is "futile to importune Heaven to change it."[‖]

The God of Israel, in contrast, is not a Law, but the Lawgiver. The order He established is not a rigid unchangeable structure, but a historic-dynamic reality, a drama. What the prophets proclaim is not His silence, but His pathos. To understand His ways, one must obey His will.

---

[*] *Tao Teh King*, I, 5, 1, in J. Legge, trans., *The Text of Taoism* (New York, 1959), p. 98.

[†] *Ibid.*, I, 25, 1, p. 115.

[‡] *Ibid.*, II, 73, 2, p. 164.

[§] *Yin Fu King*, 3, 2, in *The Text of Taoism*, pp. 703 f.

[‖] G. F. Moore, *History of Religions*, I (New York, 1949), p. 35; cf. p. 47.

## PATHOS AND KARMA

The great Hindu doctrine of karma may be cited as a profound contrast to prophetic thinking. Starting with the assumption that souls have been transmigrating from the beginning, the doctrine of karma claims that the well-being and suffering of every individual is the result of acts committed in a previous incarnation.

From the standpoint of the strict Vedantist, karma is the law of consequences by which the amount of pain is precisely equated with the amount of wrongdoing throughout the series of reincarnations. Working by its own efficacy, it operates unequivocally, inexorably, automatically; no god would have any right to come in and confound this beautiful exactitude of adjustment by freeing individual sinners from the consequences of their actions. Karma and its *vipāka*, the act and its fruit, are inextricably interwoven. With absolute necessity the effect follows upon every deed, word, and thought. The act brings forth its consequences directly. Punishment follows the crime, reward follows the good works—without the intervention of a god. There is no grace, no freedom, no repentance, no atonement. There is only an impersonal order: the inevitable, automatic retribution.

The secret meaning of Enlightenment in Buddhism is the supreme, long strife through ages of incarnation to attain release from the universal law of moral causation (karma).*

In full contrast to the doctrine of karma, retribution, according to the theology of pathos, is understood not as the blind operation of impersonal forces, but as above all determined by the freedom of the divine Person as well as by the freedom of man. Considering the depth of the people's iniquities, man may reach the conviction that the human situation could not stand the test of God's judgment. And yet even when the people seem to be doomed by their own deeds, the mercy and grace of God may save them from disaster. Divine pathos may explain why justice is not meted out in the world.

*H. Zimmer, *Philosophies of India* (New York, 1956), p. 479; H. Oldenberg, *Die Lehre der Upanishaden und die Anfänge des Buddhismus* (Göttingen, 1915), p. 1.

The way to God is mediated not only by the interplay of deed and retribution. A variety of relations between God and man— multifarious modes of approach and encounter, and also the direct orientation of the inner life of man toward God as subject—are made possible and justifiable by the conception of pathos.

> *The Lord is merciful and gracious,*
> *Slow to anger and abounding in love. . . .*
> *He does not deal with us according to our sins,*
> *Nor requite us according to our iniquities.*
> *For as the heavens are high above the earth,*
> *So great is His love toward those who fear Him;*
> *As far as the east is from the west,*
> *So far does He remove our transgressions from us.*
> *As a father pities his children,*
> *So the Lord pities those who fear Him.*
> *For He knows our frame;*
> *He remembers that we are dust.*
>
> *Psalm 103:8, 10–14*

Above reward and punishment is the mystery of His pathos. Sin does not inevitably bring about punishment. Between act and retribution stands the Lord God, "merciful and gracious, slow to anger, abounding in steadfast love and faithfulness, forgiving iniquity, and transgression, and sin" (Exod. 34:6 f.). He remembers that "man is but flesh" (Ps. 78:39).

Indeed, the central message of the prophets was the call to return.

> *Let the wicked forsake his way,*
> *And the unrighteous man his thoughts;*
> *Let him return to the Lord,*
> *And He will have mercy upon him,*
> *And to our God, for He will abundantly pardon.*
>
> *Isaiah 55:7; cf. Amos 5:14;*
> *Hosea 14:4; Jeremiah 3:14 ff.;*
> *Ezekiel 18:21 ff.; 23:11–21.*

Perhaps it was in reference to this paradox that another prophet, following his emphasis upon God's abundant power of forgiveness, reminded us:

> For My thoughts are not your thoughts,
> Neither are your ways My ways, says the Lord.
> For as the heavens are higher than the earth,
> So are My ways higher than your ways,
> And My thoughts than your thoughts.
>
> Isaiah 55:8–9

Sharp and sure is man's responsibility. "He who digs a pit will fall into it, and a stone will come back upon him who starts it rolling" (Prov. 26:27). "The nations have sunk in the pit which they made; in the net which they hid has their own foot been caught" (Ps. 9:15). And of Israel the prophet said, "They have sown the wind, and they shall reap the whirlwind" (Hos. 8:7). Yet it is within the power of man to return to God, Whose loving kindness is ever extended to the returning sinner. "Cast away from you all the transgressions which you have committed against Me, and get yourselves a new heart and a new spirit! Why will you die, O house of Israel?" (Ezek. 18:31; cf. Jer. 24:7; Ps. 51.)


## PATHOS AND *MOIRA*

To the biblical man, God is the supreme Lord Who alone rules over all things. This association of the concept of God with the idea of absolute sovereignty and supreme power may be contrasted with other ways of religious thinking. Zeus, for example, although acknowledged as the supreme god, was not regarded as having supreme power. When his son Sarpedon was about to be slain, Zeus shed a rain of blood upon the earth, but left him to his fate, knowing that even he could not snatch a man, "whose doom has long been fated, out of the jaws of death."*

*Homer, *Iliad*, XVI, 431–461.

Deeply rooted in Greek thought was the conviction that over and above the gods stood the dim impersonal figure of Fate (*Moira*) armed, or identified, with necessity (*anankē*) that defied craft (*technē*), in partnership with the Furies (*Erinyes*); perhaps endowed with sight and intelligence, perhaps not. It was a power whose fateful decrees Zeus himself feared. The Pythia declared to Croesus that "it is impossible even for a god to escape the decree of destiny." Croesus had to suffer for the sin of his fifth ancestor. "Apollo was anxious that the punishment should not happen in the lifetime of Croesus but be delayed to his son's days; he could not however persuade the fates."*

Fate was the ultimate idea and ultimate mystery to the Greeks, which, even after being divested of mythological conceptions, continued to exercise an overpowering influence. In Plato's *Timaeus,* for example, God, the Demiurge, Providence, Soul, *nous,* represents the living, intelligent, purposeful source and agencies of good; and the resistance to the divine act of creation comes from the blind, inert recalcitrance of *anankē,* or matter. *Anankē* is not a logical necessity, but an errant cause which pursues no purpose. It is the task of *nous,* of the Demiurge or Creator, to persuade *anankē,* but this can be done only imperfectly; for "there is a residuum of 'brute fact' in the world which cannot be rationalized." The power of the Creator is thus limited by irrational *anankē.*† "Even God is said not to be able to fight against necessity."‡ Plato takes for granted that there is a predetermined order of destiny, especially in relation to human affairs, without specifying by whom or what it has been determined.§

In many civilizations we find a basic awareness in man of being subject to a primeval, determining power which roots him to this very life, this very time and space. The riddle as to why one was born and why, just here and now, one's life rolls on, is insoluble; it is just one's lot. The Greeks experienced it as sheer power, power that is beyond good and evil. One cannot predict or argue with Fate. Fate is immuta-

*Herodotus, *History,* I, 91.
†W. C. Greene, *Moira* (Cambridge, 1944), pp. 203 ff.
‡Plato, *Laws,* 741a.
§See Plato, *Phaedo,* 113a; *Phaedrus,* 320d.

ble, impersonal, unseeing, and strikes like a thunderbolt. Future is like past: determined.

"Dreadful is the mysterious power of fate."* This is the keynote of Greek tragedy. Man is depicted as the victim of some dreadful power which foredooms him to disaster. "Pray not at all," chants the chorus in Sophocles' *Antigone,* "since there is no release for mortals from predestined calamity."† The Stoics maintained that Fate is a force which permeates the entire universe. While to most of them it was equated with Providence, Cleanthes, in his effort to explain the existence of evil, admitted that there was a sphere of fate over which Providence did not extend.

Similarly, the people of Mesopotamia were led to the idea of a Necessity controlling all things, superior to the gods themselves, and this Necessity, which ruled the gods, was bound, *a fortiori,* to hold sway over mankind.‡ They developed "a concept of fate which often becomes a sense of doom and a conception of suffering gods in which the richness as well as the cruelty of existence found expression."§

The Egyptians, too, had a definite concept of a predestined fate. From the Amarna period, Fate and Fortune were regarded as all-controlling, repressive deities, cutting down on the individual's freedom.‖

Astrology, first elaborated in the temples of Mesopotamia, whence it spread to Greece and Rome, was an extremely important element in ancient civilization.# Every level of society was affected by

*Sophocles, *Antigone,* 951.
†*Ibid.,* 1337 ff.
‡F. Cumont, *Astrology and Religion* (New York and London, 1912), p. 28.
§H. Frankfort, *Kingship and the Gods* (Chicago, 1948), pp. 282 f.
‖J. A. Wilson, *The Culture of Ancient Egypt* (Chicago, 1951), pp. 223, 225, 298 f.
#The conception of the heavenly bodies as endowed with life resulted in a belief in the existence of astral gods. It is blasphemous, according to Plato, to regard the sun, moon, and other stars as wanderers; however, they will be worshiped as gods in the state which the *Laws* contemplate (VII, 821). The astral gods were to play a great role in the Hellenistic and later ages. "Necessity," being something that, in the language of Plato, even God cannot "persuade," serves as the deterministic foundation of astrology, a pseudo science, the influence of which persists even in our day.

its fatalistic belief in the influence of the apparent motions of heavenly bodies on human destinies.* During certain periods of antiquity and throughout the Middle Ages, it commanded the ardent allegiance of the best minds; even emperors resorted to it. How significant it is that the biblical writers remained unaffected by this strange superstition. Scornfully the prophet declares:

> *Learn not the way of the nations,*
> *Nor be dismayed at the signs of the heavens*
> *Because the nations are dismayed at them,*
> *For the customs of the nations are false.*
> Jeremiah 10:2†

The divine pathos represents a sharp antithesis to the belief in destiny, or the idea of the inevitable necessity controlling the affairs of man. Pathos, a dynamic category which makes every decision provisional and contingent upon what man does with his existence, conquers fate. The ultimate power is not an inscrutable, blind, and hostile power, to which man must submit in resignation, but a God of justice and mercy, to Whom man is called upon to return, and by returning he may effect a change in what is decreed.

## POWER AND PATHOS

In the interpretation of religion it is generally assumed that God is, above all, "the name for some experience of power." That power is mysterious, *ne plus ultra*. Such interpretation, valid as it may be for the understanding of other types of religion, hardly applies to the prophets. Here the reality of the divine is sensed as pathos rather than as power, and the most exalted idea applied to God is not infinite wisdom, infinite power, but infinite concern. He who does not live on others, cares for others.

---

*See F. Cumont, *op. cit.,* pp. 28–35; 45–56; 66–72; 81–100; 153–161; 167–202; F. Boll, *Sternglaube und Sterndeutung* (3rd ed.; Leipzig, 1926).

†See also Isa. 47:12, Lev. 19:26, and Deut. 18:10, according to Sanhedrin 65b–66a.

The God of pathos may be contrasted with the God of Islam. For all the belief in divine mercy, Allah is essentially thought of as unqualified Omnipotence, Whose will is absolute, not conditioned by anything man may do. He acts without regard for the specific situation of man. Since everything is determined by Him, it is a monologue that obtains between Allah and man, rather than a dialogue or a mutuality as in the biblical view. Not the relation between Allah and man, but simply Allah himself is central to Islam. "The Koran does not describe Allah as the Father of mankind: He is throned too high for that."*

The power of God is not the ultimate object in the prophet's experience of the divine, nor the utter remoteness and inscrutability of the numinous—the supremely exalted—but the divine Mind whose object of attention is man and whose pathetic reactions reveal man as cause. Spirit, not power, is the ultimate reality for the prophetic consciousness.

## THE ILL WILL OF THE GODS

In primitive religion, the power of the gods is felt as a constant threat. Their dealings with man are not motivated by consideration for his welfare, and primitive man is always trying to appease them. With few exceptions, the arbitrariness of the gods is accepted as a sacred fact to which man clings with the fear and strength of religion. "Demonic dread" is the characteristic mark of the religion of the primitive man. It is "a horror of some power which concerns itself neither with my reason nor with my morals. . . . Horror and shuddering, sudden fright and the frantic insanity of dread, all receive their form in the daemon; this represents the absolute horribleness of the world, the incalculable force which weaves its web around us and threatens to seize us. . . . The malicious inadequacy of all that happens and the irrationality at the very basis of life receive their form in the

* *Enzyklopaedie des Islam*, I (Leipzig, 1913), 726.

manifold uncanny and grotesque apparitions that have inhabited the world from time immemorial."*

This "demonic dread" gives rise to fantastic images of the gods and does not disappear even in the more highly developed forms of the numinous emotion. "Even when the worship of the 'demons' has long since reached the higher level of worship of 'gods,' these gods still retain as 'numina' something of the 'ghost' in the impress they make on the feeling of the worshipper."†

"The idea of goodness as an essential attribute of God by no means prevailed everywhere even in the organized worship and established belief, not to speak of the immoralities of casual mythology."‡ The gods of the Indo-European pantheon are indifferent to morality.§ Even the supreme gods are not free of malice and cruelty, and some of the minor deities are often presented as evil gods. The same applies to the gods Rudra‖ and Indra,# e.g., in primitive Hinduism, whose images reveal a religious dimension quite different from that disclosed in the *Bhagavad Gita,* particularly in the eleventh book, with its doctrine of *bhakti* and the idea of divine grace to be bestowed by Vishnu upon those who give themselves up to him.

The Egyptian god Seth, conceived as a Red Fiend, is a power of

---

*G. van der Leeuw, *op. cit.,* pp. 134 ff.

†R. Otto, *The Idea of the Holy* (London, 1923), p. 17.

‡L. R. Farnell, *The Attributes of God* (Oxford, 1925), p. 164.

§H. Oldenberg, *Die Religion des Veda* (Berlin, 1894), p. 284.

‖Rudra, a mighty and terrible god, who under the euphemistic name of Siva became one of the greatest gods of Hinduism, is described as an impure and proud demolisher of rites, as roaming about in cemeteries, attended by ghosts and spirits. The gods themselves are afraid of his arrows, lest he should destroy them. He is implored not to slay his worshipers and their families: "Do not out of thy anger injure our children and descendants, our people, our cattle, our houses, and do not kill our men. We invoke thee always with offerings" (*Rigveda,* Mandala I, hymn 114, 8).

#Indra, the powerful lord of heaven and the chief of gods in Brahmanism, is in constant terror lest some saint, by severe austerities, wrest his power from him, and when there is a danger of this sort he sends one of his heavenly nymphs to seduce the saint from his ascetic exercises. Indra is reputed to have slain more than one saint, thus having become polluted with the heinous sin of Brahmanicide. (See H. Zimmer, *op. cit.,* pp. 536 ff.)

darkness. He murders his brother Osiris, a nature god whose original hostility to human beings has been gradually transformed into beneficence; he had taught the Egyptians agriculture.*

The Thracian god Ares, worshiped in numerous places and in the later Greek system joined to Aphrodite, who nursed a strong passion for him, delights in the slaughter of men and the sacking of towns, and loves fighting for fighting's sake.

In Greek religion, the gods are not regarded as friends of man. Vindictiveness, ill-will, niggardliness on the part of the gods were continually decried by the writers of Hellas. "The whole effect of the anthropomorphic religion reflected in the Homeric poems, in Hesiod, in the gnomic poets, and even in later literature, is to suggest that the gods are powerful, remote and not wholly kindly; they give both good and evil, and somewhat capriciously and there is little to hope for beyond the grave. . . . The result, if it is not pessimism, is at least an attitude of resignation before the inevitable; and the fear of the gods (*deisidaimonia*) may easily become mere superstition, even panic."†

When men are punished by the gods, it is not usually on moral grounds because they have sinned in our sense of the word. They are punished for personal offences against the gods. The few who are condemned to eternal torment—Ixion, Tityos, Tantalos, Sisyphus—had personally affronted Zeus. Ixion had assaulted Hera. The only immorality involved was an infringement of Zeus' prerogative. The offence of Sisyphus was actually to have given away the secret of one of Zeus' own intrigues. The myth of Prometheus, though first told for us in Hesiod, is an outstanding example of the same motive for divine punishment. His crime was that he tried to place in the hands of men powers which had been reserved for the gods. The resentment of Zeus was aroused because he feared for the

*H. Frankfort, *op. cit.,* pp. 22, 183.
†W. C. Greene, *op. cit.,* p. 48; cf. A. J. Festugiere, *Epicurus and His Gods* (Oxford, 1955), pp. 52 ff.

continuance of his tyranny. And the story of Sisyphus shows, it is not for men to criticize or interfere with the actions of the gods, be they good or bad.*

Sisyphus is one of those tormented in Hades, having eternally to roll a rock up a hill, only to have it roll down again. The reason for his damnation was his offense against Zeus in telling Aesopus where the god had forcibly carried his daughter Aegina.

In Homer, gods as well as men are indifferent to crimes committed against others than themselves. At times, the gods force men to commit crimes. What man thinks of the character of all gods is bluntly expressed. "Father Zeus, of all gods you are the most malicious. You have no pity on men though you have given them birth; you lead them into misery and wretched pains."† "It is Zeus who sends weal and woe upon mankind according to his own good pleasure."‡ "This is the lot the gods have spun for miserable men, that they should live in pain; yet themselves are sorrowless."§

The oft-cited passage in the *Iliad* concerning men who draw down the wrath of Zeus upon themselves by passing crooked judgments and defying justice, is alien to the general theme of the *Iliad*. It is a view that was prevalent in Hesiod, and since its wording is found in Hesiod,‖ the conclusion that the passage has been interpolated in the Iliad from Hesiod "would seem irrefutable."#

Plato speaks of the evil features of the gods.** Even Aeschylus, who extols the power and righteousness of Zeus, represents him in the tragedy of *Prometheus Bound* as the enemy of man. Prometheus is tortured for having saved the human race by the gift of fire, the chief

---

*W. K. C. Guthrie, *The Greeks and Their Gods* (London, 1950), p. 121.

†*Odyssey*, XX, 201–203. See above, p. 262.

‡*Odyssey*, I, 346 f.

§*Iliad*, XXIV, 525 f.

‖Hesiod, *Works and Days*, 224, 251; cf. *Iliad*, XVI, 388.

#P. von der Muehl, *Kritisches Hypomnena zur Ilias* (Basel, 1952), p. 247; S. Ranulf, *The Jealousy of the Gods and Criminal Law at Athens* (Copenhagen and London, 1933–1934), I, 9; Victor Ehrenberg, *Die Rechtsidee im fruehen Griechentum* (Leipzig, 1921), pp. 69 ff.

**Plato, *Republic*, 380.

instrument of civilization. Zeus is said to be governing gods and men arbitrarily, unjustly, and odiously.*

In the words of Sophocles, "Zeus rules the world with arbitrary power according to new-made laws." He is "the tyrant among the gods." He is "insensible to prayer," "hard, and decides at will what is to be just." According to Sophocles, Herodotus, and others, Zeus punishes men for sins which he himself has forced them to commit, or arbitrarily leads an innocent man to boundless disaster.

The Sumero-Akkadian gods, with the notable exception of the benign Enki and the ethical Shamash, were not as a rule sympathetically disposed toward man. The elements of love and compassion played hardly any role. "Man was a necessary nuisance, fashioned for the sole purpose of providing the gods with food and shelter so that they could live a life of leisure."† "Just as the serf rarely has intimate relations with the lord of the manor, so the individual in Mesopotamia looked upon the great gods as remote forces to whom he could appeal only in some great crisis and then only through intermediaries." The individual had close, personal relations to only one deity, his house god or patron divinity. To this personal god, before any other, a man owed worship and obedience. In every house there was a small chapel for the personal god where the owner of the house worshiped and brought his daily offerings. When a city was destroyed by an aggressor, its people placed the blame on the city's deity: "May his personal deity, the goddess Nidaba, bear this crime on his neck!"‡

## The Envy of the Gods

The idea of the envy or jealousy (*phthonos*) of the gods played an important role in Greek thought. It was believed that "there are times

* *Prometheus Bound,* 189, 150, 975. See also E. M. Eenigenburg, *The Experience of Divine Anger in Greek Tragedy* (New York, 1949).
† I. Mendelsohn, *Religions of the Ancient Near East* (New York, 1955), pp. xiii f.
‡ T. Jacobsen, "Mesopotamia," in H. Frankfort, ed., *The Intellectual Adventure of the Ancient Man* (Chicago, 1946), pp. 203 f.

when the gods seem to send calamities to man without just cause and to be jealous of their own superiority and prerogatives, or even to be animated by ill-will at the sight of the prosperity of others."* Penelope, excusing her caution in welcoming her husband, pleads: "Be not angry with me, Odysseus. . . . It is the gods that gave us sorrow, the gods who begrudge us that we should abide together and have joy of our youth and come to the threshold of old age."†

Many of the evils that befall man are due to the envy of the gods, who "are in a position to translate their envy into positive vindictiveness, casting down what is exalted not necessarily because prosperity has led to sin but merely because it is exalted." In one of his odes, Pindar prays that the family of the victor "may suffer no envious reversal at the hands of the gods."‡

In Herodotus, the jealousy of the gods is one of the leading motifs of his historiography. He is convinced that the gods work harm to men, and that oftentimes they give men "a gleam of happiness," and then plunge them into ruin. He makes Solon say, "I know that the deity is full of jealousy and fond of troubling our lot," and the words carry no suggestion of impiety. "The deity is utterly jealous and fond of troubling man's estate. . . . He often bestows felicity only to uproot it entirely."§ "Prosperity, not pride, eminence, not arrogance, provokes him. He does not like anyone to be great or happy but himself."‖ It is for this reason that death is a much better thing than life for man.# "The jealousy of the gods, as Herodotus understands it, therefore, has little in common with the conception of divine justice. Only as he applies the notion to his larger scheme, the conflict of

---

*W. C. Greene, *op. cit.*, p. 19. See J. Adams, *Religious Teachers* (Edinburgh, 1909), pp. 36–39; S. Ranulf, *op. cit.*, I, 20–114; 146–158; II, 28–74. H. V. Canter, "Ill Will of the Gods in Greek and Latin Poetry," *Classical Philology*, XXXII (1937), 131–143; F. Wehrli, *Lathe Biosas* (Leipzig and Berlin, 1931).

†*Odyssey* XXIII, 209–212; see IV, 181 f.; V. 118–120.

‡W. C. Greene, *op. cit.*, p. 75.

§*History*, I, 32; III, 40; VII, 10. 46. See M. Pohlenz, *Herodotus, der erste Geschichtschreiber des Abendlandes* (1937), p. 237.

‖E. H. Blakeney, ed., *The History of Herodotus* (London, 1910), I, 32, n. 1.

#*Ibid.*, I, 31.

Greece with Persia, does he begin to find in it the germ of a really ethical idea."*

"Sophocles, Herodotus, and perhaps Aeschylus also, attribute to the gods an inclination to bring ruin upon men gratuitously. They make good and bad suffer without discrimination, although such as have sinned against the gods themselves or against their fellow-creatures are more exposed to the divine wrath than others. There is, however, still another group of men, on whom the gods are supposed to visit their anger with equal predilection, namely those who are remarkable for their great riches, their power, their fame, or their happiness. Such men, said the Greeks, aroused the jealousy of the gods."†

"What man, of woman born, outwits the guile of God?" complains Aeschylus.‡ Roman poets likewise maintain that "the gods play games with men as balls."§ And Virgil speaks of "cruel Juno's unrelenting wrath."‖

In contrast, the Bible "does not reveal the ambivalence between Zeus and Prometheus of Greek tragedy. God is not unjustifiably jealous; and the defiance of God is not the tragic prerequisite of man's creativity."#

---

*W. C. Greene, *op. cit.*, p. 87. On Bacchylides, see p. 81. The doctrine of the jealousy of the gods was opposed by Plato, *Phaedrus* 247, *Timaeus* 29; Aristotle, *Metaphysics* 983a; also Aeschylus, *Agamemnon*, 750–762.

†S. Ranulf, *op. cit.*, I, 63.

‡*The Persians*, 98.

§Plautus, *The Captives*, Prologue 1, 22.

‖*Aeneid*, 1, 4.

#R. Niebuhr, *The Self and the Dramas of History* (New York, 1955), p. 80.

# The Philosophy of Pathos

## The Repudiation of the Divine Pathos

For more than two thousand years Jewish and later Christian theologians have been deeply embarrassed by the constant references in the Bible to the divine pathos. What were the reasons for that embarrassment? Why did they oppose the idea of pathos? The opposition, it seems, was due to a combination of philosophical presuppositions which have their origin in classical Greek thinking.

It will be our task to set forth these presuppositions, to examine their validity, to show that these presuppositions represent a particular philosophical perspective, and to inquire whether that perspective is the only way to truth, or whether an alternative way may not disclose a more plausible view of ultimate reality.

## The Indignity of Passivity

"The Greek had always felt the experience of passion as something mysterious and frightening, the experience of a force that was in him, possessing him, rather than possessed by him." Homer's heroes and the men of the archaic age interpreted such experience as *ate* "as the direct working of a daemon who uses the human mind and body as his instrument."* Even Xenocrates, one of the teachers of Zeno, the founder of the Stoic school, maintained that every emotion, especially that of sudden anger, is aroused by the evil spirits dwelling in the soul.†

The very word "pathos," like its Latin equivalent *passio,* from *pati* (to suffer), means a state or condition in which something happens to man, something of which it is a passive victim.‡ The term was applied to emotions such as pain or pleasure as well as to passions, since they were understood to be states of the soul aroused by something outside the self, during which time the mind is passively swayed by the emotion or passion. The person thus affected finds himself in a relation of dependence upon the agent, comparable to the relation of cause and effect. Such a state was considered a sign of weakness, since the dignity of man was seen in the activity of the mind, in acts of self-determination.

From very early times, it was felt that God could not be affected in such a way. The Deity, the Supreme Cause, could not possibly suffer from, or be affected by, something which is effected by Himself. Passivity was held to be incompatible with the dignity of the divine. It was on these grounds—the conception of a First Cause and its dignity—that pathos was rejected.

Indeed, matter *qua* matter is regarded by Aristotle as the passive principle (*pathētikon*). "It is characteristic of matter to suffer, i.e., to be moved: but to move, i.e., to act, belongs to a different power."§ The Deity is a principle whose very essence is actuality.‖ The Stoics also

---

*E. R. Dodds, *The Greeks and the Irrational* (Boston, 1957), pp. 5 ff.; 38 ff.; 185 f.; cf. Plato, *Symposium*, 202e, "Love is a great demon [*daimon*]." Euripides, *Medea*, 1079, Passion, "that cause of direst woes to mortal man. Does his own fatal passion become to each man his god?" (Virgil, *Aeneid*, IX, 185; cf. W. C. Greene, *Moira* [Cambridge, 1944], p. 101.)

†M. Pohlenz, *Vom Zorne Gottes* (Göttingen, 1909), p. 16; *idem, Die Stoa* (Göttingen, 1947), II, 77.

‡Aristotle, *Nicomachean Ethics*, 1106a, 7, "In respect of the passions we are said to be moved."

§Aristotle, *De Generatione*, 324b, 18; 335b, 29–30.

‖Aristotle, *Metaphysics*, 1071b, 19.

saw the principle of action in the Deity and the principle of passivity in matter.* Following the Stoic equation of the Deity and the active force, Philo maintains that "to act is the property of God; and this we may not ascribe to any created being; the property of the created is to suffer action."† The numerous attributes which the Bible predicates of God are reduced by him to one single attribute, that of action. In this, Philo is followed by Maimonides.

For Philo, the scriptural denial of the likeness of God to any other being implies not only the incorporeality of God, but also complete lack of emotion. Why, then, does Moses speak "of His jealousy, His wrath, His moods of anger, and the other emotions similar to them, which he describes in terms of human nature?" To this Philo replies, "He hoped to be able to eradicate the evil, namely by representing the Supreme Cause as dealing in threats and oftentimes showing indignation and implacable anger. . . . For this is the only way in which the fool can be admonished."‡ Thus Scripture describes the divine Being in human terms in order to educate man. The pedagogical interpretation of biblical anthropopathy became one of the standard solutions of the problem in Jewish and Christian literature.

## THE DISPARAGEMENT OF EMOTION

One of the major intentions in Plato's philosophy was to show that the soul is beset by a duality, having within itself a faculty which reaches upward to the divine as well as a power which pulls it downward to the contamination of the flesh. The former is identified as the rational and immortal component, and the latter as the irrational and mortal. For the soul, according to Plato, belongs both to the lower world of Becoming and to the higher realm of abiding Being. It bears in itself the traits of both worlds: the rational faculty corresponding to the world of ideas, and the irrational faculties—will and appetite—

---

*C. Baeumker, *Das Problem der Materie in der Greichischen Philosophie* (Münster, 1890), p. 331, n. 3; p. 339, n. 7.

†*De Cherubim,* XXIV, 77.

‡*Quod Deus Immutabilis Est,* XIII, 60, 68.

corresponding to the world of perception. At the close of the ninth book of the *Republic,* Plato offers a simile of man's composite nature. It is an image of a many-headed monster, a lion, and a man; the second smaller than the first, and the third smaller than the second. Combine these three into one, and you have man as he is, externally one and internally a plurality of forces. The passions in us, we are told, are like cords and strings which pull us in different and opposite ways.

Plato enumerates three faculties of the soul, namely, the appetitive, the impulsive, and the rational. The rational component of the individual soul is made by the Demiurge, whereas the irrational one is the creation of the lower gods. The former is indivisible and immortal, the latter comprises a better and a worse part: the better part manifests itself in energy, courage, and ambition; the worse part functions in desire, appetite, and nutrition.* The rational soul, which is the divine power in man, is located in the head; the heart, the impulsive soul, is the seat of emotion; while the appetitive soul with its desires and passions is relegated to the lowest part of the body—its seat is below the diaphragm. Each faculty has its own virtue, and the harmony of all is justice. Yet the supremacy must belong to reason, the charioteer of the steed, which subordinates the other faculties to its rule.

Disagreeing with Plato, Aristotle teaches the unity of the human soul. "Some say that the soul is divisible and that one part of it thinks, another desires. What is it then which holds the soul together, if naturally divisible? Assuredly, it is not the body: on the contrary, the soul seems rather to hold the body together; at any rate, when the soul is gone, the body dissolves into air and decays. If, then, the unity of soul is due to some other thing, that other thing would be, properly speaking, soul. Why not attribute unity to the soul?"† For Aristotle, as for Plato, knowledge is the highest virtue. The emotions he regards as auxiliaries or impediments to a rational form of life. None of the passions, however, are in themselves bad; they are simply natural, but in order to become ethical they require training. The ethical consists

---

*Timaeus, 35a, 69e, 72d; *Republic,* 435b ff., 438d ff., 504a ff., 580d ff.; *Laws,* 644.

†*De Anima,* I, 411b; cf. 404b, 27.

in the restraining of desire and emotion within the limits of the mean through intelligence and discipline.* Indeed, while condemning the man who is unduly passionate, Aristotle condemns equally the man who is insensitive. Neither the virtues nor the vices are passions, and we are neither praised nor blamed for our passion.†

The dualism of the soul was also denied by Strato, the Stoics, and the Epicureans. Strato regarded the soul as a single force diffused through the body.‡ The Stoics asserted the complete homogeneity of the soul. Reason, they maintained, is the primary power, of which all other faculties are parts or derivations.§ The Epicureans, on the other hand, taught that the soul is corporeal; it is a body and part of the body; there is a real unity between body and soul.‖

However, one aspect of the Platonic conception became the prevalent view of subsequent schools of thought and was further developed by the Stoics. It is the view that regards the human soul as a house of two floors, with reason dwelling upstairs, and the emotions downstairs. The two tenants have separate ways and different manners. Reason is dissociated from the emotional life and sharply contrasted with it. Emotions belong to the animal nature in man, reason to the divine in man. Emotions are unruly, fleshy, the source of evil and disaster; reason is order, light, and the power that raises man above the level of the animal.

It was such preference that enabled Greek philosophy to exclude all emotion from the nature of the Deity, while at the same time

---

* *Nicomachean Ethics,* 1108a, 30; cf. 1104b, 24. "It is not possible to perform virtuous acts without pain or pleasure . . . because virtue implies feeling, and feeling pain or pleasure. . . . Virtue is attended either with pain or with pleasure. Now if one does the right with pain, he is not good. So that virtue will not be attended with pain. Therefore with pleasure. Not only, then, is pleasure not an impediment, but it is actually an incentive to action, and generally virtue cannot be without the pleasure that comes from it." (*Magna Moralia,* II, 7, 1206a, 17 ff.)

† *Nicomachean Ethics,* 1105b, 29 ff.

‡ H. Siebeck, *Geschichte der Psychologie,* II, 165; E. Zeller, *Die Philosophie der Greichen,* II (Leipzig, 1919–20), 466.

§ M. Pohlenz, *Die Stoa,* I, 90 f., 226.

‖ G. S. Brett, *A History of Psychology,* I (London, 1912), 183; Diogenes Laertius, *Lives of Eminent Philosophers,* X, 63.

ascribing thought and contemplation to it. To Xenophanes, God set all things in motion by the power of His thought alone.* Empedocles speaks of God as "a holy and unutterable mind, darting through the whole cosmos with its swift thoughts."† He is the supreme *nous* or the Mind of the cosmos, in the language of Anaxagoras and others. And to Plato, God is *nous,* the essence of His being is thinking.‡ He is above joy and sorrow.§

The perfect example of an impassive deity is the God of Aristotle. By identifying the Deity with the First Cause, with something which, while it has the capacity of moving all things, is itself unmoved, Aristotle's Deity has no pathos, no needs. Ever resting in itself, its only activity is thinking, and its thinking is thinking of thinking. Indifferent to all things, it does not care to contemplate anything but itself. Things long for it and thus are set in motion, yet they are left to themselves.

Thus, virtues cannot be ascribed to the Deity—not even acts of justice. The circumstances of action are trivial and unworthy of God. "Still, every one supposes that they live and therefore that they are active; we cannot suppose them to sleep like Endymion. Now if you take away from a living being action, and still more production, what is left but contemplation? Therefore the activity of God, which surpasses all others in blessedness, must be contemplative."‖

Carneades used similar arguments in order to demonstrate that God cannot be thought of as a living, rational Being without attributing to Him qualities that are incompatible with His nature. If God is infinite, He cannot be thought of as possessing the qualities and living the life of a personal being, for it is impossible to apply the attributes of personal existence to God without limiting His nature. The same

---

*H Diels, *Die Fragmente der Vorsokratiker* (3rd ed.; Berlin, 1912), fragment 26. Cf. in contrast: "By the word of the Lord the Heavens were made . . . for He spoke, and it came to be; He commanded, and it stood forth" (Ps. 33.6, 9).

†Diels, *op. cit.,* fragment 134.

‡*Philebus,* 22c, 28c, *Phaedrus,* 247d f.

§*Philebus,* 33b; *Republic,* II, 377e ff.

‖*Nicomachean Ethics,* 1178b, 7 ff. See Ch. Hartshorne and W. L. Reese, *Philosophers Speak of God* (Chicago, 1953), pp. 58 ff. On the conception of God as pure thought in medieval Jewish philosophy, see Jul. Guttmann, *Die Philosophie des Judentums* (München, 1933), pp. 184, 222, 226, and 356 n.

contradiction is involved in regarding Him as a living Being, for every living being is composite, having parts and passions, and is hence destructible. For similar reason we can ascribe to Him neither virtue nor intelligence. The assumption of feeling in God is incompatible with the idea of divinity.*

Jewish scholasticism of the Middle Ages agreed with the philosophers on the impossibility of ascribing to God any human qualities in the literal sense. Even Judah Halevi maintains that mercy and compassion are in truth signs of "a weakness of the soul and irritability of nature, and cannot therefore be applied to God. He is a just judge; He ordains the poverty of one individual and the wealth of another without any change in His nature, without feelings of sympathy with one or anger against another."†

According to Maimonides, any predicate that implies corporeality or passibility must not be applied to God. For all passibility implies change; the agent producing that change cannot be the same as the one who is affected by the change, and if God could be affected in any way whatever, this would imply that another being beside Him would act on Him and cause change in Him. Maimonides, accepting the Stoic view that "all passion is evil," interprets the statements of the Bible regarding God which in their literal sense predicate certain qualities of Him as not describing characteristics of His essence, but as human ways of understanding His works. Thus when He is called compassionate, this does not mean that He feels compassion, but that He works deeds in regard to His creatures similar to those which with us would proceed from the feeling of compassion.‡ The same principle holds true of the terms "pain" or "sorrow" when applied to God.§ Love alone, according to Crescas, can be attributed to God, and just as man ought to love God, God loves man.‖

---

*E. Zeller, *The Stoics, Epicureans, and Sceptics* (London, 1870), pp. 515–518; R. Richter, *Der Skeptizismus in der Philosophie,* I (Leipzig, 1904), 85 ff.; Ueberweg-Praechter, *Grundriss der Geschichte der Philosophie der Altertums* (Berlin, 1920), p. 611. M. M. Patrick, *The Greek Sceptics* (New York, 1929), pp. 170 f.

†*Kuzari*, II, a.

‡*The Guide of the Perplexed*, I, 54–55.

§*Ibid.*, I, 29.

‖*Ibid.*, II, vi, 1.

As a corollary of his proposition that "God is free from passions, nor is He affected with any emotion of pleasure and pain," Spinoza maintains that "strictly speaking, God does not love or hate. God loves no one and hates no one."\* Therefore, if we love God, we cannot desire Him to return our love, for then He would lose His perfection by becoming passively affected by our joys and sorrows.

## PATHOS AND APATHY

The Stoics regarded passion, impulse, desire—the emotions in the widest sense—as unreasonable, unnatural, and the source of evil. To live rightly was to dominate the emotional life by reason, and so to act by will. Pathos was considered to be the chief danger to the self-determination of man, whereas "apathy"—the subduing of the emotions—was believed to be the supreme moral task.

The doctrine of *apatheia,* the great ideal of the Stoic school, seems to have been known at an earlier date. Opposition to this extreme doctrine is expressed by Plato: "I want to know whether anyone of us would consent to live, having wisdom and mind and knowledge and memory of all things but having no sense of pleasure and pain and wholly unaffected by these and the like feelings?"†

There are tendencies toward the ideal of *apatheia* in the Cynic school. But it was Zeno, the founder of the Stoa, who demanded of the sage complete freedom from the emotions. Wisdom is shown in the relation which man maintains to his passions. His overcoming of the world is his overcoming of his own impulses.

Zeno defined pathos as "a movement in the soul contrary to

---

\* *Ethics,* V, prop. XVII. See H. A. Wolfson, *Spinoza* (Cambridge, Mass., 1934), pp. 285 f. Otto von der Pfordten, *Religionsphilosophie* (Berlin, 1917), p. 100, maintains mistakenly that a wise instinct of the religious man has always prevented him from using feeling—a specifically human element—in shaping the idea of God. "The prophets in their visions preach an anthropomorphism, which, since it is not in the least likely that they themselves entertained such crude conceptions of the Deity, or that the imagination played them such gross tricks, clearly has the character of deliberate invention" (Redslob, *Der Begriff des Nabi,* [Leipzig, 1839]).

† *Philebus,* 21d, 60e, 63e.

reason and to the soul's very nature."* Whereas Zeno assumed the existence of a nonrational faculty or part of the human soul, from which pathos is derived, Chrysippus denied the existence of any such part. There is only reason in the soul, and nothing else. Pathos is due to an error in judgment, to a false notion of good and evil, for in a state of passion everything is judged from a limited perspective. The craving for money, for example, is essentially the notion that money is desirable. Such radical intellectualism supplied a psychological basis for the Socratic view that virtue is knowledge.† Upsetting the harmony of the soul and the self-determination of the mind, emotions and passions are disturbances of mental health, and if indulged in, become chronic diseases of the soul.‡

Chrysippus denied the contention of the Peripatetics that the emotions—anger or compassion, for example—are a necessary part of the life of the soul, which, if kept within proper limits, are an aid to right living. The knowledge of virtue, he claimed, is perfectly sufficient without the aid of emotion. Moreover, the suggestion that emotions be kept within proper limits overlooks the very essence of emotions, namely, that they know no limits. It is not enough to control them. They must be completely eradicated,§ for it is easier to destroy them than to keep them in check.‖ True virtue can exist only where emotions are no more. The wise man must strive to attain *apatheia*, the complete freedom from emotions.# He must be emotionless, never yielding to anger, never knowing fear or pity.**

---

*J. Arnim, ed., *Stoicorum Veterum Fragmenta* (Leipzig, 1903–1924), pp. 205–206. Diogenes Laertius, *Lives of Eminent Philosophers*, VII, 110.

†M. Pohlenz, *Die Stoa*, I, 92, 143 f.

‡Diogenes Laertius, *op. cit.*, VII, 115; Cicero, *Tusculan Disputations*, IV, 10, 23. Cf. E. Zeller, *The Stoics, Epicureans and Sceptics*, p. 235, n. 2.

§Seneca, *Epistolae* 116, 1.

‖Seneca, *De Ira* 1, 7, 2.

#Epictetus, *Discourses*, III, 62. Sextus Empiricus, *Outlines of Pyrrhonism*, III, 235. Diogenes Laertius, *op. cit.*, VII, 117. Unlike Pyrrho, to whom *apatheia* means insensitivity to the impressions of the outside world, the Stoics maintain that the wise man does at first react emotionally, when witnessing a crime, for example. (M. Pohlenz, *Die Stoa*, p. 152; on Posidonius and Seneca, see pp. 224–226, 307–309.)

**Cicero, *Tusculan Disputations*, III, 9, 20. Seneca, *De Clementia*, II, 5.

The post-Aristotelian schools, the Epicureans, Skeptics, and Stoics, agreed that happiness is entirely a state of mind, regardless of conditions and events outside the person, and that the only happiness consists of *ataraxia*, of mental imperturbability, or peace of mind. *Ataraxia* may be secured by avoiding all disturbances, those which are due to external causes and those which arise from within, namely, the emotions. The wise man must strive for both *apatheia* (absence of feeling and passion; indifference to what appeals to feelings and interest) and *autarkeia* (independence, self-sufficiency). By achieving self-sufficiency, by withdrawing within himself, he becomes immune to external circumstances and will be unaffected by the course of events around him. For wrong opinions and prejudices to which passions are due arise from one's dependence upon external things. By attaining *apatheia* the wise man has eradicated the emotions.

The classical ideal of the Greeks was the achievement of inner harmony in personal existence. It contains the demand that reason shall control impulses. This is why *sophrosyne*, the power of self-control gained by resisting immediate pleasure, was regarded as the cardinal virtue. As mentioned above, Zeno in his doctrine of *apatheia* set up as an ethical postulate the complete effacement of emotion and passion. Other schools, while opposed to this radical view, granted nevertheless that the root of evil is to be found in the irrational acts of the soul.*

The dualistic conception of the soul prevailed throughout the ages, and has deeply penetrated Western thinking.† To the degree that

---

*W. H. S. Jones, *Greek Morality* (London, 1906), pp. 26, 59 ff.; A. Bonhoeffer, *Epiktet und das Neue Testament* (Giessen, 1911), pp. 164 ff.; R. Bultmann, *Zeitschrift für die neutestamentliche Wissenschaft* (1912), p. 97; R. Hirzel, *Themis, Dike* (Leipzig, 1907), pp. 25 ff. "It was with reluctance and with fear that the Greeks learned the value of the higher meaning of pity. . . . The Homeric heroes feared it; Agamemnon bitterly reproached his brother for feeling it; and Achilles asked the spirit of his friend Patroclus to forgive him for yielding to it. The heroes had the primitive and savage dread of pity that Nietzsche expresses when he says: Pity is opposed to the tonic emotions that heighten the energy of life-consciousness, *Lebensgefühl*." (G. H. Macurdy, *The Quality of Mercy* [New Haven, 1940], p. xi.)

†On Neoplatonism, see J. Kroll, *Hermes Trismegistos* (Münster, 1938), pp. 276 ff.

theology has subscribed to this dualism of values, it has attributed to God the power of thinking, but has excluded the realm of emotion. What is postulated for man must be fulfilled in God. *Apathēs to theion* becomes a fundamental principle in the doctrine of God for both Jewish and Christian theologians. Since the passions are unnatural disturbances in man, *a fortiori* they could not exist in God.

## APATHY IN THE MORAL THEORY OF THE WEST

Plato's dualistic conception of the soul and particularly the Stoic disparagement of emotion have deeply influenced the moral and religious thinking of subsequent generations. Morality has often been equated with the suppression of passion, with the control of desire by reason. Passion and vice, emotion and weakness, have frequently been called synonymous. And there seems to be a tacit assumption that reason and ruthlessness, knowledge and evil, are mutually exclusive.

No other system in the history of moral philosophy has had such a lasting impact as the ethical ideas of the Stoics.* Jewish and Christian morality have shown a tendency to coalesce with the Stoic ideal. *Apatheia* has often been a guiding star in the moral search, both in Christian and in secular ethics. According to Clement of Alexandria, to be entirely free from passion is to be most like God Who is impassible. The perfect man, he says, is above all affections: courage, fear, cheerfulness, anger, envy, love for the creature. Clement's doctrine of *apatheia* contributed to the shaping of the Christian ideal of life.† The saint is regarded as a person who has extirpated his passions. Even Descartes regards the emotions and passions as a disturbance of the mind (*perturbationes animi*). Since in such perturbations the mind remains passive, one must strive to free the mind from such states through clear and distinct knowledge.‡

---

*W. Dilthey, *Gesammelte Schriften,* II (Leipzig and Berlin, 1914), 47. Cf. J. Macmurray, *Reason and Emotion* (New York, 1938), pp. 123 ff.

†Cf. T. Rüther, *Die sittliche Forderung der Apatheia ("Freiburger Theologische Studien,"* 63), 1949.

‡R. Falckenberg, *Geschichte der neueren Philosophie* (Berlin, 1927), pp. 89 ff.

The same Stoic ideal is taught by Spinoza, who defines emotions as "confused ideas," and to whom the overcoming of the passions is accomplished by a knowledge of them, by an understanding of the necessary system of all things. The fourth book of his *Ethics* is entitled "Of Human Bondage, or of the Strength of the Emotions."*

Kant sought to exclude impulse and inclination from the moral life. Duty must be done for duty's sake, out of respect for the law, and never from inclination or passion. Passions cause cancerous harm to the pure practical reason; they are, without exception, evil.† "The principle of apathy," says Kant, "according to which the wise man must never succumb to emotion, not even to that of sympathy for the evils that befall his best friend, is a correct and sublime moral principle of the Stoic school, for emotion makes a person [more or less] blind."‡

Kant's view was challenged by Hegel, who pointed out that "impulse and passion are the very life-blood of all action. . . . We may affirm absolutely that nothing great has been accomplished without passion." Kant's false and abstract view, he claims, is based upon the separation of the mind into independent "faculties." The "practical reason," the "categorical imperative," are here on the one side; the impulses and inclinations are over against these on the other side, usually warring against the practical reason, but in any case quite independent of it. But as soon as it is seen that these very impulses have the "practical reason" implicit in them, are themselves only an inchoate and undeveloped form of it, such an abstract view becomes impossible.§

## REASON AND EMOTION

We have been trained to draw a sharp contrast between reason and emotion. The first is pure spontaneity, the drawing of inferences,

*See W. Dilthey, *op. cit.,* II, 285 ff.
†*Anthropologie,* I, 81.
‡*Ibid.,* I, 75; cf. *Critique of Judgment,* par. 29.
§Hegel, *Philosophy of History,* Introduction.

the ordering of concepts according to the canons of logic. Emotion, on the other hand, is pure receptivity, an impression involving neither cognition nor representation of the object. such a contrast, however, is hardly tenable when applied to religious existence. Is religious thinking ever to be completely separated from the stream of emotion that surges beneath it? Religious reason is more than just thinking, and religious emotion is more than just feeling. In religious existence, spontaneity and receptivity involve each other. Is there no reason in the emotional life?

True, if emotion is unreasonable, it tends to distort a person's thinking. But emotion can be reasonable just as reason can be emotional, and there is no need to suppress the emotional roots of one's life in order to save the integrity of one's principles. Receptivity and spontaneity involve each other; the separation of the two is harmful to both.

Reason may be defined as the capacity for objectivity or as a person's ability to think in impersonal terms. To think in personal terms, or subjectively, is to be exposed to bias and error. In the light of such a definition we would have to exclude reason from the nature of God, Whose Person is the truth, and ascribe only emotion to Him. Impersonal reasoning in God would mean an operation in ideas devoid of divinity. Furthermore, pure reason comprehends a concrete fact as if it were an abstraction, a particular being in terms of a generalization. But it is the greatness of God according to the Bible that man is not an abstraction to Him, nor is His judgment a generalization. Yet in order to realize a human being not as a generality but as a concrete fact, one must feel him, one must become aware of him emotionally.

Is it more compatible with our conception of the grandeur of God to claim that He is emotionally blind to the misery of man rather than profoundly moved? In order to conceive of God not as an onlooker but as a participant, to conceive of man not as an idea in the mind of God but as a concern, the category of divine pathos is an indispensable implication. To the biblical mind the conception of God as detached and unemotional is totally alien.

## EMOTION IN THE BIBLE

The ideas that dominate the Hellenistic understanding of the emotional life of man must not affect our understanding of Hebrew thinking. The Bible knows neither the dichotomy of body and soul nor the trichotomy of body, soul, and spirit, nor the trichotomy within the soul. It sets up no hierarchy in the inner life, nor does it tend to compartmentalize the soul. The heart, regarded as "the totality of the soul as a character and operating function,"* is the seat of all inner functions, of knowledge as well as of emotion. To put it in different terms: the mind is not a member apart, but is itself transformed into passion. For the two "do not dwell separate and distinct, but passion and reason are only the transformation of the mind toward the better or the worse."† Nor does the Bible share the view that passions are disturbances or weaknesses of the soul,‡ and much less the premise that passion itself is evil, that passion as such is incompatible with right thinking or right living.

Neither in the legal nor in the prophetic writings is there a suggestion that the desires and passions are to be negated. Asceticism was not the ideal of the biblical man. The source of evil is not in passion,

---

*J. Pedersen, *Israel*, I–II (London and Copenhagen, 1926), 104.
†Lactantius, *De Ira Dei*, I, 8, 3.
‡Contrary to the view of the Stoics that the passions were not grounded in nature, but were due to wrong thinking and could and should be extirpated, the author of IV Macc. maintains that the passions were implanted in man by God and are not to be extirpated but controlled (2:21–23). The theme of the book is that reason, which is the culture acquired under the law of Moses (1:17), should be the supreme master over the passions. "Reason," the author says, "is not the extirpator of the passions but their antagonist" (3:5; cf. 1:6). Cf. Sirach 6:2 (in the translation of Box and Oesterley): "Be not a slave to thy passions, lest they consume thy strength like a bull." The reference, as the context shows, is to impure passions; see note in R. H. Charles, *The Apocrypha and Pseudepigrapha of the Old Testament*, I (Oxford, 1913), 333; *Aboth* IV, 1; *Aboth de Rabbi Nathan* A, 23. Philo engaged Moses and Aaron in a debate on the question whether virtue implies control of one's emotions or their complete extirpation, with Aaron the exponent of the Aristotelian view, and Moses representing the Stoic view. He considers complete eradication of emotion to be possible only for rare individuals like Moses; for the majority of mankind moderation of emotions is the goal. (*Legum Allegoria*, III, XLIV, 128 f.; XVI, 136; see H. A. Wolfson, *Philo* II (Cambridge, Mass., 1947), 274 f.

in the throbbing heart, but rather in hardness of heart, in callousness and insensitivity. (See p. 243.) Far from insisting upon their effacement, the biblical writers frequently regarded some emotions or passions as having been inspired, as reflections of a higher power. There is no disparagement of emotion, no celebration of apathy. Pathos, emotional involvement, passionate participation, is a part of religious existence. The utterances of the psalmist are charged with emotion, are outpourings of emotion. Reading the prophets, we are stirred by their passion and enlivened imagination. Their primary aim is to move the soul, to engage the attention by bold and striking images, and therefore it is to the imagination and the passions that the prophets speak, rather than aiming at the cold approbation of the mind.

The ideal state of the Stoic sage is apathy, the ideal state of the prophet is sympathy. The Greeks attributed to the gods the state of happiness and serenity; the prophets thought of God's relation to the world as one of concern and compassion. To quote Nietzsche, "The dignity of death and a kind of consecration of passion has perhaps never yet been represented more beautifully . . . than by certain Jews of the Old Testament: to these even the Greeks could have gone to school."*

Awe and fear of the Lord (*yirath hashem*) is for the Jew what *sōphrosynē* is for the Greek, and *bhakti* is for the Indian. "Awe and fear of the Lord is the beginning of wisdom," says the psalmist (111:10). The characterization of passion as a state of passivity would hardly be consonant with biblical experience.† Passion was regarded as a motive power, a spring, and an incentive. Great deeds are done by those who are filled with *ruah*, with pathos.

In the light of such affirmation, with no stigma attached to pathos, there was no reason to shun the idea of pathos in the understanding of God. Pathos implied no inner bondage, no enslavement to impulse, no subjugation by passion, but a willed, transitive feeling

---

* *Gesammelte Werke* (Musarion edition), XVI, 373.

† "Feelings are not characterized with the passivity which we instinctively attribute to the emotions of the heart. With the Israelites the heart is the soul, being the organ which at the same time feels and acts." (J. Pedersen, *op. cit.*, I–II, 104.)

which existed only in relation to man. An apathetic and ascetic God would have struck biblical man with a sense, not of dignity and grandeur, but rather of poverty and emptiness. Only through arbitrary allegorizing was later religious philosophy able to find an apathetic God in the Bible.

Impressive as is the thought that God is too sublime to be affected by events on this insignificant planet, it stems from a line of reasoning about a God derived from abstraction. A God of abstraction is a high and mighty First Cause, which, dwelling in the lonely splendor of eternity, will never be open to human prayer; and to be affected by anything which it has itself caused to come into being would be beneath the dignity of an abstract God. This is a dogmatic sort of dignity, insisting upon pride rather than love, upon decorum rather than mercy.

In contrast with the *primum movens immobile,* the God of the prophets cares for His creatures, and His thoughts are about the world. He is involved in human history and is affected by human acts. It is a paradox beyond compare that the Eternal God is concerned with what is happening in time.

> *For thus says the high and lofty One*
> *Who inhabits eternity, Whose name is Holy:*
> *I dwell in the high and holy place,*
> *And also with him who is of a contrite and humble spirit,*
> *To revive the spirit of the humble,*
> *To revive the heart of the contrite.*
>
> Isaiah 57:15

The grandeur of God implies the capacity to experience emotion. In the biblical outlook, movements of feeling are no less spiritual than acts of thought.

## ANTHROPOLOGICAL SIGNIFICANCE

The idea of divine pathos has also anthropological significance. It is man's being relevant to God. To the biblical mind the denial of man's relevance to God is as inconceivable as the denial of God's relevance to man. This principle leads to the basic affirmation of God's participation in human history, to the certainty that the events in the world concern Him and arouse His reaction. It finds its deepest expression in the fact that God can actually suffer. At the heart of the prophetic affirmation is the certainty that God is concerned about the world.

Beyond these implications for the meaning of history and human deeds, the idea of pathos reflects a high estimation of human nature. The consciousness of the high dignity and sanctity of man, his soul and body alike, accounts for the extreme development of anthropomorphic views in Jewish and Christian tradition, as the rejection of such consciousness played a part in the radical opposition to anthropomorphism. (See p. 291.)

The *analogia entis* as applied to man having been created in the likeness of God and as expressed in the commandment, "You shall be holy, for I the Lord your God am holy" (Lev. 19:2), points to what may be called a *theomorphic anthropology*. Soul, thought, feeling, even passion, are often regarded as states imbued by God. It is perhaps more proper to describe a prophetic passion as theomorphic than to regard the divine pathos as anthropomorphic.

## THE ONTOLOGICAL PRESUPPOSITION

Pathos denotes a change in the inner life, something that happens rather than an abiding condition. Since to the Greek philosophers the Deity was immutable, remaining absolutely and forever in its own form,* it could not be susceptible of pathos, which would contradict the transcendence, independence, and absoluteness of the Supreme Being. Indeed, to attribute any pathos to God, to assert that He is affected by the conduct of those He has brought into being, is to reject the conception of Him as the Absolute. Pathos is a movement from one state to another, an alteration or change, and as such

---

*Plato, *Republic*, II, 381.

is incompatible with the conception of a Supreme Being Who is both unmoved and unchangeable.

The static idea of divinity is the outcome of two strands of thought: the ontological notion of stability and the psychological view of emotions as disturbances of the soul. Having analyzed the psychological view, we shall now examine the ontological notion.

The idea of divine immobility seems to have originated in Xenophanes. In Homer, the gods' quickness of movement is regarded as a special sign of divine power. Xenophanes, however, insists that omnipotence implies repose, absolute calm, and immobility. "But effortlessly he sets everything in motion, by the power of his mind alone, and he always remains in the same place, not moving at all, nor is it fitting for him to change his position at different times."* Yet it was in the speculation of Parmenides of Elea (*ca.* 515–449 B.C.E.), who was perhaps a disciple of Xenophanes, that the idea of immobility gained decisive importance.

Parmenides, insisting upon the sharp alternatives of being and not-being, taught that being is, whereas not-being cannot be, nor can it be conceived of or uttered. Being, he maintained, cannot be many. It must rather be one alone; for anything manifold is subject to change and motion, and this would be contrary to the persistence that is essential to the very nature of being. Thus there are no *onta* in plural (things that are present or given), but only a single *on* (Existent, that which is)—being "unborn and imperishable, complete, immovable and without end; nor was it ever, nor will it be; but now it *is*; all at once; a continuous one."†

Parmenides stressed the concept of being to the exclusion of becoming, affirming that generation, multiplicity, change, and movement are illusory. His thought is an attempt "to strip reality of its character as a world by removing every feature that goes to make it a world at all."‡

---

*Diels, *op. cit.*, fragments 25, 26; cf. K. Freeman, *Ancilla to the Pre-Socratic Philosophers* (Oxford, 1952), p. 23.

†Diels, *op. cit.*, fragment 8; cf. K. Freeman, *op. cit.* pp. 43 f.

‡W. Jaeger, *The Theology of the Early Greek Philosophers* (Oxford, 1947), see F. M. Cornford, *Plato and Parmenides* (London, 1930), p. 36.

Zeno, a disciple of Parmenides, developed the famous arguments against the reality of movement. Immobility, changelessness, and intranscience hang together.

In contrast to the Eleatic school, Heraclitus taught: "Everything flows and nothing abides; everything gives way and nothing stays fixed." What appears to be permanent is simply an example of change in slow motion. Change, becoming, tension are essential to existence. If strife were to perish, then all things would cease to exist. Even deity is no exception. Particular gods and demigods will eventually be transformed from gods into something else.*

Almost all of Greek philosophy after Parmenides was an effort to reconcile the two points of view.† The solution that prevailed agreed with Parmenides that being, in the true sense of the word, is uncreated, indestructible, and changeless, and that becoming is the combination and separation of those eternal and changeless elements of being. There is no creation out of nothing, and no dissolution into nothing; the elements merely unite and fall asunder.‡

Plato restricted Heraclitus' theory of the eternal flux of all things to the world of sense perception, while in the realm of ideas he found Parmenides' true being. He never wearies of insisting that the objects of true knowledge, the ideas, are changeless and eternal like the being of Parmenides. The idea is that which "always is" and "never becomes"; it is "ever immutably the same."§ Aristotle, too, maintains that true being is incompatible with any change or movement, and he describes substance as that which is "eternal and immovable . . . impassive and unalterable."‖

Parmenides has been characterized as "a tinker who knows no other desire than knowledge, feels no other manacle than logic, and is left indifferent by God and by feeling." For Parmenides and his

---

*Diels, *op. cit.*, fragments 20, 27, 66; cf. P. Wheelwright, *Heraclitus* (Princeton, 1959), pp. 30–34.

†See J. Adams, *The Religious Teachers of Greece* (Edinburgh, 1909), p. 244.

‡*Cratylus*, 402a; cf. Aristotle, *Metaphysics*, 987a, 34 ff.

§*Metaphysics*, 1073a, 11.

‖K. Reinhardt, *Parmenides und die Geschichte der Griechischen Philosophie* (Bonn, 1916), p. 256.

successors in the Eleatic school, the concept of God disappears in the concept of being. Polytheism and monotheism are alike excluded.\*

Thus, while Parmenides did not explicitly identify being with God, his theory of absolute being and its predicates was again and again adopted as a basis for philosophical theology. Most speculation on the nature of God held unchangeableness to be an essential attribute.

The principle that change is incompatible with true being has led to what Sextus Empiricus called "the dogma of the philosophers that the Deity is impassible."† Indeed, as a corollary of Eleatic ontology a static view of the Deity has become the common property of most philosophers.‡ Rest and immobility are regarded as the typical features of divine preeminence. The Deity is thought of as a Being who abides in absolute calm.§

The Eleatic premise that true being is unchangeable and that change implies corruption is valid only in regard to being as reflected in the mind. Being in reality, being as we encounter it, implies movement. If we think of being as something beyond and detached from beings, we may well arrive at an Eleatic notion. An ontology, however, concerned with being as involved in all beings or as the source of all beings, will find it impossible to separate being from action or movement, and thus postulate a dynamic concept of divine Being.‖

To Jewish and Christian scholastics of the Middle Ages, divine perfection implies absolute immutability. To Thomas Aquinas, God is *actus purus*, without the admixture of any potentiality.⁑ Everything which is in any way changed is in some way in potentiality. Hence it is evident that it is impossible for God to change in any way. Passion, being a change, would be incompatible with His true Being.

\*See J. Adams, *op. cit.*, pp. 206, 244.
† *Outlines of Pyrrhonism*, I, 162.
‡ Augustine, *Confessions*, VII, 11; XII, 15.
§ We do not include the Stoics.
‖ "Wisdom is more mobile than any motion," says the author of the Wisdom of Solomon (7:24), to whom Wisdom, an intermediary between the Deity and the world, possesses all the attributes of the Deity.
⁑ *Summa Theologica*, I, 8, 1; 20, 1.

## The Ontocentric Predicament

The Greek concept of being represents a sharp antithesis to the fundamental categories of biblical thinking. Parmenides maintains, "Being has no coming-into-being. . . . For how couldst thou find a birth for it? How and whence could it have sprung? I shall not let thee say or think it came from that which is not, for that which is not can neither be thought or uttered. And what need could have stirred it up out of nothing, to arise later rather than sooner? Hence it must either be altogether or not at all."

But is being to be taken as the ultimate theme of thinking? The fact that there is being at all is as puzzling as the question of the origin of being. Any ontology that disregards the wonder and mystery of being is guilty of suppressing the genuine amazement of the mind, and of taking being for granted. It is true that being's coming-into-being "can neither be thought nor uttered." Yet a fact does not cease to be fact because of its transcending the limits of thought and expression. Indeed, the very theme of ontology, being *as* being, "can neither be thought nor uttered."

The acceptance of the ultimacy of being is a *petitio principii;* it mistakes a problem for a solution. The supreme and ultimate issue is not *being* but the *mystery of being.* Why is there being at all instead of nothing? We can never think of any being without conceiving the possibility of its not being. We are always exposed to the presence as well as to the absence of being. Thus what we face is a pair of concepts rather than one ultimate concept. Both concepts are transcended by the mystery of being.

The biblical man does not begin with being, but with the surprise of being. The biblical man is free of what may be called the ontocentric predicament. Being is not *all* to him. He is not enchanted by the given, granting the alternative, namely the annihilation of the given. To Parmenides, not-being is inconceivable ("nothingness is not possible"); to the biblical mind, nothingness or the end of being is not impossible. Realizing the contingency of being, it could never identify being with ultimate reality. Being is neither self-evident nor self-explanatory. Being points to the question of how being is possible. The act of bringing being into being, creation, stands higher in the ladder of problems than being. Creation is not a transparent concept. But is the concept of being as being distinguished by lucidity? Creation is a mystery; being as being an abstraction.

Theology dares to go behind being in asking about the source of being. It is true that the concept of that source implies being, yet it is also true that a Being that calls a reality into being is endowed with the kind of being that transcends mysteriously all conceivable being. Thus, while ontology asks about *being as being,* theology asks about *being as creation,* about being as a divine act. From the perspective of continuous creation, there is no being as being; there is only continuous coming-into-being. Being is both action and event.

For the Greek philosophers the natural world was the starting point of speculation. The goal was to develop the idea of a supreme principle—Anaximander's *apeiron* (the Boundless), the *ens perfectissimum* of Aristotle, the world-forming fire of the Stoics—of which they then asserted, "this must be the divine." The words "the divine" as applied to the first principle, current since the time of Anaximander, and "of epoch-making importance to Greek Philosophy,"* illustrates a procedure adopted by philosophers in subsequent ages. It is always a principle first, to which qualities of personal existence are subsequently attributed. Such attribution represents a concession either to one's personal religiosity or to popular religious beliefs. It is a God whose personality is derivative; an adjective transformed into a noun.

To Greek philosophy, being is the ultimate; to the Bible, God is the ultimate. There, the starting point of speculation is ontology; in the Bible, the starting point of thinking is God. Ontology maintains that being is the supreme concept. It asks about being as being. Theology finds it impossible to regard being as the supreme concept.

Biblical ontology does not separate being from doing. What *is,* acts. The God of Israel is a God who acts, a God of mighty deeds. The Bible does not say how He is, but how He acts. It speaks of His

*W. Jaeger, *op. cit.,* p. 31; p. 203, n. 44.

acts of pathos and of His acts in history; it is not as "true being" that God is conceived, but as the *semper agens*. Here the basic category is action rather than immobility. Movement, creation of nature, acts within history rather than absolute transcendence and detachment from the events of history, are the attributes of the Supreme Being.

In the intellectual climate in which this ontology developed, there was no place for the lasting significance of unique, incomparable events. Greek speculation was concerned with the cosmos, not with history, which as the sphere of contingency and change was not a proper theme for philosophy.

The prophets, on the other hand, were preoccupied with history, deeply conscious of the lasting significance of unique events, such as deliverance from Egypt, the theophany at Sinai, the conquest of the land. The call for a change in the sphere of history, for a change in the very nature of man, is the burden of their exhortation. Indeed, the very act of inspiration was a unique event.

It is of extreme importance that theology should endeavor to operate with categories indigenous to the insights of depth-theology instead of borrowing its categories from speculative philosophy or science. What is regarded as the ultimate in philosophy must not be regarded as the ultimate in theology. What man thinks or what man says is the ultimate theme of philosophical analysis. To theology, the ultimate theme is that which man is unable to objectify, which he refuses to conceptualize.

Philosophy objectifies its themes. Imagination creates an image, reason coins a concept. All conceptualization is limitation, restriction, reduction. In the question, What is the cause of being? the ultimate has been restricted to one aspect, to one category. "Cause" is one concept among many; "what" does not mean "who." There is an anticipation of a "who" in the question of religion, as there is an anticipation of a "what" in the question of speculation. Historically, we are told, the idea of God as a purely transcendent Being, a Cause or Author of the universe, entirely distinct from an effect which is spoken of metaphorically as the work of His hands carries us back to a primitive stage of pictorial thought like that of the Zulus, mentioned by Tylor, who trace their ancestry back to Unkulunkulu, the Old-old-one, who created the world. It meets us with something of a sublime simplicity in the opening words of Genesis: "In the beginning God created the heaven and the earth." Such a statement yields a temporary satisfaction to the craving for causal explanation, though it is not necessary to go beyond the child's question, "Who made God?" to become aware of its metaphysical insufficiency. As has been not unjustly said, "Contentment with regress to a God-creator or some similar notion is the true mark of speculative indolence."*

This argumentation rests upon the assumption that to the biblical mind the supreme question is, "Who made the world?" and that the essential idea of creation is the answer, "God made it." However, the Bible does not begin by saying, "God created heaven and earth"; it begins by saying, *"In the beginning."* The essential message is not that the world had a cause, but rather that the world is not the ultimate. The phrase "in the beginning" is decisive. It sets a limit to being, as it sets a limit to the mind.

The supreme question is not, "Who made the world?" but rather, "Who transcends the world?" The biblical answer is, "He Who created heaven and earth transcends the world."

It is not "the finitude of being which drives us to the question of God," but the grandeur and mystery of all being. There is no stigma in being a finite creature. Finitude is our excuse rather than our shame. We could not bear being infinite. There is a stigma in being reckless, in forgetting that we are finite, in behaving as if we were infinite.

God is a presupposition as well as a conclusion. He cannot be derived from premises, since the concept of God is not implied in any other concept. A presupposition is either arbitrary or valid. But this very distinction between true and false concerning a Being beyond

*A. S. Pringle-Pattison, *The Idea of God* (New York, 1917), p. 298.

our grasp assumes the validity of such a distinction regardless of our own predilection. But such an assumption would be absurd without a regard for truth outside man.

God is the climax if He is also the basis. You cannot find Him in the answer if you ignore Him in the question.

In asking about God, we examine our own selves: whether we are sensitive to the grandeur and supremacy of what we ask about, whether we are wholeheartedly concerned with what we ask about. Unless we are involved, we fail to sense the issue.

## THE LOGICAL PRESUPPOSITION

The idea of the unity of the Supreme Being has played an important part in the philosophical reflections about divinity since the time of Xenophanes. It precluded not only outward plurality, namely the existence of another Supreme Being besides God, but also any kind of inner plurality or complexity within the nature of God. Eventually unity was understood not only in a numerical, but also in a metaphysical sense. For this reason any statement implying an attribute in God was felt to contradict the plea of divine unity.

Euclides of Megara, an Eleatic and also an associate of Socrates, denied the realness of all sensation and called for trust in reasoning alone. Only the One, or the Whole is real; the Many and the Parts have no claim to reality. Unlike Parmenides, who regarded the One as a continuous corporeal plenum, Euclides identified it with the Good, God, Wisdom, and Mind. "It was in this way that the Absolute made its first appearance in the history of philosophy, and its claim to be the sole reality was based on the inherent contradictoriness of all appearance."*

Since all thought presupposes a duality of thinker and the object of the thinking, Plotinus denied even that God was the object which thinks itself. For him, the One contains no more than the negation of

---

*J. Burnet, *Greek Philosophy*, I (London, 1920), 230 ff.; cf. his article "Megarics," *Encyclopedia of Religion and Ethics*, VIII, 523a.

plurality, and must not be understood in a merely numerical sense. "The One is not one of the units that make up the number Two."* In calling the Absolute "One," we merely intend to exclude the note of inner divisibility.

In the language of Maimonides, "belief in unity cannot mean essentially anything but the belief in one single homogeneous uncompounded essence; not in a plurality of ideas but in a single idea." An attribute is either identical with the essence of that to which is attributed, or different from it. If it is identical, then its attribution is either a tautology (e.g., man is human), or the definition of a term (e.g., man is a reasoning animal). Such attributes are impossible with reference to God. God cannot be described by His definition because He cannot be defined. On the other hand, if the attribute is different from the thing to which it is attributed, and thus an idea added to that thing, then it denotes an accident of that essence. Yet such an attribute would imply a plurality (of essence and accidents) in the divine Being.†

These difficulties arise from the attempt to reduce the biblical insight to an exact rational category. To be sure, the rational component is central to the biblical understanding of unity. However, the biblical intention is not to stress an abstraction, an idea in general, but the fullness of the divine Being; the certainty that the Creator *is* the Redeemer, that the Lord of nature *is* the Lord of history. *God's* being One means more than just being one. It means, we may say, that He is One, not many; unique and only (one-ly), the center and the circle, all-embracing and involved.‡

---

* *Enneads,* V, 5, 7.
† *The Guide of the Perplexed* (Rabin trans.), I, 51-52.
‡ See A. J. Heschel, *Man Is Not Alone* (New York, 1951), pp. 111 ff. See also pp. 352 and 356 of the present volume.

# 4

# Anthropopathy

## ANTHROPOPATHY AS A MORAL PROBLEM

Mythopoeic thought and reflection about right and wrong represent ways of human thinking which, far from being related to each other, run in different directions and are devoid of coherence. Thus, the realm of religion is one thing and the realm of moral striving another. Even divinity does not connote decency. It was at a late date in history, when he became aware of the majesty and eminence implied in the concept of the divine, that man undertook to remove from this concept all that contradicts propriety. Sometimes the simple insight was enough; what decency forbids man is likewise unbecoming to God.

The aversion to anthropomorphism among cultured Greeks was, first of all, a reaction against conceptions offensive to their moral sensibilities. "Both Homer and Hesiod have attributed to the gods all things that are shameful and a reproach among mankind: theft, adultery, and mutual deception,"* Xenophanes complained. Plato denounced the caprice and corruptibility of the gods, from whom the

*H. Diels, *Fragmente der Vorsokratiker* (3rd ed.; Berlin, 1912), fragments 11, 12.

wicked could secure immunity from chastisement by means of sooth-ing entreaties and offerings.* The conception that jealousy or envy was inherent in the very nature of the gods was particularly repulsive to both Plato and Aristotle.†

"Thine is unwisdom, or injustice thine," says Amphitryon to Zeus. And Theseus is even more specific about the gods: "Have they not linked them in unlawful bonds of wedlock, and with chains, to win them thrones, outraged their fathers? In Olympus still they dwell, by their transgressions unabashed."‡

The prophets, the psalmist, the authors of the books of Wisdom, all of whom were powerfully sensitive to the uniqueness and transcen-dence of the living God, seem to have had no apprehension that the statements of divine pathos might impair their understanding for the one, unique, and transcendent God. One might wonder whether Xenophanes, had he been faced by the Bible instead of by Homer, would have felt compelled to protest against the humanization of divinity. The unbridled indulgence of impulses, the impassioned ego-ism and caprice of the Homeric gods called forth his criticism. He had scorn for the idea that the gods are corrupt.

As a moral problem, anthropopathy has been of very limited rele-vance to Jewish thinkers. It was due to other presuppositions that pathos became an issue in Jewish theology.

## THE THEOLOGICAL PRESUPPOSITION

A major motive for the rejection of the idea of pathos has been the fear of anthropomorphism, by which we mean the endowment of God with human attributes. The religious man denounces not only the idea that the Deity has a body or limbs like a man or an animal, but also the attribution of emotion or passion (anthropopathy) as incompatible with the nature of a Supreme Being. Since divine pathos was regarded as an aspect of anthropomorphism, or more precisely, of

---

* *Republic*, 378c.
† Plato, *Phaedrus*, 247a; *Timaeus*, 29e; Aristotle, *Metaphysics*, 983a.
‡ Euripides, *Heracles*, 345, 1316 ff., 1308.

anthropopathy, every effort was made either to disregard it or to cancel out its significance.

It is an oversimplification to assume that the prophets, who were so deeply aware of the grandeur and transcendence of the Creator of heaven and earth as well as of the failure and frailty of human nature, should have sought to invest God with human qualities. Speaking about God, the biblical man did not intend simply to describe a fact, but to praise, to extol, to celebrate. Merely to personify God would have been to disparage Him.

Anthropomorphism as a way of thinking is in harmony with the thought that man may become a god. The presence of this belief, widely held in ancient religions, may be regarded as a test for the genuineness of anthropomorphism.

Such a belief, however, was an extreme blasphemy to the biblical man. With superb irony the prophet pictures the downfall of the king of Babylon who said in his heart:

> I will ascend to heaven;
> Above the stars of God
> I will set my throne on high;
> . . . But you are brought down to Sheol,
> To the depths of the pit.
>
> Isaiah 14:13, 15

In the prophetic mind there was a disassociation of the human—of any biological function or social dependence—from the nature of God. Since the human could never be regarded as divine, there was no danger that the language of pathos would distort the difference between God and man.

There are several ways by which we can establish the presence of anthropomorphic conceptions: the equivalence of imagination and expression; the unawareness of the transcendence and uniqueness of God; the adjustment of God's moral nature to the interests of man; the endeavor to picture or to describe God in His own existence, unrelated to man.

We are inclined to question the legitimacy of applying the term anthropopathy to the prophetic statements about the divine pathos. The term applies properly to religions in which there is no discrepancy between imagination and expression: the gods are conceived of as human beings and described as human beings—in their appearance, their way of life, their passions, their occupations. There are myths and images. In contrast, the biblical man's imagination knows nothing about God, how He lives and what occupies Him. He is God and not man (Hos. 11:9; Isa. 31:3); man shall not see Him and live (Exod. 33:20); even seraphim cover their faces lest they see Him (Isa. 6:2).

> *Who in the skies can be compared to the Lord?*
> *Who among the heavenly beings is like the Lord?*
> *Psalm 89:6*

> *To whom then will you liken God,*
> *Or what likeness compare with Him?*
> *Isaiah 40:18*

Myths are disavowed, an image is an abomination.

## THE ACCOMMODATION OF WORDS TO HIGHER MEANINGS

The error in regarding the divine pathos as anthropomorphism consisted in regarding a unique theological category as a common psychological concept. This was due to the complex nature of prophetic language, which of necessity combines otherness and likeness, uniqueness and comparability, in speaking about God. One is more easily cognizant of the aspects of pathos resembling human emotions than of the aspects which set pathos apart as superhuman. Regarded as a form of humanization of God, the profound significance of this fundamental category is lost. The otherness and uniqueness of pathos can be understood only by comprehending it in its total structure, not by taking isolated traits out of context; by observing the peculiar usage of the terms as contrasted with assertions about the nature of man.

We must not fail to remember that there is a difference between anthropomorphic conceptions and anthropomorphic expressions.

The use of the latter does not necessarily prove belief in the former. God has often been pictured in human form, or as having passions just like man's. However, to picture Him as human does not mean to think of Him as human. Michelangelo in depicting the Creator in human form may continue to shock those tho are sensitive to the Second Commandment, but he can hardly be accused of believing that God possesses the shape of man.

All language is relative, adapted to the ideas and associations cherished in a particular age and capable of evoking them. But so is our understanding relative, attuned to the ideas and associations cherished in our age. In reading ancient words, it is difficult to ascertain the ideas which they represented and the thoughts which they sought to evoke in their contemporaries.

What sort of ideas were present in the prophet's mind which anthropomorphic words were supposed to convey?

The statements about pathos are not a compromise—ways of accommodating higher meanings to the lower level of human understanding. They are rather the accommodation of words to higher meanings. Words of psychological denotations are endowed with a theological connotation. In the biblical expressions of divine emotions, which are always morally conditioned and morally required, the religious consciousness experiences a sense of superhuman power rather than a conception of resemblance to man.

The idea of the divine pathos combining absolute selflessness with supreme concern for the poor and the exploited can hardly be regarded as the attribution of human characteristics. Where is the man who is endowed with such characteristics? Nowhere in the Bible is man characterized as merciful, gracious, slow to anger, abundant in love and truth, keeping love to the thousandth generation. Pathos is a thought that bears a resemblance to an aspect of divine reality as related to the world of man. As a theological category, it is a genuine insight into God's relatedness to man, rather than a projection of human traits into divinity, as found for example in the god images of mythology.

The conception of selfless pathos, synthesizing morality as a supreme, impartial demand and as the object of personal preoccupation and ultimate concern, consists of human ingredients and a superhuman *Gestalt.* Absolute selflessness and mysteriously undeserved love are more akin to the divine than to the human. And if these are characteristics of human nature, then man is endowed with attributes of the divine.

God's unconditional concern for justice is not an anthropomorphism. Rather, man's concern for justice is a theomorphism. Human reason, a feeble reflection, reminder, and intimation of the infinite wisdom deciphered in God's creation, is not the form after which our concept of God's wisdom is modeled. The language the prophets employed to describe that supreme concern was an anthropomorphism to end all anthropomorphisms.

Prophecy is essentially a proclamation that God's ways are not man's ways. He is not to be utilized. He is not a guarantee for security. The belief that ultimately there is a God of justice, a God whose concern is for justice, is anthropomorphic in the sense in which the idea of transcendence or eternity is anthropomorphic.

## The Wisdom and the Folly of Anthropomorphism

According to the celebrated statement of Xenophanes, "If oxen and horses and lions had hands or could draw with hands and create works of art like those made by men, horses would draw pictures of gods like horses, and oxen of gods like oxen. . . . Aethiopians have gods with snub noses and black hair; Thracians have gods with grey eyes and red hair."*

The essential error is not in *how* man depicts God, but in depicting Him at all. The great revolution in biblical faith was to regard any image of God as an abomination. "You shall not make yourself a graven image" (Exod. 20:4). "You saw no form on the day that the Lord spoke to you at Horeb out of the midst of the fire" (Deut. 4:15). Imagination and God are not the same.

*K. Freeman, *Ancilla to the Pre-Socratic Philosophers* (Oxford, 1952), fragments 15, 16.

Oxen, lions, and horses would depict God like one of them. We are wiser—should we then depict God unlike us? Is it true that the absolute antithesis to man is the true characteristic of the divine? If man has nothing in common with God, he will never be able to know what God is, or even to know that God is the absolute antithesis to man.

Oxen would depict God in their image; a community of triangles would worship a triangular God. The fallacy of these statements is concealed in their glibness. Do oxen depict God? Are triangles capable of worship?

The problem of anthropomorphism is an afterthought in the process of religious thinking. It is a type of reflection which stands in relation to genuine utterance as criticism stands in relation to works of creative art, testing and appraising verbal formulations in the light of conceptual criteria. However, there is an essential incongruity of creative and critical thinking, of the effort to hold up insights against words and the effort to hold up words against conceptions. Creative minds are more anxious to save what they sense than to refine and protect what they say. Translating insights into words is not done in the light of conceptual criteria, but under the impact of incomprehensible facts. Ignoring the tension of the moment and the paradox of the endeavor, one would retain the concepts, but lose the facts. Thus, in responding to facts of religious experience, the mind does not always employ the yardsticks of general rules. It is in analyzing the formulated response from a distance that one begins to measure the irregularities of religious language by the scales of general rules.

Impropriety is the mark of all expression that presumes to convey what is meant by the divine. Fortunately, creative thinking is not always hurt by the awareness of impropriety, nor does it dread the frown of the critic. In trying to set things right, we must not forget the anguish of sensing things altogether.

To speak about God as if He were a person does not necessarily mean to personify Him, to stamp Him in the image of a person. Between personifying God and speaking about Him in terms of personality lies a difference as great as between presuming to count and weigh all beings and employing the word "universe."

To most of us a person, a human being, seems to be the maximum of being, the ceiling of reality; we think that to personify is to glorify. Yet do not some of us realize at times that a person is not superlative, that to personify the spiritually real is to belittle it? A person may be both a distortion and a deprecation.*

The idea of the divine pathos is not a personification of God but an exemplification of divine reality, an illustration or illumination of His concern. It does not represent a substance, but an act or a relationship.

The fear of the fallacy of anthropomorphism could lead us to cast aspersions, for example, upon Hosea's proclaiming Israel as the consort of God and His saying: "I will betroth you to Me for ever; I will betroth you to Me in righteousness and in justice, in love and in mercy" (Hos. 2:19 [H. 2:21]). Yet the idea of God's betrothal to Israel did not represent a mental image, something imagined by the prophet. There was no picture in the mind that corresponded to the metaphor. Nor was it crystallized as a definite concept, from which logical consequences could be drawn, or raised to a dogma, to an exact formulation of a belief.

The essential function of the critic is to protect such ideas from pretension and inflation, resulting in either visible or verbal iconography. A sacred venture is always in danger of ending in a blasphemy. The sacred venture of conveying more than what minds could visualize or words could say is always in danger of being a failure. Yet the rivalry between the creative and the critical mind must not turn to antagonism. The critic may be ahead of the creative mind in clarity of conception, but remain behind in the immediacy of insight and experience.

As important as the content of our thinking about God is our way of thinking about Him. There is a reflective way, commencing in ignorance and rising from concept to concept until it arrives at the

---

*See A. J. Heschel, *The Sabbath* (New York, 1951), pp. 59 f.

idea of One Supreme Being described by the attribute of perfection. The other way begins in embarrassment, and, rising from insight to insight, arrives at a vision of one transcendent Being, Whom one acknowledges as a source of embarrassment. One cannot describe Him, one can only praise Him.*

The notion of God as a perfect Being is not of biblical origin. It is not the product of prophetic religion, but of Greek philosophy; a postulate of reason rather than a direct, compelling, initial answer of man to His reality. In the Decalogue, God does not speak of His perfection, but of His having made free men out of slaves. Signifying a state of being without defect and lack, perfection is a term of praise which we may utter in pouring forth our emotion; yet, for man to utter it as a name for His essence would mean to evaluate and to endorse Him. Biblical language is free of such pretension; it dared to call perfect (*tamim*) only "His work" (Deut. 32:4), "His way" (II Sam. 22:31), and the Torah (Ps. 19:7). We have never been told: "Hear, O Israel, God is perfect!"

## THE LANGUAGE OF PRESENCE

What do we mean when we employ the word "God"? It is a word that is used in many ways. It may denote an idea, or a force working within the universe, or wisdom as reflected in nature, or an omnipotent Ruler, or the First Cause. All these words denote ideas. They do not convey any sense of the realness of God. How does one rise from saying the word "God" to sensing His realness?

This is the most serious challenge. God is a Being hidden from the eye and removed from the mind. No image must be fashioned, no concept formed. How can His realness be felt, thought, or uttered?

Greek philosophy, groping for a rational way to comprehend the ultimate Being, was rarely able to transcend the mind's tragic uncertainty as to whether there is a God. In the memorable words of Xenophanes: "There never was, and never shall be, any man, who has

*See A. J. Heschel, *Man Is Not Alone* (New York, 1951), pp. 101 f.

sure and certain knowledge about the gods . . . and all things; for however much he may hit the mark by accident, yet he himself has no knowledge; but opinion presides over all things."* Or to quote Plato: The higher "knowledge which reason herself attains by the power of the dialectic, using the hypotheses . . . as steps and points of departure into a world which is above hypotheses, in order that she may soar beyond them to the first principle of the whole; and clinging to this and then to that which depends on this, by successive steps, she descends again without the aid of any sensible object, from ideas, through ideas, and in ideas she ends."†

Plato thinks of God *in the image of an idea;* the prophets think of God *in the image of personal presence.* To the prophets, God was not a Being of Whose existence they were convinced in the way in which a person is convinced of the truth of an idea. He was a Being Who is supremely real and staggeringly present.

They could not use the language of *essence;* they had to use the language of *presence.* They did not try to depict Him; they tried to present Him, to make Him present. In such an effort only words of grandeur and intensity, not abstractions, can be of any avail.

There is a world, and there is God. Plato planted in the Western mind the consciousness of unseen, eternal ideas, of which the visible world is but a copy. The prophets placed in the Western mind the consciousness of an unseen, eternal God, of Whose Will the visible world is a creation.

## MY PATHOS IS NOT YOUR PATHOS

There are two pitfalls in our religious understanding; the humanization of God and the anesthetization of God. Both threaten our understanding of the ethical integrity of God's will. Humanization leads to the conception of God as the ally of the people; whether they do right or wrong, God would not fail His people. The idea of the divine anger shatters such horrible complacency.

*Diels, *op. cit.,* fragment 34.
†*Republic,* 511.

The anesthetization of God would reduce Him to a mystery Whose will is unknown, Who has nothing to say to man. Such indifference was refuted by the prophets' own experiences of being addressed by Him and called upon to convey His word to the people.

We are inclined to assume that thought and sympathy, because they are found in man, are limited to man. However, with the same logic it may be maintained that being, because it is characteristic of man and matter, is limited to them. Sight, because of its being a faculty of man, is not to be denied to God. Yet, there is an absolute difference between the sight and the thought of God and the sight and the thought of man. God compared with man is like the potter compared with the clay.

> Woe to those who hide deep from the Lord their counsel,
> Whose deeds are in the dark,
> And who say, Who sees us? Who knows us?
> You turn things upside down!
> Shall the potter be regarded as the clay;
> That the thing made should say of its maker,
> He did not make me;
> Or the thing formed say of Him who made it,
> He has not understanding?
>
> Isaiah 29:15–16

The nature of the divine pathos is a mystery to man. What Isaiah (55:8 f.) said concerning the thoughts of God may equally apply to His pathos: For My pathos is not your pathos, neither are your ways My ways, says the Lord. For as the heavens are higher than the earth, so are My ways higher than your ways, and My pathos than your pathos.

The Bible speaks in the language of man. It deals with the problems of man, and its terms are borrowed from the vocabulary of the people. It has not coined many words, but it has given new meaning to borrowed words. The prophets had to use anthropomorphic language in order to convey His nonanthropomorphic Being.

The greatest challenge to the biblical language was how to reconcile in words the awareness of God's transcendence with His over-whelming livingness and concern. Had the biblical man recoiled form using anthropomorphic words, he never would have uttered: "The Lord is my shepherd, I shall not want." On the other hand, to assume that the psalmist, in using the word "shepherd," had the image of a shepherd in his mind is to misunderstand the meaning of that passage.

It is precisely the challenge involved in using inadequate words that drives the mind beyond all words. Any pretension to adequacy would be specious and a delusion.

To others, God seems to recede in a distance; to the prophets, He calls continually for participation. What the prophets experience, they demand of the people: not a fleeting experience of extraordinary surrender, but a perpetual attitude of obedience; not to stand "outside oneself," but to love Him with the whole self; not to lose one's destiny, but to remember one's destiny: being called, being chosen.

This was the central endeavor of the prophet: to set forth not only a divine law, but a divine life; not only a covenant, but also a pathos; not the eternal immutability of His Being, but the presence of His pathos in time; not only absolute Lordship, but also direct relatedness to man.

God is not a point at the horizon of the mind, but is like the air that surrounds one and by which one lives. He is not a thing, but a happening. The psalmist may ask man to meditate on God's works; the prophets call upon man to consider God's inner acts. They not only sense God in history, but also history in God.

*All expressions of pathos are attempts to set forth God's aliveness.* One must not forget that all our utterances about Him are woefully inadequate. But when taken to be allusions rather than descriptions, understatements rather than adequate accounts, they are aids in evoking our sense of His realness.

"The father and maker of all this Universe is past finding out, and even if we found him, to tell of him to all men would be impossible."* The mind of man can never go beyond the limits indicated in

---

*Plato, *Timaeus,* 28.

Plato's words. What does the mind know about God? His works. Where is His goodness to be found? In His works. There is no greater goodness than that which is already given in the universe. The prophets speak of a mercy that transcends the mercy found in the world. It was not from His works alone that they knew Him, but also from His word.

God is alive in His regard and concern for life, for man, for righteousness. Compassionate is His concern, although the form in which it is expressed may be harsh. Man is callous and deaf to God's call. It is frequently in moments of distress that he regains ultimate understanding.

> *Thou turnest man to contrition,*
> *And sayest, Turn back, O children of men!*
> Psalm 90:3

His wrath can be unbearably dreadful, yet it is but the expression and instrument of His eternal concern.

A merciful or angry God was not unknown to the Babylonians or Egyptians. New is the prophetic conception that mercy and anger are not sporadic reactions, but expressions of *a constant care and concern*. The divine pathos embraces all life, past, present, and future; all things and events have a reference to Him. It is a concern that has the attribute of eternity, transcending all history, as well as the attribute of universality, embracing all nations, encompassing animals as well as human beings.

By God's livingness the prophets did not mean living in a biological or physiological sense. They never thought of God as a thing or an organism, as a force or a cause. God's life was thought of as a unity of conscious acts, of creating, demanding, expressing, and responding. He was conceived of in terms of acts, in terms of moments, rather than in terms of thinghood. A thing may be thought of as a force or a cause. Personal life is the presence or manifestation of a will, of unity of intention, of a regard and a concern for the nonself.

Is history derelict, a mere chain of chance? Is the survival of mankind the exclusive concern of man? Is human life to be defined as life that cares for itself? Biblical religion did not simply evolve from a reflection about an ultimate cause. Its premise rather seems to be that, just as there is an ultimate origin, there is an ultimate concern. Human life is life that God cares for and that is concerned with Him.

"God is alive" does not mean He is a Person among persons. "It means," the psalmist or the prophet would say, "that more than my own life do I cherish His regard for me." "For Thy love (*ḥesed*) is better than life" (Ps. 63:3 [H. 63:4]).

> *My flesh and my heart may fail,*
> *But God is the rock of my heart*
> *And my portion for ever. . . .*
> *The Lord is my shepherd,*
> *I shall not want.*
>                                   *Psalms 73:26; 23:1*

# 5

# The Meaning and Mystery of Wrath

### The Embarrassment of Anger

Expositors of the teachings of the prophets are prone to dwell upon passages which seem to conform to their views and predilections. The prophets, we are told, spoke of a God Who stands for all the virtues we should like to see in human beings. The harsh words, the grave threats, the relentless demands, the shrieks of doom, are usually disregarded. There are hurricanes in the world as well as lilies. The prophets preached justice and celebrated God's eternal love, but they also proclaimed the danger of man's presumption, the scandal of idolatry and human ruthlessness, and above all the seriousness of divine wrath.

> *Who can stand before His indignation?*
> *Who can endure His anger?*
> *His wrath is poured out like fire,*
> *The rocks are broken asunder by Him.*
> *Nahum 1:6*

> *But the Lord is the true God;*
> *He is the living God and the everlasting King.*

*At His wrath the earth quakes,*
*And the nations cannot endure His indignation.*

*Jeremiah 10:10*

On the other hand, among those who remained open to the message of the anger of God, to which the Bible, and particularly the prophetic writing, refers again and again, some have recoiled; others have treated it allegorically; while still others have been repelled by it. It is, indeed, impossible to close one's eyes to the words of the wrath of God in Scripture.* To interpret it on allegorical lines or as a metonymy,† and to regard wrath as a synonym for punishment, is to misread the authentic meaning of the word and to misrepresent biblical thought. Are we to suppose that the ancient Hebrew excluded passions from the divine Being and yet pictured to himself divine indignation as a real fact—and felt that he was delivered over to it to the very roots of his existence? No. To experience divine anger "as if" God were provoked is a subterfuge alien to the biblical mind. Both in predictions of things to come and in descriptions of things that came to

---

*"Some people who hear these words suppose that the Existent feels wrath and anger, whereas He is not susceptible to passion of any kind. For disturbance is a mark of human weakness. To God irrational passions of the soul can no more be attributed than bodily parts or limbs. [Moses uses such expressions to admonish those who could not otherwise be brought to their senses.] Thus it is for training and admonition, not because God's nature is such, that these words are used." (Philo, *Quod Deus Immutabilis Est*, XI, 52–54.) "We shun indeed in words the monstrosity of saying that God is of human form, but in actual fact we accept the impious thought that He is of human passions. And therefore we invent for Him hands and feet, incoming and outgoing, enmities, aversions, estrangements, anger, in fact, such parts and passions as can never belong to the Cause; . . . a mere crutch for our weakness." (Philo, *De Sacrificiis Abelis et Caini*, XXI, 96.)

Some Palestinian rabbis of the third century c.e. interpreted the terms *af* and *ḥemah* (anger, wrath) to denote, not divine qualities, but angels of destruction. (*Talmud Jerushalmi, Taanith*, II, 65b.) Cf. the interpretation of Deut. 9:19, *Deuteronomy Rabba*, 3, 11; see Buber, ed., *Pesikta*, 45a. Maimonides' thesis that in the Pentateuch and the prophets, anger is applied to God only in reference to idolatry, has puzzled his commentators; cf. M. Friedlander, ed., *The Guide of the Perplexed*, I, ch. 36, p. 130, n. 2; Ibn Shmuel, *Moreh Nebukim*, I, 167.

†The substitution of one word for another suggested by it; the cause for the effect, *metonymia causae pro effectu*.

pass, the word about the divine anger points to a stark reality, to the power behind the facts, not to a figure of speech.

"The Jews have experienced wrath differently from us and pronounced it holy; for they have seen the sullen majesty of man, joined with which it manifested itself, in their own midst at a height which a European is not able to imagine."*

Is there a way for us today to relate ourselves to the prophetic understanding of divine anger? In the chapter "The Philosophy of Pathos," we attempted to analyze the reasons for opposing the idea of divine pathos. There are additional reasons for resisting the idea of divine anger.

Few passions have been denounced so vehemently by teachers of morality as the passion of anger.† It is pictured as a sinister, malignant passion, an evil force, which must under all circumstances be suppressed. The truth, however, is that these features are accretions and exuberances, not its essence. Admittedly, anger is something that comes dangerously close to evil, yet it is wrong to identify it with evil. It may be evil by association, but not in essence. Like fire, it may be a blessing as well as a fatal thing—reprehensible when associated with malice, morally necessary as resistance to malice. Both alternatives are fraught with danger. Its complete suppression, even in the face of outbursts of evil, may amount to surrender and capitulation, while its unrestrained drive may end in disaster. Anger may touch off deadly explosives, while the complete absence of anger stultifies moral sensibility. Patience, a quality of holiness, may be sloth in the soul when associated with the lack of righteous indignation. "For everything

---

*Nietzsche, *Morgenröte,* 38; W. A. Kaufmann, *Nietzsche* (Princeton, 1950), p. 263.

†Anger is defined as "the desire for retaliation" (Aristotle, *De Anima,* I, 1); as the desire for "vengeance on account of an apparent slight" (*Topica,* 156a, 33); as "the lust for revenge" (Cicero, *Tusculan Disputations,* IV, 19, 44); as "a brief madness" ("*Ira furor brevis est,*" Horace, *Epistolae,* I, 2, 62); as the desire to injure others or to inflict pain; as "uneasiness or discomposure of the mind, upon the receipt of an injury, with a present purpose of revenge" (J. Locke, *An Essay Concerning Human Understanding,* II, 20). "Nothing annihilates an inhibition as irresistibly as anger does it; for, as Moltke says of war, destruction pure and simple is its essence." (W. James, *The Varieties of Religious Experience* [New York, 1958], p. 210.) It is doubtful whether such a description sheds any light on the essence of anger.

there is a season, and a time for every matter under heaven: . . . a time to keep silence, and a time to speak, a time to love, and a time to hate" (Eccles. 3:1, 7, 8).*

## AN ASPECT OF THE DIVINE PATHOS

The major difficulty in our attempt to understand the issue is in the failure to sense the ambiguity and the homonymous aspect of the terms denoting the pathos of anger. As psychological terms, the words suggest the emotional excitement induced by intense displeasure, implying the loss of self-control, compulsiveness, temporary derangement of the mind, and the desire or intent to avenge or punish. Anger is, therefore, a passion which rightly we are urged to curb and to suppress. Jacob condemned anger in his sons Simon and Levi, although it was the outburst of righteous indignation. "Cursed be their anger, for it is fierce; and their wrath, for it is cruel" (Gen. 49:7). Edom is

---

*Moses is reported to have become angry on a number of occasions (Exod. 16:20; Lev. 10:17; Num. 31:14, etc.). This seems to have become a problem only in postbiblical times. Rabbi Eleazar ben Azariah (first century A.D.), followed by other rabbis, maintained that no man could afford to be angry, not even Moses, for on three occasions anger led him to error, Sifre Numbers, 157 (ed. H. S. Horovitz, p. 213). According to IV Macc. 2:17, Moses when he was angered against Dothan and Abiram (Num. 16:15) "did not give free course to his wrath, but controlled his anger by reason." Unqualified condemnation of anger has frequently been voiced in Jewish literature. God loves him who never gets angry, Pesahim 113b. "Do not get angry and you will not sin," Berachoth 29b. A popular epigram maintains: "He who gets angry is regarded as if he would worship an idol." (Maimonides, Mishne Torah, Deoth, II, 3.) Unqualified eradication of anger is recommended in Sefer Hasidim, Vulgata, 145, also by Maimonides, loc. cit., and by many other authorities. In later literature, anger was often described as a cardinal vice. Unqualified rejection of anger was unknown to the Septuagint which understood Ps. 4:5 to mean "Be angry and sin not." In contrast, the Aramaic version and the rabbinic interpretation read: "Tremble before God, and you will not sin." A moderate attitude is expressed by some Babylonian rabbis, see Taanith 4b; under certain circumstances indignation is permitted, Megillah 6b. According to Ibn Gabirol, The Improvement of the Moral Qualities, IV, 1, "wrath is a reprehensible quality, but when employed to correct or reprove, or because of indignation at the performance of transgression, it becomes laudable." Cf. Aristotle, Nicomachean Ethics; cf. Eph. 4:26 f.: "Be angry but do not sin; do not let the sun go down on your anger, and give no opportunity to the Devil." Here anger in itself is not considered evil. In Mark 3:5, anger is ascribed to Jesus.

denounced because "he cast off all pity, and his anger tore perpetually, and he kept his wrath for ever" (Amos 1:11). Anger, we are told in the book of Proverbs, produces strife (30:33), exalts folly (14:29). "A man of wrath stirs up strife, a man given to anger causes much transgression" (29:22). "A man of great wrath will pay the penalty" (19:19). "Cease from anger and forsake wrath" (Ps. 37:8). "Anger rests in the bosom of fools" (Eccles. 7:9). In praise of him who subdues his anger or restrains it, the book of Proverbs says: "He who is slow to anger is better than the mighty, and he who rules his spirit than he who takes a city" (16:32).

It is unlikely that the prophets, who never cease to proclaim the righteousness of God, should in the same breath ascribe to Him a morally reprehensible disposition, "a defect in His justice." As long as the anger of God is viewed in the light of the psychology of passions rather than in the light of the theology of pathos, no adequate understanding will be possible. Is this the connotation the prophetic word evokes: "Here is a God who acts compulsively, who loses self-control, and who delights in hurting man, disregarding standards of justice"—? The anger of God is one of the profound ideas in the biblical understanding of divine sovereignty, righteousness, and freedom.

The prophets never thought that God's anger is something that cannot be accounted for, unpredictable, irrational. It is never a spontaneous outburst, but a reaction occasioned by the conduct of man. Indeed, it is the major task of the prophet to set forth the facts that account for it, to insist that the anger of God is not a blind, explosive force, operating without reference to the behavior of man, but rather voluntary and purposeful, motivated by concern for right and wrong. This is the premise of biblical thinking:

> *The Lord is good to all,*
> *And His compassion is over all that He has made.*
>
> Psalm 145:9

He has a merciful purpose toward the universe which He has made. The land was His gift, rain his blessing.

The anger of God must not be treated in isolation, but as an aspect of the divine pathos, as one of the modes of God's responsiveness to man. It shares the features that are characteristic of the pathos as a whole: it is conditioned by God's will; it is aroused by man's sins. It is an instrument rather than a force, transitive rather than spontaneous. It is a secondary emotion, never the ruling passion, disclosing only a part of God's way with man.

Pathos includes love, but goes beyond it. God's relation to man is not an indiscriminate outpouring of goodness, oblivious to the condition and merit of the recipient, but an intimate accessibility, manifesting itself in His sensitive and manifold reactions.

The word "anger" is charged with connotations of spite, recklessness, and iniquity. The biblical term, however, denotes what we call *righteous indignation,* aroused by that which is considered mean, shameful, or sinful; it is impatience with evil, "a motion of the soul rousing itself to curb sins." The free, voluntary nature of divine anger is expressed in the words spoken to Moses after the people worshiped the golden calf (Exod. 32:10). Without Moses' consent, God's anger would not turn against the people.*

As a righteous Judge, righteous indignation is part of Him. "God is a righteous Judge, a God Who has indignation every day" (Ps. 7:11). Not to show partiality is an essential attribute of a judge (Exod. 23:3; Deut. 16:19). But to be impartial to people, one cannot be impartial to evil. In the Bible, a judge is not merely a person who has the cognitive faculty to examine a case and to pronounce a sentence; he is also a person who is pained and distressed when injustice is done.

God's concern is the prerequisite and source of His anger. It is

---

*The text of the Decalogue, "For I the Lord Thy God am a jealous God" (Exod. 20:5), is interpreted to mean: "I am a God above jealousy. I am the master of jealousy and jealousy is not master of Me." *(Mechilta, ad loc.)* "Man's anger controls him, but God controls His anger, as it is said, The Lord is God over jealousy and avenging" (Nah. 1:2). *Genesis Rabba,* 49, 8 (ed. Theodor, p. 509). "It is the nature of a mortal that when he is in a state of anger he is not at the same time in a state of conciliation, and when he is in a state of conciliation he is not at the same time in a state of anger. But the Holy One, blessed be He, when He is angry He is ready for conciliation in the midst of His anger, as it is said: For His anger is but for a moment, His favor is for a lifetime." (Ps. 30:6. [*The Midrash on Psalms* (trans. W. Braude), end of ch. 2].)

because He cares for man that His anger may be kindled against man. Anger and mercy are not opposites but correlatives. Thus Habakkuk prays: "In wrath remember mercy" (3:2). It is inconceivable that His love should ever cease. This is why the psalmist ponders: "Has He in anger shut up His compassion?" (77:9 [H. 77:10].)

For all the terror that the wrath of God may bring upon man, the prophet is not crushed or shaken in his understanding and trust. What is divine is never weird. This is the greatness of the prophet: he is able to convert terror into a song. For when the Lord smites the Egyptians, he is both "smiting and healing" (Isa. 19:22).

> *Come let us return to the Lord;*
> *For He has torn, that He may heal us,*
> *He has stricken, and He will bind us up.*
>
> Hosea 6:1

## THE EVIL OF INDIFFERENCE

There is an evil which most of us condone and are even guilty of: indifference to evil. We remain neutral, impartial, and not easily moved by the wrongs done unto other people. Indifference to evil is more insidious than evil itself; it is more universal, more contagious, more dangerous. A silent justification, it makes possible an evil erupting as an exception becoming the rule and being in turn accepted.*

The knowledge of evil is something which the first man acquired; it was not something that the prophets had to discover. Their great contribution to humanity was the discovery of the evil of indifference. One may be decent and sinister, pious and sinful. I am my brother's keeper (cf. Gen. 4:9).

*Plato defines education as that "which leads you always to hate what you ought to hate, and to love what you ought to love from the beginning of life to the end." (*Laws,* II, 653.) Cf. Aristotle, *Nicomachean Ethics,* 1125b, 31: "The man who is angry at the right things and with the right people and further, as he ought, when he ought, and as long as he ought, is praised." Philo speaks with approval of "righteous anger"; see H. A. Wolfson, *Philo,* II (Cambridge, Mass., 1947), 276.

The prophet is a person who suffers the harms done to others. Wherever a crime is committed, it is as if the prophet were the victim and the prey. The prophet's angry words cry. The wrath of God is a lamentation. All prophecy is one great exclamation; God is not indifferent to evil! He is always concerned, He is personally affected by what man does to man. He is a God of pathos. This is one of the meanings of the anger of God: the end of indifference!

The message of wrath is frightful, indeed. But for those who have been driven to the brink of despair by the sight of what malice and ruthlessness can do, comfort will be found in the thought that evil is not the end, that evil is never the climax of history.

This is the most vexing question in a world where the righteous suffer and the wicked prosper: Does God condone? Does God care for right and wrong? If the agony of man were a matter of discomfort, a mild condition—a word of divine commiseration, a word of reprobation—would have been adequate. To a generation afflicted by the fury of cruel men, by the outrage of abandoning God, no condemnation is too harrowing.

Man's sense of injustice is a poor analogy to God's sense of injustice. The exploitation of the poor is to us a misdemeanor; to God, it is a disaster. Our reaction is disapproval; God's reaction is something no language can convey. Is it a sign of cruelty that God's anger is aroused when the rights of the poor are violated, when widows and orphans are oppressed?

## THE CONTINGENCY OF ANGER

It is impossible to understand the meaning of divine anger without pondering the meaning of *divine patience* or forbearance. Explicitly and implicitly, the prophets stress that God is patient, long-suffering, or slow to anger (*'erekh appayim*) (Exod. 34:6; Num. 14:18; Jer. 15:15; Joel 2:13; Jonah 4:2, Nah. 1:3; Pss. 86:15; 103:8; 145:8; Neh. 9:17). Patience is one of "the thirteen attributes of

God," yet never in the sense of apathy, of being indifferent.* Contrary to their thinking was the idea of a God Who submits to the caprice of man, smiling at the hideousness of evil. The patience of God means His restraint of justifiable anger.

One must not mistake divine forgiveness for indulgence or complacency. There is a limit at which forbearance ceases to be a blessing.† Forgiveness is neither absolute nor unconditional. We may forgive the criminal; is it right to forgive the crime? I may forgive a wrong done to me; but do I have the right to forgive a wrong done to others? Unconditional forgiveness may be found in Pandora's box, a fine incentive to vice. Anger is a reminder that man is in need of forgiveness, and that forgiveness must not be taken for granted. The Lord is long-suffering, compassionate, loving, and faithful, but He is also demanding, insistent, terrible, and dangerous.

An essential feature of anger as proclaimed by the prophets is its contingency and nonfinality. It is man who provokes it, and it is man who may revoke it. One of the major tasks of the prophet is to call upon the people to repent. "Amend your ways and your doings, and obey . . . the Lord your God, and the Lord will repent of the evil which He has pronounced against you" (Jer. 26:13). Again and again we hear: "Behold, I am shaping evil against you and devising a plan against you. Return, every one from his evil way, and amend your ways and your doings" (Jer. 18:11). "If you truly execute justice one with another, if you do not oppress the alien, the fatherless or the widow, or shed innocent blood in this place, and if you do not go after other gods to your own hurt, then I will let you dwell in this

---

*In the religions of the East, patience as a human virtue is closely akin to *apatheia,* namely, complete indifference to circumstance induced by mental discipline. Patience as a positive attitude of the soul is a distinctly biblical idea. It is the enduring of suffering and privation silently, and the waiting which rests upon the assurance that God's goodness will be ultimately manifest.

†"The unrighteous and vicious are always to be pitied in any case; and one can afford to forgive as well as to pity him who is curable, and refrain and calm one's anger, not getting into a passion, like a woman, and nursing ill-feeling. But upon him who is incapable of reformation and wholly evil, the vials of our wrath should be poured out; wherefore, I say, that good men ought, when occasion demands, to be both gentle and passionate." (Plato, *Laws,* 731.)

place, in the land that I gave of old to your fathers for ever" (Jer. 7:5–7).

This is the mysterious paradox of Hebrew faith: The All-wise and Almighty may change a word that He proclaims. Man has the power to modify His design. Jeremiah had to be taught that God is greater than His decisions. The anger of the Lord is instrumental, hypothetical, conditional, and subject to His will.* Let the people modify their line of conduct, and anger will disappear.† Far from being an expression of "petulant vindictiveness," the message of anger includes a call to return and to be saved. The call of anger is a call to cancel anger. It is not an expression of irrational, sudden, and instinctive excitement, but a free and deliberate reaction of God's justice to what is wrong and evil. For all its intensity, it may be averted by prayer.‡ There is no divine anger for anger's sake. Its meaning is, as already said, instrumental: to bring about repentance; its purpose and consummation is its own disappearance.

The contingency of anger is dramatized in the story of the prophet Jonah. Jonah was called by the Lord to go to Nineveh, the capital of Assyria, there to announce her imminent downfall, "for their wickedness has come up before the Lord." Jonah tried first to evade his mission, knowing that God is "gracious, merciful, slow to anger, abounding in love," and ready "to repent of the evil" (4:2). Running away from God, Jonah soon found himself in peril on the sea. In order to save the lives of the others on the ship, he had himself thrown overboard, and was eventually rescued by the Lord. Told a second time to go to Nineveh, Jonah obeyed, and he proclaimed in the capital of Assyria: "Yet forty days, and Nineveh shall be over-

---

*"I will not execute My fierce anger" (Hos. 11:9). "For My name's sake I defer My anger, for the sake of My praise I restrain it for you, that I may not cut you off" (Isa. 48:9).

†"If any time I declare concerning a nation or a kingdom, that I will pluck up and break down and destroy it, and if that nation, concerning which I have spoken, turns from its evil, I will repent the evil that I intended to do to it" (Jer. 19:7–8).

‡Moses confesses: "I was afraid of the anger and the hot displeasure which the Lord bore against you, so that He was ready to destroy you. But the Lord hearkened to me" (Deut. 9:19). See also Exod. 32:7–11.

thrown!'' The prophet's words inspired the people to repent and to turn from their evil ways (3:8), for they said: "Who knows, God may turn and repent, and turn from His anger" (3:9). When God saw what they did, how they turned from their evil ways, "He repented of the evil He said He would do to them" (3:10) and Nineveh was saved.

God's change of mind displeased Jonah exceedingly. He had proclaimed the doom of Nineveh with a certainty, to the point of fixing the time, as an inexorable decree without qualification. But what transpired only proved the word of God was neither firm nor reliable. To a prophet who stakes his life on the reliability and infallibility of the word of God, such realization leads to despair. "O Lord, take my life from me, I beseech Thee, for it is better for me to die than to live" (4:3), was his prayer.

The prophet was now alone, angry with man and displeased with God; man is wicked, and God unreliable. He left the city and made a booth for himself outside its boundaries, where he waited to see what would become of the city. "And the Lord appointed a plant and made it come up over Jonah that it might be a shade over his head, to save him from his discomfort. So Jonah was delighted with the plant." But when the dawn came up next day God caused the plant to wither away. A sultry east wind and the sun beat upon the head of Jonah. He was faint, and said again: "It is better for me to die than to live." But God's answer was: "You pity the plant, for which you did not labor, nor did you make it grow, which came into being in a night. And should not I pity Nineveh, that great city, in which there are more than a hundred and twenty thousand persons who do not know their right hand from their left, and also much cattle?" (4:5–11).

God's answer to Jonah, stressing the supremacy of compassion, upsets the possibility of looking for a rational coherence of God's ways with the world. History would be more intelligible if God's word were the last word, final and unambiguous like a dogma or an unconditional decree. It would be easier if God's anger became effective automatically: once wickedness had reached its full measure, punishment would destroy it. Yet, beyond justice and anger lies the mystery of compassion.

## I Will Rejoice in Doing Them Good

God's anger is not a tempest in a void full of mystery and dread. The world is dark, and human agony is excruciating. But the prophet casts a light by which the heart is led into the thinking of the Lord's mind. God does not delight in unleashing anger. In what, then, does God delight? "I am the Lord Who practices kindness, justice, and righteousness in the earth, for in these things I delight, says the Lord" (Jer. 9:24 [H. 9:23]). "I will rejoice in doing them good, and I will plant them in this land in faithfulness, *with all my heart and all my soul*" (Jer. 32:41). It is only blessing that the Lord gives with all His heart and all His soul. For just as God delights in kindness done by man, He rejoices in doing kindness Himself.

Kind and compassionate in all His ways, the God of Israel chooses to bind His people in a covenant, in a reciprocal relation with Himself of rights and obligations. He will, if their deeds disturb the covenant, plead with them and go to all lengths to restore them to their loyalty. "He will and can never rest until the defaulter is brought, not to punishment (which is a minor matter) but to a re-entrance into the old personal relations."*

Although God delights in kindness, there are moments when He is led to the pathos of anger. Here is man whom God had made and to whom He had given dominion over sea and land. Here is a people whom God had chosen and redeemed from agony and slavery, a people to whom He gave His Torah, a land, prosperity, and prophets. And this people whose destiny was to be a witness to the living God and a light to the nations, betrayed His teachings, turned to idols, and abandoned Him. The Judge of the world cried His protest again and again. But the people remained deaf to the prophets. Then came a moment when His patience turned to anger.

> *Behold, the storm of the Lord!*
> *Wrath has gone forth,*
> *A whirling tempest;*

*W. F. Lofthouse, *ZAW*, LI (1933), 29 ff.

> *It will burst upon the head of the wicked.*
> *The anger of the Lord will not turn back*
> *Until He has executed and accomplished*
> *The intents of His mind.*
> *In the end of days you will understand it clearly.*
> > Jeremiah 23:19–20; cf. 30:23–24

The prophets' comparisons of anger with fire and storm have led some scholars to the idea that His anger is "like a hidden force of nature, incalculable and arbitrary," which strikes without measure or reason. Such an idea is a complete distortion of prophetic thinking. God's anger is never regarded by the prophets as either inscrutable or unaccountable. In the first word that came to Jeremiah, he was told, "I will utter My judgments against them, for all their wickedness in forsaking Me" (1:16). In forecasting the impending doom, Jeremiah heard: "I Who speak in judgment upon them" (4:12). And over the ruins and misery of Jerusalem, after disaster had set in, rose a Voice to make the darkness plain:

> *Because your guilt is great,*
> *Because your sins are flagrant,*
> *I have done these things to you.*
> > Jeremiah 30:15

Justice, *mishpat,* is the measure of His anger. Divine sympathy for the victims of human cruelty is the motive of anger. Indeed, what is God's sense of outrage at the mistreatment of the fatherless if not a sense of justice enhanced by compassion? It was concerning such a mistreatment that the Voice proclaimed:

> *Shall I not punish them for these things? says the Lord,*
> *Shall I not avenge Myself*
> *On a nation such as this?*
> > Jeremiah 5:29

God's anger is not a fundamental attribute, but a transient and reactive condition. It is a means of achieving "the intents of His mind." Inscrutable though it appears to the people, "in the end of days" they "will understand it clearly" (Jer. 23:20).

## ANGER LASTS A MOMENT

The ancient conception that the gods are spiteful seems to linger on in the mind of modern man, and inevitably the words of the Hebrew Bible are seen in the image of this conception. In gods who are spiteful, anger is a habit or a disposition. The prophets never speak of an angry God as if anger were His disposition. Even those who dwell more on His anger than on His mercy explicitly or implicitly accentuate the contrast.

*His anger passes, His love goes on for ever.* "I have loved you with an everlasting love" (Jer. 31:3). "I will betroth you to Me for ever . . . in love and in mercy" (Hos. 2:19 [H. 2:21]).

Again and again we are told that God's love or kindness (*ḥesed*) goes on forever (Jer. 33:11; Pss. 100:5; 106:1; 107:1; 118:1–4; 136:1–26; Ezra 3:11); we are never told that His anger goes on forever.\*

Is He a dreadful God, demanding terror and causing horror? The prophet Micah exclaims:

> *Who is a God like Thee, pardoning iniquity,*
> *And passing over transgression*
> *For the remnant of his inheritance?*
> *He does not retain His anger for ever*
> *Because He delights in love.*
> *He will again have compassion over us,*
> *He will tread our iniquities under foot.*
> *Thou wilt cast all our sins*
> *Into the depths of the sea.*
> *Thou wilt show faithfulness to Jacob*
> *And steadfast love to Abraham,*
> *As Thou hast sworn to our fathers*
> *From the days of old.*
>
> *Micah 7:18–20*

---

\*In Jer. 17:4, "for in My anger a fire is kindled which shall burn for ever," the reference is to the result of anger, not to anger itself. According to Mal. 1:4; Edom is "the people with whom the Lord is angry for ever."

Anger is always described as a moment, something that happens rather than something that abides. The feeling expressed by the rabbis that even divine anger must not last beyond a minute seems to be implied in the words of the prophets.

> *Come my people, enter your chambers*
> *And shut your doors behind you;*
> *Hide yourselves for a little while*
> *Until the indignation is past. . . .*
> *For a brief moment I forsook you,*
> *But with great compassion I will gather you.*
> *In overflowing wrath for a moment*
> *I hid My face from you,*
> *But with everlasting love I will have compassion on you,*
> *Says the Lord, your Redeemer.*
> > *Isaiah 26:20; 54:7–8*

> *For His anger is but for a moment,*
> *But His favor is for a lifetime.*
> *Weeping may tarry for the night*
> *But joy comes with the morning.*
> > *Psalm 30:5 [H. 30:6]*

> *For I will not contend for ever,*
> *Nor will I always be angry;*
> *For from Me proceeds the spirit,*
> *And I have made the breath of life.*
> *Because of the iniquity of his covetousness I was angry,*
> *I smote him, I hid My face and was angry;*
> *But he went on backsliding in the way of his own heart.*
> *I have seen his ways, but I will heal him;*
> *I will lead him and requite him with comfort,*
> *Creating for his mourners the fruit of the lips.*
> *Peace, peace, to the far and to the near, says the Lord;*
> *I will heal him.*
> > *Isaiah 57:16–19*

Merciful and gracious, *rahum ve-hannun* (Exod. 34:6; Pss. 86:15; 103:8, or *hannun ve-rahum* (Joel 2:13; Jonah 4:2; Pss. 111:4; 112:4; 116:5; 145:8; Neh. 9:17, 31; II Chron. 30:9),* are qualities which are never separable in the Bible from the thought of God.

> *The Lord is merciful and gracious,*
> *Slow to anger and abounding in steadfast love.*
> *He will not always chide,*
> *Nor will He keep His anger for ever.*
> *He does not deal with us according to our sins,*
> *Nor requite us according to our iniquities.*
> *For as the heavens are high above the earth,*
> *So great is His love toward those who fear Him;*
> *As far as the east is from the west,*
> *So far does He remove our transgressions from us.*
> *As a father pities his children,*
> *So the Lord pities those who fear Him.*
> *For He knows our frame;*
> *He remembers that we are dust.*
>
> *Psalm 103:8–14*

Israel's prayerful question,

> *Will He be angry for ever?*
> *Will He be indignant to the end?*

is answered decisively:

> *Return, faithless Israel, says the Lord.*
> *I will not look on you in anger,*
> *For I am merciful, says the Lord.*
> *Jeremiah 3:5, 12*

The contrast between wrath that lasts a moment and love that goes on forever is expressed in prophetic words:

---

*Also, *rahum* separately in Deut. 4:31; *hannun* separately in Exod. 22:26; Ps. 116:5.

> *In overflowing wrath for a moment*
> *I hid My face from you,*
> *But with everlasting love I will have compassion on you.*
> *Says the Lord, your Redeemer.*
>
> Isaiah 54:8

In the numerous biblical statements about the attributes of God, the adjectives used are "good," "righteous," "merciful," "gracious." Only once does the expression "angry [or wrathful] God" occur (Nah. 1:2). Anger is an act, a situation, not an essential attribute. This distinction is implied in the words which are of fundamental importance for the understanding of all biblical words: "The Lord, the Lord, a God merciful and gracious, slow to anger, long-suffering, and abundant in love and truth; keeping mercy unto the thousandth generation. Who takes away iniquity and transgression and sin; but Who will by no means clear the guilty; visiting the iniquity of the fathers upon the children, and upon the children's children, unto the third and unto the fourth generation" (Exod. 34: 6–7).

## THE SECRET OF ANGER IS CARE

The secret of anger is God's care. There is nothing greater than the certainty of His care. Anger brings about destruction and distress, but not despair. The prophet's response is not only acceptance, but also gratitude. This is the climax of faith.

> *You will say in that day:*
> *I will give thanks to Thee, O Lord,*
> *For though Thou wast angry with me;*
> *Thy anger turned away,*
> *And Thou didst comfort me.*
>
> Isaiah 12:1*

Afflicted by the anger of God, the prophet is neither indifferent to suffering nor perplexed by it. The wrath is not the end, nor is suffer-

---

*I follow the rabbinic interpretation, see Bab., *Niddah* 31a, Rashi, *Commentary, ad loc.; Leviticus Rabba*, ch. 32, beginning.

ing an absolute. The experience is dark, to be sure, but in the darkness caused by God, there is God and there is light.

> Rejoice not over me, O my enemy,*
> When I fall, I shall rise;
> When I sit in the darkness,
> The Lord will be my light.
> I will bear the indignation of the Lord
> Because I have sinned against Him,
> Until He pleads my cause
> And executes judgment for me.
> He will bring me forth to the light,
> I shall behold His righteousness,
>
> Micah 7:8–9

When Jerusalem fell, the enemy invaded the sanctuary and massacred the people.

> The Lord has destroyed without mercy
> All the habitations of Jacob;
> In His wrath He has broken down
> The strongholds; . . .
> The kingdom and its rulers.
>
> Lamentations 2:2

And yet, God's mercy is renewed every morning, and therefore man may hope in sorrow, which is only a divine method of discipline.

> The Lord is good to those who wait for Him,
> To the soul that seeks Him.
> It is good that one should wait quietly
> For the salvation of the Lord.
>
> Lamentations 3:25–26

Job's answer to his wife expresses the essential attitude: "Shall we accept good at the hand of God, and shall we not accept evil?"

---

*Anguished by the blows of enemies, Israel was the butt of stinging sneer: "Where is the Lord your God?" (Pss. 42:4; 79:10; 115:2; Joel 2:17; Obad. 12 ff.; cf. Pss. 25:2; 35:19.)

(Job 2:10.) Certain of God's faithfulness to His people, trusting in His justice, the biblical man was able to say: "Though He slay me, yet will I trust on Him" (Job 13:15).

Evil was accepted because it came from God. Then people began to wonder whether it was right to hold God responsible for all misfortunes that happen to man. One very strange adversity that happened at the time of David, described in one source as due to divine anger, is ascribed in another source to a power of darkness.* The latter conception stands in sharp contrast to the efforts of the prophets to unravel the mystery of divine wrath, to account for it in terms of a higher justice, of a more profound responsibility.

The ultimate meaning of history lies in the continuity of God's concern. His wrath is not regarded as an emotional outburst, as an irrational fit, but rather as a part of His continual care. Because the prophets could not remain calm in the face of crimes committed by men and disasters falling upon men, they had to remember and to remind others: God's heart is not of stone.

## DISTASTEFUL TO GOD

Anger is an emotion attendant upon God's judgment, but not identical with it. It is the personal dimension of God's justice. God is not only Judge, Guardian, and Lawgiver, but also the loving Father Who is intimately affected by what man does to man as well as by what He Himself does to man.

The significance of divine anger as personal participation is apparent in a careful reading of the words spoken after the people worshiped the golden calf: "Now therefore let Me alone *that my anger may turn against them,* and that I may consume them . . ." (Exod. 32:10). Let us imagine that these words had come down to us in the following version: "Now therefore let Me alone that I may consume

---

*It is told in II Sam. 24:1 that the Lord was angry with the people and prompted David to a sinful act in taking a census in order to bring disaster upon the people. Later in II Chron. 21:1 this was modified by Satan's being made responsible for inciting David to take the census.

them. . . ." and an image would emerge of an unfeeling, stony-hearted God Who, without personal involvement, is about to consume a whole people.

The situation of little children in relation to their parents may be described as one of complete dependence; children are miserable when deprived of the experience of being loved. Similarly, the situation of parents in relation to their children may be described as one of spiritual dependence; parents are in misery when unable to love. As a rule, the parent is more fully conscious of the meaning of this dependence than the child, and the parent's pain in hurting is deeper than the child's pain in being hurt.

The anger of the Lord is a tragic necessity, a calamity for man and grief for God. It is not an emotion He delights in, but an emotion He deplores. "For He does not willingly afflict or grieve the sons of men" (Lam. 3:33). "Thus says the Lord God of hosts, the God of Israel: Why do you commit this great evil against yourselves? . . . Why do you provoke Me to Anger?" (Jer. 44:7–8.)

The state of wrath is distasteful to God. This is the dream of God: to see Israel as a pleasant vineyard (Isa. 5:1 ff.), and to say of Himself: "I have no wrath."

> *In that day:*
> *A pleasant vineyard, sing of it!*
> *I, the Lord, am its keeper;*
> *Every moment I water it.*
> *Lest any one harm it,*
> *I guard it night and day;*
> *I have no wrath.*
>
> Isaiah 27:2–3

> *I will not execute My fierce anger,*
> *I will not again destroy Ephraim;*
> *For I am God and not man,*
> *The Holy One in your midst,*
> *And I will not come to destroy.*
>
> Hosea 11:9

The intention of this passage is to elucidate the nature of divine anger. Just as God is absolutely different from man, so is divine anger different from human anger. The Lord must punish, but He will not destroy, for He is the master of His anger,* in control of His anger, "for I am God and not man."

## ANGER AS SUSPENDED LOVE

As a mode of pathos, it may be accurate to characterize the anger of the Lord as *suspended* love, as mercy withheld, as mercy in concealment. Anger prompted by love is an interlude. It is as if compassion were waiting to resume. "I will pluck them up from their land . . . and after I have plucked them up, I will again have compassion on them, and I will bring them again each to his heritage and each to his land" (Jer. 12:14–15).

> *For the Lord will not*
> *Cast off for ever,*
> *But, though he cause grief, He will have compassion*
> *According to the abundance of His love.*
> Lamentations 3:31–32

Suspended mercy, or love withheld, is a term that attempts to describe what wrath may mean to God. It certainly fails to convey what His wrath means to man. Doom, destruction, agony, make us feel that mercilessness is much harsher than the mere absence of mercy. Once the fury of the events is unleashed, the innocent suffer as much as the wicked.

Does the term "suspended love" express the terrifying word?

> *So I will be to them like a lion,*
> *Like a leopard I will lurk beside the way,*
> *I will fall upon them like a bear robbed of her cubs,*
> *I will tear open their breast,*

*See Ibn Ezra and Kimhi, *Commentaries, ad loc.*

> *And there I will devour them like a lion,*
> *As a wild beast would rend them.*
>
> *Hosea 13:7–8*

What was first uttered as a threat was later experienced as a fact.

> *He is to me like a bear lying in wait,*
> *Like a lion in hiding;*
> *He led me off my way and tore me to pieces.*
>
> *Lamentations 3:10–11*

And the most bitter statement, "The Lord has become like an enemy; He has destroyed Israel" (Lam. 2:5), was not expressed as a tenet, but as an outcry of astonishment. Yet, a later prophet undertook to explain the incongruous:

> *They rebelled*
> *And grieved His holy spirit,*
> *Therefore He turned to be their enemy,*
> *And Himself fought against them.*
>
> *Isaiah 63:10*

The wrath of God is neither eerie nor weird, but justified.

A note of sorrow over the distress He brought to Israel rings in God's words: "I have dealt you the blow of an enemy, the punishment of a merciless foe, Because your guilt is great, because your sins are flagrant. . . . and all your foes . . . those who despoil you shall become a spoil" (Jer. 30:14–16).

Cruel though the wrath of God be, yet it is transcended by His love. The view that "love is nothing but quenched wrath"* exemplifies an extreme misinterpretation of biblical thought.

The anger of God may bring misery and distress. Nevertheless, there is an agony more excruciating, more loathsome: the state of being forsaken by God. The punishment of being discarded, abandoned, rejected, is worse than the punishment of exile. Anger, too, is

*See R. Otto, *The Idea of the Holy* (London, 1923), p. 24.

a form of His presence in history. Anger, too, is an expression of His concern.

This is the grandeur of God's compassion as proclaimed by the prophets. It is a love that transcends the most intense anger, a love that abides in full recognition of human weakness.

## ANGER AND GRANDEUR

Our embarrassment in reading the harsh expressions of divine wrath is also due to the general disposition of modern man. We have no sense for spiritual grandeur. Spiritual to us means ethereal, calm, moderate, slight, imperceptible. We respond to beauty; grandeur is unbearable. We are moved by a soft religiosity, and would like to think that God is lovely, tender, and familiar, as if faith were a source of comfort, but not readiness for martyrdom.

To our mind the terrible threats of castigation bespeak a lack of moderation. Is it not because we are only dimly aware of the full gravity of human failure, of the sufferings inflicted by those who revile God's demand for justice? There is a cruelty which pardons, just as there is a pity which punishes. Severity must tame whom love cannot win.

Those of us to whom the crimes of the world are mere incidents, and the agony of the poor is one of the many facts of life, may be inclined to describe the God of the prophets as stern, arbitrary, inscrutable, even unaccountable. But the thought of God and indifference to other people's suffering are mutually exclusive.

Nothing is so sweet to the heart of man as love. However, for love to function, the suppression of sympathy may be necessary. A surgeon would be a failure if he indulged his natural sympathy at the sight of a bleeding wound. He must suppress his emotion to save a life, he must hurt in order to heal. Genuine love, genuine mercy, must not be taken to be indulgence of mere feeling, excess of sensibility, which is commonly called sentimentality.

No single attribute can convey the nature of God's relationship to man. Since justice is His nature, love, which would disregard the evil deeds of man, would contradict His nature. Because of His concern for man, His justice is tempered with mercy. Divine anger is not the antithesis of love, but its counterpart, a help to justice as demanded by true love.

The end of sentimentality is the enfeeblement of truth and justice. It is divine anger that gives strength to God's truth and justice. There are moments in history when anger alone can conquer evil. It is after mildness and kindness have failed that anger is proclaimed.

## In Conclusion

To sum up, the pathos of anger is by no means regarded as an attribute, as a basic disposition, as a quality inherent in the nature of God, but rather as a mood, a state of mind or soul. In both its origin and duration, anger is distinguished from mercy. It is never a spontaneous outburst, but rather a state which is occasioned and conditioned by man. There is a biblical belief in divine grace, in a mercy which is bestowed upon man to a degree greater than he deserves. There is no belief in divine arbitrariness, in an anger which consumes and afflicts without moral justification. The pathos of anger is, further, a transient state.* What is often proclaimed about love—"For the Lord is good, for His steadfast love endures for ever" (Jer. 33:11; Ps. 100:5; Ezra 3:11; I Chron. 16:34; II Chron. 5:13; 7:3)—is not said about anger. "Will He be angry for ever? Will He be indignant to the end?" (Jer. 3:5) asked a horrified people. The answer is given in the prophet's powerful predictions of redemption. "For I will not contend for ever, nor will I always be angry" (Isa. 57:16).

The normal and original pathos is love or mercy. Anger is preceded as well as followed by compassion (Jer. 12:15; 33:26). For punishment to be imposed upon the people, God's "love and steadfast mercy" must be suppressed (Jer. 16:5). These are the words spoken to Jeremiah: "I am the merciful" (Jer. 3:12), "I am the Lord who practices kindness, justice, and righteousness in the earth; for in these

---

*In his address to God, Jeremiah speaks of "a moment of anger" (18:23; cf. 18:7 and Isa. 26:20).

things I delight, says the Lord" (Jer. 9:23). Even in moments of indignation, His love remains alive.

> *Return, faithless Israel, says the Lord;*
> *I will not look on you in anger,*
> *For I am merciful, says the Lord,*
> *I will not be angry for ever. . . .*
> *Is not Ephraim a precious son to Me?*
> *Is he not a darling child?*
> *For as often as I speak against him,*
> *I do remember him still.*
> *Therefore My heart yearns for him;*
> *I must deal with him in boundless compassion,*
> *Says the Lord.*
>
> Jeremiah 3:12; 31:20

The divine pathos, whether mercy or anger, was never thought of as an impulsive act, arising automatically within the divine Being as the reaction to man's behavior and as something due to peculiarity of temperament or propensity. It is neither irrational nor irresistible. Pathos results from a decision, from an act of will. It comes about in the light of moral judgment rather than in the darkness of passion.

It was only in the certainty that His mercy is greater than His justice that the prophet could pray:

> *Though our iniquities testify against us,*
> *Act, O Lord, for Thy name's sake.*
>
> Jeremiah 14:7

# 6

# Ira Dei

## THE GOD OF WRATH

In the history of Christian theology the implications of divine pathos have been brought into focus by the problem of divine anger (*ira dei*), which for a long time has formed the object of passionate and learned discussion. Under the influence of the philosophical doctrine of God, there arose in Gnostic circles a movement of sharpest opposition to anthropopathy. This reached its climax in the teachings of Marcion who, for a variety of reasons, affirmed an abrupt discontinuity between the gracious God and the just God. He bitterly assailed as imperfect the just world-Creator of "the Old Testament," the Demiurge, specially emphasizing His anger, but also His affections in general.

Starting with an understanding of God as love and grace, and driven by a profound aversion to the Torah, Marcion, who considered himself a faithful follower of Paul,* found it impossible to reconcile his understanding with the biblical references to the God of anger and

---

*A. Harnack remarked: "It may be said that in the second century only one Christian—Marcion—understood Paul; but it must be added that he misunderstood him." See M. S. Enslin, "The Pontic Mouse," *Anglican Theological Review*, XXVII (1945), 15.

particularly with the misery of man and the nature of this world. The world, as he saw it, was "stupid and bad, crawling with vermin, a miserable hole, an object of scorn." He found it inconceivable that the God of grace and goodness should have created "the disgusting paraphernalia of reproduction and the nauseating defilements of the human flesh from birth to final putrescence."*

"The foundation of Marcion's entire criticism of the creator or just god was the conviction that God must be impassible."† The God of the Hebrew Bible Who could say, "I create evil" (Isa. 45:7), could not Himself be good. "He was the Demiurge, the creator of the universe, but he was not the God whom Jesus had come to reveal."

He insisted that the one is "judicial, harsh, mighty in war; the other mild, placid, and simply good and excellent."‡ The God of the Hebrew Bible, Marcion further considered "to be the author of evils, to take delight in war, to be infirm in purpose, and even to be contrary to himself,"§ ignorant, cruel,‖ inconsistent, mutable,# and wicked.**

The good God, who was unknown not only to men but also to the Creator, decides to undo the works of the Creator. Jesus is His emissary whose purpose is to redeem the race of man enslaved to the Demiurge. Man must renounce his allegiance to the Creator, flee all contact with His works. It was consistent with his view of the world that Marcion condemned marriage and frowned upon the propagation of children.††

---

*A. Harnack, *Marcion, Das Evangelium vom fremden Gott* (1st ed.; Leipzig, 1921), pp. 94, 97; 144 f.; see H. R. Niebuhr, *Christ and Culture* (New York, 1951), p. 168.

†M. Pohlenz, *Vom Zorne Gottes* (Göttingen, 1909), p. 21.

‡Tertullian, *Adversus Marcionem,* I, 6.

§Irenaeus, *Adversus Haereses,* I, 27, 2; Tertullian, *op. cit.,* II, 14.

‖Tertullian, *op. cit.,* II, 11, 25.

#Tertullian, *De Idolatria,* 5.

**Hippolytus, *Refutatio Omnium Haeresium,* VII, 30, 2. See H. A. Wolfson, *The Philosophy of the Church Fathers,* I (Cambridge, Mass., 1956), 542, n. 34.

††The wrath of God is sensed as a reality in the New Testament, see, e.g., Matt. 3:7; Luke 3:7; Rom. 1:18 ff.; 3:5; 5:9; 12:19; Eph. 2:3; 5:6; Col. 3:6; I Thess. 2:16; 5:9; Rev. 14:10; ch. 15; 18:3; 19:5. For literature on the subject see *Realencyklopädie für protestantische Theologie und Kirche,* XXI (Leipzig, 1908), 722 ff. *ThWBNT,* V, s.v. *orge.*

Marcion wanted a Christianity free from every vestige of Judaism. He saw his task in showing the complete opposition between the Hebrew Bible and the Gospels. Repudiating the Hebrew Bible *in toto,* he put in its place a new Scripture, the nucleus of which was the letters of Paul. The good God, as described in Marcion's Scripture, was "incapable of anger, entirely apathetic, free from all affections."*

Marcion deeply challenged Christian thinking and precipitated a grave crisis in the history of the Church. In the year C.E. 144 the Church expelled him and anathematized his doctrines.†

## THE REPUDIATION OF MARCION

In a special work, dedicated to the refutation of Marcionism, Tertullian maintained that anger is a necessary attribute of God as a Judge. For "if He is neither jealous nor angry, if He neither harms nor injures, . . . I do not understand how the meaning of discipline can have any meaning."‡

Yet, having affirmed the idea of divine anger, he denied anger to the Father and attributed it to the Son. "Whatever, therefore, you demand as worthy of God must be found in the Father, and, as I might say, in the God of the philosophers who is invisible, inaccessible, and mild. On the other hand, whatever you reprehend as unworthy, must be imputed to the Son who has seen, heard, and spoken to, the witness and servant of the Father, uniting in himself man and God, in great deeds God, in weak ones man."§ Thus, while rejecting the dualism of the just God and the good God, he introduced another kind of dualism—"the impassible Father and the irascible Son."‖ All the pas-

---

*See A. Harnack, *Lehrbuch der Dogmengeschichte,* I (Freiburg, 1894), 260. Cf. Tertullian, *Adversus Marcionem,* I, 27: "A better god has been discovered who never takes offense, is never angry, never inflicts punishment."

†For an attempt to find echoes of the Marcionite controversy in rabbinic literature, see A. Marmorstein, *Studies in Jewish Theology* (London, 1950), pp. 1 ff.

‡*Adversus Marcionem,* I, 26.

§*Ibid.,* II, 27.

‖E. F. Micka, *The Problem of Divine Anger in Arnobius and Lactantius* (Washington, 1943), p. 30.

sages in Scripture which Marcion had found offensive, Tertullian referred to the Logos. The Logos plays almost the same part in this thought as had been fulfilled in later Platonism by "demons on whose responsibility was cast everything repulsive concerning the gods."*

In the polemic of Jews and Christians against heathendom, the passions of the pagan gods formed a favorite target of attack.† The question thus raised by Marcion brought to a head the problem of divine passibility within the Christian Church, too. In the struggle against Marcion it became necessary to deal with the problem of divine passions.

The Apologists of the second century C.E., though accepting in theory the idea that God is impassible and that anger cannot be predicated of the divine Being, continued to refer to the threat and manifestation of divine anger.‡ A detailed discussion of the problem was undertaken by Arnobius and Lactantius.

Arnobius, born about C.E. 260, a teacher of rhetoric in North Africa who was converted to Christianity late in life, stressed in his work *Adversus Nationes* the wretchedness of man and the excellence of God. Men are not the offspring of God, and whoever maintains that they are is guilty of blasphemy. They do not owe their origin to Him any more than flies, beetles, moths, and other insects do. God is too exalted to be concerned in the least with the conduct of men, with the good or the evil that befalls them. Any interest in man would be unbecoming to God. Anthropomorphism must be utterly rejected. "Would you like it if donkeys, dogs or pigs decided that they owed religious veneration to man and then proceeded to fashion him after their own likeness? Or if swallows offered him as an honorable gift the capacity to fly?" Defining anger as the "passion which approaches closest to wild animals and beasts, disturbs with misfortune those who

*M. Pohlenz, *op. cit.*, p. 29.

†"Let us grant that they have human forms, but let them be above wrath and anger." (R. Harris, *The Apology of Aristides on Behalf of Christians* [Cambridge, 1893], p. 100.)

‡M. Pohlenz, *op. cit.*, p. 44; E. F. Micka, *op. cit.*, pp. 18 f.

experience it, and leads to the danger of destruction," Arnobius considered it blasphemous to ascribe anger to God.*

A point of view opposite to Arnobius' was presented by his fellow countryman and pupil, Lactantius, who considered the subject of divine anger so important that he devoted a special treatise to it entitled *De Ira Dei*. He maintained that if God cares for man, He must regard man with love when he does good and be moved to anger when he sins, and necessarily so, for he who hates wickedness must love goodness; and, on the contrary, he who is not angry at evil does not love the good. Passions, Lactantius maintained, are not in themselves diseases, as the Stoics had taught. When kept within proper bounds, they are an occasion of virtue. God in His providence placed them in man and ordained that the passions be material of vices, and vices be the material whence virtues are drawn. He argued against those who thought "that God is moved by no feeling."

Anger, which Lactantius defined as "a motion of the soul rousing itself to curb sin," ought to be present in man, so that he can correct the vices and faults of those who are subject to him, and must be present in God. It is impossible that God not be angry when He sees His law contemned. God must be provoked by the sins of man, since He has set man in a personal relationship to Himself.

In subsequent ages, the view advanced by Clement and Origen prevailed. Anger or any other *affectus,* as predicated of God in the Bible, must not be taken literally. Since the language of the Bible is adapted to the capacity of man, its spiritual truth is to be found in the nonliteral meanings of the words.† Clement and Origen, following Philo, refused to take literally the notions of the anger, repentance, and jealousy of God. "Just as when we are talking with little children we do not aim to speak in the finest language possible to us, but say

*M. Pohlenz, *op. cit.,* pp. 47 ff.; E. F. Micka, *op. cit.,* pp. 39 ff.

†Lactantius, *De Ira Dei,* 5, 10; M. Pohlenz, *op. cit.,* pp. 48 ff.; E. F. Micka, *op. cit.,* pp. 114 ff. Lactantius composed a treatise, *De Mortibus Persecutorum,* containing a history of divine anger exercised against those who hated God and His followers; see Micka, *op. cit.,* p. 130, n. 64.

what is appropriate to the weakness of those whom we are addressing, . . .
so also the Logos of God seems to have arranged the Scriptures, using
the method of address which fitted the ability and benefit of the read-
ers."\* God's wrath is not "an emotional reaction on His part, but
something which He uses in order to correct by stern methods those
who have committed many terrible sins." It has "a corrective purpose."†

By the fourth century C.E., the theory that God was impassible
was a generally recognized principle. For Augustine, also, the
Hebrew Bible predicated passions in God "whether because of
peculiar features in the diction of the original language, or whether
mistakenly in order to speak intelligibly to men." He would "feel it
to be a desecration and blasphemy," were any one really to suppose
God passible.‡

Luther, who cherished "a certain gloomy distrust of God's readiness to come to man's assistance" and "a melancholy conception of a
stern and cruel God,"§ used to boast that he had spoken more strongly
of the divine wrath than had been done "under the Pope."

Among the enemies, or "the tyrants" from which Christ delivers
mankind are the Law and the wrath. In counting Law as a "tyrant,"
Luther follows Paul; the inclusion of wrath is remarkable. For
"though the Wrath of God is identical with His will, yet it is, according to Luther, a tyrant, even the most awful and terrible of all the
tyrants. It is a tyrant in that it stands opposed to the Divine Love. At
this point the idea of God's own conflict and victory is brought by
Luther to a paradoxical sharpness. . . . It would seem almost as if the
conflict were carried back within the Divine Being itself. . . . Luther
presents us here with an antinomy, a conflict, between the Divine
curse, the Wrath, and the Divine blessing, the Love."‖

\*Origen, *Contra Celsum*, IV, 71.
†*Ibid.*, IV, 72.
‡M. Pohlenz, *op. cit.*, p. 128; J. K. Mozley, *The Impassibility of God* (London,
1926), pp. 104 ff.
§H. Grisar, *Luther*, I (London, 1913), 113, 189.
‖G. Aulen, *Christus Victor* (London, 1950), pp. 130 f.

## THE SURVIVAL OF MARCIONISM

Marcion's proclamation about the God of Israel has been stubbornly preserved in the mind of Western man to this day. Even modern scholars have not refrained from speaking of the God of Israel as if He were Moloch. We are told that the God of Israel was thought of as the "destroyer, sinister, dangerous and unaccountably angered, as one who rejoices in destruction, ruins unexpectedly and craftily, who punishes without mercy, demands cruelty and creates evil."*

The God of Israel is consistently described as "stern, arbitrary, inscrutable, unaccountable, even frightful."† "The God of the Old Testament is a God of power, the God of the New Testament is also a God of love."‡

"Jewish theology never seems to have risen above" the vindictive theory of justice, human and divine, "in its exposition of the ultimate divine purpose. And the defect of the Jewish presentation of God in much of the Old Testament is the imputation to him of strong vindictiveness with liability to such passing human emotions as rage, fury and jealousy, hence the thoughtful and refined heretic Marcion pronounced the God of the Jews just, but not wholly good. And Christianity to our own day has been in its doctrine of judgment in bondage to the Judaic spirit, of which it inherited a large measure from the beginning."§

The Aztec god Tezcatlipoca is a despotic numen, "all-powerful in earth and sky, but more inclined to do evil than good, vengeful and pitiless, rather than just, the author of disagreements and quarrels and cursed by his victims, . . . the great enemy." This god, "who is a despotic divinity, ruthless, implacable, violent in punishing, well-pleased at inflicting pain, has the appearance, if we darken the colours, of an Old Testament God."‖ Chungichnish, a god of the Luiseno

---

*P. Volz, *Das Dämonische* (Tübingen, 1924), p. 9.
†H. J. Muller, *The Uses of the Past* (New York, 1952), p. 83.
‡B. Russell, *History of Western Philosophy* (London, 1946), p. 608.
§L. R. Farnell, *The Attributes of God* (Oxford, 1925), p. 174.
‖R. Pettazzoni, *The All-Knowing God* (London, 1956), pp. 409, 438, adopted this ingenious comparison from H. Dietschy's article in *Anthropos* (Germany, 1940–41), p. 336, who writes that *"Tezcatlipoca ist, wenn man will, ein alttestamentlicher*

Indians of southern California, has been considered as "a living god that watched and punished," a kind of God of Israel.* Similarly, we are told that because of "this character of irascibility and of vindictiveness which not even the prophets can completely transfigure into their ideal of a God of justice, . . . [the God of Israel] has been compared to the Vedic Varuna."†

The spirit of Marcion, hovering invisibly over many waters, has often been brought to clear expression. In his work on Marcion, Adolf Harnack, a leading authority on Christian history and dogma, maintains that what Marcion demanded was basically right: the Old Testament must be eliminated from the Church. The trouble with the churches is that they are too timorous to admit the truth. "The rejection of the Old Testament in the second century was a mistake which the Great Church rightly refused to make; the retention of it in the sixteenth century was a fatal legacy which the Reformation could not yet avoid; but for Protestantism since the nineteenth century to treasure it as a canonical document is the result of paralysis which affects religion and the Church. To make a clean sweep and to pay homage to truth in confession and in instruction is the heroic action demanded of Protestantism today—and it is almost too late."‡

The history of the Western world may be written and appraised by the way the various generations understood or misunderstood, revered or repudiated, the spirit of the prophets. Whether the constant harping on the subject of the God of anger is due to superficiality in the knowledge of the Bible or to a profound hostility remains a fateful issue.

---

*Gott."* The Nazi ideology which infested the scholarly output of those years should impose some caution in relying upon such sources.

    *M. Eliade and J. M. Kitagawa, eds., *The History of Religions* (Chicago, 1959), p. 6a.

    †A. Titius, *"Die Anfänge der Religion bei Ariern und Semiten,"* Studien zur systematischen Theologie, XVI (Heidelberg, 1934), p. 34. One of the three reasons for the elimination of the Hebrew Bible given in the *"Mythos des zwanzigsten Jahrhunderts"* is that the God of Israel is *"ein tyrannischer Dämon, der dem wirren religiösen Denken der Juden entsprungen ist."*

    ‡A. Harnack, *Marcion* (2nd ed.; Leipzig, 1924), pp. 127, 222. See E. C. Blackman, *Marcion and His Influence* (London, 1948), p. 122.

## DEMONIC OR DYNAMIC

Embarrassment over the emotional features of the biblical account of God induced the so-called "historical school" of Bible criticism to assume an evolutionary development. In ancient times, it was alleged, Israel knew only the terrible, mysterious God. It was only in later times that they came to think of Him as a loving and good God.

Israel, we are told, was compelled "to transfer all sinister forms to the essential nature of God, who still shared much in common with the demon."* Thus they developed the conception of the jealous, terrible, and explosive God. The demonic element, it was believed, belonged to the essential basis of "Old Testament" theism generally.† Even the rejection of magic in biblical religion is explained by the demonic nature of God. "In the presence of such a monstrous and frightful God, who united all the might of God and demons, magic completely disappeared: before such a God, who was not only a demon, but also God, no charm could avail."‡

This view, which is neither true to fact nor in line with the fundamental biblical outlook, arises from the failure to understand the meaning of the God of pathos and particularly the meaning of anger as a mode of pathos. We must not forget that the God of Israel is sublime rather than sentimental, nor should we associate the kind with the apathetic, the intense with the sinister, the dynamic with the demonic. The stormy violence of the manifestations of God in the Bible cannot be reconciled with an apathetic-harmonious divinity. These outbursts must be seen as an aspect of pathos which is characterized by the correlation of love and anger, mercy and justice.

It is incorrect to make the generalization that "it is patent from

---

*G. van der Leeuw, *Religion in Essence and Manifestation* (London, 1938), pp. 139 f.

†P. Volz, *op. cit.*, p. 5; see p. 39; G. Hölscher, *Geschichte der Israelitischen und Juedischen Religion* (Giessen, 1922), pp. 67 ff., 85–87.

‡P. Volz, *op. cit.*, p. 31. More recently scholars have been inclined to date back to an early period the tradition of God as the dispenser of the blessings of nature and as the gracious Savior God Who freed Israel from Egypt, and proved His faithfulness preeminently in the desert.

many passages in the Old Testament that [the wrath of God] has no concern whatever with moral qualities. There is something very baffling in the way in which it 'is kindled' and manifested. It is, as has been well said, 'like a hidden force of nature,' like stored-up electricity, discharging itself upon any one who comes too near. It is 'incalculable' and 'arbitrary.' "*

His anger is aroused when the cry of the oppressed comes into His ears. "You shall not wrong a stranger or oppress him, for you were strangers in the land of Egypt. You shall not afflict any widow or orphan. If you do afflict them, and they cry out to me, I will surely hear their cry; and my wrath will burn, and I will kill you with the sword, and your wives shall become widows and your children fatherless" (Exod. 22:21–24).†

---

*R. Otto, *The Idea of the Holy* (London, 1923), p. 18.

†S. D. Goitein in his article in *Vetus Testamentum,* vol. VI (1956), pp. 1–9, has suggested that the Tetragrammaton is related to the Hebrew root *hwy* (and the Arabic *hawa*), the basic meaning of which is passionate love and devotion to some aim (see Micah 7:3; Prov. 10:3). "The name has the usual form of the imperfect—as, e.g., the names of Isaac and Jacob—and means therefore *'He who acts passionately, the Passionate.'*" Such interpretation of the Name may be found in Exodus 33:19, where God says to Moses: "I will make all My goodness pass before you, and will proclaim before you My name 'the Lord'; and I will be gracious to whom I will be gracious, and will show mercy on whom I will show mercy." The Lord proclaims His name "in order to make manifest His nature: He is passionately devoted to those whom He regards as worthy." Similarly the name in Exodus 3:14 is to be understood as "I shall (passionately) love whom I love." In other words: "I shall redeem the people of Israel who worship Me." The root *kn'* implies two meanings: "The strength of emotion and the exclusiveness of its direction." Exodus 34:14, *The Lord, His name is Jealous* "should not be understood as implying that the nature of the Lord is that of a jealous God, but that His very name actually meant this." Cf. also S. D. Goitein's review of *Die Prophetie* in *Kirjath Sepher,* XIII (Jerusalem, 1936–37), 450–452.

# 7

# Religion of Sympathy

## THEOLOGY AND RELIGION

It is important to distinguish between the objective and the subjective aspect of the prophetic consciousness of God. By the objective aspect we mean that which is given to the prophet as a reality transcending his consciousness. By the subjective aspect we mean the personal attitude or the response of the prophet to that reality. The objective aspect may be properly designated as the theme of prophetic theology; the subjective aspect may be designated as the theme of prophetic religion.

The fundamental feature of divine reality, present in the prophets' consciousness, we have described as pathos. Their attitude or response to that reality we have found to be sympathy. For the understanding of prophetic religion, sympathy is as fundamental as pathos is for the understanding of prophetic theology. It is now our task to analyze the meaning of prophetic sympathy.

The nature of man's response to the divine corresponds to the content of his apprehension of the divine. When the divine is sensed as mysterious perfection, the response is one of fear and trembling; when sensed as absolute will, the response is one of unconditional obedience; when sensed as pathos, the response is one of sympathy.

Such a classification must not be taken in an absolute sense, as if the awareness of one aspect of the divine either excluded or obscured the awareness of any other aspect. However, no reality or subject matter can be apprehended simultaneously and wholeheartedly in all its aspects. To the prophet, the pathos is the predominant and staggering aspect in what he encounters. Even if in the first place the people's practical compliance with the divine demand is the purpose of his mission, the inner personal identification of the prophet with the divine pathos is, as we have shown, the central feature of his own life. Not the word and the Law in themselves, but the mode of divine involvement is the focal point in his religious consciousness. The divine pathos is reflected in his attitudes, hopes, and prayers. The prophet is stirred by an intimate concern for the divine concern. Sympathy, then, is the essential mode in which he responds to the divine situation. It is the way of fulfilling personally the demand addressed to him in moments of revelation.

It is no mere listening to, and conveying of, a divine message which distinguishes his personal life. The prophet not only hears and apprehends the divine pathos; he is convulsed by it to the depths of his soul. His service of the divine word is not carried out through mental appropriation, but through the harmony of his being with its fundamental intention and emotional content.

Any other attitude would seem preposterous to the prophet, whose mission is to proclaim the pathos to the people. How could he remain indifferent, unmoved? *Epoché* in the face of divine involvement would be callousness to the divine.

For the biblical man who has an awareness of the unity of the psychical life, and for whom the passions form an integral part of the human spiritual structure, an unemotional sobriety could not be the form of religious consciousness. An emotional religion of sympathy is more compatible with his mentality than a self-detached religion of obedience. Man is expected to love his God with all his heart, with all his soul, with all his might.

## THE PROPHET AS A *HOMO SYMPATHETIKOS*

In contrast to the Stoic sage who is a *homo apathetikos,* the prophet may be characterized as a *homo sympathetikos.** For the phenomenology of religion the prophet represents a type *sui generis.* The pathos of God is upon him. It moves him. It breaks out in him like a storm in the soul, overwhelming his inner life, his thoughts, feelings, wishes, and hopes. It takes possession of his heart and mind, giving him the courage to act against the world.

The words of the prophet are often like thunder; they sound as if he were in a state of hysteria. But what appears to us as wild emotionalism must seem like restraint to him who has to convey the emotion of the Almighty in the feeble language of man. His sympathy is an overflow of powerful emotion which comes in response to what he sensed in divinity. For the only way to intuit a feeling is to feel it. One cannot have a merely intellectual awareness of a concrete suffering or pleasure, for intellect as such is merely the tracing of relations, and a feeling is no mere relational pattern. In contradistinction to empathy, which denotes living the situation of another person, sympathy means living with another person.

The unique feature of religious sympathy is not self-conquest, but self-dedication; not the suppression of emotion, but its redirection; not silent subordination, but active co-operation with God; not love which aspires to the Being of God in Himself, but harmony of the soul with the concern of God. To be a prophet means to identify one's concern with the concern of God.

*The interpretation of the prophetic personality in terms of sympathy as developed in my book *Die Prophetie* (Krakow, 1936) has been adopted by H. Wheeler Robinson, *Redemption and Revelation* (London, 1942), p. 150 n., and in his interpretation of Hosea, *Two Hebrew Prophets* (London, 1948), pp. 21 ff.; see N. W. Porteous in H. W. Robinson, ed., *Record and Revelation* (Oxford, 1938), p. 240; C. R. North, *The Old Testament Interpretation of History* (London, 1946), pp. 172 ff. Henry Corbin applied the categories of the theology of pathos and the religion of sympathy to the religious existence of the Sufis in Islam in his illuminating essay, *"Sympathie et théopathie chez les 'fidèles d'amour' en Islam,"* *Eranos Jahrbuch,* XXIV (1956), pp. 199–301; *idem, L'Imagination créatrice dans le soufisme D'Ibn (Arabi,* Paris, 1958. Cf. also H. Knight, *The Hebrew Prophetic Consciousness* (London, 1947).

Sympathy is a state in which a person is open to the presence of another person. It is a feeling which feels the feeling to which it reacts—the opposite of emotional solitariness. In prophetic sympathy, man is open to the presence and emotion of the transcendent Subject. He carries within himself the awareness of what is happening to God.

Thus, sympathy has a dialogical structure. What characterizes prophetic existence is, indeed, an interpersonal relationship, either a relationship between the one who feels and the one who sympathizes with that feeling, or a relationship of having a feeling in common. Unlike the experience of the numinous or the feeling of sheer awe or fear, sympathy always refers to a person or to persons.

Sympathy, however, is not an end in itself. Nothing is further from the prophetic mind than to inculcate or to live out a life of feeling, a religion of sentimentality. Not mere feeling, but action, will mitigate the world's misery, society's injustice or the people's alienation from God. Only action will relieve the tension between God and man. Both pathos and sympathy are, from the perspective of the total situation, demands rather than fulfillments. Prophetic sympathy is no delight; unlike ecstasy, it is not a goal, but a sense of challenge, a commitment, a state of tension, consternation, and dismay.

The prophets did not often speak of their sympathy. Yet, though rarely expressed, it is echoed in most of their words. The prophets were not in the habit of dwelling upon their private experiences. A feeling of shyness and reticence may have inhibited them from offering more than slight indications of their private emotions.

It is such intense sympathy or emotional identification with the divine pathos that may explain the shifting from the third to the first person in the prophetic utterances.* A prophecy that starts out speaking of God in the third person turns into God speaking in the first

---

*A. R. Johnson, *The One and the Many in the Israelite Conception of God* (Cardiff, 1961), pp. 33 ff., infers from this oscillation the idea that the prophet was held to be more than the representative of God; he was an active "extension" of the Lord's personality, and as such was the Lord in Person. Such an idea is, however, absolutely contrary to all we know about the prophets' understanding of God.

person.* Conversely, a prophecy starting with God speaking in the first person turns into a declaration of the prophet speaking about God in the third person.†

## SYMPATHY AND RELIGIOUS EXISTENCE

Prophetic sympathy is one of the heights of religious consciousness of transcendent spirituality. In contrast to a one-sided emotional relationship to God, as is the case, for example, in the religion of quietude or adoration, it is an attitude of many facets, calling forth all the soul's potentialities, every capacity of thought and feeling. Facing manifold forms of pathos, corresponding modes of sympathy are evoked. Indignation and tranquility, vehemence and humility, are transposed in the service of an ultimate goal. The religion of sympathy knows no bounds within the horizontally human. The assurance of worth, the religious legitimization of feeling and affection, spring from the vertical dimension within which pathos moves. This enrichment of spiritual resources creates a marvel of intense existence.

In the prophetic consciousness, "mystical and rational thinking is combined in a way which puts to shame all slogans about rationalism and irrationalism."‡ The prophet is a riddle for which there is no explanation. We believe, however, that the key to a psychological understanding of the prophets is the phenomenon of sympathy. It enables us to understand the zeal of the prophet who knows himself to be in emotional harmony and concord with God; and the power of

*Amos 3:1a (third person) and 3:1b (first person); Isa. 3:1a (third person) and 3:4a (first person); 5:1–2 (third person), 5:3–6 (first person), and 5:7 (third person); 10:12a (third person) and 10:12b (first person); 11:3a (third person) and 11:9a (first person); 22:17 (third person) and 22:19a, 20b (first person); Jer. 11:17a (third person) and 11:17b (first person); 23:9 (third person) and 23:11 (first person); 9:1 (the prophet speaking) and 9:2 (God speaking); Isa. 53:10a (third person) and 53:12 (first person); 61:6 (third person) and 61:8 (first person).

†Isa. 1:2b–3 (first person) and 1:4 (third person); Jer. 4:1 (first person) and 4:2 (third person); 4:21 (the prophet speaking) and 4:22 (God speaking); 8:13 (first person) and 8:14 (third person); Nah. 1:12 f. (first person) and 1:13 (third person).

‡R. Kittel, *Gestalten und Gedanken in Israel* (Leipzig, 1925), p. 505.

his anger, which motivates him to turn away from his people whom he loves so dearly. He is effective, not merely by his word and deed, but also by the force of his attitude which is sensed by his contemporaries to be the manifestation of his inner accord with God.

There is a question that has occupied many thinkers both in the Middle Ages and in modern times: What quality or capacity was there in the prophets that enabled them to hear the voice of God? In truth, however, there is no explanation for that which is a divine secret; there are no keys available to open God's hidden chambers. Ecstasy is a false answer to a real problem. Nor is the theory of sympathy able to unveil the mystery. Sympathy is the result of being a prophet, but it does not bring about prophetic events. Any kind of sympathy with God presupposes some sort of knowledge of the nature or of the pathos of God. It is not through sympathy that the prophet learns of the divine pathos, for the latter must already be known in some way if the prophet is to share it.

Sympathy is a prophetic sense. Compatible with God, the prophet is sensitive to the divine aspect of events. To be sure, such sensitivity is not regarded by him as an innate faculty. Sympathy is a response, not a manifestation of pure spontaneity. The prophet has to be called in order to respond, he has to receive in order to reciprocate.

This moving awareness of God's cares and sorrows concerning the world, the prophet's communion with the divine in experience and suffering, is of such evident and striking power and authority, evincing such complete surrender and devotion, that it may offer a basic understanding of religious existence. Perhaps it is in sympathy that the ultimate meaning, worth, and dignity of religion may be found. The depth of the soul becomes the point where an understanding for God and a harmony with transcendent possibility spring to birth.

This, perhaps, is the reward and distinction of prophetic existence: to be attuned to God. No one knows the measure of such intensity, the degree of such accord. It is more than a feeling. It is a whole way of being. In contrast to ecstasy, with its momentary transports, sympathy with God is a constant attitude.

Man's love of God is among the earliest expressions of biblical religion. It is mentioned in the Decalogue: ". . . showing love to thousands of those who love me" (Exod. 20:6); in the song of Deborah: ". . . those who love Him be like the sun as he rises in his might" (Judg. 5:31).

In the words of Isa. 41:8, God speaks of Abraham as "My friend."* In Deut. 33:12, Benjamin is called "the friend (*yedid*) of the Lord." As the prophet Isaiah begins his song of the vineyard,

> *Let me sing for my friend* [yedidi]
> *A love song concerning His Vineyard.*
> Isaiah 5:1

Israel calls to God: "My father, Thou art the friend of My youth (*alluph ne'urai*)" (Jer. 3:4).

Such a relationship seemed inconceivable to the mind of a thinker like Aristotle, who held that friendship involved equality. "This is evident from cases where there is a wide disparity between two persons in respect of virtue or vice or wealth or anything else; for such persons neither are nor expect to be friends. It is most clearly seen in our relations with the gods."†

According to Aristotle, there is no friendship of man with God. "For friendship," he maintains, "exists only where there can be a return of affection, but friendship toward God does not admit of love being returned, nor at all of loving. For it would be strange if one were to say that he loved Zeus."‡

---

*This refutes the statement of G. van der Leeuw, *Religion in Essence and Manifestation* (London, 1938), p. 477: "The designation of the patriarch Abraham . . . as the friend of God probably originated from Hellenistically influenced quarters." The term occurs also in *Aboth* VI, 1; *Leviticus Rabba*, 6, 1; *Genesis Rabba*, 69, 2 (ed. Theodor, p. 792); for other references, see *Kalla* (ed. M. Higger), p. 279. For an analysis of the idea in Hellenistic Jewish literature, see E. Peterson, *"Der Gottesfreund, Beitrage zur Geschichte eines religiosen Terminus,"* Zeitschrift für Kirchengeschichte, XLII, NF 5 (1923), 172 ff.

†*Nichomachean Ethics*, VIII, 8, 158b, 33 ff.; cf. P. Wheelwright, *Aristotle* (New York, 1951), p. 243.

‡*Magna Moralia*, 1208b, 29–32. See, however, *Ethica Eudemia*, 1242a, 33.

## THE MEANING OF EXHORTATION

What is the torment that prompts the prophet to hurl bitter words at the people? Is it a feeling of alarm, the threat of disaster? What is the direct inner impact the prophet seeks to make upon his people? Does he aim to strike terror in the heart, to alarm? The prophet's purpose is to move people to repent, to convert the inner man, to revive devotion, love, to reconcile Israel with God. Is it likely that to the prophet's mind terror alone would sow the seeds of love?

Fear does not give birth to prophetic sensitivity, nor is it his own pity or his ability to mourn in advance of events that lends such sublime intensity to what he utters.

The prophet is a person who holds God's love as well as God's anger in his soul, enraptured or enfevered. It is the love that inhabits his soul together with the vision of its outpouring of blessings; it is the anger that consumes his heart together with the vision of its outpouring of horrors. The dreadful hurt to the prophet's soul comes both from realizing the effects anger may yield and from realizing the anger itself. In other words, what shocks the prophet's soul is not only what he is able to sense in anticipation, but also what he is able to sense as an immediate perception.

There are two aspects of the divine anger: how it affects God and how it may affect man. Its historical significance is the disaster that may ensue; its intrinsic significance is pain in the heart of God.

To man, the anger of God incites the fear of pain; to God, the anger *is* pain. Again and again the prophet refers to what anger means *sub specie dei,* the sorrow, the disillusionment caused by the people's disloyalty. He shares the tension between divine patience and divine indignation.

Anger meant disturbance, contention, discord. The aim in proclaiming it is to invoke contrition, pain, and woe, not only fear. The message of anger seeks to evoke the thought not only of the danger of punishment for man, but also of the presence of disturbance in God, a thought so monstrous that it strikes both fear and shock. The hope is for contrition, shame, and repentance: for the disturbance to depart.

In magic, man undertakes to control nature, to force his will upon the gods. By the aid of magic, he "takes the initiative against things, or rather he becomes the conductor in the great concert of the spirit which murmurs in his ears. To make the rain fall, he pours out water; he gives the example, he commands, and fancies he is obeyed."* Curse or blessing is a wish that becomes a fact by the sheer power of speech. It is charged with energy and its effectiveness is certain. In contrast, the word spoken by a prophet derives its power from being in agreement with the will of God, from sympathy with His pathos. Called to pronounce a curse upon the children of Israel, Balaam is forced to confess:

> *From Aram Balak has brought me,*
> *The king of Moab from the eastern mountains:*
> *Come, curse Jacob for me,*
> *Come, be incensed at Israel!*
> *How can I curse whom God has not cursed?*
> *How can I be incensed if God is not incensed?*
> *Numbers 23:7–8*

## FORMS OF PROPHETIC SYMPATHY

Sympathy, the fundamental feature of the prophet's inner life, assumed various forms. Common to them all as an essential element is the focusing of the attention on God, the awareness of divine emotion, intense concern for the divine pathos, sympathetic solidarity with God. However, following Max Scheler's classification, we may distinguish two types of sympathy: (1) community of feeling, or sympathy *with* God; (2) fellow feeling, or sympathy *for* God.†

The first type of relationship obtains when two persons are standing at the coffin of a beloved friend. They feel in common the "same" sorrow, the "same" anguish. It is not that A feels this sorrow and B

---

*Reinach, *Orpheus* (London, 1909), pp. 21 f. See E. Durkheim, *The Elementary Forms of the Religious Life* (New York, 1961), pp. 57 f.
†M. Scheler, *The Nature of Sympathy*, P. Heath, trans. (New Haven, 1954).

feels it also. What obtains here is a *feeling in common*. "A's sorrow is in no way an 'external' matter for B here, as it is, e.g., for their friend C, who joins them and commiserates 'with them' or 'upon their sorrow.' " The feeling of A and the feeling of B are independent of each other; the sorrow of one is neither caused nor reinforced by the sorrow of the other. "On the contrary, they feel it together, in the sense that they feel and experience in common, not only the self-same value-situation, but also the same keenness of emotion in regard to it." The sorrow and the grief are here one and identical.

Since the prophets are, so to speak, confronted with the same object or reality as God, namely the spiritual and moral plight of the people of Israel, and the standard and motivation of the divine pathos worked in them in similar fashion, the prophets may react in the same mode as God, in sorrow or indignation, in love or anger.

The second type of relationship is fellow feeling, or sympathy for God. It involves the prophet's intentional reference of the feeling of joy or sorrow to God's experience. Here God's pathos is first presented as A's in an act of understanding and it is to this pathos that the prophet's primary commiseration is directed. In other words, the prophet's sympathy and God's pathos are phenomenologically two different facts, not *one* fact, as in the first case.

Such sympathy for God derives from an understanding of the situation and pathos of the Lord. The divine evokes a similar pathos in the prophet. The prophet may respond to the divine pathos only by way of intuiting what the pathos might be. The prophet's personal concern for God also focused his emotions directly on the given pathos of God. Alongside his attention to the people—the occasion of divine pathos—he was also attentive to the pathos of God. This complex structure of sympathy is the prophet's typical mode of experience. This applies equally to his solidarity with the pain of God, to the echo of the divine experience in relation to an analogous object and to his compassionate communion with God.

There is in this relationship a direct correspondence between the divine pathos and the human sympathy, the character of the latter depending upon the character of the former. The prophet remains conscious of the fact that his feeling is a fellow feeling with God.

Thus the prophet is guided, not by what he feels, but rather by what God feels. In moments of intense sympathy for God, the prophet is moved by the pathos of God, Who is disillusioned by His people. The state is far from being his main concern. His declarations are made from the point of view of God.

It is rarely a personal, direct reaction to a situation, and mostly an articulation of God's view and an identification with it. Yet, in taking God's part he defends the people's position, since in truth God's pathos is compassion. For compassion is the root of God's relationship to man.

"Sympathy" as a religious category, used for the first time in this book, implies no cosmological, but an anthropological significance: man's immediate relation to the divine pathos. This idea is just as free from the pantheism of the philosophical doctrine of sympathy as it is from the pessimism of the ethical doctrine of sympathy. It is a unique category of religious anthropology, describing a singular type of religious experience and enabling us to understand the structure of the prophetic personality.

## SPIRIT AS PATHOS

The word *ruah* means, according to standard dictionaries, "air in motion, breath, wind, vain things, spirit, mind." What was not noticed is that one of the chief uses of the word *ruah* is to denote pathos, passion or emotion—the state of the soul. When combined with another word, it denotes a particular type of pathos or emotion. It is only in extremely rare cases that the word may be rendered with thought.

The wives of Esau affected Isaac with "bitterness of spirit" or grief (Gen. 26:35; cf. Prov. 14:10). The inner state of the children of Israel, enslaved in Egypt, was one of dejectedness or anguish (Exod. 6:9).* Hannah describes herself as a woman of sorrowful or troubled

---

*Here, *ruah* may possibly mean "impatience"; cf. Prov. 14:29. Contrast this use with *'erekh ruah* (Sirach 5:11).

spirit, speaking out of great anxiety or anguish (I Sam. 1:15). "For the Lord has called you like a wife forsaken and grieved in spirit" (Isa. 54:6). "A spirit of jealousy" comes over a husband whose wife has defiled herself (Num. 5:14, 30). The Lord dwells with him who is of "a contrite and humble spirit to revive the spirit of the humble, and to revive the heart of the contrite" (Isa. 57:15). He has special regard for him who is "humble, contrite in spirit, and trembles at His word" (Isa. 66:2). He is "near to the broken-hearted and saves the crushed in spirit" (Ps. 34:18 [H. 34:19]). It was the mission of the prophet "to grant to those who mourn in Zion . . . a mantle of praise instead of a faint spirit" (Isa. 61:3). The sacrifice acceptable to God is "a broken spirit" (Ps. 51.17 [H. 51:19]).

It is used in the sense of deep pain or anguish ("You shall cry out for pain of heart, and shall wait for anguish of spirit" [Isa. 65:14]). "I am full of words, the spirit within me distresses me," says Job (32:18), who speaks in the anguish of his spirit, in the bitterness of his soul (Job 7:11).

The term is used in the sense of erotic passion—"a spirit of harlotry" (Hos. 4:12; 5:4), of intense inner excitement (Ezek. 3:14), of "a downcast spirit" (Prov. 17:22; 18:14). It is employed in the general sense of intense and overpowering passion, particularly as it relates itself to anger. "He who is slow to anger is better than the mighty, and he who rules his spirit than he who takes a city" (Prov. 16:32). Control of passions is highly praised in the book of Proverbs. "He who restrains his words has knowledge, he who has a cool spirit is a man of understanding" (Prov. 17:27).

Disagreeing with the thought that man is capable of being in control of his passions, we are told in the book of Ecclesiastes: "No man has power over the spirit to retain the spirit" (8:8).

As a generic name for passion, the word also denotes anger. "Be not hasty in thy spirit to be angry" (Eccles. 7:9); "He who is slow to anger is better than the mighty, but he who has a short temper [literally: short spirit] exalts folly" (Prov. 14:29). "Their anger against him abated" (Judg. 8:3). It is also used to describe what we call "mood," a temporary state of the soul or the emotions. "A glad heart makes a cheerful countenance, but by sorrow of heart the spirit is broken" (Prov. 15:13). The psalmist has moments in which his spirit becomes languid, losing its zest and intensity: "When my spirit is faint" (Pss. 77:3 [H. 77:4]; 142:3 [H. 142:4]; 143:7). "Make haste to answer me, O Lord, my spirit fails" (Ps. 143:7). Here the term is hardly used in the sense of intelligence.*

It is as nonbiblical to separate emotion or passion from spirit as it is to disparage emotion or passion. The disparagement of emotion was made possible by ascribing to the rational faculty a power of sovereignty over the objects of its comprehension, thought being the active, moving principle, and the objects of knowledge the passive, inert material of comprehension. However, the act of thinking of an object is in itself an act of being moved by the object. In thinking we do not create an object; we are challenged by it. Thus, thought is part of emotion. We think because we are moved, a fact of which we are not always conscious. Emotion may be defined as the consciousness of being moved.

Emotion is inseparable from being filled with the spirit, which is above all a state of being moved. Often the spirit releases passion, an excessive discharge of nervous energy, enhanced vitality, increased inner strength, increased motor activity, a drive.

While spirit includes passion or emotion, it must not be reduced to either. Spirit implies the sense of sharing a supreme superindividual power, will, or wisdom. In emotion, we are conscious of its being our emotion; in the state of being filled with spirit, we are conscious of joining, sharing, or receiving "spirit from above" (Isa. 32:15). Passion is a movement; spirit is a goal.

Pathos, one of the root meanings of *ruah* when applied to man, seems to be implied in *ruah* as applied to God, at least in some pas-

---

*In this sense, *ruah* has its morphological analogy in the German word *mut*, which in old German meant the entire life of the soul (close to *gemüt*); only later did its meaning become limited to desire, and, since the sixteenth century, to courage. The original meaning is still preserved in such combinations as *froher, heiterer, leichter Mut,* and particularly in the composites: *Gross-, Lang-, Sanft-, Schwer-, Weh-, De-, Hoch-, Über-, Un-, mut.*

sages.* "They rebelled and grieved His holy spirit" (Isa. 63:10). Spirit in this context, capable of being affected by grief, has the clear connotation of pathos.

> *But as for me, I am filled with power,*
> *With the* ruaḥ *of the Lord,*
> *And with justice and might,*
> *To declare to Jacob his transgressions,*
> *And to Israel his sin.*
>
> *Micah 3:8*

The prophet is called *ish ha-ruaḥ,* a man filled with divine pathos (Hos. 9:7).

## COSMIC SYMPATHY

The idea of prophetic sympathy must not be equated with the idea of cosmic sympathy that has often been advanced in the history of philosophy.

The Stoics conceived of the cosmos as a living thing endowed with reason, in which all parts are connected in a bond of sympathy. This sympathy served as a basis for their belief in the *heimarmene* and in the possibility of foretelling future events by divination.[†] The doctrine of cosmic sympathy became the central thought in the thinking of Posidonius.[‡]

In the same way Plotinus maintains that the universe is one comprehensive, living being, encircling all the living beings within it and having a soul which extends to all its members. Every separate thing

---

*In Gen. 6:3, *ruaḥ* is used in the sense of the inner life of the Lord, according to Rashi. "My spirit shall not contend (?) for ever" he interprets as meaning: "My spirit shall not be in a state of discontent and shall not strive within Me because of man. . . . My spirit has been contending within Me whether to destroy or whether to show mercy: such contending shall not be for ever."

[†]Diogenes Laertius, *Lives of Eminent Philosophers,* VII, 149; Cicero, *De Natura Deorum,* II, 19, and *De Divinatione,* II, 33.

[‡]K. Reinhardt, *Kosmos und Sympathie* (München, 1926), pp. 92–138; I. Heinemann, *Poseidonios metaphysische Schriften* (Breslau, 1928), p. 114.

is an integral part of the universe both by belonging to its material fabric and also by participation in the All-Soul. Each thing is affected by all other things by virtue of the common participation in the universe and its soul, and to the degree of its participation.* A fellowship of feeling unites all things. Our amenability to experience is explained by our belonging to that unity, by that fellowship.† For, just as in a single organism, there obtains a sympathy and correspondence between all parts of the universe.‡

This kind of sympathy, coming to pass without active thought and without conscious intention, is totally different from the prophetic sympathy. The biblical man does not believe in an organic unity of God and man. God transcends man, and man is by nature callous to the will of God. Sympathy is not inherent in man. Plotinus' sympathy is a reflex action; it is impersonal. It is not an act by which one person enters into emotional solidarity with another person, but rather a process in which a plurality of beings is stirred by the same force. The prophetic sympathy is an act of will, an emotional identification of the human person with God.

Cosmic sympathy is, furthermore, morally neutral. Its idea is borrowed from organic life. Prophetic sympathy, on the other hand, is a moral act, motivated by considerations for right and wrong. It is related to the phenomenon of compassion.

Petrus Johannis Olivi (1248/49–1298) explained the derivation of intellectual knowledge from sense perception, which differs basically from it by the doctrine of the solidarity of the powers of the soul (*colligantia potentiarum animae*) rather than by means of causality. "If two powers are correlated with each other, a movement in the one produces a corresponding movement in the other: not because of an *actio* on the latter, but because of a *colligantia* with it, i.e., *per formalem inclinationem et unionem ipsius ad illud, cui est colligatum.*"§

---

*Enneads, IV, 4, 32 ff.
†Ibid. IV, 5, 2.
‡Ibid. II, 3, 7; cf. IV, 9, 1; 3, 8; 4, 41; 26.
§B. Geyer, *"Die patristische und scholastische Philosophie,"* in F. Ueberweg, *Grundriss der Geschichte der Philosophie,* II (Berlin, 1928), pp. 490 f.; idem, *"Die mittelalterliche Philosophie,"* in M. Dessoir, *Lehrbuch der Philosophie* (Berlin, 1926), pp. 357 f.

With Ibn Gabirol, Olivi maintains that the soul is a composite unit consisting of several forms (vegetative, sensitive, intellectual) which are united by their common relation to the same spiritual matter. "Since their matter is the same, the action of one of these forms agitates, so to speak, this matter, whose commotion is felt by the other forms and perceived by their knowing powers. There is therefore no direct action of one faculty on the others, but there is a natural solidarity between the several forms of a common matter."*

Olivi's theory is similar to Suarez' doctrine of *sympathia seu consensio potentiarum cognoscentium,* of the psychological interrelation in the exercise of the various faculties. "The wonderful harmony (*sympathia*) is explained by the fact that when the lower faculties are exercised, the higher ones produce in themselves the corresponding species, without any reciprocal causal influence."† The thought of sympathy as the basis of harmony in the pantheistic sense was also taught by Agrippa of Nettesheim (d. 1535).

## ENTHUSIASM AND SYMPATHY

The prophets were as profoundly aware of the reality of the divine pathos as they were of themselves and their own feelings. That is the true meaning of the religion of sympathy—to feel the divine pathos as one feels one's own state of the soul. In enthusiasm, man experiences himself as divine (*entheos*), in sympathy man experiences God as his own being. In enthusiasm, one attains personal exaltation; in sympathy, a sense of the divine inwardness. There is no fusion of being, *unio mystica,* but an intimate harmony in will and feeling, a

---

*E. Gilson, *History of Christian Philosophy in the Middle Ages* (New York, 1955), pp. 344 f. According to Gilson, p. 693, n. 41, the solidarity of the powers of the soul is not a theory proper to Olivi. Athenagoras admits that imitations of monotheism could be found in Greek philosophers, yet it was merely a conjecture due to the sympathy which obtained between their souls and the divine spirit. (*Intercessions for the Christians,* "The Ante-Nicene Fathers of the Church" [Grand Rapids, 1950–1951], p. 382.)

†Rösseler in *Philosophisches Jahrbuch* (1922), pp. 185–191, quoted by Ludwig, *Das akausale Zusammenwirken* (dissertation, München).

state that may be called *unio sympathetica.*\* It is an accord of human privacy and divine concern. One does not feel united with the divine Being, but emotionally identified with divine pathos. This unity in the consciousness, the unity of will and experience, of personality and inspiration, express well the very essence of the prophetic spirit.

The prophet is a person who is inwardly transformed: his interior life is formed by the pathos of God, it is *theomorphic.* Sympathy, which takes place for the sake of the divine will, and in which a divine concern becomes a human passion, is fulfillment of transcendence. Enthusiasm, which is motivated by striving for personal exaltation, seldom raises man beyond the goals he strives for.

In sympathy we find an identity between the private and the divine; the prophet is not really fused with the divine, he is but identifying himself emotionally with the divine pathos. It is a unity of will and emotion, of consciousness and message.

## PATHOS, PASSION, AND SYMPATHY

Ancient religion knew not only happy, serene gods; demonic and vicious gods; but also the myth of the suffering god, whose fate exercised a deep emotional appeal in the hearts of worshipers, symbolizing its impotence in the face of an evil power and the eventual, if only temporary, liberation. Evidence of the powerful appeal which the suffering god possessed may be seen in the fact that his cult was celebrated not only in the temple ritual but also in widespread popular observance.†

In many lands of the ancient Near East the periodic decline and renewal of the life of nature was represented by the death of a god, slain by an enemy. His death resulted in the stagnation of all natural life. A mother goddess bewailed him and set out to retrieve him. The god was found and liberated, and with his resurrection all vegetation revived. In Egypt, Osiris was the suffering god who was bewailed and

---

\*"I am not 'one with' the acrobat; I am only 'with' him" (Edith Stein, quoted by M. Scheler, *The Nature of Sympathy* [New Haven, 1954], p. 18).

†Cf. the wailings for Tammuz and Ezekiel observed in Jerusalem (Ezek. 8:14).

liberated by Isis. In Mesopotamia, the bewailing of the death of Tammuz and his liberation by Ishtar, the great mother, was the most
important celebration of the year. In Syria and in Greece, it was
Adonis (the Greek form of the Phoenician *adon,* "lord"), who was
rescued by Aphrodite.

The cult was also celebrated in Rome, where annually on October
28 the lament for Osiris, the search, the finding, and the rejoicing were
re-enacted. With loud wailing and every expression of passionate grief,
in which priests and people united, Isis, seconded by Nephtys and
Anubis, sought the slain, and, according to a later myth, dismembered
body of Osiris. With the cry of discovery, grief would turn to gladness.

The importance of these rituals centered not only on the death
and suffering of the god, but also on the mourning and wailing on the
part of a mother goddess. The image of a bereaved mother or wife was
an added factor in calling forth a deep emotion of sympathy. In public
rituals and, during the Greco-Roman period, in secret mystery cults, the
worshipers experienced the passion or suffering of the god and shared
his fate both in sorrow and in joy.

Pathos must be sharply contrasted with the theme of divine passion; prophetic sympathy must not be equated with the worshiper's
participation in divine passion. In passion, the divinity is thought of as
a martyr, the basis of whose suffering lies, in the last analysis, in the
powerlessness of the god. In pathos, God is thought of as the supreme
Master of heaven and earth, Who is emotionally affected by the conduct
of man. Thus, in the myth of the suffering god and the mourning goddess, Adonis was killed by an enemy in the guise of a boar; Osiris was
murdered by his brother Seth. The theme was one of mourning for the
death of a god. Pathos, on the other hand, is suffering in the sense of
compassion or in the sense of moral indignation. There the god was a
victim, here God is the Lord concerned for His creation; there, a feeling
of mourning and bewailing;* here, a sympathy calling for righteousness
and faithfulness to God.

---

*In the Egyptian mystery play of the succession, Horus weeps because of his
father and says: "They have put this father of mine into the earth. . . . They have made
it necessary to bewail him." (H. Frankfort, *Kingship and the Gods* [Chicago, 1948],
p. 288.)

Passion is the personal and private suffering of a deity; it all happens within the life of a deity, though it is taken as an event that affects the life of man. Pathos is a relative state, it always refers to humanity; it is a reaction to what happens within the life of humanity. "In the myth of the suffering god and the mourning goddess the complex of feelings which characterizes Mesopotamian religiosity could find adequate expression: the anxiety inherent in an uncertain destiny; the sorrow that life is transitory and death unrelieved by hope; the exultation that life knows abundance."* What is brought to expression is the natural plight of man. The prophets, on the other hand, are concerned with the moral and historical plight of man.

The passion plays are the re-enacting of a tragic destiny which was completed in the past or a ritual symbolizing its eternal recurrence. In prophetic sympathy there is no re-enacting; the divine pathos is a present situation, and, with one exception, there is no re-enacting of divine pathos,† there is only an awareness, an inner identification and an effort to put it in words. What is given to the prophets is God's pathos as a free reaction of the Lord to the conduct of man; what is given in the passion plays is a martyrdom of a god, passively endured, and brought about by an enemy; in the latter it is a physical, in the former a moral, suffering. The passion of the dying god can be the object of cultic rites; pathos can be apprehended only through emotional communion. The original purpose of the passion mysteries was to enable the dead god to rise again, a thought both absurd and repulsive to the biblical mind.‡

## IMITATION OF GOD AND SYMPATHY

In ancient Egypt it was said: The king does what Osiris does. Man must become like the god as much as possible, it is suggested in

---

* *Ibid.*, p. 283.

†The marriage of Hosea is a single act of sympathy, not a cult of sympathy.

‡"There is an element of the unpredictable in his resurrection because the return of nature's vitality lies beyond the scope of human planning. Yet the community cannot passively await a revival upon which its very existence is dependent. Hence a ritual 'search' is undertaken, and society's concern with the god's fate is expressed by procession, lament, and other appropriate rites. Mourning and search are presented in the personification of myth as the part of a goddess." (H. Frankfort, *op. cit.*, p. 288.)

Plato's *Theaetetus.* * The point of the Hellenistic mysteries was that the dedicated member should approximate the deity as closely as possible. In the Isis and Mithras cults the motif of *"imitatio dei"* was central.[†] In the religion of Zarathustra all cultivation of the soil—for example, ploughing—was regarded as an imitation of Ahura Mazda in the struggle against the evil spirit.[‡] Paul taught that Christ was the one to follow, and thus the life of Jesus became a pattern for Christian piety (Rom. 6:4 ff.; Eph. 5:1).

The forms of this religious discipline are different in the various cults, but at bottom they imply the same disposition of soul, and are at one through a common purpose: the approximation of one's own life to the life of God.

Prophetic sympathy is by no means identical with the imitation of God, which in the broadest sense is also a biblical motif (cf. Lev. 19:2). The difference is the more significant because the resemblance, too, is obvious. *Imitatio,* the pattern of which is a concrete life-history, is realized as a practical way of life. Sympathy, whose object is an inner spiritual reality, is a disposition of the soul. The prototype of *imitatio* is an unchanging model; a constant traditional knowledge of it indicates a ready path to be followed. Pathos, on the other hand, is ever changing, according to the circumstances of the given situation. The content of sympathy is not fixed by any predetermination. What is abiding in it is simply the orientation toward the living reality of God.

*Imitatio* is concerned with a past, sympathy with a present, occurrence. Mystical *imitatio* is remote from history; what is at stake in sympathy is an actual historical situation.

Just as pathos implies a relation of God to the people, so sympathy, unlike world-denying *imitatio,* which is concerned with the private destiny of divinity, is motivated by attention to human existence. Sym-

---

*"Therefore we ought to try to escape from earth to the dwelling of the gods as quickly as we can; and to escape is to become like God, so far as this is possible; and to become like him is to become righteous and holy and wise." (*Theaetetus,* 176a f.)

[†]R. Reitzenstein, *Mysterienreligion* (Leipzig and Berlin, 1927), pp. 192 ff.; F. Cumont, *Die Mysterien des Mithra* (Leipzig and Berlin, 1923), pp. 143 f.

[‡]H. Lommel, *Die Religion Zarathustras,* p. 250.

pathy, like pathos, is directed toward the people. Pathos and sympathy run parallel, but in *imitatio* man turns directly toward the pattern.

In accordance with the transcendent significance of prophetic acts and experiences, their meaning finds its fulfillment beyond the range of human action. Sympathy, likewise, is not an end in itself. *Imitatio*, on the other hand, the aim of which is personal exaltation, is itself a fulfillment. The goal of sympathy is not to become like unto God, but to become effective as a prophet through approximation to the pathos of God. In sympathy, divine pathos is actually experienced in the moment of crisis; in *imitatio*, the fixed pattern is transmitted. In the former case, an assimilation or creative understanding is necessary; in the latter, mere knowledge is sometimes sufficient.

In *imitatio*, the whole being of the deity is often taken as the pattern; in sympathy, only its aspect as pathos is taken as the pattern.*

---

*On the problem of *imitatio dei* in Judaism cf. M. Buber, *"Nachahmung Gottes,"* *Kampf um Israel,* pp. 68–83; Marmorstein, *"Die Nachahmung Gottes in der Agada,"* *Festschrift für Wohlgemut,* pp. 144–159; A. J. Heschel, *Maimonides* (Berlin, 1935), pp. 272 ff.; A. J. Heschel, *Theology of Ancient Judaism,* I (Heb.; London and New York, 1962), p. 153 f.

# Prophecy and Ecstasy

### THE SEPARATION OF THE SOUL FROM THE BODY

Of all the forms of religious experience, none has been as fascinating to both the psychologist and the historian as ecstasy. It has often been regarded as a universal phenomenon, the elucidation of which would solve the riddle of how religions have come into being. Prophetic inspiration was assumed to have been a form of ecstasy.

The theory of ecstasy accomplished two things. First, it reduced biblical prophecy as well as other phenomena in the history of religion to a common anthropological denominator; the prophets were conveniently classified as a typical phenomenon of primitive or ancient society. Second, it offered a psychological explanation of what seemed to be an enigma. Before analyzing the validity of that theory, we shall try to clarify the meaning and implications of ecstasy as well as to sketch the history of that theory in the interpretation of prophecy.

The Greeks, who coined the word "ecstasy" (*ekstasis*), understood by it quite literally a state of trance in which the soul was no longer in its place, but had departed from the body, or a state in which the soul, escaping from the body, had entered into a relationship with invisible beings or became united with a deity.* It was a way of ascending to a higher form of living, or at least a way which rendered possible the receiving of supernormal endowments.

From the viewpoint of psychology, ecstasy is a "withdrawal of consciousness from circumference to center"; a state in which the absorption of the mind in one idea, in one desire, is so profound that everything else is blotted out. A person in ecstasy is impervious to messages from without; awareness of time and space, consciousness of one's own self, disappear. Such a condition is brought about by preparation, and the means used to induce it vary: narcotics, alcohol, music, dance. But ecstasy may also be induced by techniques of contemplation and complete spiritual concentration as well as by prayer.†

There are two fundamental types of ecstasy: the wild and fervid type, which is a state of frenzy arising from overstimulation and emotional tension; and the sober or contemplative type, which is a rapture of the soul in a state of complete calmness, enabling a person to rise beyond the confines of consciousness. The motivation for ecstasy lies in the desire for communion with higher being which transcends the grasp of man in his normal condition. It seems that the type of ecstasy one strives for is determined by one's conception of the character of such being. If the god is thought of as a sensuous being, fervid ecstasy would be a way of communion. If the divinity is thought of in terms which stress invisibility, distance, mystery, or incomprehensibility, sober ecstasy would prevail. As illustrations, the Dionysiac frenzy and the Neoplatonic trance may be mentioned.

Ecstasy is a part of the belief, maintained by primitive people all over the world, in the temporary separation of the soul from the body during sleep, illness, or trance.‡

---

*E. Rohde, *Psyche*, II (Tübingen, 1925), 311 ff.; cf. Schneider, *"Die mystisch-ekstatische Gottesschau im Griechischen und Christlichen Altertum," Philosophisches Jahrbuch der Görresgesellschaft*, XXI, 24 ff.

†E. Underhill, *Mysticism* (London, 1912), pp. 363 f.; P. Beck, *Die Ekstase* (1906).

‡See J. G. Frazer, *Taboo and the Perils of the Soul* (London, 1920), ch. 2; see also Achelis, *Die Ekstase* (Berlin, 1902), p. 21.

Herodotus records that Aristeas of Proconnesus, "rapt in Bacchic fury," according to his poem, miraculously visited the northern peoples in far distant places. It is narrated of Hermotimus of Clazomenae—later considered a pre-existent form of Pythagoras—that his soul would leave his body for years at a time, to wander in space and learn secret matters, his body the while lying as though dead. Once during such disengagement of the soul, his enemies set fire to his lifeless body, thus preventing the soul's return.* Of Epimenides the Cretan who according to Plato predicted the Persian war ten years before it happened,† and who was supposed to have helped the Athenians cleanse their city of a plague by means of a sacrifice, it is said that he had the power of sending forth his soul at will from his body, to which it would afterward return.‡

## A Divine Seizure

Related to ecstasy is another phenomenon, namely, possession or enthusiasm. There is a belief, found in many parts of the world, that supernatural powers, spiritual or divine, may take possession of a person, either permanently or temporarily, for good or for evil. Sickness, for example, is thought to be caused by a demon which enters into persons and takes possession of them. Abnormal manifestations, physical or psychical, are regarded as evidence of the presence of a god or a spirit. The vast body of the cuneiform incantations that have come down to us from Babylonia are based upon the belief that some demon or ghost is plaguing the sick man, and must be expelled before the patient can be healed. The so-called Penitential Psalms presumably have their origin, not in the remorse of the suppliant, but in this actual physical malady, which he believes to be due to some supernatural blow. Just as modern medicine distinguishes one germ from another, so did the ancient Babylonians distinguish one demon from another.

---

*Herodotus, *History*, IV, 13–15; see E. Rohde, *op. cit.*, pp. 94 f.

†*Laws*, 642d.

‡E. Rohde, *op. cit.*, pp. 96 ff. According to Plutarch, *Lives*, Solon, XII, Epimenides "had the reputation of being dear to the gods and wise in divine matters with the wisdom by *enthousiasmos* and mysteries, wherefore the men of his time called him the son of a nymph named Balte, and a new Kures."

The possessed person becomes sick or delirious, but also, in certain circumstances, inspired. His utterance or action is then thought of as proceeding from, not merely prompted by, an indwelling higher power. Those under the influence of possession are regarded as sorcerers, oracles, or prophets.

"The attempt to become materially filled with the materially conceived divine or demonic beings or to become united with them is part of the earliest demonstrable phenomena from which religious feeling later emerged." It was thought possible "to be penetrated with the divine substance by a sexual union or by swallowing the object which was thought to be the seat of the demon."*

Among the Greeks, such a condition is described as a divine seizure, as the state of being filled with the god, *enthusiasm* in the original sense of the word *entheos:* having god in oneself.

Thus, possession, or enthusiasm, is basically different from ecstasy; yet since they frequently appear together, they are often confused with each other. Enthusiasm is the state of a man in whom a god dwells, while ecstasy denotes the separation of the soul from the body, and also the state in which the soul surges toward the god and strives to become one with him.† The enthusiast feels that he is being swept away by a higher force, which lifts him completely out of himself and fills him with new insight, new strength, new life. Such a state could be brought about by wild dancing with the god, by a ritual communion that used sexual symbolism, or by drinking wine, since Dionysus materializes himself in it. The Pythia was inspired by the vapor rising from a cleft in the ground. She was regarded as filled with the god who, forcing his way through the whole of her frame, compelled her to yield to his exclusive guidance.‡ The central rite of the Dionysiac orgies was that of theophagy, i.e., of eating the god. Worshipers, rapt in ecstatic trance, tore an animal—the incarnation of the god—and devoured its flesh raw. By killing the god, eating his

*Gruppe, *Griechische Mythologie* (München, 1906), p. 849.
†See A. Dieterich, *Eine Mithrasliturgie* (Leipzig, 1903), p. 98.
‡*Ibid.,* pp. 97 ff.; on the erotic union of the Delphic priestess with Apollo, see p. 14. Cf. L. R. Farnell, *Cults of the Greek States,* III (Oxford, 1896), 300.

flesh, and drinking his blood, they were filled with divine power and transplanted into the sphere of divinity.*

In order to make room for the entrance of the higher force, the person must forfeit the power over the self. He must abandon his mind in order to receive the spirit. Loss of consciousness, *ecstasy,* is a prerequisite for enthusiasm, or possession. Ecstasy is a state in which the soul is, as it were, freed from, or raised above, the body.† It is a state during which breathing and circulation are depressed. Sometimes entrancement is so deep that there is complete anesthesia.‡ This measure was always adopted by the medicine man when, in ecstatic condition, he sought to obtain a visionary understanding of illness. "As an abnormal condition ecstasy belongs to the group of hysteric-hypnotic phenomena bordering on somnambulism, and reaching its highest degree becomes obsession. As such a pathological condition ecstasy must be as old as humanity itself."§

## A SACRED MADNESS

In Greece, the Dionysus cult was the harbinger of popular ecstasy. "The worshipers of Dionysus believed that they were possessed by the god. It was a step further to pass to the conviction that they were actually identified with him, actually *became* him. This was a conviction shared by all orgiastic religions, and one doubtless that had its rise in the physical sensations of intoxication. Those who worshiped Sabazios became Saboi, those who worshiped Kubebe became Kubeboi, those who worshiped Bacchos, Bacchoi; in Egypt the worshipers of Osiris, after death became Osiris."∥ The *ekstasis,* the temporary *alie-*

---

*Bertholet-Lehmann, *Lehrbuch der Religionsgeschichte,* II (Tübingen, 1925), p. 293.

†The minds of the *mystai* first had to be freed entirely from all confusing earthly entanglements so that they might be ready for the holy things that the initiation rites would reveal. W. Wundt, *Völkerpsychologie,* V (Leipzig, 1910), 181, defines ecstasy as a temporary separation of the soul from the body, as a transplantation of the consciousness into remote places, a departure from the immediate environment.

‡E. Underhill, *op. cit.,* p. 359.

§M. Ebert, *Reallexikon der Vorgeschichte,* s. v. *Ekstase.*

∥J. Harrison, *Prolegomena to the Study of Greek Religion* (New York, 1955), p. 474.

*natio mentis* of the Dionysiac cult was not thought of as a vain, pur-
poseless wandering in a region of pure delusion, but as a *hieromania,*
a sacred madness in which the soul, leaving the body, winged its way
to union with the god. "It is now with and in the god, in the condition of the *enthousiasmos;* those who are possessed by this are the
*entheoi;* they live and have their being in the god. . . . The *entheos* is
completely in the power of the god; the god speaks and acts through
him. The *entheos* has lost his consciousness of himself."*

Asia Minor is generally regarded as the home of orgiastic religion. Dionysus was, as is now generally recognized, not originally a
Greek deity, but imported to Greece from Thrace, where he was worshiped under the name of Sabos, or Sabazios.† His cult spread through
Greece some time before the dawn of Greek history. Although it
encountered opposition at first, the new cult proved irresistible and
won its way victoriously, taking Thebes for its Hellenic metropolis
and later securing its position at Delphi, where the priesthood and
the Apolline oracle became its eager champions. All Greeks became
acquainted with the emotional experience of its ecstasies and the
feverish exaltation of a union with the god.

Clad in fawn skins, with ivy wreaths on their heads, the worshipers, led by the priest, would go to the wildest part of the mountains
to celebrate the rites. Nothing was lacking which could serve to introduce a sense of exaltation: darkness of the night, music—played on
flutes, tympana or kettle-drums—dance, the god's special gift of wine.
All this produced the state of *ekstasis* or *enthousiasmos,* which might
show itself in a wild outburst of superhuman strength, and which produced the feeling of self-abandonment.‡ Their disheveled hair stream-
ing in the wind as they carried serpents or daggers, women would
dance in wild frenzy amidst the glare of torches, whirling dizzily to
the clangor of rude music—the clashing of bronze vessels, the hollow

---

*E. Rohde, *op. cit.,* pp. 19 f.
†Herodotus, *History,* V, 7; see the notes of W. W. How and J. Wells in London,
1912, edition.
‡It is true, however, that not all who participated in the Dionysiac acts were
elevated to such an experience. "For many, as they say in the mysteries, are the thyrsus-
bearers, but few are the bacchoi." (Plato, *Phaedo,* 69.)

roll of large drums, the shrill whistling of flutes—and shouting loudly, *"Eoui!"* Escaping the limits of their own nature, the votaries would achieve a temporary sense of identity with the god, which might avail them even after death. In their frenzy they would hurl themselves upon a bull or a goat, supposed to be the incarnation of the god, tear the animal to pieces with their bare hands or teeth, and in consuming it become filled with the blood and spirit of the god, and thus acquire divine powers.\*

Even the cult of Apollo did not remain immune to the intoxication of the orgies.† Those who are inclined to regard Apollo as the god of light and beauty, of limit and "nothing too much, who is all sweet reasonableness and lucidity, ascribe the ecstatic element in his cult to the influence of Dionysus."‡ If Apollo exercised his softening influence upon the raging Bacchus, Dionysus in turn imparted a measure of ecstasy to the Pythia, the prophetess of Apollo at Delphi. It has been suggested, however, that *ekstasis* was not original in the worship of Apollo, and that the mantic *ekstasis* of Apolline religion was simply borrowed from the worshipers of Dionysus.§

Of the same orgiastic type as the cult of Dionysus was the cult of the Great Mother Deity of the Phrygians, Cybele. Her worship had its origin in Anatolia, Asia Minor, in prehistoric times, possibly prior to the advent of the Phrygians (about 900 B.C.E.), and was most strongly centralized in Phrygia. From Asia Minor the cult spread to

---

\*Euripides, *Bacchae,* 120 ff., 680–768, 1043–1147; E. R. Dodds, "Maenadism in the Bacchae," *Harvard Theological Review,* XXXIII (1940), 155–176; J. Geffcken, "Maenads," *ERE,* VIII (1908 ff.), 240 f.

†The Greek *orgia* meant primarily acts of ritual. It was applied principally to secret or mystical cults, such as the Eleusinian *mysteria* and the Dionysiac *homophagia.* From the Bacchanalia suppressed by Rome, the term derived its modern meaning of revelry, especially when marked by excessive indulgence or license. (See the *Oxford English Dictionary*).

‡Opposition to the cult of ecstasy found its expression in the following tradition or story quoted by Plato. Dionysus was robbed of his wits by his stepmother Hera. Out of revenge he inspired Bacchic furies and dancing madnesses in others, for which purpose he gave men wine (Plato, *Laws,* 672b). According to U. von Wilamowitz-Moellendorff, *Der Glaube der Hellenen,* II (Berlin, 1932), 66, n. 4, this opposition is a late ascetic tendency, corresponding to movements for prohibition in modern times.

§W. K. C. Guthrie, *The Greeks and Their Gods* (London, 1950), p. 200 f., 204; see, however, E. Rohde, *op. cit.,* pp. 56 ff.

Thrace and the islands, and finally to Greece, where it was used with the cult of Rhea, "the Mother of the gods." In the year 205 B.C.E. a Sibylline oracle was discovered directing the Romans to introduce the worship of the Great Mother (*Magna Deum Mater*). After that the cult was adopted by Rome.

The Great Mother had a train of attendant demons called Corybantes, who were supposed to accompany her with wild dances and intoxicating music, while she wandered by torchlight over the forest-clad mountains. The name was further given in Phrygia to the eunuch priest of the goddess.*

The rites of the Great Mother, in which the worshiper sought to attain a union with the deity, took the form of adoption of the worshiper as her son of sexual communion. The orgies would serve to inflame the priests and the worshipers of the goddess to the highest pitch of enthusiasm. Accompanied by clashing music, played on flutes, cymbals, tambourines, and castanets, the followers of Cybele and Rhea would yell and dance themselves into a frenzy. The curdling scream of the priestess of the Great Mother, which "makes all shudder who hear," was compared to the shrieks of a madman. The delirious excitement of the priests culminated in self-scourging, or self-laceration with knives to symbolize the supreme act of consecration to the Mother, which consisted of self-emasculation.

While it is unsafe to invest the early cult in Asia Minor with all customs practiced centuries afterward among the Romans, it is correct to state that the revolting sensual rites, and the mountain temples of the Cybele cult, all have their parallels in Semitic worship; the Great Mother's resemblance to Ashtoreth is almost complete.†

Apuleius, writing about the wandering priests of Syria in his own day, describes how they would enter a rich man's country house: "The moment they entered it, they raised a chorus of discordant howls and rushed madly through all the house, with bowed heads and necks that

---

*From that name the Greeks formed the verb "to corybant" which means to be in a state of divine madness in which hallucinations occur.

†G. Showerman, *The Great Mother of the Gods* (Bulletin No. 43 of the University of Wisconsin [Madison, 1901]), p. 238 and *passim;* E. O. James, *The Cult of the Mother-Goddess* (New York, 1959), pp. 69 ff.

writhed with snaky motion. They whirled their hanging curls, till they stood out in a circle, and ever and anon they bit their own sinews with their teeth. At last when they had done this for some time, they began each of them to slash their arms with the two-edged knives which they carried. Meanwhile one of them raved more wildly than the rest; a deep and frequent panting, that seemed to come from his very heart-strings, burst from him, as though he were filled with the breath of some divinity, and he feigned a frenzy that racked his whole being. As if, forsooth, the presence of the gods instead of making men better were wont to make them feeble and sickly!"*

## Ecstasy Among the Semites

The phenomena of ecstasy and enthusiasm do not seem to have been popular among all Semitic peoples. The Babylonians, who developed an intricate system of dealing with sicknesses thought to have been caused by the possession of demons, apparently had no belief in the possession of a man by a good spirit or by a god.† The highly developed practice of divination, which played an important role in the religious life of the Babylonians and Assyrians, was a kind of science or technique devoid of orgiastic elements.‡

From Phoenicia we hear of a case of ecstasy. In the so-called Papyrus Golenischeff, of the eleventh century, an Egyptian relates that on an occasion when the Prince of Byblos was "making offering to his gods, the god attending the ceremony seized one of the youths

---

*H. E. Butler, trans., *The Metamorphoses or Golden Ass of Apuleius of Madaura* (Oxford, 1910), VIII, 27; II, 55. In the *Aethiopica* of Heliodorus (4, 16) the hero of the story tells of a sacrifice on the part of certain Tyrian seafarers to the Tyrian God, and graphically describes the accompanying ecstatic dance: "And I left them there with their flutes and their dances which they carried out to the violent music of their pipes in Syrian fashion, hopping at one time, leaping up in easy jumps, at another limping steadily on the ground (that is, with bent knee) and twisting the whole body, like persons possessed, turning round in a circle."

†H. Junker, *Prophet und Seher in Israel* (Trier, 1927), p. 94, endeavors to prove the opposite, unconvincingly. See also R. C. Thompson, *The Devils and Evil Spirits of Babylon* (London, 1903–1904).

‡For a description of that practice, compare B. Meissner, *Babylonien und Assyrien*, II (Heidelberg, 1925), ch. 18.

and made him possessed." In a state of frenzy the youth expressed the wish of the god to the effect that the prince should show hospitality to a passing Egyptian and his god whom the Egyptian was taking along for protection on his journey, although the prince had previously dismissed him.*

About pre-Islamic Arabia we possess an account of the ecstatic inspiration of *kahin,* or soothsayer. "The form of his prophecy is rhymed prose, . . . the language peculiar to the ecstatic life. He speaks . . . to the people, not as their fellow, but directly as their God; they are his 'servants,' strictly 'slaves.' They reply with the formula used only to a God, 'With thee! O our Lord.' "†

In Egypt, Pliny reports, an ox was worshiped as a deity called Apis. During the processions connected with its cult, it was attended by a crowd of boys singing hymns in its honor. The crowds would suddenly become inspired, and predict future events.‡

We are told of enthusiasts among the Hittites who claimed that they were united with the deity, that the deity revealed itself to them and spoke through them.§

## ECSTASY IN NEOPLATONISM

As said above, ecstasies occur in a variety of forms and on different levels. They are different in a pious, sublime, noble man, such as Plotinus, and in camel drivers who smoke hashish. The most common form is the wild, artificially produced orgiastic act which, as we have seen, is at home in many cults. It may be achieved in public by mass suggestion or in private under the influence of *mystes,* by intoxication or by mimetic ritual. However, the Orphics, a small group of religious devotees, sought to achieve the same goal by different means. One might attain divine life, not in physical intoxication, but in spiritual

---

*ANET,* p. 26.

†D. B. Macdonald, *The Religious Attitude and Life in Islam* (Chicago, 1909), pp. 31 f.

‡*Naturalis Historia,* VIII, ch. 71 (46).

§*Kulturgeschichte des alten Orients* (*"Handbuch der Altertumswissenschaft"* [München, 1933]), III, 1, 3, 3, 1, p. 139.

ecstasy; the way to become divine is not through drunkenness, but by abstinence and rites of purification.* This, indeed, is the type of ecstasy which came to play an important part in the tradition of philosophical mysticism.

As an experience in which the individual feels himself to have become one with the divine, ecstasy is known to Christian mystics as well as to the Sufis in Islam. A partial analogy may be in the Yoga practices in India.

## A Source of Insight in Philo and Plotinus

As a source of mystical insight, ecstasy first appears in Philo and in Neoplatonism, though it was foreshadowed in Plato.

Philo of Alexandria was, it seems, the first thinker to use the term *ekstasis* in its technical sense. Accepting the Pythagorean assumption that the body is the prison-house of the soul and a hindrance to the perception of pure truth, and convinced that the human mind (*nous*) stands in sharp contrast to the divine Spirit, Philo maintains that the highest degree of knowledge can be attained only in an act of ecstasy. In the normal state, man can achieve only rational knowledge. "When the mind is mastered by the love of the divine, when it strains its powers to reach the inmost shrine, when it puts forth every effort and ardor on its forward march, under the divine impelling force, it forgets all else, forgets itself, and fixes its thoughts and memories on Him."† "For when the mind is divinely possessed and becomes filled with God, it is no longer within itself, for it receives the divine spirit to dwell within it."‡ "Seized by a sober intoxication, like those filled with Corybantic frenzy,"§ the soul becomes "filled with inspired frenzy, even as the prophets are inspired. For it is the mind under the divine afflatus, and no longer in its own keeping," that receives the higher knowledge.‖ "Wafted . . . to the topmost arch of the things perceptible

---

*J. Harrison, *op. cit.*, p. 476.
†*De Somniis*, II, 232.
‡*Questions in Genesin*, III, 9.
§*De Opificio Mundi*, XXIII, 71.
‖*Quis Rerum Divinarum Heres*, XIV, 69; see H. A. Wolfson, *Philo*, II (Cambridge, Mass., 1947), pp. 27 f.

to mind, it seemed to be on its way to the Great King Himself; but, amid its longing to see Him, pure and untempered rays of concentrated light stream forth like a torrent, so that by its gleams the eye of the understanding is dazzled."*

Of Abraham it is said, "about sunset there fell on him an ecstasy." When the mind comes to its setting, "naturally ecstasy and divine possession and madness fall upon us. For when the light of God shines, the human light sets; when the divine light sets, the human dawns and rises. This is what regularly befalls the fellowship of the prophets. The mind is evicted at the arrival of the divine Spirit, but when that departs the mind returns to its tenancy. Mortal and immortal may not share the same home."†

Philo describes his own experience of ecstasy.

I feel no shame in recording my own experience, a thing I know from its having happened to me a thousand times. On some occasions, after making up my mind to follow the usual course of writing on philosophical tenets, and knowing definitely the substance of what I was to set down, I have found my understanding incapable of giving birth to a single idea, and have given it up without accomplishing anything, reviling my understanding for its self-conceit, and filled with amazement at the might of Him that is to Whom is due the opening and closing of the soul-wombs. On other occasions, I have approached my work empty and suddenly become full, the ideas falling in a shower from above and being sown invisibly, so that under the influence of the Divine possession I have been filled with corybantic frenzy and been unconscious of anything, place, persons present, myself, words spoken, lines written. For I obtained language, ideas, an enjoyment of light, keenest

---

* De Opificio Mundi, loc. cit.

† Quis Rerum Divinarum Heres, LIII, 264–265. It has been suggested that Philo adopts here, as in other cases, conceptions which were common in the thinking of mystery cults. In the state of ecstasy the human mind is replaced by the divine *pneuma*. On the whole problem, cf. H. Leisegang, *Der heilige Geist* (Leipzig, 1919); J. Pascher, *Der Koenigsweg* (Paderborn, 1931).

vision, pellucid distinctness of objects, such as might be received through the eyes as the result of clearest shewing.*

Neoplatonism, which claimed to be a way of salvation, as well as a system of thought, lent new significance to the idea of ecstasy. Here the longing of the soul for liberation from the world of sense in which it is immersed, and the return of the soul to God, consist in its soaring to the source from which it came. Reflection and meditation afford only little help.

The ultimate end of philosophy is, according to Plotinus, in the attainment of complete contact and union with the divine unity. Such contact, however, can be attained only in an ecstasy,† "in which reasoning is in abeyance and all Intellection and even, to dare the word, the very self,"‡ and in which the soul is swept entirely out of itself and carried up into a realm where the One manifests itself in its majesty. "This is the true end of the soul: to see the Supreme by the Supreme and not by the light of any other principle. . . . But how is this to be accomplished? Strip thyself of everything."§ In such a condition no knowledge of the divine is imparted, since the highest cannot be grasped through knowledge. The aim of ecstasy is to dissolve the finite personality of man in order that he may be attuned to the infinity of God, and to obtain an immediate apprehension of the unfathomable ultimate. Such apprehension is possible only through absorption of the self in the divine, and in mystic union with it.

The Soul must remove from itself good and evil and everything else, that it may receive the One alone, as the One

---

* *De Migratione Abrahami,* VII, 35. "But there is a higher thought. . . . It comes from a voice in my own soul, which is God-possessed ( *theolepteisthai*) and divines where it does not know. This voice told me that while God is indeed one, His highest and chiefest powers are two, even goodness and sovereignty. Through His goodness He begat all that is, through His sovereignty He rules what He has begotten." ( *De Cherubim,* IX, 27).

†The question whether Plotinus in his doctrine of ecstasy was influenced by Philo remains unsolved. For divergent views, see E. Zeller, *Die Philosophie der Griechen,* vol. III, pt. 2 (Leipzig, 1920), p. 485; P. Wendland, *Die Hellenistisch-Roemische Kultur* (Tübingen, 1907), p. 211; F. Heinemann, *Plotinus* (Leipzig, 1921), p. 8 f.

‡*Enneads,* VI, 9, 11 (trans. By S. MacKenna and B. S. Page).

§*Enneads,* V, 3, 17.

is alone. . . . When the Soul turns away from visible things and makes itself as beautiful as possible and becomes like the One; (the manner of preparation and adornment is known to those who practise it;) and seeing the One suddenly appearing in itself, for there is nothing between, nor are they any longer two, but one; for you cannot distinguish between them, while the vision lasts; it is that union of which the union of earthly lovers, who wish to blend their being with each other, is a copy. The Soul is no longer conscious of the body, and cannot tell whether it is a man or a living being or anything real at all; for the contemplation of such things would seem unworthy, and it has no leisure for them; but when, after having sought the One, it finds itself in its presence, it goes to meet it and contemplates it instead of itself. What itself is when it gazes, it has no leisure to see. When in this state the Soul would exchange its present condition for nothing, no, not for the very heaven of heavens; for there is nothing better, nothing more blessed than this. . . . It fears no evil, while it is with the One, or even while it sees him; though all else perish around it, it is content, if it can only be with him; so happy is it.*

---

* *Enneads,* VI, 7, 34; see W. R. Inge, *Plotinus,* II (London, 1918), 134 f. "Many times it has happened: Lifted out of the body into myself; becoming external to all other things and self-centered; beholding a marvellous beauty; then, more than ever, assured of community with the loftiest order; enacting the noblest life, acquiring identity with the divine; stationing within It by having attained that activity; poised above whatsoever within the Intellectual is less than the Supreme. . . ." (*Enneads,* IV, 8, 1.) Plotinus experienced only four times, during the six years of his stay with Porphyrius, the condition of ecstasy. (Porphyry, *Vita Plotini,* p. 23.)

The semantic value of the concept of ecstasy has weakened frequently to the point of vulgarization. As an example we may cite Mantegazza, *Die Ekstasen des Menschen* (Jena, 1888). The designation of ecstasy has been given to the most diverse states of psychological tension. A promiscuous application of the idea underlies J. Hauer, *Die Religionen* (Berlin, 1923), pp. 86, 89, as well as H. Grabert, *Die ekstatischen Erlebnisse der Mystiker und Psychopathen,* p. 16. Such extravagant and frivolous use has made it very difficult to employ this concept in scientific studies. It is necessary to counteract the undue extension of the idea of ecstasy and to limit its use according to its definition and real connotation.

# 9

# The Theory of Ecstasy

## In Hellenistic Judaism

Philo of Alexandria is the first thinker known to us who developed a comprehensive approach to the understanding of biblical prophecy. In his endeavor to fuse Greek and Jewish doctrines he does not shrink from applying the ideas and the nomenclature of the Greek mystery religion to his description of biblical prophets.* His syncretistic prophetology became the cornerstone of an interpretation of prophecy which has prevailed ever since. Philo took over from Greek oracle-religion the idea of ecstasy and declared it to be the decisive mark of the prophet. For him the prophet is a hierophant, a term for the highest officer of the heathen mysteries. The prophetic state is described as "the divine possession (*entheos*) and frenzy (*mania*) to which the prophets as a class are subject;"† or as "the experience of the God-inspired and the God-possessed . . . which proves him to be a prophet."‡ Philo applies to Moses in particular his fundamental

---

*On the mystery cults see K. Pruemm, *Religiousgeschichtliches Handbuch für den Raum der altchristtichen Umwelt* (Rome, 1954).

†*Quis Rerum Divinarum Heres,* LI, 249.

‡*Ibid.,* LII, 258. See H. Leisegang, *Der Heilige Geist* (Berlin, 1919), pp. 142 ff.; H. A. Wolfson, *Philo,* II (Cambridge, 1947), 25 f.

principle: "No prophecy without ecstasy."* The prophet is a passive instrument of the Lord. He receives illumination in a condition of total passivity and unconsciousness.†

According to Philo, "a prophet possessed by God will suddenly appear and give prophetic oracles. Nothing of what he says will be his own, for he that is truly under the control of divine inspiration has no power of apprehension when he speaks, but *serves as the channel* for the insistent words of Another's prompting. For prophets are the interpreters of God, Who makes full use of their organs to set forth what He wills."‡ "His organs of speech, mouth and tongue, are wholly in the employ of Another . . . Who beats on the chords with the skill of a masterhand and makes them instruments of sweet music, laden with every harmony."§

This conception of the prophet as a mere instrument is a necessary corollary of Philo's theory that on the arrival of the divine Spirit "the mind is evicted." For "mortal and immortal may not share the same home."‖

In the Septuagint the term "ecstasy" is used to render the Hebrew words for "fear" or "horror," and never in connection with prophetic experience. However, the term does occur in the story of Abraham's prophetic vision. "And it came to pass, that, when the sun was going down, *a deep sleep* (*tardemah*) fell upon Abraham, and, lo, a dread, even a great darkness fell upon him" (Gen. 15:12). The word *tardemah* is translated in the Septuagint

---

*H. Leisegang, *op. cit.*, pp. 150 ff., 206 ff.

†"No pronouncement of a prophet is ever his own; he is an interpreter prompted by Another in all his utterances, when knowing not what he does he is filled with inspiration, as the reason withdraws and surrenders the citadel of the soul to a new visitor and tenant, the divine Spirit, which plays upon the vocal organism and dictates words which clearly express its prophetic message." (*De Specialibus Legibus,* IV, 8, 49.)

‡*De Specialibus Legibus,* I, 11, 65.

§*Quis Rerum Divinarum Heres,* LIII, 266.

‖*Ibid.*, LIII, 265. I. Heinemann traces Philo's phrase to Plato, *Ion,* 534. This is questioned by F. H. Colson, *Philo,* VIII (Loeb Classics), 430, according to whom "the idea of the prophet as a mouthpiece is self-evident throughout the prophetic books." Philo's image "that the prophet is the musical instrument on which God plays does not come . . . from Plato, at any rate not from this passage in *Ion.*"

with "ecstasy."* This rendition gives Philo the opportunity to declare that the term is used in this passage in the sense of "the divine possession or frenzy to which the prophets as a class are subject." "Sun" is a figure for the human mind. While the radiance of the mind is still all around us, when it pours as it were a noonday beam into the whole soul, we are self-contained, not possessed. But when it comes to its time of setting, naturally ecstasy and divine possession and madness fall upon us. For when the light of God shines, the human light sets; when the divine light sets, the human light dawns and rises. This is what regularly befalls the fellowship of the prophets. The mind is evicted at the arrival of the divine Spirit, but when that departs, the mind renews its tenancy. Mortal and immortal may not share the same home. And therefore the setting of reason and the darkness which surrounds it produce ecstasy and inspired frenzy.†

Josephus, who never applies to the prophets terms such as "ecstasy" or "frenzy"‡ describes the state of divine inspiration as

---

*Ecstasy may denote (1) a raving condition, (2) alarm, (3) tranquility of spirit, (4) prophetic rapture. "Since in Gen. 20:7, Abraham is called a prophet, *ekstasis* in 15:12 can only be understood in the last-named sense." (P. Heinisch, *Der Einfluss Philus auf die christliche Exegese* [Münster, 1908], p. 113.) See also Hatch and Redpath, *A Concordance to the Septuagint* (Oxford, 1892). This opinion is contradicted by the fact that the Septuagint also translates *tardemah* by *ekstasis* in the only other passage in which it occurs (Gen. 2:21). In this latter case *tardemah* denotes the sleep of Adam, and its meaning has nothing in common with prophecy. Cf. I. Heinemann, *"Philons Lehre vom heiligen Geist und der intuitiven Erkenntnis,"* MGWJ, LXIV (1920), p. 26.

†*Quis Rerum Divinarum Heres,* LI, 249; LIII, 264. "The prophet, even when he seems to be speaking, really holds his peace, and his organs of speech, mouth and tongue, are wholly in the employ of Another, to shew forth what He wills" (53, 266). Cf. IV Ezra 12:38 ff., the seventh vision: "And it came to pass on the morrow that, lo! a voice called me, saying: Ezra, open thy mouth and drink what I give thee to drink! Then I opened my mouth, and lo! There was reached unto me a full cup. . . . And I took it and drank; and when I had drunk, my heart poured forth understanding, wisdom grew in my breast and my spirit retained its memory." The apocalyptic writer who was acquainted with the phenomena of ecstasy seems to imply that Ezra's inspiration was of a higher form. Instead of a loss of consciousness and memory, Ezra experienced an intensification of his mental powers. See R. H. Charles, *Commentary* (Oxford, 1929), *ad. loc.*

‡He applies the term *enthousian* to the Roman soldiers setting fire to the Temple in Jerusalem (*Jewish War,* VI, 260). See D. A. Schlatter, *Die Theologie des Judentums nach dem Bericht des Josephus* (Gütersloh, 1932), p. 60.

*entheos.* * Balaam is characterized by him as "the inspired utterance of one who was no longer his own master but was overruled by the divine spirit to deliver it." When Balak accused Balaam, whom he had hired to curse the people of Israel, of treachery because of his singing of the praise of Israel, Balaam retorted: "Thinkest thou that it rests with us at all to be silent or to speak on such themes as these, when we are possessed by the spirit of God? For that spirit gives utterance to such language and words as it will, whereof we are all unconscious. . . . Nothing within us, once He has gained prior entry, is any more our own."†

## In Rabbinic Literature

There is no word in the Bible for ecstasy. Yet like Philo, and possibly under his influence, Rab, the celebrated Babylonian Amora and founder of the academy in Sura (d. 247 B.C.E.), seems to have interpreted the word *tardemah* in Gen. 2:21 as ecstasy. *Tardemah,* he says, is used in the Bible in three meanings:‡ (*a*) as deep sleep in the

---

* *Jewish Antiquities,* VI, 56, 76 (Saul); VIII, 346 (Elijah); IX, 35 (Elisha). Josephus claims that at the hour when he decided to surrender Jotapata to the Romans he was *enthous* (divinely inspired) to read the meaning of ambiguous utterances of the Deity which came to him in "nightly dreams." ( *Jewish War,* III, 352–353.) Of Vespasian while in Gamala, Josephus says that he was like one *enthous genomenon.* ( *Jewish War,* IV, 33.)

† *Jewish Antiquities,* IV, 118–122. See A. Poznanski, *Ueber die religions-philosophischen Auffassungen des Flavius Josephus* (dissertation; Halle, 1887), pp. 17–25.

‡ *Genesis Rabba,* XVII, 5; XLIV, 17. This Midrash is strongly reminiscent of Philo who, commenting on Gen. 15:12, distinguishes four kinds of ecstasy: (*a*) mad fury producing mental delusion, (*b*) extreme amazement, (*c*) passivity of mind, (*d*) divine possession, or frenzy to which the prophets as a class are subject. The first rabbinic type is the same as the third in Philo, with the same illustration offered. "God cast an ecstasy on Adam, and he slept" (Gen. 2:21), which means "passivity and tranquility of mind." The second rabbinic type is the same as the fourth in Philo, namely "the inspired and God-possessed experience," with the same illustrations offered, Gen. 15:12. The third rabbinic type probably corresponds to Philo's second type, a state which produces "great agitation and terrible consternation." Finally, the fourth rabbinic type seems to be the same as Philo's first type, with an illustration which resembles that in the Midrash. It is mentioned, Philo says, in the curses described in Deuteronomy. "Madness and loss of sight will overtake the impious, so that they shall differ in nought from blind men groping at noonday as in deep darkness" (Deut. 27:28 f.).

case of Adam;* (*b*) as a state of prophetic experience or ecstasy in the case of Abraham;† and (*c*) as a state of torpor or consternation.‡ Following Rab, other rabbis said that there is a fourth kind of *tardemah,* namely, madness. These rabbis do not contradict Rab's statement concerning the ecstatic type of Abraham's prophetic experience.§ They merely add that the word *tardemah* is also used in the Bible to denote a state of madness.

*Tardemah* as a state of madness‖ has been attributed to false prophets,# as in the words of Isaiah:

*"So the Lord God caused a deep sleep (*tardemah*) to fall upon the man, and while he slept took one of his ribs" and made it into a woman (Gen. 2:21).

†"As the sun was going down, a deep sleep (*tardemah*) fell on Abram; and lo, a dread and great darkness fell upon him. Then the Lord said to Abram: Know of a surety that your descendants will be sojourners in a land that is not theirs, and will be slaves there, and they will be oppressed for four hundred years" (Gen. 15:12–13). Cf. *Mishnah of Rabbi Eliezer,* ch. vi. (ed. Enelow, p. 110), where it is emphasized that this is the only passage in which *tardemah* is used in the sense of a prophetic state of experience. On the other hand, *Seder Olam Rabba,* ch. xxi, maintains that in Gen. 2:21 the term is used to denote a prophetic state. This view is also maintained by many, among them Clemens Alexandrinus, Tertullian, Aphraates, and other Church Fathers; see L. Ginzberg, *Die Haggada bei den Kirchenvaetern und in der apokryphischen Literatur* (Berlin, 1900), p. 35. An allegorical interpretation of the same term as a prophetic state is contained in the rabbinic comment on Prov. 19:15. "Slothfulness casts into *tardemah.*" The rabbis remarked: "Because Israel was slothful in repenting in the days of Elijah, prophecy increased among them," and numerous prophets arose at that time. (*Ruth Rabba,* proemium, 2; cf. *Yalkut Shimoni,* Proverbs, 958.)

‡While King Saul and his soldiers were sleeping at night in the wilderness of Ziph where they had gone in pursuit of David, the latter entered the encampment and took away the spear which was stuck in the ground at Saul's head. No one saw it, or knew it, "nor did any awake, for they were all asleep, because a *tardemah* from the Lord has fallen upon them" (I Sam. 26:12). "What is the meaning of the phrase 'the deceived and the deception' (Job 12:16)? Said Rabbi Simeon ben Lakish: Prophets and their prophecy. Rabbi Yohanan said: The madman and madness." (*Midrash Tehillim,* 7, 3, ed. Buber, p. 64.) The rabbis seem to have vocalized *mishgeh* in parallelism to *tushyyah.*

§Their remark is preceded by the word *af,* also, which in rabbinic language introduces a supplementary rather than a contradictory statement. This remark, therefore, does not warrant S. Baron's inference (*A Social and Religious History of the Jews* [New York, 1952], II, 315) that "there was even a certain revulsion against the state of ecstasy *per se.*"

‖*Shatah* and its derivatives are frequently used in the sense of "to be demented," madness. See *Toseftah, Baba Kamma,* IV, 4; *Yebamoth,* XIV, I.

#See Kimhi, *Commentary, ad loc.*

*Stupefy yourselves and be in a stupor,*
*Blind yourselves and be blind!*
*Be drunk, but not with wine;*
*Stagger, but not with strong drink!*
*For the Lord has poured out upon you*
*A spirit of deep sleep* [tardemah],
*And has closed your eyes, the prophets,*
*And covered your heads, the seers!*
                                    *Isaiah 29:9–10*

The rabbis looked with irony upon the phenomena of wild ecstasy which were common in Palestine and Syria in the third century C.E. Such an attitude of irony may be traced in the sayings of Rabbi Yohanan (d. C.E. 279), who was the head of the leading academy in Tiberias, Palestine. "From the day of the destruction of the Temple prophetic inspiration was taken away from the prophets and given to children and madmen."*

While the rabbis knew of the phenomena of prophetic ecstasy, they did not adopt Philo's view that the prophets of Israel received their inspiration in a state of ecstasy. Ecstasy, they maintained, is the mark that distinguished Moses from the pagan prophet Balaam. "Moses received his revelation while retaining his full power of consciousness, . . . whereas Balaam lost his power of consciousness in the moment of revelation, as it is said, the oracle of him who hears the words of God, who sees the vision of the Almighty, falling down, yet with opened eyes (Num. 24:4)."† To another rabbi, the absence of ecstasy is the mark that distinguished the Hebrew prophets from all other prophets. Rabbi Eleazar quotes in this connection the words of Isaiah 8:19, "And when they say unto you: 'Consult the mediums and the wizards who chirp and mutter,' the diviners chirp and mutter

---

* *Baba Bathra* 12b. *Shotim,* usually rendered "fools," is in all likelihood an allusion to those who prophesy in madness, and must be rendered "madmen." The association of so-called prophecy and madness is also reflected elsewhere in rabbinic literature.

† *Sifre Deuteronomy,* end, and the version in *Yalkut.*

without knowing what they utter."* This, indeed, seems to be the implication of the rabbis' stressing the clarity and unambiguousness of the message of the Hebrew prophets: the view that the experience from which the message stemmed did not occur while the prophet suffered a loss of consciousness.†

*Sotah, 12b. According to Rabbi Eleazar, Rabbi Yose ben Zimra (a scholar of the second century C.E.) maintained that "all the prophets prophesied without knowing what they prophesied, with the exception of Moses and Isaiah. Moses said: 'May my teaching drop as the rain, my speech distill as the dew' (Deut. 32:2). Isaiah said: 'Behold, I and the children whom the Lord has given me are signs and portents in Israel from the Lord of hosts, who dwells on Mount Zion' (Isa. 8:18). . . . Even Samuel who was master of prophets prophesied without knowing what he prophesied. He said: 'The Lord sent Jerubbaal, Barak, Jephtah and Samuel and delivered you out of the hand of your enemies' (I Sam. 12:11). He spoke of himself in the third person, because he did not know what he prophesied." (*Midrash Tehillim* 90, 4 [ed. S. Buber, p. 387]). This view does not necessarily imply that the prophets suffered a loss of consciousness during the act of inspiration, but rather that at times, words came to them or were uttered by them, the full import of which was unknown to them. According to *Mechilta, tractate shirata*, ch. x, Moses and the people Israel in singing the song at the Red Sea "prophesied without realizing what they prophesied." They sang: "Thou wilt bring *them* in, and plant *them* on Thy own mountain" (Exod. 15:17), instead of, "Thou wilt bring *us* in, and plant *us* on Thy own mountain." "They thus predicted that the children would enter the land and the fathers would not." In *Aboth de Rabbi Nathan,* B version, ch. xliii (ed. Schechter, p. 118), this passage is quoted to prove that Moses was among the ten people who prophesied without realizing what they prophesied. Indeed, among the ten people are mentioned not only prophets, but also non-prophets such as Laban. The phrase in this and in other passages in rabbinic literature refers, not to prophetic ecstasy, but to unconscious divination. According to *Sotah,* 12b, Pharaoh's daughter, who after rescuing the infant Moses from the waters of the Nile committed the child to his mother's care, uttered words which contained an unconscious divination: "Here is what is thine." L. Ginzberg, *The Legends of the Jews,* V (Philadelphia, 1909), 250, calls attention to a reference to unconscious divination in Herodotus, *History,* III, 153, and John 11:51.

†"What is the difference between the prophets of Israel and those of other nations? Rabbi Hamma ben Rabbi Hanina said: The Holy One, blessed be He, reveals Himself to heathen prophets with half-speech only. . . . But to the prophets of Israel He speaks with complete speech." According to another opinion, God appeared to the heathen prophets at night, namely in dreams (*Genesis Rabba,* L, 11, 5). "The prophecy of the nations of the world is ambiguous . . . but the prophecy of Israel is clear" (*Esther Rabba* to 3:14). In Gen. 17:1–3 we read: "The Lord appeared to Abraham and said to him, I am the God Almighty. . . . Then Abraham fell on his face. . . ." "As long as Abraham was uncircumcised, he would fall on his face whenever the Shechinah spoke to him. After he was circumcised, he was able to stand up when the Shechinah conversed with him, as it is said, and Abraham still stood before the Lord" ([Gen. 18:22],

However, the *Zohar,* the classical work of Jewish mysticism, seems to follow Philo's theory of prophecy except in its pronouncement that Moses was free of ecstasy. "Moses," it is said, "received the divine message standing and with all his senses unimpaired, and he comprehended it fully, as it is written: 'even manifestly and not in dark speeches' (Num. 12:8); whereas other prophets fell on their faces in a state of exhaustion and did not obtain a perfectly clear message."* According to Maimonides, prophetic vision is "something terrible and fearful which the prophet feels while he is awake (in contradistinction to the prophetic dream), as is distinctly stated by Daniel: 'And I saw this great vision, and no strength was left in me; my comeliness was fearfully upset, and I retained no strength' (Dan. 10:8). He continues: 'I fell in a deep sleep with my face to the ground' (10:9). Under such circumstances the senses cease to function and the Active Intellect influences the rational faculties, and through them the imaginative faculties, which become perfect and active."†

In discussing the difference between Moses and all other prophets, Maimonides avers: "All the prophets experience prophetic manifestations in dreams only, at night, or by day when deep sleep falls upon them; as it is said, 'I do make Myself known unto him in a vision. I do speak with him in a dream' (Num. 12:6). During the prophetic experience their limbs tremble, their physical strength fails them, their thoughts become confused. Thus the mind is left free to comprehend the vision it perceives, as is said in reference to Abraham, 'And lo, a horror of great darkness fell upon him' (Gen. 15:12)." Moses alone

---

*Tanhuma,* Lech, 20). Of Balaam too, it is said that "he sees the vision of the Almighty, falling down, but having his eyes uncovered" (Num. 24:4). Cf. *Agadath Bereshith* (S. Buber, ed. [Krakau, 1903]), ch. 11. See also S. Horovitz, *Das Problem der Prophetologie in der judischen Religionsphilosophie von Saadia bis Maimuni* (Halle, 1883), p. 11; Dienstfertig, *Die Prophetologie in der Religionsphilosophie des ersten nachchristlichen Jahrhunderts* (dissertation; Erlangen, 1892), pp. 25 f.

*Zohar,* I, 170b–171a; cf. III, 268b–269a.

†*The Guide of the Perplexed,* II, ch. 41. See also Maimonides' introduction to *Mishnah Sanhedrin,* ch. x, "The Seventh Principle." In his commentary on *The Guide of the Perplexed,* II, ch. 41, Asher ben Abraham Crescas (15th century, Provence) expresses his amazement at Maimonides' theory. What holds true of Daniel, who, according to Maimonides, was not a prophet in the classical sense, must not be assumed

was an exception. "All the prophets are filled with fear and consternation and become physically weak" during the experience. "Not so, our teacher Moses, of whom Scripture says, 'As a man speaks unto his neighbor' (Exod. 33:11). Just as a man is not startled when he hears the words of his fellow man, so the mind of Moses was vigorous enough to comprehend the words of prophecy while retaining his normal state."*

Yet Maimonides, far from assuming the cessation of the faculty of reasoning, emphasized, on the contrary, the role of the intellectual capacity of the prophet.

## IN THE CHURCH FATHERS

Philo's view of the ecstatic character of the prophetic state passed over to the earliest Church Fathers. Athenagoras (who lived *ca.* 177) says of the prophets that while "under the impulse of the divine Spirit and raised above their own thoughts, they proclaimed the things with which they were inspired. For the Spirit used them just as a flute player blows on a flute."† Similarly Justin Martyr maintains that the Spirit, "as a divine plectrum, descending from heaven," used the prophets "like a cither or lute."‡ In his *Dialogue with Trypho,* he maintains that the prophet Zechariah saw Joshua, Satan, and the angel (Zech.

---

of the classical prophets. The fear and darkness that came over Abraham were due to what was revealed to him in the vision, not to the vision itself.

*Mishneh Torah, Yesode Hatorah,* VII, 2, 6. Kimhi, *Commentary,* I Sam. 19:24, describes the state of prophecy as one in which all emotional powers disappear and only the power of intelligence remains. Similarly, Gersonides, *Commentary,* I Sam. 19:20.

†Athenagoras, *A Plea Regarding Christians,* IX, in C. C. Richardson, ed., "The Library of Christian Classics," I, 308. See Leitner, *Die prophetische Inspiration* (Freiburg, 1896), p. 109. See also T. W. Hopkins, *Doctrine of Inspiration* (Rochester, 1881), p. 18; K. Rahner, *Über die Schriftinspiration* (Freiburg, 1958); P. A. Bea, *"Die Instrumentalitätsidee in der Inspirationslehre,"* *Studia Anselmiana,* XXV–XXVIII (Rome, 1951), 47 f.; R. Abba, *The Nature and Authority of the Bible* (Philadelphia, 1958), pp. 104 f.

‡*Cohortatio ad Graecos,* 8. The same figure was used by Montanus. "Behold man is like a lyre and I fly to him as a plectrum. Man sleeps and I awake. Behold it is the Lord that throws the hearts of men into an ecstasy and gives them a new heart." W. Scheppelern, *Der Montanismus und die Phrygischen Kulte* (Tübingen, 1923), p. 19.

2:10–3:2), not in his waking condition, but in ecstasy.* Ecstasy was the accepted form of prophecy in the Church of the second century.†

The emergence of the Montanist movement soon after the middle of the second century C.E. brought ecstasy into the foreground. Montanus, originally a priest of the goddess Cybele in Phrygia, who had become a convert to Christianity, proclaimed that the age of the Spirit foretold in the Gospel according to John had dawned and that he was himself the Spirit's mouthpiece. In the words of an opponent: "He would fall into a state of possession, as it were, and abnormal ecstasy, insomuch that he became frenzied and began to babble and utter strange sounds, that is to say, prophesying contrary to the manner which the Church had received‡ from generation to generation by tradition from the beginning." Montanus was joined by others who also claimed to be prophets, and the movement which started in Phrygia spread rapidly throughout Asia Minor and found large numbers of followers.

By alleging ecstasy to be "an outward sign of the highest stage of revelation," the Montanists aroused the opposition of the Church and gave occasion for a sharp debate. The Montanists would not be able to prove that any prophet either in the Old or the New Testament prophesied in ecstasy, wrote an anonymous presbyter of the second century.

The Montanists rested their case on Gen. 2:21 and Ps. 116:11. Yet they could not deny the difference between ecstasy and the type of inspiration which was known from Scripture and tradition. Their opponents argued that Montanus was not a genuine prophet, for he spoke while he was actually in a state of ecstasy, whereas the true

---

*Dialogue with Trypho, ch. 115.

†"Do not test or examine any prophet speaking in spirit (i.e., in an ecstasy), for every sin shall be forgiven, but this sin shall not be forgiven" (Didache, XI, 7). See A. Harnack, Die Lehre der zwölf Apostel (Leipzig, 1884), pp. 41, 123 ff. Celsus claimed that there were prophets in his time in Syria and Palestine. (Origen, Contra Celsum, VII, 2; see VI, 9.) It is likely that wandering prophets were common in Syria, see Theologisches Wörterbuch zum Neuen Testament, II (Stuttgart, 1933 ff.), 456. On Alexander of Abonuteichos and Peregrinus Proteus, see E. Fascher, Prophetes (Giessen, 1927), pp. 190 ff.

‡H. J. Lawlor and J. E. L. Oulton, trans., Eusebius, Ecclesiastical History, bk. V, ch. 16 (London, 1927).

prophets received their message in ecstasy, but did not deliver it until they had regained their normal faculties.*

Disgusted with the character of ecstasy as presented by the Montanist prophets, the Church Fathers declared that ecstasy is incompatible with true prophecy. "How can the spirit of wisdom and knowledge deprive anyone of his senses?"†

"A false prophet falls into an ecstasy in which he is without shame or fear. Beginning with willing ignorance, he passes on, as has been stated, to involuntary madness of soul. The adherents of Montanus cannot show that anyone either of the old or of the new prophets was thus carried away in spirit."‡ On the other hand, Tertullian, the chief advocate of the Montanists, who devoted one of his writings to this problem, identified prophetic revelations with raving and delirium, and regarded ecstasy as the hallmark of the supreme prophetic state. "When a man is rapt in the Spirit, especially when he beholds the glory of God, or when God speaks through him, he necessarily loses his sensation, because he is overshadowed with the power of God."§

---

*Eusebius, *Ecclesiastical History*, II, 176. Cf. the references in bk. V, ch. 17, to the lost treatise of Miltiades devoted to the idea "that the prophets ought not to speak in ecstasy." *The Pseudo-Clementine Homilies* formulate a theory to the effect that a true prophet prophesies not darkly and ambiguously, but clearly and simply. He at all times is to be distinguished from "those who are madly inspired by the spirit of disorder, from those who are drunken beside the altars, and are gorged with fat." (*The Pseudo-Clementine Homilies*, III, 12 f.; cf. XVI, 18.)

†Basil, *Commentary on Isaiah*, Proemium, e, 5, quoted by Hengstenberg, *Christology of the Old Testament*, IV (Edinburgh, 1864), 396.

‡Eusebius, *Ecclesiastical History*, V, 17, 2. See also I Cor. 14:32; cf. N. Schepelern, *Der Montanismus und die phrygischen Kulte* (Tübingen, 1929), p. 20; N. Bontwetsch, *Die Geschichte des Montanismus* (Erlangen, 1891). The tracing of Montanist ecstasy to the Jewish idea of inspiration (Schwegler, *Das nachapostolische Zeitalter* [Tübingen, 1846], pp. 259 ff.) is untenable; see also Leitner, *op. cit.*, p. 121, and Dausch, *Die Schriftinspiration* (Freiburg, 1891), p. 54.

§*Adversus Marcionem*, IV, 22. "This power we call ecstasy, in which the sensuous soul stands out of itself, in a way which even resembles madness." Tertullian finds support for his idea in the Septuagint version of Gen. 2:21. "And God sent an ecstasy upon Adam, and he slept. The sleep came on his body to cause it to rest, but the ecstasy fell on his soul to remove rest; from that very circumstance it still happens ordinarily . . . that sleep is combined with ecstasy. In fact, with what real feeling, and anxiety, and suffering do we experience joy, and sorrow and alarm in our dreams! Whereas we should not be moved by any such emotions, by what would be the merest fantasies of

It was not the fact that Montanus was an ecstatic, but rather the character of his ecstasy that appeared offensive to his contemporaries.* Origen most emphatically asserts that while under the influence of the Holy Spirit, the will and judgment of the prophets remain in the normal state. He saw in the absence of any perturbation, alienation of mind, or loss of will the criterion of true prophecy, and the formal note of the distinction between biblical and mantic inspiration.†

Generally, the Church Fathers did not deny the existence of every kind of ecstasy in the prophets. In the language of Augustine, ecstasy as *alienatio a mente* was denied, but *alienatio mentis a sensibus corporis,* namely, "the derivation of the spiritual activity of man from some life outside his senses and its guidance towards the object of revelation," was admitted. This theory prevailed throughout the Middle Ages.

Lutheran dogmaticians of the seventeenth century developed the doctrine of verbal inspiration to the extreme: every word in Scripture was inspired and dictated by God; the prophets were merely the hands and penmen of the Holy Spirit, *God's amanuenses.* Yet this monergistic doctrine of inspiration did not imply that God dehumanized His amanuenses and reduced them to mere mechanisms. They were not "unconscious, as the enthusiasts say of themselves and as the Gentiles imagine the ecstasy in their prophets. Neither is it to be taken as if the prophets did not understand their prophecies of the things which they were to write, which was the aberration once taught by the Montanists, Phrygians, or Cataphrygians, and Priscilianists."‡ Inspiration embraces first of all a certain supernatural and extraordinary enlightenment of the mind.

---

course, if when we dream we were masters of ourselves (unaffected by ecstasy)." (*De Anima,* ch. xlv, trans. P. Holmer [Edinburgh, 1870]).

*Eusebius, *Ecclesiastical History,* p. 173. On the difference between the Phrygian Montanists and their opponents as to the nature of ecstasy, see Labriolle, *La Crise montaniste* (Paris, 1913), pp. 162–175.

†*De Principiis,* III, 4 f. (*Patrologiae Greco-Latinae,* XI, 317 f.). *Contra Celsum,* VII, chs. 3 and 4; Homil. in Ezek. 6:1, n. 9 (*Patrologiae,* XV, 735). A. Zollig, *Die Inspirationslehre des Origenes* (Freiburg, 1902), pp. 67 ff.

‡Robert Preuss, *The Inspiration of Scripture* (Edinburgh, 1955). A study of the theology of the seventeenth-century Lutheran dogmaticians. See pp. 57 f.

While the doctrine of verbal inspiration was gradually given up in the eighteenth century,* the mechanical conception of prophetic inspiration was revived in a modified form.

## IN MODERN SCHOLARSHIP

In the nineteenth century the theory of ecstasy proved to be of great value in removing the embarrassing enigma of the biblical prophets. There was nothing unique about their experience. Ecstasy was the feature

> that put the prophets on the plane as the seers of other peoples; they employ the usual means to set themselves in a condition of ecstasy. . . . Rational consciousness is only a secondary and subordinate feature with the prophets; they were rapt into a state utterly different from the normal. . . . In the eyes of the ordinary man the prophets appeared as madmen. There must therefore have been a point of contact between the prophetic state and that of madness; . . . This feature puts the prophets on the same plane as the seers of other peoples; they employ the usual means to set themselves in a condition of ecstasy.†

Attempts were made to explain the prophets of Israel by comparison with similar phenomena in other religions. On the presupposition of a basic similarity between all religious phenomena, prophetic states were equated with the raptures of Indian fakirs, the frenzy of the Greek orgiasts and Bacchantes, with the ecstasy of Arabian dervishes and the wild behavior of Syrian priests as depicted in the writings of Greco-Roman authors. By accumulating such diversified material, scholars believed that they had penetrated to the historical roots and the structure of the prophetic consciousness.

---

*"A petty way of thinking typical of former benighted ages liked to represent those inspired by the spirit as organ pipes through which the wind blows." (Herder, quoted by P. Dausch, *Die Schriftinspiration* [Freiburg, 1891], p. 125.)

†E. W. Hengstenberg, *The Christology of the Old Testament* III (Edinburgh, 1864), 161, 167.

Insofar as the prophet possessed supernatural knowledge, the prophet as an ecstatic secured this through the temporary excitation of his own mental powers in such a way as to give rise to a vision.* Numerous authors have maintained the theory of ecstasy,† some even holding the view that every prophetic message received or recorded in the Bible arose out of an ecstatic experience.‡

It is taken for granted that the prophets were men of ecstatic frenzy. In such frenzy, we are told, the nervous and emotional excitement inhibits the ordinary control of the brain, and the actions of the subject are controlled by the reflex working of lower nervous centers. In all parts of the world, people in such paroxysms have been thought to be under control of a supernatural being. "The subject has visions and dreams; he laughs, rolls on the ground, leaps about, exhibits contortions of the body, or twistings of the neck, changes color; the body shakes violently, becomes rigid; the subject falls in a fit." From the shadowy land of the subconscious "come at call many elements which make up shifting mental states and momentary conscious experiences—long-forgotten memories, impressions, convictions. And there come, too, without our willing, many factors which we cannot account for, the superstitions, fancies, impulses, dreams, that seem to belong to another personality—though they may be our very own, by brain-cell inheritance from a dim and distant animal and human past, incubated unconsciously by our own mental mechanism."§

To quote some of the leading exponents:

*G. Hölscher, *Die Profeten* (Leipzig, 1914), pp. 125 ff.

†B. Duhm, *Israels Propheten* (2nd ed.; Tübingen, 1916), p. 290; H. Gunkel in H. Schmidt, *Die Schriften des Alten Testaments,* II (Göttingen, 1917), p. xviii; H. Gunkel, *Die Propheten* (Göttingen, 1917), p. 30; H. W. Hertzberg, *Gott und Prophet* (Gütersloh, 1928); W. Jacobi, *Die Ekstase der alttestamentlischen Propheten* (München, 1923); J. Lindblom, *Die Literarische Gattung der prophetischen Literatur* (Uppsala, 1924); H. W. Robinson, *Inspiration and Revelation in the Old Testament* (Oxford, 1946), pp. 134 f.; J. G. Matthews, *The Religious Pilgrimage of Israel* (New York, 1947), p. 130.

‡F. Giesebrecht, *Die Berufsbegabung der alttestamentlichen Propheten* (Göttingen, 1897), pp. 36 ff.

§F. M. Davenport, *Primitive Traits in Religious Revivals,* a study in mental and social evolution (New York, 1905), pp. 11, 24.

The fundamental experience of all types of prophecy is ecstasy.*

The great majority of the prophetic oracles as we have them now are reports, possibly or even probably given by the prophets themselves of what they had heard in the access of the ecstasy.†

Psychologically viewed, most pre-Exile prophets were ecstatic men. At least, Hosea, Isaiah, Jeremiah, and Ezekiel professed to be and undoubtedly were. Without gross carelessness, one may safely assume that all were ecstatics, though of various kinds and in different degrees.‡

> We can now call before our minds a picture of the Prophet's activity in public. He might be mingling with the crowd, sometimes on ordinary days, sometimes on special occasions. Suddenly something would happen to him. His eye would become fixed, strange convulsions would seize upon his limbs, the form of his speech would change. Men would recognize that the Spirit had fallen upon him. The fit would pass, and he would tell to those who stood around the things which he had seen and heard. There might have been symbolic action, and this he would explain with a clear memory of all ecstasy. Such manifestations were common, and there were many who were subject to them.§

It has been maintained that ecstasy "provided a criterion without which neither the prophet nor his audience would be satisfied."‖

G. Hölscher's is the first attempt (apart from Wundt's general characterization of prophetism in his *Völkerpsychologie*) systematically to describe prophetic experiences by means of the methods of modern psychology. Applying the principles of Wundt's physiological psychology and psychology of the peoples, he tries to derive prophetism from an abnormal, physiologically definable condition and to interpret pro-

---

*H. Gunkel, quoted by H. H. Rowley, *The Servant of the Lord* (London, 1952), p. 93.

†T. H. Robinson, "The Ecstatic Elements in Old Testament Prophecy," *The Expositor*, Eighth Series, No. 123 (March, 1921), p. 235.

‡M. Weber, *Ancient Judaism* (Glencoe, 1952), p. 286.

§T. H. Robinson, *Prophecy and the Prophets* (London, 1923), p. 50.

‖See H. H. Rowley, *The Servant of the Lord*, pp. 91 f.

phetic experiences, actions, and expressions as ecstatic phenomena. The narratives of the so-called "schools of the prophets" of the time of Samuel (I Sam. 10:5 ff.; 14:18 ff.), which are said to report ecstatic movements and their typical concomitants, are supposed to support this thesis. The excited emotional behavior of the late prophets, their lively gesticulation (Ezek. 6:11; 21:17 [H. 21:19]), their violent utterance (Jer. 4:19; 6:11; 20:8 f.), the intense mental concentration (Jer. 4:23, 26; 25:15 ff.) are regarded as signs of ecstasy.*

The general mentality of the ecstatic prophet is described in much the same terms. The aim of the ecstatic is to become one with the god through rapture and trance. These ideas of union spring, according to Hölscher, from the notions underlying the magic cult.

> In all festivals, especially those of orgiastic vegetation cults, cultic actions including the mimetic dance consist in the fact that men imitate the activity of the god and thus magically support it. In proportion as the excitement of the celebrants increases and the articulation of the experience is dissolved, the dancers become increasingly one with the experience they represent. In the overflow of their feelings they are conscious of being transformed and bewitched; they feel the breath of the divine, they seem to gain contact with the god whom they believe to be present at the festival and in the tension and expansion of their being they aspire towards him in order to become one with him.†

Hölscher, who himself admits that such ideas are not compatible with the spirit of Israelite prophetism, since the Semite was strongly aware of the cleavage between God and man, and his religion was thus unfavorable to the development of notions of deification, solves this difficulty by supposing that in place of God a spirit or a demon is the operative factor in the experience of ecstasy. Although in this way the idea of a union of God and man was avoided, it emerged where ecstasy

---

*G. Hölscher, op. cit., pp. 7, 16 f., 32.
†Ibid., pp. 22 f.

arose from the depths of personal consciousness, even in classical prophetism. Accordingly, Hölscher thinks that "the prophets not only speak in the service and at the behest of God, not only repeat words and revelations which God has imparted to them or shown them in vision, but that they speak as God Himself, and in their ecstatic speech, utterly identify themselves with Him."*

The connections between the older prophecy, i.e., so-called nabi-ism, and classical prophecy are usually understood in the following way. An editorial note in I Sam. 9:9 states: "Formerly in Israel, when a man went to inquire of God, he said: 'Come, let us go to the seer'; for he who is now called a prophet was formerly called a seer (ro'eh)." This note informs us that in earlier times a distinction was made between seer and prophet. Indeed, in I Sam. 9:1–10:6, seer (9:11, 18) and prophet (10:5, 10–12) are distinguished from each other, and that distinction was still maintained in the ninth century B.C.E. On the other hand, in the writings of the great prophets of the eighth century B.C.E., the distinction has more or less disappeared. Later sources use the two notions almost interchangeably (II Sam. 14:11; II Kings 17:13; Isa. 29:10). In the old days, then, the *nabi* was the excited ecstatic who came forward as a mediator of supernatural revelations which had come to him in inner experiences, whereas *ro'eh* and *hozeh* were seers of every kind who gained supernatural knowledge, not with ecstasy, but by various external means of perception, favorite among them being the illusions of darkness, half sleep, and dreaming.†

The word *nabi* is supposed to denote a person who had the gift of tongues or glossolalia through the inspiration of a higher being. This sort of speaking is not meant to be heard by others, the obscurity of its expressions making it totally unintelligible to the bystanders. The *nabi* appear as men of occult knowledge, proclaiming future events, although prediction in itself does not necessarily belong to the essential character of the *nabi*. They are differentiated from the diviner and magician by the fact that their ecstatic experiences are rooted in

---

* *Ibid.*, p. 25.

† *Ibid.*, pp. 125 f. A similar view is held by Sanda, *"Elias und die religiosen Verhält-nisse seiner Zeit"* (*Biblische Zeitfragen* [Münster, 1914]), p. 51.

mystical dispositions, whereas divination and magic are grounded in a knowledge that has been acquired. Of course they practiced various exercises in order to induce their trances. Loud music (I Sam. 10:5) and bloody mutilation of their own bodies* were used as means for promoting ecstasy. In contrast, the seer, to whom all delirious frenzy is alien, is able to divine the will of the gods through the interpretation of various omens, for example, the rustling of trees (cf. II Sam. 5:24) and the flight of birds (cf. Gen. 15:11).†

Of these two elements, from the fusion of which later classical prophecy is considered to spring, divination is held to be an original Semitic phenomenon. Ecstatic prophetism is held to be alien to the Semites, and not to be found in the desert. Unknown in Israel during the early nomadic period, ecstasy is believed to have developed under Canaanite influence.‡ From Thrace or Asia Minor, ecstasy is supposed to have spread to both Greeks and Hebrews shortly before the year 1000 B.C.E. Nabiism "was gradually transformed by the spiritual leadership of native Israelite divination."§ R. Kittel thinks that this purifying process began under Samuel, who wished to transmute nabiism in accordance with his purely religious purposes. "Thus he guided Nabiism into new paths and began to cleanse and spiritualize the naturalistic half-heathen Dionysiac movement. In principle therefore he refashioned it into what it later became."‖ In any event, these older

---

*B. Duhm, *Die Propheten,* p. 81. The phenomenon called glossolalia is particularly known to us from the New Testament (cf. I Cor. 14:2–25). Through Torczyner's interpretation of Isa. 28:10 as containing not meaningless sounds, but clear words (*Zeitschrift der Deutschen Morgenländischen Gesellschaft,* LXVI, 393), the only text which could be adduced in support of the contention that "speaking with tongues was not foreign to Israelite and Judaic prophecy" (Hölscher, *Die Profeten,* p. 35; Volz, *Der Geist Gottes,* p. 9), loses its force as a proof.

†Cf. I Kings, 18:26 f. about the manner of the prophets of Baal.

‡R. Kittel, *Die Geschichte des Volkes Israel,* II (3d ed.; Stuttgart, 1932), p. 148; cf. Hölscher, *op. cit.,* pp. 140 f. W. Baumgartner called attention to the fact that there is no trace of ecstatic prophets in the Ugaritic documents. This is particularly significant since Ras Shamra is geographically close to Asia Minor, the home of Cybele and Attis and their ecstatic priests. Nor has any such trace been found in the Amarna archives (the first half of the 14th century). See F. M. Bohl, *Opera Minora* (Groningen, 1953), p. 69.

§H. Junker, *Prophet und Seher im alten Israel* (Trier, 1927).

‖R. Kittel, *op. cit.,* p. 150.

prophets are described as ecstatics. They formed "raving bands who travelled through the country in blustering enthusiasm—anyone who came too near them had to take care lest the fit should seize him too."* Such bands of prophets had to nurse the prophetic spirit, and they performed certain exercises until the Spirit came upon them. "Then they tore off their clothes and lay naked, all day and night" (I Sam. 19:24). This inspired condition is certainly considered by all to be ecstatic. Deliberate cultivation and preparation are its characteristic features. Thus, for example, Elijah, Amos, Hosea, Isaiah, and Jeremiah are termed ecstatic, and Ezekiel an ecstatic dervish, half terrible and half amusing.

As ecstatics "the prophets not only speak in the name and at the behest of God, repeating words and revelations divulged to them by God or shown in visions; they speak as God Himself and identify themselves completely with Him, while they speak in the state of ecstasy."† The outstanding feature of their attitude to God is their "consciousness of being one with God."‡

Much debate has been carried on about the probability and validity of the views advanced by Hölscher. Many scholars have fully accepted his views, while others have voiced complete opposition or expressed qualified agreement, regarding them as correct only in relation to the older prophets.

Criticism has exposed Hölscher's arbitrary leveling of entirely heterogeneous phenomena and historical muddles, resulting in false conclusions.§ He has in fact linked together reports about the oldest types of Hebrew prophecy, the speeches of the classical literary prophets, reports about medicine men, shamans, dervishes, oracle-givers, visionaries, divines of many different ages as well apocalyptic writings of the Hellenistic period, and has constructed from the medley a unified and

---

*H. Gunkel, *Die Propheten*, p. 3.

†G. Hölscher, *op. cit.*, p. 25.

‡H. W. Hertzberg, *Prophet und Gott* (Gütersloh, 1923), p. 12, cf. A. R. Johnson, *The One and the Many in the Israelite Conception of God* (Cardiff, 1961), pp. 33 ff.

§Baentsch, *"Pathologische Zuege in Israel's Prophetentum," Zeitschrift für Wissenschaftliche Theologie*, vol. L; J. Haenel, *Das Erkennen Gottes bei den Schriftpropheten* (Berlin, 1923); H. Junker, *op. cit.;* Auerbach, *Die Prophetie* (Berlin, 1920).

typical picture of all biblical prophecy. Apart from the unfairness of equating phenomena which are separated by several centuries (the time between the oldest prophets and the book of Revelation spans, roughly, a millennium), this procedure is incompatible with the fact that there is a gulf between the literary prophets and the older type of prophet, the so-called *nabi,* which the former expressly emphasize.

The theory of ecstasy is by no means shared by all scholars. W. Robertson Smith insists that "the prophets of the Old Testament never appeared before their auditors in a state of ecstasy, being thus clearly marked off from heathen soothsayers, who were held to be under the influence of the godhead just in proportion as they lost intelligent self-control; . . . the true prophets never seek in heathen fashion to authenticate their divine commission by showing themselves in a state of visionary ecstasy."*

Eduard König is the one who most tenaciously opposes the view that the ecstatic bands of prophets were the raw material out of which later prophecy developed through a smoothing and polishing process. He emphasizes again and again the mental clarity of the prophets and the self-consciousness which they preserved even in the moment of their call, and he denies that ecstasy had any significance for the rise of prophetism. In more recent biblical study, scholars have felt uncomfortable about the theory of ecstasy, the use of which has not proved fruitful.†

---

* *The Prophets of Israel* (New York, 1892), p. 219.
† E. König, *Geschichte der alttestamentlichen Religion* (Götersloh, 1912), p. 144; *Der Offenbarungsbegriff des Alten Testaments,* (Leipzig, 1882), I, 48; *Das alttestamentliche Prophetentum und die moderne Geschichtssauffassung* (Gütersloh, 1910), pp. 65 ff. P. Beck, *Die Ekstase* (1906), p. 148, thinks that the prophetic experience had no ecstatic elements. The almost universal tendency among British and American scholars to deny prophetic ecstasy is thoroughly discussed by T. H. Robinson, *Theologische Rundschau,* III (Tübingen, 1931), 75–104. H. W. Robinson suggests that the prophetic experience is more aptly described as "abnormal" rather than "ecstatic," "since it included many elements besides that of ecstasy proper, whilst ecstasy corresponds with Greek rather than with Hebrew psychology." (*Redemption and Revelation* [New York and London, 1942], pp. 140, 135.) A moderate view on the role of ecstasy is taken by R. S. Cripps, *A Critical and Exegetical Commentary on the Book of Amos* (London, 1929), pp. 83 ff.; cf. J. Skinner, *Prophecy and Religion: Studies in the Life of Jeremiah* (2nd ed.; Cambridge, 1930), p. 11; A. Guillaume, *Prophecy and Divination* (London, 1938), pp. 83 ff.

# 10

# An Examination of the
# Theory of Ecstasy

*Our task now is to examine the theory of ecstasy which claims that* prophecy originated in a state of trance, in undisciplined, delirious raving. Our analysis will be limited to the literary prophets, without reference to the *nebiim* of an older period.

What is involved is far more than a psychological problem, namely, the state of mind of the prophet. The issue is the uniqueness of the prophetic act and the nature of prophetic consciousness. The theory of ecstasy, in its attempt to make the prophetic act plausible by making it comparable, deprives us of an understanding of what is genuine and tends to distort the essence of prophecy. It is because of its numerous implications for the understanding of the personality of the prophet that we must examine the theory of ecstasy from the standpoint of the prophetic consciousness as a whole.

## TACIT ASSUMPTIONS

The theory of ecstasy is a combination of applying the method of the comparative study of religion and doctrines of modern psychology to the problem of biblical prophecy. It starts, then, with the assumption that the experiences of the prophets are of the same kind as those of the orgiastic cults in many primitive societies. Since hardly any undeniable signs of ecstatic experiences can be found in the utterances of the great prophets, the proponents of the theory of ecstasy seek to prove their contention by way of analogies. Such analogies are amply supplied by the mantic practices of priests, the orgiastic prophets of Baal, the enthusiastic devotees of the cults of Dionysus or Cybele, the trance state of the shaman among the Samoyeds in Siberia and among the Lapps, the phenomenon of the ecstatic women preachers in Finland or of the prophets of the Cévennes in the seventeenth and eighteenth centuries, or the experiences of the medieval mystics.* But is it admissible to equate phenomena widely separated in space and time and profoundly different in their essential nature?

The theory of ecstasy offers, furthermore, an explanation of the enigma of prophecy. The prophet is a person who when suffering the loss of consciousness becomes prey to subconscious impulses and associations. What emerges in a state of depersonalization he then ascribes to divine inspiration. He may believe himself to have been overwhelmed by God, while in truth he was the victim of inner compulsion. Such a view, which regards the prophets as victims of hallucination and autosuggestion, introduces a naturalistic bias concerning the claim of the prophets, an issue the truth of which lies beyond the grasp of scientific inquiry. And does such a view contribute to a genuine understanding of our problem? With the help of such ideas it might be possible to understand the raptures of dancing dervishes or the transports of ecstatic nuns, but never the consciousness of the great prophets.† Indeed, the theory of ecstasy has done much to obscure what is unique and relevant in the prophetic personality.

One must not disregard the presumption involved in applying the methods of modern psychology to the prophetic personalities, who lived by habits and categories basically different from those of modern man. It is a historic fallacy to assume that forms of behavior which today would be regarded as symptomatic of mental disturbance

*See N. W. Porteous, "Prophecy," in H. W. Robinson, ed., *Record and Revelation* (Oxford, 1938), p. 226.

†E. Auerbach, *Die Prophetie* (Berlin, 1920), p. 41.

have similar significance for the man of ancient Palestine. It is "a mistake to assume *a priori* that the experience of the great prophets is directly accessible to modern psychological method."* The theory of ecstasy assumes that the origin of all that appears in the field of religion, including prophetism, is to be found in the subconscious realm of the soul. Yet this is a premise which is open to question.†

## Who Is a Prophet?

Indeed, if ecstasy were essential to prophetic experience, Moses, Amos, Hosea, Isaiah, and Jeremiah would have to be disqualified as prophets, since no trace of ecstasy is found in their experiences.

It is true that the prophet is overwhelmed by the divine word that comes to him; but it is the consciousness of being overwhelmed, the consciousness of receptivity, and the ability to respond to the word that are outstanding features of his experience.

When Amos is shown in visions the punishments destined to come upon his people, he has the strength to exclaim,

*O Lord God, forgive,*
*I beseech Thee!*
*How can Jacob stand?*
*He is so small!*
*Amos 7:2*

In his vision of consecration, Isaiah (ch. 6) is conscious of being "a man of unclean lips," conscious that his guilt is being removed and his son forgiven. He is capable of saying, "Here I am! Send me," and of uttering his dismay and compassion by saying, "How long, O Lord?" Jeremiah, too, in his inaugural experience, is conscious of what the divine call implies, and he is capable of resisting it by saying, "Ah, Lord God! Behold, I do not know how to speak, for I am only a youth."

*N. W. Porteous, *op. cit.,* p. 227.
†H. Junker, *Prophet und Seher im alten Israel* (Trier, 1927), p. 13.

It is true that Ezekiel, when the vision of God was granted to him, was so struck by the glory that he fell down upon his face; yet it was not until he stood upon his feet that the word came to him. Indeed, it was the power of the spirit which entered into him that raised him up again, and he then in full consciousness received the word (1:28–2:1). The same situation is found in Daniel (10:8–10).

Originally—in the Hellenistic period—the theory of ecstasy was advanced in order to suggest that a complete change of the prophet's personality would explain his receptivity to the divine voice; and in order to stress the loss of his mental powers, thus to eliminate any share on his part in the act of inspiration and to guarantee the divine authenticity of the message received. The modern application of the theory of ecstasy was advanced in order to reduce the experience of the prophet to a mental aberration, typical of ecstatics all over the world. The kind of ecstasy which the prophets of Israel were supposed to be addicted to is the wild rather than the quiet, contemplative kind, as it occurs in the vegetation cults.*

## FRENZY

Ecstatic prophets, though unknown in Egypt and Mesopotamia, have, indeed, been a part of the cults of Syria and Canaan. In I Kings 18:26–29 we read about the prophets of Baal who took a bull, prepared it, and called on the name of Baal from morning until noon, saying, " 'O Baal, answer us!' And they cried aloud, and cut themselves after their custom with swords and lances, until the blood gushed out upon them. And as midday passed, they raved on until the time of the offering of the oblation, but there was no voice; no one answered, no one heeded." Such ecstatic phenomena fit into the orgi-

---

*"Not that there is anything whatever which depreciates the prophets or God's revelation in ecstasy." Yet "so-called explanations, 'natural laws' for physical or psychical connections, clearly give no real explanation of the inmost essence of the phenomena, of what that is which actually occurs either in nature or in the psyche; they are nothing but abstract descriptions of habitual events." (S. Mowinckel, in *JBL*, LVI [1937], 263 f.).

astic nature of the cult of the Baalim, the gods of the native population of Canaan. It was a cult in which ritualistic cohabitation on the field, sacred harlotry, and alcoholic orgies played an important role. Seeking to unite with the object of his worship, the worshiper worked himself into a state of frenzy by wild dancing, shouting, or by alcoholic stimulants.

The greatest challenge to the religion of Israel was the infatuation of many Hebrews with the cult of the Baalim. The confrontation of Elijah with the prophets of Baal dramatized not only the issue: *Who* is the true God? but also the issue: *How* does one approach Him? Elijah employs neither swords nor lances; he does not mutilate his body, nor go into frenzy. He repairs the altar of the Lord, which was broken down, arranges the offering of the sacrifice, and utters a prayer which, far from being an ecstatic ejaculation, contains an invocation as well as a declaration of purpose: "Lord God of Abraham, Isaac, and Israel, let it be known this day that Thou art God in Israel, and that I am Thy servant, and that I have done all these things at Thy word" (I Kings 18:36). It is strange that in all the discussions of prophetic ecstasy, scholars overlooked the significant fact that in the leading prophetic figures between the time of Moses and the time of Amos, no sign of ecstasy is reported.

Passionately and relentlessly, the prophets battled against the alcoholic and sexual orgiasm of the Baal cult. The fight of the Rechabites against the enjoyment of wine was no mere moral campaign; it was a struggle against alcoholic orgiasm.* Is it conceivable that the prophets should themselves succumb to a practice which they condemned? Did not Isaiah denounce prophetic ecstasy as flowing from intoxication?

> *These also reel through wine,*
> *And stagger through strong drink;*
> *The priest and the prophet . . .*

---

*See E. Busse, *Der Wein im Kult des Alten Testaments* (Freiburg, 1922); M. Weber, *Ancient Judaism* (Glencoe, 1952), p. 189; K. Kircher, *Die sakrale Bedeutung des Weines im Altertum in seiner Beziehung zur Gottheit* (Giessen, 1910).

> *They are confused because of wine,*
> *They stagger because of strong drink;*
> *They reel in vision,*
> *They totter in judgment.*
>
> Isaiah 28:7

With unconcealed irony, I Kings reports the orgiastic rites of the prophets of Baal. How could the classical prophets express more plainly their repudiation of ecstasy?

This is the premise of the ecstatic: What is inaccessible to man in the state of normal consciousness is given to him in the state of intoxication. Drunkenness elevates man to a higher level of existence and facilitates spiritual illumination. "In the drunken, my friends, you can see plainly that there is a link with God, where there is no being of one's own."* The less there is of man, the more there is of God; the less there is of the mind, the more there is of the divine.

Far from regarding drunkenness as a state inspired by God, Isaiah equates it with "a spirit of confusion": "a drunken man staggers in his vomit" (Isa. 19:14). "Woe unto them . . . that run after strong drink. . . . Woe unto them that are mighty to drink wine and valiant men in mixing strong drink" (Isa. 5:11, 22). Harlotry and wine take away the heart (Hos. 4:11). "Wine is treacherous" (Hab. 2:5). "Wine is a mocker, strong drink a brawler; and whoever is led astray by it is not wise" (Prov. 20:1). The eyes of a drunken man will not see prophetic visions, but "strange things"; his mind will utter "perverse things" rather than the word of God (Prov. 23:33).

The prophet Joel (3:3) speaks of the connection of drunkenness with licentiousness and gambling, of orgies in which the three were mingled. Approving the moderate use of intoxicants, the Bible condemns its excessive use. For the priests, total abstinence was a duty (Lev. 10:8 f.); and the Rechabites, and the Nazirites were sworn to abstain from any product of the grapevine.

---

*G. Van der Leeuw, *Religion in Essence and Manifestation* (London, 1939), p. 489.

## MERGING WITH A GOD

The root of ecstatic experiences in ancient religions lies in a thirst to become possessed with a god, or to become one with a god.* Theoretically, such a desire was hardly extravagant. To the Greeks, for example, god and man were not contrasted as being totally different from each other. The gods were creatures like men. They were taller and more beautiful, wiser and more powerful than men, and were exempt from old age and death; but otherwise they were scarcely regarded as morally or physically different.† Subject to human passion and driven by human impulses, they succumbed to follies and vices.‡ Nor was there a sharp line of demarcation between the gods and the beasts. The gods were occasionally incarnated in the beasts of the wild.§ Should not an incarnation of a god in a man be considered a possibility?

For different motives and in a different spirit the great mystics strive for *unio mystica*. In ecstasy "we have all the vision . . . of a

---

*See E. Rohde, *Psyche* II (London, 1925), 61, n. 1.

†"From one source spring gods and mortal men." (Hesiod, *Works and Days*, 107.) "One is the race of men, one the race of gods, and from one mother [Gaia, or Earth] do we both have breath." (Pindar, *Nemean Odes*.)

‡In the eyes of the aristocracy of the Homeric period, "gods and men together formed one society, organized on a basis of strongly marked class-distinctions as was the human society itself. The highest class of aristocrats were the gods, their relation to the whole of mankind is much the same as that of the king or chieftain (*basileus*) to the lower orders. . . . Certain faults are unsuited to the nobility, mainly because they detract from its dignity, but from all faults they are certainly not expected to be free. They have a certain, though by our standards a rather crude, code of conduct. On the whole they will be expected to deal fairly, since petty fraud at least is beneath their dignity, but they will not hesitate to stoop to unfairness or deceit on occasion if it suits their purpose. Again, in the sphere of sexual morality, a person of the rank of Agamemnon or Achilles felt at liberty to take any woman whom he fancied from the lower orders. It was his right, as one of kingly line, and indeed to be thus singled out was to be regarded as an honor by the recipient of his favors; . . . the loves of gods for mortals form a parallel to this. . . . The gods were captivated by mortal beauty. They mated with fair women and had offspring. . . ." (W. K. C. Guthrie, *The Greeks and Their Gods* [London, 1950], pp. 117 ff.) Cf. H. J. Rose, *Modern Methods in Classical Mythology* (St. Andrews, 1930), pp. 13 ff.

§Dionysus, for example, was regarded as incarnate in many nature-shapes, and operative on the life-processes of the vegetative world.

self wrought to splendor, unburdened, raised to godhood or, better, knowing its godhood."*

The overcoming of all the usual barriers between the individual and the Absolute is the great mystic achievement. In mystic states we both become one with the Absolute and we become aware of our oneness. This is the everlasting and triumphant mystical tradition, hardly altered by difference of clime or creed. In Hinduism, in Neoplatonism, in Sufism, in Christian mysticism, in Whitmanism, we find the same recurring note, so that there is about mystical utterances an eternal unanimity which ought to make a critic stop and think, and which brings it about that the mystical classics have . . . neither birthday nor native land. Perpetually telling of the unity with God, their speech antedates language, and they do not grow old.†

Such a thirst to become one with God—the supreme aspiration of many mystics—is alien to the biblical man. To him the term "union with God" would be a blasphemy. Great is his love of God and his craving to sense God's nearness; yet he is equally overcome by fear and trembling at the very thought of divine grandeur. In His presence, Abraham knows, "I am but dust and ashes" (Gen. 18:27). Moses is told that to see God is beyond the power of man. "Thou canst not see My face, for man shall not see Me and live" (Exod. 33:20). Even to hear His voice is more than ordinary people can bear. At Sinai the children of Israel said to Moses: "Speak thou with us, and we will hear; but let not God speak to us, lest we die" (Exod. 20:19 [H. 20:16]; cf. Deut. 4:30; 5:24–26). Even the vision of an angel of God is fraught with peril (Judg. 6:22 f.).

When, at the burning bush, Moses turned aside to see "the great sight," he heard the voice of the Lord calling: "Do not come near . . ." (Exod. 3:5). What was said of Moses was true of all the prophets of Israel: "Moses hid his face, for he was afraid to look at

---

*Plotinus, *Enneads*, VI, 9, 10.
†W. James, *The Varieties of Religious Experience* (London, 1912), p. 419.

God" (Exod. 3:6). The glimpse at the majesty of the Lord of hosts that burst upon Isaiah in his great vision was felt by him to be a presumption and encroachment, and it stunned and frightened him: "Woe is me! For I am undone; for I am a man of unclean lips, and I dwell in the midst of a people of unclean lips; for my eyes have seen the King, the Lord of hosts" (Isa. 6:5).

It is pain, not joy, to behold the majesty of God. The contrast is shattering: God is holy, holy, holy, and man is of unclean lips: he cannot join the choir of the seraphim. His lips must be cleansed with fire.

In polytheistic religions man may pay homage to a god, but he is not aware of the ultimate contrast of the human and the divine. The prophet, however, knows: "As the clay in the potter's hand, so are you in my hand, O house of Israel" is the word of the Lord (Jer. 18:6; Isa. 29:16). Osiris, Attis, and Adonis were men who died and rose again as gods. Union with gods seems, therefore, to the believer quite a practicable means of attaining immortality. Not so in Israel.*

Prophetic consciousness is marked by a shuddering sense of the unapproachable holiness of God. The prophet knows there is a chasm that cannot be bridged, a distance that cannot be conquered. As the Lord is "God and not man," so "man is flesh and not spirit" (*ruaḥ*, Hos. 11:9; Isa. 31:3), a mere breath (Ps. 144:4). The central feature of the understanding of God in the Hebrew Bible is divine superiority to nature.†

## EXTINCTION OF THE PERSON

To attain enthusiasm a person must lose his identity. He must be divested of the qualities of personality in order to become invested

---

*The view of B. Stade, *Biblische Theologie des Alten Testaments* (Tübingen, 1905), pp. 123 f., that there was such a striving at the early stage of Israelite prophetism, is without foundation. Cf. Kittel, *Die hellenistische Mysterienreligion und das Alte Testament* (Stuttgart, 1924), pp. 84 ff.

†J. Hehn, *Die Biblische und Babylonische Gottesidee* (Leipzig, 1913), p. 281; J. Hänel, *Das Erkennen Gottes bei den Schriftpropheten* (Berlin, 1923), p. 188.

with the fullness of deity. Self-extinction is the price of mystical receptivity. The concrete past is gone; only the abstract present remains.

The prophetic personality, far from being dissolved, is intensely present and fervently involved in what he perceives. The prophetic act is an encounter of a concrete person and the living God. The prophet is responsive, not only receptive. The act is often a dialogue in which consciousness of time, remembrance of events of the past, and concern with the plight of the present come into play. God as a person confronts the prophet as a person: God in His pathos, and the prophet in history with an awareness of a personal mission to a particular people.

In his visions the prophet's personal identity does not melt away, but, on the contrary, gains power under the overwhelming impact of the event. Even if the event takes him by storm, his consciousness remains undisturbed, free to observe and free to respond.

## THE WILL TO ECSTASY

The ecstatic is moved by a will to experience ecstasies. He is in quest of what is not promised and what does not spontaneously communicate itself, and he must ever anew strive to attain his goal by means of various stimulants. Dramatic gestures, dance, music, alcohol, opium, hashish, the drinking of water of a sacred well, or of the blood of an animal, induces the state of rapture which enables man to transcend the barriers of self. The prophet, on the other hand, is not moved by a will to experience prophecy. What he achieves comes against his will. He does not pant for illumination. He does not call for it; he is called upon. God comes upon the prophet before the prophet seeks the coming of God.

Ecstasy is motivated by man's concern for God, by his will to be illumined. Prophecy, to the prophet's mind, is motivated by God's concern for man, by God's will that the prophet illumine his people.

The prophet does not perform ceremonies in order to receive a revelation. We hear of no outward exercises for the purpose of inducing God to inspire the prophet. Moments of inspiration come to the prophet without effort, preparation, or inducement. Suddenly and unexpectedly, without initiative, without aspiration, the prophet is called to hear the Voice.

Unlike mystical experience, which is attained as the result of craving for communion with God, revelation occurs against the will of the prophet. It is not a favor to him, but a burden of terror. To Isaiah (6:5) the perception of God is a venture fraught with shock, peril, and dismay, something which is more than his soul can bear: Moses hid his face; he was afraid to look upon God (Exod. 3:6). When called, the prophets recoiled, resisted, and pleaded to be left alone. "O Lord, send, I pray Thee, someone else," was Moses' response to the mission.

Ecstasy presupposes an inner capacity, a disposition of the soul, a natural endowment. Among primitive peoples the office of the ecstatic seer is very often linked to a certain psychically gifted family. The office of the shaman in Siberia is hereditary, passing from father to son, sometimes also to daughter.* The gifted man must prepare for his dedication to office, by means of special ceremonies and by training his aptitude and skill.

On the other hand, prophecy is a vocation, an act of charisma and election. It presupposes neither training nor the gradual development of a talent. It comes about as an act of grace.†

## DEPRECATION OF CONSCIOUSNESS

Underlying the strivings for ecstasy there is frequently the awareness that the normal consciousness is a will-o'-the-wisp, that the finest deed is a bitter defeat. Detachment from society, separation from the world, rejection of civilization, and complete avoidance of the self are the ultimate implications of an ecstatic's way of thinking. Such deprecation of consciousness not only maintains that the mind in its conscious state is unable to produce adequate notions of higher truths,

---

*J. Hauer, *Die Religionen* (Berlin, 1923), p. 462; cf. pp. 406, 458–472.
†See B. Baentsch, *"Pathologische Züge in Israels Prophetentum,"* *Zeitschrift für Wissenschaftliche Theologie*, vol. L.

but that it is even unfit to receive divine inspiration. To be inspired, one must cease to be conscious. Coupled with the deprecation of consciousness is the high estimation of the state of trance or rapture, the belief that doors open when consciousness is lost. Elimination of all concepts, religious or profane, the emptying out of the mind of all interest in man or society, the rapturous deliverance from all ties with this world, bring about a state in which all personal identity is lost.

Such premises—the deprecation of consciousness, the high estimation of the state of trance—seem to be unknown to the prophets.* Their intense concern with man and society is incompatible with an ecstatic mentality. There is no indication in the prophets' reports of their experiences of that emptying of consciousness which is the typical preparation for ecstasy, of a loss of self-consciousness or of a suspension of mental power during the reception of revelation. Unlike mystical insight, which takes place in "the abyss of the mind," in "the ground of consciousness," prophetic illumination seems to take place in the full light of the mind, in the very center of consciousness.

There is no collapse of consciousness, no oblivion of the world's foolishness. The prophet's will does not faint; his mind does not become a mist. Prophecy is consciousness and remembrance of the scandals of priests, of the callousness of the rich, of the corruption of the judges. The intensity and violence of the prophet's emotions do not cause his intelligence to subside. The noetic character of prophecy is reflected in most of its aspects. Its message had to be relevant to the contemporary situation and capable of changing the minds of those who held the power to change the situation. The Inspirer in whose name they spoke was not a God of mystery, but a God Who has a design for history, Whose will and law are known to His people. The prophet is not a person who has had an experience, but one who has a task, and the marks of whose existence are the consistency and wholeheartedness in the dedication to it. The noetic character of the prophetic experience is, furthermore, reflected in the noetic character

---

*The prophets consider lack of knowledge the root of misery, see, e.g., Hos. 4:6; Isa. 5:13. They constantly summon the people to return and to win some insight into the meaning of the historic process.

of prophetic utterance. Unlike the stammering of the ecstatic or the language of negation of the mystic, the prophet's word is like fire, like a hammer which breaks the rock in pieces.

The paradox is that while the ecstatic disregards consciousness in order to enrich the self, the prophet disregards the self and enriches his consciousness.

## BEYOND COMMUNICATION

Ecstasy is an experience which is incommunicable. In its mystical state, the soul must rise above the level of thought and emotion in order to find a junction of the ground of the soul with absolute reality. It is a moment of speechless communion, transcending words, images, and worldly affairs—"a flight of the alone to the Alone." The content of such experience is like a mysterious gleam which shines dimly beyond the borders of consciousness. Words cannot grasp it, categories elude it; verbal articulation is an impossibility. It is a stirring of the soul rather than an engagement of the mind; an interim awareness beyond communication.*

The ecstatic, therefore, stresses constantly the ineffability of his experiences.† The impossibility of adequate verbal articulation is based on the fact that language serves only to describe the inner life of the mind and the outer life of the world, but has no words for the objectless experience of the ecstasy. There is a cleavage between consciousness and ecstasy, the contents of which do not penetrate into the memory, eluding later attempts at articulation.

If we examine the accounts and reports delivered by ecstatics, we note that their contribution to positive knowledge is slight. Astonishment has been expressed at the fact that the ecstatics really report nothing new about the divine Being and attributes.‡ The contribu-

---

*The words or ejaculations of the Pythia at Delphi were unintelligible and had to be shaped into comprehensive language by the "prophets."

†See II Cor. 12:4; cf. J. Lindblom, *Die literarische Gattung der prophetischen Literatur* (Uppsala, 1924), p. 59.

‡K. Oesterreich, *Die religiose Erfahrung als philosophisches Problem* (Berlin, 1915), pp. 17 f.

tions of the ecstatic have to do with the sphere of subjective experience, not with that of objective insight and understanding.

Prophecy, on the other hand, is meaningless without expression. Its very substance is a word to be conveyed, a message to be imparted to others. The habit of the mystic is to conceal; the mission of the prophet is to reveal.

Is it conceivable that the prophets whose main activity, as they assure us, was the communication of the insights inspired within them, should have received their speeches in a condition of ecstatic trance? If we felt obliged to accept the hypothesis of an ecstatic consciousness in the prophet, we should have to imagine in him an improbable double life, yielding both the articulated, comprehensible contents of his discourses as well as unconscious, mystical, ecstatic experiences. This dualism would be so much the more difficult to understand since the prophetic discourses, utterly dissimilar as they are to the experiences, would have to spring from ecstasy.

Ecstasy or mystical illumination is its own fulfillment; prophecy points beyond itself. Its purpose is not to bring to pass personal exaltation. The purpose of God's communion with the prophet was to bring about righteousness in history, justice in society, piety in the people. The reception of the word must be followed by the proclamation of the word. The prophet's role is that of a mediator; neither the author nor the final addressee, he stands between God and the people. In the same sense, prophetic inspiration is but a phase in a larger process, a part of a drama. It is preceded and transcended by a divine reaction to the life of the people, by a decision to reveal, and is followed by the prophet's effort to communicate and by the people's response.

Ecstasy, mystical illumination, is a consummation, a reward; prophecy is never complete in itself; it is a burden, a tension, a call, the waging of a battle, never a victory, never a consummation. Incompleteness is inherent in the prophetic act. The fact that the prophet reads the value of his experience, not in the incident itself, but in the message thereby imparted sets prophecy apart from the phenomena of ecstasy and possession.

## THE PRIVACY OF MYSTICAL EXPERIENCE

The mystic is driven into trance by a personal impulse. His own life, his concern for his own spiritual situation, form the background of his experiences. His attainment, his insight and inspiration, constitute a spiritual self-enhancement of significance to his existence as an individual. Consistent with the private nature of his endeavor, the account of his experiences bears pre-eminently an autobiographical stamp. Ecstasy is esoteric.*

In contrast, the motive, content, and aim of prophetic events have a markedly superpersonal character. Prophecy is not a private affair of the experient. The prophet is not concerned with his personal salvation, and the background of his experiences is the life of the people. The aim is not personal illumination, but the illumination of a people; not spiritual self-enhancement, but a mission to lead the people to the service of God. The prophet is nothing without his people.

## ECSTASY IS ITS OWN END

The state of ecstasy is its own end; the prophetic act is a means to an end. For the ecstatic, the experience of ecstasy is the achievement of a goal. For the prophet, the act is for the sake of acquiring a message; the experience is the vessel, the form; while the teaching is the content, the substance. Trances do not confer on the ecstatic an increase of knowledge. It is not expected that new ideas come into the world through the secret gate of mystical openings, and ecstasy as a rule takes place without the inspiration of any words or the communication of any definite message. But the prophet who tells us less about the experience than about the inspired truth to which it gives birth, seems to have regarded the word as more essential than the act.

Ecstasy is a state of being, an act of transmuting the self; the experience of the prophet is an act of receiving a word, a gift of knowledge,

*The motive which lies at the root of ecstasy is sometimes a desire for immortality. Ecstasy, which Baader has described as "anticipation of death," produced in the Dionysiac cult the belief in an immortal soul; see Rohde, *op. cit.*, II, 92.

an act of understanding. The prophetic act leaves an utterance behind; ecstasy leaves behind a memory of a moment that cannot be put into words.*

An important principle in prophetic understanding is the belief *in God's need to communicate to the prophets.*

> *Surely the Lord God does nothing*
> *Without revealing His secret*
> *To His servants the prophets.*
>
> *Amos 3:7*

"The Lord said, Shall I hide from Abraham what I am about to do?" (Gen. 18:17.) The prophets, therefore, do not regard the mystery of God's entering into communion with them as the substance of the event. The substance and worth of their experience is seen in the communicated meaning, in the content, in the word to be conveyed. In the overwhelming majority of their utterances they dwell upon the content and speak little of the act. The primary purpose of prophecy is to impart understanding rather than to bestow exaltation.

These ideas may be contrasted not only with the prophet's proclamation of the divine pathos, which is a positive affirmation about God's relation to the world, but also with the nature of the prophetic act, which is not a junction of the soul with the Supreme Being, but an encounter with the God of Israel. The prophet's experience is not one in which thought is lost and volition dissolved; the prophet receives a message which he must be able to communicate; he senses a pathos to which he responds in sympathy. A person deprived of pathos would not be in a position to experience the God of pathos. The office of a prophet, which consists of setting forth a message in blunt and clear terms rather than in dark oracles and intimations, must

---

*Compare Aristides' description of his inward state during ecstasy: "It was a sort of sense of contact and a clear realization that the god himself had come; an intermediate state between sleeping and waking, a desire to look and at the same time a fear that he would go away first; a listening and hearing half in dream, half awake; the hair on end and tears of joy and an inward swelling with delight—what human beings could find words to describe it? Those who are of the initiated will understand and recognize it." (G. Misch, *A History of Autobiography in Antiquity,* II [Cambridge, 1951], 503.)

have its source in moments of comprehension and understanding. The prophet encounters real otherness, else there would be no mission; but also retains the fullness of his own person, else there would be no vocation.

## HEAVEN AND THE MARKET PLACE

Mysticism, born in a longing for a world beyond this world, strives for a perception of timeless reality. It flourishes in a soul for which the world with its petty troubles and cares does not deserve mention. "Life here, with the things of earth is a sinking, a defeat, a failing of the wing. . . . Our good is there. . . . There the soul is Aphrodite of the heavens; here, turned harlot, Aphrodite of the public ways. . . . Here what we love is perishable, hurtful; . . . our loving is of mimicries, and turns awry because all was a mistake, our good was not here, this was not what we sought; there only is our veritable love and there we may hold it and be with it, possess it in its verity no longer submerged in alien flesh."*

In contrast, the prophet's field of concern is not the mysteries of heaven, but the affairs of the market place; not the spiritual realities of the Beyond, but the life of the people; not the glories of eternity, but the blights of society. He addresses himself to those who trample upon the needy and destroy the poor of the land; who increase the price of the grain, use dishonest scales, and sell the refuse of the corn (Amos 8:4–6). What the prophet's ear perceives is the word of God, but what the word contains is God's concern for the world.

As the God of Israel is concerned with the here and the now, the attention of the prophet is directed upon the social and political issues

---

*Plotinus, *Enneads,* VI, 9, 10. "For all is nothing but still less than nothing is everything that is transient," says St. Theresa. The view that everything earthly and temporal is valueless, the idea that the body is a prison, has in every period driven man into ecstatic states. Nietzsche once compared the Dionysiac man with Hamlet: "Both had a deep insight into the true essence of things, they recognized truth and became disgusted with action. Recognition kills action, it is of the essence of action that one should be wrapped in illusion. In the consciousness of truth once comprehended, man now sees everywhere only the horror and absurdity of existence. . . ."

of the day. The mystic is absorbed in contemplation of the infinite; the prophet's eye scans the definite and finite, the insolence and hypocrisy of man, the little cruelties, the silly idolatries. This is why it is not enough for a prophet to be inspired by God; he also must be informed about the world. The world and its fate are very dear to him. There is no hostility to civilization, only to its abuses.

## RADICAL TRANSCENDENCE

Ecstasy is often due to a theology of radical transcendence. Where God is thought of as wholly above the world, indifferent to man and absent from history, inaccessible to the mind and inconceivable in any way, ecstasy arises as an effort to force one's way toward Him, as an attempt to cross the abyss. Thus, Neoplatonism, after Epicurus had disallowed the idea that the gods had any influence on earthly life, tried to attain union with the transcendent by means of ecstasy.*

What is important in mystical acts is that *something happens;* what is important in prophetic acts is that *something is said.* Ecstasy is the experience of a pure situation, of an inner condition. It is an experience that has form, but no content. Prophecy is an experience of a relationship, the receipt of a message. It has form as well as content. Ecstasy is the perception of a Presence; prophecy, the encounter of a Person. Ecstasy is one-dimensional, there is no distinction between the subject of experience and the experience itself. The person becomes one with the divine. Prophecy is a confrontation. God is God, and man is man; the two may meet, but never merge. There is a fellowship, but never a fusion.

In the biblical tradition, God was not immured in a conception of absolute transcendence. The Lord who created the world manifests His presence within the world. He is concerned with man and is present in history. He is accessible to man's prayer, and His faithfulness is

*Cf. D. Koigen, *"Die Idee Gottes im Lichte des neuen Denkens,"* Second Conference of the World Union for Progressive Judaism (London, 1930), pp. 42–58.

a rock to be relied upon. Fundamental to biblical belief is a tradition of theophanies in which God's power and love become active and apparent in history. Prophecy must be understood, not as an individual's venture to find God in ecstasy, but within the tradition of theophanies in which God approaches man in decisive moments of history (Gen. 12:7; 18:1; 26:2; 32:31; Exod. 3:16; 24:10; 33:11, 23; cf. Judg. 5:4 ff.; Isa. 30:27; Hab. 3:6 ff.; Ps. 18:8 ff.).

Socrates is quoted as having said: "There is a madness which is a divine gift. The greatest of blessings have come to us through madness."* (See pp. 500 f.) In contrast, the prophets of Israel might have said: "The greatest of blessings have come to us through revelation."

To the Neoplatonists, who craved divine revelation, the idea of a theophany was alien. Only in Proclus do we find a belief in the manifestation of the gods.† We may, therefore, suggest the following contrast: The Neoplatonists knew of a tradition of ecstasy; the prophets knew of a tradition of theophany. Their religious experiences followed their respective traditions.

A typical ambivalence may be seen in the fact that the duality and even contrariety of the human and the divine gave rise to a belief in a complete fusion of the human and the divine. In experiencing such a fusion, the ecstatic does not have to be mindful of that duality. The principle of duality vanishes as does the whole consciousness of the ecstatic. For the prophet, on the other hand, the awareness of the distance between God and man remains vividly and painfully present even in the moment of his call.

## THE TRANS-SUBJECTIVE REALNESS

The divine Inspirer is experienced as a living reality. The prophets imply this not only in their accounts of their visions, but also in other references to their prophetic experience. "The hand of God" came upon them. The very word itself which they apprehend is palpable

---

*Plato, *Phaedrus,* 244a.
†E. Zeller, *Die Philosophie der Griechen,* V (Leipzig, 1889), 821.

reality: "Thy words were found, and I ate them" (Jer. 15:16). The emphasis is not upon visionary experience, but upon palpable truth. "They prophesy a lying vision and a thing of nought" (Jer. 14:14); "they have seen lies" (Zech. 10:2; cf. Ezek. 7:23; 13:3); "they have only dreams" (Jer. 23:25–32; 29:8; Zech. 10:2) and speak a vision of their own heart (Jer. 23:16) is the substance of their reproach to the false prophets.

In all forms of prophetic experience the content, the word, proceeds from a personal Inspirer rather than from the mysterious Unknown. Prophetic inspiration differs from both ecstasy and poetic inspiration in that it is an act in which the prophetic person stands over against the divine person. It is characterized by a subject-subject structure: the self-conscious active "I" of the prophet encounters the active, living Inspirer.

The prophet, unlike the ecstatic, is both a recipient and a participant. His response to what is disclosed to him turns revelation into dialogue. The prophets asserted that many of their experiences were not moments of passive receptivity, mere listening to a voice or mere beholding a Presence, but dialogues with God. By response, pleading, and counterspeech, the prophet reacts to the word he perceives. The prophet's share in the dialogue can often give the decisive turn to the encounter, evoking a new attitude in the divine Person and bringing about a new decision. In a sense, prophecy consists of a revelation of God and a co-revelation of man.*

Prophetic inspiration may come as a flash, but it is a flash of a perpetual light. All inspirations of all of Israel's prophets are installments of one revelation. They are not spasmodic reactions, fragmentary expressions of divine opinions. A continuity, an all-embracing meaning, welds into a totality every insight the prophet receives. The covenant of God with Israel and the demands of that covenant are reflected in every word, and, accordingly, the affairs of everyday life which form the occasion that stimulates prophetic utterance are not treated as sporadic incidents, but as parts of a great drama.

*See A. J. Heschel, *God in Search of Man* (New York, 1955), pp. 228; 234, n. 3; 260 f.

# 11

# Prophecy and Poetic Inspiration

### PROPHECY A FORM OF POETRY

What is the nature and genesis of prophecy? Where does it come from? How should one explain it? Few people have ever been brave enough to define poetry. Yet there have been scholars who did not hesitate to define prophecy as a form of poetry.

Maintaining that the experiences of the great prophets cannot be regarded as ecstasy in a technical sense, some scholars insist upon equating the inspiration of the prophets with the experience of the poets and artists in their creative moments. The prophet is like a poet who is frequently overcome by a *raptus mentis*. At times the poet is overcome unexpectedly, at other times he prepares himself for the creative moment, with a pen in his hand and an inkstand on his desk. With his attention concentrated upon a specific content, a certain excitement enters his soul, with thoughts and images flowing upon him.*

The enigma is solved. The prophet is a poet. His experience is one known to the poets. What the poets know as poetic inspiration,

---

*Lindblom, *Die literarische Gattung prophetischer Literatur* (Uppsala, 1924), p. 27; N. Micklem, *Prophecy and Eschatology* (London, 1926), p. 17.

the prophets call divine revelation.* "Psychologically considered, prophetic inspiration is not materially different from *furor poeticus* of the master-poet or artist."† "The inspiration of the artist is what is meant by 'the hand of the Lord which rests upon the prophet.' "‡

What makes the difference between the prophet and the ordinary person is the possession of a heightened and unified awareness of certain aspects of life. Like a poet, he is endowed with sensibility, enthusiasm, and tenderness, and above all, with a way of thinking imaginatively. Prophecy is the product of poetic imagination. *Prophecy is poetry,* and in poetry everything is possible, e.g., for the trees to celebrate a birthday, and for God to speak to man. The statement "God's word came to me" was employed by the prophet as a figure of speech, as a poetic image.

The issue is not the poetic nature of prophetic language, and the profound kinship of prophetic and poetic imagination, but rather the problem of prophetic experience as reflected in the prophetic consciousness. Is that experience "not materially different from *furor poeticus* of the master-poet or artist"?

## OVERSIGHT OR INATTENTION

Due to the aura of supreme sanctity surrounding the Bible, the aesthetic literary quality of biblical writing as well as the kinship of Hebrew prophecy and poetry have long remained unnoticed. Entranced with Scripture as a source of ultimate truth, of ultimate guidance and eternal life, students paid little attention to the sheer poetry and beauty found in it. Generation after generation, the Bible was read as dogma, as law, as prayer, for edification. To read the Bible as literature or as history would have been incongruous. To the mind of the faithful

---

*De Wette, *Lehrbuch der historisch kritischen Einleitung in die kanonischen und apokalyptischen Buecher des Alten Testaments* (8th ed.; Berlin, 1869), par. 249; Köster, *Die Propheten des Alten und Neuen Testaments* (Leipzig, 1838), p. 272.

†M. Buttenwieser, *The Prophets of Israel* (New York, 1914), p. 156.

‡E. Auerbach, *Die Prophetie* (Berlin, 1920), p. 32.

and particularly the mystic, any aesthetic appreciation of the Bible was regarded as a profanation.*

The earliest testimony to an appreciation of the literary quality of biblical writing is found in Longinus' treatise *On the Sublime,* probably written shortly after the death of Augustus. In illustrating his theory, Longinus, presumably a Jew who revered Moses and Homer alike,† refers to the book of Genesis: "The Jewish lawgiver, no ordinary person, since he had the capacity worthily to receive the divine power and show it forth, writes at the very beginning of his legislation: 'And God said . . .' What was it God said? 'Let there be light,' and there was light. 'Let there be earth,' and there was earth."‡ The book of Genesis is placed by Longinus beside Homer, and in some respects preferred to him. An awareness of the aesthetic excellence of the book of Genesis is implied in the writings of Philo;§ and Josephus maintains that the song of the Red Sea as well as the blessing of Moses were written in hexameter!‖ From statements found in rabbinic literature opposing the view that the Bible is to be regarded as mere poetry, we may adduce that there were exponents of such a view.

Raba expounded: "Why was David punished? Because he called words of Torah *songs,* as it is said: 'Thy statutes have been my songs in the house of my pilgrimage' (Ps. 119:54). The Holy One, blessed be He, said to Him: 'Words of Torah, of which it is written (Prov. 23:6): When your eyes light upon it, it is gone (the Torah is beyond human comprehension), you call songs! . . .' "# In opposition to the

*"TALKATIVE: If a man doth love to talk of miracles, wonders, or signs, where shall he find things recorded so delightful, so sweetly penned, as in the Holy Scripture?

"FAITHFUL: That is true; but to be profited by such things in our talk should be that which we design." (J. Bunyan, *The Pilgrim's Progress,* pt. 1, Faithful and Talkative discourse.)

†W. R. Roberts, *Longinus on Style* (Cambridge, 1899), p. 209.

‡Mommsen, *Romische Geschichte,* VI (Berlin, 1868), 494.

§Cf. Philo's statement that Moses, in contrast to other lawgivers, "introduced his laws with an admirable and most impressive exordium"; his exordium "excites our admiration to the highest degree." (*De Opificio Mundi,* 1 ff.) Cf. E. Norden, *Das Genesiszitat in der Schrift vom Erhabenen* (Berlin, 1955).

‖*Antiquities,* II, end; IV, 8, 303.

#*Sotah,* 35b.

view that the book of Daniel and possibly the Torah were mere literature, the assertion was made that the sequence of the chapters in the
book of Daniel is intentionally "disarranged so that it might not be
said that the narrative is mere poetry, and that all might know that it
was composed under divine inspiration."*

In Christian exegesis the principle prevailed that the letter of the
Bible is mere flesh, while the spiritual sense within it is divinity.
"Blessed are the eyes which see divine spirit through the letter's veil."†
Literary aspects of biblical writings were hardly relevant except when
challenged by opponents of Christianity who disputed the belief in
the inspiration of the New Testament by pointing out the barbarous
Greek in which it is written and its lack of eloquence. This roused
Augustine to claim that "all those powers and beauties of eloquence"
are to be found in sacred writings. He then cited examples from both
the prophets and the Pauline epistles.‡

An exception may be seen in the Jewish Bible exegesis developed
in Spain from the middle of the tenth to the beginning of the twelfth
centuries, which insisted that the meaning of the scriptural word is
reached by grammatical exegesis, that homiletic interpretation must
not obscure the literal sense of the word. The Spanish Hebrew grammarian Jonah Ibn Janah, Abul-Walid Ibn Merwan (b. end of tenth
century) drew upon rhetoric and upon analogies in Arabic, seeking to
explain biblical expressions as metaphors and other tropes familiar to
him from Arabic literature. The rise of linguistic studies and the
renaissance of Hebrew poetry sharpened perception for the literary
qualities of the Bible. Poets sought to wrest from the Bible the secrets
of its literary power, probing its choice of words, its style and mode
of expression. The renowned poet Moses Ibn Ezra (*ca.* 1070–1138)
called attention in his work on rhetoric and poetics to poetry in biblical writings.§

An awareness of the literary and poetic qualities of the Bible is

---

*Genesis Rabba*, 85, 2. See the note in Theodor's edition, p. 1033.

†B. Smalley, *The Study of the Bible in the Middle Ages* (New York, 1952), p. 1.

‡Augustine, *On Christian Doctrine*, quoted by S. H. Monk, *The Sublime, A Study
of Critical Theories in XVIII Century England* (New York, 1935), pp. 77 f.

§B. Halper, trans., *Shirath Israel* (Leizpig, 1924).

also expressed by Judah Halevi (d. 1149),* Samuel Ibn Tibbon (d. in Marseilles *ca.* 1230),† Jehuda Al-Harizi (d. *ca.* 1235),‡ Isaac Abravanel (d. in Venice, 1508),§ Azariah Dei Rossi (d. 1578),‖ and Samuel Arch-evolti, an Italian grammarian and poet of the sixteenth century.# However, the literary approach evoked sharp protests on the part of the mystics.

That the author of the *Zohar* was aware of scholars concerned with the literary form of biblical writing and its relevance as a record of history, is testified to by his vehement condemnation of such an approach.

> Perdition take anyone who maintains that any narrative in the Torah comes merely to tell us a piece of history and nothing more! If that were so, the Torah would not be what it assuredly is, to wit, the supernal Torah, the Torah of truth. Now if it is not dignified for a king of flesh and blood to engage in common talk, much less to write it down, is it conceivable that the most high King, the Holy One, blessed be He, was short of sacred subjects with which to fill the Torah, so that He had to collect such commonplace topics as the anecdotes of Esau, and Hagar, Laban's talks to Jacob, the words of Balaam and his ass, those of Balak, and of Zimri, and such-like, and make of them a Torah? If so, why is it called the "Law of Truth?" Why do we read "The Law of the Lord is perfect. . . . The testimony of the Lord is sure. . . . The ordinances of the Lord are true. . . . More to be desired are they than gold, yea, than much fine gold"

---

* *Kuzari* II, 70. Since the ninth century the Moslems have presented as a proof of the divine origin of Islam "the beauty of the Koran," or "the insuperability of the Koranic style"; see A. J. Heschel, *God in Search of Man* (New York, 1955), p. 248, n. 2. It is significant that the aesthetic quality of the Bible has never been used as an argument in supporting the dogma of revelation. "The proof of the influence of the divine power is not in the beauty of phrases." (*Kuzari*, II, 56.)

† *Commentary* on Ecclesiastes, introduction; quoted by J. Moscato, *Kol Jehudah*, II, 70.

‡ *Tahkemoni*, 3.

§ *Commentary* on Isaiah 5:1.

‖ *Meor Enayim*, ch. 60.

# *Arugath ha-Bosem* (Venice, 1602).

(Ps. 19:8–11). But assuredly each word of the Torah signifies sublime things, so that this or that narrative, besides its meaning in and for itself, throws light on the all-comprehensive Rule of the Torah.*

And again:

> Alas for the man who regards the Torah as a mere book of tales and everyday matters! If that were so, we, even we, could compose a torah dealing with everyday affairs, and of even greater excellence. Nay, even the princes of the world possess books of greater worth which we could use as a model for composing some such torah. The Torah, however, contains in all its words supernal truths and sublime mysteries. Observe the perfect balancing of the upper and lower worlds. Israel here below is balanced by the angels on high, of whom it says: "who makest thine angels into winds" (Ps. 104:4). For the angels in descending on earth put on themselves earthly garments, as otherwise they could not stay in this world, nor could the world endure them.
>
> Now, if thus it is with the angels, how much more so must it be with the Torah—the Torah that created them, that created all the worlds and is the means by which these are sustained. Thus had the Torah not clothed herself in garments of this world the world could not endure it. The stories of the Torah are thus only her outer garments, and whoever looks upon that garment as being Torah itself, woe to that man—such a one will have no portion in the next world. David thus said: "Open Thou mine eyes, that I may behold wondrous things out of Thy Law" (Ps. 119.18), to wit, the things that are beneath the garment. Observe this. The garments worn by a man are the most visible part of him, and senseless people looking at the man do not seem to see more in him than the garments. But in truth the pride of the garments is the body of the man, and the

*Zohar, III, 159b.

pride of the body is the soul. Similarly the Torah has a body made up of the precepts of the Torah, called *gufe torah* (bodies of the Torah), and that body is enveloped in garments made up of worldly narratives. The senseless people only see the garment, the mere narrations: those who are somewhat wise penetrate as far as the body. But the really wise, the servants of the most high King, those who stood on Mount Sinai, penetrate right through to the soul, the root principle of all, namely to the real Torah. In the future the same are destined to penetrate even to the super-soul (the soul of the soul) of the Torah. . . .*

Aesthetic essays on biblical books remained isolated ventures in the vast literature of medieval biblical exegesis. It was not until the eighteenth century in the wake of the philosophy of Enlightenment, which disputed the inspired character of the Bible, that the realization of the literary qualities of the Bible was born. Its beginnings go back to England.

The Rationalists, who no longer read the Bible as the word of God, but as the product of human composition (Spinoza had laid down the principle that Scripture must be interpreted like any other book), called for a purely historical exegesis; the romanticists called for an aesthetic understanding. In a sense, aesthetic appreciation became a substitute for the belief in divine inspiration.

## THE DISPARAGEMENT OF INSPIRATION

The Deists of the seventeenth century, with their championship of freedom of inquiry and their insistence on reason as the sole instrument for acquiring and judging the truth, regarded revelation as a more or less superfluous republication, since the essential elements of true religion could be acquired by the "natural light" of reason. In addition to voicing criticism of the traditional views about Scripture, the very concept of prophetic revelation was questioned.

Thomas Morgan (d. 1743), sometimes called "the modern Mar-

*Zohar, III, 152a.

cion," rejected the evidence and authority of prophecy, insisting on the sole supremacy and sufficiency of the moral law. He thought, with Matthew Tindal, that natural religion is perfect in itself, and denied that the prophets were inspired; their ability to predict future events, he maintained, was really due to their wisdom and fine understanding for the course of history. If they claimed to have been sent by God, it was for the purpose of making an impression upon their contemporaries who were enslaved to superstition. Thus they had to adjust to popular beliefs.* Morgan, to whom Moses was a more fanciful writer than Homer or Ovid, sought to subject the Bible to the judgment of "sense and reason."

The miraculous, mysterious, and supernatural were widely repudiated both in France and in England. In terms of rational knowledge, the Bible was discredited by Spinoza. According to John Locke (1632–1704), its value lies in its being "a collection of writings, designed by God, for the instruction of the illiterate bulk of mankind, in the way to salvation."

Anthony Collins (1676–1729), an intimate friend of Locke's, argued that all belief must be based on free inquiry, and that the use of reason would involve the abandonment of supernatural revelation. To him, prophecy (by which he meant prediction) was either nonsense or an assertion contrived after the events had occurred. Confusing the prophets of the Bible with professional diviners, Collins said that their oracles were a commodity obtainable on payment of money.† In an earlier publication, however, he likened the prophets to freethinkers who, endowed with university training, had fought the established religion.‡

* *Moral Philosopher,* I (London, 1737), 289 ff. Cf. A. S. Farrar, *A Critical History of Free Thought* (New York, 1863), pp. 140 ff. F. Mauthner, *Der Atheismus and seine Geschichte in Abendlande,* II (Stuttgart, 1922), 504 ff.

† *A Discourse of the Grounds and Reasons of Christian Religion* (London, 1724), p. 28. Cf. G. Berkeley, *Alciphron* (the Sixth Dialogue), A. C. Fraser, ed., in *The Works of G. Berkeley,* II (Oxford, 1871), 259 ff.

‡ "The prophets who had the most learned Education among the *Jews,* and were bred up in *Universities* call'd *Schools of the Prophets,* where they learn to prophesy . . . were great *Free-Thinkers,* and have written as great *liberty* against the *establish'd Religion of the* Jews (which the People look'd on as the Institution of God himself) as if

In consonance with the rationalist spirit of the age, poet and poetry had to conform to logic and clarity; inventiveness, imagination, were secondary. The concept of inspiration was rejected. The ancient poets (having been, at the same time, statesmen) were excused for claiming to be inspired, "as knowing . . . the frequent necessity of dissembling for the ease of government."* Thomas Hobbes considered it "a reasonless imitation of Custom, of a foolish custom, by which a man, enabled to speak wisely from the principles of nature and his own meditation, loves rather to be thought to speak by inspiration, like a Bagpipe."† "Poetry was chiefly to appeal to the understanding, and any attempt to reach the heart was met with ridicule; common sense reigned supreme, and any soaring of fancy, any expression of emotion was sure to be received with derision and a sneer."‡ All subjects must adapt themselves to ratiocination. Reason was the test of all truth. "No province of knowledge can be regarded as independent of reason," Locke proclaimed, and reason was identical in all men and in all realms. Communion with the spirit was neither necessary nor possible. "He therefore who claimed to hear the individual voice of the Spirit speaking inwardly to him and appointing unto him some special mission among men was suffering either from the effects of an abnormal imagination, the ravages of a diseased brain, or else

---

they believ'd it was all Imposture. . . ." (*A Discourse of Free-Thinking* [London, 1713], pp. 153 ff.) Collins adopted the image developed by A. Cowley in his epic *Davideis,* on the basis of II Sam. 19:20; Cowley speaks of a "*Prophet's College* . . . by Samuel built, and moderately endowed," resembling a British university, with "well-furnisht Chambers" for the scholars, a Hall, Schools, Library, Synagogue and "reverend Doctors," the prophet Nathan offering the course in astronomy, the prophet Gad teaching mathematics, and Samuel himself teaching Law. (*Davideis,* Bk. I, written 1656; see *The English Writings of Abraham Cowley: Poems,* ed. by A. R. Waller [Cambridge, 1905], pp. 258 ff.) *Davideis* was the first religious epic in English, anticipating Milton by several years, "hailed in Cowley's own day as one of the chief lights of English poetry," and rather quickly forgotten, according to A. H. Nethercot, *Abraham Cowley* (London, 1931), pp. 285 ff.

*Sir William Davenant, "Preface to Gondibert," in J. E. Spingarn, *Critical Essays of the Seventeenth Century,* II (Oxford, 1908), p. 25.

†"Answer to Davenant," Spingarn, *op. cit.,* p. 59.

‡C. E. De Haas, *Nature and the Country in English Poetry of the First Half of the Eighteenth Century* (Amsterdam, 1928), p. 10.

was deliberately imposing upon the credulity of the weak or the uneducated."*

Reason, respectability, and decent conformity were the watchwords of the time.

With Voltaire and Pope the celebrated figures, with classicism in literature and skepticism in philosophy, imagination, spontaneity, and emotionalism were in as much disfavor in the literary world as were enthusiasm and mysticism in religious speculation. "Mystery was hated, and Respectability exalted."

The zeal for rationality was not to last forever. While Pope and Voltaire were at their height, people began to realize that they were "creatures of emotion, not instruments of reason: they wanted an ardent religious faith, not a dead-cold philosophy." The Methodist movement began in a revival of personal religion, stressing the immediate influence of the Holy Spirit on the consciousness of the Christian. Tired of the dicta of reason in literature, the Enthusiast poets and critics of the eighteenth century attempted to reinfuse into poetry those very elements which, in the domain of religion, were most abhorrent to the rationalistic mind: inspiration, "inner light," special divine commands and revelations.

The poetic enthusiast was one who moved in a supernatural world, one to whom was imparted the divine gift of poetry, one sent into the world to lead men to the beauty of the truth. As a recipient of divine inspiration, the poetic enthusiast felt himself to be a prophet. "As a prophet he had a divinely-revealed message for mankind. Man was to abandon the paths of urban luxury and vice and to come apart among nature's beauties where peace and innocence and virtue dwelt, and where angel forms enshadowed his every footstep."†

The new appreciation of enthusiasm in poetry and religion, and, allied with it, a new understanding of the idea of sublimity in nature

*M. K. Whelan, *Enthusiasm in English Poetry of the Eighteenth Century* (Washington, 1935), pp. 22 ff.

†M. K. Whelan, *op. cit.,* pp. 10, 139, 73, 82. O. Elton, *Reason and Enthusiasm in the Eighteenth Century* ("Essays and Studies . . . of the English Association"), XI (Oxford, 1924), 122 ff. "There could be no true Poet, but must be divinely inspired,"

and poetry prepared the way for this discovery of the poetry in the Bible. Literary critics began to deal with the Bible from an aesthetic point of view, and especially to compare it with Greek poetry. Several writers extolled the poetic qualities of the Bible. Poets were advised to write on biblical themes, and the view was advanced that just as the Hebrew spirit excelled the spirit of the pagans, so did Hebrew poetry surpass the poetry of the pagans.* Thus it was that the English, often regarded as *homines unius libri,* were the first in modern times to appreciate the literary aspect of the Bible.

This new awareness was also stimulated by Longinus' celebrated essay *On the Sublime,* to which we have referred, a Latin version of which was printed 1636 in Oxford, and an English translation in 1652. This work came to exercise a powerful influence over the minds of eighteenth-century Englishmen. Its reference to Gen. 1:3 must have called attention to the sublime in the Bible. Soon books began to appear in which the eloquence and poetic qualities of the Bible were extolled.†

Henry Leslie, discussing the authority of the Bible, said in 1639: "Wee give credit unto her Report; but when we peruse it, and consider the divinity of the matter, the sublimity of the style, the efficacy of the speech, we are fully perswaded that the same is from *God* indeed." In 1715, a writer undertook to prove that in the Bible one finds "not only a body of religion, but a system of rhetoric as well, and that only an atheist could fail to see the sublimity of the sacred writings." In 1725, another author developed a defense of the sublimity of the Bible and sought to show that the writings of the Hebrew Bible exhibit the sublime par excellence, being more sublime than the

---

writes an Enthusiast essayist in the seventeenth century. (M. Casaubon, quoted by M. K. Whelan, *op. cit.,* p. 53.)

*P. Hamelius, *Die Kritik in der Englischen Literatur des 17 und 18 Jahrhunderts* (Leipzig, 1897), pp. 90 ff.

†S. H. Monk, *op. cit.,* p. 19. Boileau's controversy with Huet and Le Clerc whether Longinus was wrong in claiming sublimity for Gen. 1:3 has given publicity to the sublime style of the account of creation, Monk, *op. cit.,* pp. 33, 79.

writings of the Greeks.* It came to be generally accepted that the Bible is the most sublime of all books.

The new approach found a systematic expression in a series of lectures delivered in 1741 by the Anglican bishop Robert Lowth (1710–1787) in his capacity as professor of poetry at Oxford, and published in 1753 under the title *Praelectiones Academicae de Sacra Poesi Hebraeorum,* a work which may be regarded as the first book on the Bible as literature.† Lowth found it strange that "the writings of Homer, of Pindar, of Horace should engross our attention and monopolize our praise, while those of Moses, David and Isaiah pass totally unregarded" even though "in the sacred writings the only specimens of the primeval and genuine poetry are to be found." The mind can conceive nothing more "elevated, more beautiful, or more elegant." The *Praelectiones,* translated as *Lectures on the Sacred Poetry of the Hebrews,* exercised a great influence both in England and on the Continent.‡ Their chief importance lay in the idea of looking at Scripture as poetry, and in examining it by the ordinary standards of literary criticism.

## THE BIBLE AS LITERATURE

Lowth had called attention to the poetic qualities of the prophetic books, and advanced the thesis that the *furor poetarum* and

---

\* *Ibid.,* p. 78. Cf. S. J. Pratt, *The Sublime and Beautiful of Scripture* (New York, 1795).

† It is generally assumed that Bishop Lowth was the first to discover the *parallelismus membrorum* as a common device of biblical poetry, although this was well known to Menahem ben Saruk, Hebrew philologist of the tenth century (Filipowski, ed., *Mahbereth* [London, 1854], p. 11), Rashi (1030–1105), and his contemporary Joseph Karo (see *Nile Naamanim* [Breslau, 1847], p. 28); see E. König, *Stilistik, Rhetorik und Poetik in Bezug auf die biblische Literatur* (Leipzig, 1900), p. 307.

‡ In 1768 E. Harwood published his *Liberal Translation of the New Testament: Being an Attempt to Translate the Sacred Writings with the same Freedom, Spirit and Elegance with which other English Translations of the Greek Classics have Lately been executed;* see also M. Alpers, *Die alttestamentliche Dichtung in der Literaturkritik des 18 Jahrhunderts* (dissertation; Göttingen, 1927); H. Schoffler, *Abendland und das Alte Testament* (Bochum, 1937).

prophetic inspiration came from the same source. The next step was to regard the prophets exclusively as poets, prophetic inspiration as poetic enthusiasm, and to look upon their words, not as repository pure and simple of the divine truth, but as divine truth in the form of a human product. This was the contention of Johann Gottfried Herder (1744–1803). His essay *"Die aelteste Urkunde des Menschengeschlechts"** develops the idea that the oldest biblical poems—the stories of the Creation, of the Flood, and of Moses—are to be considered oriental national songs. The usual interpretation of the Mosaic history of Creation as a divine revelation appears to Herder not only indefensible but pernicious, since it fills the mind with false ideas and leads to persecution of the physical scientist. He compares the stories of the Garden of Eden, of the Deluge, of the Tower of Babel, with Greek stories of origins, like those of Prometheus and Pandora.† His approach is developed more fully in the *Theological Letters* and in his important but unfinished book, *The Spirit of Hebrew Poetry (Vom Geiste der Ebraeischen Poesie,* 1782–83). As Herder saw it, the human element in the Bible must be taken quite seriously. The Bible, a work of literature written at a particular time, by a particular people, in particular situations, and conditioned by race, language, thought forms, and historical and geographical milieu, must be read in a human way as we read the Greek historians and dramatists, with constant effort to interpret its contents in relation to their temporal and local setting.‡ Herder's aesthetic empathy for the poetry of the Bible opened the possibility of a secular encounter with the Bible which was particularly welcome in an age when dogmatic orthodoxy and crude rationalism were the predominant attitudes in biblical studies. His legacy was taken up a century later.

The theological idea of divine inspiration is superseded by the

---

*Riga, 1774–76.

†See H. Hettner, *Literaturgeschichte des achtzehnten Jahrhunderts,* III (Brunswick, 1894), 60 f.

‡Herder even planned to undertake a translation of the entire Bible, not as the Bible, but as a collection of ancient writings. E. Neff, *The Poetry of History* (New York, 1947), pp. 61 ff. Cf. H. J. Kraus, *Geschichte der historisch kritischen Erforschung des Alten Testaments* (Neukirchen, 1956), pp. 108 f.

romantic conception of the people as a whole spontaneously express-
ing itself in its literature. Lowth had called his book *De Sacra Poesi
Hebraeorum;* in the title of Herder's book, *The Spirit of Hebrew
Poetry,* the word "sacred" has vanished.*

Revelation occurs at all times; every period discloses and reveals.†
Thus, prophetic inspiration is not to be denied, but it is not to be
absolutized. It is the same as the inspiration of great religious thinkers
and poets through whom God is speaking everywhere in nature, philosophy, and the arts. Prophetic inspiration is simply a heightened
form of true conviction, of religious enthusiasm in the purer and
deeper sense.

The new approach to the Bible received impetus from the poets
and thinkers of the Romantic movement with their sense for the personal, historical, and individual, their plea to view each nation as a
unique entity contributing its special achievement, their desire to find
a substitute for the classical models and the overworked mythology of
Greece and Rome. They developed an appreciation of the treasures
to be found outside classical literature, resulting, for example, in the
discovery of old Scandinavian poetry and particularly in the so-called
Celtic Revival, which began about the year 1750 as a movement
among Englishmen of letters to infuse into English poetry the
mythology, the history, and the literary treasures of the ancient Celts.
English poets were searching for facts about the rites and beliefs of
the ancient Druids, Bards, and Vates.‡

In the wake of the new sensitivity to natural poetry and to the
beauty of free emotional expression in literature came the publication
of Percy's *Reliques of Ancient English Poetry* (London, 1765), which
gave a powerful impulse to many who found a wealth of traditional
poetry in their own literature, hitherto disregarded. In Germany,

---

*See D. B. Macdonald, *The Hebrew Literary Genius* (Princeton, 1933), p. xx.
†*"Offenbarung gehet durch alle Zeiten: jede Zeit enthüllet und offenbaret."*
(Herder, *"Ueber Begeisterung, Erleuchtung, Offenbarung," Werke,* XI [1852], 120.)
‡E. O. Snyder, *The Celtic Revival in English Literature* (Cambridge, 1923); cf.
also F. E. Farley, *Scandinavian Influences in the English Romantic Movement* (Boston,
1903).

Herder, influenced by Percy's publication, was one of the first to appreciate the value of what is natural and spontaneous in literature. If in the age of Puritanism the tendency had been to see a prophet in the poet, the trend now was to see a poet in the prophet.* The image of the Hebrew prophet was similar to that of a Celtic minstrel, a bard, or of an ancient Scandinavian minstrel, a scald.†

The tendency to look mainly at the aesthetic aspects of the prophetic books and to view the prophets as enlightened religious poets culminates in J. G. Eichhorn, *Die Hebraeischen Propheten* (1816–19). It prepared the way for the popular conception of the Bible as "the product of the national genius of the Jewish people."

The new trend which made it possible to read the Bible "as literature," with no religious strings attached to it, represented more than a form of study; it was an evasion of a challenge. The rationalism of the Enlightenment was modified, not abandoned; aesthetic appreciation remained the substitute for a theological approach.‡

## POETIC AND DIVINE INSPIRATION

Everywhere the gift of poetry is inseparable from divine inspiration. Everywhere this inspiration carries with it knowledge—whether of the past, in the form of history and geneal-

---

*B. Bamberger, *Die Figur des Propheten in der englischen Literatur* (Würzburg, 1933), p. 51.

†In A. Pope's "Messiah" (1712), Jesus speaks of the Hebrew prophets as the ancient bards, and of Isaiah: "Rapt into future times, the bard began. . . ." More examples are cited by Bamberger, *op. cit.*, pp. 52 ff.

‡Numerous books and articles have been written in appreciation of the literary qualities of the Bible; cf. R. Gordis, "The Bible as a Cultural Monument," in L. Finkelstein, ed., *The Jews* (New York, 1949), pp. 457 ff. Courses on "the Bible as literature" are being offered at many American colleges. However, the assumption that those who have rejected the theological claims of the Bible nevertheless continue to cherish it as a treasure house of literary masterpieces is charming but not true; cf. C. S. Lewis, *The Literary Impact of the Authorized Version* (London, 1950), pp. 22 f.; D. B. MacDonald, *The Hebrew Literary Genius* (Princeton, 1933). One might mention the emphasis upon the characterization of the Bible as the "national literature of the Jewish people." See, e.g., G. F. Moore, *The Literature of the Old Testament* (New York, 1913), pp. 24 f.; J. Pedersen, *ZAW*, LXIX (1931), 161.

ogy; of the hidden present in the form commonly of scientific information; and of the future in the form of prophetic utterance in the narrower sense. . . . Invariably we find that the poet and seer attributes his inspiration to contact with supernatural powers, and his mood during prophetic utterance is exalted and remote from his normal existence. Generally we find that a recognized process is in vogue by which the prophetic mood can be induced at will. The lofty claims of the poet and seer are universally admitted, and he himself holds a high status wherever he is found.*

"What a poet writes with enthusiasm and divine inspiration is most beautiful," said Democritus, who regarded Homer as inspired.† "Like a fountain, the poet allows to flow out freely whatever comes in," said Plato.‡ Higher inspiration (*mania*), in which intuitions flash forth, is the source of all poetic creation. "For all good poets, epic as well as lyric, compose their beautiful poems not by art, but because they are inspired and possessed."§ "Poetry demands a man with a special gift for it, or else with a touch of madness in him," says Aristotle.‖

The ancient Greek poets attributed their poetic gift directly to the Muses, sister-goddesses, the offspring of Zeus and Mnemosynē (Memory), regarded as inspirers of learning and the arts, especially of poetry and music. At Delphi they were worshiped in connection with Apollo, who is often called *Musagetes,* or leader of the Muses.# In classical poetry, the Muse is invoked for the purpose of being inspired. Thus the *Odyssey* opens with the words: "Tell me, O Muse, . . ." By

---

*N. K. Chadwick, *Poetry and Prophecy* (London, 1942), p. 14.

†Diels, *Die Fragmente der Vorsokratiker* (Berlin, 1912), fragments 17, 21; cf. K. Freeman, *Companion to the Pre-Socratic Philosphers* (Oxford, 1933).

‡*Laws,* 719.

§*Ion,* 543 f.

‖*Poetics,* transl. by Fyfe (Oxford, 1940), XVII, 2. See also A. Gudeman, *Aristoteles Poetik* (Berlin, 1934), pp. 307 ff.

#Cf. Homer, *Odyssey* VIII, 488, where Ulysses assumes that Demodocus has studied his epic song about the destruction of Troy under the Muse, Jove's daughter, and under Apollo.

the eighth century B.C.E. it had become conventional for any epic to begin with an invocation of the Muses.

Hesiod, roughly a contemporary of Amos, and, like him, a shepherd, developed this theme into a narration of a personal experience. He related that while grazing his father's flocks near his home at the foot of Helicon, the sacred mountain of the Muses, he had been inspired by them with a mission such as no poet before him had ever received: "They breathed into me the divine gift of song that I should declare the things of the future and of former times."* Thus the *Theogony* was introduced as a revelation from divine beings. It is impossible for us to ascertain whether it was Hesiod's intention to relate an actual experience or whether he was employing a poetic way of speaking. The fact is that the *Theogony,* though it was regarded as a standard authority on the genealogies of the gods, never possessed the character of a sacred book, and was never taken to be the expression of a divine will. Should the narrative about Hesiod be regarded as a description of an event or as a symbolic, mythical creation, in tune with the mythical form of the whole book?

Hesiod's conception is by no means to be equated with the prophetic consciousness of inspiration. It stemmed from the general mythical outlook that men derived all their notable inventions from the gods; for example, growing corn from Demeter, weaving and spinning from Athena, the training of the horse to human service from Poseidon. In the same way the poet received his general expertness in his art from divinity. Yet the poem itself is not a divine message, but a human work. Prophetic inspiration as a specific concern of God, aiming at more than, and something different from, the service of man's need, is not suggested in this myth.

According to Wilamowitz-Moellendorff, Hesiod's experience is "the only one truly felt poetic dedication. . . . All that follows, from Callimachus, Ennius, Propertius and many others up to the Parnassians, all the mythological talk with its distortions, imitations, and misunderstandings, depends on the verses of Hesiod. All this is sport,

---

* *Theogony,* I, 31 f.

witty and entertaining, but sport. Inwardly experienced and felt in the depth of the heart and thus sacred sport is only to be found in Hesiod."* The references to the Muses by later writers, therefore, have no relevance to our problem.

Parmenides of Elea in Italy (*ca.* 500 B.C.E.) seems to follow in Hesiod's footsteps. In the Prologue to his famous poem, Parmenides presents himself as borne on a chariot and attended by the sun maidens who guide him on his journey to the palace of a goddess. She welcomes him and instructs him in the two ways: the way of Truth; and the way of Opinion, which is no truth at all. It is generally accepted that the narration, in which he describes his ascent to the home of the goddess, who is supposed to speak the remainder of the verses, is not intended to relate an experience, but is rather a reflection of the conventional ascents into heaven which were as common as descents into hell in the literature of the period. Later imitations of this exist in the myth of Plato's *Phaedrus* and in Dante's *Divine Comedy*. Contrary to most scholars, who have either ignored the Prologue or interpreted it as an allegory, W. Jaeger insisted that Parmenides' "mysterious vision in the realm of light is a genuine religious experience . . . a highly individual inner experience of the Divine, combined with the fervour of a devotee who feels himself charged with proclaiming the truths of his own personal revelation and who seeks to establish a community of the faithful among his converts."†

---

* *"Der Berg der Musen,"* Deutsche Rundschau, L (May, 1924), 131–138. Wilamowitz declares the nine names of the Muses as given in *Theogony* 915 ff. to be Hesiod's invention. (*Glaube der Hellenen,* I [Berlin, 1931], 343.)

†W. Jaeger, *The Theology of the Early Greek Philosophers* (Oxford, 1948), p. 96; see also H. Diels, *Parmenides' Lehrgedicht* (Berlin, 1897), pp. 11 ff.; cf. H. F. Fraenkel, *Dichtung und Philosophie des fruehen Griechentums* (New York, 1951), p. 453; K. Deichgraeber, *Parmenides' Auffahrt zur Goettin des Rechts* (Mainz, 1958), p. 11. According to Sextus, "the horses which bore him and set him on the 'famous road of the goddess' were the irrational impulses of his soul which drew him into the pursuit of philosophy. The means of transport were the senses: the cart, the axle of which gave out a note like a pipe as its two wheels turned on each side, represents hearing, the wheels being the ears! The Daughters of the Sun, who had left the halls of the Night and who drove the cart towards the light, pushing aside their veils, are, Sextus says, the eyes. The cart reaches the 'gates of the paths of Day and Night,' and Justice who guards them with twin keys. The maidens with gentle words tactfully persuade her to throw open the gates; a great opening is disclosed, and the cart and its passengers go straight

In India, soma, an intoxicating drink consumed by the Vedic priests in order to induce a state of rapture, is also the name of a god. Occupying the third most important place among the Vedic gods, Soma is regarded as the force that inspires the poets. The hymns of the ninth book of the *Rigveda* are addressed directly to the deified plant, Soma, and the liquor pressed from it. Among other blessings he bestows upon man, Soma inspires the poets.

"Among the Arabs the poet (*shâ'ir*, i.e., "the knower" par excellence), as his name implies, was a person endowed with knowledge by the spirits who gave him his magic powers: his poetry was not art, it was supernatural knowledge."*

Caedmon, the earliest Christian English poet (seventh century), was a herdsman who, according to the Venerable Bede, received a divine call to poetry. It was the custom in the evening for the villagers to pass the harp around and sing in turn, accompanied by it. Caedmon, who had never been able to learn a song, quietly left the company as the harp was about to reach him. One night he dreamed that there appeared to him a stranger who commanded him to sing of "the beginning of created things." He first pleaded inability, but then found himself uttering "verses which he had never heard."†

## Accounts of Inspiration

Poets of the ancient world have given us few personal expressions about the genesis of their work or the nature of the creative act, beyond some rules of literary technique. The prophets' accounts of their experiences belong to the oldest authentic testimonies of inspiration. Only in modern times did people begin to grapple with problems of inspiration and origin. In the Renaissance, which saw the beginning

---

through. When they get inside, Parmenides is at once met and welcomed by the goddess." (K. Freeman, *Companion to the Pre-Socratic Philosophers* [Oxford, 1933], p. 147.) Cf. H. F. Fraenkel, *Wege und Formen des frühgriechischen Denkens* (New York, 1955), pp. 157 ff.

*A. Guillaume, *Prophecy and Divination* (London, 1938), pp. 243 f.

†J. E. King, trans., *Historia Ecclesiastica*, IV, 24.

of individualism and of the history of individual artists, such personal documents were not infrequent (Leonardo da Vinci, Leone Battista Alberti, Benvenuto Cellini, Michelangelo, Albrecht Dürer, among others). Since then, such testimonies have accumulated considerably.

Many artists and scientists of modern times have written about the moment of artistic activity when out of a vague creative mood there suddenly dawned, as though by illumination, the clear consciousness of the essential features of the projected work, as they have observed it in themselves.* Attempts have been made to collect, classify, and characterize their statements.† Various interpretations have been advanced. A metaphysical view emphasizes the transcendent mystery of inspiration, the rationalistic view sees in the creative process a deliberate act of consciousness, while positivist psychology would describe it as a release of fermenting associations latent in the subconscious. Among the various methods employed by modern psychologists in an attempt to elucidate the creative process are the biographical, pathographical (based upon the theory that artistic imagination and mental or physical illness reveal certain common features), psychographical (the analysis of the artist's works), experimental, biological, ethnological, and the method of systematic interrogation.

*Notable is H. Poincaré's essay on "Mathematical Creation" in his book *The Foundations of Science* (Lancaster, 1915).

†The literature on the subject is vast. A rich though by no means exhaustive listing of the material is found in R. Hennig, *Das Wesen der Inspiration* (Leipzig, 1912); R. E. M. Harding, *An Anatomy of Inspiration* and *An Essay on the Creative Mood* (Cambridge, 1948); B. Ghiselin, *The Creative Process* (Berkeley and Los Angeles, 1954); J. Portnoy, *A Psychology of Art Creation* (Philadelphia, 1942); O. Behaghel, *Bewusstes und Unbewusstes im kuenstlerischen Schaffen* (Leipzig, 1907); W. Phillips, ed., *Art and Psychoanalysis* (New York, 1957). Against the assumption that "art is not based on craft, but on sensibility; it does not live by honest labor, but inspiration" (Clive Bell, *Art*, p. 187, quoted by Portnoy, *op. cit.*, p. 95), one must cite Rodin's warning that inspired moments "by inducting a condition akin to intoxication, may cause the artist to forget the very principles on which the adequate interpretation of his plea most certainly depends." G. Flaubert wrote: "You should mistrust everything which resembles inspiration, for that is often nothing more than a deliberate determination and a forced excitement, voluntarily caused, and which did not come of itself; besides, we do not live in inspiration; Pegasus walks more often than he gallops, genius consists in

Jacob Boehme (1575–1624) wrote: "I declare before God that I do not myself know how the thing arises within me, without the participation of my will. I do not even know that when I must write. If I write, it is because the Spirit moves me and communicates to me a great, wonderful knowledge."*

William Blake (1757–1827) said about his poem "Milton": "I have written this poem from immediate Dictation, twelve or sometimes twenty or thirty lines at a time, without Premeditation, and even against my Will; the time it has taken in writing was thus render'd Non Existent. [I am] the secretary, the authors are in eternity."†

Dickens declared that when he sat down to write "some beneficent power" showed it all to him. To Thackeray it seemed as if "an occult Power" were moving the pen. And Tchaikovsky defined his creative state "as the result of that supernatural and inexplicable force we call inspiration."‡

Goethe made reference to the trancelike state in which he sometimes wrote. "In such a somnambulistic condition, it has often happened that I have had a sheet of paper before me all aslant, and I have not discovered it till all has been written, or I have found no room to write anymore. [I have written] this little work [*Sorrows of Werther*] almost unconsciously, like a sleep-walker."§ "The songs made me, not I them; the songs had me in their power." "I sing myself as carols the bird."‖ He said to Eckermann: "No productiveness of the highest kind, no remarkable discovery, no great thought which bears fruit and has results, is in the power of any one; but such things are elevated above all earthly control. Man must consider them as unexpected gifts from above, as pure children of God, which he must receive and ven-

---

showing how to make him take the pace we require." (Quoted by R. E. M. Harding, *op. cit.*, p. 22.)

*Aurora*, quoted by T. Ribot, *An Essay on the Creative Imagination* (Chicago, 1906), p. 335.

†G. Keynes, ed., *The Letters of William Blake* (London, 1956), p. 85.

‡R. E. M. Harding, *op. cit.*, pp. 14, 17.

§*Dichtung und Wahrheit*, Bk. XIII.

‖Bielschovsky, *Life of Goethe*, trans. W. A. Cooper, III (New York, 1905 ff.), 31.

erate with joyful thanks. The process savours of the daemonic element which irresistibly does with a man what it pleases and to which he surrenders himself unconsciously while believing that he is acting on his own impulses." In such cases a man is often to be considered as an instrument of higher powers, "as a vessel which has been found worthy to receive divine influence."* Goethe declared of Byron that he came upon his lines of poetry as wives produce beautiful children: they do not think of them and they do not know how it all comes about.†

"Whence and how [my ideas] come I know not; nor can I force them," said Mozart.‡ In describing the origin of *Zarathustra*, Nietzsche emphasized the completely involuntary and unconscious elements in its creation as well as its transcendent origin.

> Can any one at the end of this nineteenth century possibly have any distinct notion of what poets of a more vigorous period meant by inspiration? If not, I should like to describe it. Provided one has the slightest remnant of superstition left, one can hardly reject completely the idea that one is the mere incarnation, or mouthpiece, or medium of some almighty power. The notion of revelation describes the condition quite simply; by which I mean that something profoundly convulsive and disturbing suddenly becomes visible and audible with indescribable definiteness and exactness. One hears—one does not seek; one takes—one does not ask who gives: a thought flashes out like lightning, inevitably without hesitation—I have never had any choice about it. There is an ecstasy whose terrific tension is sometimes released by a flood of tears, during which one's progress varies from involuntary impetuosity to involuntary slowness. There is the feeling that one is utterly out of hand, with the most distinct consciousness of an infinitude of

---

* *Gespräche mit Eckermann,* March 11, 1928. Cf. Walter Jacobi, *Das Zwangmässige im dichterischen Schaffen Goethes* (Langensalza, 1915).

†M. Dessoir, *Aesthetik und allgemeine Kunstwissenschaft* (2nd ed.; Stuttgart, 1923), p. 173.

‡E. Holmes, *Life of Mozart* (New York, 1912).

shuddering thrills that pass through one from head to foot;—there is a profound happiness in which the most painful and gloomy feelings are not discordant in effect, but are required as necessary colors in this overflow of light. . . . Everything occurs quite without volition, as if in an eruption of freedom, independence, power and divinity. The spontaneity of the images and similes is most remarkable; one loses all perception of what is imagery and simile; everything offers itself as the most immediate, exact, and simple means of expression. If I may recall a phrase of Zarathustra's, it actually seems as if the things themselves come to one, and offered themselves as similes. . . . This is *my* experience of inspiration. I have no doubt that I should have to go back millenniums to find another who could say to me: "It is mine also!"*

## MODERN INTERPRETATIONS

Against the ancient view that "from heaven descends the flame of genius to the human breast, and love of beauty and poetic joy and inspiration," the view began to gain ground in the second half of the nineteenth century that the artistic conception is something that must be traced to the darkness of the unconscious mind, and that the essential element in its realization and execution is intellectual effort, taste, and skill. Psychologists as well as a number of artists, among them Edgar Allan Poe[†] and Auguste Rodin,[‡] disputed the view that a work of art might come into being purely through inspiration and without effort. A creative idea which seemingly occurs in the mind unexpectedly as if by sheer intuition is always the outcome of long reflection and intensive mental labor.[§] The divine or transcendent aura surrounding inspiration was dispelled. What is unknown must not be equated with the divine. The mysterious origin of a work of art; the

---

*Nietzsche, "Composition of *Thus Spake Zarathustra*" from *Ecce Homo*.
†Cf. the essay by Poe on "The Raven," "The Philosophy of Composition."
‡See Ziehen, *Vorlesungen über Aesthetik*, II (Halle, 1925), 311.
§See Lange, *Das Wesen der Kunst* (Berlin, 1907), p. 458.

exaltation, emotional rapture, and enthusiasm which attend its coming into being are no reason for assuming the presence of a divine factor.* Others considered inspiration to be an act of unconscious and purely physiological nature. In every case the decisive moment remains that of creative, imaginative activity, "a synthesis released in a moment of rapt emotion, and determined by and combining anew in selective fashion latent conceptions and emotionally charged complexes."†

According to Eduard von Hartmann's metaphysical theory, inspiration is to be explained by an involuntary emergence of a psychological factor (feeling, thought, desire) out of the unconscious. For Hartmann, the unconscious is identifiable with the Absolute. Thus, in the mystic or the poet, the Absolute, which is unconscious, rises into consciousness. Hartmann sees in this process "an intuitive tearing aside of the veil of Maya or the emotional transcendence of the barriers of individuality."‡ William James explains inspiration as the interruption of the causal series in the surface mind by the transcendent. In the view of Ribot, the creative imagination is a composite phenomenon, the constituent elements of which are the intellectual factor, the effective or emotional factor, and the unconscious factor. By the last term he designates what ordinary speech calls "inspiration," which he defines as the result of an imperceptible process. It marks either the end of an unconscious elaboration or the beginning of a conscious elaboration.§

The main features of the creative state seemed to be suddenness, passiveness, involuntariness (it does not depend on the will; it cannot be called forth), obscurity of origin ("the poem seems to issue forth from the dark of the mind, without much awareness of how it comes"), impersonality or the consciousness of being subject to a power superior to the conscious individual, strange to him although acting through him; a state which many inventors have expressed in

---

*K. Köstlin, *Aesthetik* (Tübingen, 1869), p. 971.
†Ziehen, *op. cit.*, II, 305–327.
‡*Die Philosophie des Unbewussten* (Berlin, 1869), XI, 1, p. 314.
§*An Essay on the Creative Imagination* (Chicago, 1906), pp. 12, 50 ff.

the words, "I counted for nothing in that." There is a feeling of not sharing consciously in the generation of ideas; "the experience of will and initiative, the sense of being bound to the ego is lacking." It is the consciousness of being merely the stage of thoughts, "of playing, as it were, a merely passive role"; the impression or conviction that "it is not I who think; it thinks in me, without or even against my will."*

The most prevalent trend in the last sixty years has been to explain the creative process by the existence of an activity of the mind which is analogous to consciousness, though hidden from direct observation, variously described as a semiconscious, semi-unconscious or subconscious state. The poet is "a man of an extraordinarily sensitive and active subconscious personality, fed by, and feeding, a nonresistant consciousness."† The material of ideas and thoughts apprehended in inspiration, is such as to produce impressions which are repressed before they can be properly grasped. Many of these impressions live on in the subconscious, forming therein more or less extensive complexes. When the latter attain sufficient intensity, they burst all barriers and demand release.‡

Plausible as this view appears to be, it hardly offers an explanation. The nature of the subconscious being one of the enigmas of psychology, any reference to it amounts to shifting the puzzle from one realm of the unknown to another. Nor are we entitled to ascribe a power of creativity to the subconscious which we deny to the conscious mind. Why only in rare cases does the subconscious give rise to poetry?

Sigmund Freud maintains that works of art are analogous in their

*Gruhle, *"Psychology des Abnormen,"* in G. Kafka, *Handbuch der vergleichenden Psychologie,* II (München, 1922), 66. Cf. Lehmann, *Die Poetik* (München, 1919), pp. 22–42; Utitz, *Grundlegung der allgemeinen Kunstwissenschaft,* II (Stuttgart, 1914), pp. 237–249; Mueller-Freienfels, *Psychologie der Kunst,* II (Leipzig, 1920); Konrad, *Religion und Kunst* (Tübingen, 1929), p. 94; R. E. M. Harding, *Towards a Law of Creative Thought* (London, 1936).

†Amy Lowell, "The Process of Making Poetry," *Poetry and Poets* (Boston, 1930), p. 25.

‡M. Nachmansohn, *"Zur Erklaerung der durch Inspiration entstandenen Bewusstseinserlebnisse,"* *Archiv für die gesamte Psychologie,* XXXVI, 255–280.

mode of creation to dreams, to daydreaming. Just as dreams afford us the experience of satisfying our desires in a world of fantasy, so the artist achieves his wish-fulfillment through his creation. The *libido,* or sexual wish, operates as a source of a never-ending striving for expression. This is why the artist, unlike the dreamer, communicates his wishes, desires, and frustrations through works of art which symbolize his repressions and aspirations. Thus, art is regarded as a substitute gratification of repressed desires in disguised form.

As for the nature or origin of the artistic gift, Freud admitted that psychoanalysis has no special explanation of this mysterious force, nor of the means by which the artist works. At the end of his essay on Leonardo da Vinci, Freud confessed that the nature of artistic attainment is psychoanalytically inaccessible to us. Psychoanalysis cannot really elucidate the nature of the artistic gift, nor can it explain the means by which the artist works. Whence comes the artist's ability to create? is not the question of psychology. Admittedly, psychoanalysis must lay down its arms before the problem of the poet. Many of Freud's followers, however, did not agree with him.

Just as Freud saw the cause of neurosis in certain childhood experiences and in the individual's particular reaction to them, so did his school claim to see in those same childhood impressions the experiences which led to artistic activity. The artistic reaction differs from the neurotic "by an *overcoming of the trauma* or of the potentiality of inhibition resulting therefrom."

## EITHER–OR

The mind's hankering for simplicity has always made it attractive to think in terms of either–or. A phenomenon had to be either natural or divine. To satisfy theology, inspiration had to be exclusively supernatural, and the prophet a mere instrument, a vessel; to satisfy psychology, inspiration had to be exclusively natural, on a par with other phenomena. In antiquity, the theory that regarded the prophetic act as a state of ecstasy eliminated the role of any human spontaneity in order to safeguard the conception of superhuman inspiration; in modern times, the theory that regards the prophetic act as an act of poetic creation eliminates the concept of superhuman inspiration in order to establish it as an act of human spontaneity. Both theories offer a solution by destroying the enigma, trying to "explain" what is far from being plain.

These theories would set the prophet straight, prove to him that he was the victim of an illusion. But can these theories be tested and verified? Does ecstasy prove an Isaiah? Does poetic inspiration account for a Jeremiah or a Moses?

In Israel, too, poetry was regarded as a gift of the spirit (II Sam. 23:2). Moses Ibn Ezra even maintained that "a poet is called in Hebrew a prophet."* Yet he certainly did not intend to equate prophecy and poetry. Indeed, Ezekiel complained about the fact that his contemporaries accepted his prophecy as "poetry." "Ah Lord God, they are saying of Me: 'Is he not a maker of allegories?' " (Ezek. 20:49 [H. 21:5].) "You are to them like one who sings love songs with a beautiful voice and plays well on an instrument, for they hear what you say, but they will not do it" (Ezek. 33:32).†

## THE ELUSIVENESS OF THE CREATIVE ACT

The analogy from poetic inspiration has had fewer exponents among students of prophecy than has the theory of ecstasy. Perhaps this is because no unequivocal scheme of ideas is associated with the creative state of the poet. All the same, an analysis of the divergencies between the two phenomena remains necessary.

What meaning does the word "inspiration" hold for the poet's consciousness? Let us sum up the content of the statements made by the poets themselves as well as the essentials contained in the interpretations of the psychologists. It is remarkable how they abound in negatives. Just as the idea of ecstasy is often related to a negative theology, so the circle of ideas underlying the apprehension of poetic inspiration

---

* *Shirath Israel* (Berlin, 1924), p. 45.
† Cf. the title of G. Hölscher's book: *Hesekiel: der Dichter und das Buch* (Giessen, 1924).

seems to depend utterly on "a negative psychology." The net result of nearly all pronouncements is not an affirmation or elucidation, but a direct or indirect confession: *ignoramus*. The perplexing elusiveness of the phenomenon is in the very essence of the poet's experience, and the poet does not even attempt to solve the riddle. He undergoes a psychological change, a shift into a new stream of consciousness, the origin or source of which remains in obscurity. The exact nature of the creative act continues to elude the human understanding. It can be described only in its manifestations; it can be vaguely sensed, but neither grasped nor explained.

"One does not ask who gives," declared Nietzsche. His inspirations come to him from no identifiable source. The inspiration is here; its source is unknown. What is encountered is an influence, a flow, not the source of the flow. The act itself appears to be a sort of automatism; it is not susceptible of conscious control. To quote Nietzsche again, "There is a feeling that one is utterly out of hand." It is as if one's personal power were suspended, one's identity immaterial. It is not as a subject or as a person that the poet faces the moment of inspiration; he faces the moment incognito, as a "mere vessel," in Goethe's words; "one is the mere incarnation, or mouthpiece, or medium of some almighty power," said Nietzsche.

In contrast, the prophetic act takes place in clear self-consciousness. The prophet is not a riddle to himself; he is not baffled or left in the dark about the source of his experience; he knows Who confronts him. The stern and steadfast certainty of being inspired by God, of speaking in His Name is derived from the unequivocal awareness of the Source of his experience.

## THE NEUTER PRONOUN

An outstanding feature of the poet's consciousness is a sense of being passive at the moment of inspiration. The ego sinks into passivity by a force which has seized the soul. The production of poetry, we are told, is less an active than a passive and involuntary process. It is said of many poets that in their highest creative state it is not they who use their imaginations, but they are used by their imaginations.

The poet's consciousness of being inspired, for all its passivity, implies no experience of the initiative of another subject acting in the place of the poet. An outstanding feature of the act is its being indeterminate, indefinite, vague; neither one's own "I" nor a transcendent "I" is present to the poet's mind. A common phrase among poets is, "It came to me." In their descriptions, the neuter pronoun of the third person prevails. Impersonal and anonymous are the images employed: "A light, a stream flooded into my consciousness."

"I soon found," said Socrates, "that it is not by wisdom that the poets create their works, but by a certain natural power and by inspiration, like soothsayers and prophets, who say many fine things, but who understand nothing of what they say."* Goethe, speaking of *Faust* to Eckermann, said: "They come and ask me what idea I meant to embody in my *Faust;* as if I knew myself, and could inform them. . . . It was in short not in my line, as a poet, to strive to embody anything abstract. I received in my mind impressions . . . and I had as a poet nothing more to do than to round off and . . . to bring them forward that others might receive the same impressions. . . ."†

The prophet, on the other hand, definitely knows what his utterance implies. The intention is more important than the impression. His purpose is not to elaborate his views artistically, but to set them forth effectively. His primary concern is the message rather than the form.

In contrast to the inspiration of the poet, which each time breaks forth suddenly, unexpectedly, from an unknown source,‡ the inspiration of the prophet is distinguished, not only by an awareness of its source and of a will to impart the content of inspiration, but also by

*Plato, *Apology,* 22.
†O. Pniower, *Goethes Faust* (Berlin, 1899), p. 187.
‡Plato spoke of the illumination which suddenly lights up the soul, "as when a light is kindled by a spark that is struck." (Epistles, VII.) See Stenzel's remarks in *Jahresbericht der Philologischen Gesellschaft zu Berlin,* XLVII, 63 ff. Plaut, *Psychologie der schöpferischen Persönlichkeit* (Stuttgart, 1929), sees in the Platonic ideas about artistic creation the scientific foundation for later theories of genius.

the coherence of the inspired messages as a whole (with their constant implication of earlier communications), by the awareness of being a link in the chain of the prophets who preceded him, and by the continuity which links the revelations he receives one to another. The words that come to him form a coherence of closely related revelations, all reflecting the illumination and the sense of mission shed by the call. There is both a thematic and a personal unity of experience.

Thus, common to the utterances of the poet and the definitions of aesthetics and psychology is the peculiar stress upon the impersonal nature of the poetic inspiration. This applies to the poet's own self-awareness as a recipient as well as to his awareness of the source of inspiration.

The poet's inspiration seems, therefore, to be a subjectless experience, a condition in which no personal agent is apprehended. The source he is exposed to is unknown, devoid of personal identity, and his own role is one of passive receptivity, of being a receptacle, a mere object. Structurally, the experience may be described as an *object–object–relationship*. Out of such inspiration, mysterious and overwhelming as it may be, no poet can derive the power of prefacing his words with the statement: "Thus says the Lord."

In prophetic inspiration, on the other hand, the knowledge and presence of Him who imparts the message is the central, staggering fact of awareness. There is a certainty of having experienced the impingement of a personal Being, of another I; not an idea coming from nowhere or from a nameless source, but always a communication reaching him from the most powerful Subject of all, confronting the prophet, who is responsive and often participates in the act. Structurally, it may be described as a *subject–subject–relationship*.

Poetic inspiration, though of great importance for the understanding of the poet's consciousness and the secret of creativity, is of no intrinsic significance for the evaluation of the work itself. For the prophet, on the other hand, inspiration is the very essence, the justification of what he is and for what he does.

# 12

# Prophecy and Psychosis

## POETRY AND MADNESS

Among the strange legacies that have come down to us from Greek civilization is the belief that great poetry comes into being through a state of madness. The oldest known exponent of this most influential conception is Democritus, who praised Homer as inspired and held that the finest poems were those written by a poet when driven by a god and a holy breath. He "denied that anyone can be a great poet without madness [*sine furore*]."* Similarly, Plato declared with assurance "that the poet, according to the tradition which has ever prevailed among us, and is accepted by all men, when he sits down on the tripod of the Muse, is not in his right mind."† He spoke of "the madness of those who are possessed by the Muses. . . . But he who, having no touch of the Muses' madness in his soul, comes to the door and thinks that he will get into the temple by the help of art—he, I say, and his poetry are not admitted; the sane man disappears and is nowhere when he enters into rivalry with the madman."‡

---

*Diels, *Die Fragmente der Vorsokratiker* (Berlin, 1912), fragments 17, 18, 21.
†*Laws*, 719.
‡*Phaedrus*, 244; cf. *Timaeus*, 71–72.

Plato further said: "All good poets, epic as well as lyric, compose their beautiful poems not by art, but because they are inspired and possessed. And as the Corybantian revellers when they dance are not in their right mind, so the lyric poets are not in their right mind when they are composing their beautiful strains; but when falling under the power of music and metre they are inspired and possessed. . . . For the poet is a light and winged and holy thing, and there is no invention in him until he has been inspired and is out of his senses, and the mind is no longer in him. . . . For not by art does the poet sing, but by power divine."*

Plato's notion that the creative process of the poet resembles or actually is a state of madness, was expanded to the claim that the poet as a person is afflicted with madness; he is a *manikos*.† This idea that the poet composes in a state of frenzy was echoed by Seneca, Cicero, and other thinkers of antiquity. "There is no great genius without a touch of madness";‡ "no man can be a good poet who is not on fire with passion, and inspired by something very like frenzy."§ Such terms as ecstasy, inspiration, poetic fury, Dionysiac frenzy, *raptus, afflatus,* and possession have all been attributed synonymously to the poet.

## The Appreciation of Madness

That the great fathers of intellectualism—Democritus, Socrates, Plato, whom we revere as models of sanity—should have expressed profound appreciation of insanity is a powerful expression of their awareness of the deficiency of pure intellectualism. Their attitude was not owing to ignorance of madness as a curse and a disease. This is testified to by the Greek epigram, "Whom the gods destroy, they first make mad"; by Plato's reference to madness as a divine punishment; and by his discussion of various types of madness, some arising out of

---

* *Ion,* 533 f.
†Aristotle, *Poetics,* 1455a, 33.
‡*"Nullum magnum ingenium sine mixtura dementiae fuit."* (Seneca, *De Tranquilitate Animi,* I, 15.) Seneca ascribes the statement to Aristotle.
§Cicero, *De Oratore,* II, 46, 194.

disease, others originating "in an evil and passionate temperament" and increased by bad education.* The insane, too, although they were shunned, were regarded as being filled with numinous powers; they were thought to be in contact with the supernatural world, and they could on occasion display powers denied common men. Ajax in his madness spoke a sinister language "which no mortal taught him, but a daemon."† On the stage again and again individuals appearing in a state of insanity are depicted as awe-inspiring figures.

According to Plato, "no man, when in his wits, attains prophetic truth and inspiration; but when he receives the inspired word, either his intelligence is enthralled in sleep, or he is demented by some distemper or possession."‡ When inspired and possessed of a god, diviners and prophets "say many grand things, not knowing what they say."§ "Bacchic maidens draw milk and honey from the rivers when they are under the influence of Dionysus, but not when they are in their right mind."‖ As quoted above, the Muses take possession of the poet's mind and drive him mad, that without this divine madness it is vain for the aspirant to knock at the gate of poetry; for the poetry of the sober sense will always be eclipsed by the poetry of frenzy.

It is such profound appreciation that explains their conception of the mystery of the creation of poetry as arising out of madness. Another example is Socrates' startling statement:

> There is a madness which is a divine gift; *the greatest of blessings have come to us in madness.* For prophecy is a madness, and the prophetess at Delphi and the priestess at Dodona when out of their senses have conferred great benefits on Hellas, both in public and in private life, but when in their senses few

---

* *Laws,* XI, 934d.

†Sophocles, *Ajax,* 243 f. On the entire problem, cf. E. R. Dodds, *The Greeks and the Irrational* (Berkeley, 1951), pp. 64 ff.; O'Brien-Moore, *Madness in Ancient Literature* (Weimar, 1924).

‡*Timaeus,* 71.

§Plato, *Meno,* 99.

‖Plato, *Ion,* 534.

or none. And must I also tell you how the Sibyl and other inspired persons have given to many an intimation of the future which has saved them from falling? . . . And as the act of the prophet is more perfect and venerable than the act of the augur, by so much the more, as the ancients testify, *is madness superior to reflection, for reflection is only human, but madness springs from the gods.* \*

Why should madness be regarded as a state of the highest spiritual receptivity? Why must a person descend to the pit in order to attain exaltation?

Following Socrates, philosophers had taken for their motto "Know thyself," but the golden cage of self-knowledge was too narrow for man to live with his own self. Madness in its essence may be described as stemming from an experience of dismay at living with oneself, leading to the alienation of a person from his own self. Madness is man's desperate attempt to reach transcendence, to rise beyond himself.

The Dionysiac frenzy, which found so many devotees, with its striving to destroy all codes and crystallizations, was more than a "return to nature," or a recrudescence of passions, or a surrender to the emotions in reaction to rationalism. Time and again man discovers how blank, how dim and abrupt, is the light that comes from within. He does not have sufficient strength within his own power to transcend himself, to ensoul his deeds. It is in the state of frenzy that he hopes to encounter a power great enough to carry his person away from himself, that he hopes to be touched by what lies beyond form, order, limit, and self.

There is a deeply rooted fascination for the abyss which has often led to the veneration of the sinister, to the sanctification of the monstrous. Exaltation is sought in war, violence, destruction.

---

\* *Phaedrus,* 244 f. (Italics mine. A. J. H.) Socrates maintained that the Greek word for prophecy ( *mantike* ) and the word for madness ( *manike* ) were really the same, "and the letter *t* is only a modern and tasteless insertion." Horace declared, "It is pleasant to go mad ( *insanire juvat* )." ( *Odes,* Bk. III, Ode 4, line 18.)

The fascination for the abyss has colored our understanding of life in art and religion. It seems inconceivable for a person to be both sober and inspired, normal and holy. The mind must be overthrown to be illumined, an object must look sinister to be acknowledged as sacred. Monstrosity rather than consistency seems to go well with mystery. Gods are often depicted as hideous and repulsive figures. Indian art delights to represent its deities as many-headed or many-armed. The head of Medusa, or Gorgon—a terrible monster—adorned the aegis of Zeus and also of Athena.

## GENIUS AND INSANITY

The problem was revived and brought within the realm of scientific inquiry by psychiatrists in the second half of the nineteenth century. Influenced by Auguste Comte's exaggerated tendency to refer all mental facts to biological causes, they sought to explain the gifts of the mind by abnormalities of brain anatomy. Moreau, in a work published in 1859, was the first to investigate the problem systematically; he advanced the view that genius is a neurosis, and often a psychosis, a pathological state of the brain, an *organic* abnormality. A heightened irritability of the nervous system was declared to be the source of either greater spiritual energy (genius) or of mental disease. Both forms are present in the state of inspiration. A perfectly normal state of the brain and superior mental endowments are mutually exclusive.

The idea that insanity, or some form of mental abnormality, is related to, or even identical with, the mental conditions which promote genius, found its classical exposition in the work of Cesare Lombroso (1836–1909), one of the earliest efforts to present empirical data on the association between psychopathology and creativity.

Genius, according to Lombroso, is the manifestation of a diseased mind. The affinity between genius and insanity is proved by the frequency of pathological signs, of neurosis, insanity, melancholy, megalomania, and hallucinations among men of genius. Lombroso's *The Man of Genius* (*L'Homo di Genio*, 1888) attained wide popularity, was translated into many languages, and stimulated a vast body of literature on the subject.* The view became popular that the effusions of genius are often the effect of distempered nerves and complexioned spleen, as pearls are morbid secretions, that creative individuals are victims of a manic-depressive psychosis, which provides the motive force for their creation.

The literature on the subject has since grown considerably, without succeeding in any way in solving the problem. According to a more moderate view, genius is related genetically to insanity, but is not a product of an insane mind; insanity, in fact, operates against creativity; men of genius have been most creative when they were sanest.† Although psychiatric investigation has shown that, among geniuses, psychologically healthy individuals, as defined by this moderate view, are in the minority, there is no unanimity of opinion about the association between insanity and genius.‡ Some scholars point to factors that release genius, stimulating both its birth and its decay. Others deny any internal or causal relation between creativity and mental abnormality, and maintain that the personality factors predisposing one to creativity are antithetical to pathology.§ Indeed, numerous attempts to examine the data available about outstanding men of genius in the past as well as numerous surveys of contemporary men of creative ability have not confirmed with any degree of certainty the

*A theory of the pathological constitution of genius was developed by Schopenhauer. A life of powerful cerebration results in abnormal irritability. Detachment of intelligence from the service of the will brings about total loneliness and deep melancholy. A person's rising above time and causal relations brings him close to insanity, which is a disease of memory. (*The World as Will and Idea*, I, 36; II, 31, 32.) Schiller spoke of the *"voruebergehenden Wahnwitz"* found in all creative people.

†A. C. Jacobson, *Genius: Some Revaluations* (New York, 1926).

‡W. Lange-Eichbau, *Genie, Irrsinn und Ruhm* (3rd ed.; München, 1942), pp. 62 ff.; cf. the survey (not comprehensive) of the vast literature on Lombroso's view, pp. 49 ff.

§A. Anastas and J. P. Foley, "A Survey of the Literature on Artistic Behaviors in the Abnormal, II. Approaches and Interrelationships," *Abstracts of the New York Academy of Sciences*, XLII (August, 1941), pp. 1–111.

view that genius is linked to insanity, a view which may reflect the failure to distinguish an unstable nervous temperament from actual mental disease.* Nor is Lombroso's thesis that genius is manifested in epilepsy borne out by careful study. Disease is not a determining factor. However, it may act on occasion as a ferment to the genius already expressing itself.

Genius is neither a psychosis nor a neurosis, but is a phenomenon *sui generis*. Indeed, genius undeniably suffers greatly from "minor nervous disorders."† However, such disorders may be due to the structure of a society indifferent or even hostile to what a creative soul is trying to convey. Rejection or false recognition, together with the mental stresses and strains, the acts of self-denial necessitated by complete dedication, the effort and agony experienced in trying to bring intuition to expression, are too severe not to affect the sensitive balance of a human being. It is a miracle that a creative person manages to survive.

It has been argued that genius is the product of health rather than sickness, that similarity of symptoms is no sign of identity, that genius is not a psychological concept, that there is no causal nexus between psychosis and genius. Madness, however, may be the effect of genius. It seems too hard for a man of genius to live in an insane world and remain unscathed.

The fallacy of Lombroso's doctrine consists in mistaking a result for the cause. It is true that the man of genius pays for this gift in some abstention or affliction; but the affliction is the result rather than the cause or the essence of genius.

---

*A psychological survey of four hundred "eminent" men and women of the twentieth century showed that only two of them were insane, the late Vaslav Nijinsky and Clara Barton, founder of the American Red Cross, who regained her sanity after three years of "unreality." Four more of the four hundred committed suicide, including Vachel Lindsay, the poet, who was mentally ill, but was never treated or committed to an institution. When this survey was presented to the eighth annual meeting of the National Association for Gifted Children, it was said: "The frequency of mental illness among the eminent is far below that of the general population. The popular association of 'genius' and 'madness' is not supported."

†N. D. M. Hirsch, *Genius and Creative Intelligence* (Cambridge, 1931), pp. 282 ff.

## PROPHECY AND MADNESS

Echoing the equation of genius and madness, scholars have insisted that prophecy was due to a morbid condition, resulting from perturbations of the growth of the psyche, or from derangement of the nervous system. "There is a close relationship between prophecy and insanity. The kind of temperament that lends itself to psychic experience, to automations, may result in genius or it may become psychopathic and lead to melancholy and outright insanity."*

The etymology of the word *"nabi"* and certain manners of the prophets' behavior have been cited in support of this theory. (For fuller discussion of *nabi,* see p. 518.) It was suggested that *nabi* denoted a man who poured out his utterances loudly and madly with deep breaths,† that the original meaning of the stem was "madness," "insanity." *Nabi* meant, therefore, originally, one who is carried away by a supernatural power. Thus "insanity was sacred to the Israelites, the insane man being believed to be possessed by a supernatural power."‡

"Isaiah's and Jeremiah's consecration-visions are pathological phenomena, akin to the ecstatic visions of the seers and diviners."§ "Men like Amos and Jeremiah were not readily distinguishable by their contemporaries from the Ecstatics whose symptoms resembled those of the epileptic, or even the insane."‖ Ezekiel, according to E. C. Broome, exhibits behavioristic abnormalities consistent with paranoid schizophrenia. "A true psychotic, his characteristics include "periods of catatonia," "an influencing machine," "a narcissistic-masochistic conflict, with attendant phantasies of castration and unconscious sexual regression, schizophrenic withdrawal, delusions of persecution and

---

*T. J. Meek, *Hebrew Origins* (New York, 1936), p. 152.

†G. Hoffmann, *"Versuche zu Amos," Zeitschrift für die alttestamentliche Wissenschaft,* III, 87 ff. "The term *nabi* is perhaps derived from the ecstatic incoherent cries." (J. Pedersen, *Israel,* III–IV [Copenhagen, 1940], p. 111.)

‡J. A. Bewer, *American Journal of Semitic Languages and Literatures,* XVIII (1901–1902), 120.

§R. Kittel, *Geschichte des Volkes Israel,* II (2nd ed.; Gotha, 1903), sec. 46, p. 449.

‖T. H. Robinson, *Prophecy and the Prophets* (London, 1923), p. 36.

grandeur." However, Broome assures us that Ezekiel's "religious significance is by no means impaired by our diagnosis of a paranoic condition."* Other scholars have advanced the view that Ezekiel was subject to cataleptic fits.†

## PROPHECY AND NEUROSIS

Psychoanalysis "did not succeed in surmounting Lombroso's materialist theory of insanity or supplementing his rational explanation by a spiritual one. All it did was to substitute neurosis for insanity [which was at bottom Lombroso's own meaning], thus tending either to identify . . . the artist with the neurotic (Sadger, Stekel) or to explain the artist on the basis of an inferiority feeling (Adler)."‡

Applying the principles of psychoanalysis, writers have frequently advanced the view that prophetic inspiration was a state of mind due to some distortion of experience, traceable to neurosis. In the visionary experiences of the prophets, in their unmannerly appearance and sensational behavior, scholars sought to discover features of an abnormal mentality. The secret of prophetic experiences was felt to lie in their tendency to ecstatic possession, in mental derangement.

Psychoanalysis, we are told, offers an explanation of the prophet Hosea. From his marrying a promiscuous woman we may infer that he was a person of sensuous disposition and unusually passionate temperament. One gains the impression from the book of Hosea that the feelings of the prophet were especially implicated in sexual matters.

---

*"Ezekiel's Abnormal Personality," *JBL*, LXV (1946), 277–292. See also K. Jaspers, *"Der Prophet Ezechiel, eine pathologische Studie,"* Festschrift fur Kurt Schneider (1947), pp. 77–85. For a critique of Broome's theory, see C. G. Howie, *The Date and Composition of Ezekiel* (Philadelphia, 1950), pp. 69–84.

†Klostermann, Bertholet, Kraetzschmar, and H. Schmidt, among others; see M. Buttenwieser, "The Date and Character of Ezekiel's Prophesies," *HUCA*, VII (1930), p. 3.

‡O. Rank, "Life and Creation," in W. Phillips, ed., *Art and Psychoanalysis* (New York, 1957), p. 311.

Hosea's sexual life was carried on in the subconscious: Hosea himself was not conscious of it and so in his book . . . it finds expression in an oblique manner. The sexual impulse had been repressed in him. His sexuality was seeking some point through which it could find release. And such a point was discovered in the obligation he felt, in the interests of the majesty of God, to denounce somehow or other, the harlotry of the country and to bring it vividly before his contemporaries as sin. Thus his sexuality could express itself out of the depths of the unconscious.*

Hosea suffered from sex-obsession, which drove him into the thing of which he had the greatest horror. He was subject to "a sex-complex" and had "a peculiar intensity and passion" which in people of this sort "run through all their life, and often, when duly sublimated, give them an extraordinary power and impressiveness. [In Hosea, then,] we have the struggle between the subconscious obsessions and the purity of conscious thought. . . . He found himself swept away by an overwhelming love for a woman who belonged to a class against which his better nature revolted. . . . So in the agony of his own spirit, and in the deathless love he knew, he found an image of the heart of God.†

According to another view, the marriage of Hosea has its psychological roots in a so-called *anima*-experience. Jung defines *anima* as a feminine symbol for the collective unconscious, which represents the attitude adopted by a certain person to what approaches it from within. Thus Gomer would really be "a sort of Sibyl for the prophet."‡

*A. Allwohn, *Die Ehe des Propheten Hosea in psychoanalytischer Beleuchtung* (Giessen, 1926), p. 60.
†W. O. E. Oesterley and T. H. Robinson, *An Introduction to the Books of the Old Testament* (London, 1934), pp. 350 ff.
‡F. Häussermann, *Wortempfang und Symbol in der alttestamentlichen Prophetie* (Giessen, 1932).

## The Hazards of Psychoanalysis by Distance

The scientific hazards involved in the attempt to expose, on the basis of literary remains, the subconscious life of a person who lived thousands of years ago are so stupendous as to make the undertaking foolhardy. These efforts, tempting as they seem to be, are reminiscent of the medical diagnosis on the basis of literary symptoms, frequently employed by some physicians in the nineteenth century; they proved, for example, from a study of Byron's poetry that he must have had gallstones; and, similarly, that Pope had high blood pressure. In addition to the chasm that normally yawns between the realm of the subconscious and the level of literary articulation, one would have to take into account in the analysis of the prophetic personalities the tremendous distance and dissimilarity in relation to words, in historic perspective, in intensity of emotion, and in spiritual sensitivity.

A reliable diagnosis of the prophet's mental health remains beyond our scope. The prophet cannot be brought to the laboratory for tests and interviews, nor do we possess the subtlety required for asking the right questions about experiences totally beyond our range of perception, nor the empathy required for an understanding of the sensitivity of the prophet's soul that would be implied in his answers. A spectrum analysis, clearly applicable to the sun and other celestial bodies, a fine method of investigating the chemical nature of distant substances, is hardly effective in the understanding of spiritual moments of a distant past.

The tendency to treat the prophet as a candidate for hospitalization, the interpretation which seeks to dissect the prophet and find him wanting, represents a procedure which most effectively makes us inattentive to what is essential and creative in the prophetic consciousness. It operates with generalizations that have a tendency to wander so far from the subject matter as to make it sound more like an explanation of dervishes. Instead of subordinating oneself to the object of investigation in order to come upon the unique and singular features which constitute and characterize the personality of the prophet, this technique seeks to fit the prophet into a ready-made scheme. Unique values which creation brings forth can be deduced from a psychological formula only by a process of destroying them.

The one respectable justification for employing such procedures would be that of self-defense: the inability of a civilization to take prophetic inspiration seriously. However, inability to take the prophet seriously is an attitude, not an explanation.

## PATHOLOGICAL SYMPTOMS IN THE LITERARY PROPHETS

What is the evidence to justify such a diagnosis? The two following expositions will supply some answers.

Hosea, Isaiah, Jeremiah, and Ezekiel, we are told (see p. 510n), "professed to be and undoubtedly were" ecstatics, and their "ecstasy was accompanied or preceded by a variety of pathological states and acts." What were these states and acts?

1. Jeremiah, upon the Lord's command, remained solitary because disaster was anticipated.

2. Isaiah, upon the Lord's "command (?) had intercourse with a prophetess whose child he then named as previously ordained (Isa. 8:3). Strange, symbolic names of children of prophets generally were found."

3. "When the spirit overcame them, the prophets experienced facial contortions, their breath failed them, and occasionally they fell to the ground unconscious, for a time deprived of vision and speech, writhing in cramps (cf. Isa. 21)."

4. Isaiah "walked naked and barefoot for three years as a sign and portent against Egypt and Ethiopia, so shall the king of Assyria lead away the Egyptians captives and the Ethiopians exiles . . . naked and barefoot (cf. Isa. 20:3–4)."

5. Jeremiah was "like a drunken man," and all his bones shook (Jer. 23:9).

6. "Jeremiah was split into a dual ego. He implored his God to absolve him from speaking. Though he did not wish to, he had to say what he felt to be inspired words not coming from himself. Indeed,

his speech was experienced by him as a horrible fate. Unless he spoke he suffered terrible pains, burning that seized him and he could not stand up under the heavy pressure without relieving himself by speaking. Jeremiah did not consider a man to be a prophet unless he knew this state and spoke from such compulsion rather than 'from his own heart.' "*

Let us now examine the evidence:

1. Is it correct to characterize "being alone" as a pathological state? Is not solitude a state needful to both imagination and contemplation? Has anything of significance in the realm of spirit been achieved without the protection and the blessings of solitude? Elijah seems to have lived alone on the top of a hill (II Kings 1:9), at Mt. Carmel (II Kings 4:25). But is solitude a state characteristic only of prophets? "To be alone is the fate of all great minds—a fate deplored at times, but still always chosen as the less grievous of two evils," wrote Schopenhauer. Is it not true that the superior instants of a lifetime occur when the soul is alone? Jeremiah was overcome by a desire to withdraw from society; this is hardly a sign of psychosis. In the light of his experience, he was presumably most alone with people and least alone in solitude. Is there any wonder that he dreamed of a lodge in a wilderness, when he could not endure any longer the complacency of his people?

2. The importance attached to name-giving, richly testified to in the Bible, extended not only to descendants but to the community at large. Hagar was told by an angel: "You are with child, and shall bear a son; you shall call his name Ishmael. . . . He shall dwell over against all his kinsmen" (Gen. 16:11–12). Numerous names in the Bible are "strange, symbolic," and some of them are "prophetic," foretelling events, as in the case of Lamech who called his son Noah, saying:

---

*This first exposition is based on M. Weber, *Ancient Judaism* (Glencoe, 1952), pp. 286 f., and on his *Wirtschaft und Gesellschaft* (2nd ed.; Chicago, 1925), pp. 140 ff., 250 ff. The quoted material is from these sources. The paragraphing and numbering are mine, done in order to facilitate the analysis, in the following paragraphs, of the points raised by Weber.—A.J.H.

"This one shall bring us relief from our work and from the toil of our hands" (Gen. 5:29), a name which, as in the case of Isaiah, signified what was in store for the people.

3. Some prophets make mention of their consternation and agitation at the time of inspiration. Such a reaction, however, is hardly a sign of either a state of ecstasy or a condition of mental disturbance. Consternation seems to occur frequently in the life of a prophet. People are calm, while the prophet is a person who lives in dismay, appalled by the vision of disaster. We should regard him as abnormal, heartless, callous, were he to remain unshocked, unruffled, when overwhelmed by a stern vision of agony. The language in which Isaiah describes his anguish is used by other biblical writers as well.

4. When the prophet was told to go naked (literally: "loose the sackcloth from your loins"), he was being instructed to remove his outer garment, to be clad only in the scanty loincloth, to dress like a slave. (Cf. Isa. 3:17; 47:2–3.) To walk about without the outer garment was also a sign of mourning. (Cf. Mic. 1:8.)* Similarly, to walk about without sandals was a sign of great poverty or of deep mourning. (Cf. II Sam. 15:30; Ezek. 24:17, 23.) Removing the shoes as a sign of mourning is observed to this day by traditional Jews. Two ways of interpreting this episode may be cited. "Isaiah's going exposed about the streets of Jerusalem is a clear case of exhibitionism, a tendency which may be observed at any bathing beach, or track meet." According to another view, we have here an act of complete submission under the will of the Lord. "The prophet threw his whole self into his prophecy, and made not his lips alone, but his whole personality, the vehicle of the divine 'word.' "†

5. The condition described in Jer. 23:9 has been discussed above, p. 150.

6. Is inner conflict, "a split into a dual ego," to be regarded as a pathological state? Did not Goethe express a common phenomenon in the famous lines:

---

*See Kissane, *The Book of Isaiah,* I (Dublin, 1941–43), 224.
†See H. H. Rowley, *The Servant of the Lord* (London, 1954), p. 118, n. 2.

> *Two souls, alas! reside within my breast,*
> *And each withdraws from and repels his brother.*
>
> *Faust, I, 2*

The second exposition states:

> In all likelihood, the prophets and the *bene nebi'im* were, for the most part, psychically abnormal: men of wild imagination, visionaries, *neurotics, epileptics*. Like men of God everywhere they differed from the rest of the people in behavior, dress, and speech. They wore a hairy mantle (Zech. 13:4), and a leather-girdle (II Kings 1:8). It was not unusual for them to appear bruised and bleeding (Zech. 13:6; I Kings 20:35). . . . They were popularly regarded as madmen and fools (II Kings 9:11; Hos. 9:7; Jer. 29:26). But this madness had its method; it made an impression and inspired fear as well as scorn. Notwithstanding the prophet's madness, the people believed and feared him.*

Let us now consider the points made in this exposition:

1. Do not many rabbis, ministers, priests, and monks to this day differ "from the rest of the people in behavior, dress ["men of the cloth"], and speech"? Priests, according to biblical law, were subject to special rules and regulations. According to Maimonides, "just as a sage is recognized by his wisdom and moral principles which distinguish him from other people, so he ought to be recognized in all his activities, in his food and drink, . . . in his talk, walk, dress. . . ."

2. Nor is the wearing of a hairy mantle or a leather girdle a sign of disturbed mentality. The use of linen came later than the use of wool, and garments made of goatskin or camel's hair were probably worn by people who were averse to modern customs. Anchorites often wore a tunic made of goatskin or camel's hair. Members of certain monastic orders are prescribed similar garments to this day.†

---

*Kaufmann, *The Religion of Israel* (Eng.; Chicago, 1960), p. 275. Italics mine, A.J.H.

†The use of haircloth as a sign of mourning is frequently mentioned, e.g., II Sam. 3:31; II Kings 6:30; Ps. 30:11. In Jonah 3:6–8 it is a sign of repentance; see also Amos 8:10. Of Esau we are told that all his body was like a hairy mantle (Gen. 25:25).

3. Self-mutilation is spoken of as a practice peculiar to the prophets of Baal, from whom Elijah very sharply distinguishes himself (I Kings 18:28). In another, often misunderstood, narrative (I Kings 20:35–47) it is reported that a prophet, at God's behest, said to his friend: "Strike me!" This strange action (which was not the same thing as self-mutilation) can scarcely be classified as a symptom of insanity or as a technique of bringing about ecstatic frenzy. The prophet wished to be bruised so that he "could face the king with his example as martyr to the word of God."*

The scars or wounds on the back of "the prophet," of which Zechariah (13:3–6) speaks, are often regarded as stigmata typical for the character of Israelite prophecy. "The Israelite ecstatics cut and hew themselves with knives and swords just like the ecstatics of other cults in Syria and Asia Minor."† However, Zechariah's illustration intends to set forth most strikingly the complete revulsion to prophetic pretenders, filled with "the unclean spirit," which would take place in the popular feeling. The evil spirit which had stirred up so many pretenders should be so radically exorcised that pretension to divine inspirations would prove a sure path to ruin. The scars are inflicted as signs of condemnation and punishment. (Cf. Num. 25:8).‡

4. Let us analyze the passages in which the prophet is called a madman.

> The days of punishment have come,
> The days of recompense have come;
> Israel shall know it.
> The prophet is a fool,
> The man of the spirit is mad,
> Because of your great iniquity
> And great hatred.
>
> *Hosea 9:7*

If this passage is taken as an affirmation that the prophet is a madman, then it must also be taken as an affirmation and confession by Hosea

---

*J. A. Montgomery, *The Books of Kings* (New York, 1951), p. 325.
†G. Hölscher, *Die Profeten* (Leipzig, 1914), p. 19.
‡See C. H. H. Wright, *Zechariah and His Prophecies* (London, 1879), pp. 418 f.

that he is a fool. The passage is, on the contrary, a repudiation by Hosea of any such impression that his extremely bitter pronouncements might have evoked in the people.

Shemaiah of Nehelam, one of those self-styled "prophets" whom Jeremiah had publicly condemned as liars, addressed a letter to the chief overseer of the Temple, asking him why he did not rebuke Jeremiah "who is prophesying to you," since it was his duty to put "every madman who prophesies in the stocks and collar" (Jer. 29:24 ff.). The use of the word "madman" here reveals, indeed, the hatred of Shemaiah and his indignation at Jeremiah's defamation of the "prophets," but certainly it is of no significance in explaining the mentality of Jeremiah. The same applies to the question which the commander of the army of the Northern Kingdom was asked by his servants: "Why did this mad fellow come to you?" (2 Kings 9:11.)

It is not at all correct to base one's conclusions on the opinion of the people who were accustomed to view the prophets as madmen, and thus to infer from them the abnormal nature of the prophetic consciousness. People like to think of men of genius as madmen, and to see in every form of possession and rapturous emotion a mysterious disturbance of the mind.

> *Demens judicio vulgi,*
> *Sanus fortasse tuo.*
>
> *Mad in the judgment of the mob,*
> *Sane perhaps in yours.*
> Horace, *Satires,* Bk. I, 6.

The impression a person makes upon other people is hardly to be taken as a completely reliable diagnosis. Hannah, when praying before the Lord, "was speaking in her heart; only her lips moved, and her voice was not heard" (Judg. 1:12)—and she was taken by the priest Eli for a drunken woman. In the eyes of society everywhere any person who refuses ever to compromise with mediocrity, commonplace, self-approval, is considered mentally awry, half-crazy, a crackpot or monomaniac.

To Antiochus, the preference of the priest Eleazar and others to be tormented to death rather than to eat of the flesh of the swine was madness (IV Macc. 8:5; 10:13).

Aulus Gellius (d. c.e. 163) tells us that the famous grammarian Domitius of Rome was given the surname *Insanus,* the Madman, "because he was by nature rather difficult and churlish." Complaining about his contemporaries, he said: "There is absolutely no hope left of anything good, when even you distinguished philosophers care for nothing save words and the authority for words. . . . For I, a grammarian, am inquiring into the conduct of life and manners, while you philosophers are nothing but *mortualia,* or 'winding sheets.' "*

A major premise of the theory that the prophet was a psychopath is the view, often repeated, that "in Israel, as throughout antiquity, psychopathic states were valued as holy. Contact with madmen was still taboo in rabbinic times,"† and madness was commonly regarded in the East and therefore also in Israel "as a mark of contact with the divine (or the demonic) world."‡ But this view is unfounded; see above, p. 432. Evidence there is none; only occurrence in other cultures pleads in favor of this view. However, the underlying assumption of sweeping religious uniformity that would lend strength to such a view is rather precarious when applied in the study of the religion of Israel. Madness (*shiggaon*), far from being regarded as holy, is mentioned as one of the plagues with which Israel is threatened in the event of disobedience (Deut. 28:28; Zech. 12:4; I Sam. 20:30; 28:30; Dan. 4). References to insanity occur rarely (only two cases are mentioned in the Hebrew Bible)—which stands in sharp contrast to the preoccupation with the phenomena of madness and possession in Greek literature.§

---

*Attic Nights, XVIII, 7.* See also John 10:20; Acts 12:15.

†M. Weber, *op. cit.,* p. 288.

‡A. R. Johnson, *The Cultic Prophet in Ancient Israel* (Cardiff, 1944), p. 19.

§Cf. T. Hobbes, *Leviathan,* I, ch. 2: "The Romans in this held the same opinion with the Greeks, so also did the Jews; for they called madmen prophets or, according as they thought the spirits good or bad, demoniacs; and some of them called both prophets and demoniacs madmen; and some called the same man both demoniac and madman. But for the gentiles it is no wonder, because diseases and health, vices and

## RELATIVITY OF BEHAVIOR PATTERNS

The views cited above are based on the obsolete assumption that the fundamental psychology of human beings will everywhere be reflected by similar customary behaviors, or, conversely, that similar behaviors always have the same implications, regardless of the context in which they appear. Many anthropological studies have indeed failed to appreciate the profound dissimilarities in patterns of behavior and ways of thinking between ancient and modern man.* Cultural and spiritual distance is not easily conquered. Thus we must not hastily assume that symptoms of behavior regarded as neurotic in our society would be neurotic in ancient Israel. Neurosis and psychosis are concepts we form in terms of cultural patterns of our particular society. What is considered strange and abnormal according to the manners and conventions of the Western world in the twentieth century may be considered entirely proper and normal in southeast Asia in the same century.

Even if it were proved that the behavior of the prophets manifested symptoms of neurosis, the question would still remain open whether these symptoms were the results or the cause of their experi-

---

virtues, and many natural accidents were with them termed and worshiped as demons. So that a man was to understand by demon as well sometimes an ague as a devil. But for the Jews to have such opinion is somewhat strange. For neither Moses nor Abraham pretended to prophecy by possession of a spirit but from the voice of God or by a vision or dream; nor is there anything in his law, moral or ceremonial, by which they were taught there was any such enthusiasm or any possession. . . . Neither did the other prophets of the Old Testament pretend enthusiasm or that God spoke in them; but to them, by voice, vision, or dream; and the 'burthen of the Lord' (II Kings 9:25) was not possession but command. How then could the Jews fall into this opinion of possession?"

In Babylonia, mental disorder was attributed to the influence of evil spirits, and on this account the medical texts are frequently interspersed with incantation formulae. F. Delitzsch, *Mehr Licht* (Leipzig, 1907), p. 51, found it surprising that, though the Hebrews were surrounded by peoples more or less allied to them, who shared the Babylonian and Egyptian belief in demons and evil spirits, hardly a trace of such powers of darkness is evident in the religious literature of ancient Israel.

*A. Jeremias, *Juedische Froemmigkeit* (Leipzig, 1929), p. 53, infers the presence or danger of homosexualism from the fact that in their social gatherings the *hasidim* observe complete separation of the sexes.

ence. Neurosis will not make a person a prophet, just as malaria will not make him a millionaire. On the other hand, the manner in which the prophets dealt with the issues of their own time and the fact that the solutions they propounded seem to be relevant for all times have compelled people in every generation to repeat a commonplace: The prophets were among the wisest of all men. Their message being ages ahead of human thinking, it would be hard to believe in the normalcy of our own minds if we questioned theirs. Indeed, if such is insanity, then we ought to feel ashamed of being sane.

We must not try to interpret the experiences and attitudes of the great prophets in the pattern of our own scope of experience, in the image of our own attitudes and conceptions. To us it is inconceivable to go on living and not be aware of the outside world; to the prophets it is inconceivable to go on living and not be aware of the Creator of the world. What we think is due to mental disorder may have been due to a higher spiritual order. Whatever departs from the normal is not necessarily pathological. From the fact that the prophet exhibits features which differentiate him from the average we must not deduce any conclusions about his total personality.*

One should be surprised not to come upon "eccentricities" in the behavior of a prophet. Would one expect a human being of flesh and blood to remain robust, smug, and calm when overwhelmed by the presence of God? Is it possible to carry God's indignation without being crushed by the burden, to live through cruel frustrations and to sustain sublime expectations? And granted, unlikely as it is, that signs of sickness should be traced in the lives of the prophets, as indeed Nietzsche stated in his famous generalization, "It does not seem possible to be an artist and not to be sick," it would still be absurd to

---

*Tchaikovsky describes the state in which "a new idea awakens in me and begins to assume a definite form. I forget everything and behave like a madman. Everything within me starts pulsing and quivering. . . . If that condition of mind and soul, which we call inspiration, lasted long without intermission, no artist could survive it. The strings would break and the instruments be shattered into fragments." (Rosa Newmarch, *The Life and Letters of Peter Ilich Tchaikovsky* [London, 1906], pp. 274–275.) " 'There are moments when I lose the feeling of things around me,' said Debussy." (R. E. M. Harding, *op. cit.*, p. 9.)

reject their claim. Is it not more meaningful to maintain that a person has to be sick in order to see what those who are benighted by their robustness and complacency fail to perceive?*

## The Etymology of *Nabi*

The etymology and exact meaning of *nabi* and its verb forms, *nibba'*, hitnabbe', a matter of much dispute, remain obscure in some points. The verb seems to be connected with the Akkadian *nabū*, "to call."† *Nabi*, a passive like *māshiah*, "anointed one," *nathin*, "one given to the Temple as a servant," *'āsir*, "a prisoner," seems to denote a person who is the passive object of an action from without. *Nabi*, then, would mean, literally, one who is called (by God), one who has a vocation (from God), as well as one who is subject to the influence of a demon or a false god, and who retains the condition imposed upon him by that call or influence.

Corresponding to the meaning of the verb, "to call, to announce," *nabi* denotes a spokesman, a person charged with delivering a message and who speaks under the authority of someone else.‡ Moses, on refusing to go before Pharaoh, is referred to his brother Aaron, who is to speak in his name. Hence Aaron is called Moses' *nabi*, prophet (Exod. 7:1).§

However, this meaning, which implies a mode of communication

---

*See A. J. Heschel, *God in Search of Man*, pp. 223 f.

†H. Torczyner, *Zeitschrift der Deutschen Morgenlaendischen Gesellschaft*, LXXXV (1931), 322. W. F. Albright, *From the Stone Age to Christianity* (Baltimore, 1940), pp. 231 f., stresses the Akkadian connection and maintains that it denotes one who has been "called" by God to communicate the divine will.

‡The verb in Old Arabic likewise denotes "to speak out," "to speak for another; and in Ethiopic, "to call," "to proclaim," "to speak." According to Moses Ibn Ezra, *Shirath Israel*, B. Halper, trans. (Berlin, 1924), p. 44, *nabi* derived from the root *nba*, which means in Arabic "to inform," because he informs in the name of God what is revealed to him secretly. In another instance, this noun is derived from the root *nb'a*, which means rising and being lifted.

§Onkelos renders *nabi* here with "interpreter." According to Rashi, *Commentary, ad loc.*, wherever this term is mentioned it refers to a man who publicly proclaims and utters to the people words of reproof.

or relation between the prophet and God, does not seem to be adequate as an explanation of the verbal forms *hithnabbe'* and *nibba'* in Hebrew. These denominative verbs seem to connote a mode of behavior, a special intensity or state of the prophet in the moment of conveying or uttering the message. This is why some scholars have suggested that there was a connection with the stem *naba'a,* which means "to bubble up," "to flow." But this view rightly failed to gain acceptance.

It is clear that the verbs denote not only the claim—to utter words in the name of God—but also the state in which the words are uttered. The prophet hardly spoke as an impartial, calm, detached messenger in a state of tranquility. He spoke in intense excitement, in inner identification with the pathos and intensity of the message itself. But such sympathy or emotional solidarity has only superficial resemblance with frenzy or genuine ecstasy. This applies equally to the moments in which inspiration came to the prophet.*

Abraham is called a *nabi* (Gen. 20:7) although he does not prophesy, but he knows of Abimelech's dream. Eldad and Medad prophesy (Num. 11:25). In Num. 12:6 God speaks to the *nabi* in a dream. In Deut. 13:1, 5 the *nabi* is placed on the same level as the dreamer of dreams. Moses is called *nabi* only after his death (Deut. 34:10). Samuel is consistently called seer (*ro'eh*), not prophet (I Chron. 9:22; 26:28; 29:29).

It is far from certain that the verb *hitnabbe'* means "to behave in an uncontrolled manner." The verb simply means "to act as *nabi*" (I Sam. 10:5, 6, 10, 13) and is applied to the wild prophets of Baal (I Kings 18:28 f.) and to the unbalanced King Saul (I Sam. 18:10; 19:24).†

The word "prophet," used to translate the Hebrew *nabi,* is a Greek word, *prophetes.* In the classical period it denoted a person who disclosed or spoke forth to others the thought of a god; a person who

---

*A. Guillaume, *Prophecy and Divination* (New York, 1938), pp. 112 f., suggested that the Hebrew *nabi* denotes a person who is in the state of announcing a message which has been given to him. Cf. H. H. Rowley, *op. cit.,* pp. 96 ff.

†H. H. Rowley, *op. cit.,* p. 97.

spoke for a god, an interpreter, as Tiresias was of Zeus, Orpheus of Bacchus, Apollo of Zeus, the Pythia of Apollo. In later times it was applied especially to those who expounded the unintelligible oracles of the Pythia of Delphi or the rustling of the leaves of Dodona. In a metaphorical sense it was used of poets as interpreters of gods or Muses.

The etymology of *prophetes* is uncertain. It is not clear whether the fix "pro" means "out of" or "fore." Since prophecies constantly dealt with future events, the notion developed of prophecy being essentially prediction.* From the vocabulary of Greek religion the word was adapted by the Hellenistic Jews and the Septuagint to render the Hebrew *nabi* (pl. *nebiim*). The Greek word was adopted in Latin as *propheta,* chiefly in postclassical times under Christian influences, and from ecclesiastical Latin it passed into modern European languages. In actual usage, the idea conveyed by the word "prophet" never quite corresponded with its historical prototype.

Even the Hebrew word *nabi* is not free of ambiguity. Applied as it is in the Bible indiscriminately to the prophets of the Lord (I Kings 18:4, 13; 19:10, 14), to the 450 prophets of Baal (I Kings 18:19, 22, 25, 40), to the four hundred prophets of the goddess Asherah (I Kings 18:19), as well as to the so-called false prophets "who prophesy lies . . . the deceit of their own heart" (Jer. 23:26).

## Transcendence Is Its Essence

The error in the psychological approach has been in its prejudgment; it has denied in advance that which it is supposed to explore. Thus, instead of elucidating the prophetic experience, it has tried to explain it away.

Consistent with its view of the inner life as a continuum or as a process, it has tried to regard prophetic inspiration as the continuation of a process that started in the imagination or in the subconscious. It has tried to explain it as the product of the personal experiences of the

---

*E. Fascher, *Prophetes* (Giessen, 1927), pp. 206, 148.

prophet, scenes, passions, tension, frustrations; to trace it back to what is called complexes. Prophecy, then, was merely a way of making peculiar connections between the different elements of the prophet's experience, a unique organization of the impulses which his sensations aroused.

While it is true that personal factors and psychic dispositions influence the prophet's experience, it is precisely the ability to stand above all personal dispositions, inclinations, and vested interests that marks the essence of prophetic consciousness.

What is the factor that makes a person a prophet? Is prophecy due to psychological repressions of instinctual needs? Should we assume that, being a failure in society, the prophet invents stories of occult experiences? Or that thwarted in the external world, he takes refuge in his own dream world?

Prophecy, like art, is not an outburst of neurosis, but involves the ability to transcend it when present. It is not simply self-expression, but rather the expression of an ability to rise far above the self or personal needs. Transcendence is its essence. The significance, therefore, is not in the presence of neurosis, but in what a person does with it; one person may end in an asylum, another become an artist. Neurosis should be regarded as that which challenges an artist rather than as that which makes him an artist. It was not Isaiah who produced prophecy; it was prophecy which produced Isaiah.

## THE PROPHETS ARE MORALLY MALADJUSTED

The prophet is a person who suffers from a profound maladjustment to the spirit of society, with its conventional lies, with its concessions to man's weakness. Compromise is an attitude the prophet abhors. This seems to be the implication of his thinking: Compromise has corrupted the human species. All elements within his soul are insurgent against indifference to aberrations. The prophet's maladaptation to his environment may be characterized as *moral madness* (as distinguished from madness in a psychological sense).

The mind of the prophet, like the mind of a psychotic, seems to live in a realm different from the world which most of us inhabit. Yet what distinguishes the two psychologically is most essential. The prophet claims to sense, to hear, and to see in a way totally removed from a normal perception, to pass from the actual world into a mysterious realm, and still be able to return properly oriented to reality and to apply the content of his perception to it. While his mode of perception may differ sharply from the perceptions of all other human beings, the ideas he brings back to reality become a source of illumination of supreme significance to all other human beings. Once the psychotic crosses the threshold of sanity to take refuge in a world of his imagination, he finds it difficult to return to reality, if to return he wishes. The delusions and hallucinations to which he is subjected can in no way be relevant to the lives of those who are not disoriented.

## LIMITS OF PSYCHOLOGY

It is not for any psychological analysis, nor for any sociological or anthropological reasoning, however profound and imaginative, however patient and exact, to have the last word about the nature of prophecy. Such analysis or reasoning is prone to reduce prophecy to a commonplace too irrelevant to justify the effort of analysis. And yet the phenomenon of the prophets continues to remain provocative, alarmingly relevant despite its incomprehensibility.

The claim that there are no significant questions so profound that they cannot be solved by exact sciences raises a question that seems to defy solution: How does one account for the dogmatic and monstrous presumption implied in such a claim?

In the mystery of prophecy we are in the presence of the central story of mankind. So many of the ideas that count ultimately, so many of the moments we cherish supremely, we owe to the prophets. In decisive hours of history it dawns upon us that we would not trade certain lines in the book of Isaiah for the Seven Wonders of the World.

One must not rule out the possibility that either the perception or the enunciation of the prophetic word was accompanied by excitation. The prophet was an intensely passionate man, and both the contents of his message and the nature of his perceptions were hardly conducive to placidity. It is sympathy with God that characterizes the total personality of the prophet, his inner state as manifested in his utterances, a state not limited to some moments, but affecting all his existence.

# 13

# Explanations of
# Prophetic Inspiration

### OUT OF HIS OWN HEART

In the profound embarrassment caused by the prophets' claim to have received the word of God, persistent efforts have been made to interpret that claim in a way which would take from it all element of mystery. It is one thing to reject the prophets' claim to inspiration; it is quite another to conclude from the prophets' own words that what they called inspiration was really an act of their own imagination. Stealthily this is what Spinoza did in advancing his own theory of prophecy, while maintaining that whatever can be said concerning prophecy must be concluded from Scripture.

Denying the uniqueness of the Hebrew Bible, he maintained that the superiority of Israel consisted, not in any special relation of God to the people or in any religious vocation, but in "their successful conduct in matters pertaining to government," in their social organization and the good fortune they enjoyed for many years. Their relation to God was not different from that of any other nation. The Israelites, we are told, held very ordinary ideas about God, and it is hardly likely that Moses should have taught them anything beyond a rule of right living. Indeed, "scriptural doctrine contains no lofty speculations nor philosophic reasoning, but only very simple matters, such as could be understood by the slowest intelligence. I should be surprised if I found [the prophets] teaching any new speculative doctrine which was not a commonplace to Gentile philosophers." "Thus to suppose that wisdom and knowledge of spiritual and natural things can be gained from the prophets' books, is to be utterly mistaken."

Spinoza furthermore expanded the notion of revelation in order to deny it. All ideas, true or false, must in one sense be "revelations," inasmuch as all knowledge, like anything else, is from "God." Thus, ordinary knowledge acquired by natural faculties has as much right as any prophetic knowledge to be called divine. The prophet has no peculiar source or means of knowledge, and there is nothing supernatural about prophecy. A revelation consists of the prophet's own thought, and is from "God" only in the sense that the prophet himself is "God," namely a part of *deus sive natura.**

Schleiermacher, often called the father of modern Protestant theology, and in his doctrine of God greatly indebted to Spinoza, not only remained entangled in many of the prejudices of the Rationalist school in respect to the prophets, but also harbored an unflinching bias against the Hebrew Bible.† The great exponent of the theory that Christianity was not a body of doctrine but a condition of the heart, a mode of consciousness making itself known in devout feeling, failed to sense any special consciousness in the prophets of Israel and limited their theological import to their universal ethical-religious convictions. He finds that the prophets' predictions were of two kinds. One kind was directed to particular events, and the ideas and views thus expressed were derived from general principles, namely, from "the two chief concepts of Jewish religion, the divine election of the Jewish people and divine retribution." "These utterances were for the most part hypothetical." The other kind was messianic prediction, and it spoke "of the future of God's true messenger which involved the end of the two Jewish conceptions of retribution and election."‡ "This is

---

* *Tractatus Theologico-Politicus,* chs. I–III.

† F. Schleiermacher, *The Christian Faith* (Edinburgh, 1922), par. 132, 1; par. 27, 3; par. 12, 1–3.

‡ *Ibid.,* 103, 3.

the real significance of messianic prophecies, wherever they appear and in however obscure presentiments they are shrouded: they disclose to us a striving of human nature towards Christianity."* "What is revelation? Every original and new communication of the Universe to man is a revelation. . . . What is inspiration? It is simply the general expression for the feeling of true morality and freedom."†

The prophets' claims to inspiration became increasingly strange if not preposterous to modern man. Curiously, even the poet Blake, to whom mystical visions were familiar, was inclined to deny to the prophets the claim to the experience of the divine.

"The Prophets Isaiah and Ezekiel dined with me," relates William Blake in *The Marriage of Heaven and Hell*, "and I asked them how they dared so roundly to assert that God spoke to them; and whether they did not think at the time that they would be misunderstood, and so be the cause of imposition?" To which Isaiah answered: "I saw no God nor heard any, in a finite organical perception; but my senses discover'd the Infinite in everything, and as I was then persuaded and remained confirm'd that the voice of honest indignation is the voice of God, I cared not for consequences, but wrote." The view Blake supposedly heard from Isaiah he must have read first in the popular literature of his time in which the prophets' claim was described as an invention.

The certainty that there is no supernatural element in the prophets became a principle of major importance to critical scholarship. "So long as we derive a separate part of Israel's religious life directly from God, and allow the supernatural or immediate revelation to intervene in even one single point, so long also our view of the whole continues to be incorrect. . . . It is the supposition of a natural development alone which accounts for all phenomena."‡

---

* *Ibid.*, 14, 3.
†F. Schleiermacher, *On Religion*, J. Oman, trans. (New York, 1958), p. 89.
‡A. Kuenen, *The Prophets and Prophecy in Israel* (London, 1877), p. 585. Cf. L. Dietsel, *Geschichte des Alten Testaments in der Christlichen Kirche* (Jena, 1869), pp. 627 ff.

## THE SPIRIT OF THE AGE

Owing to a bias against any experience that eludes scientific inquiry, the claim of the prophets to divine inspiration was, as we have seen, *a priori* rejected. Regarding them as no more than great moral teachers, with a noble zeal and profound conviction of the moral purpose and government of men, it was assumed that their correct insight into the truth that national sin would bring about a national disaster was derived from their vivid apprehension of the principle of righteousness. Little, if any, importance was attached to the prophets' own insistence on having received "the word of God" and on having been called by Him.

History has shown us how men are influenced in their thinking and feeling by "the spirit of the age" in which they live. In the age in which the prophets lived, the belief was common that the deities revealed themselves to men. The prophets' claims, then, were due to their being subject to the common religious limitations of their age, and are signs rather of their human weakness than of any guidance by a higher power. "In its essence prophecy is neither magical nor unnatural, but a conviction of a really moral religious nature." Prophecy, then, is defined as "the prophets' application to the future, of his certainty as to the eternal laws of the Divine Being and Will and as to the final goal of salvation. . . . This certainty can of itself arise quite as well in a condition of spiritual excitement and enthusiasm, as in the tranquil course of spiritual meditation."* At one time after long reflection and by gradual development; at another, suddenly and apparently without preparation, some great thought comes before his soul with such vividness and power that in this moment of conception his creative mind already bears within it, in its fully completed state, the work on which he may perhaps still have to labor for years.†

"Prophecy, from this point of view, may be defined as a system of thought *(a)* intended to lift the people to an ethical conception

---

*H. Schultz, *Old Testament Theology*, I (Edinburgh, 1898), 282.
†E. Graf, *Studien und Kritiken* (Paris, 1859), no. 2, p. 272.

of the Deity; *(b)* advocated by men of various degrees of moral and intellectual attainment, some of whom were fanatics, others men of great spiritual endowment; *(c)* including coarse and extravagant pictures of the people's sins, and varied by prognostications of the future which were more likely to prove false than true."*

In more recent times the view has been expressed that

> the Prophet was in some sort a spiritual scientist. It was his province to study the mind of God in His dealings with men. He had to discover the divine attitude towards human relationships, an attitude expressed not in an arbitrary system of rewards and punishments, but in a reasonable chain of cause and effect. To him was granted the insight, born of direct communication with God, to see with startling clarity that a given type of conduct, still more a given attitude of the soul, carried within itself the seeds of prosperity and disaster. . . . Crime and penalty are not two distinct and separable facts—they are one and the same, seen merely from different angles and on different sides. It was from this knowledge of the law that the prophet was able to predict the future. An astronomer who is familiar with the "law" of gravitation can foretell for thousands of years the exact movement of the heavenly bodies. A chemist will state with unfailing accuracy the reaction which will take place when certain substances are combined. In just the same way the Prophet, an earnest and faithful student of God's laws in religion and ethics, will state with equal accuracy the issue of social condition or a spiritual attitude.†

We are told at the same time that "men like Amos and Jeremiah were not readily distinguishable by their contemporaries from the Ecstatics, whose symptoms resembled those of the epileptic or even the insane."

The premise must be granted: It is always easy to fall victim to

---

*W. R. Harper, *The Prophetic Element in the Old Testament* (Chicago, 1905), p. 15, who cites Spinoza, Hitzig, Renan, and, with some reservations, Kuenen, as representatives of this view.

†Th. H. Robinson, *Prophecy and the Prophets* (London, 1923), pp. 46 f., 36.

an illusion. Yet, why did "the spirit of the age" produce no prophets in Assyria and Babylonia, among the Phoenicians or Canaanites? Knowing the old Oriental literature as we do today, it is easy to imagine how the life and letters of ancient Israel might have been had no prophets arisen.

When the northern neighbors of Israel, the Moabites, were engaged in a war and their king, Mesha, saw that the battle was going against him, "he took his eldest son who was to reign in his stead, and offered him for a burnt offering upon the wall" (II Kings 3:27). Israel's kings, Ahaz and Manasseh, too, sacrificed their sons as offerings "according to the abominable practices of the nations" (II Kings 16:3; 21:6). If the prophets were inspired by "the spirit of the age," why did they express horror at such acts of "supreme piety"? Why was not the worship of the God of Israel like the worship of Baal or Tammuz?

Indeed, the nature of the Bible is precisely something which is not consistent with everything else we know about the historical circumstances under which it evolved. It would have been more consistent with our general understanding had the great religious insights been given to the sages of Egypt or Athens rather than to a homeless people roaming and starving in the wilderness of the Sinai peninsula. The wonder of the Bible is against all human expectations, and if it had not been for the book's apparent spiritual glory and for the inexplicable power of human faith, it would have been rejected as absurd and unlikely.*

## A LITERARY DEVICE

Another view regards the prophets' claim to have received a divine call as a literary device;† their utterances were the product of a free, spontaneous decision rather than the result of a divine call.‡ Even the visions described by the prophets do not represent experiences,

---

*See A. J. Heschel, *God in Search of Man* (New York, 1955), pp. 230 f.
†Redslob, *Der Begriff des Nabi* (1839), p. 29.
‡W. Knobel, *Der Prophetismus der Hebraeer*, I (Breslau, 1837), 14, 40.

but rather literary devices, forms of imaginative writing.* They are "only a poetic dress consciously adopted, that is to say, poetry is purposely employed in order to present a spiritual truth clearly to the people in the form in which they understand and like. . . . In such cases, therefore, the revelations are not conceived in the imagination as pictures, but are recombined by it into pictures. They are akin to the parable."†

"Not seldom, when a prophet utters the words 'Thus saith the Lord' his meaning might be expressed in a modern way, 'It is my profound conviction that such and such is God's thought (or will or purpose).' "‡ The very phrase "the word of God," which the prophets so often make use of, is a metaphor, the child of intense religio-ethical feeling, the highest and boldest poetic expression.§

The source of the prophet's utterances, we are told, is his own mind. Moses' "prophetic career may be traced back directly to spiritual curiosity. . . . Interest, then, is the factor which most truly portrays the nature of inspiration. . . . It is the persistent and intense interest in God and spiritual reality that moves the prophetic nature to secure results." Elijah's still, small voice was "clearly the result of original meditation," while "the manner in which Jeremiah expressed his inspiration is illustrative of the general prophetic habit to sublimate the facts of their inspiration. This deliberate subtilization of inspirational power does not mark some very extraordinary and unusual manner of divine communication between the deity and prophet, but rather it tends to cover up the commonplace nature of inspiration, or at any rate, to conceal the prophet's own psychological ignorance of the source of his prophetic calling."‖ The prophet is simply a person

---

*A. Kuenen, quoted by A. Lods, *The Prophets and the Rise of Judaism* (London, 1937), pp. 61 ff.

†H. Schultz, *Old Testament Theology,* I (Edinburgh, 1898), pp. 278 f. Similarly, K. Cramer, *Amos* (Stuttgart, 1930), pp. 207, 215.

‡R. S. Cripps, *A Critical and Exegetical Commentary on the Book of Amos* (London, 1929), p. 79.

§P. Schwartzkopff, *Die prophetische Offenbarung* (Giessen, 1896), p. 96.

‖H. C. Ackerman, "The Nature of Hebrew Prophecy," *Anglican Theological Review,* IV (1921–22), 97–127.

of mental alertness and breadth, ethical depth and religious exaltation, who has "a conscious intuition of truth."*

Is it plausible to regard an utterance such as "thus says the Lord" or "the word of the Lord is like a burning fire in my bones" as a literary device?† Is it historically correct to regard the prophet as a demagogue who did not hesitate to condemn others for proclaiming words in the name of God which were born in their own minds, while he himself was using the same device?

## A TECHNIQUE OF PERSUASION

And this, too, is a theory: The prophets, like the philosophers of Greece, arrived at their insights by speculation or intuition, but in their desire to impress the people with their authority, they invented a story about revelation. The distinct theological features, the references to the divine origin of their insights, are the result of subsequent literary elaboration.‡ The prophets were poets who "invested their narratives about the past with the form of a prediction of the future."§ Out of a desire to impress the people and to bring about a moral or spiritual improvement, and realizing that only a message bearing the stamp of the divine would be effective with their contemporaries, the prophets ascribed their insights to God. *Finis sanctificat media.* Ezekiel's ability to tell in Babylonia what happened in Jerusalem at the exact moment it happened, and to foretell political events, is explained by asserting that "the entire first part of his book, that is chapters 1–31, are not real prophecies but are only disguised as such. They are,

---

*D. E. Thomas, "The Psychological Approach to Prophecy," *American Journal of Theology*, XVII (1914), 255.

†See F. Giesebrecht, *Die Berufungsbegabung der alttestamentlichen Propheten* (Göttingen, 1897); O. Eissfeldt, "Das Berufungsbewusstsein als theologisches Gegenwartsproblem," *Theologische Studien und Kritiken*, CVI (1934–35), 124–156; A. Weiser, *Die Profetie des Amos* (Giessen, 1929), pp. 296 f.

‡P. Schwarzkopff, *op. cit.*, p. 98.

§N. G. Eichhorn, *Einleitung in das Alte Testament;* cf. Dienstfertig, *Die Prophetologie* (Erlangen, 1892), p. 1; G. W. Meyer, *Geschichte der Schrifterklärung*, II (Göttingen, 1802 ff.), 401; H. Ewald, *Die Propheten des Alten Bundes*, I (Stuttgart, 1840), 54 ff.; A. Krochmal, *Theologie der Zukunft* (Lemberg, 1872), pp. 42 f.

without exception, *vaticinia post eventum*," a prediction uttered in full knowledge of what had already happened. The same opinion is held in regard to the "prophecies" of Second Isaiah.*

So, also, Hosea married Gomer with no intention of prophecy, expecting a happy marriage. "Then, when he realized that he was not holding the affections of Gomer, he rationalized his inferiority complex, his jealousy, and his desire for revenge, by recognizing in his experience the hand of God. Therefore he understood his wish for Gomer as the word of God and in her unfaithfulness found the text for his first preaching."†

Machiavelli praised the Romans because they understood how to make religion politically useful. They always availed themselves of religion in reforming their state, in prosecuting their wars, and in fomenting tumults. As an example of great political wisdom he cites Numa Pompilius (the second king of Rome, traditionally 715–673 B.C.E.) "who feigned that he held converse with a nymph, who dictated to him all that he wished to persuade the people to do. . . . In truth, there never was any remarkable lawgiver amongst any people who did not resort to divine authority."‡

No one acquainted with the spiritual rigorism and lack of self-righteousness of the prophets could conceivably ascribe to them such a way of thinking. Could a man like Isaiah, who felt shattered by the overwhelming power of God's holiness, have fabricated a story like the one of his vision (ch. 6)? The fear of God was too constricting to allow the prophets to take the name of God in vain. Is this not the gist of all their thoughts: Above all, God abhors deceit.

Is it conceivable that men who placed God's demand for righteousness even above the interests of their own country and above the glory of their own sanctuary—and who condemned the lie as a fundamental evil—should have lived by a lie?

---

*M. Buttenwieser, "The Date and Character of Ezekiel's Prophecies," *HUCA*, VII (1930), 7; cf. p. 6, n. 15.

†O. Sellers, "Hosea's Motives," *American Journal of Semitic Languages*, XLI (1924–25), 243–247.

‡*Discourses*, Bk. I, ch. 11.

Moreover, prophecy was not an episode in the life of a few individuals, and it would be most fantastic to assume that, generation after generation, men of highest passion for truth, of deepest contempt for sham, all schemed and conspired to deceive the people of Israel. Did Moses pray for a company of connivers when he said, "Would that all the people were prophets"?*

It requires something more than the magic of pretension to have the power to overwhelm men of all ages with the earnestness of one's claim. Can there be any doubt about the intensity of the prophet's certainty? Many of our own convictions seem faint and timid compared with this certainty.

## CONFUSION

According to yet another view, the prophets' claims must be explained as the result of their inability to analyze their inner life correctly, of their mistaking a feeling born in the heart for an idea bestowed upon them from without. Prophecy, then, was the result of mental confusion. Here are typical examples of such an explanation. Prophetic visions were due to hyperaemia of the covering membrane of the brain, to the influence of toxic substances or to anemia of the brain; they are to be regarded as hallucinations, resulting from the combination of normal perceptions and wistfulness (*gruebelnde Gedanken.)*[†] All prophetic vision is finally the rectilinear continuation of a process, the ultimate foundation of which is in the normal activity of the imagination.[‡]

As we have seen earlier, the prophets asserted that many of their experiences were not moments of passive receptivity, or mere listening to a voice, but dialogues with God, and in recording their experiences they clearly distinguished between the words they heard and the words they uttered (Amos 7:2–9; Mic. 7:1–10; Isa. 6:5–12; Jer. 1:6–14). Does not this fact testify to their ability for discernment?

*See *God in Search of Man,* pp. 227 f.
[†]G. Hölscher, *Die Profeten* (Leipzig, 1914).
[‡]Hänel, *Das Erkennen Gottes bei den Schriftpropheten* (Berlin, 1923), p. 92.

Moreover, circumstances compelled the prophets clearly to discern between the voice of the heart and the voice of God. Something happened:

> *An appalling and horrible thing*
> *Has come to pass in the land:*
> *The prophets prophesy falsely,*
> *And the priests rule at their beck.*
> *And my people love to have it so.*
> *Jeremiah 5:31*

Jeremiah, for example, did not question the sincerity of the so-called false prophets. He condemned them for mistaking "a dream" for a divine message. For thus says the Lord: "I have heard what the prophets have said, those who prophesy lies in My name, saying, I have dreamed, I have dreamed. How long shall this be? . . . The prophet who has a dream, let him tell a dream; and he who has a word, let him speak My word faithfully, says the Lord. . . . Is not My word like fire? says the Lord; and like a hammer which breaks the rock in pieces?" (Jer. 23:25–29.)

It is beyond doubt that men like Jeremiah and Ezekiel manifested a critical attitude toward prophecy by false prophets. They condemned "the false prophets who prophesy out of their own heart" (Ezek. 13:17). For thus said the Lord: "You say: the Lord saith, and I have not spoken" (Ezek. 13:7), "the [false] prophets prophesy lies in My name: I sent them not, neither have I commanded them, neither spoke I unto them: they prophesy unto you a lying vision, divination, a thing of nought, the deceit of their own heart" (Jer. 14:14). Since they argued not only against the ideas but primarily against the false prophets' claim to have received the word of God, they must have had a criterion for distinguishing between experience and illusion. There are always imitators, but the worth of the genuine is never impaired by the abundance of imitation and forgery.

The word of the prophets was not proclaimed to a gullible, primitive society. The people of Israel, who felt the impact of the great neighboring civilization of Egypt and Babylonia, knew of the life and wisdom of other nations. They were far from being predisposed to accept the prophetic claim. The story of the prophets' activity is one of encountering constant rivalry, opposition, or disbelief. Had the story of prophecy been an invention of the biblical writer, it would have been a story of a people swept into faith by the power of prophecy. Instead, the opposition to the prophets is recorded with reckless honesty.

What gave the prophets the certainty that they witnessed a divine event and not a figment of their own imagination? The mark of authenticity of the divine character of revelation was not in outward signs, visible or sonorous; revelation did not hinge upon a particular sense perception, upon hearing a voice or seeing a light. A thunder out of a blue sky, a voice coming from nowhere, an effect without a visible cause, would not have been enough to identify a perception as a divine communication. Immense chunks of natural reality, showers of light thrust upon the mind, would, even if they were not phantasmagorial, manifest only a force of nature, not God.

This, it seems, was the mark of authenticity: the fact that prophetic revelation was not merely an act of experience, but an act of being an object of an experience, of being exposed to, called upon, overwhelmed, and taken over by Him who seeks out those whom He sends to mankind. Here it is not God who is an experience of man; it is man who is an experience of God.

## "A Very Simple Matter Indeed"

Jeremiah would impress upon his hearers, that God reveals himself not to the prophet alone, but to every individual—reveals himself immediately and unmistakably in the moral consciousness of each. . . .

Thus reduced to its essence, divested of all the miraculous features and supernatural accompaniments which the primitive mind had associated with it, prophetic inspiration seems a very simple matter indeed. Yet this view of inspiration was the view, not of Jeremiah alone, but of all the great literary prophets;

only Jeremiah being the most subjective and analytic of them, he naturally gave it the most reasoned out and definite expression. Amos, Hosea, Micah, Isaiah, Deutero-Isaiah, every one of them, there is evidence, when he spoke of revelation, meant the divine force or voice which he felt within his heart. None of them claimed anything else than the impulsion of this force, the authority of this voice. It was so simple, so elemental, so self-evident to them, that any particular explanation or demonstration would have seemed superfluous. They all refer to their inspiration in the most matter-of-fact way—God spoke to them. The earnest man of today might ponder over the initial mystery of man's moral consciousness—not so the prophets. For them it was no mystery, it was an *a priori* fact, the manifestation of God. It was the source from which they derived the moral vision and the moral energy, which constituted their prophetic gift. . . .

The great basic truths or principles of which they were cognizant through their moral consciousness, and which [constituted] their revelation from God, formed the centre and essence of their prophecy.*

## THE GENIUS OF THE NATION OR THE POWER OF THE SUBCONSCIOUS

Prophecy was also seen as a particular manifestation of a general power inherent in the human mind, characteristic of the great personality or hero. "The hero can be Poet, Prophet, King, Priest, or what you will, according to the kind of world he finds himself born into. I confess, I have no notion of a truly great man who could not be all sorts of men."† Prophet and genius are closely related. Just as the history of Greece shaped the Greek genius into sculptor and philosopher,

*M. Buttewieser, *The Prophets of Israel* (New York, 1914), pp. 150–152.
†T. Carlyle, *Heroes and Hero-Worship*, Lecture II.

and the history of Rome shaped the Roman genius into soldier and statesman, so the history of Israel shaped the Hebrew genius into prophet.*

Above all, it is the idea of the unconscious and later the subconscious that since the latter part of the nineteenth century has come to serve as a solution of the enigma of prophecy. William James proposed

> as an hypothesis, that whatever it may be on its *farther* side, the "more" with which in religious experience we feel ourselves connected is on its *hither* side the subconscious continuation of our conscious life. Starting thus with a recognized psychological fact as our basis, we seem to preserve contact with "science" which the ordinary theologian lacks. At the same time the theologian's contention that the religious man is moved by an external power is vindicated, for it is one of the peculiarities of invasions from the subconscious region to take on objective appearances, and to suggest to the Subject an external control. . . . This doorway into the Subject seems to me the best one for a science of religions, for it mediates between a number of different points of view. Yet it is only a doorway, and difficulties present themselves as soon as we step through it, and ask how far our transmarginal consciousness carries us if we follow it on its remoter side. Here the over-beliefs begin: here mysticism and the conversion-rapture and Vedantism and transcendental idealism bring in their monistic interpretations and tell us that the finite self rejoins the absolute self, for it was always one with God and identical with the soul of the world. Here the prophets of all the different religions come with their visions, voices, raptures, and other openings, supposed by each to authenticate his own peculiar faith.†

The prophet frequently has been regarded as an individual who brought to expression the collective genius of Israel.

*J. Kaplan, *The Psychology of Prophecy* (Philadelphia, 1908), pp. 68 ff.
†*The Varieties of Religious Experience* (London, 1911), pp. 512 ff.

If there is present in every human soul somewhat of the collective powers of the soul of his nation and of the soul of all mankind, nay, of the soul of the world; and if, in the matter of prophesying, as in every great matter of human life, the individual soul is immersed in the universal soul, in the great and universal meaning of nature and the world, and is thence born again with renovated powers; it is conceivable that, as the present is as substantially connected with the future as it is with the past, each individual soul may foresee not only its own future, but also that of its nation, nay, of all mankind. From the depths of the soul and from the creative power of God therein arise all great thoughts, all that is new or extraordinary, all that leads mankind toward its eternal destination.*

The prophetic vision is undoubtedly a creation of the subconscious mind, working uncontrolled by voluntary reflexion, and producing subjective images which have something of the vividness and reality of actual sense perception. . . . Whether, as Professor James taught, the sub-consciousness be open to the direct influx of the divine, or whether . . . it is but the lumberroom of the soul, . . . on either theory the revelation wells up from the hidden depth of his [the prophet's] being, and clothes itself in symbols before his inner eye.†

Was it then the subconscious that acted as a prompter in the experiences of the prophets? Did the Bible arise from the vortex of

---

*E. Lasaulx, *Die prophetische Kraft der menschlichen Seele in Dichtern und Denkern* (München, 1858), pp. 43 f. See G. F. Oehler, *Theology of the Old Testament* (New York, 1883), p. 483, n. 2. S. Dubnow, *Nationalism and History* (Philadelphia, 1958), p. 279, says that the spirit of the people became flesh in its noblest sons, i.e., the prophets.

†J. Skinner, *Prophecy and Religion* (Cambridge, 1922), pp. 11 ff. C. G. Carus (1789–1869), whose works are thoroughly influenced by Schelling, begins *Psyche* (Jena, 1846) with the statement: "The key to the knowledge of the essence of the conscious life of the soul lies in the realm of the unconscious." And Nietzsche in *Antichrist:* "We deny that something could be made perfect as long as it is made with consciousness." See O. Kandeleit, *Das Unbewusste als Keimstaette des Schoepferischen* (Basel, 1959), p. 16; S. Klink, *Das Prinzip des Unbewussten bei Carl Gustav Carus* (dissertation; Wuerzburg, 1933).

psychic power, generated by yearning and imagination? Such a view, while not questioning the integrity or sanity of the prophets, would stamp them as deceived deceivers; while not bringing us closer to an understanding of what really took place, it would merely substitute an enigma for the mystery. The subconscious is a hypothesis so wide and so vague that it is hardly more positively known to us than is the idea of the supernatural. How strange that the cunning demon of the subconscious, in spite of its omnipresence and relentless vitality, has not produced elsewhere works of such sublime power! The paths of imagination opened by mythologies were certainly unbounded, but where did they lead to? Where else did a divine idea sanctify history? Where else did the history of a people become sacred Scripture?

To assume that prophetic revelation was the expression of an urge, hidden in the heart of the prophet, of which he not only was unaware but to which he was resistant, would presuppose the action of a spiritual power so wise and so holy, that there would be no other name for it but God.*

## THE PROPHETS WERE FOREIGN AGENTS

The prophets have also been viewed as foreign agents or professional agitators. This is how the picture of an Isaiah or Jeremiah is painted: Kept on the payroll of the imperialist kings of Assyria and Babylonia, the prophet, who had access to the king of Judah, had the task of working for the interests of his masters, the kings of Assyria and Babylonia. The content of his speeches, which were delivered in the name of God, was in fact prepared for him in the Assyrian and Babylonian capitals. Elijah received his instructions from Tyre, Elisha from Damascus, Isaiah from Nineveh, and Jeremiah from Babylon.† Thus Amos did for Judah and Ahaz what Elisha once did for Jehu. As an aide *(Gefolgsmann)* of Ahaz, his aim had been to incite the people

*A. J. Heschel, *God in Search of Man*, p. 231.
†"Der Grosskönig unterhält in Jerusalem seine Aufpasser" and "Berufsmässige Agitatoren," Winckler and Zimmern, *Die Keilinschriften und das Alte Testament*, 3rd ed. (Leipzig, 1903), pp. 170 ff.

against Pekah and to win them over for the ideal union with Judah.*
Isaiah knew that behind the stirrings for independence there was
nothing but the desire on the part of those in power to divert the
attention of the discontented people from the true causes of the miserable situation of the country. It was this knowledge that determined
Isaiah's attitude to Assyria.†

Jeremiah's persistent advocacy of a "defeatist" policy has led
some historians to represent him as an agent of the Babylonian government who, under the cloak of religion and prophetic inspiration,
carried on an insidious propaganda in the interest of his country's
foes. In the words of the leading exponent of the general view of
prophecy on which this opinion rests:

> If a Jeremiah was consulted by the king about the line of
> conduct to be followed towards Nebuchadnezzar, the reason is
> not that he was a "prophet" or a wise man of any kind. As a
> man of property and influence and as one of the leaders of the
> Chaldean party, Jeremiah had communications with Babylon
> which enabled him to form a clearer judgment of the political
> situation than the king, who, surrounded by the anti-Babylonian
> and pro-Egyptian party, was not in a position to arrive at a clear
> decision. Standing outside the court-camarilla, Jeremiah as a
> *politician* had a more comprehensive outlook on international
> affairs, because he had the necessary diplomatic connexions,
> and was able to maintain uninterrupted intercourse with the
> influential Babylonian circles, whether in Babylon itself or in
> the immediate vicinity, where Samaria was already the seat of a
> Chaldean viceroy.‡

*H. Winckler, *Geschichte Israels in Einzeldarstellungen,* I (Leipzig, 1895), pp.
91, 95; E. Schrader, *Die Keilinschriften und das Alte Testament* (Berlin, 1903), p. 267.

†H. Winckler, *op. cit.,* pp. 108 f.; see W. Erbt, *Die Hebraeer* (Leipzig, 1906), pp.
134, 128 ff., 172 ff.

‡E. Schrader, *op. cit.,* p. 170, quoted in J. Skinner, *Prophecy and Religion: Studies
in the Life of Jeremiah* (Cambridge, 1955), p. 264. It has been suggested that Second
Isaiah stayed at the Persian headquarters in order to affect the king with his oracles; see
M. Haller, *Eucharistion für H. Gunkel,* I (Göttingen, 1923), pp. 272 ff.

The prophets were skillful politicians who understood how to dominate the people and the kings; sometimes, in fact, they were demagogues of the worst sort. Their interference helped to undermine the authority of the kingship, which alone could have preserved the state.*

## THE PROPHETS WERE PATRIOTS

It has often been maintained that the prophets were, above all, patriots, namely, men who loved their country and were zealously devoted to its interests; patriotism, indeed, was their compelling motivation. "Patriotism was the spirit of their speeches, and morality their purpose."† They have therefore been described as "above all, *political demagogues* (namely, speakers) and, on occasion, pamphleteers. . . . The predominant concern of the prophet was the destiny of the state and the people. This concern always assumed the form of emotional invectives against the overlords. It is here that the 'demagogue' appeared for the first time in the records of history, at about the period when the Homeric songs threw the figure of Thersites [an ugly, foul-tongued fellow, who rails at Agamemnon until beaten into silence by Odysseus]‡ into relief."§

This characterization tends to obscure the peculiar traits of prophetic consciousness. The fact that they were, above all, speakers is obvious. What requires elucidation is their own motivation and consciousness, and how they were regarded by their contemporaries. Their concern for the people was never detached from their concern for God.

The prophet does not regard himself as a spokesman for the peo-

*F. Delitzsch, *Die Grosse Täuschung* (Stuttgart, 1920–21).
†Herder, *Ueber Begeisterung, Erleuchtung, Offenbarung,"* Werke, XI (Stuttgart, 1852), 128. The conception of the prophets as patriots is maintained by N. Schmidt, ed., *Die Schriften des Alten Testaments in Auswahl* (Göttingen, 1915), II, 2, p. 327. G. Stosch, *Das Wesen der Inspiration* (Gütersloh, 1912), p. 222, asserts of the prophets: "Their religion was patriotic."
‡Homer, *Iliad*, II, 212 ff.
§M. Weber, *Ancient Judaism* (Chicago, 1952), pp. 267 ff.

ple. Even when calling for justice, mercy, or kindness to the poor, he does not do so in the capacity of a people's tribune. He never declares that the poor and oppressed have commissioned him to speak, or that the people's moral or political plight has directly occasioned his intervention to set matters right. He speaks at all times in the name of God.

Sheer attachment to the people does not make a person a prophet. What motivates the prophet is God's attachment to Israel, and Israel's failure to reciprocate. To save the country was the aim of their mission, but the mission itself was to re-establish the relationship between Israel and God. Naïve or vulgar patriotism pandering to the natural instincts of the masses, the attitude of "My country, right or wrong," was precisely what the prophets condemned. In a moment of extreme despondency, Jeremiah exclaimed: "O that I had in the desert a wayfarer's lodging place, that I might leave my people and go away from them!" (Jer. 9:1). There are moments when he is told by the Lord: "Do not pray for the welfare of this people" (Jer. 14:11); "Do not pray for this people, or lift up cry or prayer for them, and do not intercede with Me, for I do not hear you" (Jer. 7:16). Indeed, *vox populi*, at least during the lifetime of the prophets, seems to have questioned their loyalty to state and country. Amos and Jeremiah, for example, were decried as traitors and exposed to abuse and attack.

Pure patriotism may be an apt characterization of the so-called false prophets. These reassuring seers of good things were minions of monarchs and favorites of the people. The confidence with which they predicted peace, if it cannot be traced to their flattery of princes or to their corruptibility (Mic. 3:5), must have had its roots deep in the instincts and affections, in a certainty of divine protection for what normal man cares most about: life, country, security.

Samuel, Nathan, and Elijah had already declared that God was no patron of kings, and the great prophets uttered threats not only against kings, but against country and nation, thus challenging the conception of God as the unconditional protector and patron.*

---

*See F. Noetscher, *Die Gerechtigkeit Gottes bei den vorexilischen Schriftpropheten* (München, 1915), p. 93.

There is a prophetic ring in the words of Thomas Jefferson: "Indeed, I tremble for my country when I reflect that God is just."*

## DEROGATING THE PROPHETS

According to Renan, the prophet of the eighth century was

an open-air journalist, reciting his own article, adding to and often interpreting it by some symbolic act. His great object was to impress the people and to assemble a crowd. With that view, the prophet did not scruple to resort to any of the tricks which modern publicity believes to be its own invention. He placed himself in a well-frequented thoroughfare, usually near the gate of the city. Then, in order to secure a group of listeners, he made use of the boldest means to attract attention, simulated madness, employed neologisms and peculiar words, and displayed written placards (Isa. 8:1 ff.) which he carried with him. The group being formed, he declaimed his vibrating phrases, obtaining his effects at times by speaking in a familiar strain, at others by bitter jests. The type of popular preacher was created. Buffoonery, oddly associated with a vulgar exterior, was placed at the service of piety. The Neapolitan friar, an edifying variety of Punch and Judy, has also in some respects his prototype in Israel.†

G. P. Gooch writes:

Renan often declares that the Jews stood for religion as the Greeks for intellect; but though admitting that Israel owes them its historic importance, he finds as much to blame as to praise. Amos is sombre and narrow, passionately threatening the day of wrath, urging men to rend their hearts, not their garments (Joel 2:3). Hosea is like a preacher of the *Ligue* or a Puritan pamphleteer. Isaiah's reputation is largely due to his

---

*T. Jefferson, *Notes on the State of Virginia: Manners* (Boston, 1829).
†E. Renan, *History of the People of Israel*, II (Boston, 1896), 356 ff.

supposed authorship of the writings of the far greater genius who lived during the Exile. The prophet was the conscience of his people; but he was a publicist not less than a preacher, a politician not less than a theologian, a forerunner of Calvin, Knox and Cromwell. Renan cannot conceal his contempt for the shrill intolerance of Jeremiah, whom he pillories as one of the founders of religious persecution and an enemy of the Monarchy and the State. Ezekiel suggested the *"Chatiments"* of Victor Hugo and the social visions of Fourier. Exclusive pre-occupation with moral standards does not tend either to culture or to national strength, and the Prophets hastened the doom of a people who had in any case no talent for politics.*

They "established religion and ruined the state."†

---

* *History and Historians in the Nineteenth Century* (London, 1913), pp. 485 f. See also Hegel, *Early Theological Writings* (Chicago, 1948), pp. 203 f.

† L. F. Mott, *Ernest Renan* (New York, 1921), p. 423. For an interpretation of the political views of the prophets, see E. Troeltsch, *"Das Ethos der Hebräischen Prophe-ten"* in *Logos*, VI (1916–17), 1 ff., who suggested that the prophets' "political" views were utopian and inapplicable. A similar view was maintained by H. Gressmann, *Der Messias* (Göttingen, 1929), p. 238; see also M. Weber, *Ancient Judaism* (Glencoe, 1952), p. 275. For a criticism, see B. Kellermann, *Der ethische Monotheismus der Prophe-ten* (Berlin, 1917); K. Elliger, *"Prophet und Politik,"* ZAW, LIII (1935), 20 ff.

# 14

# Event and Experience

## THE CONSCIOUSNESS OF INSPIRATION

The certainty of being inspired by God, of speaking in His name, of having been sent by Him to the people, is the basic and central fact of the prophet's consciousness. Other people regard *experience* as the source of certainty; what singles out the prophet in the world of man is that to him *the source of his experience* is the source of his certainty. To his mind, the validity and distinction of his message lie in the origin, not only in the moment of his experience.

When Moses was challenged by the rebellion of Korah and his followers, he called for a miracle to prove his prophetic call. "Hereby you shall know that the Lord has sent me to do all these works, and that it has *not* been *out of my own mind*" (Num. 16:28). It was, first of all, this negative certainty—that the word they proclaimed was not the product of their own minds, that was fundamental to the consciousness of the prophet. It came to expression in the polemics against the prophetic pretenders, the false prophets who were again and again condemned as people who prophesy "a lying vision, worthless divination, the deceit of their own minds" (Jer. 14:14; cf. 23:26). "They speak visions of their own minds, not from the mouth of the Lord" (Jer. 23:16). This seems to have been a synonym for lying prophets: "those who prophesy out of their own minds" (Ezek. 13:2).

Militantly, Ezekiel proclaimed: "Thus says the Lord God, Woe to the foolish prophets who follow their own spirit, and have seen nothing! . . . They have spoken falsehood and divined a lie; they say, Says the Lord, when the Lord has not sent them, and yet they expect Him to fulfill their word. Have you not seen a delusive vision, and uttered a lying divination, whenever you have said, Says the Lord, although I have not spoken?" (Ezek. 13:3, 6–7; cf. 13:17.) "They have spoken in My name lying words which I did not command them" (Jer. 29:23). "Thus says the Lord concerning Shemaiah of Nethelam: Because Shemaiah has prophesied to you when I did not send him, and has made you trust in a lie, therefore thus says the Lord: Behold, I will punish Shemaiah . . ." (Jer. 29:31–32). And to Hananiah, Jeremiah said: "Listen, Hananiah, the Lord has not sent you, and you have made this people trust in a lie. Therefore, says the Lord, Behold, I will remove you from the face of the earth. This very year you shall die, because you have uttered rebellion against the Lord" (Jer. 28:15–16). "The Lord said to me: The prophets are prophesying lies in My name; I did not send them, nor did I command them or speak to them. They are prophesying to you a lying vision, worthless divination, and the deceit of their own minds" (Jer. 14:14).

In a variety of ways, in utterance and in action, the prophets stressed their staggering claim. It was such certainty of being inspired that enabled the prophet to proclaim again and again: "Thus says the Lord"; "Hear the word of the Lord" (Hos. 4:1; Isa. 1:10; 28:41; 39:5; Jer. 2:4; 7:2; 9:20; 29:20; Ezek. 13:2). Balaam could speak only the word which he believed the Lord to have "put in his mouth" (Num. 22:38; 24:12 f.).

To use such expressions without being inspired was condemned by the prophets as "a falsehood," a lie. Should we assume that what the prophets reproved in others, they themselves were guilty of? There is no doubt that the prophets were conscious of their own sincerity; that their tongues were not confuted by their consciences.

"What I heard from the Lord of hosts, . . . I announce to you," said
Isaiah (21:10). And Jeremiah insisted:

> *I have not pressed Thee to send evil,*
> *Nor have I desired the day of disaster,*
> *Thou knowest;*
> *That which came out of my lips*
> *Was before Thy face.*
>
> *Jeremiah 17:16*

The prophet does not speak of a resolution or a purpose, framed
by himself, to devote himself to his vocation, but describes a decisive
moment in which he received a call. He thinks of himself as "a messenger of God" (Hag. 1:13), sent by Him to His people (Jer.
26:12–14; Isa. 49:5 f.). Moreover, he does not speak on the strength
of a single experience or sporadic inspirations. His entire existence is
dedicated to his mission. Jeremiah was chosen even before he was
born (Jer. 1:5). "For twenty-five years . . . the word of the Lord came
to me" (Jer. 25:3). When the priests and prophets pronounced him
publicly worthy of death, because he dared to prophesy against the
Temple, the only plea he entered was: "The Lord sent me to prophesy
against this house and this city all the words which you have heard. . . .
But, as for me, behold, I am in your hand. Do with me as is good and
right in your eyes" (Jer. 26:12, 14).

> *I have heard what the prophets have said who prophesy lies in My*
> *name, saying, I have dreamed, I have dreamed! How long shall there be*
> *lies in the heart of the prophets who prophesy lies, and who prophesy the*
> *deceit of their own heart? . . . Let the prophet who has a dream tell the*
> *dream, but let him who has My word speak My word faithfully. What*
> *has chaff in common with wheat? says the Lord. Is not My word like fire,*
> *says the Lord, and like a hammer which breaks the rock in pieces? . . .*
> *Behold, I am against the prophets, says the Lord, who use their tongues*
> *and say, Says the Lord. Behold, I am against those who prophesy lying*
> *dreams, says the Lord, and who tell them and lead My people astray by*
> *their lies and their recklessness, when I did not send them or charge them;*
> *so they do not profit this people at all, says the Lord.*
>
> *Jeremiah 23:25–26, 28–29, 31–32*

Jeremiah, to whom the authenticity of prophetic experience was a matter of life and death, not only for his own survival, but for Israel's, must have been in possession of criteria by which to distinguish between "chaff" and "wheat," between a prophet who had "a dream" and a prophet who received "the word of God." After announcing the word of God concerning an issue of great importance (Jer. 32:15), he was still in doubt over its full meaning, and prayed for illumination in order to understand it (Jer. 32:16 f.). The voice visited him, it did *not* dwell in him. He remained dependent in his illuminations as he was in his supplications. Some of his prayers were accepted (Jer. 7:3, 6), others were rejected (Jer. 11:14; 14:11; 15:1). The prophet was asked by the people, "What has the Lord answered?" or "What has the Lord spoken?" (Jer. 23:35.) But did he always receive an answer? Implored by the people to pray for guidance, Jeremiah, on one occasion we know of, had to wait ten days for the word to come to him (42:7).

In his anxiety to find an answer to the question: "Why is the land ruined and laid waste like a wilderness, so that no one passes through?" Jeremiah pondered: "Who is the man so wise that he can understand this? To whom has the mouth of the Lord spoken, that he may declare it?" (Jer. 9:12.)

Was the word the prophet proclaimed the product of wishful thinking? The content of his message was often in direct opposition to his own hopes and inclinations. Jeremiah wished that the message of the false prophet Hananiah might be true (Jer. 28:6). The Lord's answer to his prayers was quite different from what he expected (Jer. 12:1 ff.; 13:1 ff.).

The conflict between the voice of the Lord and the desire of his heart is illustrated in his prayers. Jeremiah implored mercy for the people, but the word he received said: "The Lord does not accept them, now He will remember their iniquity and punish their sins" (Jer. 14:10). The prophet persisted: "We acknowledge our wickedness, O Lord. . . . Do not spurn us for Thy name's sake." And the Lord said to him: "Though Moses and Samuel stood before Me, yet My heart would not turn toward this people . . ." (Jer. 14:19–15:3).

When "Jeremiah's harsh word of judgment against the Temple of Jerusalem provoked the priests . . . that they wanted to kill him," Jeremiah had nothing to say in his defense before the royal officials except: "The Lord has sent me" (Jer. 26:1), and then, once again, "of a truth, the Lord has sent me to you, to say all these words in your ears" (Jer. 26:15).

What was it that transpired in the life of a prophet to enable him to assert such a claim? What gave him the certainty to regard his experiences as divine inspirations? The fact that the illumination came without preparation, unexpectedly, as a sudden invasion of consciousness, was no basis for the assertion that it was God Who spoke to him.

That the prophets themselves were convinced of the divine origin of their pronouncements is beyond dispute. For the understanding of the prophet's mind this central conviction must be regarded as the fundamental quality, and has therefore served as a starting point for this inquiry into the essential structure of the prophetic personality.

It is not within our power to decide about the nature of the visions and voices perceived by prophets: whether they were real or merely subjective phenomena; whether the voice was perceived in trance or in a waking state. It is vain to speculate how the divine mind coalesces with the human, or to ask at what point the divine begins to operate; whether the formula "thus says the Lord" introduced a verbally inspired message; or whether only the thought was revealed, the language being the prophet's own.

We will use the idea of inspiration as a general designation of all acts and experiences in which the prophet is aware of a transcendent activity, directly or indirectly, sensuously or spiritually turned toward him. We will not be able to analyze the empirical content and the manifold modes and aspects of his experiences, and will dwell on inspiration in its essential givenness as the determinative factor in the prophetic consciousness.

## CONTENT AND FORM

In preceding chapters, we have described the content of the prophetic act as divine pathos and prophetic sympathy. We now know something about the *what* of prophetic experience. We have left untouched the question of the *how*. The problem, to which we now wish to turn our attention, is: What *form* does the prophet's experience assume?*

To the consciousness of the prophet, the prophetic act is an act of communication, in which a message is conveyed by words, thoughts, or signs. The decisive elements in the prophetic act of communication are the prophet's understanding and appropriation of the contents, his awareness of its being communicated to him, and the intercourse or encounter between him and the divine, that is, the form in which the message comes to his attention. It is the encounter which lends the character of prophecy to the experience.

In order to comprehend the form or the essential structure of that encounter, it will be necessary to subtract from it its accidental aspects, or whatever does not belong indispensably to it. In other words, we must disregard all features not essential to revelation as such. We are therefore excluding from our present consideration not only the substantial elements (e.g., the pathos motive), but also all contingent formal elements, such as the outward form of the experience (e.g., whether it was an act of hearing or of seeing).

The usual definitions seek to understand revelation and inspiration from the psychological or at best the anthropological standpoint. Yet an intelligent understanding of the prophetic consciousness of inspiration will never be possible as long as the immanent meaning of inspiration is overlooked. Our question, then, is: What is, to the mind of the prophets, the ultimate, irreducible form or essential structure of the prophetic act?

The prophetic act comprises a transpersonal fact which we call *inspiration* and a personal fact which we call *experience*. We will not

*The separation of form and content which we assume in regard to inspiration as well as in regard to experience is not something that can be accepted as a matter of course. From the standpoint of dogmatic theology, every revelation is indivisible. Even in modern discussions of the philosophy of religion, any divisibility of revelational experience is often disregarded. And when we purpose such an analysis, it is not because of the logical dogma of the correlation of content and form. Rather, the idea was inferred from a phenomenological examination of the prophets' accounts of their experiences.

be able to apprehend the meaning of the experience until we gain an insight into what inspiration meant to the prophet. For it is on the certainty of the objective or transpersonal aspect of the act that the whole meaning and relevance of the experience depend. From a phenomenological point of view, we can do justice to the essence of the experience only when we include in our discussion the awareness of that which is given *to* experience. We must, therefore, examine the structure of the inspiration in its objectivity, which is a given fact for experience, in order that we may be in a position to grasp the character of the experience which it initiates.

In accordance with our procedure in the analysis of prophetic experience, we shall take as our point of departure *the form of inspiration* corresponding to *the form of experience*. What does the prophet—apart from all factual content—view and experience as the essentially characteristic form of the act of inspiration?

## INSPIRATION AN EVENT

To the consciousness of the prophet, the prophetic act is more than an experience; it is an objective *event*. This is its essential form. Whatever be the motive or content, and whatever be the mode in which inspiration is apprehended, there remains always its character as an event, not as a process. What is the difference between process and event? A process happens regularly, following a relatively permanent pattern; an event is extraordinary, irregular. A process may be continuous, steady, uniform; events happen suddenly, intermittently, occasionally. Processes are typical; events are unique. A process follows a law, events create a precedent. The term "continuous revelation" is, therefore, as proper as a "square circle."

We must admit that revelation is remote from "the daily experience of modern man today"; even the thought of it is intellectually embarrassing. Yet, to identify it with our own intellectual preference is to distort it before we explore it; is to abuse what we are supposed to understand. We must be ready to go beyond the categories of our own experience, even though such a procedure may upset our mental routine and ease.*

Inspiration, then, is not a process that goes on all the time, but an event that lasts a moment. The term used in the Bible to describe general events in history, *vayehi,* "it happened," is employed to describe prophetic inspiration, *vayehi dvar Adonai eilai,* particularly in Jeremiah and Ezekiel.

God is not simply available once and for all, to be found whenever man so desires. There is an alternative to God's presence, namely, His absence. God may withdraw and detach Himself from history. While exposed to the overwhelming presence, the prophets predict the absence.

> *With their flocks and their herds*
> *They shall go to seek the Lord,*
> *But they will not find Him;*
> *He has withdrawn from them.*
>
> Hosea 5:6

> *Then they will cry to the Lord,*
> *But He will not answer them;*
> *He will hide his face from them at that time,*
> *Because they have made their deeds evil.*
>
> Micah 3:4

> *I will wait for the Lord, who is hiding His face from the house of Jacob, and I will hope in Him.*
>
> Isaiah 8:17

*A. J. Heschel, *God in Search of Man* (New York, 1955), p. 209. An example of conceiving prophecy as a process is Maimonides' theory, according to which prophecy (with the exception of Moses) is a continuous emanation from the divine Being, and is transmitted to all those who are endowed with certain qualities (innate superiority with the imaginative faculty, moral and mental perfection) through the medium of the Active Intellect, a superhuman spirit, first to his rational faculty and then to the imaginative faculty. Accordingly, prophetic illumination occurs in conformity with natural law or with the order or emanation, while the failure to be inspired is regarded as a miracle, for "we believe that, even if one has the capacity for prophecy and has duly prepared himself, he may yet not actually prophesy. The will of God prevents it." (*The Guide of the Perplexed,* II, ch. 32 ff.)

> *Behold, I go forward, but He is not there;*
> *And backward, but I cannot perceive Him;*
> *Bending to the left, I cannot take hold of Him;*
> *Turning to the right, I cannot see Him.*
>
> *Job 23:8–9*

Receiving the word of God is a wonder that does not always come to pass.

> *Behold, the days are coming, says the Lord God,*
> *When I will send a famine on the land;*
> *Not a famine of bread, nor a thirst for water,*
> *But of hearing the words of the Lord.*
> *They shall wander from sea to sea,*
> *And from north to east;*
> *They shall run to and fro, to seek the word of the Lord,*
> *But they shall not find it.*
>
> *Amos 8:11–12*

Prophetic experience, then, is not the perception of vistas or the perception of sounds that persist all the time. It is not a discovery, a coming upon something permanently given by the mind of the prophet. The prophet encounters, not something given, a timeless idea, *mishpat*, justice, a law, but something dynamic, an act of giving; not an eternal word, but a word spoken, a word expressed, springing from a Presence, a word in time, a pathos overflowing in words. His experience is a perception of an act that happens rather than a perception of a situation that abides.

## AN ECSTASY OF GOD

There is another sense in which prophetic inspiration must be described as having been an event to the consciousness of the prophets. It is in the sense of having been more than an inner experience. What happened in the decisive moments in the life of the prophet did not burst out of him, but upon him. Furthermore, inspiration is an act that happens to him and beyond him.

To the prophet the supremely real is not his experience, but that which is given *to* his experience, that which surpasses his power of experience. To him, God is not an object, but a subject, and his perceiving of the event matters less than God's uttering of His word. (See p. 621.) He is not the agent, the moving force; he stands within the event, not above it.

No perception is as plain, direct, and infallible as eating food. What we see or touch remains outside us, what we consume becomes a part of us. "Thy words were found, and I ate them . . ." (Jer. 15:16). His was not an experience of God, but an experience of a divine experience.

Prophecy is a personal event. It happens to the divine Person Who does not merely send forth words, but becomes involved and engaged in the encounter with man.

Thus, to the prophetic consciousness, inspiration is more than an emotional experience, a consciousness of inner receptivity. It is experienced as a divine act which takes place *not within* but *beyond*, as an event which happens in one's view rather than in one's heart. The prophet does not merely feel it; he faces it.

The decisive mark of the prophetic act is in its transcendent aspect. To the prophet, the overwhelming fact is not only that he hears, but that God speaks; something happens to him, and something happens to God. What makes possible the prophetic act within his consciousness is an act that happens beyond his consciousness, a transcendent act, *an ecstasy of God*. To the prophet, it is as though God stepped forth from the silence, aloofness, and incomprehensibility of His being to reveal His will to man. In its depth and intensity the act takes place in the transcendent subject, but is directed toward the experiencing prophets.

Prophecy cannot be forced. The prophet does not assume that abandonment of consciousness brings about inspiration, as though one had only to leave "the self" in order to be able to receive the word. Prophecy comes about by the grace of God. Ecstasy is something which happens to the person; inspiration happens to the Inspirer as well as to the human person. Ecstasy is a psychological process; prophecy has its origin in a transcendent act.

## BEING PRESENT

The prophets tell us little of how the divine word came to them or how they knew it to be the word of the very God. Perhaps it was the discovery of being present at a divine event, "of standing at the council of the Lord" that was the essence of their experience and the source of evidence. Prophetic inspiration involved participation, not merely receptivity to communication.

The term "visions," generally applied to some of the descriptions of prophetic experience, is a metonymy. Seeing is but a part of the experience. What stands out as essential, unique, and decisive is *the prophet's participation*, his affecting and witnessing the thinking of the Lord. Witness some of the visions that came to Amos. Once a cloud swept down and devoured every blade of grass in the fields; again, a fire appeared, so fierce that it licked up the great deep and threatened the land. That was the vision. The people were ripe for severe punishment. Had the record finished here, its meaning would be limited to foreseeing a coming disaster. Yet, the prophet did not accept what he saw; he did not say, "Thy will be done." He prayed:

> *O Lord God, forgive [or, cease], I beseech Thee!*
> *How can Jacob stand?*
> *He is so small!*
>
> *Amos 7:2*

The Lord repented concerning this:

> *It shall not be, says the Lord, . . .*
> *This also shall not be, says the Lord.*
> *Amos 7:3, 6*

Others may be granted ultimate insights, may perceive the imperceptible. What the prophet speaks of is not a personal experience but a startling event, the least important aspect of which is its effect upon the prophet. What he speaks of is an event that must affect heaven and earth.

> *Hear, you peoples, all of you;*
> *Hearken, O earth, and all that is in it.*
> *Micah 1:2*

> *Hear, O heavens, and give ear, O earth,*
> *For the Lord has spoken.*
> *Isaiah 1:2*

> *The Lord roars from Zion,*
> *And utters His voice from Jerusalem*
> *And the heavens and earth shake.*
> *Joel 4:16*

It takes great inner power to address a nation; it takes divine strength to address heaven and earth.

The prophets do not speak in the name of a personal experience, of an inner illumination. They speak in the name of a divine experience, of a divine event. Inspiration is more than an act that happens to the prophet; inspiration is a moment of the prophet's being present at a divine event.

"The mouth of the Lord has spoken" (Isa. 1:20; 40:5; Mic. 4:4). "The Lord has spoken this word" (Isa. 24:3; Jer. 46:13), "has sworn in my hearing" (Isa. 5:9), "has revealed Himself in my ears" (Isa. 22:14).

## THE EVENT AND ITS SIGNIFICANCE

Two subjects are involved in the act of inspiration: a giver of revelation and a recipient. In order to grasp the essential character of inspiration, its significance for both partners must be elucidated. Principally: How did the prophet conceive of the significance of the revelational event for the divine Being? Before attempting to answer this question, it should be explained what significance the idea of divinity has in prophetic thought.

In our section on the prophet's understanding of God, it has been pointed out that the prophet rarely speaks of God as He is in Himself, as ultimate Being. (See p. 620.) It is God in relation to humanity, in relation to the world, Who is the theme of his words.

It is improper to employ the term "self-revelation" in regard to biblical prophecy. God never reveals Himself. He is above and beyond all revelation. He discloses only a word. He never unveils His essence; He communicates only His pathos, His will. Consequently, the question of significance which we raised must be framed in the following terms: What does the event of revelation imply as regards divine pathos? At the same time the question must be asked: What does the event of revelation signify for the prophetic partner? Here again the qualification must be made that we are not now concerned with the entire existence of the prophet, but with the significance for his own understanding of his experience.

## ANALYSIS OF THE EVENT

Every event is essentially made up of two phases. Since an event is limited in time, it must have a beginning, and since it is not indefinitely continuous, it must run a certain course. The beginning and the course of development together constitute the characteristic structure of every event. The first phase is effected by a change in the prior, original condition; the second by a tendency to evolve according to a certain momentum. In the first phase we have an interruption and ceasing; in the second, a continuance and progress. The first we term a *turning*, or a *decision;* the second, a *direction*. Thus there are two aspects to inspiration as seen from the prophet's point of view; a moment of decision, or a turning, and a moment of expression, a direction.

What do we mean by *turning*, or decision?

Every event starts out as a change, as a turning point; a turning away from a stable condition must take place for the event to happen. In the change lies the transition from motive to initiative, the birth of the event out of the motive.

The moment of turning is that which has an immediate nexus with what precedes the event; it is that which takes place at the source: the origination of an event. Because it introduces or is the genesis of the event, it is rooted in the interior, intimate life of him who bears the event. At this stage the event carries a maximum of motivation and a minimum of happening.

In the critical turning we see the initiating and generating factor behind the event, we see the dynamic and potential quality of the latter: the impulse to the opening up of a new direction. The act of turning is the first result of the initiative. At that point we have to grasp the principle which shapes the total structure of the event before the latter is completely realized as fact.

As a rule, God is silent; His intention and design remain hidden from the mind of man. What comes to pass is a departure from the state of silence and aloofness, God's turning from the conditions of concealment to an act of revealment.

This change brings about the transition from a state or a condition which seems permanent and timeless to a moment of encounter which is always unique in time. *Eternity enters a moment.* The uniqueness of the latter interrupts what at a distance seems to be uninterrupted uniformity. Timeless silence we can only conceive in the image of impersonality. It is an order, perhaps a principle, unrelated; it has no face and no regard. Turning is personal; it involves initiative, will. It is the beginning of communion.

A turning is always pivoted upon the will. The prophets knew no manifestation of God which was passive, unwilled or unintentional. It was not thought of as proceeding out of God like rays out of the sun. It was an act proceeding from this will and brought about by a decision to disclose what otherwise would remain concealed. In this sense, it was an act within the life of God.

Revelation was more than a miracle or an acting upon the prophet. The word was not spoken in the way that it was when the world came into being. God did not say, "Let there be a word!" and there was a word reaching the prophet's ear. God did not create the word out of nothing; He spoke it out of his own Being.

The prophetic event impresses itself on the prophet as a happening that springs exclusively from the will and initiative of God. He cannot himself control or call forth inspiration; it must proceed from God and therefore depends utterly on God's willing it. He is unable to conjure it up by human means, not even by prayer.

The fact that inspiration is independent of the will of the prophet expresses negatively and indirectly its transcendent nature. Positively, the moment of turning is understood as an expression of God's will to communicate. The statement, "Surely the Lord does nothing without revealing His secret to His servants the prophets" (Amos 3:7), contains a thought which lies at the very root of biblical religion: "The Lord said: Shall I hide from Abraham what I am about to do?" (Gen. 18:17.)

The decision to communicate is an event in the life of God. It arises directly from divine motivation; for it belongs to the very nature of God to declare His thoughts to the prophets. Inspiration as a crucial event is conditioned both by the history of man and by the character of God.

What do we mean by *direction*?

A personal event is an act of communication in which an intention is conveyed to another person. It means addressing a person. An act of communication has a direction. The turning is the genesis of the event, the direction its realization. It is a moment in which an act within a person becomes an act for the sake of another person. A relationship is established; the event has reached its end; it has assumed form; it is a maximum of eventuation.

A distinction must be made between a divine manifestation and a divine communication. A divine manifestation which may be either directly evident (Exod. 24:9–11) or sensed in its effects upon nature and history (Judg. 5:4 f.; Hab. 3:3) is not directed to the prophet and does not accost him. An essential moment in prophecy is direction. Amos' word, "The Lord roars from Zion, and utters His voice from Jerusalem; the pastures of the shepherds mourn, and the top of Carmel withers" (1:2), describes a call not directed to any particular person (cf. Joel 3:16). Likewise the call in Isaiah's inaugural vision, "And

I heard the voice of the Lord saying: Whom shall I send, and who will go for us?" (6:8), is not directed to any particular person; it contains a decision, not a direction. It is in verse 9 that the address begins: "And He said: Go and say to this people." Yet it is those words of decision that suggest how much the mission of the prophet means to God Himself.

Revelation is not a voice crying in the wilderness, but an act of received communication. It is not simply an act of disclosing, but an act of disclosing *to* someone, the bestowal of a content, God addressing the prophet. There is no intransitive aimless revelation in prophecy. God's word is directed to man.

The situation of God's turning and presence in which there is no direction to man is described in the book of Job:

> *Lo, He passes by me and I see Him not;*
> *He moves on, but I do not perceive Him.*
>
> *Job 9:11*

There is no revelation here.

Unlike the voice, the *bath kol,* spoken of in old rabbinic literature, the voice the prophet hears is calling upon him. It is only marginal to the prophet's experience to overhear words not addressed to him.* The word is always spoken to him, addressed to him. The standard formula is: *"The word of the Lord came to me"* (Jer. 1:9). It is placed in his mouth.

The idea of God's turning *(tropos)* to man is a fundamental presupposition of biblical prophecy. The idea of pathos is an answer to the question of content only, not to that of form, and it by no means implies the event of revelation. Pathos is the object of communication, but it does not necessarily of itself engender the latter. The need to reveal itself is not intrinsic to it.

Hence, we must seek the primary presupposition of prophecy in

---

*"And I heard the voice of the Lord saying: Whom shall I send, and who will go for us?" (Isa. 6:8.) The statement "The Lord of hosts has sworn in my ears" (Isa. 5:9) is ambiguous; cf I Kings 22:18–24. Apocalyptic visionaries read the words written in heavenly books.

some other category. This category is to be inferred from the act itself, from the character of eventuation. It is the inclination to *tropos*, the *tropos* tendency of the Eternal, which is the ultimate ground of prophecy.

## HERE AM I, HERE AM I . . .

All of human history as seen by the Bible is the history of *God in search of man*. In spite of man's failure, over and over, God does not abandon His hope to find righteous men. Adam, Cain, the generation of the flood, the generation of the Tower of Babel—it is a story of failure and defiance. And yet, God did not abandon man, hoping against hope to see a righteous world. Noah was saved in the expectation that out of his household generations would not corrupt their ways, and a covenant was established with him and his descendants after him. But it was Noah himself who planted a vineyard and then became drunk. It was Noah himself who set brother against brother, blessing Shem and Yapheth, and cursing Canaan to be a slave to his brothers. The arrogance of those who built the Tower of Babel paved the way for greater tension and confusion. But the Lord did not abandon man, and in His search determined to choose Abraham, so that in him might "all families of the earth be blessed."

Israel's faith is not the fruit of a quest for God. Israel did not discover God. Israel was discovered by God. The Bible is a record of God's approach to man.*

> *Like grapes in the wilderness,*
> *I found Israel.*
> *Like the first fruit on the fig tree,*
> *I saw your fathers.*
>
> Hosea 9:10

> *He found him in a desert land,*
> *In the howling waste of the wilderness;*

---

*"I have found David, My servant" (Ps. 89:20).

> He encircled him, He cared for him
> He kept him as the apple of His eye.
>
> Deuteronomy 32:10

This is the biblical conception of God's relationship to man: God would call, and man would answer. God is longing for the work of His hands (Job 14:15; cf. 7:21). That relationship is distorted when the call goes forth, and man fails to answer.

> Why, when I came, was there no man?
> When I called, was there no one to answer? . . .
> I was ready to be sought by those who did not ask for Me;
> I was ready to be found by those who did not seek Me.
> I said: Here am I, here am I,*
> To a nation that did not call on My name.
> I spread out My hands all the day
> To a rebellious people,
> Who walk in a way that is not good,
> Following their own devices, . . .
> I will choose affliction for them,
> And bring their fears upon them;
> Because, when I called, no one answered,
> When I spoke they did not listen.
>
> Isaiah 50:2; 65:1–2; 66:4

I sought for a man among them who should build up the wall and stand in the breach before Me for the land, that I should not destroy it; but I found none.

> Ezekiel 22:30

## ANTHROPOTROPISM AND THEOTROPISM

In the light of these structural categories, religious events must be divided into two types. They are experienced either as a turning of

---

*"Here am I" is a phrase of humble readiness and consent, uttered by Abraham (Gen. 22:1), Jacob (Gen. 46:2), Moses (Exod. 3:5), Samuel (I Sam. 3:4).

a transcendent Being toward man, or as a turning of man toward a transcendent Being. The first may be called *anthropotropic,* the second *theotropic.*

To the first category belongs the consciousness of being approached by God, directly or indirectly, of receiving teaching or guidance, a word or an intimation; the consciousness of living under a God Who calls upon man, turns to him, is in need of him. In anthropotropic experience, man is affected by the impact of events which he does not initiate, but which are addressed to him or relate to his existence, and in which he feels a transcendent attentiveness focused upon himself.

Prophetic inspiration as a pure act may be defined as anthropotropism, as a turning of God toward man, a turning in the direction of man.

The call that comes to the prophet to accept the prophetic mission is the outstanding example of anthropotropism (Amos 7:14 f.; Isa. 6; Jer. 1:3 ff.; Ezek. 9:2 ff.; Hos. 1:2). Such a call is not reported of the Buddha, who attains insight through personal striving, but is claimed by prophetic men like Muhammad and Zarathustra; it belongs to the fundamental features of their religious consciousness. This is an essential characteristic of the prophetic act: Not only does it come from the initiative of God, but it is directed toward man.

The unique quality of the awareness that characterizes biblical religion goes beyond what Schleiermacher called "absolute dependence." It is rather an awareness of a God who helps, demands, and calls upon man. It is a sense of being reached, being found, being sought after; a sense of being pursued: *anthropotropism.*

While the prophets of Israel may be regarded as the classical example of anthropotropism, not all anthropotropic experiences are prophetic in character; they occur in a variety of forms in the lives of individuals who lay no claim to prophecy, and seem to be particularly prevalent in theistic religions.

Theotropism, man's turning to God, is a structure of experience that may be attained through the performance of ritual acts, prayer, meditation. It is characteristic of exercises performed in order to induce the state of ecstasy and communion with God; of efforts of a magic nature aimed at establishing contact with the sphere of the divine.

Prayer, too, is an act consisting of a moment of decision or turning, and of a moment of direction. For to be engaged in prayer and to be away from prayer are two different states of living and thinking. In the depth of the soul there is a distance between the two. The course of consciousness which a person pursues, the way of thinking by which he lives most of the time, are remote from the course and way of thinking peculiar to prayer. To be able to pray, one must alter the course of consciousness, one must go through moments of disengagement, one must enter another course of thinking, one must face in a different direction.

The course one must take in order to arrive at prayer is on the way to God. For the focus of prayer is not the self. A man may spend hours meditating about himself, or be stirred by the deepest sympathy for his fellow man, and no prayer will come to pass. Prayer comes to pass in a complete turning of the heart toward God, toward His goodness and power. It is the momentary disregard of one's personal concerns, the absence of self-centered thoughts, which constitute the art of prayer. Feeling becomes prayer in the moment in which one forgets oneself and becomes aware of God. When we analyze the consciousness of a supplicant, we discover that it is not concentrated upon his own interests, but on something beyond the self. The thought of personal need is absent, and the thought of divine grace alone is present in his mind. Thus, in beseeching Him for bread, there is one instant, at least, in which the mind is directed neither to one's hunger nor to food, but to His mercy. This instant is prayer.

In prayer we shift the center of living from self-consciousness to self-surrender. God is the center toward which all forces tend. He is the source, and we are the flowing of His force, the ebb and flow of His tides.*

Just as the prophet is the supreme example of anthropotropism,

*See A. J. Heschel, *Man's Quest for God* (New York, 1954), pp. 7, 15, 24.

so is the priest the outstanding exponent of theotropism. The difference between them must be understood in terms of the different experiences they represent. The prophet, speaking for God to the people, must disclose; the priest, acting for people before God, must carry out the will of God. The prophet speaks and acts by virtue of divine inspiration, the priest performs the ritual by virtue of his official status. In the earliest times nonpriests could perform cultic actions.* If subsequently this privilege became confined to the priest, it was rarely assumed that the priest was called by God to perform this task. The transference of the control of the cultic domain to the priest was based, not upon a consideration of his calling, but upon a consideration of his gifts. This is confirmed by the fact that the priestly vocation was hereditary (Exod. 28:1).† Magic and exorcism—the art of healing and divination, sacrifice and prayer—are acts which proceed from man and are directed toward God.

The two types differ not only in inner experience but also in outward action, in the modes of service. The sphere in which theotropism finds expression is *the cult;* the emotions with which it is charged are those of aspiration and devotion, the soul's longing for God; the course of its piety proceeds from man to God. The point of departure is the sphere of man, the end is the sphere of the divine. What is hoped for is divine aid, protection or intervention. God is called upon to answer, to send relief in distress. Conversely, the sphere in which prophetic anthropotropism finds expression is *history;* the emotions with which it is charged are sympathy for God, sympathy for man; the course of its piety runs from God to man. The point of departure is the divine pathos, the end is the sphere of man. What is hoped for is repentance, human action. Man is called upon to answer, to mend his ways.

The priest, guardian of sacred traditions and master of sacred technique, of formulae and rites, often a diviner who ascertains the

---

*In ancient Israel, one was not required to be specially consecrated in order to perform sacrificial functions: anyone might approach the altar and offer sacrifices; cf. Judg. 6:26 ff.; 13:16, 19; I Sam. 2:13–16; II Sam. 24:25.

†Cf. A. Erman, *Die Ägyptische Religion* (2nd ed.; Berlin, 1909), p. 67.

decrees and the will of the gods, presents a social and stable order, and stands in contrast to the prophet whose activities and appearance are unpredictable, individual, and incalculable.

Theotropic experience may be an end in itself, whereas anthropotropism is only a means to an end. The former is conceivable as an isolated episode in the life of man; the latter happens as a part of a relationship embracing all of life.

Anthropotropism finds its supreme expression in prophecy; theotropism, in psalmody. Characteristic of the former is the election or the call that comes to a prophet from above; characteristic of the latter is repentance and conversion. One must not assume, however, that both types are mutually exclusive. The existence of the prophet, for example, is sustained by both kinds of events. And conversion, the structure of which is theotropic, is often accompanied by an anthropotropic experience as though, in the words of William James, "a higher power streamed in from without and attained the mastery within man."

Anthropotropism and theotropism are far more than categories describing formal structures of inner events; they affect and shape the substance of religious thinking.

Anthropotropism, the thought of God approaching man, willing, needing, and requiring his work, carries not only a supreme affirmation of values encountered here and now, but also the assurance of the ultimate significance of history. The directedness of the divine upon man sets forth the supreme relevance and urgency of what man must do, of how man may fail, of how his acts affect the course of history.

Where theotropic moments determine the ultimate image of existence, directedness of the mind upon the divine may become, in extreme cases, the exclusive standard and principle of judgment. Focused upon the Beyond, the mind begins to disregard the demands and values of here and now, sliding into resignation and withdrawal from action, moral indifferentism, and world denial.

To sum up, these seem to be the outstanding features of prophetic inspiration as seen from the perspective of the prophetic consciousness:

1. It is not brought about by the prophet, but comes about without and even against his will. It presupposes neither training nor the gradual development of a talent. It comes about as an act of election and grace.

2. It is not an absolutely mysterious, numinous, wholly other source from which inspiration comes to the prophet; it proceeds from the known God.

3. It is an event, not part of a process; it is not a constant, it happens.

4. It is an event in the life of God; it happens in God in relation to the prophet; it is an event in which both decision and direction come upon a person as a transcendent act.

5. It is not an act of imparting general information. Prophecy is God's personal communication to man. It deals with what concerns God intimately.

6. It is more than a state of mind; it is the apprehension of a divine state of mind, being present at a divine event. What the prophet senses as time is not a passive, quiet presence, but an approach, an imminence.

The prophetic act, as said above, comprises a transpersonal fact which we call inspiration and a personal fact which we call experience. Having characterized the form of inspiration as anthropotropism, it is now our task to describe the form of experience. What is the relationship of the prophet to the event?*

## THE FORM OF PROPHETIC EXPERIENCE

The element of will which is effective in every event is always expressed in the initial decision: the subsequent direction and development is merely the unfolding of what is given in the moment of

---

*Sympathy, it will be recalled, is the response, not to the event, but to the content of the event.

decision. In the prophetic event, where the moment of decision is experienced solely as a transcendent act which the prophet can neither determine nor occasion, no scope is given for the exercise of the prophet's will. His awareness is one of being subject to a transcendent intensity, to overpowering force, so that he does not merely listen to inspiration but feels compelled to listen to it. He experiences power, not only a word, and is swept into a position in which he can do no other than experience and accept. The prophet does not receive the word of inspiration because he wishes to, but because he feels compelled to, though this of course does not exclude the possibility that his sense of compulsion can be transformed into free identification and acceptance.

The unwilled nature of his experience is for the prophet part of his inner evidence that the message does not spring from his own heart. But the prophet's sense of authenticity is more positive and emphatic than that. It is not the impact of an unknown, anonymous, mysterious incident, but a divine anthropotropism which he confronts.

The prophetic moment, as said earlier, was not experienced as the prophet's long-coveted opportunity to attain knowledge which is otherwise concealed. He does not seize the moment, he is seized by the moment. The word disclosed is not offered as something which he might or might not appropriate according to his discretion, but is violently, powerfully urged upon him. The impact of the anthropotropic event was reflected in the prophet's awareness of his being unable either to evade or to resist it.

Prophecy is more than knowledge acquired by inspiration. It is not a quiet insight, a simple act of apperception. It is a startling event: a thunder in the world and a lightning in the soul.

"The hand of God," a synonym for the manifestation of His strength and power (Isa. 10:10; 28:2; Deut. 32:36), is the name the prophet uses to describe the urgency, pressure, and compulsion by which he is stunned and overwhelmed. "For the Lord spoke thus to me with His strong hand upon me" (Isa. 8:11). "I sat alone, because Thy hand was upon me" (Jer. 15:17). "The Hand of the Lord was upon me" (Ezek. 37:1, 3:14, 24). "The hand of the Lord was on Elijah" (I Kings 18:46). The prophet very rarely speaks of God's face; he feels His hand.

The prophet does not volunteer for his mission; it is forced upon him. He is seduced, he is overwhelmed. There is no choice. Yoked in the knowledge he is compelled to receive, he is also under stress of the necessity to declare it.

> *The lion has roared,*
> *Who will not fear?*
> *The Lord God has spoken,*
> *Who can but prophesy?*
>
>               *Amos 3:8*

> *As for me, I am filled with power,*
> *With the spirit of the Lord,*
> *With justice, with might,*
> *To declare to Jacob his transgression,*
> *To Israel his sin.*
>
>               *Micah 3:8*

Isaiah heard the voice of God saying, "Go and say to this people . . ." (6:9). "Go, set a watchman, let him declare what he sees" (21:6). The word came to Jeremiah: "Speak to all the cities of Judah which come to worship in the house of the Lord all the words that I command you to speak to them; do not hold back a word" (26:2).

The compulsion to proclaim the word of God to the people is stronger than all attempts to restrain oneself from doing so.

> *Thou hast seized and overpowered me. . . .*
> *If I say: I will not mention Him,*
> *Or speak any more in His name,*
> *There is in my heart as it were a burning fire*
> *Shut up in my bones,*
> *And I am weary of holding it in,*
> *And I cannot.*
>
>               *Jeremiah 20:7,9*

Thus even beyond the moment of the encounter, the prophet remains subject to the compelling power of his experiences. To reiterate, the significance of prophecy lies not in those who perceive it, as happens in mystical experience, but in those to whom the word is to be conveyed. The purpose is not in the perception of the voice, but in bringing it to bear upon the reality of the people's life. Apart from, and often against, his own will the prophet must take over and fulfill his task; he must both apprehend and preach inspired truth. Thus he knows a twofold necessity—that of accepting and experiencing and that of announcing and preaching.

We have seen that there are two aspects to the prophetic act: *form* and *content;* something happens, and something is said. A dialectic tension in the prophet's consciousness has its source in the dualism of his experience. He is both active and passive, free and forced. He is free to respond to the content of the moment; he is forced to experience the moment, to accept the burden of his mission. Thus the effect of the impact of inspiration is to evoke in him both a sense of freedom and a feeling of coercion, an act of spontaneity and an awareness of enforced receptivity. This note of dialectic tension is of essential significance in the structure of the prophetic personality.

Prophetic experience is more than an encounter or a confrontation. It is a moment of being overwhelmed by the tremendous arrival. From a distance, the word surges forth to land in the prophet's soul. It is more than the sense of being addressed, of receiving a communication; it is more accurate to describe it as *the sense of being overpowered* by the word. Inspiration is a momentous event, directed exclusively to the prophet. The divine voice is audible to none save the prophet himself (I Sam. 3:8). The prophet experiences the pointing of the divine will toward himself, a coercion to encounter God, to appropriate the word, to bring it to the people.

There is no need to emphasize here that the prophet's experience is not a state of depersonalization, of inner dissolution, as is often asserted.* Though acted upon and affected by the presence of God,

*G. van der Leeuw, *Einführung in die Phänomenologie der Religion* (Munich, 1925), p. 106.

the prophet does not simply endure the event without emotional reaction. He is not merged in rapture, he surrenders neither his emotion nor his outlook. At the very moment of inspiration he may take issue, pleading or contending with God. Being inspired does not mean being reduced to a state of passivity, a mere vessel or an instrument. The prophet overcome by the hand of God may lose the power of the will; he does not lose the power of the mind.

# 15

# Prophets Throughout the World

## The Occurrence of Prophetic Personalities

There is hardly a people on the earth, at least no Oriental people, which in some form or other does not know revelations of its gods.* In almost every age and every land, inspired people emerge who are believed to be endowed with a spiritual strength not given to other men or who even claim to have access to occult sources of knowledge. No student of religion will, however, be satisfied with such a generalization. He will try to ascertain the heterogeneity of claims and experiences behind the homogeneity. The question that concerns us here is not primarily whether claims to having received divine revelations have been made in other religions, but rather whether prophetic personalities or persons endowed with prophetic consciousness are to be found in antiquity outside Israel.

A widely held view maintains that "prophecy of the Hebrew type has not been limited to Israel; it is indeed a phenomenon of almost world-wide occurrence; in many lands and in many ages the wild, whirling words of frenzied men and women have been accepted as the

---

*See E. Sellin, *Der alttestamentliche Prophetismus* (Leipzig, 1912), p. 201.

utterances of an indwelling deity."* "On the subject of inspiration, Egyptians, Hebrews and Greeks thought much alike, from the earliest times to which we can trace back their thoughts; and in the time of the Roman Empire, Pagans, Jews, and Christians spoke of it in similar terms."† "We have, in fact, a belief which goes back to primitive man all the world over, and persists in the various civilizations which have grown out of primitive society, not only in . . . the Egyptian, Hebrew and Greek, but in all civilizations which have existed. Everywhere we find diviners and prophets carrying on the functions of the primitive medicine-man; everywhere there is the belief in the possession of certain men by spirits which have entered their bodies and use their tongues, a belief resting largely on the actual pathological peculiarities which mark the insane."‡

These statements contain an impressive half-truth. There are phenomena in many lands which bear a strong superficial similarity to biblical prophecy. A careful analysis, however, will reveal their essential dissimilarity, and compel us to qualify these statements. Indeed, most of the phenomena usually cited fail to corroborate them. The belief in possession by spirits or demons, soul journeys, telepathic communication, forewarnings of death and disaster, crystal-gazing in which all lands and events are disclosed in the translucent stone; talking skull-bones; predictions by means of a dish concerning the coming harvest and the cattle-breeding, are not parallels to biblical prophecy.§

*J. G. Frazer, *The Golden Bough,* V (London, 1911–15), 74.
†W. Scott, *Hermetica,* III (Oxford, 1924 f.), 5.
‡E. Bevan, *Sibyls and Seers* (London, 1928), p. 13.
§The widely maintained view that considers prophecy to be a universal phenomenon is not shared by all scholars. E. Sellin challenged F. Delitzsch to mention a parallel to the prophets out of the entire history of the ancient Orient. *(Das Alte Testament und die evangelische Kirche der Gegenwart* [Leipzig, 1921], pp. 30 f.) According to A. Jirku, *Altorientalischer Kommentar zum Alten Testament* (Leipzig, 1923), p. 187, we stand before a phenomenon which is unique in world history. Sellin summed up the matter thus: "Not the faintest hint of an analogy to revelation as we know it in the Israelite writing prophets, has so far been discovered in the sphere of ancient Oriental religion." *(Der alttestamentliche Prophetismus* (Leipzig, 1912), p. 221.

COMPARISONS

The prophets of Israel have been equated with various Babylonian orders of priests (the bārū and mahū guilds), who were technicians in divination, either by hepatoscopy or by some other specialized technique.* They have been compared to many groups: the wandering "priests" of the Dea Syria described by Apuleius; the so-called wizards of Patagonia in the eighteenth century; the *dugganawa* among the Veddas of Ceylon;† medieval mystics, such as Theresa, Mechthild, Birgitta of Vadstena;‡ with the ecstatics and shamans found among the Ural-Altaic peoples from the Bering Straits to the borders of the Scandinavian countries (persons who ascend to the spirit world, to the land of the dead, learn the secrets of the gods and spirits, and can then overcome or drive out hostile spirits or powers);§ with the *kāhins* among the pre-Islamic Arabs;‖ with the dervishes of Moslem orders; with the *tâng ki* in China ("youths who have divinity in themselves," who are easily stirred to ecstasy by their conviction that gods descend into them, causing them to act as possessed mediums, exorcists, and seers);# with the so-called prophets in Africa, particularly the Zulu prophets (who claim to experience visions and, conscious of having a special mission, bring to the community messages of an apocalyptic nature

*A. Haldar, *Associations of Cult Prophets among the Ancient Semites* (Uppsala, 1945). According to M. Bic, *Vetus Testamentum,* I (1951), 293 ff., Amos was a *hepatoscopos.*

†A. R. Johnson, *The Cultic Prophet in Ancient Israel* (Cardiff, 1944), p. 21.

‡J. Lindblom, *Die literarische Gattung der prophetischen Literatur* (Uppsala, 1924): W. Baumgartner, *Archiv für Religionwissenschaft* (1928), pp. 95 f.

§A. F. Puuko, *"Ekstatische Propheten mit besonderer Beruecksichtigung der Finnisch-Ugrischen Parallelen," ZAW,* LIII (NF, 12), 28 f.

‖J. Pedersen, "The Role Played by Inspired Persons among the Israelites and the Arabs," in *Studies in Old Testament Prophecy,* presented to T. H. Robinson (Edinburgh, 1950), pp. 127 f.

#See J. J. M. DeGroot, *The Religious System of China,* vol. VI, Bk. 11 (Leyden, 1910), pp. 1269 f. See J. Lindblom in *Von Ugarit nach Qumran, Festschrift für Otto Eissfeldt* (1958), pp. 96 f.; DeGroot, *Die Grundlage der Religion und Ethik, des Staatswesens und der Wissenschaft Chinas* (Berlin, 1918), pp. 356 f.

from an invisible world);* with Greek orators† and demagogues.‡

Others have attempted to understand the prophets "in terms of
the psychology of mysticism," and suggested that the prophets
belong "psychologically in the great family of mysticism."§

Biblical prophecy has even been compared to the Oxford Group.
"That which the Group calls guidance is exactly that which the prophets experienced and taught with their expression 'The word of (the
Lord) came to me. . . .' Their conception of the actuality itself, the
guidance itself, is exactly the Prophets' conception of the word of
(the Lord) which came to them. Merely to read the short brochures
produced by the Group about the 'Quiet Time' and about the way in
which God (or the Holy Spirit) speaks to us therein, will convince
anyone of this."‖

The ability to compare, an outstanding function of the mind, is
more easily developed than the ability to differentiate. Qualities that
things have in common are outstanding; the uniqueness of each thing
is frequently imperceptible.

The comparative method in the study of religion, for all its value
in stressing the features that various religions have in common and in
setting forth the unity of all human experience, must be supplemented
by an *immanent method,* by the attempt to go beyond the general
features of incidental externals to the unique aspects of religious phenomena. The placing together of similar phenomena irrespective of
age and context tends to ignore essential though subtle differences. A

---

*K. Schlosser, *Propheten in Afrika* (Braunschweig, 1949); B. Sundkler, *Bantu
Prophets in South Africa* (London, 1948), pp. 109 f.; Will-Erich Peuckert, *"Deutsche
Volkspropheten," ZAW,* LIII (1935), pp. 35 ff.

†B. Duhm, *Theologie der Propheten* (Bonn, 1875), pp. 22 f.

‡M. Weber, *Ancient Judaism* (Glencoe, 1952), pp. 267 ff.

§H. W. Hines, "The Prophet as Mystic" in the *American Journal of Semitic
Languages,* XI, 37 ff.; "The Development of the Psychology of Prophecy" in the *Journal of Religion,* VIII (1928), 212 ff. On the difference between prophetic and mystical
experience, see F. Heiler, *Das Gebet* (2nd ed.; München, 1920), pp. 248 ff. See also
above, pp. 460 ff.

‖S. Mowinckel, *JBL,* LVI (1937), 261 f.

careful analysis of the various phenomena will prevent us from hastily identifying the great prophets of Israel and the corresponding figures in other religions of antiquity.

We will examine phenomena in the history of religion which bear resemblance to the prophets of Israel.* Such an examination is important, and the wider the field of study, the better, but, regretfully, we must limit ourselves to the most outstanding examples.

Clearly the theme to be compared is not revelation in the wider sense—of a divine influence upon human intelligence or action—but in the sense of a personal disclosure of a word or a thought.

## OLDER VIEWS

Biblical sources, far from maintaining that prophecy is the monopoly of Israel, record with respect the utterances of the non-Hebrew diviner Balaam (Num. 22–24). Long before Abraham, the word of God came to Noah; and at the time of Moses, to Balaam. About Cyrus, the founder of the Persian empire, a prophet related:

> *Thus says the Lord to His anointed, to Cyrus, . . .*
> *I Myself will go before you and level the mountains, . . .*
> *I will give you the treasures of darkness, . . .*
> *That you may know that it is I, the Lord,*
> *The God of Israel, who call you by your name. . . .*
> *I call you by your name,*
> *I surname you, though you do not know Me.*
>
> Isaiah 45:1–4

---

*We must not compare the prophets of the Bible with the men of subsequent ages who have claimed to be inspired. The latter were obviously influenced by biblical examples, and, significantly, the spiritually powerful in their message was inspired by the Bible, and what was original with them was hardly of great power. On prophecy among the Jews in the Middle Ages, cf. A. J. Heschel, "Did Maimonides Strive for Prophetic Inspiration?" in *L. Ginzberg Jubilee Volume* (Heb.; New York, 1945), pp. 159–188; *idem*, "Inspiration in the Middle Ages," in *Alexander Marx Jubilee Volume* (Heb.; New York, 1950), pp. 175–208. N. Söderblom, *The Living God* (London, 1933), pp. 374 f., quotes approvingly an opinion that puts Grundtvig of Denmark (d. 1872) in the row of the prophets of all time, such as the four great and the twelve minor prophets.

Heathen kings had dreams of divine significance (Gen. 20:6; 41:1 ff.). The soothsayers of the Philistines offered the right advice (I Sam. 6:2 ff.). On the other hand, the prophets regarded pagan gods as gods of stone and wood, described the manufacture of idols with irony, and seemed to identify the idols with the divinities they represented. These gods were certainly incapable of communicating anything to their worshipers. "They have mouths, but do not speak; eyes, but do not see . . ." (Ps. 115:5). In I Kings 18, the conduct of the prophets attached to the cult of Baal is described. Jeremiah referred to prophets, diviners, and sorcerers among the neighboring nations of Israel (27:9), and he condemned "the prophets of Samaria" who "prophesied by Baal, and led my people Israel astray" (23:13; cf. 2:8).

Just as the great prophets distinguished between true and false prophets in Israel, they may have distinguished between true and false prophets among other nations. It is obviously not within our scope to investigate the "truth" or "untruth" of a prophetic experience. We can only analyze the consciousness of "prophets" as reflected in their own utterances.

It is a well-established tradition in Jewish literature that the Lord sent prophets to the nations, and even addressed Himself directly to them.*

Commenting on Deut. 33:2, a Tannaitic source maintains that the mention in this text of God's appearance at Sinai and at other places is taken to mean that He offered the Torah to all the nations of these and other places in turn, but that they refused to accept it.†

A phrase that occurs twelve times in the description of the offerings brought by the princes of the Twelve Tribes of Israel at the dedication of the Tabernacle (Num. 7:13–79) is celebrated as an emphatic

---

*Rabbi Simeon ben Gamliel (*ca.* C.E. 140) refers to seven non-Jewish prophets (*Leviticus Rabba,* ch. 2; *Seder Eliahu Rabba,* ch. 7 [ed. Friedmann, p. 35]). Their names are enumerated in *Seder Olam Rabba,* 21, and *Baba Bathra,* 15b. When the nations of the world were about to go astray, God sent two prophets, Shem and Eber, to admonish them, *Genesis Rabba,* 52, 13. See also *Berachoth,* 7a.
†*Sifre Deuteronomy,* 343.

declaration that God had sent Gentile prophets to the Gentiles just as He had sent Hebrew prophets to Israel ". . . 'both of them full of fine flour mingled with oil for a meal-offering *(minhah)*': This signifies that both to the nations and to Israel the Holy One, blessed be He, sent prophets from their own stock. The meaning of the expression for a *minhah*\* can be illustrated by the text, 'And the spirit of the Lord shall rest *(wenahah)* upon him' (Isa. 11:2), and by the text, 'And the spirit rested *(wattanah)* upon them' (Num. 11:26)."† The apologists of the early church speak of the *logos spermatikos,* the Word in embryonic form, which always and everywhere has been active in the world.‡

Before the building of the Tabernacle, the nations shared the gift of prophecy with Israel.§ The subsequent restriction of prophecy to Israel was due to Moses' prayer.‖

In a highly respected source we read: "I call upon heaven and earth to witness that both Jew and non-Jew, both man and woman, both manservant and maidservant, everybody according to his deeds the Holy Spirit rests upon him."# The influence of the Holy Spirit comes to all men at all ages.

Though the universality of the gift of prophecy is maintained, the uniqueness of the Torah is beyond question. "He declares His word to Jacob, His statutes and ordinances to Israel. He has not dealt thus with any other nation; they do not know His ordinances" (Ps. 147:19–20). This was not due to a refusal on the part of God to give them the Torah, but to a refusal on their part to accept it.\*\*

---

\*The noun *"minhah,"* derived from the verb *"noah,"* which is used for the resting of the divine spirit upon a prophet, is taken to denote the gift of prophecy.
†*Numbers Rabba,* 14, 10.
‡These partial revelations of truth growing from the implanted seed of the logos in the human consciousness are so fragmentary as to contradict each other. See Justin Martyr, *Apologia,* I, 32:46; II, 10.
§*Leviticus Rabba,* I, 12.
‖*Berachoth,* 7a.
#*Seder Eliahu Rabba* (ed. M. Friedmann; Wien, 1902), p. 48.
\*\*According to Rabbi Jose the Galilean, *Mekilta de Rabbi; Ishmael, Bahodesh,* I (ed. Lauterbach, II, 199 f.). See also p. 577 n.

## THE EXPERIENCE OF *MANA* AND *TABU*

There is a widely held belief among the so-called primitive peoples that a mysterious, all-pervading power operates within the life of both man and nature. Among the American Indians, the Iroquois call it *orenda,* the Algonquins *manitou,* and the Sioux *wakanda.* The Melanesians call it *mana,* the term *mana* having been accepted by students of comparative religion as denoting the notion so important to the mentality of primitive man everywhere.* Is it proper, as is occasionally done, to characterize these experiences of numinous power as revelation?

*Mana* means "occult power." It implies the mysteriously efficient, transferable force recognized in all remarkable, impressive, wonderworking things as well as in striking human personalities. An indwelling, occult potency, it reveals itself in effects that can only be ascribed to its presence.

Hidden and vague as *mana* is, it may at times discharge itself, favorably or unfavorably, and become operative. Such manifestations occur when the substances which embody it, certain things or personalities such as the king or the medicine man, are touched or desecrated.†The *mana* may electrify or electrocute him who is exposed to it, the operation being a sort of reflex automatic reaction, effecting either an infusion of power or a resistance offered by the numinous power itself immediately, therefore, as what it is, as power or energy. Its effects are physical: it metes out no retribution; it merely sets up a counteraction. Eternally silent, it does not impart to man its intentions and wishes. In this silence lies the endless mystery felt by helpless man as a constant menace.

---

*  *Mana* is a Melanesian word used in the language of the people of the South Seas, and was first described by R. H. Codrington, *The Melanesians: Anthropology and Folklore* (Oxford, 1891). As a general category, it was first used by R. R. Marett, "Mana," *Encyclopaedia Britannica,* XIV (1945), 770 f. See N. Söderblom, *Das Werden des Gottesglaubens* (Leipzig, 1926), p. 37.

†The awful power lurking in the occult may manifest divine and diabolic effects alike. Rites duly performed by the experts bring *mana* into play. The initiation of youth, puberty, marriage, a battle, a hunt may enable a person to acquire *mana,* "a strong heart," "uplift"; see R. R. Marett, *op. cit.,* p. 771.

An object or a person endowed with *mana* is *tabu*, "marked off." The two notions refer to two aspects, *mana* to the positive, *tabu* to the negative aspect. *Tabu* implies that certain things or individuals are unsafe for casual conduct or use in ordinary life, "not to be lightly approached," because they are charged with *mana*. The *tabu* preserves the *mana* intact; while the sanction behind *tabu* is *mana*.

In sharp contrast to revelation, to the moment of turning and the decision to mediate, or to communicate not the selfhood of God but His thought or intention, stands the immediacy in which the *mana* discharges itself, its incommunicability and silence.

Primitive man does not assert that a god is revealed through an experience of *mana* or *tabu*. The *tabu* object is not equated with the god, but is thought to be possessed by him, and possession by the god is a notion totally different from incarnation of a god. The thought of regarding the object itself as an expression of the god is certainly alien to the mind of the primitive man. An object is *tabu*, not because it is an expression of the god, but because of its being possessed by the god.

What happens between the *tabu* object and the person who approaches it, is part of a process; it is not an event. There is no decision, but only a reaction, an outburst; direct manifestation, not communication; a release of power rather than a grant of meaning. Revelation is a leap, a disclosure of the divine in terms intelligible to man; in the experience of *mana* the numinous force does not cease to be less occult and mysterious, it merely becomes perceptible.

To sum up: primitive man experiences possessions, not revelations; a mysterious process, not a divine event; effects, not utterances; a reaction, not a communication. The scope of ideas relating to *mana* and *tabu* revolves around the sheer fact of numinous power. That power is ambivalent, it may serve or destroy, bring advantage or misfortune. Thus, the world is divisible for him into two aspects: the world as a menace and the world as a source of enhancement. "Ethical distinction does not exist for primitive man."* The notion of divine

---

*B. Ankermann, *"Die Religion der Naturvoelker,"* in Bertholet-Lehmann, *Lehrbuch der Religions Geschichte,* I (Tübingen, 1925), see also G. van der Leeuw, *Religion in Essence and Manifestation* (London, 1939), pp. 24 ff.

power enters the mind of man long before the notion of divine goodness dawns upon him, whether displayed as justice or compassion. Prophetic revelation, on the other hand, is essentially motivated by the divine pathos, which is charged with ethos and relates itself to human conduct seen in terms of good and evil.

## THE ART OF DIVINATION

Divination, the effort to obtain information about future happenings or things otherwise removed from ordinary perception by consulting informants other than human, is found all over the world and is still practiced even among civilized people today. Some primitive peoples would do nothing without consulting an oracle first. Highly regarded in the Greek and Roman world, as well as in the ancient Near East, divination has often been cited as the closest analogy to biblical prophecy.

Among the Babylonians and Assyrians the practice of divination formed one of the most important activities of the national religion. No other people had such an elaborate and highly complicated system of public and private divination. Every great temple had in the course of time accumulated a store of recorded portents, with notes about the events which had been observed to follow them. The principal method of divination was hepatoscopy, or divination by the liver of a sacrificial sheep. The diviner, called *bārû*, was both priest and interpreter or foreteller of the purpose of the gods. He was a professional seer, whose art of hepatoscopy was said to be "the secret knowledge of heaven and earth," and whose office was hereditary. After the due performance of certain rites and the slaughter of the animal, the diviner exposed its liver, and by an examination of its parts or the markings on its surface, was able to predict the future. Definite questions were addressed to the god before the sacrifice and were then answered by the priests according to the omens presented by the sacrificial victims. Some kings consulted the oracle on every occasion of importance, such as the appointment of a high official or the giving of a daughter in marriage. Other means of foretelling future events were dreams, the flight of birds, the movement of animals, and astral signs.*

In Greece there were special places, oracles, where a deity was supposed to respond, by the mouth of an inspired priest, to the inquiries of his votaries. The methods of divination were of great variety, but may be divided into two types. One was the "sane" form of divination, "inductive" and "scientific," the diviner *(mantis)* interpreting signs and omens according to fixed principles of interpretation, telling the will of the gods from the flight of birds or the entrails of a sacrificial victim. The seer remained completely human and self-possessed, but, because instructed, claimed to be able to read what the god had to say. The other type of divination was the ecstatic, enthusiastic, intuitive, or "insane" form, as exemplified by "the prophet," shaman, or the pythoness, who was possessed and overpowered by the deity, and in a state of frenzy served as a mouthpiece through which the god himself spoke.†

The Greek *prophetes* is properly used only of seers and functionaries attached to an established oracular shrine; the unattached seer is called *mantis. Mantis* is one who sees, who knows; *prophetes* is one who proclaims, who interprets. In many of the Greek city states, new appointments were made to the prophetic office every year, the candidates having been taken from certain specific families.‡

At the oracle of Zeus at Olympia, soothsayers prophesied, for

*See M. Jastrow, *Die Religion Babyloniens und Assyriens,* II (Giessen, 1905), 138 ff.; *ANET,* pp. 441 ff. "For the king of Babylon stands at the parting of the way . . . to use divination; he shakes the arrows, he consults the teraphim, he looks at the liver. Into his right hand comes the lot for Jerusalem . . ." (Ezek. 21:26 f.). On divination among the Hittites, see O. R. Gurney, *The Hittites* (Penguin Books, 1961), pp. 158 f.

†See E. Rohde, *Psyche* (Eng.; London, 1925), pp. 290 f. The distinction goes back to Plato, *Phaedrus,* 244, and to Cicero, *De Divinatione,* 1, 11; 2, 26. Inspired prophecy goes back to the chthonian cults which—in contrast to the Olympian religion with its human, comprehensible, and businesslike atmosphere of daylight—lead to mysterious and incomprehensible gods, to be approached at night and often in the darkness of an underground cavern or pit. "They possessed prophets and made them their mouthpiece. Some of them possessed ordinary men too, who thus became *enthoi,* filled with the god, caught up into a new nature." (W. K. C. Guthrie, *The Greeks and Their Gods* [London, 1950], p. 256.)

‡E. Fascher, *Prophetes* (Giessen, 1927), pp. 12, 44.

example, by the inspection of the entrails of the animal sacrificed. At Dodona, the oldest oracle of Zeus in Epirus, where the ecstatic method of divination was never used, stood the "talking oak" of Zeus, which delivered messages concerning the future. It was believed that the tree gave utterance to the thought of Zeus through the whispering of its foliage, and these sounds were interpreted by skilled priests who made the meaning known to consultants by inscribing them on small plaques of lead.* Zeus could further reveal his will through the flight of birds, particularly the eagle, his special bird, across the sky. The will of the gods could also be determined by all sorts of omens and prognostications.

The most important oracular centers, particularly on the Greek mainland, were connected with Apollo, the god of prophecy.† It was not considered possible to approach a specific god or goddess directly, instead, one would apply to one of the established centers, preferably Delphi, and ask Apollo for information about the will of the gods on the subject. Presumably it was taken for granted that members of the polytheistic society of Olympus knew each other's wishes and used Apollo as their general spokesman, in view of his special function as the mouthpiece of Zeus.‡ At Delphi, a woman known as Pythia was believed to be inspired by the god when she was seated on a tripod

---

*A. B. Cook, *Zeus,* I (Cambridge, 1914), 162. According to J. G. Frazer, the oak was the special tree of Zeus because it was more often struck by lightning than any other tree of the forest. Zeus had the power "to foretell at least the immediate future by means of the thunder and the lightning. . . . A shepherd feeding his sheep in the marshes of Dodona stole the finest of his neighbor's flocks and kept it penned in his own fold. The story goes that the owner sought among the shepherds for the stolen sheep, and, when he could not find them, asked the gods who the thief was. They say that the oak then for the first time uttered a voice and said—'The youngest of thy followers.' He put the oracle to the proof, and found them with the shepherd who had but recently begun to feed the flock in that district." (Proxenos, *History of Epeiros,* quoted in A. B. Cook, *op. cit.,* p. 367).

†It is said that Glaucus, a fisherman, having eaten a magical herb, leaped into the sea; there he was changed into a sea god, endowed with the gift of unerring prophecy, and then instructed Apollo and Nereus. Apollo endowed Cassandra with the gift of foreseeing the future, but later added to it the penalty that her predictions would never be believed.

‡H. W. Parke, *A History of the Delphi Oracle* (Oxford, 1939), p. 325. The Pythia is regarded as the bride of Apollo, see A. B. Cook, *op. cit.,* II, 207–9. According to

placed over the rock sacred to him in the inner shrine of the temple. Her words or murmurs, spoken in a state of frenzy, were believed to be the voice of Apollo, expressing the mind of Zeus, and her oracles were so highly respected that Plato allowed the Pythia's Apollo a function in his ideal state.* Yet it was not the frantic priestess, but the guardians of the shrine who were called "prophets," ostensibly shaping her frenzied ejaculations into comprehensible replies.

Another form of divination was the dream, which was believed to be a communion with the spiritual world or an intercourse with a departed spirit. Some dreams would be attained by the method of incubation, by going to sleep in some holy place, after being prepared by a course of ritualistic purification.

Divination, according to Plato, is a divine gift to men. "The prophetess at Delphi and the priestesses at Dodona, when they have been made mad, have conferred many splendid benefits upon Greece both in private and in public affairs."†

The Romans assumed that all nations knew and respected the predictions of soothsayers, the interpreters of prodigies and lightnings, of augurs, or of astrologers, or of oracles.‡ Chrysippus defined divination as "the power to see, understand and explain premonitory signs given to men by the gods. Its duty is to know in advance the disposition of the gods toward men, the manner in which that disposition is shown and by what means the gods may be propitiated and their threatened ills averted."§

Among the ancient Gauls, seers (*vates, manteis*) claimed to have the power of foretelling the future. The *file* among the Celts appears to have been originally a diviner and magician, corresponding to *vates*

---

Plutarch, Themis on the Delphic tripod is impregnated by the central pillar of light, namely, Apollo. (*Ibid.*, p. 1216.)

   * *Republic,* 427b, 470a; *Laws,* 738b, 759c, 865b, 988a. on Socrates' respect for the oracle at Delphi, see *Apology,* 20e. The oracle is to be an authority from which detailed regulations can be sought on the founding of temples and sacrifices and other worship of gods, demigods, and heroes. In the *Laws,* Dodona and Ammon are mentioned together with Delphi as sources of guidance.

   † *Phaedrus,* 244b.

   ‡ Cicero, *De Divinatione,* I, 6, 12.

   § *Ibid.,* II, 63, 130.

of the ancient Gauls. In the course of time the office of the *fili* became extinct, and from the thirteenth to the sixteenth centuries the bard filled its place.

"From both Wales and Ireland we have life-histories of mantic persons, composed in saga-form, and a rich wealth of poetry attributed to seers and sages, which claims to have been recited by them during their periods of inspiration."* Celtic and Norse literature is rich in information about the seer's technique for bringing himself into the inspired condition as well as about mantic practices. Mantic accessories included a preserved human head which was consulted as an oracle.

## PROPHECY AND DIVINATION

The biblical attitude to Semitic divination was one of uncompromising antagonism. Its practice was unequivocally forbidden. "You shall not practice augury or witchcraft. . . . Do not turn to mediums or wizards; do not seek them out, to be defiled by them" (Lev. 19:26, 31; cf. 20:6, 27). "There shall not be found among you . . . any one who practices divination, a soothsayer, or an augur, or a sorcerer, or a charmer, or a medium, or a wizard, or a necromancer. For whoever does these things is an abomination to the Lord; and because of these abominable practices the Lord your God is driving them out before you" (Deut. 18:10–12). However, no prohibition could prevail against the desire to attain knowledge of what the future held in store, and so the practice of divination was not easily eliminated.

Isaiah denounced his people for being like the Philistines in encouraging soothsayers (Isa. 2:6). He knew that in the hour of distress there would be a cry in the land: "Consult the mediums and the wizards! . . . consult the dead on behalf of the living" (Isa. 8;19).†

To be sure, the prophets of Israel, particularly in earlier times, were consulted both on state and on private matters for guidance

---

*N. K. Chadwick, *Poetry and Prophecy* (Cambridge, 1942), pp. 5 f.
†On the legitimate means of obtaining oracles, cf. Y. Kaufmann, *The Religion of Israel* (Eng.; Chicago, 1960), pp. 87 ff.

where human skill had failed to find an answer (I Sam. 9:6; I Kings 14:1 ff.; 22:6; II Kings 19:2). However, such activity on the part of the prophets, particularly in the case of the literary prophets, was accidental to their vocation, and, in contrast to divination, did not involve any technique, fetish, or oracle.

The contrast between prophecy and divination was stressed in the book of Deuteronomy. "For these nations . . . give heed to soothsayers and to diviners; but as for you, the Lord your God has not allowed you to do so. The Lord your God will raise up for you a prophet like me . . ." (18:14 f.). And Jeremiah equated the diviners with the false prophets (Jer. 27:9; 14:14; 29:8; Ezek. 13:6, 9; 21:26; Zech. 10:2).

Phenomenologically, divination is lacking in the fundamental characteristics which, to the mind of the prophet, are decisive for the prophetic event. Divination is never felt to be an event in which a god directs himself to man, nor is it experienced as an act that follows from a divine decision or a turning. It is man who is approaching a god or some occult power. What is sought is information about the future, believed to be indicated in certain signs. The acts of divination are not understood to be a divine inspiration directed to the diviner. The secret is unveiled, but the discovery is not taken to be a communication to man. The signs disclosed, by the inspection of the liver, for example, are there, and do not come about with the intention of disclosing information to the diviner. There is no transcendent event corresponding to the human experience. The act of disclosure is unrelated to the person; it has no direction, in contrast to prophetic inspiration which is experienced as God's free grant to the prophet.

The same situation obtains in acts of divination derived from manifestations in nature. The god speaking in the thunder, in the rustling of the leaves or in the cooing of doves is not believed to be directing himself to man, to be addressing himself to a particular person.

Divination, which is an act initiated by man, is often accompanied by the feeling of wringing a secret from the gods. In earlier periods the knowledge obtained by seers was often felt to be esoteric, and seers were punished by the gods for having revealed their secret to men. The daughter of Cheiron was turned into a mare, the daughters of Dion were turned into rocks, the seers Teiresias and Phineus were blinded for revealing such secrets.* Such antagonism to communication is of course alien to biblical prophecy.

The premise of biblical prophecy is that God is One Who demands and judges, and the prophet is sent to convey the demand and the judgment. The premise of divination seems to be that nature is a storehouse of hidden knowledge that may be unlocked by the diviners. The birds, for example, are more knowing than men. The diviner holds a key; he is not a messenger. He explores at the behest of those who seek guidance, in contrast to the prophet whose experiences are believed to come about at the initiative of God. The former is an act of theotropism; the latter, an act of anthropotropism.

The diviner seeks to obtain God's answer to man's questions; the prophet seeks man's answer to God's question.

In divination, I repeat, the disclosure does not come about as a result of a transcendent initiative or decision; origin and initiative lie with man, who seeks to achieve his aim by means of methods and techniques, or by the performance of certain ascetic or ecstatic exercises.

Foreknowledge of the future is disclosed even without man's initiative or inquiry through signs and omens. Certain natural phenomena were regarded as portents by which the deity intimated to men the evils that were about to befall them. Thunder, especially on a cloudless day, was the omen of Zeus. If heard on the right, it was favorable, and therefore unfavorable to the enemy, who would hear it on the left. Prodigies and portents have been cited as parallels to biblical prophecy.

However, to regard the thunder as "the word from above" or a "a revelation that teaches" and thus bring it into parallel with biblical prophecy is an example of how a metaphor can effectively serve to obscure salient differences. Is there no difference between noise and

*See W. R. Halliday, *Greek Divination* (London, 1913), pp. 71 f.

words, between the rattle of thunder and the language of the prophets?*

Direct intercourse of the gods with man was not an experience claimed in historical times; it belonged, Greek writers maintained, to a happier age when gods and men had lived together in more intimate and unconstrained manner. The whole of antiquity thirsted for divine revelation, and listened and looked for every intimation of the Deity. Yet where, outside Israel, arose men who believed themselves to have been spoken to by God and who, in spite of the bitter and fateful content of their message, made a deep impact on their contemporaries as well as on generations to come?

## Ecstatic Diviners

Besides the inductive and technical form of divination, we occasionally come upon diviners who claim to foretell the future or the will of a god by an intuitive or ecstatic method. The language of the oracles ascribed to the priestesses of the goddess Ishtar of Arbela, a city northeast of Nineveh, implies an ecstatic element.[†]

In an Assyrian oracle dating back to the seventh century, the person who foretells victory and prosperity to the king Esarhaddon feels himself to be one with the god and speaks as the god. "I am the great divine lady, I am the goddess Ishtar of Arbela, who will destroy your enemies before your feet."[‡] What we find here is an oracle rather than a prophetic message.

---

*"In the voice of the thunder the Greeks recognized the warning of a god which the wise understand, and they worshipped it as 'the Word, messenger of Zeus.' The Romans worshipped it as a goddess, Fama; India adores it as 'the Voice in the cloud' which issues from the waters, from the forehead of the father, and hurls the deadly arrow against the foe of Brahman. *So the word from above is either a weapon that kills, or a revelation that teaches.*" (J. Darmsteter, *The Zend Avesta,* "The Sacred Books of the East," IV [Oxford, 1880], p. lxxviii.)

[†]A. Guillaume, *Prophecy and Divination* (London, 1938), p. 43.

[‡]*ANET,* p. 449; H. Gressmann, *Altorientalische Texte zum Alten Testament* (2nd ed.; Berlin, 1926), pp. 281–83.

Wen-Amon, an Egyptian official of the eleventh century B.C.E., tells how he was sent to Byblos on the Phoenician coast to procure lumber for the ceremonial barge. His situation, however, grew precarious when he became embroiled in an argument over money. The prince of Byblos sent to him daily for nearly a month the message: "Get out of my harbor!" While the prince "was making offerings to his gods," the god seized one of his youths and made him possessed. And he said to him, "Bring up [the] god! [namely, the image carried by Wen-Amon for his protection]. Bring the messenger who is carrying him! Amon is the one who sent him out. He is the one who made him come!" We have here a kind of messenger of god who, unasked and unbidden, suddenly appears with some definite divine charge.*

The remarkable feature of this report is that the young man apparently was not asked for his views, that the seizure and the utterance came about suddenly and spontaneously. It is not, however, a prophetic experience that is described here. Here is not a person speaking in the name of a deity, but rather a person speaking as one who is possessed with a deity. (See p. 422.)†

Merlin, the famous bard and seer of Welsh tradition, enchanter and counselor of Arthurian romance, fled in frenzy to the Caledonian forest after learning of the death of his sister's son; and there he prophesied to his pig under an apple tree.‡

---

*ANET, p. 26. According to J. A. Wilson, the determinative of the words "prophetically possessed" shows a human figure in violent motion or epileptic convulsion. Cf. the remarks of A. Schraff in *Zeitschrift für Aegyptische Sprache und Altertumsteunde*, LXXIV (1938), p. 147.

†The sibyls—women supposedly possessed with an occult power that enabled them to predict the future while in a state of frenzy—were connected with many different towns and localities. Heraclitus refers reverently to the sibyl who speaks "with raving mouth," driven by the god. (Diels, *Fragmente der Vorsokratiker*, Heraclitus, 92.) "But the prophetess, not yet able to endure Apollo, raves in the cavern, swollen in stature, striving to throw off the god from the breast; he all the more exercises her frenzied mouth, quelling her wild heart, and fashions her by pressure." (Virgil, *Aeneid*, VI.) See E. Rohde, *op. cit.*, pp. 351 ff. The earliest sibyl was apparently that of Erythrae in Asia Minor; see H. C. O. Lanchester, "Sibylline Oracles," in *ERE*, XI, 496 f.; and E. Bevan, *Sibyls and Seers* (London, 1928), pp. 135 f.

‡J. A. Macculloch, "Celtic Mythology," *The Mythology of All Races*, III (Boston, 1918), 201.

## DREAMS

Closely related to our theme was the almost universal belief in the divine and prophetic character of dreams. In Homer, the sender of dreams was Zeus. Socrates maintained that the dreams of the good man are pure and prophetic.* The Babylonians believed that the deity revealed himself in the dream, declaring the will of heaven and predicting the future. It was particularly the king to whom such knowledge would be conveyed, although prophetic dreams could come to ordinary individuals as well.

While there are in the Bible abundant examples of the belief in divine communication that comes to man in a dream,† the distinction between dream and prophecy is stressed (I Sam. 28:6, 15; Joel 3:1; Job 4:12–16; 7:13–14; 33:14–16). Addressing Aaron and Miriam, who had spoken against Moses, the Lord said to them: "Hear My words. If there is a prophet among you, I the Lord make Myself known to him in a vision, I speak with him in a dream. Not so with My servant Moses. . . . With him I speak mouth to mouth . . ." (Num. 12:6 f.). The statement seems to be intended to minimize the degree of the prophetic gifts of Aaron and Miriam. While the importance of the dream is frequently acknowledged, it is sharply differentiated from prophetic experience (Deut. 13:1 ff.). Jeremiah drew a sharp distinction between a prophet who had the word of God and him who had "a dream. What has chaff in common with wheat?" (Jer. 23:28–32); dreamers are on a par with diviners, soothsayers, sorcerers (Jer. 27:9).

> For the teraphim utter nonsense,
> The diviners see lies;
> The dreamers tell false dreams,
> And give empty consolations.
> Therefore the people wander like sheep;
> They are afflicted for want of a shepherd.
>                         Zechariah 10:2

---

*Plato, *Republic,* 571c.
†In the case of Abimelech, Gen. 20:3; of Jacob, Gen. 31:10 f.; of Solomon, I Kings 3:5, 15.

Even as the night visions of the postexilic Zechariah are not to be understood as dreams. Only in Daniel (2:1 ff.) do we find prophecy through the medium of the dream.*

## SOCRATES' DAIMONION

"How prophetic is the human soul!" said Socrates.† At sundry times and in divers places he spoke of an oracle or a sign coming to him. It was a common experience to him to hear a mysterious inner voice—"the usual prophetic sign from the Daimonion on my behalf"—which he accepted as divine instruction. It did not come to him as a result of deliberation or preparation; he took no steps to bring it about. It was something that fell upon him when exercising his vocation. Significantly, Socrates maintained, "It always forbids, but never commands me to do anything which I am going to do."‡ It came in the form of warnings even in reference to trifles if he were on the verge of making a slip or an error in any matter. Once when about to cross a river, he heard a voice saying in his ear that he had been guilty of impiety, and that he must not go away until he had made an atonement.§ The Daimonion made him feel certain that he was the object of divine care, a certainty which was intimately connected with his uprightness and submission to the good.

Socrates considered this Daimonion to be a unique phenomenon. By his own admission, "rarely, if ever, has such a monitor been given to any other man."‖ The Athenians had never heard of such an experience and therefore regarded it as a new divinity, while Xenophon considered it akin to the art of divination.#

*E. L. Ehrlich, *Der Traum im Alten Testament* (Berlin, 1953), pp. 151 ff.
†*Phaedrus,* 242.
‡*Apology,* 31, 40.
§*Phaedrus,* 242.
‖*Republic,* 496.
#Xenophon, *Memorabilia,* IV, 3, 12; N. Söderblom, *op. cit.,* p. 241. Generalizing some passages in Xenophon and Plato, where Daimonion is employed metaphorically, as a symbolic expression for the inner conviction, "the attempt has been made to deliver Socrates from an embarrassing and, for a wise man and pattern of virtue, unworthy eccentricity by explaining the Daimonion as a figure of speech." (K. Joel, *Der Xenophon-*

"Socrates," it may be maintained, "had indeed an auditory perception unknown to other people. The peculiar phenomenon was a reality, not a way of speaking."* Yet it differed basically from what transpired in the life of the prophet—in what it conveyed, in how it transpired, and in whom it made present. It did not convey a way of living or a vision of history, but rather a warning or a premonition. It concerned Socrates personally rather than the people of Greece. The experience he claimed was the perception of a voice; the prophet's experience was the encounter with God. To hear a voice of an anonymous deity is not the same as being overcome by the presence of the Creator of heaven and earth. The Daimonion was a sign from an anonymous divinity; the prophetic word came from the God of Israel. The Daimonion was a guide, a friend who warned him of danger, rather than the Creator, Judge, King, and Savior of all men.

Related to Socrates' claim was the belief that man had the capacity of hearing the voice of the Deity within his own soul.

"There is a god within us; we are in touch with heaven: from celestial places comes our inspiration." "There is a god within us. It is when he stirs us that our bosom warms; it is his impulse that sows the seeds of inspiration."†

## THE CODE OF HAMMURABI

It is often assumed that the sculptured relief at the head of the stele bearing the Code of Hammurabi shows a picture of the god Shamash giving the laws to Hammurabi. We see Hammurabi standing before the deity, who holds in his hands a staff and a ring.‡ Such a

---

tische und der echte Socrates [Berlin, 1893], pp. 67 ff.) This is rejected by N. Söderblom, op. cit., p. 240.

*Ibid.

†Ovid, Ars Amatoria, III, 549 ff.; Fasti, vi, 5 f.

‡Significantly, there is a discrepancy between the image and the text of the Prologue, in which there is no reference to Shamash, and according to which it is Marduk who is said to have ordered Hammurabi to set forth justice in the land. See F. M. T. Boehl, "King Hammurabi of Babylon in the Setting of His Time," Mededeelingen der Koninklijke Nederlandsche Akademie van Wetenschappen, IX (new series; 341 ff.)

picture is found elsewhere showing a king in the performance of a ritual and the god holding the ring, the staff, and the measuring line. However, the ring and the staff are emblems of sovereignty. It is these that the god is handing to Hammurabi. The relief expresses in design what the prologue of the Code expresses in words: that Hammurabi's power is from heaven. A fundamental belief of the Babylonians and Assyrians was that kingship came down from heaven, and the power of kingship included the power to give laws to the land and its people. But the picture does not represent the giving of the laws. How little the conferring of these insignia implies the giving of the laws or the notion of a just rule may be gathered from a wall painting, contemporary with Hammurabi, found at Mari, where the king, with a similar gesture, receives these tokens from an armed goddess.*

The text of the Code falls into three parts: the prologue, the corpus of the laws, and the epilogue. The prologue, written in the language of poetry, tells of the call of Hammurabi to be king of Babylon and to give justice to the people entrusted to his care. It begins by saying that Anum, the father of the gods, and Enlil, the god of heaven, had given lordship over all things to Marduk, the tutelary god of Babylon and patron deity of the dynasty of Hammurabi, and that they had called Hammurabi "to cause justice to prevail in the land, to destroy naughty and wicked men so that the strong might not afflict the weak." The prologue concludes with Hammurabi's announcement that "when Marduk commissioned me to guide the people aright, to direct the land, I established law and justice in the language of the land and prospered the people."†

There is no reference in the text itself to a revelation. On the contrary, in the prologue he seems to attribute the laws to himself, stating that he was commanded by Marduk, "to make justice shine in the land" (1, 27–34). Hence, "I established law and justice in the

---

*C. J. Gadd, *Ideas of Divine Rule in the Ancient Near East* (London, 1948), pp. 90 f.

†"The Code of Hammurabi," trans. by T. J. Meek, in *ANET,* pp. 163 ff.; G. R. Driver and J. C. Miles, *The Babylonian Laws* (Oxford, 1955–56), I, 36 f.; II, 7–13.

land" (5, 20 f.). And so, his long list of statutes are laws of justice which Hammurabi, the efficient king, set up, and by which he "caused the land to secure firm guidance and good government" (24, 1–8). No one shall alter "the Law of the land which I enacted and the ordinances of the land which I prescribed; let him not scorn my statutes" (25, 68).

Far from considering himself a recipient of revelation, he calls himself "the powerful king, the sun of Babylon who causes light to go forth over the lands of Sumer and Akkad; the king who has made the four quarters of the world subservient, the favorite of Inanna am I" (5, 3–9).

The people of Babylonia and Assyria thought that certain facts and ideas were communicated to them by the gods in the days of old.* The statement, "I, Hammurabi, the king of justice, to whom Shamash committed law" (25, 95), expresses a belief in a general divine influence rather than the claim of a particular revelation.

What the god "gives" the king is not "laws," but the gift of the perception of *kittum* (cosmic truths), by virtue of which the king, in distinction from any other individual, becomes capable of promulgating laws that are in accord or harmony with the cosmic principle of *kittum*.†

The ancients said their laws came from the gods. The Cretans attributed their laws, not to Minos, but to Jupiter.‡ The Lacedaemonians believed that their legislator was not Lycurgus, but Apollo. The Romans believed that Numa wrote under the dictation of one of the most powerful divinities of ancient Italy—the goddess Egeria. The

---

*E. Schrader, *Die Keilinschriften und das Alte Testament* (3rd ed.; Berlin, 1905), pp. 534 ff.

†See M. Greenberg, "Some Postulates of Biblical Criminal Law," *Yehezkel Kaufmann Jubilee Volume* (Jerusalem, 1960), pp. 9 f., and the statement by J. J. Finkelstein, quoted in n. 8.

‡According to a myth, Minos, the son of Zeus, consorted and discoursed with Zeus in the ninth year, and went regularly to be educated by Zeus as though he were a Sophist. Among the Cretans it was believed that every ninth year Minos would go up to the cave of Zeus and receive decrees from him and carry them to the people. Cf. Homer, *Odyssey* XIX, 179; Plato, *Minos*, 319c; Plato, *Laws*, 624d; Strabo, *Geography*, 16, 2, 38.

Etruscans had received their laws from the god Tages.* Yet such belief did not claim that the laws were given to a prophet at a particular moment in history. It expressed mythically the idea that the laws were not invented by man.

## "Prophets" in Egypt

For a time the claim was made that a number of Egyptian texts show such a close kinship to biblical prophecy that they must be regarded as a source and model for biblical prophecy.† Today the prophetic character of these texts is generally denied.‡

In one of these texts, a certain Ipu-wer condemns the past and present administration of Egypt. The country, it seems, had suffered a breakdown of government, resulting in social and economic chaos. Yet the Pharaoh appeared indifferent to what was happening. ". . . poor men have become the possessors of treasures. He who could not make himself a pair of sandals is (now) the possessor of riches . . . nobles are in lamentation, while poor men have joy. . . . Behold, noble ladies are (now) gleaners, and nobles are in the workhouse. (But) he who never (even) slept on a *plank* is (now) the owner of a bed . . . How is it that every man kills his brother?" Ipu-wer, who was at first inclined to absolve the Pharaoh of his guilt, ends his speech by denouncing the king for evading his responsibilities.§

In the remarkably outspoken way in which social conditions are denounced and the fearlessness with which the king is criticized to his face, the text shows affinity with prophetic writing. Bewailing chaos and confusion and reminding the king of his responsibilities, the author, however, does not rise from the awareness of the collapse of

---

*F. de Coulanges, *The Ancient City* (New York, 1955), p. 189.

†E. Meyer, *Die Israeliten und ihre Nachbarstaemme* (Halle, 1906), pp. 451 ff.; J. H. Breasted, *The Dawn of Conscience* (New York, 1933), pp. 193–200.

‡H. Bonnet, *Reallexikon der Aegyptischen Religionsgeschichte* (Berlin, 1952), pp. 608 f. Cf., however, G. Lanczkowski, *"Aegyptischer Prophetismus in Lichte des alttestamentlichen,"* ZAW, LXX (1958, NF, 29), pp. 31 ff.

§*ANET*, pp. 441 f. J. A. Wilson, *The Culture of Ancient Egypt* (Chicago, 1958), pp. 2, 107–110.

the social and administrative order to an understanding of a moral or spiritual failure. The author decries the end of prosperity for the rich, while the prophets of Israel condemn the deprivation of the poor in the midst of prosperity. Ipu-wer's "anger and sympathy are aroused, indeed; not so much, however, because the weak are oppressed as because the established order of society is overthrown. Whereas the Hebrew prophet was the champion of the poor, the Egyptian is, in this case at least, the defender of law and order. It is unseemly in his eyes that the conditions should be reversed as they have been so that poor and rich have changed places."* The Egyptian speaker pleads for stability, the prophets call for a change. Far from searching for the roots of the crisis in the human condition, as the prophets of Israel consistently do, the author blames the gods, especially the god Re, for the calamities and misery that befall man. Indeed, along with the description of the disorder, the complaint against the gods emerges as the main theme.†

The so-called Papyrus Golenischeff, "the prophecy of Nefer-rohu," relates how the Pharaoh, seeking to be entertained, called in Nefer-rohu in order to be told about events to come. Nefer-rohu then predicted the coming age of happiness and light, to be brought about by a certain King Ameni.‡

Apart from the much-debated resemblance of the prediction of an age of happiness to the messianic idea in Israel, it is difficult to discern any kinship with the prophets. Nefer-rohu is a priest, seer, and magician, "a scribe competent with his fingers; he is a man of rank, who has more property than any peer of his"; a wise man whose wisdom enables him to perform deeds of magic as well as to predict what is going to happen. He is not an inspired man but a diviner.

Moreover, the text intends to relate how "a prophet" foretold the collapse of the Old Kingdom in the presence of King Snefru of the Fourth Dynasty (2650 B.C.E.), whereas in actuality the document

*J. M. P. Smith, *The Prophet and His Problems* (New York, 1916), pp. 26 f.
†O. Eberhard, B. Spuler, eds., in *Handbuch der Orientalistik,* Vol. I, *Aegyptologie,* Pt. II, *Literatur* (Leiden, 1952), p. 113.
‡*ANET,* pp. 444 f.; J. A. Wilson, *op. cit.,* pp. 106–8.

seems to have been produced five centuries later at the time of Amen-em-het I (1991–1961 B.C.E.), first ruler of the Twelfth Dynasty of the Middle Kingdom. The Middle Kingdom delivered Egypt from civil war and anarchy which had followed the Old Kingdom, and the early pharaohs of the Middle Kingdom sought to foster a feeling of salvation which their rule has established. The text of the prophecy of Nefer-rohu was apparently designed to reinforce their pretensions.*

Last but not least, neither Ipu-wer nor the author of the prophecy of Nefer-rohu speaks in the name of a god, as a person called by a higher being to convey his will to the king; both speak as critics of society, not as communicators of a divine word.

## Revelation and Prophecy in India and China

Indian religion makes no claim to a revelation, to an event that happened at a particular moment in time in which a personal God who transcends man as well as nature addressed Himself to a particular person who actually lived. It is rather a revelation of what is latent in man, a revelation that is timeless, not restricted to a real person in history. The theophany described in the Bhagavad-Gita, for example, is not intended to be taken as an event that actually happened, nor as an account of a revelation of God. Krishna, who appears to Arjuna in the disguise of a charioteer, speaks not as a deity but as an incarnation of a deity, as one who has passed through many births and who is born for the protection of good people and the destruction of evildo-ers. Krishna, believed by some to have been either a tribal leader or a wise man inquiring into the highest truth, became a hero of his people, a demigod and later a god, and still later in Brahmanism an incarnation of Vishnu. At one time in the Bhagavad-Gita he says of himself that he is the one sole, supreme god, creator and ruler of the universe; at another time, the impersonal world-soul (Brahman) is presented as the supreme first principle.† "Verily I am the Author of Vedanta and the knower of Vedas am I."‡

---

*See J. A. Wilson, *ANET,* p. 444.
†*ERE,* VII, pp. 194 f.; R. Garbe, *Bhagavad-Gita* (Leipzig, 1905), ch. 2.
‡*Bhagavad-Gita,* vi, 15.

Most of the religions of India accept as authoritative certain sacred writings which are believed to be not purely human productions, but to derive from a superhuman source. Such writings are called *sruti,* that which is heard, for example, the Vedas. There are two trends of thought concerning their origin. According to the school of Mimāmsā, the Veda in the form of eternal words is, like the world, without beginning or end. It was intuited by the sages without any revealer. The authority of the Veda is beyond doubt because it is not composed by anyone, and so there is no likelihood of falsehoods in it. According to the school of Nyāya, the Veda was composed by God at the beginning of creation, and was revealed by God to the first-born Brahmā, to sages and gods.

The first school argues that since nobody is remembered as the author of the Veda, and since it is unique and therefore no one could have composed it, it is eternal and not composed by anyone. There are no prophets. According to the second school, the Veda itself mentions God as its author. If it is asked, How did God, who has no body, compose and teach the Veda? We can suppose that he embodies himself whenever necessary. Thus, while some authorities do not expressly mention God as its author, later Nyāya writers assert that God is its author.*

This voluminous ancient literature, however, occupies a rather different place in the life of Hinduism from the place the Torah has in the life of the Jew, or the Koran in the life of Islam. While the theory of the inspiration and inerrancy of the sacred writings is universally taught and accepted, its effect on the life and thought of the Hindu is slight. Like the books themselves, which are unknown except in name to any but a very few, the subtleties of the doctrine are the possession of a learned class.

More important is the fact that most of these writings do not impress the reader as having been intended as revelations; no such claim seems to be asserted. Thus, a Christian writer remarks,

*K. S. Murty, *Revelation and Reason in Advaita Vedanta* (New York, 1959), pp. 212–239.

Brahmanas, which are reckoned as sruti, or revelation of
the first order, in content appear to be very human discussions
of the ritual of sacrifice, which might be classed as technical
theological discussion, but which makes in itself little claim to
be divine. The oldest section of the Vedic literature, the
Rigveda, consists of hymns, the aspiration of men towards
God, or the gods, rather than God's impartation of Himself to
men. . . . In the Upanishads, which are the fount and origin of
the higher thought of later Hinduism, we seem to have for the
most part acute insights or intuitions into truth, rather than
divine revelation. . . . The situation changes when we come
to the Bhagavadgita, although according to theory this is only
revelation of the second rank. In it we have not merely the
conveyance of doctrine by a divine teacher, but at the climax of
the work there is the revelation of Krishna as the supreme God.
We find an equally definite claim to revelation in sectarian
works which are entirely outside the Vedic category.*

The Buddha disclaimed any revelation in the sense of receiving
knowledge from a source of wisdom higher than his own. "That
which behooves the world to learn, but through the world no learner
found, I now myself and by myself have learned throughout," he said.

In China, Confucianism and Taoism have each their Scriptures
or classics *(king)* which are authoritative over every detail of Chinese
life. However, the authority of these classics is not due to any special
inspiration, but to their connection with sages who comprehended
the ideal development of human nature.

"The ancient books of China do not profess to have been
inspired, or to contain what we should call a revelation. Historians,
poets, and others wrote them as they were moved in their own
minds."† No Hebrew prophet would venture to prophesy without an

---

*M. H. Harrison, "Christian Apologetic and the Claims of the Non-Christian
Religions in Regard to Revelation," *International Review of Missions,* XXXVIII (Oct.,
1949), pp. 458–459.

†James Legge, *The Sacred Books of China* (Oxford, 1879), p. xv.

initial experience of an extraordinary character. "Of the Chinese sages we have no record of similar memorable experiences in which they heard the voice of God summoning them to their task," though Confucius, Mencius, and Mo-tzu were not "without the consciousness that their mission had been laid upon them." Although they have shared with the Hebrew prophets "a passion to reform men and so to reform the world, a vision of a world marked by righteousness and a sense of mission divinely given," they could not be characterized as prophets in the sense of men who, conscious of being inspired by God, convey to the people what was given to them.*

## The Prophets of Mari

French excavations at Tel-el-Hariri, the seat of the ancient kingdom of Mari, on the Middle Euphrates, have brought to light very many cuneiform tablets once in the public record office of the royal palace, of which only a small portion has been published. Three texts seem to contain parallels to biblical prophecy.†

In one of these texts, Itur-ashdu, the governor of the royal city, Mari, reports to the king, who is in the field with his army, as follows: A man, whose name and town are given, has come to him and informed him that he has had a dream in which he was transported into the sanctuary of the god Dagan in the city of Tirqa, and that he was instructed by the god, saying: "Go now; I send you to Zimrilim (the king of Mari): (to him) you yourself shall say: 'Send me thy messengers, and lay all thy affairs before me.'" As a reward, the god will grant him victory over his foes.

The diviner delivers the message to the governor rather than

---

*See H. H. Rowley, *Prophecy and China* (New York, 1956), pp. 5, 121 ff., 142 f.; see p. 2, n. 1.

†A. Lods, in *Studies in Old Testament Prophecy*, "T. H. Robinson Festschrift," ed. by H. H. Rowley (Edinburgh, 1950), pp. 103 ff. M. Noth, *Bulletin of the John Rylands Library, XXXII* (1949–50), 194 ff.; M. Noth, *Geschichte und Gotteswort im Alten Testament* (Krefeld, 1949), pp. 12–13. G. E. Mendenhall, "Mari," *The Biblical Archaeologist*, XI (1948), 2–19; A. Malamat, "Prophecy in Mari Documents," *Eretz-Israel*, IV (1956), 74 ff.; F. M. Röhl, *Opera Minora* (Groningen, 1953), pp. 63 ff.

directly to the king. The message from the god Dagan is said to have come in a dream.

In a letter to the king we read: "To my Lord (i.e., King Zimri-lim) speak. Thy servant Kibri-Dagan (has spoken) as follows: The god Dagan and the god Ikrub-il are safe and sound. The city Tirqa and district are safe and sound. Moreover on the day on which I dispatched this tablet to my lord on the way, a man of the god Dagan came and spoke the following word to me: The god has sent me (with the following instruction): Send speedily to the king! Offerings for the dead shall they offer to the spirit of Jahdun-lim. This has the man spoken to me. I communicate it to my lord. May my lord do whatever he thinks right."

In a second letter the same writer reports to the king a similar message of "a prophet" concerning sacrificial offerings.

The striking feature in these documents is the use of the expressions "the god has sent me," "Dagan has sent me," reminiscent of Moses' statement to Pharaoh: "The Lord, the God of the Hebrews, sent me to you" (Exod. 7:16) and of Jeremiah saying: "The Lord sent me" (Jer. 26:12). It would appear that the message came by divine initiative, and not in response to a question, and that "the prophet" felt that he had been sent by the god,* a feeling which is one of the main characteristics of the biblical prophet (see Jer. 6:8; 23:21; 29:19).

What is the nature of the exhortation to keep the god informed ("send me thy messengers, and lay all thy affairs before me") or that sacrifices be brought for the dead spirit of the previous king? It is in substance similar to the command given to Esarhaddon, one of the bloodiest of Assyrian kings, in connection with a military campaign, by a prophetess of Ishtar of Arbela: "I am the Ishtar of Arbela. I have made Ashur gracious unto thee. . . . Fear not, but glorify me."† To

---

*In ancient Elam the highest title in the land was *sukkalmah*, "exalted messenger," presumably in the sense of "divine messenger" or angel. See G. G. Cameron, *History of Early Iran* (Chicago, 1936), p. 71.

†L. Waterman, *Royal Correspondence of the Assyrian Empire*, Pt. I (Chicago, 1892); R. H. Pfeiffer, *State Letters of Assyria* (New Haven, 1935), pp. 179 ff. At times

glorify Ishtar meant hardly more than, "See that the priests of the sanctuary are lavishly rewarded and that the temple worship is adequately provided for from the treasury."*

The bearers of the Mari messages speak in the name of gods whose primary concern is with the upkeep of the sanctuaries with which they, and presumably the messengers as well, are associated. These are messages which are literally *pro domo*. The god feels neglected because he is not consulted which, of course, means that the priests feel neglected. The Mari "prophet" speaks for the sake of priests and sanctuaries.

Letters and reports from diviners conveying directions for the king to carry out ceremonies of propitiation were common in Mesopotamia. The only novel element in these records that go back to pre-Israelite times is the claim that the message came by the initiative of the god rather than as a response to an inquiry, as is the case in divination, and that furthermore the person appears as a messenger of the god, sent to deliver a message to the king, a messenger with a specific divine mission to fulfill. This information is particularly important since it refers to a region from which, according to the biblical account, Abraham migrated to Canaan.

Indeed, it would be strange if men living in genuine dedication to the gods and maintaining cults and sanctuaries to their benefit should assume that the gods never communicate at least with certain individuals. These gods depend upon man, upon his gifts and homage, and are, in fact, very much like human beings, except for their being immortal and their possession of superior powers. If they may be appeased and their will manipulated, if the gods may be influenced and turned by sacrifices, by soothing entreaties and offerings,† why should there not be a way of causing them to communicate with some individuals? The Mari "prophet" is the extension of an institution rather than the spokesman of a transcendent Deity. His inspiration is

---

the king became impatient at the prolongation of a fast enjoined upon him by the diviners; see L. Waterman, *op. cit.*, no. 78.

*A. Guillaume, *op. cit.*, p. 44.

†See Plato, *Republic*, II, 365.

devoid of the sublime. There is no intrusion of the transcendent in his experience. He is being addressed by a god, experiencing a divine direction, but there is no awareness of "a turning."

Neither prediction nor speaking in the name of God is the most important feature of biblical prophecy. The prophet is not sent to the people in order to demand that some particular act be done; he is sent because of a divine concern for the total existence of the people; he does not convey primarily a command *ad hoc,* but a message that relates to the total existence of the people.

The prophets of Israel do not claim that a god spoke to them, a god among many gods, a local deity, an oracle, a force among many forces in the world; it is the Creator of heaven and earth, the One and Unique Who transcends the world and Whose wisdom no one can fathom, Whose word the prophets claim to have heard. It seems likely that to the consciousness of the Hebrew prophets the difference between their own experiences and the experiences of the pagan prophets was as absolute as the difference between the God of Israel and the gods of the pagans.

Both have received an insight into the will of a deity they worship. The man of Mari receives the god's appeal for information; the god feels neglected, he is not kept informed about the king's affairs; in the dream the god inquires whether a certain tribe had come to terms with the king of Mari. The prophet of Mari speaks for the god and for the benefit of the god: the prophets of Israel speak for God, but for the benefit of the people. Both claim to be sent, to be messengers, but there is a radical difference between the consciousness of being sent by the god Dagan and the consciousness of being sent by the Holy One of Israel.* The man of Mari is sent because of the god's impotence and dependence upon man for food, information, and prestige. The prophet of Israel is sent because of man's sins and total dependence upon God Who demands righteousness. "As the clay in

---

*I do not agree with the view of M. Noth, *op. cit.,* p. 200, that the difference "lies not in the manner of occurrence, but in the content of that which is announced as the divine message. . . . The message deals with cult and political matters of very limited and ephemeral importance."

the potter's hand, so are you in My hand, O house of Israel" is the word of the Lord (Jer. 18:6).

## THE BIBLICAL PROPHET A TYPE *SUI GENERIS*

Are prophets to be found everywhere in the world?

It is not within the power or concern of critical scholarship to suggest and to prove who is to be called a prophet. The first and main feature of a prophet is his own claim to be a prophet; his own testimony to an experience of the Supreme Being addressing Himself to him for the purpose of conveying a message to others; his own consciousness of an event in which both decision and direction come upon him as a transcendent act.

Other ancient religions had their shamans and diviners, their priests and oracles, their wise and inspired men, but what have most shamans and diviners left to posterity? Where else has a revelation come with a claim to be the word and the truth for all men? Or to be the voice of Him Who created heaven and earth?

Prophecy in Israel was not an episode in the life of an individual, but an illumination in the history of the people. A chain of experiences that held together events extending over centuries was an unparalleled fact in the history of mankind.

Thus, the prophet is not an isolated figure; he feels himself to be a link in the succession of the prophets (Amos 3:7 f.; cf. 2:12); "from the day that your fathers came out of the land of Egypt to this day, I have persistently sent all my prophets to them, day after day" (Jer. 7:25; cf. 11:7; 25:4; 26:15; 29:19). The consistency with the experience and message of his predecessors is such that each prophet regards the revelations he receives as a continuation of what is given to earlier prophets. The Hebrew prophet is not a pioneer; he hears Him Who spoke to Abraham.

Prophetic incidents, revelatory moments, are believed to have happened to many people in many lands. But a line of prophets, stretching over many centuries, from Abraham to Moses, from Samuel to Nathan, from Elijah to Amos, from Hosea to Isaiah, from Jeremiah to Malachi, is a phenomenon for which there is no analogy.

Zoroaster was obviously an inspired man, and so was Balaam; but it was a spark lost in the darkness. What followed them was superstition or complete oblivion. There were men elsewhere who were inspired and were able to inspire their fellow men. But where else was there a nation which was able to emulate the prophetic history of Israel?

Thus it is not accurate to say that biblical inspiration simply followed a conception already found in many earlier religions, or that its difference from the spells used by shamans to force the spirits to do their behests, the incantations so common with medicine men, is one of degree rather than of kind.

Neither Lao-Tzu nor Buddha, neither Socrates nor Plotinus, neither Confucius nor Ipu-wer spoke in the name of God or felt themselves as sent by Him; and the priests and prophets of pagan religions spoke in the name of a particular spirit, not in the name of the Creator of heaven and earth.

It is true that man everywhere and at all times seeks guidance and help from the divine world, aspires to visionary experience and to the acquisition of supernatural powers, and longs to behold in dreams and visions the mysteries which are veiled from the common eye. Yet the prophets of Israel did not seek such experiences; they resisted their call. In contrast to the apocalyptic visionaries, the pre-exilic prophets are shown the confusions on earth rather than the glories in heaven. Their distinction was to sense the human situation as a divine emergency.

It may be true that almost everywhere some sort of revelation is regarded as the primary source of religious truth. Yet the supernatural means by which such truth is communicated are omens, dreams, divination, inferences from strange happenings, utterances of shamans and priests. The biblical prophet is a type *sui generis*.

# 16

# Prophet, Priest, and King

## THE DEIFICATION OF KINGS

"God and king are two conceptions so nearly coupled in the oriental mind that the distinction is constantly blurred."* The god Re, according to mythology, was the first king in Egypt, and gods were among the rulers in Sumeria after the Flood. Thus, in historic times the king's majesty was equaled to that of a god. The king was held to be a god, begotten by his heavenly father, the sun god Re, who assumed the form of the living king for the purpose of procreation of an heir to the throne.

The kings were regarded as gods, sacrifices were offered to them, and their worship was celebrated in special temples by special priests. Indeed the worship of the kings sometimes cast worship of the gods into the shade. Thus, in the reign of Merenra a high official declared that he had built many holy places in order that the spirits of the king, the ever-living Merenra, might be invoked "more than all the gods." The king was also the high priest of each god, who for practical pur-

*C. J. Gadd, *Ideas of Divine Rule in the Ancient Near East* (London, 1948), p. 33. Cf. I. Engnell, *Studies in Divine Kingship in the Ancient Near East* (Uppsala, 1943).

poses delegated his functions to the professional priesthood.* In Mesopotamia, the king, while not begotten by a god, was regarded as a man made divine, as the adopted "son" of the god, nursed, reared, and educated by the different gods and goddesses. It was not uncommon for rulers of Sumerian cities to claim that a god was their parent, and the belief in having been nourished by the holy milk of a divine nurse was professed by rulers as far apart as Eannadu (probably before 4000 B.C.E.) and Ashurbanipal (d. 633 B.C.E.). A few kings called themselves "husbands" of goddesses. The king, who was also a priest, was "always upon the point of stepping over into the god, and yet he is always subordinate." The courtly phrase for the demise of the crown was the late king "became a god."†

Among the Hittites, the king was also the high priest. He sustained the cult, deposed and instituted priests. Though not recognized as a god during his lifetime, he was deified after his death.‡ Similarly, Parthian monarchs of an Arsacid dynasty called themselves brothers of the moon and sun, and they were worshiped as gods.§

This conception of kingship going back to primitive times, when the chief was regarded as charged with mysterious *mana, orenda,* or *dynamis* and was *tabu* to his subjects, has remained a potent motive in political and religious history in many civilizations down to the twentieth century.‖ According to Shinto doctrine, the emperor of Japan was descended from heaven, divine and sacred. Not only should he not be the subject of derogatory comment, he should not be a topic of discussion. He was the sole owner of the empire, the author

*H. Jacobsohn, *Die dogmatische Stellung des Königs in der Theologie der alten Aegypten* (Glueckstadt, 1939).

†C. J. Gadd, *op. cit.,* pp. 17 f. A. Jeremias, *"Die Vergoettlichung der Babylonisch-Assyrischen Koenige,"* *Der Alte Orient,* XIX, 3–4. (Leipzig, 1919). H. Frankfort, *Kingship and the Gods* (Chicago, 1948). M. Buber, *Königtum Gottes* (3rd ed.; Heidelberg, 1956), pp. 39 ff.

‡R. de Vaux, *Ancient Israel* (New York, 1961), p. 112. See, however, Engnell, *op. cit.,* pp. 52, 62, 173.

§J. G. Frazer, *The Golden Bough* (abr. by Th. H. Gaster; New York, 1959), pp. 66 ff.

‖See *The Sacred Kingship* ("Studies in the History of Religions," IV, supplements to *Numen* [Leiden, 1959]).

of law and justice.* Through the apotheosis of the Roman emperor as *Dominus et Deus* and medieval traditions, down to modern times, one may trace the tendency to deify the king or to garb him with the trappings of divinity. One may cite as an example the frequent allusions made by Henry VIII's contemporaries to his "sun-like nature whose flaming beams the lowly subject can in no wise steadfastly behold."† Absolute nonresistance to the king was enjoined because he "representeth as it were the image of God upon earth," and must be obeyed "yea, though he were an infidel."‡ Views have been expressed that "absolute princes, such as the sovereigns of England, were a species of divinity," that kings "represent unto us the person even of God Himself."§

As a consequence of this conception it was assumed that the king stood above the law. According to the fourteenth-century Italian jurist Baldus, the prince had *plenitude potestatis,* and he could therefore do anything *supra jus et contra jus, et extra jus.* From the time of the English Reformation we have Tyndale's statement that "the King is, in this world, without law; and may at his lust do right or wrong, and shall give account but to God only."‖ James I (1567–1625) declared that "the King is above the Law." "That the king can do no wrong is," according to the famous jurist Sir William Blackstone (1723–1780), "a necessary and fundamental principle of the English constitution."#

Some German scholars have held that the state was creator of the

---

*P. Wheeler, *The Sacred Scriptures of the Japanese* (New York, 1952), p. xiii. In Lamaism, the Dalai Lama is the incarnation of the great bodhisattva Avalokiteśvara, the ancestor of the Tibetans, and the Tashi Lama is an earthly reflex of Amitābha, one of the Buddhas of the ten directions of space.

†F. L. Baumer, *The Early Tudor Theory of Kingship* (New Haven, 1940), p. 86; cf. p. 89.

‡*Ibid.,* p. 121.

§*Ibid.,* p. 96; see also F. D. Wormuth, *The Royal Prerogative* (Ithaca, 1939), pp. 83 ff.

‖Tyndale, *Obedience of a Christian Man* (1528), quoted in F. L. Baumer, *op. cit.* (New Haven, 1940), pp. 121–164. Cf. the saying of Bracton in the 13th century: *Rex non debet esse sub homine sed sub deo et lege.* Even the French political philosopher, Jean Bodin (1530–96) argued that only when the king possesses "an unlimited right to make, interpret, and execute law" can anarchy be averted. (Baumer, *op. cit.,* p. 124.)

#W. C. Jones, ed., W. Blackstone, *Commentaries* (San Francisco, 1916), Bk. III, ch. 17.

law, and thus superior to the law, and that acts of government officials were therefore not subject to the jurisdiction of the courts. Opposing such executive despotism, others insisted that the state was bound by law.*

## THE SEPARATION OF POWERS

Deification of kings was unthinkable in Israel. Any attempts to attribute divinity to a human being would have evoked horror and outrage. If "elsewhere the king was a god, in Israel it was God who was king."† For the land is Mine; for you are strangers and sojourners with Me" (Lev. 25:23). The arguments adduced in support of the theory that the ancient Hebrews adhered to the divinity of kings, but that this conception was suppressed in biblical records,‡ "are extremely flimsy."§

How the prophets felt about the deification of kings may be deduced from Ezekiel.

> *Son of man, say to the prince of Tyre*
> *Thus says the Lord God:*
> *Because your heart is proud*
> *And you have said, I am a god,*
> *I sit in the seat of the gods,*
> *In the heart of the seas,*
> *Yet, you are but a man, and no god,*
> *Though you consider yourself as wise as a god—*
> *Therefore, behold, I will bring strangers upon you,*

*Vecchio, *Justice* (New York, 1953), p. 135.

†E. Jacob, *Theology of the Old Testament* (New York, 1958), pp. 238 f.

‡See, e.g., Engnell, *op. cit.*, pp. 174 ff. In the Jerusalem cultus, the king was regarded as the "son" of the national God. (A. R. Johnson, *The Cultic Prophet in Ancient Israel* [Cardiff, 1944], p. 32). .

§"If popular religion or the royal ideology had accepted such a divine character of the king, we should find traces of it in the prophets, who are anything but lenient towards unfaithful kings. They accuse the kings of many crimes, but never of claiming divinity. Israel never had, never could have had, any idea of a king who was a god." (R. de Vaux, *op. cit.*, p. 112). See also G. von Rad, *Theologie des Alten Testaments,* I (München, 1957), p. 318.

> *The most terrible of the nations; . . .*
> *And you shall die the death of the slain*
> *In the heart of the seas.*
> *Will you still say, I am a god,*
> *In the presence of those who slay you?*
>           *Ezekiel 28:1–2, 7, 8–9; cf. Isaiah 14:13–14*

The king is neither the son nor an incarnation nor a representative of God. He is the ruler appointed by God who must reign according to the will and the *mishpat* of God. The heart of the social order was neither king nor priest, but the covenant between God and the people. The king, to be sure, was an exalted figure, wielding considerable influence and power, the protector and guardian of the people, "The breath of our nostrils, the Lord's anointed . . . of whom we said, Under his shadow we shall live among the nations" (Lam. 4:20). And yet, with the exception of David, no king seems to have been an object of veneration. Solomon achieved fame for his wisdom rather than for his character. Suspicion of monarchy, and opposition to the very institution of kingship, powerfully expressed in the word of Gideon when kingship was offered to him—"I will not rule over you; . . . the Lord will rule over you" (Judg. 8:22)— seem never to have died out in the people, an attitude so different from that encountered elsewhere. Where God alone ought to be the ruler no man could, theoretically at least, claim more than a limited authority. In actuality, however, the drive for power and the readiness to submit to its glory knew no bounds. What were the safeguards that kept alive that attitude and prevented the king from ever assuming the mysterious nimbus that goes with the power of sovereignty?

The answer may lie in the separation of powers and authority within the religious and social order: the separation of kingship, prophecy, and priesthood,* a fact of the highest importance for the understanding of the religion of Israel.†

---

*On the fundamental importance of the idea of theocracy in Israel, see M. Buber, *Königtum Gottes* (3rd ed., Heidelberg, 1956), pp. 115 ff.

†After the Persian period, the position of a high priest in Jerusalem was not very different from that of a king. According to Josephus, the high priest and Maccabean leader, Aristobulus, was the first of his line to adopt the royal title.

## KING AND PRIEST

The kings of Egypt, Assyria, and Phoenicia possessed priestly authority and acted as priests. The combination of royal and priestly functions in one person was common in primitive society. In the Bible, Melchizedek, king of Salem, was priest of El-Elyon (Gen. 14:8). Indeed, the position of priest, side by side with that of the king, is a differentiation of power that has never become universal or incontestable. In Rome, for example, the ruler was both king and priest *(pontifex maximus)*.

Canaanite kings generally possessed priestly authority and acted as priests. In Moab, the king was the leader in religious affairs. King Balak presided when sacrifices were offered before Balaam was called upon to curse the Israelites. At a later period, King Mesha claims to have been instructed by the god to go to battle against Israel. It is not mentioned that this instruction was mediated by a diviner. When he sacrificed his firstborn son, it is stated that the king conducted the sacrifice.*

In Israel, the king was not a priest. He was sanctified by his anointing, appointed by God; in his person centered the hopes of the people, yet sacerdotal functions were regarded as the heritage of the tribe of Levi (Deut. 33:8); in earlier times, the king had performed actions which were properly sacerdotal, even offering sacrifices, yet those actions were "all very special or exceptional." Ordinarily, the conduct of worship was left to the priest.†

Some kings, however, did attempt to arrogate to themselves priestly prerogatives, for example, when Uzziah entered the Temple to burn incense on the altar and was told by the high priest, "It is not for you, Uzziah, to burn incense to the Lord, but for the priests, the sons of Aaron, who are consecrated to burn incense. Go out of the

---

*J. Gray, "Canaanite Kingship in Theory and Practice," *Vetus Testamentum*, II (1952), pp. 193–220.

†"The part played by the king in the regulation and supervision of worship or the nomination of the clergy does not mean that he was himself a priest; it does not exceed the prerogatives which the head of the State may have over the State religion." (R. de Vaux, *op. cit.*, pp. 113 f.)

sanctuary . . ." (II Chron. 26:16 ff.). Interference of the kings in the affairs of the temple at Bethel seems to be reported of the Northern Kingdom, with Jeroboam burning incense on the altar (I Kings 12:33). It was the subordination of the Temple to the court or the alliance of king and priest that made it dangerous for Amos to prophesy at Bethel. "O, seer," said the priest to him, "go, flee away to the land of Judah, eat bread there, and prophesy there; but never again prophesy at Bethel, *for it is the king's sanctuary, and it is a temple of the kingdom*" (Amos 7:12–13).

## PROPHET AND KING

Of paramount importance in the history of Israel was the freedom and independence enjoyed by the prophets, their ability to upbraid the kings and princes for their sins. From the beginning of the monarchy, the king was at any moment in peril of rebuke, even of rejection, by the prophets, who reminded him that the king's sovereignty was not unlimited, that over the king's *mishpat* stood the *mishpat* of the Lord—an idea that frequently clashed with the exigencies of government.

A striking contrast to the prophets' threats of doom, hurled against kings and princes, was the anxiety often shown by Assyrian diviners "to explain away for their masters' comfort the threatening signs which they cannot deny having observed."*

It was such independence that enabled the prophet Nathan to hurl rebuke in King David's face for his crime against Uriah (II Sam. 12:1–13). The supremacy of Nathan's advice extended to matters which directly affected the activities of the priests. It was upon Nathan's prophetic word that David abstained from building the Temple, it was also his intervention that secured Solomon's accession to the throne.

*C. J. Gadd, *Ideas of Divine Rule in the Ancient Near East* (London, 1948), p. 42. Cf. L. Waterman, *Royal Correspondence of the Assyrian Empire* (Chicago, 1892), Nos. 137, 355; *Orientalia* (1939), p. 306; R. C. Thompson, *Reports of the Magicians and Astrologers* (London, 1900), No. 268.

The prophets led the opposition to King Ahab and the fight against the cult of the Baalim sponsored by the court (I Kings 20:13–35); some of them were slain by the queen, Jezebel (I Kings 18:4, 13, 22; 19:10–14; II Kings 9:7).

Ahab and Jezebel, king and queen of the Northern Kingdom, having failed to persuade one of their citizens, Naboth, to sell them his vineyard, had by false accusation put him to death. In the very flush of Ahab's satisfaction, the prophet Elijah appeared proclaiming in the name of God: "In the place where dogs licked the blood of Naboth shall dogs lick your blood!" (I Kings 21.)

The charge falsely brought against Naboth and for which he was condemned to be stoned to death, "Naboth cursed [God and] the king" (I Kings 21:13), could not have been brought rightly against Elijah. To curse "a ruler of your people" was considered a crime in biblical law (Exod. 22:27), just as offending the dignity of a sovereign is regarded as an act of high treason in Roman and modern law.*

It was, indeed, an act of high treason when Amos stood at Bethel, the temple of the Northern Kingdom, and publicly prophesied: "Jeroboam shall die by the sword, and Israel must go into exile away from this land" (Amos 7:11). Yet the great prophets persisted in condemning the leaders—the kings, princes, priests, and false prophets—even more vehemently than the common people.

> O, My people, your leaders mislead you,
> And confuse the course of your paths.
> The Lord enters into judgment . . .
> With the elders and princes of his people:
> It is you who have devoured the vineyard,
> The spoil of the poor is in your houses.
> What do you mean by crushing My people,
> By grinding the face of the poor?
> Says the Lord of hosts.
>
> *Isaiah 3:12, 14–15*

---

*Maiestatem laedere* or *minuere, crimen maiestatis* in Roman law; *laesa maiestas* in modern law.

Micah asked "the heads of Jacob and rulers of the house of Israel: Is it not for you to know justice?" (3:1.) And the anonymous prophet condemned the watchmen as "blind and without knowledge; they are dumb dogs; . . . the shepherds also have no understanding; they have all turned to their own way, each to his own gain, one and all" (Isa. 56:10–11).

While the prophets did not go so far as to call for the abolition of the monarchy, they insisted that human pretension to sovereignty was dangerous, a fake and a caricature, "for dominion belongs to the Lord, and He rules over the nations," says the psalmist (22:29). The prophets were awaiting the day "when the Lord will become king over all the earth" (Zech. 14:9). Even when His kingship was denied by the nations of the world, the prophets reminded the people: "For the Lord is our judge, the Lord is our ruler, the Lord is our king; He will save us" (Isa. 33:22).

What is more, the prophet was not a *primus inter pares,* first among his peers. By his very claim, his was the voice of supreme authority. He not only rivaled the decisions of the king and the counsel of the priest, he defied and even condemned their words and deeds.

## THE PROPHETS AND THE *NEBIIM*

There were also efforts on the part of both kings and priests to avail themselves of the power exercised by prophets. We find, therefore, kings who surrounded themselves with false prophets, and there were false prophets attached to the Temple.

The prophets in Greece, the diviners in Babylonia, the Canaanite *nebiim* * stood in close association with the cult, and belonged in a sense to the staff of the sanctuary. Since the cult and the sanctuaries were subordinate to the kings, all three powers were united in the person of the king.

---

*For all the denunciations of the *nebiim,* they do not go so far as to condemn the office. On the contrary, the presence of the *nebiim* in Israel is regarded as a divine blessing (Amos 2:11); what is bewailed is the fact that they failed in their task.

Though such centralization never fully materialized in Jerusalem, the priests seem at times to have succeeded in establishing an alliance with the *nebiim,* with both groups abandoning the position of independence in relation to the court.*

What the nature and function of the *nebiim* was in earlier times is obscure. From references of the literary prophets we may gather that they were regarded as inspired, consecrated like the Nazirites to the service of God (Amos 2:11), and that their functions may have included teaching ("the prophet who teaches" [Isa. 9:15])—interpreting and proclaiming the will of God. Endowed with spiritual power, they were called upon to answer questions affecting the fortunes of the king and the nation. In the period of the great prophets, this ancient calling seems to have lost its spiritual power and even its integrity. Devoid of divine inspiration, they uttered, instead, visions of their minds, we are told; they flattered the kings and inspired them with a sense of security. Instead of being free and capable of defiance, the *nebiim* became professionals, amenable to the wishes of the court (I Kings 18:19–40; II Kings 10:19).

The prophets raised their voices against these *nebiim* again and again, charging that they "divine for money"; they "cry 'Peace' when they have something to eat, but declare war against him who puts nothing into their mouth. . . . yet they lean upon the Lord and say, Is not the Lord in the midst of us? No evil shall come upon us" (Mic. 3:5, 11). It may be deduced from Micah's prediction of the total

*In complete reversal of the older view that the literary prophets stood in sharp opposition to priest and cult, Scandinavian scholars have advanced the theory that the literary prophets, not only the *nebiim,* were attached to the sanctuaries in the capacity of diviners, and are to be regarded as members of cultic prophetic associations. Prophet and priest, far from being exponents of opposite types of religion, were both officials of the cult. This theory, first advanced by S. Mowinckel, *Psalmenstudien,* III (Kristiania, 1923), was further developed by A. Haldar, *Associations of Cult Prophets among the Ancient Semites* (Uppsala, 1945), who interpreted Hebrew prophecy in terms of the Babylonian *bârû* and *mahhu* guilds. A. R. Johnson, *op. cit.,* p. 29, maintains that "the part played by the prophet in the drama of Israelite religion was primarily that of a cultic specialist." There is, however, no evidence to justify such a sweeping allegation. Cf. the criticism of H. H. Rowley, *The Servant of the Lord* (London, 1954), pp. 109 f.; E. Jacob, *Theology of the Old Testament* (New York, 1958), pp. 239 f.; G. von Rad, *Theologie des Alten Testaments,* II (Müchen, 1960), 63 f.; R. de Vaux, *op. cit.,* pp. 384 f.

destruction of both Jerusalem and the Temple (3:12) that the source of their confidence was reliance upon the sanctuary, to which they were probably attached. The *nebiim* as well as the priests were condemned by Hosea (4:5, 8–10; 6:9). The degeneration of both groups was depicted by Isaiah:

> *The priest and the prophet reel with strong drink,*
> *They are confused with wine,*
> *They stagger with strong drink; they err in vision,*
> *They stumble in giving judgment.*
> *For all tables are full of vomit,*
> *No place is without filthiness.*
>
> Isaiah 28:7–8

Mercilessly Jeremiah condemned the kings, the princes, the priests, and the *nebiim* (2:26; 4:9; 8:1; 13:13; 32:32; cf. 14:18; 29:1). Of the *nebiim* of Samaria he maintained that "they prophesied by Baal and led My people astray" (Jer. 23:13; cf. 2:8). Of the prophets in Jerusalem he said: "They commit adultery and walk in lies; they strengthen the hands of evil-doers, so that no one turns from his wickedness" (Jer. 23:14). "Both prophet and priest have become polluted, even in My house I have found their wickedness, says the Lord" (Jer. 23:11). "From the *nebiim* of Jerusalem pollution has gone forth into all the land. . . . They proclaim visions of their own minds, not from the mouth of the Lord" (Jer. 23:13–16). And according to the author of the book of Lamentations, the great calamity came over Jerusalem "because of the sins of her *nebiim* and the iniquities of her priests" (Lam. 4:13).*

> *From prophet to priest,*
> *Every one deals falsely;*
> *They have healed the wound . . . lightly,*
> *Saying, Peace, Peace,*

---

*E. F. Siegman, *The False Prophets of the Old Testament* (Washington, 1939); G. Quill, *Wahre und falsche Propheten* (Gütersloh, 1952); G. von Rad, *Theologie des Alten Testaments*, II, pp. 222 f.

*When there is no peace. . . .*
*The priests did not say, Where is the Lord?*
*Those who handle the Torah did not know Me;*
*The rulers transgressed against Me;*
*The prophets prophesied by Baal,*
*And went after things that are worthless.*
                    *Jeremiah 6:13–14; 2:8; cf. 5:13*

It is unlikely that the false prophets were shameless charlatans. They were presumably sincere patriots, ardent lovers of the people and zealous in their devotion to state and sanctuary. They as well as the leaders of the state, who had the interest of the country at heart, resented the invectives and exaggerated accusations of Jeremiah and entertained a profound trust in God's attachment to Israel.

# 17

# Conclusions

## INVOLVEMENT AND CONCERN

Pathos is always disclosed as a particular mode or form. There are, as we have seen, many and variable modes of pathos, such as love and anger, grief and joy, mercy and wrath. What is the basic feature they have in common? What is the ultimate significance of pathos?

Pathos in all its forms reveals the extreme pertinence of man to God, His world-directness, attentiveness, and concern. God "looks at" the world and is affected by what happens in it; man is the object of His care and judgment.

The basic feature of pathos and the primary content of the prophet's consciousness is a *divine attentiveness and concern*. Whatever message he appropriates, it reflects that awareness. It is a divine attentiveness to humanity, an involvement in history, a divine vision of the world in which the prophet shares and which he tries to convey. And it is God's concern for man that is at the root of the prophet's work to save the people.

The great secret is God's hidden pathos. A divine attachment concealed from the eye, a divine concern unnoticed or forgotten, hovers over the history of mankind. Yet there are moments when attachment turns to detachment, when concern is overshadowed by anger.

For biblical theology these ideas are as basic as the ideas of being and becoming are for classical metaphysics. They mark the difference between pagan and prophetic experience. There, existence is experiencing being; here, existence is experiencing concern. It is living in the perpetual awareness of being perceived, apprehended, noted by God, of being an object of the divine Subject. This is the most precious insight: to sense God's participation in existence; to experience oneself as a divine secret (see Ps. 139:7–18).

Yet even here we must not think that we reach God's essence. Transcendent attentiveness merely defines the limits of the prophet's understanding of God. God in Himself, His Being, is a problem for metaphysics. The theme and claim of prophetic theology is God's concern for man, and man's relevance to God. Only one aspect of His Being, His directedness to man, is known to man.

This, then, is the ultimate category of prophetic theology: involvement, attentiveness, concern. Prophetic religion may be defined, not as what man does with his ultimate concern, but rather *what man does with God's concern.*

He whose thinking is guided by the prophets would say: God's presence is my first thought; His unity and transcendence, my second; His concern and involvement (justice and compassion), my third. Upon deeper reflection, however, he will realize that all three thoughts are one. God's presence in the world is, in essence, His concern for the world. One word stands for both. And both are expressions of His unity. Divine unity implies concern. For unity means love.

The fundamental thought in the Bible is not creation, but God's care for His creation. The sense of wonder for His creation is common to all men. The sense of care for His care is the personal prerequisite for being a prophet. All men care for the world; the prophet cares for God's care. In the process of such redirection, he may be driven to be careless about everything else.

Sympathy opens man to the living God. Unless we share His concern, we know nothing about the living God.

## GOD IN RELATIONSHIP

What was the prophetic way of thinking about God?

Overwhelmingly, mysteriously different from man, God was not the object of imagination. He could not be captured in a myth or comprehended in a concept or a symbol. Challenging, involved, and concerned, His presence pierced the impregnable walls of His otherness. The dilemma was overcome by abstaining from any claim to comprehend God's *essence,* His inmost being, or even to apprehend His inscrutable thoughts, unrelated to history, and by insisting upon the ability to understand His presence, expression or manifestation. The prophets experience what He *utters,* not what He *is.*

Ontologically, the distinction between being and expression is rooted in the distinction between essence and relation. The theme of prophetic understanding is not the mystery of God's essence, but rather the mystery of His relation to man. The prophet does not speculate about God in Himself; in thinking about Him, the world is always present. His message does not seek to disclose or to impart new truth concerning the divine Being. What the prophet knows about God is His pathos, His relation to Israel and to mankind. God can be understood by man only in conjunction with the human situation. For of God we know only what He means and does in relation to man. The prophet reflects, not on heavenly or hallowed mysteries, but on the perplexities and ambiguities of history. He never discloses the life of the beyond, but always speaks of an appearance, God as turned toward man. The anthropotropic moment is the object of his experience; God in His eternal self-existence, never. The prophet refers to God, not as absolute, but always as related to the people. It is an interpretation, not of divine Being, but of the divine interaction with humanity. Revelation means, not that God makes Himself known, but that He makes His will known; not God's disclosure of His Being, His self-manifestation, but a disclosure of the divine will and pathos, of the ways in which He relates Himself to man. Man knows the word of revelation, but not the self-revelation of God. He experiences no vision of God's essence, only a vision of appearance. A subject of pathos, God Himself is not pathos. His insight always contains, together with the *subjectum relationis,* a *fundamentum* and a *terminus relationis.* The ground of the relation is moral, and from God's point of view, objective and impersonal. The goal of the relation is man. The divine pathos is transitive.

## GOD AS SUBJECTIVITY

The subjectivity of God epitomizes our conclusion. The term is used in two senses. In the first sense He is the supreme Subject, the One to Whom all prophetic events are referred as their source and initiator; the "I" Who calls, questions, demands, and acts. In the second sense, He is a God Who is involved and concerned rather than detached, absolute, and unrelated.

To the prophet, God is always apprehended, experienced, and conceived as a *Subject,* never as an object. He appears as One Who demands, as One Who acts, Whose intention is to give righteousness and peace rather than to receive homage or adoration, Whose desire is to bestow rather than to obtain. In all that the prophet knows about God, he never finds in God a desire which does not bear upon man.

The prophet does not find God in his mind as object, but finds himself an object in God's mind. To think of Him is to open the mind to His all-pervading, all-penetrating presence. To think of things is to have a concept within the mind, while to think of Him is like being surrounded by His thinking. Thus, to know Him is to be known by Him.

Prophetic experience was not a feeling of objective presence, a perception of what has been called "something there," but rather a feeling of subjective presence, a perception of what may be called *Someone here.* He is all-personal. He is all-Subject, not the object of man's quest, but He Who is in search of man.

There is a profound difference between this mode of thought

and the philosophical approach to the knowledge of God, which arises, for instance, *via eminentiae* and takes place as an unfoldment of ideas. For prophetic apprehension, God is never an "it," but is constantly given as a personal spirit, manifesting Himself as subject even in the act of thought addressed to Him. Those who objectify Him falsify Him. Those who surrender to Him are approached by Him.

Is it proper to apply the term "personal" to God? We have suggested that the outstanding feature of a person is his ability to transcend himself, his attentiveness to the nonself. To be a person is to have a concern for the nonself. It is in this limited sense that we speak of God as a personal Being: He has concern for nondivine being.

He is always felt as He Who feels, thought of as He Who thinks, never as object, always as a Being Who wills and acts.

He is encountered not as universal, general, pure Being, but always in a particular mode of being, as personal God to a personal man, in a specific pathos that comes with a demand in concrete situation. Prophetic thought is not focused upon His absoluteness, as indeterminate being, but upon His "subjective" being, upon His expression, pathos, and relationship. The dichotomy of transcendence and immanence is an oversimplification. For God remains transcendent in His immanence, and related in His transcendence.

## TRANSCENDENT ANTICIPATION

In the light of prophetic insights, we are faced not merely with a relation to God, but also with a living reality which is a relationship, having its origin in God. The *a priori* of man's relationship to Him is the fact of His relationship to man.

Although the prophet remains open to the totality of the divine as Subject, it is God's relationship to man which occupies his attention. Keeping steadily in view the fundamental interrelation between God and history, he seems to conceive of it as the relation between man in himself and man in God. Concern for man as he is in God's vision and anticipation, on the one hand, and, on the other, a regard

for man as he is in his own situation, are the two terms of this relationship. Prophetic consciousness, it must be stressed again, does not
spring from the depths of the human spirit; it is based upon anticipation or inclusion of man in God.

The datum of the experience is not something given, but Someone Who gives; not a fact, but an act. Prophetic activity itself is determined by the transcendent Subject. The object here manifests itself as
Subject, anticipating man, revealing, indicating, opening the mind.
Prophecy arises not from any sudden, spontaneous feeling awakened
by an indeterminate, silent, and numinous image, but from an experience of inspiration which has its source in the revelation of a divine
pathos.

The natural movement of the soul has been compared to a circle
around its center. We always move around the One. The One does
not strive to encircle us, but we strive to encircle It. In the spirit of
prophetic thinking we might say that God is the circle moving around
humanity. His knowledge of man precedes man's knowledge of Him,
while man's knowledge of Him comprehends only what God asks
of man.

In view of the gulf which yawns between divine infinitude and
the limitations of the human situation, a divine-human understanding
is ultimately contingent upon an awareness of a divine anticipation
and expectation. The inclusion of man in God is the life "bound in
the bundle of living in the care of the Lord" (II Sam. 25:29).* Not
human love reaching out to God, but divine love or concern focused
upon man—a central feature of the prophetic consciousness—is the
basis of such religious communion. Man's turning to God is thus no
longer a point of departure without a background of presuppositions.
Prophetic experience is the experiencing of a divine experience, or a
realization of having been experienced by God.

We live in the universe of His knowing, in the glory of attachment. "Before I formed you in the womb I knew you" (Jer. 1:5).
This is the task: to sense or to discover our being known. We approach

---

*Kimhi, *Commentary, ad loc.*

Him, not by making Him the object of our thinking, but by discovering ourselves as the objects of His thinking.

## THE DIALECTIC OF THE DIVINE–HUMAN ENCOUNTER

A specific aspect of prophetic religion or of the religious phenomenon in general, as opposed to the purely psychological, lies in the fact of a mutual inherence of the "I" and the object of religious experience, for an intention of man toward God produces a counteracting intention of God toward man. Here all mutual relations end, not in the original decision, but in a relationship which represents a counteraction. In turning toward God, man experiences God's turning toward him. Man's awareness of God is to be understood as God's awareness of man, man's knowledge of God is transcended in God's knowledge of man, the subject—man—becomes object, and the object—God—becomes subject. Not a reciprocal succession of acts, not a distinguishable alteration of sound and echo, but rather in every event of the religious consciousness it is a question of a dual mutual operation, a twofold mutual initiative. Every apprehension of God is an act of being apprehended by God, every vision of God is a divine vision of man. A mere human aspiration toward God, apart from God's loving election of man, is wide of the mark. For we can think of God only insofar as He thinks of us. The primary factor is our being seen and known by Him for that constitutes the essential content of our vision of God. And so the ultimate element in the object of theological reflection is transcendent divine attention to man, the fact that man is apprehended by God.

In the mysticism of Yoga, the apprehension of the divine is attained only by the complete surrender and dissolution of the ego and without any sense of encounter. In prophetic thinking, man is the object of God's vision, concern, and understanding. It is man's vision, concern, and understanding for God that is the goal.

This is the test of the uniqueness of religious experience. Unlike other types of experience, there is no clear and distinct separation of object and comprehension, of reality and response. The religious person is not always confronted by a silent, aloof object to which his feeling reacts autonomously. In the prophetic type of experience, the object is not to be sought in the "I," but the "I" in the object. What is experienced is the attention of the Transcendent.

"Know thy God" (I Chron. 28:9) rather than "Know Thyself" is the categorical imperative of the biblical man. There is no self-understanding without God-understanding.

# Appendix

## A Note on the Meaning of Pathos

The sense in which the word "pathos" is employed in this volume differs from the meaning most frequently encountered in common usage. Let us briefly review some of the changes in significance which the word has undergone.

Pathos, according to Liddel-Scott in *A Greek-English Lexicon*, means *that which happens* to a person or thing; *what one has experienced,* good or bad; *emotion, passion; state, condition.* In general, the ancient classical idea of pathos included all conditions of feeling and will in which man is dependent on the outer world. See p. 319 of the present volume.

Ancient rhetoricians have always stressed the role of the emotions in the art of persuasion. To stir the emotions is one of the three aims of the orator. Aristotle, *Rhetoric,* I, II, 1356A; Cicero, *De Oratore,* II, 43, 185.) Oratory, Cicero claims, has three functions: *docere, conciliare, movere,* and the distinction must be made between *ethos* and *pathos.* Through *ethos* the orator conciliates his audience and wins their confidence in his own integrity. The grand style has as its purpose the awakening of emotions in the audience; through *pathos* he excites their feelings by impassioned speaking.

Thus the power of pathos was considered weak in Andokles and

Lysias (whose ethos, on the contrary, was famous), stronger in Isaios, and masterly in Demosthenes. (F. Bass, *Die Attische Beredsamkeit* [2nd ed.; Leipzig, 1887], I, 304, 400; II, 534 f.; III, 190. See also W. Suess, *Ethos, Studien zur älteren Griechischen Rhetorik* [Leipzig, 1910], pp. 129 ff.) Jaeger refers to "the style that we call Demosthenic in the strict sense—the style truly passionate, which comes from the soul and is no mere matter of words . . ." (*Demosthenes, the Origin and Growth of His Policy* [Berkeley, 1938], p. 124.)

The idea of the exhibition and evocation of feeling was carried over from rhetoric into poetry. Aristotle (*Poetics*, XVII, 1455A) advises the poet to act out the part and feel the emotions of his characters in order to represent them more convincingly. Horace (*Ars Poetica*, II, 102) maintains: *Si vis me flere, dolendum est primum ipsi tibi.*

In English the word "pathos" came to mean "that quality in speech, writing, music, or artistic representation (or *transferred* in events, circumstances, persons, etc.) which excites a feeling of pity or sadness; power of stirring tender or melancholy emotion; pathetic or affecting character or influence." In rare cases it also means suffering, bodily or mental (*A New English Dictionary on Historical Principles* [Oxford, 1909], VII, 554). Denoting the quality found in human situations—or especially in works of art or literature—which moves one to pity or sorrow, it has early been used as an aesthetic term and often "implies not so much an effect produced on the person who sees, hears, or reads, as the art, device, or trick employed by the writer, speaker, artist, or other person seeking to produce such an effect" *(Webster's Dictionary of Synonyms).*

Under the impact of Longinus' celebrated essay on the sublime, *Peri Hupsos,* and its emphasis upon the importance of passion, this term came to play an important role in the aesthetic theories of eighteenth-century England. Paradoxically it was Boileau, author of the neoclassic code as well as translator of Longinus into French, who gave impetus to the consideration of the aesthetic value of emotions and the emotional effect of the sublime. Pathos and the pathetic were discussed in relation to the sublime.

In the aesthetic treatises of the eighteenth century the semantic status of this term was highly respectable. John Dennis (1657–1734) regards art as the expression of passion and maintains that the highest art—the sublime—is the expression of greatest passion. "The sublime and the pathetic begin their long journey in each other's company." (S. H. Monk, *The Sublime, A Study of Critical Theories of Eighteenth-Century England* [New York, 1935], p. 46.) Poetry is defined by Dennis as "an Imitation of Nature by a pathetick and numerous Speech." The sublime and the pathetic go together (*ibid.,* p. 53).

By contrast, John Baillie, in *An Essay of the Sublime* (London, 1747), maintains that the two qualities have nothing to do with each other. The sublime composes rather than agitates the mind, "whilst the very Essence of the Pathetick consists in the Agitation of the Passions."

R. P. Knight (*An Analytical Inquiry into the Principles of Taste* [3rd ed.; London, 1806], III, p. 313) distinguishes between "those tender feelings which are called pathetic, or those exalted or enthusiastic sentiments, which are called sublime." He maintains that in real life the sublime and pathetic may be separated and opposed (as the tender to the exalted), whereas "in all the fictions, either of poetry or imitative art, there can be nothing truly pathetic unless it be, at the same time, in some degree, sublime. for, though, in scenes of real distress, pity may so far overcome scorn, that we may weep for sufferings, that are feebly or pussillanimously borne; yet, in fiction, scorn will always predominate, unless there be a display of vigour, as well as tenderness and sensibility of mind" *ibid.,* p. 358). See also D. Stewart, *Philosophical Essays,* V (Edinburgh, 1855), 444, 449 f.

Pathos came to denote more specifically passions which fill the mind with terror, dismay, and gloom—for which, it was said, there was no equivalent in the German language. Johann George Sulzer, in *Allgemeine Theorie der schönen Kunste,* a four-volume dictionary of esthetic terms first issued in 1771–1774, says in his article on *Pathos: Pathetisch,* "Yet it seems at times that the meaning of the word is extended to cover the passions in general, which as a result of their intensity and seriousness grip the soul with a kind of awe."

The apostle of romanticism in Sweden, Thomas Thorild (1759–

1808) maintains that the greatest impression of the beauty of literature—the greatest in the world in degree, as in reach—is made upon
the populace through ballads. "And I, dear Sir, can myself solemnly
assure you that I have never found in the world's great poetry that
intrinsic pathos I once found [in certain medieval tales]. . . ." (G. W.
Allen and H. H. Clark, *Literary Criticism; Pope to Croce* [New York,
1941], p. 127.)

Schiller, in his essay "On the Pathetic," believes it is impossible
"to represent moral freedom, except by expressing passion, or suffering nature with the greatest vividness. . . . Therefore the *pathetic* is
the first condition required most strictly in a tragic author. . . . The
pathetic only has esthetic value insofar as it is sublime."

Hegel (1770–1831) speaks of the difficulty in translating the
word "pathos." "Passion almost always implies as its concomitant an
element of meanness or baseness. We contend in ordinary parlance
that a man should not surrender himself to his passions. It must therefore be understood that we use the expression pathos in a nobler and
more universal sense than this without the slightest implication of anything blameworthy or egotistic . . . Pathos in this sense is a power of
the emotional life which completely justifies itself, an essential part of
the content of rationality and the free will . . . Thus understood we
may add that it is impossible to say that the gods possess pathos . . .

". . . Pathos moves us because it is that which is essentially the
vital force of our human existence."*

The Scottish poet Robert Burns (1759–1796) says in his "Epistle
to Dr. Blacklock":

> To make a happy fire-side clime
> To weans and wife,
> That's the true pathos and sublime
> Of human life.

The beginning of the nineteenth century witnesses a change in
the conception of the nature of poetry and the role of the emotions

---

* *The Philosophy of Fine Art*, F. P. B. Osmaston, trans. (London, 1920), I, 308 f.

in art. The display of emotion is frowned upon; pathos and the pathetic are deprived of their respectable semantic status. Pathos came to be associated with the false or the disingenuous rather than with the noble, tragic or sublime. It even has a comic connotation. (See E. von Hartmann, *Die Philosophie des Schönen* [Leipzig, 1887], p. 314; see also J. Volkelt, *System der Aesthetick* [München, 1910], II, 179, n. 1; 183 ff.)

John Ruskin (1819–1900) designates the literary device by which external and nonhuman objects are credited with human feelings as a *pathetic fallacy*, "caused by an excited state of feelings, making us, for the time, more or less irrational . . . that which the mind admits when affected strongly by emotion" (*Modern Painters*, III, pt. IV, ch. 12).

In his "Richard Wagner in Bayreuth," Nietzsche says that before Wagner's time "music for the most part moved in narrow limits: it concerned itself with the permanent states of man, or with what the Greeks call *ethos*. And only with Beethoven did it begin to find the language of *pathos*, of passionate will, and of the dramatic occurrences in the souls of men." About refraining from pathetic feelings, see *The Dawn of the Day* (Edinburgh, 1910), pp. 386–508. "Pathetisch werden heisst: eine Stufe zurücktreten," he says elsewhere (Musarion ed., XI, p. 78). "Pathetic attitudes are not in keeping with greatness," he declares in *Ecce Homo*.

"In ordinary modern use *pathos* and *pathetic* are limited to the idea of painful emotion" (H. W. Fowler, *A Dictionary of Modern English Usage* [Oxford, 1926], p. 425 f.).

A contemporary writer maintains that "pathos is a queer ghoulish emotion, and some failure of expression, real or simulated, seems to be peculiar to it. . . . Highly articulated emotion is apt to become a factitious appeal to self-pity, or tear-jerking" (N. Frye, *Anatomy of Criticism* [Princeton, 1957], p. 39).

We are told that, although in its strict meaning pathos "is closely associated with the pity which tragedy is supposed to evoke, in common usage it describes an acquiescent or relatively helpless suffering or the sorrow occasioned by unmitigated grief, as opposed to the stoic grandeur and awful justice of the tragical hero. In this distinction, Hamlet is a tragic figure and Ophelia a pathetic one. Lear's fate is tragic, Cordelia's pathetic" (W. F. Thrall and A. Hibbard, *A Handbook to Literature* [rev. by C. H. Holman; New York, 1961], pp. 345 f.).

# Index of Passages

## I. HEBREW BIBLE

## II. APOCRYPHA AND PSEUDEPIGRAPHA

## III. RABBINICAL WRITINGS

## IV. NEW TESTAMENT

# V. OTHER SCRIPTURES

# Index of Subjects and Names

# ABOUT THE AUTHOR

Abraham Joshua Heschel was the foremost Jewish theologian of his day. Born in 1907 into a distinguished family of Hasidic rebbes in Warsaw, he completed his doctorate at the University of Berlin just as the Nazis came to power. Arriving as a refugee in the United States in 1940, he taught for five years at Hebrew Union College, then at the Jewish Theological Seminary until his death in 1972.

His study of the prophets inspired his conviction that religiosity demands involvement in political affairs and led to his engagement in the Civil Rights movement. Strongly opposed to the war in Vietnam, he founded Clergy and Laymen Concerned About Vietnam. In addition, he served as the Jewish representative to the Second Vatican Council during its deliberations on Catholic-Jewish relations.

Heschel's scholarship includes numerous distinguished works of Jewish theology, including *God in Search of Man*, *Man Is Not Alone*, *The Sabbath*, *Man's Quest for God*, and *A Passion for Truth*. He is also the author of a three-volume Hebrew study of rabbinic thought, several essays on medieval Jewish philosophy, and a two-volume study in Yiddish of the Kotzker rebbe.

Theologians and religious people of all faiths have embraced Heschel's work as an authentic expression of spiritual experience.